2010

Dedicated to the glory of God
in whose name and by whose grace
the work described in this volume
has been accomplished

Annual reports in this edition mostly cover the period 1 May 2008 to 30 April 2009. The staff lists and details of centres of work are generally accurate to 30 September 2009.

Statistics are those for the year ending 31 December 2008.

Officers and lay staff serving in countries other than their own are counted in the statistics of the territory/command in which they are serving.

The 'Biographical Information' section is as accurate as possible at the time of going to press.

THE
SALVATION ARMY
YEAR BOOK

THE SALVATION ARMY YEAR BOOK

2010

INTERNATIONAL MISSION STATEMENT

The Salvation Army, an international movement, is an
evangelical part of the universal Christian Church.
Its message is based on the Bible. Its ministry is motivated by
love for God. Its mission is to preach the gospel of Jesus Christ
and meet human needs in his name without discrimination.

THE SALVATION ARMY
INTERNATIONAL HEADQUARTERS
101 QUEEN VICTORIA STREET, LONDON EC4V 4EH, UNITED KINGDOM

First published 2009

Copyright © 2009 The General of The Salvation Army

ISBN 978-0-85412-819-8

Editor: Major Trevor Howes

Desktop publishing support: Nathan Sigauke

Cover design: Berni Georges

Published by Salvation Books
The Salvation Army International Headquarters
101 Queen Victoria Street, London EC4V 4EH, United Kingdom

Printed in the United Kingdom by Page Bros Ltd, Norwich, Norfolk, England
using paper from sustainable sources

Contents

Foreword by the General 1

Articles of special interest

Who We Are Meant To Be – the focus of the World Youth Convention
                                    by Colonel Birgitte Brekke 3

We Must Go On – 100 years of women preaching in The Salvation Army
                                    by Colonel Prema Wilfred Varughese 5

Good Health For Everyone – the International Health Services
                                    by Major Dean Pallant 7

Responding To Global Recession   *by Commissioner Ann Woodall* 9

Facts and figures

What is The Salvation Army? 11
The Doctrines of The Salvation Army 12
Founders of The Salvation Army 13
Glossary of Salvation Army terms 14
Salvation Army History (chronological table) 16
Significant Events 2008-2009 21
The High Council 22
Generals Elected by a High Council 23
Countries where The Salvation Army is at work 27
International Statistics 29
Salvation Army Periodicals 31
Books Published 2008-2009 32
Ministries and Fellowships 34
Salvation Army Honours 35

Reports, staff lists and addresses

International Headquarters 38
    International College for Officers and Centre for
                                   Spiritual Life Development 41
    International Social Justice Commission 42
    The Africa Development Centre 43
    International Administrative Structure 44
    The Salvation Army International Trustee Company 45
    Reliance Bank Limited 45
    Overseas Service Funds 46
    Community Development Projects 48

(Continued on next page)

Angola	49	Mexico	178
Australia		Mozambique	182
National Secretariat	51	Netherlands, The, and Czech	
Eastern	52	Republic	184
Southern	60	New Zealand, Fiji and Tonga	189
Bangladesh	72	Nigeria	196
Brazil	74	Norway, Iceland and	
Canada and Bermuda	78	The Færoes	199
Caribbean	88	Pakistan	203
Congo (Brazzaville)	93	Papua New Guinea	206
Democratic Republic of Congo	96	Philippines, The	209
Denmark	100	Portugal	214
Eastern Europe	103	Rwanda and Burundi	216
Finland and Estonia	106	Singapore, Malaysia and	
France and Belgium	109	Myanmar	218
Germany and Lithuania	114	South America	
Ghana	117	East	222
Hong Kong and Macau	120	West	225
India		Southern Africa	231
National Secretariat	126	Spain	235
Central	128	Sri Lanka	237
Eastern	132	Sweden and Latvia	240
Northern	135	Switzerland, Austria and	
South Eastern	139	Hungary	245
South Western	142	Taiwan	249
Western	145	Tanzania	251
Indonesia	149	Uganda	253
Italy	153	United Kingdom	255
Japan	155	USA	
Kenya		National	263
East	158	Central	265
West	161	Eastern	271
Korea	164	Southern	279
Latin America North	169	Western	285
Liberia	174	Zambia	294
Malawi	176	Zimbabwe	297

Biographical Information	300
Retired Generals and Commissioners	330
Retirements from Active Service	338
Promotions to Glory	343
Abbreviations	348
International direct dialling	349
Index	350

IT ALL BELONGS TO GOD
Foreword by General Shaw Clifton
International leader of The Salvation Army

IN presenting this latest edition of *The Year Book* I give thanks to God for his ongoing, unfailing guidance to The Salvation Army and for every expression of Christian witness and service recorded in these pages. It is divine help and strength that keeps us going. It is energy from Heaven that fuels the work. It is the Holy Spirit who directs and leads. Everything described and recorded in these pages should be read in that light.

It has ever been thus. Every Christian believer knows that when we trust in our own strength, our own wisdom, we will not succeed – at least, not in Heaven's terms. We might somehow and superficially impress a few folk, but what is that compared with doing the will of our Father in Heaven?

The four articles that immediately follow this foreword illustrate powerfully aspects of Salvationist life and endeavour that would simply fail but for the help of God.

General Shaw Clifton and Commissioner Helen Clifton

How can you reach modern young people without relying upon divine insight and wisdom? Youth culture is now so diverse and so rapidly changing that just keeping up with it demands huge commitment. I thank God for every Salvation Army person working with passion and skill to reach young people. That work will bear fruit that will last.

The women of the Army exemplify a reliance on God that can be found in every corner of the still-expanding Salvation Army world. Army women engage in selfless service. They lead, hold authority, preach and teach – in local, national and international settings.

More and more women officers, married and single, are being

Foreword

Children excitedly greet the General during his visit to Pakistan (*see page 203*)

placed into senior roles. We cannot, dare not, hold them back.

Our health services seek always to express the compassion of Christ. Medical mission is part of our Movement's DNA. We are called to continue the healing work of Christ, and to do it in a modern, professional manner. Modern challenges are very great, not least when it comes to funding, but we reassess and redeploy under God's guiding hand.

The global financial recession impacts The Salvation Army directly. I thank God for faithful stewards of the past and for skilful, knowledgeable Army professionals of today. Friends of the Army can still be sure that their precious monetary gifts will be faithfully used in keeping with our commitment to serve others in Christ's name.

I thank readers and users of *The Year Book*. I pray the blessing of God upon you as you ponder the content of these pages. It all belongs to God, who has never forsaken those who are faithful to him. My prayer is that in his mercy, and by grace, he will count the Army faithful.

International Headquarters,
London

WHO WE ARE MEANT TO BE

Colonel Birgitte Brekke outlines the focus of the 2010 World Youth Convention

'WE need, in each succeeding generation, to understand who we are in the light of God's special dealings with us as a people. We are not in the business of proclaiming ourselves better than others, or pointing a finger at anyone. However, we are most definitely in the business, first of all, of knowing who we are meant to be and, secondly, of obeying God.' These are words from General Shaw Clifton's book, *New Love*.

A clear definition of who we are meant to be as Salvationists and the implications of that in every young person's life will be the focus of the World Youth Convention, being held from 15 to 18 July 2010. With 'Raised Up' as its title and 'Salvationism' as its theme, the event will be led by General Clifton and has been planned around the first chapter in *New Love*: 'Salvationism – Holiness and the non-negotiables of Salvationism'.

One thousand delegates aged from 18 to 28 – representatives from every territory and command – will gather in Sweden on the campus of Stockholm University. Thousands of other young people will take part in the convention as 'virtual' delegates through interactive links and live webcasts accessed through www.raisedup.org

The interactive links will help form a global network that will unite, across borders, the Army's young people. They will share with each other the realities of their lives and circumstances, along with their hopes, concerns and achievements.

This will lead them to a greater understanding of the world's many complex issues, enabling young Salvationists to work together in a more-informed way, to disseminate their knowledge and insight, and become advocates for justice and equity in their local communities.

The World Youth Convention will be truly global.

Questions

Who are we meant to be? What was The Salvation Army raised up to be? What is Salvationism? These questions are to be the convention's main focus.

In the first chapter of *New Love* we find eight key elements that describe who we are:

Realistic – we are down-to-earth about human nature and sin.

Idealistic – we can live a holy life day by day.

Inclusive – our arms are wide open to others.

Compassionate – we have 'the smell of the streets' on us.

Simple – we reveal the truth in language that's accessible and in a style that does not threaten.

International – the whole globe is

What We Are Meant To Be

our arena, no person is an enemy.

Visible – we want to be seen as a witness to Christ, available to others.

Audible – we are a voice for the voiceless.

Salvationism is more than methods, programmes, music, language, ranks and so on. It is a way of life. When we describe Salvationism, we describe what each young Salvationist is meant to be, and the personal implications for every young person in the Army. Salvationism at its best is radical and challenging. When lived out it is a perfect fit to young people's interests and lifestyle.

So the World Youth Convention is not about the Army as an organisation. It is not about what God and the Army can do for young Salvationists, but what each young person is called to be and do for God and the Army's mission – for them, individually, to discover God's call and his plan for their lives.

Writes General Clifton: 'If he [God] has called us out to be a distinctive people for him, we cannot risk disobedience. If he wants us to be thoroughly Salvationist, then we are going to be just that. We will persist in bearing the hallmarks of Salvationism, resisting attempts to trivialise or erase them.'

May each young person in The Salvation Army know who and what they are meant to be and do – and then go and be and do that!

Colonel Brekke is World Youth Convention Organiser, IHQ.

Vibrant young Salvationists from Germany – some will be delegates at the 2010 World Youth Convention in Sweden

WE MUST GO ON

Colonel Prema Wilfred Varughese acknowledges 100 years of women preaching in The Salvation Army

GENERAL Evangeline Booth said in her book titled *Woman*, published in 1930: 'We must light new lamps. We must tread new paths. We must go on.' She was remembering the new path for women preaching in public, which was trodden for the first time by her mother – and our Army Mother – Catherine Booth, in The Salvation Army.

This began for Mrs Booth when she received an inward urge on a fine morning of Whit Sunday, 27 May 1860. It astonished the congregation and even her husband, William. This brave woman of God walked up the aisle as William Booth was concluding his sermon and told him that she desired to speak.

That was a new beginning in the history of women sharing the same platform with men in ministering the Word of God. This bold act inspired many other women evangelists especially in preaching God's Word.

Evangeline Booth was influenced by her mother. She walked on that path and urged many other women to tread new paths and to go forward in our mission in preaching the Word of God. Many dedicated women risked their lives to lead the desperate into the fullness of life – a mission that has now reached 118 countries.

In every generation God has raised up gifted and passionate women in the Army from different nations and backgrounds. They stood as unbeatable. They carried the mission of God as evangelists and travelled the world. General Eva Burrows is an outstanding figure in the Army's history; the World Presidents of Women's Ministries and the first woman Chief of the Staff (pictured here preaching during a visit to Portugal Command) are other examples.

The talented single and married women officers in leadership and many other gifted women are proving that they are effective in preaching the Word of God. Hundreds and thousands of men and women have been won to Christ through their

We Must Go On

An artist's impression (circa 1890) of Catherine Booth preaching during a Salvation Army meeting held in a theatre in the north of England

ministries. In 2010, the celebration of 150 years of women in preaching will doubtless give more strength and courage and will inspire every Salvation Army woman of God to tread new paths and to reach the unreached.

Every opportunity

The apostle Paul declared: 'There is neither Jew nor Greek, slave nor free, male nor female, for you are all one in Christ Jesus' (Galatians 3:28, *New International Version*). Christian women are not to be entangled in a yoke of cultural bondage but to make use of every opportunity to preach God's Word for the extension of his Kingdom.

The great command and commission of Jesus is for all who believe in Christ to proclaim the gospel and make disciples (Matthew 28:19, 20). This was the basic principle established and followed by The Salvation Army.

We, we have chosen our path –
Path to a clear purposed goal,
Path of advance!

(Matthew Arnold – Rugby Chapel, November 1857, quoted by Evangeline Booth in *Woman*, 1930)

Let us go on preaching to win the lost and worst souls for Christ until he comes.

Colonel Varughese is Territorial Secretary for Women's Ministries, Zimbabwe

GOOD HEALTH FOR EVERYONE

Major Dean Pallant writes about the International Health Services

GOOD health is the desire of every person on Earth. Around the world increasingly large amounts of money are invested in the search for good health. Some people are enjoying the benefits. Many richer people are living longer but, sadly, millions of poorer people are struggling.

More than 100 million people fall into poverty each year paying for health care. Millions more are unable to access any health care. The global recession is making it harder for billions of people to enjoy a healthy life.

The World Health Organisation defines health as 'a state of complete physical, mental and social well-being, and not merely the absence of disease'. This is a useful definition but it lacks one essential word – spiritual. The Salvation Army has always believed that everyone requires spiritual transformation in order to enjoy full health.

Benefits

A comprehensive transformation enables people – and the wider society – to experience the benefits of healthier bodies, healthier minds and healthier souls. The Salvation Army believes transformation is best achieved through the life and power of God – Father, Son and Spirit.

The pages of *The Year Book* are full of Salvation Army programmes that offer opportunities for people to develop healthier bodies, minds and souls. Almost every programme has a health dimension because Army programmes aim to help people discover health in all its fullness.

When some people hear about good health they think only about better hospitals, doctors, nurses, drugs and equipment. Of course these are necessary and The Salvation Army is proud to have more than 300 hospitals and clinics worldwide serving people who would otherwise struggle to access health care.

Attitudes

However, good health requires much more than doctors and nurses doing more with better drugs and more complex technology. The transformation to a healthier society full of healthy people needs right attitudes, not simply right actions.

Perhaps a line from a secular song sums it up: 'It's not what you do it's the way that you do it, that's what gets results.'

The way health care is 'done' needs urgent review. Despite more money being spent, health indicators for the poorest people are not improving. Even in economically developed countries, health costs are spiralling out of control.

More effort needs to be put into preventing disease rather than just spending more on treatment. People

Good Health For Everyone

need to be given (and accept) more ownership of their health because good health is everyone's responsibility and not something left to doctors, nurses and governments.

Health ministry needs to be integrated into a continuous chain of education, prevention, treatment and care from home to hospital and back – the closer the interventions are to the home the better.

The work of faith-based organisations, like The Salvation Army, is increasingly being seen by governments and health strategists as vital in improving the health of the poorest people. People of faith are present in every community around the world – they are often the most active members of the community in caring for the less fortunate. People of faith are members of the community, often struggling with their own health while seeking to help their neighbours.

Salvation Army health programmes are making a real difference in the lives of the poorest people. I have seen inspiring work that improves the health of people in all corners of the world.

Good health requires an integrated understanding of body, mind and soul. Good health for poor and marginalised people requires services as close to the family as possible. Salvation Army health ministry encourages every person to take responsibility for their own health as well as caring for the health of others.

Vision Statement for Salvation Army Health Services

The Salvation Army seeks to be a significant participant in faith-based, integrated, quality primary health care as close to the family as possible, giving priority to poor and marginalised members of society

Major Pallant is International Health Services Coordinator, IHQ

The entrance to Begora Clinic in Ghana where the medical services offered by The Salvation Army are used by Christians and Muslims

RESPONDING TO GLOBAL RECESSION

Commissioner Ann Woodall tells how Salvationists worldwide are playing their part

THE Salvation Army exists in the real world, and so the lives of individual Salvationists as well as the life of the organisation are affected by world events. The present downturn in the world economy is clearly such an event.

Most of the impact is first felt in the territories: through the fall in standards of living of the Salvationists and donors that can lead of necessity to a reduction in giving; through a falling off in investment and bank income; and through added demands on programmes.

This is all basic to charity finance, and the level of impact felt in each of the 118 countries where The Salvation Army operates will be of a different degree. However, just as the international spirit of the Army adds a new dimension to the Movement, the international financing is more than just a summation of the financial activities in each country.

Expertise

Much of what we do builds on the experience and expertise of other religious and charitable bodies and companies, as well as our own history. Sometimes one of our number has a bright idea that takes off and adds a new dimension to our financial health – and I think the best idea the Army had was the Self-Denial Appeal.

It grew out of the desire of one early-day officer to give up some of his food and offer the money saved to help the Army's work among people who were poorer. From that simple idea grew the International Self-Denial Fund (ISDF) which still today is the backbone of all our international financing.

Schemes

The appeal itself has other names in different countries, such as World Services, but the central idea remains the same. Around it has grown much more international funding and movement of funds. There are project funds from money given by Salvationists and external donors. Many of the larger projects are for community development, including micro-finance schemes and self-help groups that become even more vital in the present economic climate.

However, holding the international Army united financially is the ISDF. Grants from the fund provide the infrastructure that enables both the central mission and the innovative projects to be effective in so many countries.

This becomes even more crucial in a global economic downturn,

especially because reserves have been built up specifically to fulfil a levelling role for the grants paid out.

All Salvationists in every country are given the opportunity to give to this fund. The giving is the most sacrificial in some of those countries where the absolute figures raised are the smallest. Giving to the fund enables contributors to be part of a spiritual exercise that is more than merely giving to charity.

At its best the act of giving is a gift to God that does not seek recognition or credit but is, in the phrase of theologian and social activist Charles Ringma, 'the generosity of forgetfulness'. Again, at its best, the receipt of money from the ISDF in those countries where there is the most need speaks of 'remembered generosity – a celebration of the acts of kindness of others'.

This generosity is celebrated by the continuation of The Salvation Army's global mission.

Commissioner Woodall is International Secretary for Business Administration, IHQ

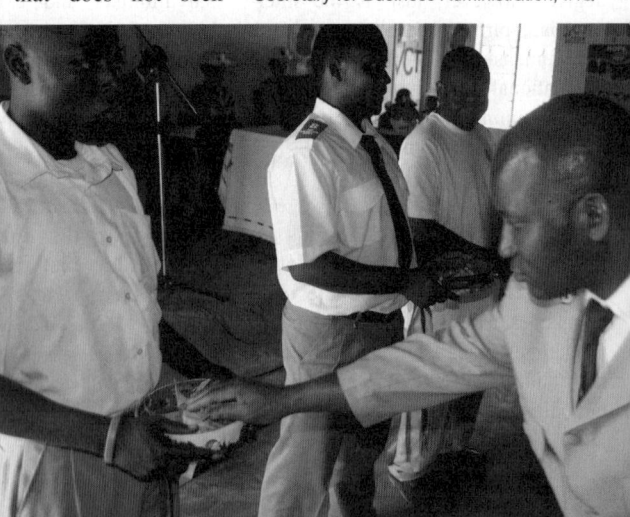

Top: Joyful Salvationists in Zambia prepare for their territory's Self-Denial Appeal ingathering

Right: A Self-Denial Appeal altar service at a corps in Malawi

WHAT IS THE SALVATION ARMY?

RAISED up by God, The Salvation Army is a worldwide evangelical Christian church with its own distinctive governance and practice. The Army's doctrine follows the mainstream of Christian belief and its articles of faith emphasise God's saving purposes.

Its religious and charitable objects are 'the advancement of the Christian religion ... and, pursuant thereto, the advancement of education, the relief of poverty, and other charitable objects beneficial to society or the community of mankind as a whole'.*

The Army (then known as The Christian Mission) was founded in London, England, in 1865 by William and Catherine Booth and has spread to many parts of the world.

The rapid deployment of the first Salvationists was aided by the adoption of a quasi-military command structure in 1878 when the title 'The Salvation Army' was brought into use. A similarly practical organisation today enables resources to be equally flexible.

Responding to a recurrent theme in Christianity which sees the Church engaged in spiritual warfare, The Salvation Army has used to advantage certain soldierly features such as uniforms, flags and ranks to identify, inspire and regulate its endeavours.

Evangelistic and social enterprises are maintained, under the authority of the General, by full-time officers and employees, as well as soldiers who give service in their free time. The Army also benefits from the support of many adherents and friends, including those who serve on advisory boards.

Leadership in The Salvation Army is provided by commissioned and ordained officers who are recognised as fully accredited ministers of religion.

Salvationists commit to a disciplined life of Christian moral standards, compassion toward others, and witnessing for Christ.

From its earliest days The Salvation Army has accorded women equal opportunities, every rank and service being open to them, and from childhood the young are encouraged to love and serve God.

Raised to evangelise, The Salvation Army spontaneously embarked on schemes for the social betterment of the poor. Such concerns develop, wherever the Army operates, in practical, skilled and cost-effective ways. Evolving social services meet endemic needs and specific crises worldwide. Highly trained staff are employed in up-to-date facilities.

The need for modernisation and longer-term development is under continual review. Increasingly The Salvation Army's policy and its indigenous membership allow it to cooperate with international relief agencies and governments alike.

The Army's partnership with both private and public philanthropy will continue to bring comfort to the needy, while the proclamation of God's redemptive love revealed in Jesus Christ offers individuals and communities the opportunity to know spiritual fulfilment here on earth and a place in Christ's eternal Kingdom.

*Section 3 of the Salvation Army Act 1980

THE DOCTRINES OF THE SALVATION ARMY

We believe that the Scriptures of the Old and New Testaments were given by inspiration of God, and that they only constitute the Divine rule of Christian faith and practice.

We believe that there is only one God, who is infinitely perfect, the Creator, Preserver and Governor of all things, and who is the only proper object of religious worship.

We believe that there are three persons in the Godhead – the Father, the Son and the Holy Ghost, undivided in essence and co-equal in power and glory.

We believe that in the person of Jesus Christ the Divine and human natures are united, so that he is truly and properly God and truly and properly man.

We believe that our first parents were created in a state of innocency, but by their disobedience they lost their purity and happiness, and that in consequence of their fall all men have become sinners, totally depraved, and as such are justly exposed to the wrath of God.

We believe that the Lord Jesus Christ has by his suffering and death made an atonement for the whole world so that whosoever will may be saved.

We believe that repentance towards God, faith in our Lord Jesus Christ, and regeneration by the Holy Spirit, are necessary to salvation.

We believe that we are justified by grace through faith in our Lord Jesus Christ and that he that believeth hath the witness in himself.

We believe that continuance in a state of salvation depends upon continued obedient faith in Christ.

We believe that it is the privilege of all believers to be wholly sanctified, and that their whole spirit and soul and body may be preserved blameless unto the coming of our Lord Jesus Christ.

We believe in the immortality of the soul; in the resurrection of the body; in the general judgment at the end of the world; in the eternal happiness of the righteous; and in the endless punishment of the wicked.

FOUNDERS OF THE SALVATION ARMY

William Booth

The Founder of The Salvation Army and its first General was born in Nottingham on 10 April 1829 and promoted to Glory from Hadley Wood on 20 August 1912. He lived to establish Salvation Army work in 58 countries and colonies and travelled extensively, holding salvation meetings. In his later years he was received in audience by emperors, kings and presidents. Among his many books, *In Darkest England and the Way Out* was the most notable; it became the blueprint of all The Salvation Army's social schemes. It was reprinted in 1970.

Catherine Booth

The Army Mother was born in Ashbourne, Derbyshire, on 17 January 1829 and promoted to Glory from Clacton-on-Sea on 4 October 1890. As Catherine Mumford, she married William in 1855. A great teacher and preacher, she addressed large public meetings in Britain with far-reaching results, despite ill health. Her writings include *Female Ministry* and *Aggressive Christianity*.

William Bramwell Booth

The eldest son of the Founder, and his Chief of the Staff from 1880 to 1912, Bramwell (as he was known) was born on 8 March 1856. He was largely responsible for the development of The Salvation Army. His teaching of the doctrine of holiness and his councils with officers and young people were of incalculable value. In 1882 he married Captain Florence Soper (organiser of the Women's Social Work and inaugurator of the Home League), who was promoted to Glory on 10 June 1957. During his time as General (1912-1929), impetus was given to missionary work. Published books include *Echoes and Memories* and *These Fifty Years*. He was appointed a Companion of Honour shortly before his promotion to Glory from Hadley Wood on 16 June 1929.

GLOSSARY OF SALVATION ARMY TERMS

Adherent: A member of The Salvation Army who has not made a commitment to soldiership.

Advisory Board: A group of influential citizens who, believing in the Army's programme of spiritual, moral and physical rehabilitation and amelioration, assist in promoting and supporting Army projects.

'Blood and Fire': The Army's motto; refers to the blood of Jesus Christ and the fire of the Holy Spirit.

Cadet: A Salvationist who is in training for officership.

Candidate: A soldier who has been accepted for officer training.

Chief of the Staff: The officer second in command of the Army throughout the world.

Chief Secretary: The officer second in command of the Army in a territory.

Citadel: A hall used for worship.

Colours: The tricolour flag of the Army. Its colours symbolise the blood of Jesus Christ (red), the fire of the Holy Spirit (yellow) and the purity of God (blue).

Command: A smaller type of territory, directed by an officer commanding.

Command leaders: An officer commanding and spouse in their joint role of sharing spiritual leadership and ministry, providing pastoral care and exemplifying the working partnership of officer couples.

Commission: A document conferring authority upon an officer, or upon an unpaid local officer, eg, secretary, treasurer, bandmaster, etc.

Congress: Central gatherings often held annually and attended by most officers and many soldiers of a territory, command, region or division.

Corps: A Salvation Army unit established for the preaching of the gospel and to provide Christian-motivated service in the community.

Corps Cadet: A young Salvationist who undertakes a course of study and practical training in a corps, with a view to becoming efficient in Salvation Army service.

Corps Sergeant-Major: The chief local officer for public work who assists the corps officer with meetings and usually takes command in his/her absence.

Dedication Service: The public presentation of infants to the Lord. This differs from christening or infant baptism in that the main emphasis is upon specific vows made by the parents concerning the child's upbringing.

Division: A number of corps grouped together under the direction of a divisional commander (may also include social service centres and programmes), operating within a territory or command.

Divisional Commander: The officer in charge of the Army in a division.

Envoy: A Salvationist whose duty it is to visit corps, societies and outposts, for the purpose of conducting meetings. An envoy may be appointed in charge of any such unit.

General: The officer elected to the supreme command of the Army throughout the world. All appointments are made, and all regulations issued, under the General's authority (see under High Council – p 22).

General Secretary: The officer second in charge of the Army in a command (or, in some territories, a large division).

Halfway House: A centre for the rehabilitation of alcoholics or parolees (USA).

Harbour Light Centre: A reclamation centre, usually located in inner city areas.

High Council: See p 22

Home League: See p 34

International Headquarters (IHQ): The offices in which the business connected with the command of the worldwide Army is transacted.

International Secretary: A position at IHQ with responsibility for the oversight and coordination of the work in a specific

Salvation Army Terms

geographical zone or functional category, and for advising the General on zonal and worldwide issues and policies.

Junior Soldier: A boy or girl who, having accepted Jesus as their saviour, has signed the junior soldier's promise and become a Salvationist.

League of Mercy: Salvationists who visit prisons, hospitals and needy homes, in their own time, bringing the gospel and rendering practical aid (see p 35).

Local Officer: A soldier appointed to a position of responsibility and authority in the corps; carries out the duties of the appointment without being separated from regular employment or receiving remuneration from the Army.

Medical Fellowship: See p 35

Mercy Seat or Penitent Form: A bench provided as a place where people can kneel to pray, seeking salvation or sanctification, or making a special consecration to God's will and service. The mercy seat is usually situated between the platform and main area of Army halls as a focal point to remind all of God's reconciling and redeeming presence.

Officer: A Salvationist who has left secular concerns at God's call and has been trained, commissioned and ordained to service and leadership. An officer is a recognised minister of religion.

Officer Commanding: The officer in charge of the Army in a command.

Order of Distinguished Auxiliary Service: See p 37

Order of the Founder: See p 36

Outpost: A locality in which Army work is carried out and where it is hoped a society or corps will develop.

Pastoral Care Council: Established in each corps for the care of soldiers, etc, and maintenance of the membership rolls. Previously called the census board.

Promotion to Glory: The Army's description of the death of Salvationists.

Ranks of Officers: Lieutenant, captain, major, lieut-colonel, colonel, commissioner, General.

Red Shield: A symbol identifying a wide range of Army social and emergency services.

Red Shield Appeal: A financial appeal to the general public; also known as the Annual Appeal in some countries.

Red Shield Centre: A club for military personnel.

Salvation: The work of grace which God accomplishes in a repentant person whose trust is in Christ as Saviour, forgiving sin, giving meaning and new direction to life, and strength to live as God desires. The deeper experience of this grace, known as holiness or sanctification, is the outcome of wholehearted commitment to God and enables the living of a Christlike life.

Self-Denial Appeal: An annual effort by Salvationists and friends to raise funds for the Army's worldwide operations.

Sergeant: A local officer appointed for specific duty, usually in a corps.

Society: A company of soldiers who work together regularly in a district, without an officer, but with the approval of the divisional commander.

Soldier: A converted person at least 14 years of age who has, with the approval of the pastoral care council, been enrolled as a member of The Salvation Army after signing the Soldier's Covenant.

Soldier's Covenant: The statement of beliefs and promises which every intending soldier is required to sign before enrolment. Previously called 'Articles of War'.

Territorial Commander: The officer in command of the Army in a territory.

Territorial leaders: A territorial commander and spouse in their joint role of sharing spiritual leadership and ministry, providing pastoral care and exemplifying the working partnership of officer couples. The chief secretary is the second-in-command of the territory.

Territory: A country, part of a country or several countries combined, in which Salvation Army work is organised under a territorial commander.

Young People's Sergeant-Major: A local officer responsible for young people's work in a corps, under the commanding officer.

Chronological Table of Important Events in Salvation Army History

1829 Catherine Mumford (later Mrs Booth, 'the Army Mother') born at Ashbourne, Derbyshire (17 Jan); William Booth born at Nottingham (10 Apr).

1844 William Booth converted.

1846 Catherine Mumford converted.

1855 Marriage of William Booth and Catherine Mumford at Stockwell New Chapel, London (16 Jun).

1856 William Bramwell Booth (the Founder's eldest son and second General of the Army) born in Halifax (8 Mar).

1858 William Booth ordained as Methodist minister (27 May). (Accepted on probation 1854.)

1859 *Female Teaching*, Mrs Booth's first pamphlet, published (Dec).

1860 Mrs Booth's first public address (27 May, Whit Sunday).

1865 **Rev William Booth began work in East London** (2 Jul); The Christian Mission, founded; Eveline (Evangeline) Cory Booth (fourth General) born in London (25 Dec).

1867 First Headquarters (Eastern Star) opened in Whitechapel Road, London.

1868 *The East London Evangelist* – later (1870) *The Christian Mission Magazine* and (1879) *The Salvationist* – published (Oct).

1874 Christian Mission work commenced in **Wales** (15 Nov).

1875 *Rules and Doctrines of The Christian Mission* published.

1876 *Revival Music* published (Jan).

1878 First use of the term 'Salvation Army' – in small appeal folder (May); 'The Christian Mission' became **'The Salvation Army'**, and the Rev William Booth became known as the General; deed poll executed, thus establishing the doctrines and principles of The Salvation Army (Aug); first corps flag presented by Mrs Booth at Coventry (28-30 Sep); *Orders and Regulations for The Salvation Army* issued (Oct); brass instruments first used.

1879 First corps in **Scotland** opened (24 Mar) and **Channel Islands** (14 Aug); cadets first trained; introduction of uniform; first corps band formed in Consett; issue No 1 of *The War Cry* published (27 Dec).

1880 First training home opened, at Hackney, London; first contingent of SA officers landed in the **United States of America** (10 Mar); SA work commenced in **Ireland** (7 May); children's meetings commenced at Blyth (30 Jul); SA work extended to **Australia** (5 Sep).

1881 Work begun in **France** (13 Mar); *The Little Soldier* (subsequently *The Young Soldier*) issued (27 Aug); *The Doctrines and Disciplines of The Salvation Army* prepared for use at training homes for Salvation Army officers; Headquarters removed to Queen Victoria Street, London (8 Sep).

1882 The Founder's first visit to France (Mar); former London Orphan Asylum opened as Clapton Congress Hall and National Training Barracks (13 May); work begun in **Canada** (21 May), **India** (19 Sep), **Switzerland** (22 Dec) and **Sweden** (28 Dec).

1883 Work begun in **Sri Lanka** (26 Jan), **South Africa** (4 Mar), **New Zealand** (1 Apr), **Isle of Man** (17 Jun) and **Pakistan** (then a part of India); first prison-gate home opened in Melbourne, Australia (8 Dec); *The Doctrines and Disciplines of The Salvation Army* published in a public edition.

1884 Women's Social Work inaugurated; *The Soldier's Guide* published (Apr); work begun in **St Helena** (5 May); *The Salvation Army Band Journal* issued (Aug); *All the World* issued (Nov).

1885 Commencement of the Family Tracing Service, known as Mrs Booth's Enquiry Bureau; *Orders and Regulations for Divisional Officers* published (10 Jun); *The Doctrines of The Salvation Army* published; Purity Agitation launched; Criminal Law Amendment Act became law on 14 Aug; trial (began 23 Oct) and acquittal of Bramwell Booth – charged, with W. T. Stead, in connection with the 'Maiden Tribute' campaign.

1886 Work begun in **Newfoundland** (1 Feb);

Salvation Army History

first International Congress in London (28 May-4 Jun); *The Musical Salvationist* issued (Jul); first Self-Denial Week (4-11 Sep); first slum corps opened at Walworth, London, by 'Mother' Webb (20 Sep); work begun in **Germany** (14 Nov); *Orders and Regulations for Field Officers* published; the Founder first visited the United States and Canada.

1887 Work began in **Italy** (20 Feb), **Denmark** (8 May), **Netherlands** (8 May) and **Jamaica** (16 Dec); the Founder's first visit to Denmark, Sweden and Norway.

1888 Young people's work organised throughout Great Britain; first food depot opened, in Limehouse, London (Jan); work begun in **Norway** (22 Jan); first junior soldiers' brass band (Clapton); the Army Mother's last public address at City Temple, London (21 Jun).

1889 Work begun in **Belgium** (5 May) and **Finland** (8 Nov); *The Deliverer* published (Jul).

1890 Work begun in **Argentina** (1 Jan); *Orders and Regulations for Soldiers of The Salvation Army* issued (Aug); the Army Mother promoted to Glory (4 Oct); *In Darkest England and the Way Out*, by the Founder, published (Oct); work begun in **Uruguay** (16 Nov); banking department opened (registered as The Salvation Army Bank, 1891; Reliance Bank Ltd, 28 Dec 1900).

1891 The Founder publicly signed 'Darkest England' (now The Salvation Army Social Work) Trust Deed (30 Jan); £108,000 subscribed for 'Darkest England' scheme (Feb); Land and Industrial Colony, Hadleigh, Essex, established (2 May); International Staff Band inaugurated (Oct); work begun in **Zimbabwe** (21 Nov) and **Zululand** (22 Nov); the Founder's first visit to South Africa, Australia, New Zealand and India; the charter of The Methodist and General Assurance Society acquired.

1892 Eastbourne (UK) verdict against Salvationists quashed in the High Court of Justice (27 Jan); Band of Love inaugurated; League of Mercy begun in Canada (Dec).

1893 Grace-Before-Meat scheme instituted; *The Officer* issued (Jan).

1894 Second International Congress (Jul); work begun in **Hawaiian Islands** (13 Sep) and **Java** (now part of **Indonesia**) (24 Nov); naval and military league (later red shield services) established (Nov); Swiss Supreme Court granted religious rights to SA (Dec).

1895 Work begun in **British Guiana** (now **Guyana**) (24 Apr), **Iceland** (12 May), **Japan** (4 Sep) and **Gibraltar** (until 1968).

1896 Young people's legion (Jan) and corps cadet brigades (Feb) inaugurated; work begun in **Bermuda** (12 Jan) and **Malta** (25 Jul until 1972); first SA exhibition, Agricultural Hall, London (Aug).

1897 First united young people's meetings (later termed 'councils') (14 Mar); first International Social Council in London (Sep); first SA hospital founded at Nagercoil, India (Dec).

1898 *Orders and Regulations for Social Officers* published; work begun in **Barbados** (30 Apr) and **Alaska**; first united corps cadet camp at Hadleigh (Whitsun).

1899 First bandsmen's councils, Clapton (10 Dec).

1901 Work begun in **Trinidad** (7 Aug).

1902 Work begun in **St Lucia** (Sep) and **Grenada**.

1903 Migration Department inaugurated (became Reliance World Travel Ltd, 1981; closed 31 May 2001); work begun in **Antigua**.

1904 Third International Congress (Jun-Jul); Founder received by King Edward VII at Buckingham Palace (24 Jun); Founder's first motor campaign (Aug); work begun in **Panama** (Dec).

1905 The Founder campaigned in the Holy Land, Australia and New Zealand (Mar-Jun); first emigrant ship chartered by SA sailed for Canada (26 Apr); opening of International Staff Lodge (later College, now International College for Officers) (11 May); work begun in **St Vincent** (Aug). Freedom of London conferred on the Founder (26 Oct); Freedom of Nottingham conferred on the Founder (6 Nov).

1906 *The YP* (later *The Warrior*, then *Vanguard*) and *The Salvation Army Year Book* issued; Freedom of Kirkcaldy conferred on the Founder (16 Apr).

1907 Anti-Suicide Bureau established (Jan); Home League inaugurated (28 Jan); *The Bandsman and Songster* (later *The*

Salvation Army History

Musician) issued (6 Apr); honorary degree of DCL, Oxford, conferred on the Founder (26 Jun); work begun in **Costa Rica** (5 Jul).
1908 Work begun in **Korea** (Oct).
1909 Leprosy work commenced in **Java** (now part of **Indonesia**) (15 Jan); SA work begun in **Chile** (Oct).
1910 Work begun in **Peru**, **Paraguay** and **Sumatra** (now part of **Indonesia**).
1912 Founder's last public appearance, in Royal Albert Hall, London (9 May); **General William Booth promoted to Glory** (20 Aug); **William Bramwell Booth appointed General** (21 Aug).
1913 Inauguration of life-saving scouts (21 Jul); work begun in **Celebes** (now part of **Indonesia**) (15 Sep) and **Russia** (until 1923).
1914 Fourth International Congress (Jun).
1915 Work begun in **British Honduras** (now **Belize**) (Jun) and **Burma** (now **Myanmar**); life-saving guards inaugurated (17 Nov).
1916 Work begun in **China** (Jan until 1951), in **St Kitts** and in **Portuguese East Africa** (now **Mozambique**) (officially recognised 1923).
1917 Work begun in **Virgin Islands** (USA) (Apr); chums inaugurated (23 Jun); Order of the Founder instituted (20 Aug).
1918 Work commenced in **Cuba** (Jul).
1919 Work begun in **Czechoslovakia** (19 Sep until 1950).
1920 Work begun in **Nigeria** (15 Nov) and **Bolivia** (Dec).
1921 Work begun in **Kenya** (Apr); sunbeams inaugurated (3 Nov).
1922 Work begun in **Zambia** (1 Feb), **Brazil** (1 Aug) and **Ghana** (Aug); publication of a second *Handbook of Salvation Army Doctrine*.
1923 Work begun in **Latvia** (until 1939).
1924 Work begun in **Hungary** (24 Apr until 1950), in **Surinam** (10 Oct) and **The Færoes** (23 Oct).
1927 Work begun in **Austria** (27 May), **Estonia** (31 Dec until 1940) and **Curacao** (until 1980); first International Young People's Staff Councils (May-Jun).
1928 General Bramwell Booth's last public appearance – the stonelaying of the International (William Booth Memorial) Training College (now William Booth College), Denmark Hill, London (10 May).
1929 First High Council (8 Jan-13 Feb); **Comr Edward J. Higgins elected General**; General Bramwell Booth promoted to Glory (16 Jun); Army work begun in **Colombia** (until 1965).
1930 Inception of goodwill league; Order of the Silver Star (now Fellowship of the Silver Star) inaugurated (in USA, extended to other lands in 1936); work begun in **Hong Kong**; Commissioners' Conference held in London (Nov).
1931 Work begun in **Uganda** and the **Bahamas** (May); The Salvation Army Act 1931 received royal assent (Jul).
1932 Work begun in **Namibia** (until 1939).
1933 Work begun in **Yugoslavia** (15 Feb until 1948), Devil's Island, **French Guiana** (1 Aug until closing of the penal settlement in 1952) and **Tanzania** (29 Oct).
1934 Work begun in **Algeria** (10 Jun until 1970); second High Council elected Commander Evangeline Booth General (3 Sep); work begun in **Congo (Kinshasa)** (14 Oct); **General Evangeline Booth took command of The Salvation Army** (11 Nov).
1935 Work begun in **Singapore** (28 May).
1936 Work begun in **Egypt** (until 1949).
1937 Work begun in **Congo (Brazzaville)** (Mar), **The Philippines** (6 Jun) and **Mexico** (Oct).
1938 Torchbearer group movement inaugurated (Jan); *All the World* re-issued (Jan); work spread from Singapore to **Malaysia**.
1939 Third High Council elected Comr George Lyndon Carpenter General (24 Aug); **General George Lyndon Carpenter took command of The Salvation Army** (1 Nov).
1941 Order of Distinguished Auxiliary Service instituted (24 Feb); International Headquarters destroyed in London Blitz (10 May).
1943 Inauguration of The Salvation Army Medical Fellowship (16 Feb) (SA Nurses' Fellowship until 1987).
1944 Service of thanksgiving to mark centenary of conversion of William Booth (in 1844) held in St Paul's Cathedral, London (2 Jun).
1946 Fourth High Council elected Comr Albert Orsborn General (9 May); **General Albert Orsborn took command of The Salvation Army** (21 Jun).
1948 First Army worldwide broadcast (28 Apr).

Salvation Army History

1950 Work begun in **Haiti** (5 Feb); first TV broadcast by a General of The Salvation Army; official constitution of students' fellowship; first International Youth Congress held in London (10-23 Aug); reopening of Staff College (later International College for Officers) (10 Oct).

1954 Fifth High Council elected Comr Wilfred Kitching General (11 May); **General Wilfred Kitching took command of The Salvation Army** (1 Jul).

1956 Work begun in Port Moresby, **Papua New Guinea** (31 Aug); first International Corps Cadet Congress (19-31 Jul).

1959 Over-60 clubs inaugurated (Oct).

1962 Work begun in **Puerto Rico** (Feb).

1963 Sixth High Council elected Comr Frederick Coutts General (1 Oct); Queen Elizabeth the Queen Mother declared International Headquarters open (13 Nov); **General Frederick Coutts took command of The Salvation Army** (23 Nov).

1965 Queen Elizabeth II attended the International Centenary commencement (24 Jun); Founders' Day Service held in Westminster Abbey, London (2 Jul); work re-established in **Taiwan** (pioneered 1928) (Oct).

1967 Work begun in **Malawi** (13 Nov).

1969 Seventh High Council elected Comr Erik Wickberg General (23 Jul); *The Salvation Army Handbook of Doctrine* new edition published (Aug); **General Erik Wickberg took command of The Salvation Army** (21 Sep); work begun in **Lesotho.**

1970 Cyclone relief operations in East Pakistan (later **Bangladesh**) (25 Nov) lead to start of work in 1971.

1971 Work begun in **Spain** (23 Jul) and **Portugal** (25 Jul).

1972 Work begun in **Venezuela** (30 Jun).

1973 Work begun in **Fiji** (14 Nov).

1974 Eighth High Council elected Comr Clarence Wiseman General (13 May); **General Clarence Wiseman took com-mand of The Salvation Army** (6 Jul).

1976 Work begun in **Guatemala** (Jun); **Mexico and Central America Territory** (now **Latin America North Territory** and **Mexico Territory**) formed (1 Oct).

1977 Ninth High Council elected Comr Arnold Brown General (5 May); **General Arnold Brown took command of The Salvation Army** (5 Jul).

1978 Fifth International Congress (Jun-Jul), with opening ceremony attended by HRH the Prince of Wales.

1979 The Salvation Army Boys' Adventure Corps (SABAC) launched (21 Jan).

1980 Inauguration of International Staff Songsters (8 Mar); The Salvation Army Act 1980 received royal assent (1 Aug); work begun in **French Guiana** (1 Oct).

1981 Tenth High Council elected Comr Jarl Wahlström General (23 Oct); **General Jarl Wahlström took command of The Salvation Army** (14 Dec).

1984 International Conference of Leaders held in Berlin, West Germany (May).

1985 Work begun in **Colombia** (21 Apr) and **Marshall Islands** (1 Jun); second International Youth Congress (Jul) held in Macomb, Illinois, USA; work begun in **Angola** (4 Oct) and **Ecuador** (30 Oct).

1986 Work begun in **Tonga** (9 Jan); *Salvationist* first issued (15 Mar); 11th High Council elected Comr Eva Burrows General (2 May); **General Eva Burrows took command of The Salvation Army** (9 Jul); International Development Conference held at Sunbury Court, London (Sep).

1988 Work begun in **Liberia** (1 May); International Conference of Leaders held in Lake Arrowhead, California, USA (Sep).

1989 Work begun in **El Salvador** (1 Apr).

1990 Work begun in **East Germany** (Mar), **Czechoslovakia** (May), **Hungary** (Jun) and re-established in **Latvia** (Nov); sixth International Congress held in London (Jun-Jul); **United Kingdom Territory** established (1 Nov).

1991 Restructuring of **International Headquarters** as an entity separate from UK Territory (1 Feb); work reopened in **Russia** (6 Jul); International Conference of Leaders held in London (Jul-Aug).

1992 Opening of new **USA National Headquarters** building in Alexandria, Virginia (3 May).

1993 The 12th High Council elected Comr Bramwell H. Tillsley General (28 Apr); **General Bramwell H. Tillsley took command of The Salvation Army** (9 Jul); work begun in **Micronesia**.

1994 First International Literary and Publications Conference held at Alexandria,

Salvation Army History

Virginia, USA (Apr); General Bramwell H. Tillsley resigned from office (18 May); 13th High Council elected Comr Paul A. Rader General (23 Jul); **General Paul A. Rader took command of The Salvation Army immediately**; work begun in **Guam**.

1995 International Conference of Leaders held in Hong Kong (Apr); all married women officers granted rank in their own right (1 May); work begun in **Dominican Republic** (1 Jul); work reopened in **Estonia** (14 Aug); following relief and development programmes, work begun in **Rwanda** (5 Nov).

1996 Work begun in **Sabah (East Malaysia)** (Mar); first meeting of International Spiritual Life Commission (Jul).

1997 International Youth Forum held in Cape Town, South Africa (Jan); first-ever congress held in Russia/CIS; Salvation Army leaders in Southern Africa signed commitment to reconciliation for past stand on apartheid; work begun in **Botswana** (20 Nov).

1998 International Conference of Leaders held in Melbourne, Australia (Mar), receives report of International Spiritual Life Commission; publication of a fourth Handbook of Doctrine entitled *Salvation Story* (Mar); International Commission on Officership opened in London (Oct).

1999 International Education Symposium held in London (Mar); work begun in **Romania** (May); 14th High Council elected Comr John Gowans General (15 May); **General John Gowans took command of The Salvation Army** (23 Jul).

2000 International Commission on Officership closed and subsequent Officership Survey carried out (Mar-May); work begun in **Macau** (25 Mar); The Salvation Army registered as a denomination in **Sweden** (10 Mar); International Conference of Leaders held in Atlanta, Georgia, USA (Jun); seventh International Congress held in Atlanta, Georgia, USA (28 Jun-2 Jul) (first held outside UK); work begun in **Honduras** (23 Nov).

2001 International Conference for Training Principals held in London (Mar); International Theology and Ethics Symposium held in Winnipeg, Canada (Jun); International Music Ministries Forum held in London (Jul); International Poverty Summit held on the Internet and Lotus Notes Intranet (Nov 2001-Feb 2002).

2002 The 15th High Council elected Comr John Larsson General (6 Sep); **General John Larsson took command of The Salvation Army** (13 Nov).

2004 International Conference of Leaders held in New Jersey, USA (29 Apr-7 May); International Music and Other Creative Ministries Forum (MOSAIC) held in Toronto, Canada (Jun); New International Headquarters building at 101 Queen Victoria Street, London, opened by Her Royal Highness, The Princess Royal (9 Nov); IHQ Emergency Services coordinates disaster relief work after Indian Ocean tsunami struck (26 Dec).

2005 Eastern Europe Command redesignated Eastern Europe Territory; Singapore, Malaysia and Myanmar Command redesignated Singapore, Malaysia and Myanmar Territory (both 1 Mar); International Literary and Publications Conference held at Alexandria, Virginia, USA (Apr); European Youth Congress held in Prague, Czech Republic (4-8 Aug); All-Africa Congress held in Harare, Zimbabwe (24-28 Aug); work in **Lithuania** officially recognised by IHQ, and Germany Territory redesignated Germany and Lithuania Territory (Sep); 'Project Warsaw' launched to begin Army's work in **Poland** (23-25 Sep); East Africa Territory redesignated Kenya Territory, with Uganda Region given command status (1 Nov)

2006 The 16th High Council elected Comr Shaw Clifton General (28 Jan); **General Shaw Clifton took command of The Salvation Army** (2 Apr); Salvation Army Scouts and Guides World Jamboree held in Almere, Netherlands (Aug); 2nd International Theology and Ethics Symposium held in Johannesburg, South Africa (Aug)

2007 Website for Office of the General launched (Feb); first of General's pastoral letters to soldiers dispatched electronically (15 Mar); first International Conference of Personnel Secretaries held in London (27 May-3 Jun); International Social Justice Commission established (1 Jul), headed by an International Director for Social

Justice; work begun in **Burundi** (5 Aug) and **Greece** (1 Oct)

2008 Work recommenced in **Namibia** (3 Jan); new opening begun in **Mali** (7 Feb); ICO renamed International College for Officers and Centre for Spiritual Life Development (Jul); first officers appointed to **Kuwait** (1 Aug); work begun in **Mongolia** (13 Oct); first International Women Leader Development Programme held at Sunbury Court, UK (18 Nov-6 Dec)

SIGNIFICANT EVENTS 2008-2009

2008

September
Hong Kong and Macau: Commissioning of the Hong Kong Staff Band (6 Sep)

Korea: Centenary Congress led by the General and Commissioner Helen Clifton (29 Sep-5 Oct)

October
SPEA Zone: The Army 'opened fire' in Mongolia (13 Oct), linked to Korea Territory

Australia Eastern: Chinese-speaking Salvationists in Australia held their first national congress in Sydney

November
IHQ: China Task Force met in Hong Kong under the leadership of the Chief of the Staff (6-7 Nov) to evaluate Salvation Army relief work and development services in mainland China

IHQ: First-ever International Women Leader Development Programme held at Sunbury Court, UK (18 Nov-6 Dec)

December
Pakistan: 125th anniversary celebrations led by the General and Commissioner Helen Clifton (1-3 Dec)

2009

January
IHQ: *Global Exchange*, IHQ's magazine for women in ministry and mission, relaunched with a fresh look and new title – *Revive*

IHQ: International College for Officers welcomed 200th session

April
Eastern Europe: Registration of the Moscow Branch of The Salvation Army in Russia completed (6 Apr) after a lengthy refusal to be granted legal status.

South Asia Zone: Salvation Army work expanded to 118 countries with the official opening in Nepal (15 Apr), linked to India Eastern Territory

IHQ: The General presided at first video conference call from the IHQ boardroom (23 Apr), held with Australia Eastern and Southern territorial leaders in Sydney and Melbourne

July
IHQ: Largest-ever assembly of Salvation Army leaders met in London, UK (7-13 July) for the International Conference of Leaders, presided over by the General

August
IHQ: The General attended the United Nations in New York, USA (4 Aug), for a meeting with Secretary-General Ban, Ki-moon (pictured)

UN Photo by Paulo Filgueiras

THE HIGH COUNCIL

THE High Council was originally established by William Booth in 1904 as a safeguard to allow the removal from office of an incumbent General who had become, for whatever reason, unfit to continue to exercise oversight, direction and control of The Salvation Army. Should such an allegation be made and receive significant support from officers of the rank of commissioner, a High Council would be called to decide upon the matter and to appoint a successor should the General be found unfit.

The Founder intended, however, that the normal method of appointment would be for the General in office to select his or her successor, but only one General – Bramwell Booth in 1912 – was ever selected in this way.

By November 1928, Bramwell Booth had been absent from International Headquarters for seven months on account of illness, and a High Council was called. The 63 members, being all the commissioners on active service and certain territorial commanders, gathered at Sunbury Court near London on 8 January 1929 and eventually voted that the General, then aged 73, was 'unfit on the ground of ill-health' to continue in office. On 13 February 1929 the High Council elected Commissioner Edward Higgins as the Army's third General.

Subsequently, a commissioners' conference agreed to three major constitutional reforms later passed into law by the British Parliament as the Salvation Army Act 1931, namely:

i. the abolition of the General's right to nominate his or her successor, and the substitution of the election of every General by a High Council;

ii. the fixing of an age limit for the retirement of the General;

iii. the creation of a trustee company to hold the properties and other capital assets of the Army, in place of the sole trusteeship of the General.

The High Council is currently constituted under provisions of the Salvation Army Act 1980 as amended by deeds of variation executed in 1995 and 2005.

Since 1929, High Councils have been held in 1934 (electing General Evangeline Booth), 1939 (General Carpenter), 1946 (General Orsborn), 1954 (General Kitching), 1963 (General Coutts), 1969 (General Wickberg), 1974 (General Wiseman), 1977 (General Brown), 1981 (General Wahlström), 1986 (General Burrows), 1993 (General Tillsley), 1994 (General Rader), 1999 (General Gowans), 2002 (General Larsson) and 2006 (General Clifton). The next is currently scheduled to convene in January 2011.

High Councils are normally called by the Chief of the Staff and have usually met at Sunbury Court but can meet anywhere in the United Kingdom. Since 1995 the High Council has been composed of all active commissioners except the spouse of the General, and all territorial commanders.

GENERALS ELECTED BY A HIGH COUNCIL

The place and date at the beginning of an entry denote the corps from which the General entered Salvation Army service and the year

Edward J. Higgins

Reading, UK, 1882. General (1929-34). b 26 Nov 1864; pG 14 Dec 1947. Served in corps and divisional work, British Territory; at the International Training Garrison, as CS, USA; as Asst Foreign Secretary, IHQ; Brit Comr (1911-19); Chief of the Staff (1919-29). CBE. Author of *Stewards of God*, *Personal Holiness*, etc. m Capt Catherine Price, 1888; pG 1952.

Evangeline Booth

General (1934-39). b 25 Dec 1865; pG 17 Jul 1950. Fourth daughter of the Founder, at 21 years of age she commanded Marylebone Corps, its Great Western Hall being the centre of spectacular evangelistic work. As Field Commissioner this experience was used to advantage throughout Great Britain (1888-91). The Founder appointed her to train cadets in London (1891-96); then as TC, Canada (1896-1904); Commander of The Salvation Army in the United States of America (1904-34). Author of *Toward a Better World*; *Songs of the Evangel*, etc.

George L. Carpenter

Raymond Terrace, Australia, 1892. General (1939-46). b 20 Jun 1872; pG 9 Apr 1948. Appointments included 18 years in Australia in property, training and literary work; at IHQ (1911-27) for most part with General Bramwell Booth as Literary Secretary; further service in Australia (1927-33), including CS, Australia Eastern; as TC, South America East (1933-37); TC, Canada (1937-39). Author of *Keep the Trumpets Sounding*; *Banners and Adventures*, etc. m Ens Minnie Rowell, 1899; pG 1960. Author of *Notable Officers of The Salvation Army*; *Women of the Flag*, etc.

Albert Orsborn

Clapton, UK, 1905. General (1946-54). b 4 Sep 1886; pG 4 Feb 1967. Served as corps officer and in divisional work in British Territory; as Chief Side Officer at ITC (1925-33); CS, New Zealand (1933-36); TC, Scotland & Ireland (1936-40); Brit Comr (1940-46). CBE, 1943. Writer of many well-known Army songs. Author of *The House of My Pilgrimage*, etc. m Capt Evalina Barker, 1909; pG 1942. m Maj Evelyn Berry, 1944; pG 1945. m Comr Mrs Phillis Taylor (née Higgins), 1947; pG 1986.

Wilfred Kitching

New Barnet, UK, 1914. General (1954-63). b 22 Aug 1893; pG 15 Dec 1977. Served in British Territory corps, divisional and NHQ appointments, then as CS, Australia Southern (1946-48); TC, Sweden (1948-51); Brit Comr (1951-54). Composer of many distinctively Salvationist musical works. Hon LLD (Yonsei, Seoul, Rep of Korea), 1961; CBE, 1964. Author of *Soldier of Salvation* (1963) and *A Goodly Heritage* (autobiography, 1967). m Adjt Kathleen Bristow (Penge, 1916), 1929; pG 1982.

Generals of The Salvation Army

Frederick Coutts

Batley, UK, 1920. General (1963-69). b 21 Sep 1899; pG 6 Feb 1986. Served in British Territory in divisional work (1921-25) and as corps officer (1925-35); for 18 years in Literary Dept, IHQ; writer of *International Company Orders* (1935-46); Editor of *The Officers' Review* (1947-53); Asst to Literary Secretary (1947-52); Literary Secretary (1952-53); Training Principal, ITC (1953-57); TC, Australia Eastern (1957-63). Author of *The Call to Holiness* (1957); *Essentials of Christian Experience* (1969); *The Better Fight* (1973); *No Discharge in this War* (1975), *Bread for My Neighbour* (1978); *The Splendour of Holiness* (1983), etc. Order of Cultural Merit (Rep of Korea), 1966; Hon Litt D (Chung Ang, Rep of Korea), 1966; CBE, 1967; Hon DD (Aberdeen), 1981. m Lt Bessie Lee, BSc, 1925; pG 1967. m Comr Olive Gatrall (Thornton Heath, 1925), 1970, pG 1997.

Erik Wickberg

Bern 2, Switzerland, 1925. General (1969-74). b 6 Jul 1904; pG 26 Apr 1996. Served as corps officer in Scotland; in Germany as Training (Education) Officer, and Private Secretary to CS and TC (1926-34); at IHQ as Private Secretary to IS and Asst to Under Secretary for Europe (1934-39); in Sweden as IHQ Liaison Officer (1939-46) and DC, Uppsala (1946-48); as CS, Switzerland, (1948-53); CS, Sweden (1953-57); TC, Germany (1957-61); Chief of the Staff (1961-69). Commander, Order of Vasa, 1970; Order of Moo Koong Wha (Rep of Korea), 1970; Hon LLD (Rep of Korea), 1970; Grand Cross of Merit, Fed Rep of Germany, 1971; King's Gold Medal (Grand Cross) (Sweden), 1980. Author of *Inkallad* (*God's Conscript*) (autobiography, Sweden, 1978) and *Uppdraget* (*The Charge – My Way to Preaching*) (1990). m Ens Frieda de Groot (Berne 1, Switz, 1922), 1929; pG 1930. m Capt Margarete Dietrich (Hamburg 3, Ger, 1928), 1932; pG 1976. m Major Eivor Lindberg (Norrköping 1, Swdn, 1946), 1977.

Clarence Wiseman

Guelph, Ont, Canada, 1927. General (1974-77). b 19 Jun 1907; pG 4 May 1985. Served in Canada as corps officer and in editorial work; chaplain with Canadian forces overseas (1940-43); Senior Representative, Canadian Red Shield Services Overseas (1943-45); back in Canada as divisional commander (1945-54), Field Secretary (1954-57) and CS (1957-60); as TC, East Africa (1960-62); Training Principal, ITC (1962-67); TC, Canada & Bermuda (1967-74). Order of Canada, 1976, Hon LLD, Hon DD (Yonsei, Seoul, Rep of Korea). Author of *A Burning in My Bones* (1980) and *The Desert Road to Glory* (1980). m Capt Jane Kelly (Danforth, Ont, Can, 1927), 1932; pG 1993. Author of *Earth's Common Clay*; *Bridging the Year*; *Watching Daily*.

Arnold Brown

Belleville, Canada, 1935. General (1977-81). b 13 Dec 1913; pG 26 Jun 2002. Served in Canada in corps, editorial, public relations and youth work (1935-64); as Secretary for Public Relations at IHQ (1964-69); Chief of the Staff (1969-74); TC, Canada & Bermuda (1974-77). MIPR, Hon LDH (Asbury, USA); Freeman, City of London; Hon DD (Olivet, USA), 1981; Officer, Order of Canada, 1981. Author of *What Hath God Wrought?*; *The Gate and the Light* (1984); *Yin – The Mountain the Wind Blew Here* (1988); *With Christ at the Table* (1991); *Occupied Manger – Unoccupied Tomb* (1994). m Lt Jean Barclay (Montreal Cit, Can, 1938), 1939. Author of *Excursions in Thought* (1981).

Generals of The Salvation Army

Jarl Wahlström

Helsinki 1, Finland, 1938. General (1981-86). b 9 Jul 1918. pG 3 Dec 1999. Served in corps, youth and divisional work in Finland; as Second World War chaplain to Finnish armed forces; in Finland as a divisional commander (1960-63), Training Principal, Secretary of Music Dept (1963-68) and CS (1968-72); as CS, Canada & Bermuda (1972-76); TC, Finland (1976-81); TC, Sweden (1981); Knight, Order of the Lion of Finland, 1964; Order of Civil Merit, Mugunghwa Medal (Rep of Korea), 1983; Hon DHL (W Illinois), 1985; Paul Harris Fellow of Rotary International, 1987; Commander, Order of the White Rose of Finland, 1989. Author of *A Traveller's Song* and *A Pilgrim's Song* (autobiography, Finnish/ Swedish, 1989). m Lt Maire Nyberg (Helsinki 1, 1944).

Eva Burrows

Fortitude Valley, Qld, Australia Eastern, 1951. General (1986-93). b 15 Sep 1929. Appointed to corps in British Territory, before post-graduate studies; served at Howard Institute, Zimbabwe (1952-67), Head of Teacher Training (1965), Vice-Principal (1965-67); as Principal, Usher Institute (1967-70); Asst Principal, ICO (1970-74), Principal (1974-75); Leader, WSS (GBI) (1975-77); TC, Sri Lanka (1977-79); TC, Scotland (1979-82); TC, Australia Southern (1982-86). BA (Qld); M Ed (Sydney); Hon Dr of Liberal Arts (Ehwa Univ, Seoul, Rep of Korea), 1988; Hon LLD (Asbury, USA), 1988; Paul Harris Fellow of Rotary International, 1990; Hon DST (Houghton), 1992; Hon DD (Olivet Nazarene Univ), 1993; Hon Dr Philosophy (Qld), 1993; Hon Dr of University (Griffith Univ), 1994; Companion of Order of Australia, 1994; Living Legacy Award from Women's International Center, USA, 1996.

Bramwell Tillsley

Kitchener, Ont, Canada, with wife née Maude Pitcher, 1956. General (1993-94). b 18 Aug 1931. Served in Canada in corps, youth, training college and divisional appointments, including Training Principal (1974-77), Provincial Commander in Newfoundland (1977-79) and DC, Metro Toronto (1979-81); as Training Principal, ITC (1981-85); CS, USA Southern (1985-89); TC, Australia Southern (1989-91); Chief of the Staff (1991-93). Resigned from the office of General in 1994. BA University of Western Ontario. Has written extensively for SA periodicals. Author of *Life in the Spirit*; *This Mind in You*; *Life More Abundant*; *Manpower for the Master*.

Paul Rader

Cincinnati Cit, USA Eastern, w wife née Frances Kay Fuller, BA (Asbury), Hon DD (Asbury Theol Seminary) 1995, Hon LHD (Greenville) 1997, 1961. General (1994-99). b 14 Mar 1934. Served in corps prior to transfer to Korea in 1962; in Korea in training work (1962-73), as Training Principal (1973), Education Secretary (1974-76), Asst Chief Secretary (1976-77) and CS (1977-84); in USA Eastern as Training Principal (1984-87), DC, Eastern Pennsylvania (1987-89) and CS (1989); as TC, USA Western (1989-94). BA, BD (Asbury); MTh (Southern Baptist Seminary); D Miss (Fuller Theological Seminary); Hon LLD (Asbury); 1984 elected to board of trustees of Asbury College; 1989 elected Paul Harris Fellow of Rotary International; Hon DD (Asbury Theol Seminary), 1995; Hon LHD (Greenville), 1997; Hon DD (Roberts Wesleyan), 1998.

Generals of The Salvation Army

John Gowans

Grangetown, UK, 1955. General (1999-2002). b 13 Nov 1934. Served in British Territory as corps officer, divisional youth secretary, National Stewardship Secretary and divisional commander; as Chief Secretary, France (1977-81); in USA Western as Programme Secretary (1981-85) and DC, Southern California (1985-86); TC, France (1986-93); TC, Australia Eastern & Papua New Guinea (1993-97); TC, UK (1997-99). Paul Harris Fellow of Rotary International; Hon DLitt (Yonsei, Seoul, Rep of Korea); Freedom of the City of London (2000). Songwriter. Author of *O Lord!* series of poetry books and *There's a Boy Here* (autobiography, 2002). Co-author with John Larsson of 10 musicals. m Lt Gisèle Bonhotal (Paris Central, France, 1955) 1957.

John Larsson

Upper Norwood, UK, 1957. General (2002-06). b 2 Apr 38. Served in corps; at ITC; as TYS (Scotland Territory); NYS (British Territory); CS, South America West (1980-84); Principal, ITC (1984-88); Assistant to Chief of the Staff for UK Administrative Planning, IHQ (1988-1990); TC, UK (1990-93); TC, New Zealand & Fiji (1993-96); TC, Sweden & Latvia (1996-99); Chief of the Staff (1999-2002). BD (London). Author of *Doctrine without Tears* (1964); *Spiritual Breakthrough* (1983); *The Man Perfectly Filled with the Spirit* (1986); *How Your Corps Can Grow* (1989), and *Saying Yes to Life* (autobiography, 2007). Composer of music and co-author with John Gowans of 10 musicals. m Capt Freda Turner (Kingston-upon-Thames, UK, 1964) 1969.

Shaw Clifton

Edmonton, UK, with wife née Helen Ashman, 1973. General (2006-present). b 21 Sep 45. Served as corps officer in British Territory; in Literary Department, IHQ (1974); in Zimbabwe as Vice Principal, Mazoe Secondary School (1975-77) and CO, Bulawayo Citadel (1977-79); in further BT corps appointments (1979-82, 1989-92); at IHQ as Legal & Parliamentary Secretary (1982-89); in UK as divisional commander (1992-95); in USA Eastern as DC, Massachusetts (1995-97); as TC, Pakistan (1997-2002); TC, New Zealand, Fiji & Tonga (2002-04); TC, UK (2004-06). LLB (Hons), AKC (Theol), BD (Theol) (Hons), PhD. Freedom of the City of London (2007). Author of *What Does the Salvationist Say?* (1977); *Growing Together* (1984); *Strong Doctrine, Strong Mercy* (1985); *Never the Same Again* (1997); *Who are these Salvationists?* (1999); *New Love – Thinking Aloud About Practical Holiness* (2004), etc.

COUNTRIES WHERE THE SALVATION ARMY IS AT WORK

THE Salvation Army is at work in 116 countries. A country in which the Army serves is defined in two ways:
  (i) Politically
  (ii) Where the General has given approval to the work, thus officially recognising it, ensuring it has legal identity and a Deed Poll is published to acknowledge this.

As far as political status is concerned, for the Army's purposes, three categories are recognised:
  (a) Independent countries, eg USA and New Zealand;
  (b) Internally independent political entities which are under the protection of another country in matters of defence and foreign affairs, eg The Færoes, Isle of Man, Puerto Rico;
  (c) Colonies and other dependent political units, eg Bermuda, French Guiana, Guernsey, Jersey.

Administrative subdivisions of a country such as Wales and Scotland in the UK are not recognised as separate countries for this purpose. The countries fulfilling the quoted criteria, with the date in brackets on which the work was officially recognised, are as follows:

Angola ....(1985)
Antigua ....(1903)
Argentina ....(1890)
Australia..............(1881)
Austria ....(1927)

Bahamas..............(1931)
Bangladesh..........(1971)
Barbados ....(1898)
Belgium ....(1889)
Belize ....(1915)
Bermuda..............(1896)
Bolivia ....(1920)
Botswana ....(1997)
Brazil ....(1922)
Burundi ....(2007)

Canada ....(1882)

Chile....................(1909)
China ....(1916)
Colombia ....(1985)
Congo, Republic of
  (Brazzaville) ....(1937)
Congo, Democratic
  Republic of (Kinshasa)
  ....(1934)
Costa Rica ....(1907)
Cuba....................(1918)
Czech Republic ..(1919)
  ....(reopened 1990)

Denmark ....(1887)
Dominican Republic
  ....(1995)

Ecuador ....(1985)

El Salvador ....(1989)
Estonia ....(1927)
  ....(reopened 1995)

Færoes, The ....(1924)
Fiji ....(1973)
Finland................(1889)
France ....(1881)
French Guiana ....(1980)

Georgia ....(1993)
Germany ....(1886)
Ghana..................(1922)
Greece ....(2007)
Grenada ....(1902)
Guam ....(1994)
Guatemala ....(1976)
Guernsey ....(1879)

27

Countries where The Salvation Army is at work

Guyana ....(1895)
Haiti ....(1950)
Honduras ....(2000)
Hong Kong ....(1930)
Hungary ....(1924)
............(reopened 1990)

Iceland ....(1895)
India ....(1882)
Indonesia ....(1894)
Ireland, Republic of
  (Eire) ....(1880)
Isle of Man..........(1883)
Italy ....(1887)

Jamaica ....(1887)
Japan ....(1895)
Jersey ....(1879)

Kenya..................(1921)
Korea ....(1908)
Kuwait ....(2008)

Latvia ....(1923)
............(reopened 1990)
Lesotho ....(1969)
Liberia ....(1988)
Lithuania ....(2005)

Macau ....(2000)
Malawi................(1967)
Malaysia..............(1938)
Mali ....(2008)
Marshall Islands..(1985)
Mexico ....(1937)
Micronesia ....(1993)
Moldova..............(1994)
Mongolia ....(2008)
Mozambique ......(1916)
Myanmar ....(1915)

Namibia ....(1932)
............(reopened 2008)
Nepal ....(2009)

Netherlands, The (1887)
New Zealand ......(1883)
Nigeria ....(1920)
Norway ....(1888)

Pakistan ....(1883)
Panama................(1904)
Papua New Guinea
............................(1956)
Paraguay ....(1910)
Peru ....(1910)
Philippines, The..(1937)
Poland ....(2005)
Portugal ....(1971)
Puerto Rico ....(1962)

Romania..............(1999)
Russia..................(1913)
............(reopened 1991)
Rwanda ....(1995)

St Christopher Nevis
  (St Kitts) ....(1916)
St Helena ....(1884)
St Lucia ....(1902)
St Maarten ....(1999)
St Vincent ....(1905)
Singapore ....(1935)
South Africa........(1883)
Spain ....(1971)
Sri Lanka ....(1883)
Suriname ....(1924)
Swaziland............(1960)
Sweden................(1882)
Switzerland ....(1882)

Taiwan ....(1965)
Tanzania..............(1933)
Tonga ....(1986)
Trinidad and Tobago
............................(1901)

Uganda................(1931)

Ukraine ....(1993)
United Kingdom (1865)
United States of
  America ....(1880)
Uruguay ....(1890)

Venezuela ....(1972)
Virgin Islands ....(1917)

Zambia................(1922)
Zimbabwe ....(1891)

Below: The General prays with Captain Lee, Min-ho and Captain Chang, Mi-hyun before they leave Seoul, Korea, to begin the Army's ministry in Mongolia (*see pages 164-165*)

INTERNATIONAL STATISTICS
(as at 1 January 2009)

Countries and territories where SA serves (at 30 September 2009, see pp 27-28) 118
Languages used in SA work, including some tribal languages....................175
Corps, outposts, societies, new plants and recovery churches....15,478
Goodwill centres................................261
Officers 26,128
    Active..16,938
    Retired..9,190
Auxiliary-captains...............................209
Envoys/sergeants, full-time 941
Cadets 1,126
Employees....................................104,977
Senior soldiers 1,122,326
Adherents.....................................189,176
Junior soldiers 378,009
Corps cadets...................................39,071
Senior band musicians...................25,377
Senior songsters............................94,090
Other senior musical group members.....................................83,498
Senior and young people's local officers 136,929
Women's Ministries (all groups) – members 599,904
League of Mercy – members......141,882
SAMF – members...........................5,618
Over-60 clubs – members 110,124
Men's fellowships – members......59,390
Young people's bands – members 12,239
Young people's singing companies – members..............80,940
Other young people's music groups – members.....................85,000
Sunday schools – members........413,431
Junior youth groups (scouts, guides, etc) and clubs – members 235,214
Senior youth groups – members....128,949
Corps-based community development programmes.............................17,347
Beneficiaries/clients 992,733
Thrift stores/charity shops (corps/territorial) 1,255
Recycling centres 46

Social Programme

Residential
Hostels for homeless and transient....441
    Capacity 26,355
Emergency lodges............................350
    Capacity 17,248
Children's homes 224
    Capacity 10,474
Homes for the elderly.......................118
    Capacity 6,110
Homes for the disabled 46
    Capacity 1,768
Homes for the blind 12
    Capacity 1,065
Remand and probation homes.............57
    Capacity 1,209
Homes for street children...................39
    Capacity 806
Mother and baby homes.....................48
    Capacity 1,077
Training centres for families 12
    Capacity 146
Care homes for vulnerable people 103
    Capacity 2,435
Women's and men's refuge centres 71
    Capacity 2,477
Other residential care homes/hostels 71
    Capacity 4,002

Day Care
Community centres...........................576
    Beneficiaries 213,520
Early childhood education centres....107
    Capacity 4,033

International Statistics

Day centres for the elderly 134
    Capacity 33,639
Play groups 179
    Beneficiaries 4,590
Day centres for the hearing
    impaired 53
    Capacity 1,756
Day centres for street children 12
    Capacity 715
Day nurseries 151
    Capacity 9,200
Drop-in centres for youth 68
    Beneficiaries 22,181
Other day care centres 441
    Beneficiaries 26,271

Addiction Dependency

Non-residential programmes 127
    Beneficiaries 5,109
Residential programmes 198
    Capacity 14,939
Harbour Light programmes 28
    Capacity 2,487
Other services for those with
    addictions 1,780
    Capacity 11,354

Service to the Armed Forces

Clubs and canteens 45
Mobile units for service personnel 35
Chaplains 38

Emergency Disaster Response

Disaster rehabilitation schemes 155
    Participants 20,889
Refugee programmes –
    host country 9
    Participants 7,170
Refugee rehabilitation programmes 39
    Participants 8,605
Other response programmes 193
    Participants 57,503

Services to the Community

Prisoners visited 325,629
Prisoners helped on discharge 190,861
Police courts – people helped 223,978
Missing persons – applications 9,797
    Number traced 3,544
Night patrol/anti-suicide –
    number helped 450,860
Community youth programmes 1,506
    Beneficiaries 276,875
Employment bureaux –
    applications 131,205
    initial referrals 213,915
Counselling – people helped 394,916
General relief – people
    helped 13,194,173
Emergency relief (fire, flood,
    etc) – people helped 2,583,708
Emergency mobile units 5,564
Feeding centres 967
Restaurants and cafes 33
Thrift stores/charity shops
    (social) 1,113
Apartments for elderly 883
    Capacity 12,514
Hostels for students, workers, etc 205
    Capacity 2,983
Land settlements (SA villages,
    farms etc) 5
    Capacity 523
Social Services summer camps 237
    Participants 19,989
Other services to the community
    (unspecified) 484
    Beneficiaries 8,404,709

Health Programme

General hospitals 29
    Capacity 2,588
Maternity hospitals 25
    Capacity 1,379
Other specialist hospitals 19
Capacity 1,051
Specialist clinics 56
    Capacity 105
General clinics/health centres 135
    Beneficiaries 8,678
Mobile clinics/community health
    posts 64
Inpatients 263
Outpatients 947,878
Doctors/medics 3,744
Invalid/convalescent homes 12

Capacity 1,090
Health education programmes
(HIV/Aids, etc) 648
Beneficiaries............................565,396
Day care programmes.........................31

Education Programme

Kindergarten/sub primary...................504
Primary schools 957
Upper primary and middle schools ..180
Secondary and high schools...............169
Colleges and universities 7

Vocational training schools/centres ...134
Pupils..513,639
Teachers 16,492
Schools for the blind (included in
above totals)....................................10
Schools for the disabled (included in
above totals)......................................7
Boarding schools (included in
above totals)....................................53
Colleges, universities, staff training
and development study and distance
learning centres................................14

SALVATION ARMY PERIODICALS
BY TERRITORY/COMMAND

International Headquarters: *All the World*, *Revive*, *The Officer*

Australia National: *Kidzone*, *Warcry*

Australia Eastern: *Creative Ministry*, *Pipeline*, *Venue*, *Women in Touch*

Australia Southern: *Kidzone*, *On Fire*, *Warcry*

Brazil: *O Oficial*, *Rumo* and *Ministério Feminino – Devocionais* (Women's Ministries magazines)

Canada and Bermuda: *Edge for Kids*, *Faith & Friends*, *Foi & Vie*, *Salvationist*

Caribbean: *The War Cry*

Congo (Brazzaville): *Le Salutiste*

Democratic Republic of Congo: *Echo d'Espoir*

Denmark: *Mennesker & Tro*, *Vision-Mission*

Eastern Europe: *Vestnik Spaseniya* (*The War Cry*), *The Officer* (both Russian)

Finland and Estonia: *Krigsropet* (Swedish), *Nappis*, *Sotahuuto* (both Finnish)

France and Belgium: *Avec Vous*, *Le Bulletin de la Ligue du Foyer*, *Le Fil*, *Le Magazine*, *L'Officier*, *Quand Même*

Germany and Lithuania: *Danke*, *Heilsarmee-Forum*, *Heilsarmee-Magazin*

Ghana: *Salvationist Newsletter*

Hong Kong and Macau: *Army Scene*, *The War Cry*

India National: *The War Cry* (English)

India Central: *Home League Magazine*, *Udyogasthudu*, *Yovana Veerudu*, *Yudha Dwani*

India Eastern: *Sipai Tlangau* (*The War Cry*), *The Officer*, *Young Salvationist*, *Chunnunpar* (all Mizo)

India Northern: *Home League Yearly* (Hindi and English), *Mukti Samachar* (Hindi and Punjabi), *The Officer*, *Yuva Sipai* (both Hindi)

India South Eastern: *Chiruveeran* (Tamil), *Home League Quarterly*, *Poresathan*, *The Officer* (both Tamil)

India South Western: *Home League Quarterly* (Malayalam/English), *The Officer*, *Youdha Shabdan*, *Yuva Veeran* (all Malayalam)

India Western: *Home League Quarterly*, *The Officer*, *The War Cry*, *The Young Soldier* (all Gujarati and Marathi)

Italy: *Il Bollettino dell' Unione Femminile*, *Il Grido di Guerra*

Salvation Army Periodicals

Japan: *Home League Quarterly, The Officer, The Sunday School Guide, Toki-no-Koe, Toki-no-Koe Junior*

Kenya East: *Sauti ya Vita* (English and Kiswahili)

Kenya West: *Sauti ya Vita* (English and Kiswahili)

Korea: *Home League Programme Helps, Loving Hands* (sponsorship magazine), *The Officer, The War Cry*

Latin America North: *Voz de Salvación* (*Salvation Voice*), *Arco Iris de Ideas* (*Rainbow of Ideas*)

Mexico: *El Grito de Guerra* (*The War Cry*), *El Eslabon* (*The Link*)

Mozambique: *Devocionias para Encontros da Liga do Lar* (Home League resource manual)

The Netherlands and Czech Republic: *Dag in Dag Uit, Heils-en Strijdzangen, InterCom, Strijdkreet* (all Dutch), *Prapor Spásy* (Czech)

New Zealand, Fiji and Tonga: *War Cry*

Nigeria: *Salvationist, The Shepherd, The War Cry*

Norway, Iceland and The Færoes: *FAbU nytt, Krigsropet, Uni-form* (all Norwegian), *Herópid* (Icelandic)

Pakistan: *Home League Quarterly, The War Cry* (Urdu)

Papua New Guinea: *Tokaut*

The Philippines: *The War Cry*

Portugal: *O Salvacionista*

Rwanda: *Salvationist News*

Singapore, Malaysia and Myanmar: *The War Cry*

South America East: *El Oficial, El Salvacionista*

South America West: *El Grito de Guerra, El Trébol* (Women's Ministries magazine)

Southern Africa: *Echoes of Mercy, Home League Highlights, Home League Resource Manual, Outer Circle Newsletter, SAMF Newsletter, The Reporter, The War Cry*

Sri Lanka: *Yudha Handa* (*The War Cry*)

Sweden and Latvia: *Stridsropet*

Switzerland, Austria and Hungary: *Espoir* (French), *Dialog* (German), *Dialogue* (French), *IN* (French and German), *Just 4 U* (French), *Klecks* (German), *Trampoline* (French), *Trialog* (German)

Taiwan: *Taiwan Regional News*

United Kingdom with the Republic of Ireland: *Kids Alive!, Salvationist, The War Cry*

USA National: *The War Cry, Word and Deed – A Journal of Theology and Ministry, Women's Ministries Resources, Young Salvationist*

USA Central: *Central Connection*

USA Eastern: *¡Buenas Noticias!, Cristianos en Marcha* (both Spanish), *Good News!* (English and Korean), *Priority!, Ven a Cristo Hoy* (Spanish)

USA Southern: *Southern Spirit*

USA Western: *Caring, New Frontier, Nuevos Fronteras* (Spanish)

Zimbabwe: *Zimbabwe Salvationist, ZEST* (women's magazine)

Books Published during 2008-09

International Headquarters: *An Army Needs an Ambulance Corps* by Harry Williams (jointly with USA National); *Born Again in the Spirit* by Kapela Ntoya; *The Rapture* by Phil Layton; *1929, A Crisis That Shaped The Salvation Army's Future* by John Larsson; *The Salvation Army Year Book 2009*; *Words of Life*; 'Classic Texts' reprints: *Essential Measures* by William Booth; *The Desert Road to Glory* by Clarence D. Wiseman; *What And Why We Believe* by Harry Dean; International Literature Programme: *Adventurers* Junior Soldiers Training Course; *Discovery* Discipling Programme for Young People; *International Bible Lessons for Children*

Books Published 2008-09

Australia Eastern: *More Stories that are Seen* by Doug Clarke

Australia Southern: *Bystander* by Michael Wright; *Famous Last Words* by Kim Haworth (ed); *In The Zone* by Cheryl Tinker; *On a Winter's Mourning* by Lucille Turfrey; *One Thing* by Jim Knaggs and Stephen Court

Denmark: *Create Relationships* anthology edited by Levi Giversen

Finland and Estonia: *Never the Same Again* by Shaw Clifton (Finnish)

Hong Kong and Macau: *Holiness Unwrapped* by Robert Street

India Eastern: *Bru Song Book*; *Home League Lessons*; *Sanctify Yourself* study book; *SAY Lesson Book*; *Senior Sunday Bible Lessons*; *Soldiers Meeting Lessons*

Japan: *Guidance for Local Officers*; *Orders and Regulations for Local Officers* (both Japanese)

Korea: *In Darkest England and the Way Out* by William Booth; *Mustard Seed Notes (1) and (2)* by Kang, Sung-hwan; *One Hundred Sermons from Seniors* (a favourite sermon from 100 retired officers); *One Hundred Years' History of The Salvation Army, Korea Territory* by Kim, Joon-chul; *Corps Cadet Lessons*; *Corps Cell Group Study Manual 2009*; *Daily Devotions for Salvationist Families 2009*; *Summer Bible School 2009* (handbook and workbooks); *Young People's Company Lessons 2008-09* (manual and workbooks)

New Zealand, Fiji and Tonga: *Heart of the City: Auckland Congress Hall Stories 1883-2008*; *Think On These Things: The Salvation Army Christchurch City Corps 1883-2008* by H. Bramwell Cook; *White Cloud Soaring: The Story of 24/7 Prayer in Aotearoa* by Judith Bennett

Sri Lanka: *General in the Jungle*; *Home League Resource Book*; *Officers' Resource Book*

Sweden and Latvia: *Our World for God* by Inger Lundin (Swedish)

United Kingdom: *The Time . . . The Place* edited and compiled by Philippa Smale; Available on UKT website: *Words Of William Booth* by Cyril Barnes; *No Discharge In This War* by Frederick Coutts

USA National: *An Army Needs An Ambulance Corps* by Harry Williams (jointly with IHQ); *No Longer Missing* compiled by Judith Brown and Christine Poff; *101 Everyday Sayings From the Bible* by Ed Forster

USA Western: *A View from the Corner* by Bob Docter

Published with the assistance of grants from the International Literature Programme, IHQ:

Brazil: *11km para Emaús* (meditations) by Carl Eliasen; *Creed and Deed* (both Portuguese)

Caribbean: *Adventurers*; *International Bible Lessons for Children*

Congo Brazzaville: *Kikongo Song Book*; *Women's Ministries Manual*

Eastern Europe: *Adventurers*; *Never the Same Again* by Shaw Clifton; *To Love and to Cherish*; *Salvation Story Study Guide* (all Russian)

Ghana: *Adventurers*; *Discovery*; *International Bible Lessons for Children*; *The Song Book of The Salvation Army*

India National: *Family Treasure* (Women's Ministries booklet)

India Central: *Discovery*; *Never the Same Again* by Shaw Clifton; *Vacation Bible School Manual*

India Eastern: *Discovery*; *YP Sunday Bible Lessons* (Senior, Intermediate, Junior, Primary, Beginners) (all Mizo)

India Western: *International Bible Lessons for Children*

Italy: *An Illustrated History of The Salvation Army* (Greek)

Nigeria: *Discovery*; *The Guide*; *The Song Book of The Salvation Army*

Papua New Guinea: *Adventurers*

The Philippines: *Adventurers*; *Child Protection Manual*; *Discovery*; *International Bible Lessons for Children*

South America West: *Discovery*; *Heroes of the Faith* by Derek Elvin; *In Darkest England and the Way Out* by William Booth; *Never the Same Again* by Shaw Clifton; *Nothing Without Love* by Kenneth Lawson (all Spanish)

Southern Africa: *Sesotho Song Book*; *Women's Ministries Resources*

Zimbabwe: *Indebele Song Book*; *Shona Song Book*

MINISTRIES AND FELLOWSHIPS

WOMEN'S MINISTRIES

THE ideal basic unit of society is the home and family, where women play a vital and definitive role. Furthermore, as natural providers of hope, women play an important part in shaping society. Therefore, any fellowship of women in which Christian influence is exerted and practical help given benefits not only the individual and the family but also the nation.

Women's Ministries provide a programme of meetings and other activities based on the fourfold aim of the Army's international women's organisation, the Home League, which was inaugurated in 1907. Those aims are worship, education, fellowship, service. The motto of the Home League is: 'I will live a pure life in my house' (Psalm 101:2 *Good News Bible*).

The mission of Women's Ministries is to bring women into a knowledge of Jesus Christ; encourage their full potential in influencing family, friends and community; equip them for growth in personal understanding and life skills; address issues which affect women and their families in the world.

THE LEAGUE OF MERCY AND COMMUNITY CARE MINISTRIES

THE League of Mercy, which began in 1892 in Canada, is made up of people of all ages whose mission is to engage in a caring ministry. The main objective of the League of Mercy is to respond to the spiritual and social needs of the community. The ministry is adapted according to the local situation, the size of its membership and the skill of its members, and endeavours to follow Christ's injunction, 'Inasmuch as ye have done it unto one of the least of these my brethren, ye have done it unto me' (Matthew 25:40 *Authorised Version*).

THE SALVATION ARMY MEDICAL FELLOWSHIP

THE Salvation Army Medical Fellowship, instituted in 1943 by Mrs General Minnie Carpenter, is an international fellowship of dedicated medical personnel. Physical suffering in the world challenges both the medical and the physical and emotional resources of medical personnel. The fellowship encourages a Christian witness and application of Christian principles in professional life while at the same time being involved with practical application in hospitals, clinics and various other places of medical care.

THE FELLOWSHIP OF THE SILVER STAR

THE Fellowship of the Silver Star, inaugurated in the USA in 1930 and extended worldwide in 1936, expresses gratitude to parents or other significant life mentors of Salvation Army officers.

THE SALVATION ARMY STUDENTS' FELLOWSHIP

THIS fellowship started in Norway in 1942 and later spread to other countries, receiving an official constitution in 1950. It comes under the world presidency of the General. The aim of the fellowship is to unite Salvationist students and graduates of universities, colleges and other centres of higher education in Christian fellowship and such Salvation Army service as may be appropriate.

THE SALVATION ARMY BLUE SHIELD FELLOWSHIP

IN 1974 the Blue Shield Fellowship was formed by two British Salvationist policemen to provide friendship and support to Christian policemen as they face present-day challenges. Membership is open to active and retired police officers; there are members in many countries.

SALVATION ARMY HONOURS

ORDER OF THE FOUNDER

Instituted on 20 August 1917 by General Bramwell Booth, the Order of the Founder is the highest Salvation Army honour. It marks 'outstanding service rendered by officers and soldiers such as would in spirit and achievement have been specially commended by the Founder'.

Recipients of the Order of the Founder 1920-2009

1920 – **BOURN, Herbert J.,** British Territory
HOWARD, Comr T. Henry, British Territory
BOOTH-TUCKER, Comr Frederick, India
CARLETON, Comr John A., British Territory
TOFT, Mrs Col Ester, British Territory
McKENZIE, Lt-Col William, Australia Southern
HED, Brig Per, Sweden
WILLE, Maj Vilhelm, Denmark
BOIJE, Staff-Capt Helmy, Finland
CARREL, Adj Francoise, France
HINE, Adj Catherine, British Territory
STEWART, Ens Christine, British Territory
PURIUS, Ens Daniel, British Territory
MANSON, Capt William, British Territory
BENACK, Capt George, USA Eastern
GAUGLER, Capt Lucie, France
1923 – **STICKELLS, Mrs Elizabeth,** Canada
OUCHTERLONY, Comr Hannah, Sweden
SMITH, Col J. Allister, British Territory
PATHAM, Lt-Col Yesu (Walter Keil), India
SLATER, Lt-Col Richard, British Territory
IWASA, Adj (Dr) Rin, Japan
WELLS, Adj Bertram, British Territory
GREEN, Ens Thomas, British Territory
1924 – **MATSUDA, Dr Sanya,** Japan
JOHANSSON, Gustaf, Sweden
BOMAN, Gustaf E., Sweden
GORE, Adj John, Australia Southern

1925 – **HODGE, CSM Thomas,** Australia Eastern
SHEPHERD, Env William, Australia Eastern
BUICK, Env Steven, New Zealand
OVESEN, Staff-Capt Emil, Norway
1926 – **ALEXANDER, Maj Alex,** British Territory
1927 – **DAVIES, Mrs Bessie,** British Territory
1928 – **PESATORI, Staff-Capt Mario,** Italy
1929 – **SOUTER, Col George,** British Territory
1930 – **BOOTH, Cmndr Evangeline,** British Territory
1931 – **COXHEAD, CSM Frederick,** British Territory
BROUWER, Lt-Col Jacob G., The Netherlands
1932 – **CANNELL, C/S Thomas,** British Territory
1933 – **BOOTH-HELLBERG, Comr Mrs Lucy STIMPSON, C/T Alfred,** British Territory
1933 – **BRENGLE, Comr Samuel,** USA Eastern
1937 – **BLOWERS, Comr Arthur R.,** British Territory
PUNCHARD, Nat B/M Alfred W., British Territory
YAMAMURO, Comr Gunpei, Japan
1939 – **SIBILIN, CSM Marie,** Switzerland
TWITCHIN, B/M Herbert, British Territory
RÖMHILD, YPSM E., Denmark
LAMB, Comr David C., Scotland and Ireland
1940 – **PEETERMAN, Env Gerardus,** Holland
BRAUND, YPSM Ralph C., Canada
WHITE, Sis Polly, British Territory
1942 – **COX, B/M Sydney W.,** British Territory
MILANS, Henry F., USA
MATUNJWA, Maj Joel Mbambo, South Africa

Salvation Army Honours

1943 – **FULLER, Col George,** British Territory
  FITCH, Sis Polly, Canada
  COLLEY, Env William, New Zealand
1944 – **HODGEN, Maj Jeanetta,** USA Western
  ANDERSON, Maj Mary, Australia Southern
  DINSDALE, CSM George, Canada
  WILLCOX, Sgt Harvey Stanley, British Territory
  LEWIS, Mother Ida, USA Central
1945 – **PEDLAR, Env Edwin,** Canada
  GORDON, Maj Annie, New Zealand
1946 – **TURNER, B/M John,** Australia Southern
  NEWTON, Field-Adj Charles, Canada
  DUNLAP, Eva, USA Eastern
  SU Chien-Chi, Maj, Northern China
1947 – **GOVAARS, Col Gerrit J.,** Holland
  BROWN, Maj Cecil, USA Southern
  OZANNE, Maj Marie, British Territory
1949 – **VALLENTGOED, Helena Dehaas,** Holland
  CHANDLER, CSM W. George, British Territory
  STEVENS, Div B/M Arthur J., Australia Southern
  LARSSON, Comr Karl, Sweden
1951 – **THOMPSON, Mrs Joseph,** New Zealand
  FOSTER, B/M George, USA Eastern
  MARSHALL, B/M George, British Territory
1952 – **PALMER, Env Robert,** Australia Southern
  LJUNGQVIST, CSM Erik, Sweden
  CROCKER, Sen-Capt Tom, USA Central
1953 – **KUNZ, CSM (Dr) Victor,** Switzerland
  FAGERLIE, Brig Martin, Norway
1954 – **SATTERFIELD, Brig Julius,** USA Southern
  HIGGINS, Lt-Col Ernest D., USA Western
1955 – **BECQUET, Lt-Comr Henri L.,** Belgium
  CARROLL, CSM Mary Jane, British Territory
  McLEOD, Staff B/M Norman, Australia Southern
1955 – **SCHRALE, Env Ids Klaas,** The Netherlands
1956 – **SIGSWORTH, Sen-Maj Alice,** British Territory
1957 – **NOBLE, Col (Dr) William** USA Southern
1958 – **GOGIBUS, Maj Georgette,** France
1959 – **SMITH, Mrs Jane,** Scotland
1960 – **CROCKER, Env James,** Australia Eastern
  WARREN, Mary, British Territory
  THÖRNKVIST, Brig Hubert, Sweden
1960 – **MEECH, C/T Alice,** British Territory
  OHARA, Env Tamokichi, Japan
  JEWKES, Col Frederick E., British Territory
1962 – **JENSON, B/M Henry Kragh,** Denmark
  ORELLANA, Env Luis, South America West
  BOSSHARDT, Maj Alida M., The Netherlands
1963 – **RUSSELL, Env Mrs Ruth,** Ireland
  WALKLEY, C/S Mrs Maud, British Territory
1964 – **BROKENSHIRE, Brig Nora,** Canada
  von WATTENWYL, Lt-Col Christine, Switzerland
1965 – **STYLES, Brig Mary,** South Africa
  CASTILLO, Sgt Ambrose, South America East
1966 – **KHUMA, Lt-Col Kawl,** India North Eastern
  FULLER, C/S Mrs Rebecca, South Africa
1967 – **DEGOUMOIS, Sgt Lydia,** France
  McILVEEN, Brig Arthur W., Australia Eastern
1968 – **THAIN, B/M Alex,** Scotland
  SINCLAIR, CSM John, Scotland
  SEGAWA, Col Yasowa, Japan

1969 – **LORD, Env Olive,** New Zealand
  DEWE, CSM Herbert, New Zealand
1970 – **IRWIN, Brig John,** Australia Eastern
  JOSEPH, Env Hendrik Mangindaan, Indonesia
1971 – **WHANG, Sook Hyun, Env,** Korea
  BLANCO, Env Atanasio, South America East
  MOORE, Mrs Sen Field-Capt May, Canada
1972 – **KIVINIEMI, C/S Julia,** Finland
  MARSDAL, CSM Bard, Norway
  SORENSON, C/T Mrs Helen J., USA Central
  KIRBY, Maj Leonard, Canada and Bermuda
  GEBBIE, Brig Eleanor, British Territory
1974 – **KRISTANO, CSM Ajub,** Indonesia
  POTTINGER, Guard Ldr Hester, USA Central
  NELANDER, CSM Eric, Sweden
1975 – **ADAMS, Col Bernard,** British Territory
  MacFARLANE, CSM James, Canada and Bermuda
1976 – **RICHES, Lucy,** British Territory
  GEDDES, Brig Charles M., Australia Eastern
  NHARI, Brig Mrs Lilian, Rhodesia
  CHU Suet-King, Env, Hong Kong
  ROSTETT, Lt-Col Henry T., USA Central
  GALE, Brig Laura, British Territory
1977 – **JONSSON, Brig Hulda,** Sweden
1978 – **HOPPER, Env Keith,** Australia Eastern
  GREEN, B/M Jack, Canada and Bermuda
  BROWN, Env Mrs Jean, Canada and Bermuda
  BYWATERS, Brig Stella, Australia Southern
  NERY, Lt-Col Jorge, South America West
1979 – **NISIEWICZ, Brig Mary,** USA Eastern
  FRASER, Rtd CT Jeannie, Scotland
  VENABLES, YPSM Lily, British Territory
1980 – **GOODING, CSM Edward,** USA Eastern
  O'NEIL Sen-Maj Elsie, Australia Southern
  HILE, Rtd C/T Kenneth, Australia Eastern
  VIVANTE, Env (Dr) Armand, SouthAmerica East
1981 – **BOYD, Sir John,** British Territory
  RIDGERS, Over-60s Sec Mrs Pam, British Territory
  SIMMONS, Rtd CSM Cyril, Canada and Bermuda
  STAIGER, Rtd CSM Frank O., USA Central
  RANDALL, Env Edward G., Australia Eastern
  MORGAN, Rtd B/M Harold, Australia Eastern
1982 – **BENJAMIN, Mrs Maj Ruth,** Bermuda
  KIRBY, Col Leonard, Canada and Bermuda
1983 – **LAUNDUN, Sis Mrs Ferraez,** USA Southern
  STILLWELL, Rtd BM Harry B., USA Western
  BRAMWELL-BOOTH, Comr Catherine,
  British Territory
  COOK, Lt-Comr (Dr) A. Bramwell, New
  Zealand and Fiji
1984 – **KJØLNER, CSM Egil,** Norway
  PARSELL, CSM Mrs Lily May, Australia Southern
  RADER, Lt-Col Lyell, USA Eastern
1985 – **KRIDER, C/T George,** USA Eastern
1986 – **SEILS, Mrs Col Else,** Germany
1987 – **HOLZ, Mrs Brig E. R.,** USA Southern
1988 – **RIVE, Lt-Col Philip,** New Zealand and Fiji
  McCLINTOCK, Env Walter, USA Central
  BROWN, Maj Jean, Canada and Bermuda
  SUGHANANTHAM, Mrs Comr Grace, India
  South Eastern

Salvation Army Honours

McBRIDE, CSM Donald G., Canada and Bermuda
McBRIDE, Mrs H. Joan, Canada and Bermuda
1989 – PERJESWAMI, Lt-Col Saratha, Burma
PAIGE, YPSM Clara, USA Southern
1990 – THANGKIMA, CSM C., India Northern
KROEKER, Lt-Col Levina, Canada and Bermuda
BEEK, Col Anna M. J. A., The Netherlands
YIN Hung-Shun, Maj, China
KORBEL, Brig Josef, Czechoslovakia
KIM, Hyun-Sook, Env, Korea
WALKER, Env Wilbur, Australia Eastern
1990 – HOLLAND, Comr Arthur, British Territory
de NESFIELD, CSM Mrs Odessa Marshall, Latin America North
GORSKA, Maj Marija, Sweden and Latvia
SERVAIS, CSM Muilton Eli, USA Southern
1992 – RASMUSSEN, Maj Tora E., Denmark
DeARMAN, Maj Billie Jean, USA Southern
RUSSELL, Lt-Col Mina, USA Eastern
DOCTER, CSM (Dr) Robert, USA Western
1993 – LALZUALA, CSM, India Eastern
HAZELL, Env George, Australia Eastern
FURSENKO, Vladimir Mikhailovich, Russia
BRADWELL, Rtd CSM Cyril, New Zealand and Fiji
1996 – SCHOCH, Maj Ruth, Switzerland
SIPLEY, Brig Clifton, USA Eastern
1997 – YEE, Lt-Col Check, USA Western
NDODA, Env David Elijah Zenzeleni, Zimbabwe
1998 – NGUGI, Comr Joshua, East Africa
1999 – PEDERSEN, Brig Victor, Australia Southern
2000 – MERRITT, Brig Violet, British Territory
SAULNIER, Mrs Mary, Canada and Bermuda
HIMES, B/M William F., USA Central
HAEFELI, Maj Rosa Maria, Caribbean
ZIMMERMAN, Maj Emma, Caribbean
CODOY, Mrs Carolina, The Philippines
COX, Maj Kathryn, USA Southern
DARTHUAMA, CSM Pu, India Eastern
LAUTIER, Maj Marguerite, France
PEACOCKE, Brig Elizabeth, Canada and Bermuda
RIVITT, Maj Dolores, Canada and Bermuda
2001 – GUERRERO, Raul, USA Western
GOKSOYR, Maj Jorun, Norway, Iceland and The Færoes
HARTMAN, Lt-Col Karin Elisabet, Sweden and Latvia
ROBB, Mrs Col Anita, USA Central
LUCAS, Col Bramwell, Australia Eastern
KHUMALO, S/L Mzilikazi Southern Africa
2002 – RADER, Lt-Col Damon, USA Eastern
GRIFFITHS, Brig Doreen, Australia Southern
LANGSTON, Brig Dorothy, USA Southern
COLLIER, Mrs Delilah, USA Eastern
2003 – GERMANY, Mrs Pat, USA Southern
RODIN, CSM Bertil, Sweden and Latvia
2004 – BURTON, CSM Kenneth, USA Eastern
RIVE, Lt-Col Lance, New Zealand, Fiji and Tonga
RIVE, Lt-Col Faye, New Zealand, Fiji and Tonga
RICE, Lt-Col R. Eugene, USA Western
WEBB, Maj Joy, United Kingdom
KNIGHTLEY, Lt-Col Brian, United Kingdom
KNIGHTLEY, Lt-Col Dorothy, United Kingdom
HERJE, Maj Anne Kristine, Norway, Iceland and The Færoes
SIGLEY, Maj Hilda, Australia Eastern
2005 – DALZIEL, Geoffrey John, Australia Southern
DAVIDOVITCH, Nina Sergeevna, Eastern Europe
STEADMAN-ALLEN, Lt-Col Ray, United Kingdom
PURDUE, Brig Gertrude McClennan, USA Southern
WILLIAMS, Comr (Dr) Harry, United Kingdom
2006 – PACQUETTE, Maj Catherine, Caribbean
2007 – SAWICHHUNGA, Col, India Eastern
GARIEPY, Col Henry, USA Eastern
COLLETT, Env Richard, Australia Southern
STAINES, Env Alan, Australia Eastern

There were no admissions to the Order of the Founder in the year under review (1 May 2008-30 April 2009)

ORDER OF DISTINGUISHED AUXILIARY SERVICE

On 24 February 1941 General George Carpenter instituted this order to mark the Army's appreciation of distinguished service rendered by non-Salvationists who have helped to further its work in a variety of ways

Recipient of the Order of Distinguished Auxiliary Service 2008-09

Alain Raoul (France and Belgium Territory) has completed 35 years' service with The Salvation Army and been influential in strategic financial and administrative roles. His work with 'Inspection Générale des Affaires Sociales' led to the establishment of the various 'foundations' of The Salvation Army in France. His service has been characterised by his professional, Christian spirit and loyalty to Salvation Army values. Admitted to the Order of Distinguished Auxiliary Service on 1 April 2009.

INTERNATIONAL HEADQUARTERS

The Salvation Army, 101 Queen Victoria Street,
London EC4V 4EH, United Kingdom

Main entrance: Peter's Hill, London EC4

Tel: (020) 7332 0101 (national)
[44] (20) 7332 0101 (international);
fax: (020) 7192 3413; email: websa@salvationarmy.org;
website: www.salvationarmy.org

General
SHAW CLIFTON
(2 April 2006)

Chief of the Staff
COMMISSIONER ROBIN DUNSTER
(2 April 2006)

INTERNATIONAL Headquarters exists to support the General as he leads The Salvation Army to accomplish its God-given worldwide mission to preach the gospel of Jesus Christ and meet human need in his name without discrimination. In so doing, it assists the General:

- To give spiritual leadership, promote the development of spiritual life within the Army, and emphasise the Army's reliance on God for the achievement of its mission.
- To provide overall strategic leadership and set international policies.
- To direct and administer the Army's operations and protect its interests – by means of appointments and delegation of authority and responsibility with accountability.
- To empower and support the territories and commands, encourage and pastorally care for their leaders, and inspire local vision and initiatives.
- To strengthen the internationalism of the Army, preserve its unity, purposes, beliefs and spirit, and maintain its standards.
- To promote the development, appropriate deployment and international sharing of personnel.
- To promote the development and sharing of financial resources worldwide, and manage the Army's international funds.
- To promote the development and international sharing of knowledge, expertise and experience.
- To develop the Army's ecumenical and other relationships.

The General directs Salvation Army operations throughout the world through the administrative departments of International Headquarters, which are headed by international secretaries. The Chief of the Staff, a commissioner appointed by the General

International Headquarters

to be second-in-command, is the Army's chief executive whose function is to implement the General's policy decisions and effect liaison between departments.

The Christian Mission Headquarters, Whitechapel Road, became the Army's first International Headquarters in 1880. However, the Founder soon decided that a move into the City of London would be beneficial and in 1881 IHQ was moved to 101 Queen Victoria Street. Sixty years after this move the IHQ building was destroyed by fire during the Second World War. The rebuilt International Headquarters was opened by Queen Elizabeth, the Queen Mother, in November 1963.

When it was decided to redevelop the Queen Victoria Street site, IHQ took up temporary residence at William Booth College, Denmark Hill, in 2001. Three years later IHQ returned to 101 Queen Victoria Street and the new building was opened by Her Royal Highness The Princess Royal in November 2004.

Website of the Office of the General:
www.salvationarmy.org/thegeneral

INTERNATIONAL MANAGEMENT COUNCIL

The International Management Council (IMC), established in February 1991, sees to the efficiency and effectiveness of the Army's international administration in general. It considers in detail the formation of international policy and mission. It is composed of all London-based IHQ commissioners, and meets monthly with the General taking the chair.

Sec: Lt-Col Rob Garrad
Asst Sec: Maj Richard Gaudion

GENERAL'S CONSULTATIVE COUNCIL

The General's Consultative Council (GCC), established in July 2001, advises the General on broad matters relating to the Army's mission strategy and policy. The GCC is composed of all officers who qualify to attend a High Council, and operates through a Lotus Notes database. Selected members also meet three times a year in London with the General taking the chair.

Sec: Lt-Col Rob Garrad
Asst Sec: Maj Richard Gaudion

ADMINISTRATION DEPARTMENT

The Administration Department is responsible for all matters with which the Chief of the Staff deals; for the effective administration of IHQ; for IHQ personnel; for international external relations; for providing legal advice; and for ensuring that the strategic planning and monitoring process is implemented and used effectively.

International Secretary to the Chief of the Staff

COMR WILLIAM COCHRANE (1 Jun 2009)

Under Sec for Administration (Admin): Lt-Col Christine Rees
Under Sec for Administration (Personnel): Lt-Col Wendy Caffull
Executive Sec to the General/Research and Planning Sec: Lt-Col Rob Garrad
P/S to the General: Maj Richard Gaudion
P/S to the Chief of the Staff: Maj Mark Watts
Sec for International Ecumenical Relations: Lt-Col Richard Munn
Sec for Spiritual Life Development: Lt-Col Janet Munn
International Director for Social Justice: Comr M. Christine MacMillan
International Doctrine Council: Chair: Comr William Francis
International Moral and Social Issues Council: Chair: Comr M. Christine MacMillan
IHQ Chaplain and City of London Liaison Officer: Comr Shona Forsyth
Legal and Constitutional Adviser to the General: Comr Kenneth G. Hodder
Special Assignment – The Salvation Army Song Book: Lt-Col Charles King
World Youth Convention Organiser: Col Birgitte Brekke

WOMEN'S MINISTRIES

World President of Women's Ministries

COMR HELEN CLIFTON (2 Apr 2006)

World Secretary for Women's Ministries and World President,

International Headquarters

SA Scouts, Guides and Guards
COMR LYN PEARCE (1 Jun 2009)

Administrative Asst: Maj Lynn Gibbs

INTERNATIONAL PERSONNEL DEPARTMENT

The International Personnel Department works in the interests of international personnel in support of the Chief of the Staff and the zonal international secretaries. Responsibilities include facilitating the personal and vocational development of all personnel, their pastoral care and physical well-being. The department exists to encourage and facilitate the sharing and appropriate deployment of personnel resources on a global basis; to assist in the identification of officers with potential for future leadership; to monitor training and development; to register and coordinate all offers for international service.

International Secretary for Personnel
COMR KENNETH G. HODDER (1 Jun 2009)

Associate Int Sec for Personnel: Comr Jolene Hodder

Sec for International Training and Leader Development: Lt-Col Wayne Pritchett

Medical Consultant: Dr John Thomlinson

BUSINESS ADMINISTRATION DEPARTMENT

The Business Administration Department is responsible for international accounting, auditing, banking, property and related matters. The International Secretary for Business Administration has the oversight of the finance functions in territories and commands.

International Secretary for Business Administration
COMR ANN WOODALL (1 Mar 2008)

Finance Sec: tba

Chief Accountant: Maj Jeffrey Wills

Chief International Auditor: Lt-Col Edmund Chung
  Auditors: Maj Samuel Amponsah, Maj Alan Milkins, Maj Francis Nyakusamwa, Maj João Paulo Ramos, Capt Emerald Urbien, Miss Karen Dare

Facilities Manager Coordinator: Mr Andrew Holden

Information Technology Manager: Mr Mark Calleran

Property Manager: Mr Howard Bowes

Travel Manager: Mr Mark Edwards

PROGRAMME RESOURCES DEPARTMENT

The mission of the Programme Resources Department is to participate with others in envisioning, coordinating, facilitating and raising awareness of programmes that advance the global mission of The Salvation Army.

International Secretary for Programme Resources
COMR ROBIN FORSYTH (1 Jul 2008)

Under Sec: Lt-Col Michael Caffull

International Emergency Services:
  IES Coordinator (Acting): Lt-Col Mike Caffull

International Health Services:
  IHS Coordinators: Majs Dean and (Dr) Eirwen Pallant

International Projects and Development Services:
  IPDS Sec: Maj Ted Horwood
  Mission Support Projects and Feeding Programmes: Maj Deborah Horwood

Communications:
  Editor-in-Chief and Literary Sec: Maj Laurie Robertson
  Editor *All the World*: Mr Kevin Sims
  Editor *Revive*: tba
  Editor *The Officer*: Maj Leanne Ruthven
  Editor *The Year Book*: Maj Trevor Howes
  Writer *Words of Life*: Maj Evelyn Merriam
  International Literature Programme Officer: Maj Simone Robertson
  Editorial fax: (020) 7332 8079

ZONAL DEPARTMENTS

The zonal departments are the main administrative link with territories and commands. The international secretaries give oversight to and coordinate the Army's work in their respective geographical areas.

AFRICA
International Secretary
COMR AMOS MAKINA (1 Jul 2004)

Under Sec: Lt-Col David Burrows
  fax: (020) 7332 8231

Sec WM: Comr Rosemary Makina

AMERICAS AND CARIBBEAN
International Secretary
COMR LARRY BOSH (1 Oct 2008)

International Headquarters

Under Sec: Lt-Col Susan McMillan
Sec WM: Comr Gillian Bosh

EUROPE
International Secretary
COMR BARRY POBJIE (1 Jun 2009)
Under Sec: Lt-Col David Shakespeare
 fax: (020) 7332 8209
Sec WM: Comr Raemor Pobjie
Officer for EU Affairs: Maj Göran Larsson

SOUTH ASIA
International Secretary
COMR LALKIAMLOVA (1 Jan 2004)

Under Sec: Lt-Col David Rees
 fax: (020) 7332 8219
Sec WM: Comr Lalhlimpuii

SOUTH PACIFIC AND EAST ASIA
International Secretary
COMR ROBERT STREET (1 Jun 2009)
Under Sec: Lt-Col Gillian Downer
 fax: (020) 7332 8229
Sec WM: Comr Janet Street

STATISTICS Officers 68 Employees 70

International College for Officers and Centre for Spiritual Life Development

The Cedars, 34 Sydenham Hill, London SE26 6LS, UK
Tel: [44] (020) 8299 8450; fax: [44] (020) 7192 3056; website: www.salvationarmy.org/ico

Principal: Lieut-Colonel Richard Munn (1 Jul 2008)

During the International Congress held at the Crystal Palace, Sydenham, London, in 1904, Commissioner Henry T. Howard voiced what he saw as the young Salvation Army's need for leaders inspired with the aggressive spirit of Salvationism. William Booth took up the idea and the International Staff Training Lodge was opened at Clapton on 11 May 1905.

Following the purchase of The Cedars in Sydenham – formerly used to house orphaned children at the end of the Second World War – the International Staff College started in 1950. Four years later it became the International College for Officers, with General Albert Orsborn declaring it to be 'an investment in the great intangibles without which our cogs and wheels would soon be rusty and dead'.

In July 2008 the role of the college was broadened to include aspects of spiritual life development that go beyond officers' attendance at the eight-week sessions, and the college was renamed International College for Officers and Centre for Spiritual Life Development.

MISSION STATEMENT

The Salvation Army's International College for Officers and Centre for Spiritual Life Development exists to further develop officers by:
- nurturing personal holiness and spiritual leadership
- providing opportunity to experience the internationalism of the Army
- encouraging a renewed sense of mission and purpose as an officer

JANUARY 2009 witnessed the arrival at the college of the 200th session – thus marking more than 5,000 officers from around the world appointed to the ICO in its history. Congratulations from General Shaw Clifton, previous principals and numerous 'Cedarlights' were delivered during a celebratory event.

German, Spanish and Kiswahili translation sessions continued to reflect the ICO's flexible and multi-national emphasis. Session 203 was designated a 'Holiness Session' with Commissioners William and Marilyn Francis (Canada and Bermuda), Major Melvin Jones (UK), Major Alan Harley (Australia

Eastern) and Dr David Rightmire (USA Eastern) serving as guest lecturers.

The missional expansion projected through the Centre for Spiritual Life Development commenced with The Cedars hosting an International Prayer Leaders' gathering and the International Doctrine Council. Additionally, the ICO curriculum now includes several periods of 24/7 prayer and varied 'rhythms of prayer' systematically interwoven throughout the daily schedule.

The appointment of an Executive Assistant to the Secretary for Spiritual Life Development reflects the further expansion of the Centre for Spiritual Life Development.

STATISTICS
Officers 6 **Employees** 5

STAFF
Associate Principal and Secretary for Spiritual Life Development: Lt-Col Janet Munn
Executive Asst to the Secretary for Spiritual Life Development: Lt-Col Karen Shakespeare
Programme Sec: Maj Rosemarie Brown
Business Sec: Maj Peter Forrest
Personnel Sec: Maj Julie Forrest

International Social Justice Commission
221 East 52nd Street, New York, New York 10022, USA
Tel: [1] (212) 758-0763; website: www.salvationarmy.org/isjc
Director: Commissioner Christine MacMillan (1 Jul 2007)

The International Social Justice Commission (ISJC) came into being on 1 July 2007. Its secretariat is in New York, with the commission and its director being attached to the Administration Department of IHQ. The ISJC advises the General and other senior leaders at IHQ in matters of social justice. The director and staff are the Army's principal international advocate and adviser on social, economic and political issues and events giving rise to the perpetuation of social injustice in the world. They assist the Army in addressing social injustice in a systemic, measured, proactive and Christian manner.

The commission has absorbed and extended the current work of the Moral and Social Issues desk at IHQ, reintroducing an International Moral and Social Issues Council (IMASIC).

THE ISJC is now well established at the United Nations (UN) in New York, with representatives also in Vienna, Geneva, Nairobi and Jakarta. The UN representatives are active on significant committees and boards and speak into UN policy with resultant documentation. The status of The Salvation Army's membership at the UN has now been lifted to Economic and Social Council (ECOSOC) designation.

The ISJC works and reports against a strategic direction that is approved and over sighted by the General. The strategies are:

☐ Raise strategic voices to advocate with the world's poor and oppressed.

☐ Be a recognised centre of research and critical thinking on issues of global social justice.

☐ Collaborate with like-minded organisations to advance the global cause of social justice.

☐ Exercise leadership in determining social justice policies and practices of The Salvation Army.

☐ Live the principles of justice and compassion and inspire others to do likewise.

STATISTICS
Officers 3 **Employees** (full time) 1 (part time) 4
Policy Interns 4

STAFF
Deputy Director: Lt-Col Geanette Seymour
Personal Asst to Director and UN Rep: Maj Victoria Edmonds (New York)
UN Reps: Maj Elisabeth Frei (Vienna) Maj Sylvette Huguenin (Geneva) Lt-Col Julius Mukonga (Nairobi) and Jakarta

International Headquarters

The Africa Development Centre

Moi Avenue, Nairobi, Kenya
Postal Address: PO Box 40575, Nairobi, Kenya 00100 GPO
Tel: [254] (020) 221 2217

On 17 April 2009, IHQ gave approval for the relocation of The Salvation Army Leadership Training College (SALT College) of Africa to Nairobi, and the establishment of the Central Africa Development Office, the Central Africa Women's Development Office and the Zonal Facilitation Resource Office, to operate under the title of the Africa Development Centre. Each office retains its individual title and role, but will be a central focal point from where the established offices will coordinate their activities for the Africa Zone on behalf of IHQ, reporting to the International Secretary for Africa. Operations carried out through the Africa Development Centre became effective 1 January 2010.

STATISTICS Officers 7 Employees 1

The Salvation Army Leadership Training College (SALT College) of Africa

Prompted by the request of territorial leaders of Africa, The Salvation Army Leadership Training College of Africa was established in 1986. Its purpose is to coordinate officer and local officer in-service training across Africa through distance-learning courses and seminars, monitored by an extension training officer in each territory. An IHQ-sponsored education and training facility, SALT College offers distance learning in 15 countries across the African continent. Its students include officers, envoys, local officers, candidates and soldiers.

Principal: Maj Kapela Ntoya
Director of Studies: Maj Juliana Musilia
Director of Special Studies: Maj Rose-Nicole Ntoya
Office Administrator: Maj Benjamin Musilia
tel: [254] (020) 221 2217;
email: leadcoll_africa@sal.salvationarmy.org

Central Africa Development Office

The office is under the leadership of the Central Africa Programme Development Secretary. Its purpose is to help implement the policies and strategies of the Central Africa territories, commands and region in relation to community development. Its role includes giving support to senior leadership and project officers in project design, reporting and implementation. Also, in collaboration with IHQ (Africa Zone and International Projects and Development Services) and in conjunction with local headquarters leadership it will pursue external donor potential and the training and development of staff.

Programme Development Sec: Lt-Col Joseph Lukau
email: Joseph_Lukau@salvationarmy.org

Central Africa Women's Development Office

Under the leadership of the Central Africa Women's Development Secretary, the office helps implement policies and strategies for developing the skills of potential women leaders, in collaboration with and on behalf of the Zonal Secretary for Women's Ministries and headquarters leadership throughout Africa. The Women's Development Secretary works alongside the Programme Development Secretary in matters where the role and participation of women relates to community development.

Women's Development Sec: Lt-Col Angelique Lukau
email: Angelique_Lukau@salvationarmy.org

Zonal Facilitation Resource Office

The office is under the leadership of the Zonal Facilitation Resource Officer who reports to the Under Secretary for Africa (IHQ) and the Women's Development Secretary, and who has a technical relationship to the International Health Services Coordinator. The office enables territories, commands and regions in Africa to better use facilitation as a way of working both internally and in the wider community. This will help people to respond more faithfully to challenges and result in more sustainable, integrated mission and ministry.

Zonal Facilitation Resource Officer: Capt Lena Wanyonyi

International Administrative Structure

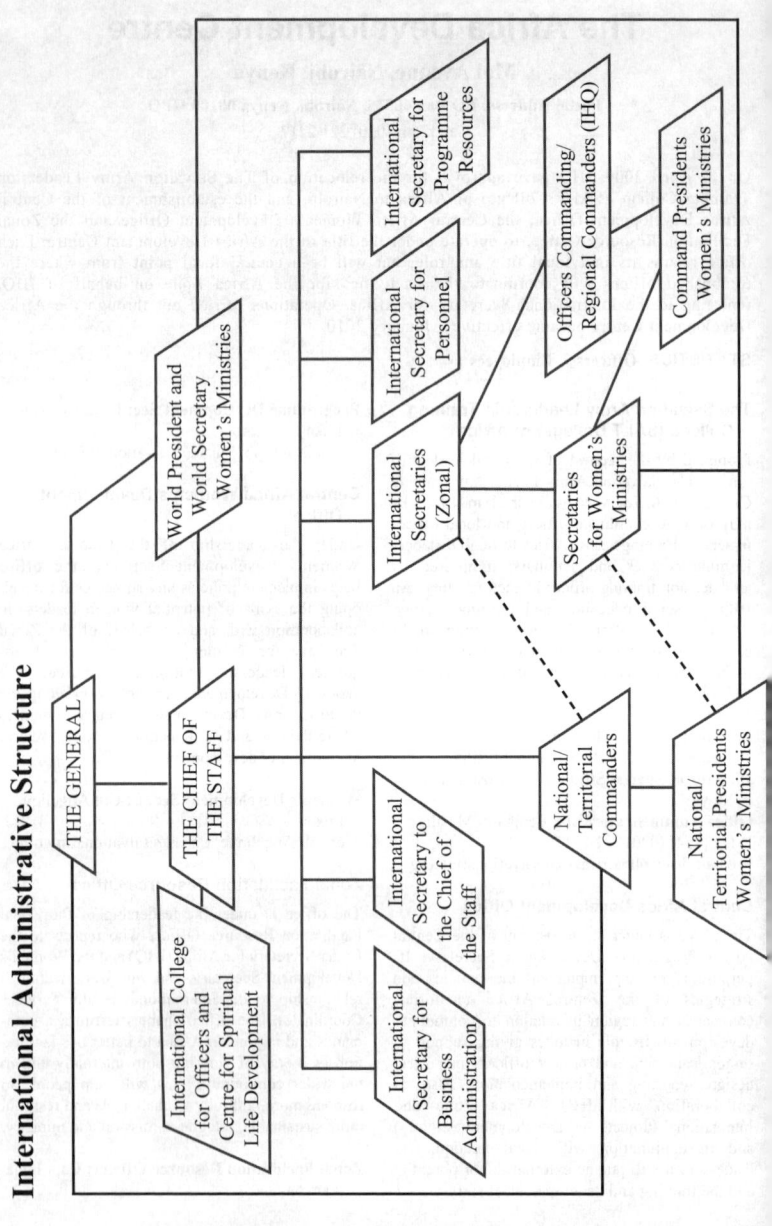

International Headquarters

- THE GENERAL
  - World President and World Secretary Women's Ministries
  - THE CHIEF OF THE STAFF
    - International College for Officers and Centre for Spiritual Life Development
    - International Secretary for Business Administration
    - International Secretary to the Chief of the Staff
    - International Secretaries (Zonal)
      - Secretaries for Women's Ministries
    - International Secretary for Personnel
    - International Secretary for Programme Resources
    - Officers Commanding/Regional Commanders (IHQ)
      - Command Presidents Women's Ministries
    - National/Territorial Commanders
      - National/Territorial Presidents Women's Ministries

International Headquarters

The Salvation Army International Trustee Company

Registered Office: 101 Queen Victoria Street, London EC4V 4EH
Registration No 2538134. Tel: (020) 7332 0101
Company Secretary: Lieut-Colonel Edmund Chung

DIRECTORS: Comr Robin Dunster (Chair), Comr Ann Woodall (Managing Director and Vice Chair), Mr Andrew Axcell, Comr Larry Bosh, Comr William Cochrane, Comr Robin Forsyth, Comr Kenneth Hodder, Mr David Kidd, Comr Lalkiamlova, Comr Amos Makina, Comr Lyn Pearce, Comr Barry Pobjie, Mr Trevor Smith, Comr Robert Street.

The company is registered under the Companies Acts 1985 and 1989 as a company limited by guarantee, not having a share capital. It has no assets or liabilities, but as a trustee of The Salvation Army International Trusts it is the registered holder of Salvation Army property both real and personal including shares in some of the Army's commercial undertakings. The company is a trust corporation.

Reliance Bank Limited

Faith House, 23-24 Lovat Lane, London EC3R 8EB
Tel: (020) 7398 5400; fax: (020) 7398 5401; email: info@reliancebankltd.com;
website: www.reliancebankltd.com
Chairman: Commissioner Ann Woodall
Managing Director: Trevor J. Smith, ACIB
Finance Director: Kevin Dare, BA(Hons), CIMA
Banking Lending Manager and Company Secretary: Paul Underwood, ACIB
Banking Services Manager: Andrew Hunt, ACIB
Business Development Manager: Nichola Keating

DIRECTORS: Comr Ann Woodall (Chairman), Comr William Cochrane, Col Brian Peddle, Lt-Col Ed Chung, Maj David Hinton, Maj Alan Read, Maj Jeffrey Wills, Mr Trevor Smith, Mr Kevin Dare, Mr Philip Deer, Mr Edward Ashton, Mr Gerald Birkett, ACIB.

Reliance Bank Ltd is an authorised institution under the Banking Act 1987, regulated by the Financial Services Authority and registered under the Companies and Consumer Credit Acts.

OWNED by The Salvation Army through its controlling shareholders – The Salvation Army International Trustee Company and The Salvation Army Trustee Company – Reliance Bank accepts sterling and foreign currency deposits, carries on general banking business, and provides finance for Salvation Army corporate customers and private and business customers.

The bank can grant mortgages, personal loans and overdrafts, and also provides travel currency, cheques and safe custody facilities. It offers current accounts, together with a Reliance Bank Visa debit card, fixed deposits and savings accounts, and provides money transmission transactions both within the UK and abroad. Internet banking and telephone banking services are also offered.

The bank pays at least 75 per cent of its taxable profits by means of Gift Aid donation to its controlling shareholders.

Brochures are available on request, or visit www.reliancebankltd.com

STATISTICS Employees 22

International Headquarters

OVERSEAS SERVICE FUNDS 2008-2009 INCOME

	International Self-Denial Contributions £	International Self-Denial Special £	Special Projects £	Donations via IHQ £	Total £
Australia Eastern	462,206	-	955,308	648,002	2,065,516
Australia Southern	456,586	-	844,736	168,503	1,469,825
Bangladesh	759	-	-	-	759
Belgium	2,536	-	-	2,013	4,549
Brazil	15,244	-	-	-	15,244
Canada	1,044,386	-	1,911,356	133,503	3,089,245
Caribbean	19,969	-	4,424	1,078	25,471
Congo (Brazzaville)	-	-	-	-	-
Democratic Republic of Congo	40,568	-	-	-	40,568
Czech Republic	813	-	-	-	813
Denmark	50,000	-	17,405	13,806	81,211
Eastern Europe	11,475	-	-	-	11,475
Finland	57,781	-	28,214	60,084	146,079
France	16,706	-	13,028	5,193	34,927
Germany	54,400	-	-	85,191	139,591
Ghana	9,000	-	-	-	9,000
Hong Kong	74,125	-	70,873	18,324	163,322
India Central	25,861	-	-	-	25,861
India Eastern	25,304	-	-	-	25,304
India Northern	16,423	-	-	-	16,423
India South Eastern	32,943	-	-	-	32,943
India South Western	21,114	-	-	-	21,114
India Western	16,260	-	-	-	16,260
Indonesia	25,618	-	-	-	25,618
Italy	12,039	-	-	5,527	17,566
Japan	69,055	-	20,751	19,143	108,949
Kenya East	23,182	-	-	621	23,803
Kenya West	15,271	-	-	-	15,271
Korea	52,008	-	2,982	16,162	71,152
Latin America North	7,895	-	-	-	7,895
Liberia	1,278	-	-	5,033	6,311
Malawi	3,285	-	-	-	3,285
Mexico	17,759	-	-	-	17,759
Mozambique	609	-	-	-	609
Myanmar	1,018	-	-	-	1,018
Netherlands	177,056	-	712,844	113,055	1,002,955
New Zealand	293,349	-	136,892	27,978	458,219
Nigeria	8,909	-	-	-	8,909
Norway	342,037	-	2,164,215	459,558	2,965,810
Pakistan	1,798	-	-	-	1,798
Papua New Guinea	5,093	-	-	491	5,584
Philippines	3,563	-	-	761	4,324
Portugal	2,013	-	-	-	2,013
Rwanda	3,752	-	-	-	3,752
Singapore & Malaysia	68,419	-	29,992	145,841	244,252
South America East	7,688	-	-	-	7,688
South America West	22,246	-	-	1,864	24,110
Southern Africa	23,505	-	-	1,985	25,490
Spain	4,701	-	-	21,873	26,574
Sri Lanka	1,275	-	-	-	1,275
Sweden	79,316	-	297,572	187,230	564,118
Switzerland	476,363	-	1,300,334	147,533	1,924,230
Taiwan	3,158	-	5,019	-	8,177
Tanzania	3,585	-	-	-	3,585
Uganda	683	-	-	-	683
United Kingdom	1,579,928	-	1,683,155	164,753	3,427,836
USA Central	2,010,444	636,537	1,511,585	581,954	4,740,520
USA Eastern	2,305,048	223,242	1,527,853	1,069,316	5,125,459
USA Southern	2,488,028	279,286	2,734,170	205,888	5,707,372
USA Western	1,577,914	93,218	2,902,929	13,676	4,587,737
USA SAWSO	-	-	440,081	85,007	525,088
Zambia	25,775	-	-	-	25,775
Zimbabwe	16,894	-	-	1,000	17,894
	14,216,016	1,232,283	19,315,718	4,411,946	39,175,963

International Headquarters

OVERSEAS SERVICE FUNDS 2008-2009 EXPENDITURE

	Support of Overseas Work £	Special Projects £	Donations via IHQ £	Total £
Africa, General	2,728	19,986	-	22,714
Americas, General	12,118	948	850	13,916
Angola	102,364	37,968	288	140,620
Austria	29,497	-	8,102	37,599
Bangladesh	121,931	318,686	2,605	443,222
Brazil	652,219	584,933	36,544	1,273,696
Burundi	24,521	-	1,065	25,586
Caribbean	591,107	986,238	31,245	1,608,590
Congo (Brazzaville)	482,161	121,758	48,777	652,696
Democratic Republic of Congo	437,295	511,046	32,773	981,114
Czech Republic	368,058	3,183	7,542	378,783
Eastern Europe	1,721,626	897,333	89,673	2,708,632
Estonia	109,932	65,824	13,066	188,822
Europe, General	11,567	54,387	7,148	73,102
Fiji & Tonga	-	131,848	2,023	133,871
France	-	-	2,860,562	2,860,562
Germany & Lithuania	231,238	146,691	4,039	381,968
Ghana	145,152	303,605	15,141	463,898
Hong Kong	8,333	353,667	4,466	366,466
Hungary	55,541	33,034	500	89,075
India National Secretariat	58,475	134,611	30	193,116
India Central	192,356	535,727	14,040	742,123
India Eastern	90,242	349,819	55,751	495,812
India Northern	244,219	127,867	68,980	441,066
India South Eastern	203,961	302,636	13,680	520,277
India South Western	307,143	276,685	11,939	595,767
India Western	209,055	197,771	17,957	424,783
Indonesia	40,489	556,161	112,374	709,024
Italy and Greece	197,934	118,195	30,508	346,637
Kenya East	364,124	653,772	13,128	1,031,030
Kenya West	295,814	376,834	11,739	684,387
Korea	2,267	147,786	2,135	152,188
Kuwait	-	130,462	-	130,462
Latin America North	584,816	333,141	16,512	934,469
Latvia (Sweden)	110,134	36,371	20,644	167,149
Liberia	159,023	248,306	3,249	410,578
Malawi	163,198	294,900	18,479	476,577
Mali	27,771	-	15,278	43,049
Mexico	357,978	1,275,392	4,909	1,638,279
Mozambique	138,605	115,792	23,445	277,842
Myanmar	86,710	426,705	500	513,915
Nigeria	139,976	233,130	22,939	396,045
Pakistan	426,665	404,566	28,665	859,896
Papua New Guinea	397,724	76,520	4,675	478,919
Philippines	342,082	1,533,988	18,981	1,895,051
Poland	13,373	33,850	31,357	78,580
Portugal	269,446	148,262	1,326	419,034
Rwanda	110,359	338,735	45,407	494,501
SALT College	36,721	-	24	36,745
Singapore & Malaysia	36,062	289,165	15,512	340,739
South America East	494,105	582,774	43,273	1,120,152
South America West	390,147	939,097	128,889	1,458,133
South Asia, General	13,119	7,133	-	20,252
Southern Africa	177,734	617,944	23,065	818,743
SPEA, General	9,070	6,772	2,071	17,913
Spain	291,679	200,025	23,184	514,888
Sri Lanka	74,992	862,642	153,545	1,091,179
Taiwan	52,444	179,214	194	231,852
Tanzania	154,860	474,168	10,464	639,492
Uganda	116,682	379,932	4,680	501,294
Zambia	418,207	379,260	12,706	810,173
Zimbabwe	412,303	418,467	76,425	907,195
Central Pension Scheme	1,000,000	-	-	1,000,000
Other International Operations	1,284,889	-	-	1,284,889
	15,604,341	19,315,718	4,269,068	39,189,127

International Headquarters

COMMUNITY DEVELOPMENT PROJECTS

THE Salvation Army thanks those listed below who, during 2008, assisted in its ministry to some of the world's most vulnerable people. This was done through community development projects overseen by the International Projects and Development Services (IPDS) at IHQ. These involved:

Combating the HIV/Aids pandemic; developing savings and loans groups; promoting healthy communities; supporting educational services; improving access to safe water and sanitation; supporting social service programmes to the aged, the marginalised and the young; responding to disaster-hit areas

Country	*Donor*	US $*
Australia	Eastern Territory (AusAID)	828,447
Canada	CIDA (Canada)	1,587,631
Germany	Christoffel Blindenmission	207,985
	Kindernothilfe	634,740
Netherlands	The Netherlands and Czech Republic Territory	2,785,749
Norway	NORAD	1,997,475
Sweden	Dispurse Foundation	203,000
	Radio Help	65,000
Switzerland	Switzerland, Austria and Hungary Territory	2,264,749
	Accentus Foundation	13,869
	Bread for All	195,555
	Government grants in kind: milk products	761,338
	Lord Michelham of Hellingly Foundation	71,095
	Solidarity Third World	43,270
	Swiss Government Grants	230,442
	Swiss Solidarity	48,078
	Various foundations	117,273
United Kingdom	Allan & Nesta Ferguson	20,000
	Beit Trust	20,000
	Count Zoltan Trust	4,650
	Douglas Investment Trust	10,000
	Hope HIV	243,733
	SMB Charitable Trust	1,000
USA	National Headquarters (SAWSO and USAID)	4,050,363
TOTAL		**US$ 16,405,442**

*As per exchange rate at time amounts recorded by the IPDS at IHQ

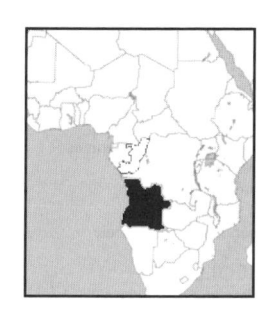

ANGOLA COMMAND

Command leaders:
Lieut-Colonels Ambroise and Alphonsine Zola

Officer Commanding:
Lieut-Colonel Ambroise Zola
(1 Mar 2008)

**Command Headquarters: Igreja Exército de Salvação,
Bairo Marçal - Rangel 2 MA nº 15, Luanda, Angola**
Postal address: Caixa Postal 1656-C, Luanda, Angola
Tel: [00244] 928-570867; email: angosalvo@yahoo.com

Salvation Army work in Angola was officially established in 1985. Having been part of the Congo (Kinshasa) and Angola Territory, it became a separate command on 1 March 2008.
In 1974, two officers originally from Angola but trained and serving in Congo (Kinshasa) entered Angola by Uige Province to commence Salvation Army meetings in that part of the country. In 1978, other Salvationists from Kinshasa met in Angola's capital, Luanda, and 'opened fire'. The Salvation Army was officially recognised by the Angola Government on 14 February 1992.

Zone: Africa
Country included in the command: Angola
'The Salvation Army' in Portuguese: Exército de Salvação
Languages in which the gospel is preached: Humbundu, Kikongo, Kimbundu, Lingala, Ngangela, Portuguese

WITHIN the first 15 months of the command's existence five sections were opened and are operating well. Officers and soldiers are very committed to develop this new command.

During the year under review three officer-couples were appointed as reinforcements from Democratic Republic of Congo Territory. Some envoys were trained but, with many outposts now established in areas where there had been no Salvation Army presence, there is a need for more leaders. In June 2008 five new lieutenants were ordained and commissioned, and appointed to corps.

Timbrelists participated at a Government-organised arts and music competition. They attracted everyone's attention and were chosen as the best display. Plans are in place to create a National Band, Songsters, Timbrelists, and Arts and Theatre Group.

The establishment of a Command and Women's Ministries Advisory Board is sparking new fire in the hearts of Salvationists as they discuss matters concerning the growth of God's Kingdom. The sectional directors for women's ministries are developing many programmes and activities for their groups.

Although faced with limited resources and difficult working

Angola Command

conditions, Angola's Salvationists continue to move forward by God's grace. Development of the work is quick; relationships with the Government and other churches are good.

STATISTICS
Officers 37 (active 33 retired 4) **Cadets** 5
Employees 8
Corps 15 **Outposts** 13 **Schools** 2
Senior Soldiers 2,467 **Junior Soldiers** 570

STAFF
Women's Ministries: Lt-Col Alphonsine Zola (CPWM) Maj Mamie Makuntima (HL)
Candidates: Maj Isabella Vuanza
Extension Officer: Capt Daniel Diantelo
Finance: Capt Sergio Nsumbu
Property: tba
Social: tba
Statistics: Capt Daniel Diantelo
Training: Majs Norbert and Isabelle Vuanza (Asst Officers)
Youth and Music: Capt Timothée Lukanu

SECTIONS
Cabinda: Maj Antoine Kupesa
Luanda 1: Maj Joâo Mpembele; tel: (00244) 923-748074
Luanda 2: Maj Domingo Makuntima; tel: (00244) 923-742759
Uige: Capt Antonio Nsingi; tel: (00244) 924-118717;
Zaire: Maj Joâo Batista Ndombele

TRAINING COLLEGE
Rua Capola, Casa no 5/Bis, Q9/SAPU, Kilamba Kiaxi; tel: (00244) 926-842134

SECONDARY SCHOOL
Rua da Esquarda Intealao dos Moradores (Antigo Empromac), Bairo Hoji ha Yenda, Municipio do Cazenga;
tel: (00244) 928-138191; Mr Paulo Mafuta (Director)

SCHOOL NZOANENE
Rua 21 de Janeiro, Bairo Rocha Pinto, Municipio de Maianga; tel: (00244) 923-607311;
Sgt Nsumbu Mavug (Director)

SOCIAL SERVICES
Development and Emergencies
Moxico (vaccination programme and water supplies); Luena 1 Corps (polio project); Luao Corps (polio project and water supplies)

BANGLADESH: Cadets of the Witnesses For Christ Session make their entry ready for their ordination and commissioning conducted by General Shaw Clifton and Commissioner Helen Clifton. It was the first commissioning to be led by a General in the command (*see page 72*).

AUSTRALIA NATIONAL SECRETARIAT

Offices: 2 Brisbane Ave, Barton, Canberra, ACT 2600
Postal address: PO Box 4256, Manuka, ACT 2603, Australia
Tel: [61] (02) 6273 3055; fax: [61] (02) 6273 1383; email: Peter.Holley@aue.salvationarmy.org

Two Christian Mission converts, John Gore and Edward Saunders, pioneered Salvation Army operations on 5 September 1880 in Adelaide. These were officially established on 11 February 1881 by the appointment of Captain and Mrs Thomas Sutherland. In 1921 the work in Australia was organised into Eastern and Southern Territories with headquarters in Sydney and Melbourne.

A National Secretariat serving the whole of Australia and funded jointly by both territories was established in 1987.

Periodicals: *Kidzone*, *Warcry*

THE National Secretariat represents the views of The Salvation Army's two Australian territories to Government. It addresses issues of spiritual, moral, ethical and social welfare by means of submissions, personal dialogue with members of parliament and attendance at open forums.

Maintaining a watching brief over legislation related to Salvation Army programmes, the Secretariat works towards creating warm, workable relationships with parliamentarians, Government departments, not-for-profit organisations and the diplomatic corps.

The National Secretary is responsible for the operations of the Red Shield Defence Services (RSDS), is a member of the National Moral and Social Issues Council (MASIC) and Employment Plus, and chairs the National Red Shield Appeal Media Advisory Committee.

The RSDS is a philanthropic support group within the Australian Defence Force (ADF). Its officers are appointed from both Australian territories and become Accredited Representatives in the ADF, having the privilege of wearing military uniform. They exercise a pastoral and welfare role but are not military chaplains. Some RSDS officers are currently supporting units that have be deployed overseas in a peacekeeping role.

Responsibility for negotiating funding from the Australian Government for overseas development transferred from the Secretariat on 1 January 2009 to Australia Eastern Territory with the establishment of the Salvation Army International Development office (SAID). Its predecessor, the Salvation Army Australia Development Office (SAADO), was commenced in 1991 with an Overseas Development Consultant and managed more than 300 projects in 25 developing countries.

National Sec: Maj Peter Holley

Editorial Department: 95-99 Railway Rd, Blackburn, Vic 3130 (PO Box 479); tel: 03 8878 2303; fax: 03 8878 4816
National Editor-in-Chief: Capt Mal Davies
Red Shield Defence Services: PO Box 3246, Manuka, ACT 2603; tel: (02) 6273 2280; fax: (02) 6273 1383
Chief Commissioner: Maj Barry Nancarrow

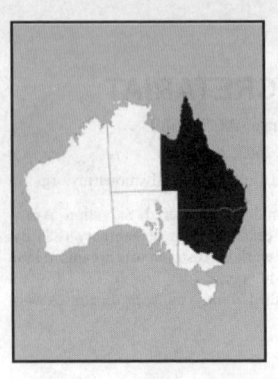

AUSTRALIA EASTERN TERRITORY

Territorial Commander:
Commissioner Linda Bond
(1 May 2008)

Chief Secretary:
Colonel James Condon (1 Mar 2008)

Territorial Headquarters: 140 Elizabeth Street, Sydney, NSW 2000
Postal address: PO Box A435, Sydney South, NSW 1235, Australia
Tel: [61] (02) 9264 1711 (10 lines); fax: [61] (02) 9266 9638; website: www.salvos.org.au

Two Christian Mission converts having pioneered Salvation Army operations in Adelaide in September 1880, the work in Australia was organised into Eastern and Southern Territories in 1921, with headquarters for the Eastern Territory being set up in Sydney.

Zone: South Pacific and East Asia
States included in the territory: New South Wales, Queensland, The Australian Capital Territory (ACT)
Languages in which the gospel is preached: Cantonese, English, Korean, Mandarin
Periodicals: *Creative Ministry*, *Pipeline*, *Venue*, *Women in Touch*

SEEKING to build upon past years in regard to mission, an invitation was given to all Salvationists, employees and friends to advise the territorial commander on what they saw were the priorities the territory needed to address to advance the mission. As a result of those submissions, and the recommendations from the seven previous years, the following mission priorities were set:

A territory marked by prayer and holiness; the whole territory, in every place, involved in evangelism; corps healthy and multiplying; people equipped and empowered to serve the world; a territory passionate about bringing children to Jesus; youth trained and sent out to front-line mission; a significant increase of new soldiers and officers.

A 2020 summit was convened in September 2008 to consider the suggestions and develop a strategy to make the mission priorities a reality. Action groups have been established; this is a work in progress.

History was created when Chinese-speaking Salvationists in Australia held their first national congress in Sydney. Attendees came from across Australia; there were also guests from Taiwan and Hong Kong. The Hong Kong Staff Band played at many venues around the city, culminating at Sydney Congress Hall.

'Hope For Life' – a new initiative – offers people new hope in overcoming the tragedy of suicide. At the launch it was stated that one person

Australia Eastern Territory

died by suicide in Australia every five hours. Also introduced were a website to help people understand suicide and identify signs in potential victims, and a training programme to assist professionals to support the bereaved.

The Hope Line telephone service was established for people bereaved by suicide to discuss their issues with qualified counsellors.

Rural Australia having been in the grip of a severe drought for some time, Christmas 2008 saw the launch of a DVD – *Braver, Stronger, Wiser* – which aimed to celebrate the resilience of the farming community and also help counter a disturbing suicide rate in these areas.

Some 130,000 remote households who have access to few or no medical or counselling services received a copy of the DVD. Copies also went to doctors' networks, Salvation Army centres and rural chaplains.

The DVD features stories of people in remote areas who have struggled with various forms of depression, plus a range of resources including emergency contact numbers. The purpose is to save lives and get across the message that there is hope and that help is available.

STATISTICS
Officers 938 (active 520 retired 418) **Cadets** (1st Yr) 14 (2nd Yr) 17 **Employees** 3,680
Corps 174 **Outposts/Corps Plants** 16 **Social Centres/Programmes** 230 **Community Services** 178 **Thrift Stores/Charity Shops** 217
Senior Soldiers 8,698 **Adherents** 2,761 **Junior Soldiers** 490
Personnel serving outside territory Officers 34 Layworkers 5

STAFF
Women's Ministries: Comr Linda Bond (TPWM) Col Jan Condon (TSWM)
Business: Lt-Col Peter Laws
Personnel: Lt-Col Philip Cairns
Programme: Lt-Col Miriam Gluyas
Social Programme: Maj Cec Woodward
Asst Chief Sec (Governance): Lt-Col Jan Laws
Asst Sec for Business (Legal): Maj Mervyn Holland
Asst Sec for Business (Administration): Capt Stuart Evans
Aged Care Plus: Ms Sharon Callister
Audit: Mr Tim Green
Booth College: Lt Col John Hodge
Candidates: Capts Craig and Donna Todd
Communications and Public Relations: Maj Philip Maxwell
Counselling Service: Maj Christine Unicomb
Emergency Services: Maj Lyall Reese
Finance: Mr Ian Minnett
Information Technology: Mr Wayne Bajema
Mission and Resource Team:
  Territorial Mission Directors: Majs Neil and Sharon Clanfield
  Music and Creative Arts: Mr Graeme Press
Moral and Social Issues Council: Maj Colin Lingard
Property: Maj Edwin Cox
Red Shield Defence Services: Maj Barry Nancarrow
Salvation Army International Development Office (SAID): Lt Col Pamela Hodge
Salvationist Supplies: Mr Graham Lang
Salvos Stores: Mr Neville Barrett
Sydney Staff Songsters: S/L Graeme Press

DIVISIONS
Australian Capital Territory and South NSW: 2-4 Brisbane Ave, Barton, ACT 2600; PO Box 4224, Kingston, ACT 2604; tel: (02) 6273 2211; fax: (02) 6273 2973; Majs Rodney and Leonie Ainsworth
Central and North Queensland: 54 Charles St, North Rockhampton, QLD 4701; PO Box 5343, CQMC, Rockhampton, QLD 4702; tel: (07) 4999 1999; fax: (07) 4999 1915
Newcastle and Central NSW: 94-96 Parry St, PO Box 684, The Junction NSW 2291; tel: (02) 4926 3466; fax: (02) 4926 2228; Maj Kerry Haggar
North NSW: cnr Taylor and Beardy Sts, PO Box 1180, Armidale NSW 2350; tel: (02) 6771 1632; fax: (02) 6772 3444; Majs Gary and Judith Baker

Australia Eastern Territory

South Queensland: 342 Upper Roma St, Brisbane QLD 4000; GPO Box 2210, Brisbane, QLD 4001; tel: (07) 3222 6666; fax: (07) 3229 3884; Majs Wayne and Robyn Maxwell

Sydney East and Illawarra: 61-65 Kingsway, Kingsgrove NSW 2208; PO Box 740, Kingsgrove, NSW 1480; tel: (02) 9336 3320; fax: (02) 9336 3359

The Greater West: 93 Phillip St, Parramatta, NSW 2150; PO Box 66, Parramatta, NSW 2124; tel: (02) 9635 7400; fax: (02) 9689 1692; Majs John and Narelle Rees

BOOTH COLLEGE

Bexley North, NSW 2207: 32a Barnsbury Grove, PO Box N63; tel: (02) 9502 0400 fax: (02) 9502 4177

SCHOOL FOR OFFICER TRAINING

Bexley North, NSW 2207: 120 Kingsland Rd, PO Box N63; tel: (02) 9502 1777; fax: (02) 9554 3298

SCHOOL FOR CHRISTIAN STUDIES

Bexley North, NSW 2207: 32a Barnsbury Grove, PO Box N63; tel: (02) 9502 0432; fax: (02) 9502 0476

SCHOOL FOR LEADERSHIP TRAINING

Stanmore, NSW 2048: 97 Cambridge St; tel: (02) 9557 1105; fax: (02) 9519 7319

SCHOOL FOR YOUTH LEADERSHIP

Lake Munmorah, NSW 2259: 42 Greenacre Ave; tel: (02) 4358 8886; fax: (02) 4358 8882

HERITAGE PRESERVATION CENTRE

Bexley North, NSW 2207: 32a Barnsbury Grove, PO Box N63; tel: (02) 9502 0424; fax: (02) 9502 0481; email: AUEHeritage@aue.salvationarmy.org; Maj Ken Sanz

EMPLOYMENT PLUS

National Support Office: Level 3, 10 Wesley Ct, East Burwood, VIC 3151; tel: 136 123 Australia Wide

RECOVERY SERVICES DEPARTMENT

Sydney: 85 Campbell St, Surry Hills 2010; tel: (02) 9212 4000; fax: (02) 9212 4032; Maj Glenn Whittaker

BRIDGE PROGRAMME – ADDICTION RECOVERY
(Alcohol, other drugs and gambling)

Brisbane: Brisbane Recovery Services Centre, Moonyah, 58 Glenrosa Rd, PO Box 81, Red Hill QLD 4059; tel: (07) 33690922; fax: (07) 3369 9294 (acc men 84, detox unit 12, halfway house 9)

Canberra: Canberra Recovery Services Centre, 5-13 Mildura St, Fyshwick ACT 2609, PO Box 4181, Kingston ACT 2604; tel: (02) 6295 1256; fax: (02) 6295 3766 (acc men 38, halfway house 3)

Central Coast: Central Coast Recovery Services Centre, Selah, 60 Berkeley Rd, Berkeley Vale, PO Box 5019, NSW Chittaway 2261; tel: (02) 4388 4588; fax: (02) 4389 1490 (acc women 36, halfway house 4)

Gold Coast: Gold Coast Recovery Services Centre, Fairhaven, 168 Macdonnell Rd, Eagle Heights, QLD 4271; tel: (07) 3173 6215; fax: (07) 5526 3989 (acc men 36, detox unit 11, women 18)

Hunter Region Recovery Services:
  Lake Macquarie Recovery Services Centre, 93 Russell Rd, PO Box 93, Morisset, NSW 2264; tel: (02) 4973 1495; fax (manager): (02) 4970 5807
  Miracle Haven Bridge Programme (acc 78 men)
  Endeavour Duel Diagnosis Bridge Programme (acc 27 men)
  Newcastle Bridge Youth and Family Drug and Alcohol Support Programme (Bridge House): 100-102 Hannell St, PO Box 125, Wickham, NSW 2293; tel: (02) 4961 1257 (acc halfway house 3 males)

Leura: Blue Mountains Recovery Services Centre, 6 Eastview Ave, Leura NSW 2780; PO Box 284, Wentworth Falls, NSW 2782; tel: (02) 4782 7392; fax: (02) 4782 9127 (acc men 17, halfway house 3)

Nowra: Shoalhaven Bridge Programme, cnr Salisbury Rd and St Anns St, Nowra, NSW 2541; tel: (02) 4422 4604; fax: (02) 4422 4672

Penrith: Involuntary Care Trial, After-care Service and The Salvation Army Problem Gambling Service, 3/76 Henry St, Penrith, NSW 2750; PO Box 702, Penrith B/C 2751

Sydney:
  William Booth House Recovery Services Centre, 56-60 Albion St, Surry Hills, NSW 2010; PO Box 209, Surry Hills, NSW 2010; tel: (02) 9212 2322; fax: (02) 9281 9771 (acc men and women 131)
  Alf Dawkins Detoxification Unit, 5-19 Mary St, Surry Hills, NSW 2010; tel: (02) 8218 1209;

Australia Eastern Territory

fax: (02) 9211 0455 (acc 10 men)
Townsville:
Townsville Recovery Services Centre,
312-340 Walker St; PO Box 803,
Townsville, QLD 4810; tel: (07) 4772 3607;
fax: (07) 4772 3174 (acc men 30)
Townsville Recovery Services Women's
out-Client Service, Grace Cottage

SALVOS STORES
General Manager: Mr Neville Barrett
Head Office: 4 Archbold Rd, Minchinbury, NSW 2770; tel: (02) 9834 9030, fax: (02) 9677 1782
ACT and Monaro Area: 5-15 Mildura St, Fyshwick, ACT 2609; PO Box 4181, Kingston; tel: (02)6239 0117; fax: (02) 6295 9788 (retail stores 8)
Brisbane: 80 Glenrosa Rd, PO Box 81, Red Hill, QLD 4059; tel: (07) 3369 0222; fax: (07) 3368 6344 (retail stores 18)
Central Coast Area Administration Office: 348 Mann St, Gosford, NSW 2250; tel: (02) 4325 3101; fax: (02) 4325 4879 (retail stores 4)
Gold Coast:3-9 Precision Drive, Molendinar, QLD 4214; tel: (07) 5571 5777; fax: (07) 5574 4893 (retail stores 12)
Illawarra Area: 29 Ellen St, Wollongong, NSW 2500; tel: (02) 4228 5644; fax: (02) 4228 1040 (retail stores 7)
Newcastle: 900 Hunter St, Newcastle, NSW 2300; tel: (02) 4961 3889; fax: (02) 4961 2623 (retail stores 9)
Sydney: 7 Bellevue St, St Peters, NSW 2044; tel: (02) 9516 5089; fax: (02) 9519 2924 (retail stores 12)
Sydney West: 4 Archbold Rd, Minchinbury, NSW 2770; tel: (02) 9834 9030; fax: (02) 9677 1782 (retail stores 10)
Townsville: Suite 2, 216-230 Woolcock St, Currajong, QLD 4812; PO Box 803, Townsville, QLD 4810; tel: (07) 4725 7360, fax: (07) 4725 7370 (retail stores 5)

RURAL CHAPLAINS
ACT and South NSW Div: c/o DHQ Canberra; tel: (02) 6273 2211; fax: (02) 6273 2973
Longreach, QLD 4730: 149 Eagle St, PO Box 127; tel: (07) 4658 3590
Newcastle and Central NSW Div: c/o DHQ Newcastle; tel: (02) 4926 3466; fax: (02) 4926 2228
North NSW Div: c/o DHQ Armidale; tel: (02) 6771 1632; fax: (02) 6772 3444
South Queensland Div: c/o DHQ Brisbane; tel: (07) 3222 6666; fax: (07) 3229 3884

AERIAL SERVICE
Flying Service Base: 10 Steelcon Parade, Mt Isa QLD 4825; tel: (07) 4749 3875; fax: (07) 4749 3870

CONFERENCE AND HOLIDAY HOUSES/UNIT
Collaroy, NSW 2097: The Collaroy Centre, Homestead Ave, Collaroy Beach, PO Box 11; tel: (02) 9982 9800 (office), (02) 9982 6570 AH; fax: (02) 9971 1895; website: www.collaroycentre.org.au
Budgewoi, NSW 2262: 129 Sunrise Ave; bookings through THQ; tel: (02) 9266 9595 (holiday cottage acc 6)
Monterey NSW 2217: 3/34 Burlington Ave; bookings through THQ; tel: (02) 9266 9595
Cairns, QLD 4870: 281-289 Sheridan St; bookings through DHQ Rockhampton; tel: (07) 4999 1902 (5 units)
Caloundra, QLD 4551: 4 Michael St, Golden Beach; bookings through DHQ Brisbane; tel: (07) 3222 6666 (holiday house)
Margate, QLD 4019: 2 Duffield Rd; bookings through DHQ Brisbane; tel: (07) 3222 6666 (3 holiday units)
Tugun, QLD 4224: 3/15 Elizabeth St; bookings through DHQ Brisbane; tel: (07) 3222 6666 (holiday unit)

RED SHIELD DEFENCE SERVICES
RSDS Administration: Canberra ACT; tel: (02) 6273 2280; fax: (02) 6273 1383
Gallipoli Barracks, Brisbane, QLD: RSDS representative; tel: (07) 3332 7684;i fax: (07) 3851 3979
Holsworthy Military Camp, Sydney, NSW: RSDS representative; mobile: 0417 796 973; fax: (02) 8782 2016
Lavarack Barracks, Townsville, QLD: RSDS representative; tel: (07) 4771 8571
Royal Military College, Duntroon, ACT: RSDS representative; mobile: 0407 830 488
Singleton Infantry Centre, NSW: RSDS representative; tel: (02) 6575 0279; fax: (02) 6573 4512

SOCIAL SERVICES
Residential Aged Care
Arncliffe, NSW 2205: Macquarie Lodge, 171 Wollongong Rd; tel: (02) 9556 6900; fax: (02) 9567 5043 (acc nursing home 65, hostel 49)
Balmain, NSW 2041: Montrose, 13 Thames St, PO Box 2; tel: (02) 9818 2355; fax: (02) 9818 5062 (acc hostel men 44)

Australia Eastern Territory

Bass Hill, NSW 2197: Weeroona Village;
14 Trebartha St; tel: (02) 9645 3220;
fax: (02) 9645 1390 (acc hostel 45, nursing home 60)

Canowindra, NSW 2804: Moyne, 161 Nangar Rd, PO Box 156; tel: (02) 6344 1475; fax: (02) 6344 1902 (acc nursing home 29, hostel 44)

Chelmer, QLD 4068: Warrina Village, 35 Victoria Ave, PO Box 239, Indooroopilly; tel: (07) 3379 9800; fax: (07) 3379 7839 (acc nursing home 40, hostel 42)

Dee Why, NSW 2099: Pacific Lodge, 15 Fisher Rd, PO Box 109; tel: (02) 9982 8090; fax: (02) 9982 9174 (acc hostel 59)

Dulwich Hill, NSW 2203: Maybanke, 80 Wardell Rd, PO Box 286; tel: (02) 9560 4457; fax: (02) 9569 1301 (acc nursing home 25, hostel 38)

Erina, NSW 2250: Woodport Village, 120-140 The Entrance Rd; tel: (02) 4365 2660; fax: (02) 4365 1812 (acc units 73, nursing home 96)

Goulburn, NSW 2580: Gill Waminda, Mary St, PO Box 233; tel: (02) 4823 4300; fax: (02) 4823 4317; (acc hostel 63, nursing home 40)

Merewether, NSW 2291: Carpenter Court, 46 John Pde, PO Box 246; tel: (02) 4963 4300; fax: (02) 4963 6489 (acc 42)

Narrabundah, ACT 2604: Mountain View, Goyder St, PO Box 61; tel: (02) 6295 1044; fax: (02) 6295 1473 (acc 67)

Parkes, NSW 2870: Rosedurnate, 46 Orange St, PO Box 100; tel: (02) 6862 2300; fax: (02) 6862 3756 (acc nursing home 29, hostel 46)

Port Macquarie, NSW 2444: Bethany, 2-6 Gray St, PO Box 2016; tel: (02) 6584 1127; fax: (02) 6584 1045 (acc nursing home 50, hostel 40)

Riverview, QLD 4303: Moggill Ferry Rd, PO Box 6042; tel: (07) 3282 1000; fax: (07) 3282 6929 (acc nursing home 50, hostel 143)

Rockhampton, QLD 4700: Bethesda, 58 Talford St, PO Box 375; tel: (07) 4922 3229; fax: (07) 4922 3455 (acc hostel 50)

Independent Living Retirement Villages

Arncliffe, NSW 2205: Macquarie Lodge, 171 Wollongong Rd; tel: (02) 9556 6900; fax: (02) 9567 5043 (acc units 82)

Bass Hill, NSW 2197: Weerona Village, 14 Trebartha St, Bass Hill, NSW 2197; tel: (02) 9645 3220; fax: 9645 1390 (acc units 44)

Burwood, NSW 2134: Shaftesbury Court, 75a Shaftesbury Rd; tel: (02) 9560 4457 (acc units 35)

Chelmer, QLD 4068: Warrina Village, 35 Victoria Ave, PO Box 239; tel: (07) 3379 9800; fax: (07) 3379 7839 [Indooroopilly, QLD 4068] (acc units 12)

Collaroy, NSW 2097: Warringah Place, 1039 Pittwater Rd, PO Box 395; tel: (02) 9971 1933; fax: (02) 9971 4155 (acc self-care units 64, serviced apartments 44)

Erina, NSW 2250: Woodport Village, 120-140 The Entrance Rd; tel: (02) 4365 2660; fax: (02) 4365 1812 (acc units 64)

Narrabundah, ACT 2604: Karingal Court, 11 Boolimba Cresc:; tel: (02) 6295 1044; fax: (02) 6295 1473 (acc 36)

Parkes, NSW 2870: Rosedurnate, 46 Orange St, PO Box 100; tel: (02) 6862 2300; fax: (02) 6862 3756 (acc units 17)

Riverview, QLD 4303: Moggill Ferry Rd, PO Box 6042; tel: (07) 3282 1000; fax: (07) 3282 6929 (acc units 26)

Aged Care Respite and Day Care

Rivett, ACT 2611: Burrangiri, 1-7 Rivett Place, PO Box 8065; tel: (02) 6288 1488; fax: (02) 6288 0321 (acc 15, respite day care 20)

Children's Services
(including Day Care and After School)

Carina, QLD 4152: 202 Gallipoli Rd; tel: (07) 3395 0744

Gladstone, QLD 4680: Family Day Care, 198 Goondoon St; tel: (07) 4972 2985; fax: (07) 4972 7835

Macquarie Fields, NSW 2564: Eucalyptus Dr, PO Box 1; tel: (02) 9605 4749; fax: (02) 9618 1492

Slacks Creek, QLD 4127: Communities for Children, 123 Paradise Rd, PO Box 998; tel: (07) 3290 5200; fax: (07) 3290 5394

Counselling Service

Head Office: Rhodes, NSW 2138: 15 Blaxland Rd, PO Box 3096; tel: (02) 9743 4535

Brisbane, QLD 4122: 5/46 Mt Gavatt-Capalaba Rd, Upper Mount Gravatt, PO Box 6266, Upper Mt Gravatt; tel: (07) 3349 5046

Campbelltown: refer to Penrith Office

Gosford, NSW 2250: 59 Mann St, Gosford; tel: (02) 9743 2831

Canberra (North Lyneham), ACT 2602: Ste 3, Southwell Park Offices, Montford Cresc: tel: (02) 6248 5504

Fairfield – refer to Penrith Office

Penrith, NSW 2751: Ste 15, Lethbridge Ct,

Australia Eastern Territory

20-24 Castlereagh St, PO Box 588;
tel: (02) 4731 1554
Stafford, QLD 4053: 32 Hayward St; refer to Brisbane Office
Sydney, NSW 2138: 15 Blaxland Rd, PO Box 3096, Rhodes; tel: (02) 9743 2831
Tuggeranong, ACT 2900: refer to Canberra (North Lyneham) Office

Moneycare Financial Counselling Services
Brisbane, QLD 4001: 342 Upper Roma St, PO Box 2210, tel: (07) 3222 6666; fax: (07) 3229 3884
Campbelltown, NSW 2560: 27-31 Rudd Rd, PO Box 2041 Leumeah; tel: (02) 4620 7482
Campsie, NSW 2194: 30 Anglo Rd, PO Box 399; tel: 9787 5375; fax: 9718 6775
Central QLD 4701: 54 Charles St, North Rockhampton, PO Box 5343, CQMC 4702; tel: (07) 4999 1999; fax: (07) 4999 1915
Dickson, ACT 2602: 4 Hawdon Pl, PO Box 1038; tel: (02) 6247 1340 (Direct Line), (02) 6247 3635; fax: (02) 6257 2791
Hurstville, NSW 2220: 23 Dalcassia St; appointments through Kingsgrove; tel: (02) 9336 3320; fax: (02) 9336 3359
Kingsgrove, NSW 1480: 61-65 Kingsway, PO Box 740; tel: 9336 3320; fax: 9336 3359
Lethbridge Park, NSW 2150: 2-6 Bougainville Rd; tel/fax: (02) 9835 2756
Newcastle West, NSW 2302: refer to DHQ, Union and Parry Sts; tel: (02) 4926 0231; fax: (02) 4926 2228
North NSW: inland outreach service, 2-6 Gray St, Port Macquarie; tel: (02) 6583 5963
Parramatta; NSW 2150: Ste 1, 2nd Fl, 95 Phillip St, PO Box 3681; tel: (02) 9633 5011; fax: (02) 9633 5214
Taree, NSW 2430: Suite 1, 10 Pulteney St; tel: (02) 6552 6237; fax: (02) 6892 4405
Tuncurry, NSW 2428: 7 South St; tel: (02) 6554 6101; fax: (02) 6555 3347
Box Hill, VIC 3128: 17 Nelson Rd; tel: (03) 9890 2993

Crisis and Supported Accommodation (homelessness services)
Adults (singles)
Cairns North, QLD 4870: Centennial Lodge, 281 Sheridan St, PO Box 140N; tel: (07) 4031 4432; fax: (07) 4031 9473 (acc men 25, women 20, women with children 6; patient transfer scheme men 5, women 5)
Campbelltown, NSW 2560: Shekinah, 127b Lindesay St; PO Box 662; tel: (02) 4625 9022 (acc women and children 4 units)
Carrington, NSW 2294: The Anchor, PO Box 73, cnr Young and Cowper Sts; tel: (02) 4961 6129; fax: (02) 4961 4038 (acc men 21)
Griffith, NSW 2680: cnr Binya and Anzac Sts; tel: (03) 6964 3388 (acc hostel 5 + 6 men in units within the community)
Leeton, NSW 2705: 9 Mulga St; tel: (02) 6953 4941 (family units 3)
Mount Isa, QLD 4825: Serenity House, 4 Helen St; PO Box 2900; tel: (07) 4743 3198 (acc women and children 11)
Newcastle, NSW 2293:
 Clulow Court, PO Box 414, the Junction, NSW 2291 (acc single women, crisis hostel beds 8)
 The Ark, 116-120 Hannell St, PO Box 94, Wickham; tel: (02) 4969 8066; fax: (02) 4969 8073 (acc 24)
Southport, QLD 4215: Still Waters, 173 Wardoo St, PO Box 888, Ashmore City 4214; tel: (07) 5591 1776 (acc crisis beds women 20, women and children 7 units, single women medium-term 16)
Spring Hill, QLD 4004: Pindari, 28 Quarry St, PO Box 159;
 (men's programme) tel: (07) 3832 1491 (acc hostel 120, units 9);
 (women's programme) tel: (07) 3832 6073 (acc crisis beds single women 18)
Surry Hills, NSW 2010:
 Foster House, 5-19 Mary St; tel: (02) 9212 1065; fax: (02) 9218 1248 (acc men's hostel 96 beds; Knudsen Place, IPU 21 beds; community places 85)
 Samaritan House, 348 Elizabeth St, PO Box 583; tel: (02) 9211 5794; fax: (02) 9212 5430 (acc single women crisis beds 24, medium-term beds 20, Glebe units 8)
Tewantin, QLD 4565: 26 Donella St, PO Box 671; tel: (07) 5447 1184; fax: (07) 5447 1854 (acc families)
Toowomba, QLD 4350: 5 Russell St, PO Box 2527; (acc men's crisis) tel: (07) 4632 5239; fax: (07) 4639 1821 (acc family crisis) tel: (07) 4639 1998

Youth Services
Bundaberg QLD 4670: Youth Refuge, 71 Woongarra St, Bundaberg 4670; tel: (07) 4151 3400; fax: (07) 4152 6044 (acc 16)
Canberra, ACT 2601: Oasis Support Network, PO Box 435; tel: (02) 6248 7191; fax: (02) 6249 8116

Australia Eastern Territory

Canberra, ACT 2601: Oasis Youth Residential Service, Canberra, PO Box 63; tel: (02) 6288 6248; fax: (02) 6288 0646

Canley Vale, NSW 2166: Youth link, 214 Sackville St, PO Box 188W, Fairfield West, NSW 2165; tel: (02) 9725 7779; fax: (02) 9725 7781

Fortitude Valley, QLD 4006: Youth Outreach Service, 20 Baxter St, PO Box 248; tel: (07) 3854 1245; fax: (07) 3854 1552

Minchinbury NSW 2770: Joblink, Unit 31b, 40 Sterling Rd; tel: (02) 9675 5972; Mt Druitt office tel: (02) 9625 8533; fax: (02) 9625 4933

Newcastle, NSW 2293: Newcastle Youth Crisis and Training Service; The Ark, 116-120 Hannell St, PO Box 94, Wickham; tel: (02) 4969 8066; fax: (02) 4969 8073 (acc 24)

Surry Hills, NSW 2010: Oasis Youth Support Network; 365 Crown St, PO Box 600, Darlinghurst 1300; tel: (02) 9331 2266

Wyong, NSW 2259: Oasis Youth Centre, 5 Hely St, PO Box 57, Wyong; tel: (02) 4353 9799; fax: (02) 4353 9550

Intellectually Disabled Persons Services

Bardon, QLD 4065: SAILSS (Salvation Army Individual Lifestyle Support Service), 3/63 Macgregor Tce; tel: (07) 3368 0700; fax: (07) 3367 1844 (home support services 31 adults)

Broken Hill NSW 2880: LISK, 633 Lane St, PO Box 477; tel: (08) 8088 2044; fax: (08) 8087 7669

Toowoomba, QLD 4350: Horton Village, 2 Curtis St, PO Box 289; tel: (07) 4639 4026; fax: (07) 4638 3248 (acc 28)

Family Tracing Service

Brisbane, QLD 4000: 342 Upper Roma St, PO Box 2210, Brisbane 4001; tel: (07) 3222 6661; fax: (07) 3229 3884

Sydney, NSW 2000: PO Box A435, Sydney South 1235; tel: (02) 9211 0277; fax: (02) 9211 2044

Sydney, NSW 2000: Special Search, PO Box A435, Sydney South 1235; tel: (02) 9211 6491; 1300 667 366 Australia Wide; fax: (02) 9211 2044

Telephone Counselling Service

Five Dock, NSW 2049: Salvo Care Line, NSW 2046; 1 Barnstaple Rd, PO Box 178; tel: (02) 8736 3297 (office); fax: (02) 8736 3278

Brisbane, QLD 4001: Salvo Care Line; QLD 4000; 342 Upper Roma St, GPO Box 2210; tel: (07) 3222 6666

Domestic Violence Programme*

Chatswood, NSW 2067: cnr Johnson and Archer Sts; tel: (02) 9411 7728; fax: (02) 9411 7174

Hostels for Students

Marrickville, NSW 2204: Stead House, 12 Leicester St, PO Box 3015; tel: (02) 9557 1276 (acc women 25)

Toowong, QLD 4066: 15 Jephson St, PO Box 1124; tel: (02) 3371 1966 (acc 66)

Employment Preparation and Skills Training

Bundaberg, QLD 4670: Tom Quinn Community Centre; 8 Killer St, Bundaberg 4670; tel: (07) 4153 3557; fax: (07) 4151 1746

Canley Vale, NSW 2166: YouthLink, 214 Sackville St, Canley Vale; PO Box 188W, Fairfield West, NSW 2165; tel: (02) 9725 7779

Fortitude Valley, QLD 4006: Youth Outreach Service, 20 Baxter St, PO Box 248; tel (07) 3854 1245

Hamilton, NSW 2303: This Way Up Furniture Company, 3/24 Hudson St, Hamilton North, PO Box 162; tel: (02) 4969 5695; fax (02) 4969 5665

Minchinbury, NSW 2770: Job Link, 6 Colyton Rd; PO Box 55, Mt Druitt 2770; tel: (02) 9625 8533; fax (02) 9625 4933

Riverview, QLD 4304: Work for the Dole, 29 Riverview Rd; PO Box 359, Booval QLD 4304; tel: (07) 3282 1300; fax: (07) 3816 2903

Surry Hills, NSW 2010: Oasis Youth Support Network, 365 Crown St, PO Box 600, Darlinghurst; tel: (02) 9331 2266; fax: (02) 9331 2200

Wickham, NSW 2293: Newcastle Youth Crisis and Training Service, 116-120 Hannell St, PO Box 94, Wickham; tel: (02) 4969 8066; fax: (02) 4969 8073

Court and Prison Ministry

ACT and South NSW Div, ACT 2604: (ACT Corrective Services, Goulburn and Berrima Prisons, Bowral, Belconnen and Alexander Maconachie Centres, Symonston Remand Centres) PO Box 4224, Kingston; tel: (02) 6273 2211; fax: (02) 6273 2973

Central and North Queensland Div, QLD 4702: (Townsville Court, Townsville, Capricornia and Lotus Glenn Correctional Centres) PO Box 5343 CQMC, Rockhampton; tel: (07) 4999 1999; fax (07) 4999 1915

Greater West Div, NSW 2124: (Parramatta, Penrith, Campbelltown Region, Bathurst and Parramatta Family Courts, Silverwater, Emu

Australia Eastern Territory

Planes, Bathurst, Kirkconnell, Oberon Correctional Centres and MRRC) PO Box 66, Parramatta; tel: (02) 9635 7400; fax: (02) 9689 1692

Newcastle and Central NSW Div, NSW 2291: (Newcastle, Wyong and Dubbo Courts, Cessnock Correctional Centre) PO Box 684, The Junction; tel: (02) 9426 3466; fax: (02) 9426 2228

South Queensland Div, QLD 4001: (Brisbane, Ipswich, Beenleigh, Southport and Caloundra Courts, Arthur Gorrie, Borrallon, Wolston, Woodford Brisbane Women's, Numinbah and Palen Creek Correctional Centres, Brisbane Police Watch House and Remand Centre) PO Box 2210, Brisbane; tel: (07) 3222 6670; fax (07) 3229 3884

Sydney East and Illawarra Div, NSW 1480: (Sydney Children's Courts and Sydney Metropolitan Juvenile Justice Centres, Downing Centre Courts) PO Box 740, Kingsgrove; tel: (02) 9336 3320; fax: (02) 9336 3359

Chaplains to Statutory Authorities

New South Wales Fire Brigades, NSW 2000: City of Sydney Fire Stn, Level 211-213 Castlereagh St, Sydney; tel (02) 9265 2736; fax: (02) 9718 9837

New South Wales Rural Fire Service, NSW 2142: 15 Carter St Homebush Bay, Locked Mail Bag 17, Granville NSW 2142; tel: (02) 8741 5555; fax: (02) 9553 1854

Queensland Fire and Rescue Service, QLD 4005: Kemp Place Fire Stn, Ivory St, Fortitude Valley, PO Box 1472, New Farm; tel (07) 3406 8322; fax (07) 3406 8328

Community Service

Auburn, NSW 2144: Auburn Community Services Centre, 5-7 Mary St; tel: (02) 9749 7150

Brisbane, QLD 4003: 97 Turbot St, PO Box 13688, George St 4003; tel: (07)3211 9230; fax: (07) 3211 9234

Broken Hill, NSW 2880: Algate House Community Centre, 633 Lane St, PO Box 477; tel: (08) 8088 2044; fax: (08) 8087 7669

Campsie, NSW 2194: 30 Anglo Rd, PO Box 399, tel: (02) 9787 2333; fax: (02) 9718 6775

Canberra, ACT 2602: 4 Hawdon Pl, Dickson; PO Box 1038, Dickson; tel: (02) 6247 3635; fax: (02) 6257 2791

Dee Why, NSW 2099: Northern Beaches Centre, 1 Fisher Rd, PO Box 210; tel: (02) 9981 4472; fax: (02) 9972 9976

Dulwich Hill: 54 Dulwich St; tel: (02) 9569 4511; fax: (02) 9569 4677

Greenslopes, QLD 4120: 481 Logan Rd; PO Box 221, Stones Corner; tel: (07) 3394 4184; fax: (07) 3324 2409

Hurstville, NSW 2220: St George Centre; 23 Dalcassia St, PO Box 930, Kingsgrove, NSW 2220; tel: (02) 9579 3897; fax: (07) 9579 6094

Inala, QLD 4077: 83 Inala Ave, PO Box 1050; tel: (07) 3372 1889

Ipswich, QLD 4305: 14 Ellenborough St, PO Box 227; tel: (07) 3812 2462; fax: (07) 3812 3818

Logan City, QLD 4114: Shop 5, 41 Station Rd, Woodridge, PO Box 816; tel: (07) 3808 2564; fax: (07) 3290 0310

Macquarie Fields, NSW 2564: cnr Eucalyptus and Peppermint Crscnt, PO Box 1; tel: (02) 9605 4717

Maroubra, NSW 2035: Eastern Beaches Centre, 100 Boyce Rd, PO Box 209; tel: (02) 9314 2166

Nerang, QLD 4211: Shop 5, Dulmar Centre, 43-45 Price St, PO Box 599; tel: (07) 5596 0764; fax: (07) 5527 4681

Newcastle West, NSW 2302: 96 Parry St, PO Box 2364, Dangar, NSW 2309; tel: (02) 4929 2300

North Brisbane, QLD 4018: cnr Roghan and Lemke Rds, PO Box 155, Taigum; tel: (07) 3173 6309; fax: (07) 3265 5841

Parramatta NSW 2150: 30-32 Smith St; PO Box 6178, Parramatta BC; tel: (02) 9891 4526; fax: (02) 9891 6089

Southport, QLD 4215: 3/80 Davenport St, PO Box 1680; tel: (07) 5591 2729; fax: (07) 5591 1216

Sydney, NSW 2010: Inner City (Streelevel) Centre, 339 Crown St, Surry Hills 2010; tel: (02) 9360 1000; fax: (02) 9331 7276

Townsville, QLD 4810: 54 Charles St, North Rockhampton, PO Box 5343; CQMC 4702; tel: (07) 4999 1999; fax: (07) 4999 1915

Wollongong, NSW 2500: 29 Ellen St, PO Box 6102; tel: (02) 4225 1372; fax (02) 4225 3509

Wynnum, QLD 4178: 107 Akonna St, PO Box 701; tel: (07) 3393 4713; fax: (07) 3393 5066

The territory also has 5 women's refuge centres which include accommodation for mothers and children. Addresses and telephone numbers are confidential.

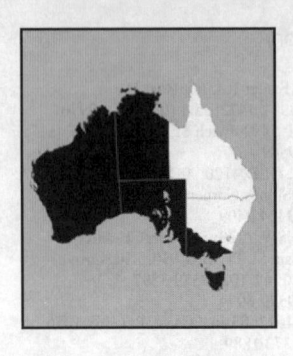

AUSTRALIA SOUTHERN TERRITORY

Territorial leaders:
Commissioners James and Carolyn Knaggs

Territorial Commander:
Commissioner James Knaggs (1 Aug 2006)

Chief Secretary:
Colonel Raymond Finger (1 Dec 2007)

Territorial Headquarters: 95-99 Railway Road, Blackburn 3130, Victoria

Postal address: PO Box 479, Blackburn 3130, Victoria, Australia

Tel: [61] (03) 8878 4500; fax: [61] (03) 8878 4841; email: Salvosaus@aus.salvationarmy.org; website: www.salvationarmy.org.au

Two Christian Mission converts having pioneered Salvation Army operations in Adelaide in September 1880, the work in Australia was organised into Eastern and Southern Territories in 1921, with headquarters for the Southern Territory being set up in Melbourne.

Zone: South Pacific and East Asia
States included in the territory: Northern Territory, South Australia, Tasmania, Victoria,
  Western Australia
Languages in which the gospel is preached: Cantonese, English, Korean, Mandarin, local aboriginal
  languages
Publications: *Kidzone*, *On Fire*, *Warcry*

THE territory saw many victories and advances during 2008-09. Arguably, the year's highlight was 'Insane' – the Territorial Youth Conference held in Melbourne in January 2009. More than 600 delegates spent a week together enjoying a range of workshops, electives, worship rallies, social events and public demonstrations.

On a 'Break the Slave Chain' protest against human trafficking, they marched holding hands through Melbourne in silence. The march concluded with a rally in Federation Square, in the heart of the city, where Steve Chalke (international chairman of Stop the Traffik) addressed more than 1,000 people.

As a result of 'Insane' more than 100 young people became Christians, more than 60 indicated they would become senior soldiers, and more than 20 said they wanted to explore Salvation Army officership.

In November 2008 commissioning weekend of the Witnesses For Christ Session also served to draw attention to Salvationists' creative talents in the Onfire Festival Exhibition. The performance and display area of Melbourne Convention Centre saw a range of art and crafts on display as well as musical, dramatic and puppetry performances. A 'soapbox' corner saw some fiery preaching and poetry readings.

In May 2008 the Army released a report called *Finding My Place*, in response to a National Youth Commission inquiry into youth homelessness. Two months later a further report, *A Raw Deal*, highlighted the impact of pharmaceutical costs on drug users trying to become clean.

Then in September the Army launched the 'Hope For Life' programme, which aimed to help prevent suicide and give bereavement support to people affected by someone taking their own life.

The territory's *War Cry* magazine celebrated its 125th year of circulation and in October received the Gutenberg Award from the Australasian Religious Press Association (jointly with the New Zealand *War Cry*). It is the most celebrated national award for religious magazines and newspapers.

Another cause for celebration was the release of the four-DVD set *Boundless Salvation*. Ten years in the making, the DVDs are a superb resource charting the Army's origins, commencement in Australia, culture, theology and mission. With high production standards and supported by study guides for small group use, they will be a valuable resource in the territory for years to come.

The year under review concluded with the Army's full focus on crisis relief after the nation's worst natural disaster ever. In the second week of February more than 1,000 homes in rural areas not far from Melbourne were lost to bush fires. Some 400,000 hectares of land were damaged and, most alarmingly, nearly 200 people lost their lives, with many other hundreds injured.

The Army took a key role in providing material, emotional and spiritual support; its relief stations in key areas were manned 24 hours a day. The public were incredibly supportive and generous, leading the territory to find several large warehouses that could be used to store donated goods for distribution among fire victims and survivors.

Government officials, community and business leaders and the public thanked The Salvation Army for the vital role it played in providing crisis support and relief.

STATISTICS
Officers 892 (active 494 retired 398) **Cadets** (1st Yr) 26 (2nd Yr) 16 **Employees** 4,964
Corps 170 **Outposts** 19 **Social Centres/Programmes** 256 **Salvos Stores** 192 **Community Support Centres** 128 **Outback Flying Service** 1
Senior Soldiers 8,709 **Adherents** 2,725 **Junior Soldiers** 1,009
Personnel serving outside territory Officers 32 Layworkers 5

STAFF
Women's Ministries: Comr Carolyn Knaggs (TPWM) Col Aylene Finger (TSWM) Lt-Col Jennifer Walker (Director) Maj Lorraine Daddow (Child Sponsorship)
Asst Chief Sec: Maj Allan Daddow
  Asst to the CS: Maj Dennis Rowe
  Asst to Asst CS: Maj Kaylene Fyfe

Australia Southern Territory

Executive Support Officer: Capt Kerryn Roberts
Training Principal: Maj Stephen Court
National Editor-in-Chief: Capt Malcolm Davies
Business Administration: Lt-Col Peter Walker
Asst Business Sec and Overseas Development Director: Maj Gary Hart
Audit: Mr Cameron Duck
Salvo Stores: Mr Allen Dewhirst
Finance: Mr Gregory Stowe
Salvationist Supplies: Mrs Karen Newton
Information Technology: Mr Larry Reed
Legal: Capt Malcolm Roberts
Property: Mr David Sinden
Public Relations: Maj Neil Venables
Personnel: Maj Frank Daniels
Asst Sec for Personnel: Maj Winton Knopp
Asst Sec for Personnel – Leader Development: Maj Christine Faragher
Candidates Sec: Maj Len Turner
Overseas Personnel Officer: Lt-Col Julie Spiller
Human Resources: Mr John Cullinan
Pastoral Care: Maj Graeme Faragher
Spiritual Development: Maj Robert Paterson
Programme: Lt-Col Ian Hamilton
Asst Sec for Programme: Lt-Col Marilyn Hamilton
Family Tracing: Maj Sophia Gibb
Melbourne Staff Band: B/M Ken Waterworth
Melbourne Staff Songsters: S/L Brian Hogg
Social Programme: Maj David Eldridge
Youth: Capt David Collinson

DIVISIONS

Eastern Victoria: 347-349 Mitcham Rd, Mitcham, Vic 3132; tel: (03) 8872 6400; Lt-Col Jocelyn Knapp and Maj Cilla Bone
Melbourne Central: 1/828 Sydney Rd, North Coburg 3058; tel: (03) 9353 5200; Majs Rodney and Jennifer Barnard
Northern Victoria: Bramble St, Bendigo, Vic 3550; tel: (03) 5443 4288; Majs Graeme and Karyn Rigley
South Australia: 39 Florence St, Fullarton, SA 5063; tel: (08) 8408 6900; Maj Winsome Mason
Tasmania: 27 Pirie St, New Town, Tas 7008; tel: (03) 6278 7184; Majs Graeme and Helen McClimont
Western Australia: 333 William St, Northbridge, WA 6003; tel: (08) 9227 7010; Majs Iain and Dawn Trainor
Western Victoria: 102 Eureka St, Ballarat, Vic 3350; tel: (03) 5337 1300; Majs Kelvin and Winsome Merrett

REGION

Northern Territory: Level 2 Suite C, Paspalis Centre, 48-50 Smith St, Darwin, NT 0800; tel: (08) 8944 6000; Majs John and Wendy Freind

OFFICER TRAINING COLLEGE

Parkville, Vic 3052: 303 Royal Parade; tel: (03) 9347 0299

ARCHIVES AND HERITAGE CENTRES

Melbourne, Vic 3000: Territorial Archives and Museum, 69 Bourke St, PO Box 18187, Collins St E, Melbourne, Vic 8003; tel: (03) 9639 3618
Nailsworth, SA 5083: Heritage Centre, 2a Burwood Ave; tel: (08) 8342 2545
Northbridge, WA 6003: Historical Society Display Centre, 3rd Floor, 333 William St; tel: (08) 9227 7010

CONFERENCE AND HOLIDAY CENTRES

Bicheno, Tas 7215: Holiday Home, 11 Banksia St
Busselton, WA 6280: Holiday Unit 2, 12 Gale St; tel: (08) 9227 7010/7134
Daylesford, Vic 3460: Holiday Flat, Unit 5/28, Camp St
Geelong, Vic 3219: Conference Centre, Adams Court, Eastern Park; tel: (03) 5226 2121
Mount Dandenong, Vic 3767: Holiday Home, 6 Oakley St
Ocean Grove, Vic 3226: Holiday Home, 4 Northcote Rd
Victor Harbor, SA 5211: Encounters Conference Centre, 22 Bartel Blvd; tel: (08) 8552 2707 (acc 148)
Weymouth, Tas 7252: Holiday Camp, Walden St; tel: (03) 6382 6359 (acc 32)

EMPLOYMENT PLUS

National Office: Level 3, 10 Wesley Court, Burwood, Vic 3151; tel: (03) 9847 8700; Maj John Simmonds
Service Delivery Centres: New South Wales 24; Queensland 15; South Australia 7; Tasmania; Victoria 27; Western Australia 7
Enquiries: tel: 136 123

Australia Southern Territory

FLYING PADRE AND OUTBACK SERVICES
PO Box 43289, Casuarina, NT 0811;
tel: (08) 8945 0176; Capt David Shrimpton

RED SHIELD DEFENCE SERVICES
Puckapunyal Representative; tel: (03) 5793 1294
Robertson Barracks Representative;
tel: (08) 8935 2526/8981 7663

SOCIAL SERVICES
Aboriginal Ministry
Alice Springs, NT 0870: Aboriginal Programme,
88 Hartley St; tel: (08) 8951 0207

Aged Care Non-Residential Services
Healthlink – Aged Care Day Therapy Services:
  138 Reservoir Rd, Modbury SA 5092;
  tel: (08) 8264 8300
  cnr Lindisfarne and Melsetter Rds, Huntfield Heights SA 5163; tel: (08) 8186 6987
  West Melbourne, Vic 3003; Community Aged Care Programme, 9 Roden St;
  tel: (03) 9329 5777
  New Town, Tas 7008: Accommodation and Housing for the Aged, 115 New Town Rd;
  tel: (03) 6278 3256
  Ulverstone, Tas 7315: Community Aged Care, 14 Grove Rd; tel: (03) 6425 6004

Alcohol, Other Drugs and Corrections
Burnie, Tas 7320: Court Mandated Diversion, Drug and Alcohol Day Programme with Outreach, 24 View St, tel: (03) 6431 6706
Darwin: Drug and Alcohol Services, Lot 5043 Salonika St, Stuart Park 0820;
tel (08) 8981 4199
Howrah, Tas 7018: Crime Prevention Programme, 135 Clarence St; tel: (03) 6244 4615
Launceston, Tas 7250:
  Bridge Outreach Service, 109 Elizabeth St; tel: (03) 6331 6760
  Drug and Alcohol Day Programme, 109 Elizabeth St; tel: (03) 63316760
  Court Support, Magistrates Court, Charles St; tel: 0409 773 401
  Breakfree Crime Prevention Programme, 109 Elizabeth St; tel: (03) 6331 6760
  Needle Syringe Programme, 109 Elizabeth St, tel: (03) 6331 6760
  Transitional Housing Support for Prionsers, 109 Elizabeth St, tel: (03) 63316760
New Town, Tas 7008:
  Bridge Programme, Creek Rd; tel: (03) 6278 8140
  Drug and Alcohol Day Programme with Outreach, Creek Rd; tel: (03) 6278 8140
  XCELL Prison Support Service, Creek Rd; tel: (03) 6278 8140
  Transitional Housing Support for Prisoner, 117 New Town Rd; tel: (03) 6278 2817

Chaplaincy – Police, Fire and Emergency Services
Darwin: Police, Fire and Emergency Services Chaplain, PO Box 39764, Winnellie 0821;
tel: (08) 8999 4154
Kununurra: Fire and Emergency Services Chaplain, PO Box 1367, Kununurra, WA 6743;
tel: 9169 2344
Perth, WA 6000: FESA chaplain; tel: 0407 294 312

Child Care and Family Services
Balga, WA 6061: Long Day Care, 10-18 Lavant Way; tel: (08) 9349 7488
Ballarat, Vic 3550: Karinya Occasional Childcare, 6 Crompton St; tel: (03) 5329 1100
Bendigo, Vic 3552: Fairground Family Access Programme, 65-71 Mundy St;
tel: (03) 5442 7699
Burnie, Tas 7320: Parenting Partners Programme, 24 View St; tel: (03) 6432 4511
Devonport, Tas 7310: Parenting Partners Programme, 166 William St;
tel: (03) 6424 9211
Hobart, Tas 7000: Communities for Children, 250 Liverpool St; tel: (03) 6234 2299
Hobart, Tas 7000: Early Support Programme and Family Pathways, 250 Liverpool St;
tel: (03) 6236 9933
Howrah, Tas 7018: Parenting Partners Programme, 135 Clarence St;
tel: (03) 6244 4615
Kingborough, Tas 7052: Parenting Partners Programme, 3 Opal Dr; tel: (03) 6229 8058
Moonah, Tas 7009: Parenting Partners Programme, 73 Hopkins St; tel: 6278 1648
North Coburg, Vic 3031: Crossroads Youth and Family Services, 2/828 Sydney Rd;
tel: (03) 9353 1011
Sunshine, Vic 3020: Westcare Child and Adolescent Services, Home-Based One-to-One Care, Intensive Case Management Services, 34 Devonshire Rd;
tel: (03) 9312 3544
Ulverstone, Tas 7315: Parenting Partners Programme, 21 Victoria St; tel: (03) 6425 5382

Court and Prison Services
Alice Springs, NT 0870: 88 Hartley St;
tel: (08) 8951 0200
Ballarat, Vic 3350: tel: (03) 5226 6239

Australia Southern Territory

Bendigo, Vic 3552: Bramble St; tel: (03) 5443 4288

Darwin, Anula, NT 0812: cnr Lee Point Rd and Yanula Dr; tel: (08) 8927 5189

Geelong, Vic 3220: Gordon St; tel: (03) 5225 3353

Hobart, Tas 7000: Prison Support Service, 250 Liverpool St; tel: (03) 6234 1870

Horsham, Vic 3400: 12 Kalkee Rd; tel: (03) 5382 1770

Manningham, SA 5086: 109 Hampstead Rd; tel: (08) 8368 6800

Northbridge, WA 6003: 333 William St; tel: (08) 9260 9500

Sale, Vic 3869: PO Box 45, Yinnar, Vic; tel: (03) 5169 1503

Stuart Park, NT 0820: Lot 5043 Salonika St; tel: (08) 8981 4199

Swan Hill, Vic 3583: 190 Beveridge St; tel: (03) 5033 1718

Wangaratta, Vic 3677: 13-17 Garnet Ave; tel: (03) 5722 1129

West Melbourne, Vic 3033: Senior Courts and Prisons Chaplain, 9 Roden St; tel: (03) 9329 6022

Wodonga, Vic 3690: PO Box 130, Beechworth, Vic 3747; tel: (03) 5728 3245

Intensive Living and Learning Environments – ILLE Programmes

St Albans; Taylors Lakes; Sunshine; North Altona; Kealba; Melton: contact through Westcare, 34 Devonshire Rd, Sunshine; tel: (03) 9312 3544

Children's Homes and Cottages

Sunshine, Vic 3020: Westcare, 34 Devonshire Rd, Sunshine; tel: (03) 9312 3544

Community Programmes

Alice Springs: 88 Hartley St, Alice Springs 0870; tel: (08) 8951 0206

Bendigo, Vic 3552: Community Programmes including Youth Ministries, Personal Support Programme, Creative Arts and Technology, Gravel Hill Community Gardens, HillSkills Workshop, Hilltop Café, Fairground Children's Contact Service, 65-71 Mundy St; tel: (03) 5442 7699

Berri, SA 5343: Riverland Community Services, 20 Wilson St; tel: (08) 8582 3182

Brunswick, Vic 3056: 256 Albert St; tel: (03) 9387 6746

Flinders and Riverland Community Service, 35 Flinders Tce; tel: (08) 8641 1021

Hawthorn, Vic 3122: Hawthorn Project, Homeless Outreach Project, Community Connection Project, Equity and Access Project, 16 Church St; tel: (03) 9851 7800

Kununurra, WA 6743: Community Outreach Centre, 106 Coolibah Drive; tel: 0429 802 885

Melbourne, Vic 3000: Melbourne Corps Project 614 and Life Centre, 69 Bourke St; tel: (03) 9650 4851

Mornington, Vic 3931: PYFS, Reconnect Programme, Shop 9, 234 Main St; tel: (03) 5976 2231

Rosebud, Vic 3939: Peninsula Community Support Programme, 17-19 Ninth Ave; tel: (03) 5986 7268

Family Violence Services

Adelaide, SA 5000: Central Violence Intervention Project, 440 Morphett St; tel: (03) 8231 0655

Ballarat, Vic 3350: Karinya; tel: (03) 5329 1100 (acc 8)

Belmont, Vic 3216: Kardinia Women's Services; tel: (03) 5241 9149

Darwin, NT 0801: Catherine Booth House, PO Box 189; tel (08 8981 5928 (acc 8)

Fullarton, SA 5063: Bramwell House, PO Box 305; tel: (08) 8379 7223 (acc 5 adults and children); providesWomen's and Children's Domestic Violence Programme, Central Violence Intervention Programme, Non-Residential Domestic Violence Programme

Karratha, WA 6714: tel:(08) 9185 2807 (acc 16)

New Town, Tas 7008: McCombe House; tel: (03) 6228 1099 (acc 16)

Onslow, WA 6710: tel: (08) 9184 6481

Perth, WA 6000: Graceville Centre, PO Box 8025, Perth Business Centre 6849; tel: (08) 9328 8529 (acc 43)

Crisis Services

Balga, WA 6061: Family Accommodation Programme, 10-18 Lavant Way; tel: (08) 9349 7488

Croydon, Vic 3136: Gateways Crisis Services, PO Box 1072; tel: (03) 9725 8455

Frankston, Vic 3199: Peninsula Counselling Service, Peninsula Crisis Centre, 37 Rossmith Ave East; tel: (03) 9784 5050

Geraldton, WA 6530: Family Crisis Accommodation, 42 Ainsworth St; tel: (08) 9965 3627

Leongatha, Vic 3953: GippsCare Domestic Violence Outreach Service, 51 McCartin St; tel: (03) 5662 4502

New Town, Tas 7008: SA Supported Housing, 117 New Town Rd; tel: (03) 6278 2817

St Kilda, Vic 3128:

Australia Southern Territory

Inner South Domestic Violence Service,
27 Grey St; tel: (03) 9536 7730,
toll free 1800 627 727
Verve Programme, 31 Grey St;
tel: (03) 9536 7780
Crisis Accommodation, 31 Grey St;
tel: (03) 9536 7730, toll free 1800 627 727
Health and Information, 29 Grey St;
tel: (03) 9536 7703, toll free 1800 627 727
Access Health Service, 31 Grey St;
tel: (03) 9536 7780
Inner South Domestic Violence Services,
29 Grey St; tel: (03) 9536 7720

Ingle Farm Community Services Programme

Emergency Relief, Family Supported
Accommodation, Youth Outreach Services,
Community Work Programme, Substance
Abuse Support Service For Youth,
Communities For Children, Community Work
Programme, Community Work Programme:
cnr Bridge and Maxwell Rds, Ingle Farm 5098;
tel: (08) 8397 9333
Burlendi Youth Shelter: 22 Spains Rd, Salisbury
5108; tel: (08) 8281 6641
Muggy's Accommodation Service Youth Hostel
and Outreach Services: 88 Henderson Ave,
Pooraka; tel: (08) 8260 6617
Muggy's Accommodation (Southern Campus):
Unit 2, 424 Marion Rd, Plympton;
tel: (08) 8371 2080

Emergency Accommodation

Alice Springs, NT 0870: 11 Goyder St;
tel: (08) 8952 1434 (acc service, single men,
dual diagnosis)
Ballarat, Vic 3350: Karinya, 6 Crompton St;
tel: (03) 5329 1100 (acc women with
children 8)
Belmont, Vic 3350: Kardinia Women's Services;
tel: (03) 5241 9149 (acc women with children 6)
Berri, SA 5343: Riverland Community Services,
20 Wilson St; tel: (08) 8582 3182 (acc 30)
Bunbury, WA 6230: cnr Bussell H'way and
Timperly Rd; tel: (08) 9721 4519 (acc family
units 2)
Burnie, Tas 7320: 24 View Rd;
tel: (03) 6431 5791 (acc 61)
Geraldton, WA 6530: Ainsworth St;
tel: (08) 9964 3667 (acc family units 3)
Grovedale, Vic 3216: Kardinia Men's Services;
tel: (08) 5274 9550
Horsham, Vic 3400: 12 Kalkee Rd;
tel: (03) 5382 1770 (acc family units 3,
single 3)
Jacana, Vic 3047: 23 Sunset Blvd;
tel: (03) 9309 6289 (acc family units 4,
community houses 6)
Kalgoorlie, WA 6430: Oberthur St;
tel: (08) 9021 2255 (acc family units 2)
New Town, Tas 7008: McCombe House,
63 Creek Rd; tel: (03) 6228 1099 (accom 8,
exit houses 4)
Sale, Vic 3850: cnr Cunningham and Marley Sts;
tel: (03) 5144 4564 (acc 6)
Stawell, Vic 3380: 26-30 Ligar St;
tel: (03) 5358 4072 (acc youth and singles)
Sunbury, Vic 3429: 27-37 Anderson St;
tel: (03) 9740 8844
Sunshine, Vic 3020: 1 St Andrew St;
tel: (03) 9364 9744

Emergency Family Accommodation

Berri SA 5343; Riverland Community Services –
Supported Accommodation for Families and
Personal Support Programme: 20 Wilson St;
tel: 8582 3182
Burnie, Tas 7320: Oakleigh House, 24 View Rd;
tel: (03) 6431 5791 (acc 61)
Darwin, NT 0800: 49 Mitchell St;
tel: (08) 8981 5994 (family units 5)
Horsham, Vic 3400: 12 Kalkee Rd;
tel: (03) 5382 1770 (acc family units 3, single 3)
New Town, Tas 7008: McCombe House,
Swanston St Family Units;
tel: (03) 6229 1099
Port August, SA 5700: 35 Flinders Tce;
tel: (08) 8641 1021 (acc 65)
St Kilda, Vic 3182: 27 Grey St;
tel: (03) 9536 7730 (acc 20)

Emergency Services

Darwin, NT 0800: tel (08) 8981 2500/4199
Eltham, Vic 3095: Lower Factory 5,
266 Bolton St; tel: (03) 9439 7786
Hobart, Tas 7000: tel: (03) 6278 7184
Malaga, WA 6944: PO Box 2131;
tel: 0407 611 466
Pooraka, SA 5095: Units 7 & 8, 95 Research Rd;
tel: (08) 8262 7834

Family Outreach (Community Programme)

Brunswick, Vic 3056: 256 Albert St;
tel: (03) 9387 6746
Jacana, Vic 3047: 23 Sunset Blvd;
tel: (03) 9309 6289
Moonah, Tas 7008: 73 Hopkins St;
tel: (03) 6228 0910
Port August, SA 5700: 35 Flinders Tce;
tel: (08) 8641 1024

Australia Southern Territory

Seymour, Vic 3660: Pathways, 6 Tallarook St;
tel: (03) 5799 1581

Salvos Stores
Administration: 233-235 Blackburn Rd,
Mt Waverley 3149; tel: (03) 9845 4000
Stores: Northern Territory 6; South Australia 36;
Tasmania 10; Victoria 96; Western Australia 44

Community Support Services
Northern Territory Region
Alice Springs, Nthn Terr 0807: 88 Hartley St,
Alice Springs; tel (08) 8951 0206
Darwin, Nthn Terr 0812: cnr Lee Point Rd and
Yanyula Dr, Anula; tel (08) 8927 9566
Katherine Community Outreach Ministry;
tel: (08) 8971 2265
Palmerston, NT 0830: cnr Temple Tce and
Woodroffe Ave; tel: (08) 8932 2103

South Australia Division
Aberfoyle Park, SA 5159: The Hub Worship and
Community Complex; tel: (08) 8370 5003
Adelaide, SA 5000: 277 Pirie St;
tel: (08) 8227 0199
Arndale, SA 5009: 1-7 Gray St, Kilkenny;
tel (08) 8445 2044
Cambelltown, SA 5074: cnr Roma Grv and
Florentine Ave; tel: (08) 8365 2301
Gawler, SA 5118: 150 Murray St;
tel: (08) 8523 4844
Golden Grove, SA 5127: 99 Wynn Vale Dr,
Wynn Vale; tel (08) 8289 4784
Ingle Farm, SA 5098: cnr Bridge and Maxwell
Rds; tel (08) 8397 9333
Kapunda, SA 5373: Jeffs St; tel: (08) 8566 3388
Marion, SA 5047: cnr Sturt and Morphett Rds,
Seacombe Gdns; tel: (08) 8377 0001
Millicent, SA 5280: Bramwell St;
tel: (08) 8733 3642
Mount Gambier, SA 5290: cnr Gray and Wyatt
Sts; tel: (08) 8725 9900
Noarlunga, SA 5162: 186 Elizabeth Rd,
Morphett Vake; tel: (08) 8384 6014
Norwood, SA 5067: 55 George St;
tel: (08) 8332 0283
Playford, SA 5112: Kinkaid Rd, Elizabeth East;
tel: (08) 8255 8811
Peterborough, SA 5422: 139 Main St;
tel: (08) 8651 3426
Port Augusta, SA 5700: 35 Flinders St;
tel: (08) 8641 1021
Port Lincoln, SA 5606: 41 Marine Ave;
tel: (08) 8682 4296
Renmark, SA 5341: 104-109 Renmark Ave;
tel: (08) 8586 4109
Tea Tree Gully, SA 5092: 138 Reservoir Rd,
Modbury; tel: (08) 8360 6444
Victor Harbour, SA 5211: Crozier St;
tel: (08) 8552 7474
Whyalla, SA 5608: 5 Vicount Slim Ave,
Whyalla Norrie; tel: (08) 8645 7101

Tasmania Division
Burnie, Tas 7320: 99 Wilson St;
tel: (03) 6431 8722
Launceston, Tas 7250: 7 Cameron St;
tel: (03) 6334 2950
Hobart, Tas 7000: 250 Liverpool St;
tel: (03) 6231 1345

Victoria – Melbourne Central Division
Altona, Vic 3018: 108 Queen St;
tel (03) 9398 1750
Brunswick, Vic 3056: 256 Albert St;
tel: (03) 9387 6746
Coburg North, Vic 3058: 828 Sydney Rd;
tel: (03) 9354 3266
Glenroy, Vic 3046: 2 Finchley Ave;
tel: (03) 9300 4099
Greensborough, Vic 3088: 2 Flodden Way;
tel: (03) 9434 6990
Keilor, Vic 3037: 2a Roseleigh Blvd;
tel: (03) 9390 6111
Melbourne, Vic 3000: 69 Bourke St;
tel: (03) 9653 3259
Moonee Ponds, Vic 3040: cnr Mount Alexander
Rd and Buckley St; tel: (03) 9375 3249
Plenty Valley, Vic 3075: cnr Morang Dr and
Fred Hollows Way, Mill Park;
tel: (03) 9436 9200
Preston, Vic 3072: 263 Gower St;
tel: (03) 9471 9111
Richmond, Vic 3121: cnr Lennox and Garfield
Sts; tel: (03) 9429 2117
Rosebud, Vic 3940: 2 Melaleuca Ave;
tel: (03) 5986 4206
Rowville, Vic 3178: Police Rd;
tel: (03) 9701 0491
St Kilda, Vic 3182: Crisis Contact Centre,
29 Grey St; tel: (03) 9536 7777,
toll free 1800 627 727
Sunbury, Vic 3429: 27-37 Anderson Rd;
tel: (03) 9744 2095
Sunshine, Vic 3020: 34 Devonshire Rd;
tel: (03) 9312 4624
Werribee, Vic 3030: 1-3 Thames Blvd;
tel: (03) 9731 1344

Victoria – Eastern Victoria Division
Bairnsdale, Vic 3875: 63 McLeod St;
tel: (03) 5152 4201

Australia Southern Territory

Bentleigh, Vic 3204: 87 Robert St;
tel: (03) 9557 2644
Berwick, Vic 3806: cnr Parkhill Dr and Ernst Wanke Rd; tel: (03) 9704 1940
Box Hill, Vic 3128: 17-23 Nelson Rd;
tel: (03) 9890 2993
Carrum Downs, Vic 3201: 1265 Frankston-Dandenong Rd; tel: (03) 9782 0383
Camberwell, Vic 3124: 7 Bowen St;
tel: (03) 9889 2468
Chelsea, Vic 3196: 4 Swan Walk;
tel: (03) 9773 1027
Cranbourne, Vic 3977: 1 New Holland Dr;
tel: (03) 5991 1777
Dandenong Vic 3175: 55 James St;
tel: (03) 9793 3933
Doncaster, Vic 3109: 37 Taunton St;
tel: (03) 9842 4744
Doveton, Vic 3177: 1a Frawley Rd;
tel: (03) 9793 3933
Ferntree Gully, Vic 3156: 37 Wattletree Rd;
tel: (03) 9752 3604
Frankston, Vic 3200: 15 Forest Dr;
tel: (03) 9776 9155
Glen Waverley, Vic 3150: 958 High St Rd;
tel: (03) 9803 2587
Healesville, Vic 3777: 114 Maroondah Hwy;
tel: (03) 5962 2486
Moe, Vic, 3825: 37 Elizabeth St;
tel: (03) 5726 2845
Mooroolbark, Vic 3138: 88 Brice Ave;
tel: (03) 9727 4777
Morwell, Vic 3840: cnr Bridle Rd and Laurel St;
tel: (03) 5133 3966
Leongatha, Vic 3953: 52 Anderson St;
tel: (03) 5662 4670
Mooroolbark, Vic 3138: 55 Manchester Rd;
tel: (03) 9727 4777
Moe, Vic 3825: 18-22 George St;
tel: (03) 5126 1683
Morwell, Vic 3840: 160 Commercial Rd;
tel: (03) 5133 9366
Mountain View, Vic 3154: 1 Basin-Olinda Rd;
tel: (03) 9762 3490
Noble Park, Vic 3174: 12 Buckley St;
tel: (03) 9548 5022
Oakleigh, Vic 3166: 50 Atherton Rd;
tel: (03) 9563 0786
Pakenham, Vic 3810: 51 Bald Hill Rd;
tel: (030) 5941 4906
Ringwood, Vic 3134: 47 Wantirna Rd;
tel: (03) 9879 2894
Sale, Vic 3850: 139 Cunningham St;
tel; (03) 5144 6374
Traralgon, Vic 3844: Lot 1, Cross's Rd;
tel: (03) 5174 1998

Warragul, Vic 3820: 120 Burke St;
tel: (03) 5623 1090
Waverley, Vic 958 High St, Glen Waverley;
tel: (03) 9803 2587
Wonthaggi, Vic 3995: McKenzie St;
tel: (03) 5672 1228

Victoria – Western Victoria Division
Ballarat, Vic 3350: 102 Eureka St;
tel: (03) 5337 0600
Colac, Vic 3250: 100 Bloomfield St;
tel: (03) 5231 1178
Geelong, Vic 3220: 26-28 Bellerine St;
tel: (03) 5223 2434
Hamilton Vic 3300: 89 Kennedy St;
tel: (03) 5572 1907
Stawell, Vic 3380: 50 Main St;
tel (03) 5358 2657
Warrnambool, Vic 3280: cnr Lava and Henna Sts;
tel: (03) 5561 6792

Victoria – Northern Victoria Division
Beechworth, Vic 3747: 35 Ford St;
tel: (03) 5728 3245
Benalla, Vic 3672: 72 Fawkner Dr;
tel: (03) 5762 6396
Bendigo, Vic 3550: 65-71 Mundy St;
tel: (03) 5442 7699
Broadford, Vic 3658: 25-27 Powlett St;
tel: (03) 7584 1635
Castlemaine, Vic 3450: 47 Kennedy St;
tel: (03) 5470 5389
Echuca, Vic 3564: 50-52 Sturt St;
tel: (03) 5482 6722
Kyabram, Vic 3620: 24 Unit St;
tel: (03) 5853 2684
Maryborough, Vic 3465: 58 High St;
tel: (03) 5461 2789
Mildura, Vic 3500: 1401-1415 Etiwanda Ave;
tel: (03) 5021 2229
Red Cliffs, Vic 3496: 16 Heath St;
tel: (03) 5024 2110
Rochester, Vic 3561: cnr Elizabeth and Ramsay Sts; tel: (03) 5484 1364
Seymour, Vic 3660: Victoria St;
tel: (03) 5799 2583
Shepparton, Vic 3630: 43a Wyndham St;
tel: (03) 5831 1551
St Arnaud, Vic 3478: 14 Queens Ave:
tel: (03) 5495 1385
Swan Hill, Vic 3585: 190 Beveridge St;
tel: (03) 5033 1718
Wangaratta, Vic 3677: 13-17 Garnet Ave;
tel: (03) 5722 1129
Wodonga, Vic 3690: 210 Lawrence St;
tel: (03) 6024 2886

Australia Southern Territory

Western Australia Division
Albany, WA 6330: 152-160 North Rd;
 tel: (08) 9841 1068
Armadale, WA 6997: 57 Braemore St;
 tel: (08) 9497 1803
Balga, WA 6024: 10-18 Lavant Way;
 tel: (08) 9349 7488
Bentley, WA 6102: Dumond St; tel: (08) 9458 1855
Busselton, WA 6280; tel: (08) 9754 2733
Ellenbrook, WA 6069: cnr Highpoint and
 Woodlake Blvds; tel: (08) 9296 7197
Geraldton, WA 6530: 42 Ainsworth St;
 tel: (08) 9964 3627
Heathridge, WA 6919: 36 Christmas Ave;
 tel: (08) 9401 3408
Kalgoorlie, WA 6430: Oberthur St;
 tel: (08) 9021 2255
Karratha, WA 6714: 2 Bond Pl; tel: (08) 9185 2148
Kwinana, WA 6167: cnr Medina Ave and
 Hoyle Rd; tel: (08) 9439 1585
Mandurah, WA 6210: Lot 5, Lakes Rd;
 tel: (08) 9535 4951
Morley, WA 6943: 565 Walter Rd;
 tel: (08) 9279 4500
Narrogin, WA 6312: Doney St; tel: (08) 9881 4004
Northam, WA 6401: Wellington St;
 tel: (08) 9622 1228
Northbridge, WA 6003: 333 William St;
 tel: (08) 9328 1690
Merriwa, WA 6030: 26 Jenola Way;
 tel: (08) 9305 2131
Rivervale, WA 6103: 96 Norwood Rd;
 tel: (08) 9355 2799
Swan View, WA 6056: 371-379 Morrison Rd;
 tel: (08) 9294 2811

Units for Intellectually Disabled Persons
Ottoway, SA 5013: Centennial Court,
 30-32 Edward St; tel: (08) 8341 0413

Red Shield Housing Network Association
Manningham, SA 5086: 109 Hampstead Rd;
 tel: (08) 8368 6800 (administers properties in
 Adelaide for disadvantaged lower-income,
 homeless people)
Hobart, Tas 7008: 223 Macquarie St;
 tel: (03) 6223 8050

Family Tracing Service
Adelaide, Fullarton, SA 5063: 39 Florence St;
 tel: (08) 8379 9388
Darwin, Anula, NT 0812: cnr Lee Point Rd and
 Yanyula Dr; tel: (08) 8927 6499
Hobart, New Town, Tas 7008: 27 Pirie St;
 tel: (03) 6278 7184

Perth, Northbridge, WA 6003: 333 William St;
 tel: (08) 9227 7010
Victoria and Inter-Territorial enquiries only:
 Blackburn, Vic 3130: 95-99 Railway Rd;
 tel: (03) 8878 4500

Home and School Support Service
Broadford, Vic 3658: 25-27 Powlett St;
 tel: (03) 5784 1635

Hostels for Homeless Men
Abbotsford, Vic 3067: Anchorage Hostel,
 81 Victoria Cres; tel: (03) 9417 5820
Adelaide, SA 5000: Towards Independence,
 277 Pirie St; tel: (08) 8223 4911 (acc 75)
Alice Springs, NT 0870: 11 Goyder St;
 tel: (08) 8952 1434 (acc 27)
Darwin, NT 0820: Sunrise Centre, Lot 5344
 Salonika St; tel: (08) 8981 4199 (acc 26)
Mount Lawley, WA 6050: Tanderra Hostel,
 68 Guildford Rd; tel: (08) 9271 1209 (acc 27)
North Melbourne, Vic 3051: The Open Door,
 166 Boundary Rd; tel: (03) 9329 6988
 (acc 45)
Perth, WA 6000: Lentara, cnr Short and
 Nash Sts; tel: (08) 9328 3102 (acc 55)
St Kilda, Vic 3182: St Kilda Crisis
 Accommodation Centre, 31 Grey St;
 tel: (03) 9525 4473 (acc 20)
West Melbourne, Vic 3003: Flagstaff Crisis
 Accommodation, 9 Roden St;
 tel: (03) 9329 4800 (acc 64)

Hostels for Homeless Youth
Fitzroy, Vic 3065: 12 Tranmere St;
 tel: (03) 9489 1122
Frankston, Vic 3199: 37 Rossmith Ave East;
 tel: (03) 9784 5050 (4 houses)
Kalgoorlie, WA 6430: 10 Park St;
 tel: (08) 9091 1016 (acc 12)
Karratha, WA 6714; tel: (08) 9144 1881 (acc 8)
Lansdale, WA 6065: Lansdale House,
 460 Kingsway; tel: (08) 9302 1433 (acc 8)
Leongatha, Vic 3953: GippsCare Cross-target
 Transitional Support, 51 McCartin St;
 tel: (03) 5662 4502
Mirrabooka, WA 6061: Oasis House, 68-70
 Honeywell Blvd; tel: (08) 9342 6785 (acc 8)
Pooraka, SA 5095: Muggy's, 88 Henderson Ave;
 tel: (08) 8260 6617 (acc 10)
Salisbury, SA 5108: Burlendi, 22 Spains Rd;
 tel: (08) 8281 6641 (acc 8)
Shepparton, Vic 3630: Brayton, 360 River Rd;
 tel: (03) 5823 2277
St Kilda, Vic 3182: 27 Grey St;
 tel: (03) 9536 7730

Australia Southern Territory

Hostels for Intellectually Disabled Persons
Manningham, SA 5086: Red Shield Housing Network Services, 109 Hampstead Rd; tel: (08) 8368 6800 (properties 310)

Social Housing – SASHS
Alice Springs, NT 0870: Towards Independence, 88 Hartely St; tel: (08) 8951 0203
Box Hill, Vic 3128: 31-33 Ellingworth Pde; tel: (03) 9890 7144
Darwin, Anula, NT 0812: Towards Independence, Top End, cnr Lee Point Rd and Yanyula Dr; tel: (08) 8927 5189
Grovedale, Vic 3216: Barwon South-West Region, 142 Torquay Rd; tel: (03) 5244 2500
Hawthorn, Vic 3122: EastCare Housing Services, 16 Church St; tel: (03) 9851 7800
Leongatha, Vic 3953: Gippsland Region, 51a McCartin St; tel: (03) 5662 4538
Manningham, SA 5086: Red Shield Housing Network Services, 109 Hampstead Rd; tel: (08) 8368 6800
Melbourne, Vic 3000: SACHS, 69 Bourke St; tel: (03) 9653 3288
New Town, Tas 7008: 117 Main Rd; tel: (03) 6278 2817
Sunshine, Vic 3020: Western Metropolitan Region, 27 Sun Cres; tel: (03) 9312 5424
Warragul, Vic 3820: 64 Queen St; tel: (03) 5622 0351
Warrnambool, Vic 3280: 70 Henna St; tel: (03) 5561 6844

Mobile Ministry
Karratha, WA 6714: (Mobile Ministry) 1 Nelson Ct, Peggs Creek; tel: (08) 9144 2985
Darwin, Jingili, NT 0810: (Flying Padre) 5 Murphy St; tel: (08) 8945 0176

Independent Units for Intellectually Handicapped Persons
Ottoway, SA 5013: Centennial Ct, 30-32 Edward St; tel: (08) 8341 0413 (acc 18)

Men's Support Service
Medina, WA 6167: cnr Hoyle Rd and Median Ave; tel: (08) 9439 1585

Migrant and Refugee Services
Brunswick, Vic 3056: 12-14 Tinning St; tel: (03) 9384 8334
Doveton, Vic 3177: 1a Frawley Rd; tel: (03) 9793 3933

Red Shield Hostels
Alice Springs, NT 0870: 11 Goyder St; tel: (08) 8952 1434 (acc 27)
Darwin, NT 0800: 49 Mitchell St; tel: (08) 8981 5994 (acc 64 family units 5)

Rehabilitation Services
Abbotsford, Vic 3067: Detox Unit, 81 Victoria Cres; tel: (03) 9495 6811
Adelaide, SA 5000:
   Bridge Drug and Alcohol Outreach Programme (inc Police and Drug Court Diversion initiative), 62 Whitmore Sq; tel: (08) 8211 8423
   'IT' Futures Initiative (computer-based support programme); tel: (08) 8227 0893
   Sobering Up Unit: 62a Whitmore Sqr; tel: (08) 8212 2855
   Supported Accommodation Services, 3/2 Dawkins Pl; tel: (08) 8227 0349
   Warrondi Transitional Support Programme (inc Warrondi Engage and Link initiative), 146 Gilbert St, Adelaide 5000; tel: (08) 8212 1251
   Warrondi Stabilisation Unit, 146 Gilbert St; tel: (08) 8212 1215 (acc 22)
Bendigo, Vic 3550:
   Northern Victoria Drug and Alcohol Coordinator, 5-67 Mundy St; tel (03) 5442 7931
   Bendigo Bridge Community Outreach, 65-71 Mundy St; tel: (03) 5442 8558
Box Hill, Vic 3128: Aurora Women's Accommodation Service, 310 Elgar Rd; tel: (03) 9890 4549
Brunswick, Vic 3056: Outreach Service, 256 Albert St; tel: (03) 9387 6746
Corio, Vic 3214: Geelong Adult Withdrawal Unit; tel: (03) 5243 3364
Darwin, Sturt Park, NT 0829: Sunrise Centre, Lot 5034 Salonika St; tel: (08) 8981 4199
Geelong, Vic 3220: Geelong Withdrawal Unit, Goldsworthy St; tel: (03) 5275 3500
Gosnells, WA 6110: Harry Hunter Adult Rehabilitation, 2498 Albany H'way; tel: (08) 9398 2077
Hawthorn, Vic 3122: Aurora Women's Accommodation Service, Drug and Alcohol Counselling Programme, 16 Church St; tel: (03) 9851 7800
Highgate, WA 6003: Bridge House, 15 Wright St; tel: (08) 9227 8086 (acc 27)
Kilmore, Vic 3664: Overdale Rural Residential Programme, 455 O'Grady's Rd; tel: (03) 5782 2744 (acc 10)

Australia Southern Territory

New Town, Tas 7008: The Bridge Programme, Creek Rd; tel: (03) 6278 8140

Preston, Vic 3072: Bridgehaven, 1a Jackman St; tel: (03) 9480 6488 (acc 15)

St Kilda, Vic 3182: The Bridge Centre, 12 Chapel St; tel: (03) 9521 2770

Stuart Park, NT 0820: Drug and Alcohol Services – Top End, Lot 5344, Salonika St; tel: (08) 8981 4199 (acc 26)

Swan Hill, Vic 3585: 190 Beveridge St; tel: (03) 5033 1718

The Basin, Vic 3154: New Hope Rehabilitation Centre, Basin-Olinda Rd; tel: (03) 9762 1166

Warrnambool, Vic 3280: 52-54 Fairy St; tel: (03) 5561 4453

Rural Outreach and Drought Relief

Bendigo, Vic 3550: Drought Response Programme, 76 Strickland Rd; tel: (03) 5441 7959

Geraldton, WA 6530: Drought Relief, PO Box 167; tel: (08) 9964 3627

Hobart, Tas 7000: Drought Relief, 250 Liverpool St; tel: (03) 6236 9933

Horsham, Vic 3440: Drought Relief, 12 Kalkee Rd; tel: (03) 5382 1770

Kaniva, Vic 3419: Drought Releif, 34 Progress St; tel: (03) 5392 2304

Senior Citizens' Residences

Angle Park, SA 5010: Linsell Lodge Residential Aged Care Facility; tel: (08) 8231 4687 (acc 53)

Clarence Park, SA 5034: Jean McBean Ct, 35 Mills St; tel: (08) 8231 4687 (acc single units 10, double 4)

Footscray, Vic 3011: James Barker House, 78 Ryan St; tel: (03) 9689 7211 (acc 45)

Gosnells, WA 6110: Seaforth Gardens, 2542 Albany H'way; tel: (08) 9398 5228 (acc hostel 53, units 50)

Lenah Valley, Tas 7008: MacFarlane Ct, 16-22 Ratho St (acc units single 22, double 8)

New Town, Tas 7008: Barrington Lodge, 21 Tower Rd; tel: (03) 6228 2164 (acc res beds 10)

Soup Runs

Adelaide, SA 5000: 277 Pirie St (c/o Adelaide Congress Hall; tel: (08) 8223 7776

Melbourne, Vic 3000: 69 Bourke St; tel: (03) 9653 3222

Northbridge, WA 6003: 333 William St; tel: (08) 9227 8655

Telephone Counselling Service

Perth, WA 6000: Salvo Care Line, PO Box 8498, Perth Business Centre 6849; tel (08) 9442 5777

Youth and Family Services

Alice Springs, NT 0870: Towards Independence, 88 Hartley St; tel: (08) 8951 0203

Box Hill, Vic 3128:
Intensive Case Management Service, Specialist Consulting and Assessment Service, Children in Residential Care Education Support, Work and Recreation Programme with Education, Residential Youth Services, Leaving Care, 31-33 Ellingworth Pde; tel: (03) 9890 7144

JJHIP (Juvenile Justice Housing Initiative Pathways); tel: (03) 9890 7144

Brunswick, Vic 3056: Brunswick Youth Services Creative Opportunities, 10-18 Tinning St; tel: (03) 9386 7611

Kew, Vic 3101: The Hawthorn Project, 85 High St; tel: (03) 9851 7800

Leongatha, Vic 3953: GippsCare Adolescent Community Placement, 51 McCartin St; tel: (03) 5662 4502

Melbourne, Vic 3000: Melbourne Counselling, 69 Bourke St; tel: (03) 9653 3250

Moonee Ponds, Vic 3039: Crosslink Employment Services, 33a Taylor St; tel: (03) 9372 0675

Mornington, Vic 3931:
Peninsula Home and Community-Based Care Services, Shop 9, 234 Main St; tel: (03) 5976 2231

Peninsula Adolescent Community Placement, Peninsula High Risk Adolescent Programme, Peninsula Special Support Unit, Peninsula Supported Independence, Reconnect Programme, Shop 9, 234 Main St; tel: (03) 5976 2747

Northbridge, WA 6003: Crosssroads West – Perth, 333 William St; tel: (08) 9260 9551

North Coburg, Vic 3058: Transitional Support, Independent Living Programmes including Youth Services, Transitional Support Accommodation for Youth (TSAY), Anger Management, Reconnect, 2/828 Sydney Rd; tel: (03) 9353 1011

Salisbury, SA 5108: CHIPS Internet Cafe, 20b John St, Salisbury; tel: (08) 8285 9406

Shepparton, Vic 3630:
Brayton Young Activities Service, Brayton Young Offenders' Pilot Programme,

Australia Southern Territory

Strengthening Families and Sexual Abuse Prevention, 360 River Rd;
tel: (03) 5823 2277

JPET, 360 River Rd; tel: (03) 5821 8144

Pathways Accommodation and Support (inc Personal Support Programme, Community Connections Programme, and Homeless Services), 43b Wyndham St;
tel: (03) 5833 1099

Seymour, Vic: Pathways Accommodation and Support; tel:(03) 5799 1581

Swan Hill, Vic 3585: Y-Space, 5 Campbell St; tel: (03) 5033 1411

Youth Centres for Homeless Unemployed

Mornington, Vic 3931:
  Peninsula JPET, Shop 8, 234 Main St;
  tel: (03) 5976 5500
  Burnt Toast Cyber Cafe, Shop 7, 234 Main St;
  tel: (03) 5976 5500

North Coburg, Vic 3058: 2/828 Sydney Rd;
tel: (03) 9353 1011

St Kilda, Vic 3182: Crisis Centre, 29 Grey St;
tel: (03) 9536 7777

Wonthaggi, Vic 3995: GippsCare Cyber Café Net, 59 McBride Ave; tel: (03) 5672 5506

During 'Insane' – the Australia Southern Territorial Youth Conference held in Melbourne – more than 600 delegates spent a week taking part in workshops, electives, worship rallies, social events and public demonstrations. On a 'Break the Slave Chain' protest against human trafficking, the young Salvationists and their leaders marched holding hands through Melbourne in silence. The march concluded with a rally in Federation Square, in the heart of the city, where Steve Chalke (international chairman of Stop the Traffik) addressed more than 1,000 people.

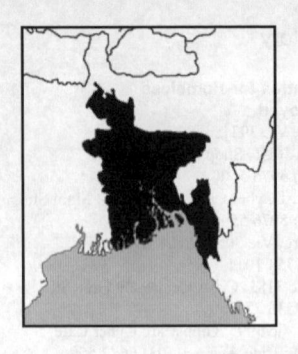

BANGLADESH COMMAND

Officer Commanding:
Lieut-Colonel Ethne Flintoff (1 Jul 2002)

General Secretary:
Major Leopoldo Posadas (1 Aug 2008)

Command Headquarters: House 96, Road 23, Banani, Dhaka

Postal address: GPO Box 985, Dhaka 1000, Bangladesh

Tel: [880] (2) 9882836/7; email: banleadership@ban.salvationarmy.org

Work in Bangladesh began immediately after the Liberation War with Pakistan in 1971. Thousands of people moved from refugee camps in Calcutta, where Salvationists had served them, and a team of Salvationists accompanied them. A year earlier, relief operations had been carried out by The Salvation Army in East Pakistan (later Bangladesh) following a severe cyclone. On 21 April 1980, The Salvation Army was incorporated under the Companies Act of 1913. Bangladesh was upgraded to command status on 1 January 1997.

Zone: South Asia
Country included in the command: Bangladesh
'The Salvation Army' in Bengali: Tran Sena
Languages in which the gospel is preached: Bengali, English

THE ordination and commissioning of eight cadets of the Witnesses For Christ Session, conducted by General Shaw Clifton and Commissioner Helen Clifton in December 2008, was the first to be led by a General in the command. Although the country was under State of Emergency restrictions, around 450 people were present for the weekend of celebration.

Commissioner Clifton admitted 14 parents of new lieutenants to the Fellowship of the Silver Star. For the first time in the command's still relatively short history the mother of one of the new officers received a second Silver Star and the lieutenant's father received two stars, the first being in recognition of fathers who were not included in the fellowship before 2002.

Continued emphasis on youth capacity development has seen exciting results. Seven young Salvationists were chosen to form a team to participate in six weeks' intensive training in a rural area where cross-border trafficking is prevalent.

Under guest team leader Meble Birengo from Kenya, the team learned how to interact with communities and helped to identify their most urgent needs. Returning to their corps to share their experiences, team members are now leading other young Salvationists in community

Bangladesh Command

outreach in their own areas.

Weekend training camps for young Salvationists were held bi-monthly. There is a growing number of youth groups in the command.

Bangladesh is in the frontline of countries most affected by global warming due to its low-lying land combined with high population density. In July 2008 the command embarked on a community-based Disaster Management Preparedness pro-gramme, targeting five communities in the three most disaster-prone areas of the country where The Salvation Army is working.

STATISTICS
Officers active 82 **Cadets** (1st Yr) 6
Employees 318
Corps 30 **Outposts** 18 **Institution** 1 **Schools** 17
Clinics 9 **HIV/Aids Counselling Centres** 2
Senior Soldiers 1,688 **Adherents** 674 **Junior Soldiers** 211

STAFF
Women's Ministries: Lt-Col Ethne Flintoff (CPWM) Maj Evelyn Posadas (CSWM)
Director of Finance: Mrs Sarah Biswas
Information Technology Development: Mr Palash (Paul) Baidya
Projects: Capt Elizabeth Nelson
Training: Maj Heather Randell
Youth and Candidates: Capt Stephen Baroi

DISTRICTS
Dhaka: Hse 96, Rd 23, Banani, Dhaka 1213; tel: (0171) 1546012; Maj Alfred Mir
South Western: PO Box 3, By-Pass Rd, Karbala, Jessore 7400; tel: (0421) 68759; Maj Ganendro Baroi

TRAINING COLLEGE
Genda, Savar, Dhaka; tel: (02) 7712614

COMMUNITY WORK
HIV/Aids Counselling Centres: Jessore, Old Dhaka
Training and Counselling Programme: Kalaroa, Satkhira

Micro-Credit Projects: Dhaka Mirpur, Jessore, Khulna
Income-generating Cooperatives: Jessore, Khulna

EDUCATIONAL WORK
Adult Education
Jessore, Khulna

Schools for the Hearing Impaired
Dhaka (acc 30); Jessore (acc 30)

Primary Schools
(pupils 2,122)
Jessore: Arenda, Bagdanga, Fatepur, Ghurulia, Kholadanga, Konejpur, Ramnagar, Sitarampur, Suro
Dinajpur: Shahargachchi
Gopalgonj: Bandhabari, Rajapur
Joypurhat: Vanuikushalia
Khulna: Andulia, Komrail, Krisnanagar

Integrated Education for Sighted and Visually Impaired
Savar (pupils 280)

Vocational Training
Dhaka, Jessore, Khulna

MEDICAL AND DEVELOPMENT WORK
Urban Health and Development Project (UHDP)
Dhaka: Mirpur Clinic, with Leprosy and TB Control Programmes

Community Health and Development Projects (CHDP)
Jessore: New Town and Kholadanga Clinics, with Leprosy and TB Control Programmes
Khulna: Andulia Clinic
Village Clinics: Fatepur, Ghurulia, Konejpur, Ramnagar, Sitarampur

SOCIAL WORK
Integrated Children's Centre (ICC)
Savar (acc 44)

'SALLY ANN' PROGRAMME
'Sally Ann' Bangladesh Ltd (employees 23 production workers 950)
email: sallyann@ban.salvationarmy.com
website: www.sallyann.com
Manager: Mr Utpal Halder
Chair of Board: Capt Elizabeth Nelson
Shop: House 96, Road 23, Banani, Dhaka; Satu Barua (shop manager)

BRAZIL TERRITORY

Territorial leaders:
Commissioners Peder and Janet Refstie

Territorial Commander:
Commissioner Peder Refstie (1 Dec 2006)

Chief Secretary:
Lieut-Colonel Alfred Ward (1 Mar 2008)

**Territorial Headquarters: Rua Juá 264 - Bosque da Saúde,
04138-020 São Paulo-SP**

Postal address: Exército de Salvação; Caixa Postal 46036, Agência Saúde
04045-970 São Paulo-SP, Brazil

Tel: [55] (011) 5591 7070; fax: [55] (011) 5591 7075; email: exercitodesalvacao@salvos.org.br;
website: www.exercitodesalvacao.org.br

Pioneer officers Lieut-Colonel and Mrs David Miche unfurled the Army flag in Rio de Janeiro on 1 August 1922. The Salvation Army operates as a national religious entity, Exército de Salvação, having been so registered by Presidential Decree 90.568 of 27 November 1984. All its social activities have been incorporated in APROSES (Assistência e Promoção Social Exército de Salvação) since 1974 and have had Federal Public Utility since 18 February 1991.

Zone: Americas and Caribbean
Country included in the territory: Brazil
'The Salvation Army' in Portuguese: Exército de Salvação
Language in which the gospel is preached: Portuguese
Periodicals: *O Oficial (The Officer)*, *Rumo* and *Ministério Feminino – Devocionais* (Women's Ministries magazines)

TRADITIONALLY the main emphasis of Salvation Army social work in Brazil has been directed towards children. In the past, large children's homes were established around the country. The policies of both The Salvation Army and government authorities have lately focused more on building family relationships and establishing conditions for needy children to grow up in a family environment rather than an institution.

This has led to many successful placements of children from the Army's homes into functional family units. Consequently the majority of the Army's residential children's homes have become day centres, enabling the Army to give care and support to a much larger number of children and families.

Here the children receive, among other things, nourishing food, support with their school work and, in many places, education to prepare them for a future professional life. They also benefit from spiritual teaching and a Christian influence on their lives.

Brazil Territory

The aim of this ministry, mainly concentrated in the slums of the *favelas*, is to give children and young people the vision of a better life and tools for achieving it. An important part of this policy was the reopening after extensive renovations of the mother and baby home in São Paulo.

Here, pregnant girls among the street children environments, some as young as 11 or 12 years old, find shelter, care and support during their pregnancy and the first few months after childbirth. At the same time they learn important, practical skills which enable them to cope better with motherhood and life in general.

An important aspect of all this work is its anti-trafficking component. Human trafficking, sexual exploitation and domestic violence are major concerns in Brazilian society. The Salvation Army is working conscientiously with these issues, trying to make an impact that will heighten public awareness and change attitudes.

Time and again the impact of the gospel, the experience of conversion and the continuous work of the Holy Spirit prove to be the most effective weapons in this fight. God is to be praised for every person who, through the work and testimony of Salvationists in social institutions and corps, receives the transforming touch of divine grace on their lives.

The theme adopted for the year 2009 was 'Growing In Compassion'. It summarises well the intention of Salvation Army work in Brazil.

STATISTICS
Officers 173 (active 126 retired 47) **Cadets** (1st Yr) 3 (2nd Yr) 4 **Employees** 321
Corps 47 **Outposts** 7 **Social Institutions** 31
Senior Soldiers 1,738 **Adherents** 63 **Junior Soldiers** 493
Personnel serving outside territory Officers 6

STAFF
Women's Ministries: Comr Janet Refstie (TPWM) Lt-Col Mary Ward (TSWM) Maj Iolanda Camargo (TSAWM & TSLM)
Personnel: Maj Verônica Jung
Editor-in-Chief/Communications: Maj Paulo Soares
Education: Maj Wilson Strasse
Finance: Maj Joan Burton
Legal/Property: Maj Giani Azevedo
Music: Maj Paulo Soares
National Band: B/M João Carlos Cavalheiro
National Songsters: S/L Vera Sales
Social: Mrs Marilene Oliveira
Training: Maj Wilson Strasse
Youth and Candidates: Maj Elisana Lemos

DIVISIONS
North East: Rua Carlos Gomes, 1016, 50751-130 Recife, PE; tel/fax: (81) 3227-7513; email: regional-ne@bra.salvationarmy.org; Majs Maruilson and Francisca Souza

Paraná and Santa Catarina: Rua Mamoré 1191, 80810-080 Curitiba, PR; tel/fax: (041) 3336-8624; email: regional-pr@bra.salvationarmy.org; Majs Miguel and Angélica Aguilera

Rio de Janeiro and Minas Gerais and Centre West: Rua Visconde de Santa Isabel no 20, salas 712/713, 20560-120, Rio de Janeiro, RJ; tel/fax: (21) 3879-5594; email: regional-rj@bra.salvationarmy.org; Majs Edgar and Sara Chagas

Rio Grande do Sul: Rua Machado de Assis 255, 97050-450, Santa Maria, RS; tel/fax: (55) 3026-1935; email: regional-rs@bra.salvationarmy.org; Capts Adão and Vilma Gonçalves

São Paulo: Rua Taguá 209, Liberdade 01508-010, São Paulo-SP; tel/fax: (11) 3207-3402; email: regional-sp@bra.salvationarmy.org; Majs Márcio and Jurema Mendes

TRAINING COLLEGE
Rua Juá 264, Bosque da Saúde, 04138-020, São Paulo-SP; tel: (11) 5071-5041

Brazil Territory

SOCIAL WORK

Children's Homes and Day Centres
Arco Verde: 'Maria Felisbina de Souza' Home,
Av Antonio Pires 1790, 35715-000,
Prudente de Moraes-MG; tel: (31) 3711-1370
(acc 50)

Joinville: 'João de Paula', Rua 15 de Novembro
3165, 89216-201, Joinville-SC;
tel: (47) 453-0588 (acc 50)

Paranaguá: 'Honorina Valente', Rua Manoel
Jordão Cavalheiro s/no, 83200-000,
Paranaguá-PR; tel: (41) 423-6115 (acc 36)

Pelotas: Av Fernando Osório, 6745,
96065-000, Pelotas-RS; tel: (53) 273-6909
(acc 30)

Rio de Janeiro: Méier, Rua Garcia Redondo 103,
20775-170, Rio de Janeiro-RJ;
tel: (21) 2595-5694 (acc 50)

Suzano: 'Lar das Flores', Rua Gal. Francisco
Glicério 3048, 08665-000, Suzano-SP;
tel: (11) 4747-1098 (acc 30)

Uruguaiana: Rua Gal. Câmara 1403, 97500-281,
Uruguaiana-RS; tel: (55) 3412-4930
(acc 50)

Clinics (medical and dental)
Porto Alegre: 'Dr Leopoldo Rössler', Av São
Pedro 1116, 90230-123, Porto Alegre-RS;
tel: (51) 3342-4170

Itinerant Dental Clinic in needy areas: 'Sorrindo
com Cristo', via THQ

Community Centres
*Cubatão: 'Vila dos Pescadores', Rua Amaral
Neto 211, 11531-070, Cubatão-SP;
tel: (13) 3363-2111

*Curitiba: 'Núcleo Sócio-Educativo de Apoio à
Criança', Rua Manoel de Abreu 274,
80215-430, Curitiba-PR; tel: (41) 3363-1537

Guarulhos: Rua NS Aparecida 10, 07191-190,
Guarulhos-SP; tel: (11) 6409-1500

*Itaquaquecetuba: Av Antônio Fugas 190,
08572-730, Itaquaquecetuba-SP;
tel: (11) 4640-4304

*Recife: 'Centro Comunitário Integração', Rua
Conde de Irajá 108, 50710-310, Recife-PE;
tel: (81) 3228-4740

*Rio de Janeiro: 'Nova Divinéia', Rua Bambuí 36,
20561-210, Rio de Janeiro-RJ;
tel: (21) 2298-2574

* *These centres have programmes for children at risk*

Crèches and Kindergartens
Carmo do Rio Claro: 'Recanto da Alegria',
Rua Luiz Amélio Freire 250, 37150-000,
Carmo do Rio Claro-MG; tel: (35) 3561-2175
(acc 100)

Cubatão: 'Recanto dos Sirizinhos', Rua Amaral
Neto 211, 11531-070, Cubatão-SP;
tel: (13) 3363-2111 (acc 300)

Guarulhos: Rua NS Aparecida 10, 07111-190,
Guarulhos-SP; tel: (11) 6409-1500
(acc 50)

Recife: 'Centro Comunitário Integração', Rua
Conde de Irajá 108, 50710-310, Recife-PE;
tel: (81) 3228-4740 (acc 420)

São Gonçalo: 'Arca de Noé', Rua Rodrigues da
Fonseca 315, 24.610-000, São Gonçalo-RJ;
tel: (21) 2604-9821 (acc 150)

São Paulo: 'Ranchinho do Senhor', Rua Bertioga
470/480, 04141-100, São Paulo-SP;
tel: (11) 5589-4609 (acc 60)

Suzano: 'NUDI - Lar das Flores', Rua Gal.
Francisco Glicério, 3048, 08665-000,
Suzano-SP; tel: (11) 4747-1098 (acc 160)

Centres for Street Children
Curitiba: Rua Bartolomeu Lourenço de Gusmão
5167, 81730-040, Curitiba-PR;
tel: (41) 286-3662 (acc 11)

São Paulo: 'Projeto Três Corações – Fase 1',
Rua Taguá 209, Liberdade, 01508-010,
São Paulo-SP; tel: (11) 3275-0644 (acc 50)

Mother and Baby Home
São Paulo: Rancho do Senhor, Rua Caramurú 931,
04138-020, São Paulo-SP; tel: (11) 2275-4487
(acc mothers 25 babies 18)

Old People's Home
Campos do Jordão: Lar do Outono, Rua João
Rodrigues Pinheiro 335, 12460-000,
Campos do Jordão-SP; tel: (12) 3662-2154
(acc 24)

Prison Work
Piraí do Sul and Carmo do Rio Claro

Social Services Centres
Santa Maria: Rua Jerônimo Gomes 74, 97001-970,
Santa Maria-RS; tel: (55) 3221-8922

São Paulo: Rua Taguá 209, 01508-010, São
Paulo-SP; tel: (11) 3209-5830

Students' Residences
Brasília: Av L2 Sul, 610B Mod 69,
70259-970, Brasília-DF; tel: (61) 443-3332
(acc 20)

Santa Maria: Rua Jerônimo Gomes, 74,
97050-350, Santa Maria-RS;
tel: (55) 3222-1935 (acc 26)

Brazil Territory

Territorial Camp
Suzano: Rua Manuel Casanova 1061, 08664-000, Suzano-SP; tel: (11) 4476-3843

Thrift Stores
São Paulo:
Salvashopping I, Av Santa Catarina 1781, 04378-300, São Paulo-SP;
tel: (11) 5562-2285

Salvashopping II: Av Cupecê 3254, 04366-000, São Paulo-SP;
tel: (11) 5563-9937
Rio de Janeiro: Breshopping, Blvd 28 de Setembro 354, 20551-031, Rio de Janeiro-RJ;
tel: (21) 3879-9600

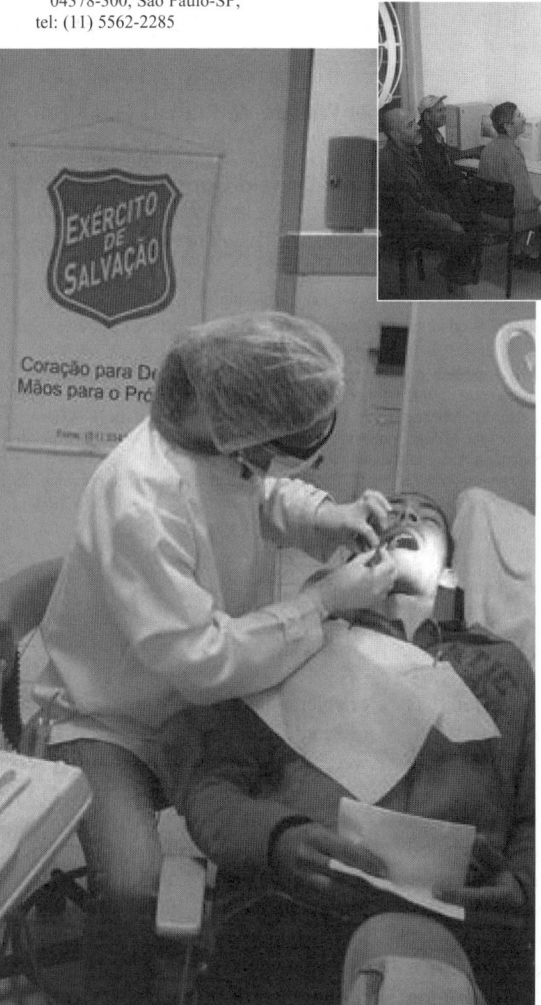

In Porto Alegre, Brazil, the Army operates 'Recovering the Hope' – a programme created to offer medical assistance (including dental treatment), professional orientation (such as information technology classes, above) and other basic needs to adults who are living on the streets. It aims to help them recover their dignity and self-esteem, and then reintegrate them into the community.

CANADA AND BERMUDA TERRITORY

Territorial leaders:
Commissioners William W. and Marilyn D. Francis

Territorial Commander:
Commissioner William W. Francis (1 Jul 2007)

Chief Secretary:
Colonel Donald Copple (1 Mar 2008)

Territorial Headquarters: 2 Overlea Blvd, Toronto, Ontario M4H 1P4, Canada

Tel: [1] (416) 425-2111; fax: [1] (416) 422-6201; email: can_leadership@can.salvationarmy.org; websites: www.salvationarmy.ca; www.salvationist.ca; www.SendTheFire.ca; www.faithandfriends.ca

There are newspaper reports of organised Salvation Army activity in Toronto, Ontario, in January 1882, and five months later the Army was reported holding meetings in London, Ontario. On 15 July the same year, Major Thomas Moore, sent from USA headquarters, established official operations. In 1884 Canada became a separate command. The League of Mercy originated in Canada in 1892. An Act to incorporate the Governing Council of The Salvation Army in Canada received Royal Assent on 19 May 1909.

The work in Newfoundland was begun on 1 February 1886 by Divisional Officer Arthur Young. On 12 January 1896 Adjutant (later Colonel) Lutie Desbrisay and two assistant officers unfurled the flag in Bermuda.

Zone: Americas and Caribbean
Countries included in the territory: Bermuda, Canada
Languages in which the gospel is preached: Creole, English, French, Indian languages (Gitxsan, Nisga'a, Tsimshian), Korean, Lao, Portuguese, Spanish, Thai
Periodicals: *Edge for Kids*, *Faith & Friends*, *Foi & Vie*, *Salvationist*

'FOR the past two years, God has been shaping your heart so that it conforms to the heart of Jesus,' the Territorial Commander told cadets of the God's Fellow Workers Session as Salvationists in Winnipeg gathered to say farewell and express their appreciation for the cadets' ministry during their training period.

Two public meetings took place during the annual commissioning weekend (13-15 June 2008). Moments of solemn dedication were mixed with joy and celebration as the new officers were appointed to various ministry settings throughout the territory.

Despite inclement weather, the spirits and expectations of Newfoundlanders and Labradorians were not dampened as they arrived for their annual congress (27-29 June) in the twin cities of St John's and Mount Pearl. Delegates gave an enthusiastic welcome home to guests

Commissioners Max and Lennie Feener, Canadian officers serving as the USA Southern territorial leaders.

A variety of activities, including men's and women's rallies, allowed participants to share in fellowship and be blessed by inspirational music and messages from the Word.

In July the Bermuda Divisional Band and Divisional Youth Band travelled to the Caribbean island of Antigua to share in Salvation Army Week celebrations. In addition to conducting a number of open-air meetings and participating in Sunday worship, band members gave practical help by painting classrooms and tiling the kitchen in the Army's pre-school facility.

The 2008 Territorial School of Music and Gospel Arts, held in August, had the highest enrolment in recent years. For the first time it included French-speaking delegates from the province of Quebec, as well as international students from England, the USA, Germany, The Netherlands and Mexico.

In September a team of Canadian women travelled to Tanzania for a 10-day 'Partners In Peace' mission trip. The group shared in spiritual and practical ministry at various Army centres, including participation in a coastal district home league rally where almost 100 women sought closer communion with Jesus.

The 'Harvest Of Hope' Congress, held in Toronto in October, brought together thousands of Salvationists and friends from wide-ranging regions of the newly created Ontario Central-East Division. Under the ministry of the territorial leaders, and with support from divisional music sections and the USA Eastern Territorial Arts Ministry team, delegates enjoyed memorable moments of fellowship and inspiration and were challenged to reach out in faith to claim a spiritual harvest.

More than 150 Salvationists from across the territory met at Jackson's Point Conference Centre in November for 'Symposium 2008'. The event was planned to follow up a similar occasion in 2005 and allowed officers and soldiers to meet informally to discuss the future direction of the territory.

Delegates developed a series of five statements outlining priorities for the territory, later endorsed by the Cabinet and shared with Salvationists, who were encouraged to implement them in their various local settings. The priorities included an increased emphasis on uniform wearing, discipleship, youth and children's ministry, community outreach and integrated mission.

Recognising the growing need for Salvation Army leaders, a group of Salvationists from across the territory has met to discuss a territorial leadership development strategy. Participants acknowledged that future leadership may be in short supply if the Army does not adapt to changing needs.

With this in mind, a new strategy

emerged to be proactive in appointing a growing diversity of leaders in terms of gender, age and ethnicity among all levels of administration. Individualised personal development plans and career paths would be developed for all officers and lay employees, reflecting individuals' aspirations as well as the Movement's leadership needs.

STATISTICS

Officers 1,806 (active 877 retired 929) **Cadets** (1st Yr) 19 (2nd Yr) 16 **Employees** 10,346
Corps 311 **Outposts** 9 **Institutions** 116 **Bible College** 1
Senior Soldiers 18,866 **Adherents** 44,151 **Junior Soldiers** 3,067
Personnel serving outside territory Officers 53 Layworkers 5

STAFF

Women's Ministries: Comr Marilyn Francis (TPWM) Col Ann Copple (TSWM)
Personnel: Lt-Col Sandra Rice
  Officer Personnel Dept: Maj Douglas Hefford
  Leadership Development: Maj Mona Moore
Programme: Lt-Col David Hiscock
Business: Lt-Col Neil Watt
Asst Chief Sec: Maj Alison Cowling
Corps Ministries: Maj Everett Barrow
Editor-in-Chief and Literary Sec: Maj James Champ
Finance: Mr Paul Goodyear
Information Technology: Mr Robert Plummer
National Recycling Operations: Mr John Kershaw
Property: Maj Shawn Critch
Public Relations and Development: Mr Graham Moore
Social: Mrs Mary Ellen Eberlin
Training: Maj Eric Bond (Winnipeg)
WCBC Bible College: Dr Donald Burke

DIVISIONS

Alberta and Northern Territories: 9618 101A Ave NW, Edmonton, AB T5H OC7; tel: (780) 423-2111; fax: (780) 425-9081; Majs Frederick and Wendy Waters
Bermuda: PO Box HM 2259, 76 Roberts Ave, Hamilton, HM JX Bermuda; tel: (441) 292-0601; fax: (441) 295-3765; Majs Douglas and Elizabeth Lewis
British Columbia: 103-3833 Henning Dr, Burnaby, BC V5C 6N5; tel: (604) 299-3908; fax: (604) 299-7463; Maj Susan van Duinen
Maritime: 282-7071 Bayers Rd, Halifax, NS B3L 2C2; tel: (902) 455-1201; fax: (902) 455-0055; Majs Larry and Velma Martin
Newfoundland and Labrador: 21 Adams Ave, St John's, NF A1C 4Z1; tel: (709) 579-2022/3; fax: (709) 576-7034; Lt-Cols Alfred and Ethel Richardson
Ontario Central-East: 1645 Warden Ave, Scarborough, ON M1R 5B3; tel: (416) 321-2654; fax: (416) 321-8136; Lt-Cols Floyd and Tracey Tidd
Ontario Great Lakes: 371 King St, London, ON N6B 1S4; tel: (519) 433-6106; fax: (519) 433-0250; Lt-Cols Lee and Deborah Graves
Prairie: 203-290 Vaughan St, Winnipeg, MB R3B 2N8; tel: (204) 946-9101; fax: (204) 946-9169; Majs Junior and Verna Hynes
Quebec: 1655 Richardson St, Montreal, QC H3K 3J7; tel: (514) 288-2848; fax: (514) 288-4657; Majs Kester and Kathryn Trim

COLLEGE FOR OFFICER TRAINING

Winnipeg Campus: 100-290 Vaughan St, Winnipeg, MB R3B 2N8; tel: (204) 924-5606; fax: (204) 924-5603

EDUCATION

The William and Catherine Booth College, 447 Webb Pl, Winnipeg, MB R3B 2P2; tel: (204) 947-6701/6702/6950; fax: (204) 942-3856
President: Dr Donald Burke

ETHICS CENTRE

447 Webb Pl, Winnipeg, MB R3B 2P2; tel: (204) 957-2412; fax: (204) 957-2418; email: ethics_centre@can.salvationarmy.org; Dr James Read

SALVATION ARMY ARCHIVES

Archives: 26 Howden Rd, Scarborough, ON M1R 3E4
Museum: 2 Overlea Blvd, Toronto, ON M4H 1P4; tel: (416) 285-4344; fax: (416) 285-7763; email: Heritage_Centre@can.salvationarmy.org
Col John Carew

Canada and Bermuda Territory

NATIONAL RECYCLING OPERATIONS
2 Overlea Blvd, Toronto, ON M4H 1P4;
tel: (416) 425-2111; fax: (416) 422-6167

Alberta Region: 37-2355 52nd Ave SE, Calgary, AB T2C 4X7; tel: (604) 944-8747; fax: (604) 944-3158

Atlantic Region: 2 Overlea Blvd, Toronto, ON M4H 1P4; tel: (416) 425-2111; fax: (416) 422-6353

British Columbia Region: 2520 Davies Ave, Port Coquitlam, BC V3C 4T7; tel: (604) 944-8747; fax: (604) 944-3158

Montreal Region: 1620 Notre Dame W, Montreal, QC H3J 1M1; tel: (516) 935-7128; fax: (514) 935-6093

Ontario Central Region: 2360 South Service Rd W, Oakville, ON L6L 5M9; tel: (905) 825-9208; fax: (905) 825-8953

Ontario East Region: 6-1280 Leeds Ave, Ottawa, ON K1B 3W3; tel: (613) 247-1435; fax: (613) 247-2243

Prairie Region: 1-111 Inksbrook Dr, Winnipeg, MB R2R 2V7; tel: (204) 953-1508; fax: (204) 953-1505

SOCIAL SERVICES (UNDER THQ)
Hospitals (public)
Rehabilitation
Montreal, QC H4B 2J5, Catherine Booth Hospital, 4375 Montclair Ave; tel: (514) 481-2070

General (B Class)
Windsor, ON N9A 1E1, Hotel-Dieu Grace Hospital, 1030 Ouellette Ave; tel: (519) 973-4444

Complex Continuing Care
Toronto, ON M4Y 2G5, Toronto Grace Health Centre, 650 Church St; tel: (416) 925-2251

Family Tracing Services
2 Overlea Blvd, Toronto, ON M4H 1P4; tel: (416) 422-6219; fax: (416) 422-6221

SOCIAL SERVICES (UNDER DIVISIONS)
Hospices
Calgary, AB T2N 1B8, Agape Hospice, 1302 8th Ave NW; tel: (403) 282-6588 (acc 20)

A moment of prayerful commitment for two cadets during their ordination and commissioning as officers in Canada

Canada and Bermuda Territory

Regina, SK S4R 8P6, Wascana Grace Hospice, 50 Angus Rd; tel: (306) 543-0655 (acc 10)
Richmond, BC V6X 2P3, Rotary Hospice, 3111 Shell Rd; tel: (604) 244-8022 (acc 10)

Adult Services to Developmentally Handicapped

Fort McMurray, AB T9H 1S7, 9919 MacDonald Ave; tel: (780) 743-4135
Hamilton, ON L8S 1G1, Lawson Ministries, 1600 Main St W; tel: (905) 527-6212 (acc 21)
Toronto, ON M4K 2S5, Broadview Village, 1132 Broadview Ave (Residential Living for Developmentally Handicapped Adults); tel: (416) 425-1052; fax: (416) 425-6579 (acc 160)
Winnipeg, MB R3A 0L5, 324 Logan Ave; tel: (204) 946-9418

Adult Services Mental Health

Toronto, ON M6K 1Z3, Liberty Housing, 248 Dufferin St; tel: (416) 531-3523 (acc 23)

Sheltered Workshops

Etobicoke, ON M8Z 4P8, Booth Industries, 994 Islington Ave; tel: (905) 255-7070 (acc 160)
Toronto, ON M3A 1A3, 150 Railside Rd; tel: (416) 693-2116 (acc 44)

Addictions and Rehabilitation Centres (Alcohol/Drug Treatment)
Men

Calgary, AB T2G 0R9, 420 9th Ave SE; tel: (403) 410-1150 (acc 34)
Edmonton, AB T5H 0E5, 9611 102 Ave NW; tel: (780) 429-4274 (acc 158)
Glencairn, ON L0M 1K0, PO Box 100; tel: (705) 466-3435/6 (acc 35)
Hamilton, Bermuda HM JX, PO Box HM 2238; tel: (441) 292-2586 (acc 10)
Kingston, ON K7L 1C7, 562 Princess St; tel: (613) 546-2333 (acc 24)
Mission, BC V2V 4J5, PO Box 3400; tel: (604) 826-6681 (acc 171)
Montreal, QC H3J 1T4, 800 rue Guy; tel: (514) 932-2214
Sudbury, ON P3E 1C2, 146 Larch St; tel: (705) 673-1175/6 (acc 45)
Toronto, ON M5B 1E2, 160 Jarvis St; tel: (416) 363-5496 (acc 80)
Vancouver, BC V6A 1K8, 119 East Cordova St; tel: (604) 646-6800 (acc 70)
Victoria, BC V8W 1M2, 525 Johnson St; tel: (250) 384-3396 (acc 109)

Winnipeg, MB R3B 0A1, 72 Martha St; tel: (204) 946-9401 (acc 32)

Women

Toronto, ON M5R 2L6, The Homestead, 78 Admiral Rd; tel: (416) 921-0953 (acc 18)
Vancouver, BC V6P 1S4, The Homestead, 975 57th Ave W; tel: (604) 266-9696 (acc 32)

Residential Services (Hostels, Emergency Shelters)
Men

Barrie, ON L4M 3A5, Bayside Mission Centre, 16 Bayfield St; tel: (705) 728-3737 (acc 32)
Brampton, ON L6T 4X1, Wilkinson Road Shelter, 15 Wilkinson Rd; tel: (905) 452-1335 (acc 85)
Brantford, ON N3T 2J6, Booth Centre, 187 Dalhousie St; tel: (519) 753-4193/4 (acc 38)
Calgary, AB T2G 0J8, Booth Centre, 631 7 Ave SE; tel: (403) 262-6188 (acc 276)
Campbell River, BC, 291 McLean St; tel: (250) 287-3720 (acc 27)
Chilliwack, BC V2P 2N4, 45746 Yale Rd; tel: (604) 792-0001 (acc 11)
Fort McMurray, AB T9H 1S7, 9919 MacDonald Ave; tel: (780) 743-4135 (acc 32)
Halifax, NS B3K 3A9, 2044 Gottingen St; tel: (902) 422-2363 (acc 49)
Hamilton, ON L8R 1R6, Booth Centre, 94 York Blvd; tel: (905) 527-1444 (acc 99)
Iqaluit, NU X0A 0H0, Box 547; tel: (867) 975-2605 (acc 20)
Mississauga, ON L5C 1T9, Mavis Shelter, 3190 Mavis Rd; tel: (905) 848-8922 (acc 24)
Montreal, QC H3J 1T4, Booth Centre, 880 Guy St; tel: (514) 932-2214 (acc 133)
Nanaimo, BC V9R 4S6, 19 Nicol St; tel: (250) 754-2621 (acc 31)
New Westminster, BC V3L 2K1, 32 Elliot St; tel: (604) 526-4783 (acc 33)
Ottawa, ON K1N 5W5, Booth Centre, 171 George St; tel: (613) 241-1573 (acc 213)
Pembroke, Bermuda HM JX, 5 Marsh Lane; tel: (441) 295-5310 (acc 83)
Penticton, BC V2A 5J1, 2469 South Main St; tel: (250) 492-6494 (acc 20)
Prince Rupert, BC V8J 1R3, 25 Grenville Court; tel: (250) 624-6180 (acc 20)
Quebec City, QC G1R 4H8, Hotellerie, 14 Côte du Palais; tel: (418) 692-3956 (acc 60)
Regina, SK S4P 1W1, 1845 Osler St; tel: (306) 569-6088 (acc 75)
Regina, SK S4P 1W1, Waterston Centre, 1865 Osler St; tel: (306) 566-6088 (acc 40)

Canada and Bermuda Territory

Richmond, BC V6X 2P3, Richmond House Emergency Shelter, 3111 Shell Rd; tel: (604) 276-2490 (acc 10)
Saint John, NB E2L 1V3, 36 St James St; tel: (506) 634-7021 (acc 75)
St Catharine's, ON L2R 3E7, Booth Centre, 184 Church St; tel: (905) 684-7813 (acc 21)
St John's, NL A1E 1C1, Wiseman Centre, 714 Water St; tel: (709) 739-8355/8 (acc 30)
Saskatoon, SK S7M 1N5, 339 Avenue CS; tel: (306) 244-6280 (acc 50)
Thunder Bay, ON P7A 4S2, CARS, 545 Cumberland St N; tel: (807) 345-7319 (acc 46)
Toronto, ON M5T 1P7, Hope Shelter, 167 College St; tel: (416) 979-7058 (acc 108)
Toronto, ON M5C 2H4, The Gateway, 107 Jarvis St; tel: (416) 368-0324 (acc 100)
Toronto, ON M5A 2R5, Maxwell Meighen Centre, 135 Sherbourne St; tel: (416) 366-2733 (acc 378)
Vancouver, BC V6A 1K7, James McCready Residence, 129 East Cordova St; tel: (604) 646-6800 (acc 44)
Vancouver, BC V6A 1K7, The Haven, 128 East Cordova St; tel: (604) 646-6800 (acc 40)
Windsor, ON N9A 7G9, 355 Church St; tel: (519) 253-7473 (acc 111)

Women

Brampton, ON L6X 3C9, The Honeychurch Family Life Resource Center, 535 Main St N; tel: (905) 451-4115 (acc 73)
Brampton, ON L6T 4M6, Wilkinson Road Shelter, 15 Wilkinson Rd; tel: (905) 452-6335 (acc 24)
Mississauga, ON L5C 1T9, Mavis Shelter, 3190 Mavis Rd; tel: (905) 848-8922 (acc 24)
Montreal, QC H3J 1M8, L'Abri d'Espoir, 2000 Notre Dame W; tel: (514) 934-5615 (acc 36)
Quebec City, QC G1R 4H8, Maison Charlotte, 14 Cote du Palais; tel: (418) 692-3956 (acc 25)
Toronto, ON M6P 1Y5, Evangeline Residence, 2808 Dundas St W; tel: (416) 762-9636 (acc 77)
Toronto, ON M6J 1E6, Florence Booth House, 723 Queen St W; tel: (416) 603-9800 (acc 60)
Vancouver, BC V5Z 4L9, Kate Booth House, PO Box 38048 King Edward Mall; tel: (604) 872-0772 (acc 12)

Mixed (male and female)

Abbotsford, BC V2S 2E8, 34081 Gladys Ave; tel: (604) 852-9305 (acc 34)
Calgary, AB T2G 0R9, Centre of Hope, 420 9th Ave; tel: (403) 410-1111 (acc 295)
Courtney, BC V9N 2S2, 1580 Ftizgerald Ave; tel: (250) 338-5133 (acc 9)
Fort St John, BC, 10116 100th Ave; tel: (250) 785-0506 (acc 20)
London, ON N6C 4L8, Centre of Hope, 281 Wellington St; tel: (519) 661-0343 (acc 253)
Maple Ridge, BC V2X 2S8, 22188 Lougheed Hwy; tel: (604) 463-8296 (acc 43)
Medicine Hat, AB T1A 1M6, 737 8th St SE; tel: (403) 526-9699 (acc 30)
Oakville, ON L6L 6X7, Lighthouse Shelter, 750 Redwood Sq; tel: (905) 339-2918 (acc 25)
Sudbury, ON P3A 1C2, 146 Larch St; tel: (705) 363-5496
Vancouver, BC V6A 4K9, Grace Mansion, 596 East Hastings St; tel: (778) 329-0674 (acc 85)
Vancouver, BC V6B 1K8, Belkin House, 555 Homer St; tel: (604) 681-3405 (acc 257)
Vancouver, BC V6B 1G8, The Crosswalk, 138-140 W Hastings St; tel: (604) 669-4349
Winnipeg, MB R3B 0J8, Booth Centre, 180 Henry Ave; tel: (204) 946-9460 (acc 208)

Family

Mississauga, ON L5R 4J9, Angela's Place, 45 Glen Hawthorne Rd; tel: (905) 791-3887
Mississauga, ON L5A 2X3, SA Peel Family Shelter, 2500 Cawthra Rd; tel: (905) 272-7061 (acc 148)
Montreal, QC H3J 1M8, L'Abri e'Espoir, 2000 rue Notre-Dame oust; tel: (514) 934-5615 (acc 25)

Youth

Sutton, ON L0E 1R0, 20898 Dalton Rd, PO Box 1087; tel: (905) 722-9076

Community and Family Services

Alberta: Calgary, Cranbrook, Drumheller, Edmonton, Fort McMurray, Grande Prairie, High River, Lethbridge, Lloydminster, Medicine Hat, Peace River, Red Deer, St Albert.
Bermuda: Hamilton.
British Columbia: Abbotsford, Campbell River, Chilliwack, Courtenay, Duncan, Dawson Creek, Fernie, Fort St John, Gibsons, Kamloops, Kelowna, Maple Ridge, Naniamo, Nelson, New Westminster, North Vancouver, Parksville, Penticton, Port Alberni, Powel River, Prince George, Prince Rupert, Quesnel, Richmond, Salmon Arm, Surrey, Terrace, Trail, Vancouver, Vernon, Victoria, White Rock, Williams Lake.

Canada and Bermuda Territory

Manitoba: Brandon, Dauphin, Flin Flon, Portage La Prairie, Thompson, Winnipeg (2).
New Brunswick: Bathurst, Campbelltown, Fredericton, Miramichi, Moncton, Saint John, Sussex.
Newfoundland and Labrador: Corner Brook, Gander, Grand Falls-Windsor, Labrador City/Wabush, Pasadena, Springdale, St Anthony, St John's, Stephenville.
Nova Scotia: Bridgewater, Glace Bay, Halifax, Kentville, New Glasgow, Sydney, Truro, Westville, Yarmouth.
Ontario: Ajax, Belleville, Bowmanville, Brampton, Brantford, Brockville, Burlington, Cambridge, Chatham, Cobourg, Collingwood, Cornwall, Essex, Etobicoke (2), Fenelon Falls, Fort Frances, Gananoque, Georgetown, Goderich, Gravenhurst, Guelph, Hamilton, Huntsville, Ingersoll, Jacksons Point, Kemptville, Kenora, Kingston, Kirkland Lake, Kitchener, Leamington, Lindsay, Listowel, London, Midland, Milton, Mississauga (3), Napanee, New Liskeard, Newmarket, Niagara Falls, North Bay, North York (2), Oakville, Orillia, Oshawa, Ottawa, Owen Sound, Pembroke, Perth, Peterborough, Renfrew, Ridgetown, Sarnia, Sault Ste Marie, Scarborough, Simcoe, Smiths Falls, St Catharines, St Marys, St Thomas, Stratford, Strathroy, Sudbury, Thunder Bay, Tillsonburg, Toronto (3), Trenton, Wallaceburg, Welland, Whitby, Windsor, Woodstock.
Prince Edward Island: Charlottetown, Summerside.
Quebec: Montreal, Quebec City, Sherbrooke, St-Hubert, Trois-Rivieres.
Saskatchewan: Moose Jaw, Prince Albert, Regina.
Yukon Territory: Whitehorse.

Correctional and Justice Services
Community Programme Centres
Barrie, ON L4M 5A1, 400 Bayfield St, Ste 255; tel: (705) 737-4140

Chilliwack, BC V2P 2N4, 45742B Yale Rd; tel: (604) 792-8581

Guelph, ON N1L 1H3, 1320 Gordon St; tel: (519) 836-9360

Halifax, NS B3J 1Y9, 1329 Barrington St; tel: (902) 429-6120

Hamilton, ON L7R 1Y9, 2090 Prospect St; tel (905) 634-7977

Kingston, ON K7K 4B1, 472 Division St; tel: (613) 549-2676

Kitchener, ON N2H 2M2, 151 Frederick St, Ste 502; tel: (519) 742-8521

London, ON N6B 2L4, 281 Wellington St; tel: (519) 432-9553

Medicine Hat, AB T1A 0E7, 874 2 St E; tel: (403) 529-2111

Moncton, NB E1C 1M2, 68 Gordon St; tel: (506) 853-8887

Ottawa, ON K1Y K1N, 171 George St; tel: (613) 725-1733

Peterborough, ON K9H 2H6, 219 Simcoe St; tel: (705) 742-4391

Prince Albert, SK S6V 4V3, 900 Central Ave; tel: (306) 763-6078

Regina, SK S4P 3M7, 2240 13th Ave; tel: (306) 757-4711/2

Saint John, NB E2L 1V3, 36 St James St; tel: (506) 634-7021

St Catharines, ON L2R 3E7, 184 Church St; tel: (905) 684-7813

St John's, NL A1C 4Z1, 21 Adams Ave; tel: (709) 726-0393

Saskatoon, SK S7M 1N5, 339 Avenue C S; tel: (306) 244-6280

Thunder Bay, ON P7A 4S2, 268 Pearl St; tel: (807) 344-0683

Toronto, ON M5A 3P1, 77 River St; tel: (416) 304-1974

Winnipeg, MB R3A 0L5, 324 Logan Ave, 2nd Floor; tel: (204) 949-2100

Adult/Youth Residential Centres
Brampton, ON L6X 1C1, 44 Nelson St W; tel: (905) 453-0988

Dartmouth, NS B3A 1H5, 318 Windmill Rd; tel: (902) 465-2690

Dundas, ON L9H 2E8, 34 Hatt St; tel: (905) 627-1632

Ilderton, ON N0M 2A0, PO Box 220; tel: (519) 666-0600

Kitchener, ON N2G 2M4, 657 King St E; tel: (519) 744-4666

Milton, ON L9P 2X9, 8465 Boston Church Rd; tel: 905 875-1775

Moncton, NB E1C 8P6, 64 Gordon St, PO Box 1121; tel: (506) 858-9486

Thunder Bay, ON P7A 4S2, 268 Pearl St; tel: (807) 344-0683

Toronto, ON M4X 1K2, 422 Sherbourne St; tel: (416) 964-6316/967-6618

Whitehorse, YT Y1A 6E3, 91678 Alaska Highway; tel: (867) 667-2741

Yellowknife, NT X1A 1P4, 4927 45th St; tel: (867) 920-4673

Health Services
Long-Term Care/Seniors' Residences
Brandon, MB R7A 3N9, Dinsdale Personal

Canada and Bermuda Territory

Care Home, 510 6th St; tel: (204) 727-3636 (acc 60)

Calgary, AB T3C 3W7, Jackson/Willan Seniors' Residence, 3015 15 Ave SW; tel: (403) 249-9116 (acc 18)

Edmonton, AB T5X 6C4, Grace Manor, 12510 140 Ave; tel: (780) 454-5484 (acc 100)

Kitchener, ON N2H 2P1, A. R. Goudie Eventide Home, 369 Frederick St; tel: (519) 744-5182 (acc 80)

Montreal, QC H4B 2J4, Montclair Residence, 4413 Montclair Ave; tel: (514) 481-5638 (acc 50)

New Westminster, BC V3L 4A4, Buchanan Lodge, 409 Blair Ave; tel: (604) 522-7033 (acc 112)

Niagara Falls, ON L2E 1K5, The Honourable Ray and Helen Lawson Eventide Home, 5050 Jepson St; tel: (905) 356-1221 (acc 100)

Ottawa, ON K1Y 2Z3, Ottawa Grace Manor, 1156 Wellington St; tel: (613) 722-8025 (acc 128)

Regina, SK S4R 8P6, William Booth Special Care Home, 50 Angus Rd; tel: (306) 543-0655 (acc 81)

Riverview, NB E1B 4K6, Lakeview Manor, 50 Suffolk St; tel: (506) 387-2012/3/4 (acc 50)

St John's, NL A1A 2G9, Glenbrook Lodge, 105 Torbay Rd; tel: (709) 726-1575 (acc 114)

St John's, NL A1A 2G9, Glenbrook Villa, 107 Torbay Rd; tel: (709) 726-1575 (acc 20)

Toronto, ON M4S 1G1, Meighen Retirement Residence, 84 Davisville Ave; tel: (416) 481-5557 (acc 84)

Toronto, ON M4S 1J6, Meighen Manor, 155 Millwood Rd; tel: (416) 481-9449 (acc 168)

Vancouver, BC V5S 3T1, Southview Terrace, 3131 58th Ave E; tel: (604) 438-3367/8 (acc 57)

Vancouver BC V5S 3V2, Southview Heights 7252 Kerr St; tel: (604) 438-3367/8 (acc 47)

Victoria, BC V9A 7J6, Matson Sequoia Residence, 554 Garrett Pl Ste 211; tel: (250) 383-5821 (acc 30)

Carol Jaudes, with other members of the USA Eastern Territorial Arts Ministries team, participates in the 'Harvest Of Hope' Congress in Toronto

Canada and Bermuda Territory

Canadian Staff Band members visit Mexico to help conduct that territory's annual music institute

Victoria, BC V9A 4G7, Sunset Lodge,
952 Arm St; tel: (250) 385-3422 (acc 108)
Winnipeg, MB R2Y 0S8, Golden West
Centennial Lodge, 811 School Rd;
tel: (204) 888-3311 (acc 116)

Immigrant and Refugee Services
Toronto, ON M5B 1E2, 160 Jarvis St;
tel: (416) 360-6036

Women's Multi-Service Programmes (and unmarried mothers)
Hamilton, ON L8P 2H1, Grace Haven,
138 Herkimer St; tel: (905) 522-7336 (acc 12)
London, ON N6J 1A2, Bethesda Centre,
54 Riverview Ave; tel: (519) 438-8371 (acc 14)
Ottawa, ON K1Y 2Z3, Bethany Hope Centre,
1140 Wellington St; tel: (613) 725-1733
Regina, SK S4S 7A7, Grace Haven, 2929 26th
Ave; tel: (306) 352-1421 (acc 7)
Saskatoon, SK S7K 0N1, Bethany Home,
802 Queen St; tel: (306) 244-6758 (acc 15)

Children's Treatment Facilities
Calgary, AB T3C 1M6, Children's Village,
1731 29 St SW; tel: (403) 246-1124 (acc 40)
Regina, SK S4S 0X5, Gemma House, 3820 Hill
Ave; tel: (306) 586-5388 (acc 8)

Child Day Care/Pre-schools
Barrie, ON L4V 5X5, Sonlight Child Care Centre,
151 Lillian Cres; tel: (705) 734-9080 (acc 93)
Brampton, ON L6S 4B7, Noah's Ark Day Care
Centre, 9395 Bramalea Rd N;
tel: (905) 793-5610 (acc 46)
Chilliwack, BC V2P 1C5, Happy Hearts Day
Care, 46420 Brooks Ave; tel: (604) 792-5285
(acc 23)
Guelph, ON N1L 1H3, Salvation Army Nursery
School, 1320 Gordon St; tel: (519) 836-9360
(acc 121)
London, ON N6J 1A2, Cantara, 54 Riverview
Ave; tel: (519) 438-8371 (acc 20)
London, ON N5W 2B6, The Salvation Army
Village Day Nursery, 1340 Dundas St E;
tel: (519) 455-8155 ext 308 (acc 75)
Medicine Hat, AB T1B 3R3, Rise and Shine Day
Care, 164 Stratton Way SE;
tel: (403) 529-2003 (acc 58)
Mississauga, ON L5L 1V3, Erin Mills Day Care,
2460 The Collegeway; tel: (905) 820-6500
(acc 32)
Mississauga, ON L5N 4W8, Gentle Guidance
Day Care, 3025 Vanderbilt Rd;
tel: (905) 785-0522 (acc 24)
Mississauga, ON L5A 2X4, Mississauga Temple
Day Care, 3173 Cawthra Rd;
tel: 905-275-8430 (acc 82)
Moncton, NB E1E 4E4, Small Blessings,
20 Centennial Dr; tel: (506) 857-0588 (acc 95)
New Westminster, BC V3L 3A9, Kids Place Day
Care, 325 6th St; tel: (604) 521-8223 (acc 20)
Owen Sound, ON N4K 2X9, Salvation Army
Day Care, 365 14th St W;
tel: (519) 371-9540 (acc 99)
Peace River, AB T8S 1E1, School Readiness,
9710-74 Ave; tel: (780) 624-2370 (acc 43)
Scarborough, ON M1W 3K3, Agincourt Temple
Child Care, 3080 Birchmount Rd;
tel: (416) 497-0329 (acc 94)
Scarborough, ON M1R 2Z2, Scarborough
Citadel Child Care, 2021 Lawrence Ave E;
tel: 416-759-5340 (acc 36)
Windsor, ON N8T 2Z7, Learning Corner Day
Care Centre, 3199 Lauzon Rd;
tel: (519) 944-4051 (acc 111)
Winnipeg, MB R3E 1E6, Weston Child Care,
1390 Roy Ave; tel: (204) 786-5066 (acc 59)

Parent Child Resource Centres
Courtney, BC V9N 2S2, 1580 Fitzgerald Ave;
tel: (250) 338-6200
Kitchener, ON N2E 3T1, 75 Tillsley Dr;
tel: (519) 745-3351

China Task Force plots progress

SALVATION Army relief work and development services in mainland China were examined and evaluated when the China Task Force met in Hong Kong under the leadership of Chief of the Staff Commissioner Robin Dunster. Experiences of work in mainland China were shared, opportunities and challenges for ministry examined and strategies for the way forward explored.

For many years The Salvation Army has fulfilled a significant ministry through emergency and poverty alleviation projects. This work continues as the Hong Kong and Macau Command, which oversees the work in China, is committed to serving suffering humanity in Christ's name in mainland China.

Task force members represented Hong Kong and Macau Command and the South Pacific and East Asia Zonal Office, IHQ.

Top: Members of the China Task Force (from left) – Major Tommy Chan and Major On, Dieu-Quang (Hong Kong and Macau Command), Lieut-Colonel Gillian Downer (Under Secretary for South Pacific and East Asia, IHQ), Major Priscilla Nanlabi (General Secretary, HK&M), the Chief of the Staff, Envoy Simon Wong (HK&M) and Commissioner Barry Pobjie (then International Secretary for SPEA, IHQ)

Left: Survivors of severe floods in mainland China receive rice from a Salvation Army relief team

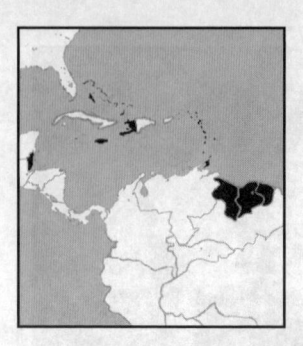

CARIBBEAN TERRITORY

Territorial leaders:
Colonels Onal and Edmane Castor

Territorial Commander:
Colonel Onal Castor (1 May 2009)

Chief Secretary:
Lieut-Colonel Lindsay Rowe (1 May 2009)

Territorial Headquarters: 3 Waterloo Rd, Kingston 10, Jamaica

Postal address: PO Box 378, Kingston 10, Jamaica, WI

Tel: [1876] 929 6190/91/92; fax: [1876] 929 7560; email: car_leadership@car.salvationarmy.org; website: www.salvationarmycarib.org

In 1887 The Salvation Army 'opened fire' in Kingston, and thence spread throughout the island of Jamaica and to Guyana (1895), Barbados (1898), Trinidad (1901), Grenada (1902), St Lucia (1902), Antigua (1903), St Vincent (1905), Belize (1915), St Kitts (1916), Suriname (1924), the Bahamas (1931), Haiti (1950), French Guiana (1980) and St Maarten (1999). The General of The Salvation Army is a Corporation Sole in Jamaica (1914), Trinidad and Tobago (1915), Barbados (1917), Belize (1928), Guyana (1930), the Bahamas (1936) and Antigua (1981).

Zone: Americas and Caribbean
Countries included in the territory: Antigua, Barbados, Belize, French Guiana, Grenada, Guyana, Haiti, Jamaica, St Kitts, St Lucia, St Maarten, St Vincent, Suriname, Trinidad and Tobago
'The Salvation Army' in Dutch: Leger des Heils; in French: Armée du Salut
Languages in which the gospel is preached: Creole, Dutch, English, French, Surinamese
Periodical: *The War Cry*

THE Salvation Army in the Caribbean continues to grow, especially in Haiti and in French Guiana. Other areas that make up the territory also report numerical and spiritual progress.

At the ordination and commissioning of cadets of the God's Fellow-Workers Session, conducted by then Territorial Commander Commissioner Raymond Houghton, the 11 new lieutenants received appointments to serve in Haiti, Jamaica and Barbados.

The Caribbean Music Institute was held again after a lapse of five years. It was a very effective means of bringing together young people from across the territory for a week of music-making, Bible study and leadership training.

National television coverage was given to a football tournament in Jamaica that attracted many young people to The Salvation Army.

Missions teams and workforces, including cadets from USA Southern and Canada and Bermuda Territories, made regular visits and undertook several projects. The Falmouth Corps building in Western Jamaica Division and seven officers' quarters within the territory were refurbished.

Following hurricane damage in Haiti a number of halls, school buildings and officers' quarters are undergoing repair and refurbishment. The territory is grateful to partner territories for funding this work, and for the relief services given in Haiti and other islands severely hit by hurricanes in summer 2008.

For the first time funds from the Home League Helping-Hand Scheme were given to support Salvation Army work in another territory rather than being used locally, so helping Caribbean people to see and respond to the needs of others beyond their own area.

In October 2008 the territory's first Caribbean Advisory Organisations Conference, attended by 80 delegates, gave new stimulus to advisory boards and should result in more-effective boards.

Holiness conventions continue to be an annual feature in most parts of the terriory. Antigua Division and French Guiana Area Command held their first, and there are plans for such conventions to become annual events.

Leadership training seminars are being encouraged in many divisions. In addition, the newly appointed Territorial Secretary for Leader Development is beginning to stimulate leadership training – seen as vital for the territory's future.

STATISTICS

Officers 299 (active 223 retired 76) **Cadets** (1st Yr) 8 (2nd Yr) 10 **Employees** 1,017
Corps 129 **Outposts** 47 **Institutions** 59
Schools 164
Senior Soldiers 9,692 **Adherents** 1,336 **Junior Soldiers** 2,714
Personnel serving outside territory Officers 10

STAFF

Women's Ministries: Col Edmane Castor (TPWM) Lt-Col Lynette Rowe (TSWM) Lt-Col Trypheme McKenzie (TLOMS & TWAS)
Personnel: Lt-Col Sydney McKenzie
Programme: Maj Devon Haughton
Business: Maj Edwin Masih
Editor: Maj Molvie Graham
Leader Development: Maj Verona Haughton
Pastoral Care: Maj Keith Graham
Prayer Coordinator: Maj Keith Graham
Projects/Sponsorship: Mr Stephen Williamson
Spiritual Life Development: Maj Verona Haughton
Territorial Development and Disaster Services Coordinator: Envoy John Williamson
Training: Maj Ronald Millar
Youth and Candidates: Capt Sherma Evelyn

DIVISIONS

Antigua: PO Box 2, 36 Long St, St John's; tel: [1268] 562-5473; fax: [1268] 462-9134; Majs Stanley and Hazel Griffin
Bahamas: PO Box N 205, Nassau, NP; tel: [1242] 393-2340; fax: [1242] 393-2189; Maj Lester and Capt Beverley Ferguson
Barbados: PO Box 57, Reed St, Bridgetown; tel: [1246] 426-2467; fax: [1246] 426-9369; Majs Dewhurst and Vevene Jonas
Guyana: PO Box 10411, 237 Alexander St, Lacytown, Georgetown; tel: [592] 22 72619/54910; fax: [592] (22) 50893; Majs Sinous and Marie Theodore
Haiti: PO Box 301, Port-au-Prince; tel: [509] 510-3671; Majs Lucien and Marie Lamartiniere
Jamaica Eastern: PO Box 153, Kingston; 153b Orange St, Kingston; tel: [1876] 922-6764/0287; fax: [1876] 967-1553; Majs Kervin and Lucia Harry
Jamaica Western: PO Box 44, Lot #949 Westgreen, Montego Bay, St James; tel: [876] 952-3778; Majs Allen and Esther Satterlee

Caribbean Territory

Trinidad and Tobago: 154a Henry St, Port-of-Spain, Trinidad; PO Box 248, Port-of-Spain; tel: [1868] 625-4120; fax: [1868] 625-4206; Majs Darrell and Joan Wilkinson

REGIONS

Belize: PO Box 64, 41 Regent St, Belize City; tel: [501] 2273 365; fax: (501) 2278 240; email: Belize_HQ@CAR.salvationarmy.org; Maj Brenda Greenidge

Suriname: PO Box 317, Henck Arron Straat 172, Paramaribo; tel: [597] 47-3310; fax: [597] 41-0555; email: Suriname_HQ@CAR.salvationarmy.org; Maj Miller Cantave

COUNTRIES NOT IN DIVISIONAL OR REGIONAL LISTS

French Guiana: Route de la Madeleine, Cite Mortin, Boite Postale 329, 97327 Cayenne Cedex, Guyane Francaise; tel: [594] 594-315832

Grenada: Grenville St, St George's, Grenada; tel: [1473] 440-3299

St Kitts: PO Box 56, Cayon Rd, Basseterre, St Kitts; tel: [1869] 465-2106; fax: [1869] 465-4429

St Lucia: PO Box 6, High St, Castries, St Lucia; tel: [1758] 452-3108; fax: [1758] 451-8569

St Maarten: 59 Union Rd, Cole Bay, PO Box 5184, St Maarten, Netherlands Antilles; tel: [599] 580-8588

St Vincent: Melville St, PO Box 498, Kingstown, St Vincent; tel: (809) 456-1574; fax: [1784] 456-1082

TRAINING COLLEGE

GPO Box 437, 174 Orange St, Kingston, Jamaica; tel: [1876] 922-2027; fax: [1876] 967-7541

CITY WELFARE OFFICES

Bahamas: 31 Mackey St, Nassau NP
Jamaica: 57 Peter's Lane, Kingston

COMMUNITY CENTRES

Bahamas: Freeport, Grantstown
Barbados: Checker Hall, St Lucy, Wellington St, Bridgetown, Wotton, Christchurch
Jamaica:
Rae Town Goodwill Centre, 24 Tower St, Kingston; tel: [1876] 928-5770/930-0028
Allman Town, 18-20 Prince of Wales St, Kingston 4; tel: [1876] 92-27279

FEEDING CENTRES

Antigua: Meals on wheels
Bahamas: Mackey St and Grantstown, Nassau
Barbados: Reed St, Bridgetown
Belize: 9 Glynn St, Belize City (acc 50)
Guyana:
237 Alexander St, Georgetown; Third Avenue, Bartica; Rainbow City, Linden
Haiti: Port-au-Prince (Nutrition Centre)
Jamaica: Peter's Lane, Kingston; Jones Town, Kingston; Spanish Town, St Catherine; May Pen, Clarendon; St Ann's Bay, St Ann; Port Antonio, Portland; Montego Bay, St James; Savanna-La-Mar, Westmoreland
St Lucia: High St, Castries
Suriname: Gravenstraat 126, Paramaribo

For Children
Bahamas: Nassau, Mackey St
Grenada: St Georges
Guyana: Georgetown, Bartica, Linden
St Vincent: Kingstown

MEDICAL WORK

Haiti: Bethel Maternity Home and Dispensary, Fond-des-Negres
Bethesda TB Centre, Fond-des-Negres
Primary Health Care Centre and Nutrition Centre, Port-au-Prince
Jamaica: Rae Town Clinic, 24 Tower St, Kingston; tel: (876) 928-1489/930-0028

PRISON, PROBATION AND AFTERCARE WORK

Antigua, Grenada, Guyana (Georgetown, Bartica, New Amsterdam), Jamaica, St Kitts, Suriname, Tobago, Trinidad

Prison Visitation Services
Belize: directed by Regional Commander

RETIRED OFFICERS' RESIDENCES

Jamaica: Francis Ham Residence, 57 Mannings Hill Rd, Kingston 8; tel: (876) 924-1308 (acc 7)
Barbados: Long Bay, St Phillip
Guyana: East La Penitence

SOCIAL SERVICES
Blind and Handicapped
Adults
Bahamas: Visually Handicapped Workshop, Ivanhoe Lane, PO Box N 1980, Nassau NP; tel: (242) 394-1107 (acc 19)
Jamaica: Francis Ham Residence (home for senior citizens), 57 Mannings Hill Rd, Kingston 8; tel: (876) 924-1308 (acc 37)

Caribbean Territory

Children (schools)
Bahamas: School for the Blind, 33 Mackay St, PO Box N 205, Nassau NP; tel: (242) 394-3197 (acc 15)
Jamaica:
School for the Blind and Visually Impaired, 57 Mannings Hill Rd, PO Box 562, Kingston 8; tel: (876) 925-1362 (residential acc 120)

Women (vocational training)
Jamaica: Evangeline Residence, Kingston; Port Antonio, Portland

SOCIAL SERVICES
Children
Day Care Centres (nurseries)
Barbados: Wellington St, Bridgetown (acc 50) Wotton, Christchurch (acc 50)
Grenada: St Georges (acc 25)
Jamaica: Allman Town, Kingston (acc 40) Havendale, Kingston (acc 16) Lucea, Hanover (acc 30) Montego Bay, St James (acc 40)
St Lucia: Castries (acc 50)
St Vincent: Kingstown (acc 20)
Trinidad: San Juan (acc 20)

Homes
Antigua: St John's Sunshine Home (acc 12)
Haiti: Bethany, Fond-des-Negres (acc 22) La Maison du Bonheur, Port-au-Prince (acc 52)
Jamaica:
Hanbury Home, PO Box 2, Shooter's Hill PO, Manchester; tel: [1876] 603-3507 (acc 90)
The Nest, 57 Mannings Hill Rd, Kingston 8; tel: [1876] 925-7711 (acc 45)
Windsor Lodge, PO Box 74, Williamsfield PO, Manchester; tel: [1876] 963-4031 (acc 80)
Suriname: Ramoth, Henck Arron Straat 172, PO Box 317, Paramaribo; tel: [597] 47-3310 (acc 62)

Playgrounds
Jamaica: Rae Town, Kingston; Lucea, Hanover; Montego Bay, St James
Suriname: Henck Arron Straat 126, Paramaribo

Schools
Basic (kindergartens)
Antigua: St John (acc 150)
Barbados: Checker Hall (acc 50) Wellington St (acc 10)
Guyana: Bartica (acc 90)
Haiti: Abraham (acc 63) Aquin (acc 112) Arcahaie (acc 45) Balan (acc 30) Bainet (acc 32) Bellamie (acc 35) Bellegarde (acc 40) Belle Riviere (acc 24) Bocolomond (acc 47) Bodoin (acc 17) Brodequin (acc 64) Campeche (acc 43) Cayot (acc 70) Couyot (acc 65) Deruisseaux (acc 10) Dessources (acc 30) Duverger (acc 77) Fond-des-Negres (acc 96) Fort National (acc 26) Gardon (acc 40) Gros-Morne (48) Guirand (acc 12) Jacmel (acc 34) Kamass (acc 12) L'Azile (acc 51) L'Homond (acc 75) La Colline (acc 21) Laferonnay (acc 34) Lafosse (acc 82) Lajovange (acc35) Le Blanc (acc 34) Lilette (acc 37) Limbe (acc 20) Montrouis (30) Moulin (acc 75) Perigny (acc 25) Petit Goave (acc 53) Plaisance (acc 15) Port-de-Paix (acc 14) Puit Laurent (acc 36) Rossignol (acc 53) St Marc (acc 91) Verena (acc 211) Vieux Bourg (acc 175) Violette (acc 42)
Jamaica: Bath (acc 25) Bluefields (acc 49) Cave Mountain (acc 30) Cave Valley (acc 75) Falmouth (acc 86) Great Bay (acc 40) Kingston Allman Town (acc 150) Kingston Havendale (acc 90) Kingston Rae Town (acc 100) Linstead (acc 65) Lucea (acc 200) May Pen (acc 60) Montego Bay (acc 240) Port Antonio (acc 50) St Ann's Bay (acc 36) Savanna-la-mar (acc 110) Top Hill (acc 93)
St Kitts: Basseterre (acc 80)
St Lucia: Castries (acc 100)
Trinidad and Tobago: San Fernando (acc 80) Scarborough, Tobago (acc 70) Tragarette Rd, Port-of-Spain (acc 20)

Home Science
Barbados: Project Lighthouse (acc 12)
Haiti: Aquin, Carrefour, Desruisseaux, Duverger, Fond-des-Negres, Gros Morne, Vieux Bourg

Primary Schools
Belize: 12 Cemetery Road, Belize City; tel: (501) 227-2156 (acc 250)
Haiti: Abraham (acc 165) Aquin (acc 229) Arcahaie (acc 131) Bainet (acc 168) Balan (acc 162) Bas Fort National (acc 198) Bellamie (acc 115) Bellegarde (acc 198) Belle Riviere (acc 198) Boco Lomond (acc 205) Bodoun (acc 52) Brodequin (acc 149) Campeche (acc 99) Carrefour/Desruisseaux (acc 235)

Caribbean Territory

Cayot (acc 174) Couyot (acc 235)
Deruisseaux (acc 220) Dessources (acc 131)
Duverger (acc 188) Fond-des-Negres (acc 520)
Fort National (acc 178) Gardon (acc 110)
Gros Morne (acc 285) Guirand (acc 94)
Jacmel (acc 65) Kamass (acc 21)
L'Azile (acc 127) Laferonnay (acc 166)
L'Homond (acc 165) La Jovange (acc 173)
La Zandier (acc 170) La Colline (acc 125)
La Fosse (acc 276) Lilette (acc 143)
Limbe (acc 55) Luly (acc 169)
Montrouis (acc 131) Moulin (acc 121)
Peirigny (acc 135) Petit Goave (acc 135)
Petite Riviere (acc110) Plaisance (acc 135)
College Verena (acc 696)
Port-de-Paix (acc 71) Puits Laurent (acc 151)
Rossignol (acc 120) St Marc (acc 118)
Vieux Bourg (acc 483) Violette (acc 98)

Evening Schools
Guyana: Happy Heart Youth Centre, New Amsterdam (acc 20)
Haiti: Port-au-Prince (acc 83)

Secondary Schools
Haiti: Port-au-Prince (acc 450) Gros-Morne (acc 85)

SOCIAL SERVICES
Men and Women
Centre for Homeless
Belize: Raymond A. Parkes Home, 18 Cemetery Rd, Belize City; tel: [501] 207-4309 (acc 24)

Eventide Home
Trinidad: Senior Citizens' Centre, 34 Duncan St, Port-of-Spain; tel: [868] 624-5883 (acc 57)

SOCIAL SERVICES
Men
Guyana: MacKenzie Guest House, Rainbow City, PO Box 67, Linden Co-op MacKenzie, Guyana; tel: [592] 444-6406 (acc 30)

Hostels and Shelters
Guyana:
Men's Hostel, 6-7 Water St, Kingston, Georgetown; tel: [592] 226-1235 (acc 40)
Drug Rehabilitation Centre, 6-7 Water St, Kingston, Georgetown; tel: [592] 226-1235 (acc 20)

Jamaica:
Men's Hostel, 57 Peter's Lane, Kingston; tel: [1876] 922-4030 (acc 25)
William Chamberlain Rehabilitation Centre, 57 Peter's Lane, Kingston (acc 25)
Suriname: Night Shelter, Ladesmastraat 2-6, PO Box 317, Paramaribo; tel: [597] 4-75108 (acc 31)

SOCIAL SERVICES
Women
Eventide Homes
Belize: Ganns Rest Home, 60 East Canal St, Belize City; tel: [501] 227 2973 (acc 12)
Guyana: 69 Bent and Haley Sts, Wortmanville, Georgetown; tel: [592] 226-8846 (acc 22)
Suriname:
Elim Guest House, Gravenstraat 126, PO Box 317, Paramaribo; tel: [597] 47-2735 (acc 15)
Emma House, Dr Nassylaan 76, PO Box 2402, Paramaribo; tel: [597] 4-73890 (acc 22)

Hostels and Shelters
Bahamas: Women and Children's Emergency Residence, Grantstown, PO Box GT 2216, Nassau NP; tel: [242] 323-5608 (acc 21)
Jamaica: Evangeline Residence, 153 Orange St, Kingston; tel: 922-6398 (acc 50)
Trinidad:
Geddes Grant House, 22-24 Duncan St, Port-of-Spain; tel: 623-5700 (acc 34)
Josephine Shaw House, 131-133 Henry St, Port-of-Spain; tel: 623-2547 (acc 106)

Sunbeams from Top Hill Corps, Jamaica

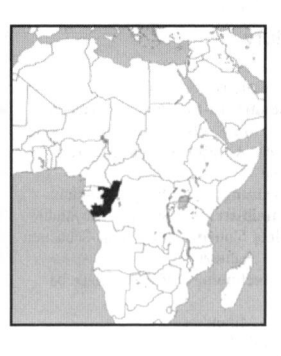

CONGO (BRAZZAVILLE) TERRITORY

Territorial leaders:
Commissioners Mfon J. and Ime Akpan

Territorial Commander:
Commissioner Mfon J. Akpan (1 Apr 2004)

Chief Secretary:
Lieut-Colonel Gerrit Marseille (1 Mar 2008)

Territorial Headquarters: Rue de Reims, Brazzaville,
République du Congo

Postal address: BP 20, Brazzaville, République du Congo; or c/o Africa Department,
International Headquarters, 101 Queen Victoria St, London EC4V 4EH, United Kingdom

Tel: [242] 2811144; email: CON_leadership@con.salvationarmy.org

In 1937 The Salvation Army spread from Léopoldville to Brazzaville, and in 1953 French Equatorial Africa (now Congo) became a separate command. Commissioner and Mrs Henri Becquet were the pioneers. The command was upgraded to a territory in December 1960.

Zone: Africa
Country included in the territory: The Republic of Congo
'The Salvation Army' in French: Armée du Salut; in Kikongo: Nkangu a Luvulusu; in Lingala: Basolda na Kobikisama; in Vili: Livita li Mavutsula
Languages in which the gospel is preached: French, Kikongo, Kituba, Lingala, Vili
Periodical: *Le Salutiste*

THIRTY-ONE cadets of the Witnesses For Jesus Session were ordained and commissioned in June 2008. It was a joyful event, held in the 3,000-seat Moungali Corps hall which was packed to capacity for the occasion.

The training of the next session of cadets having been postponed for a year, the college hosted 'Capacity Building' seminars for 87 officers who have given five to 15 years' service. From February to April 2009 three seminars took place dealing with such subjects as leadership, doctrine, ethics and African theology, orders and regulations, women's ministries, youth work, community development and finance.

In March more than 100 of the territory's women officers crossed the mighty Congo river to pay a return visit to their sisters in Kinshasa. Their days were packed with various presentations, demonstrations and discussions. The inspirational tour was enhanced by the presence of Commissioners Janet Street (then World Secretary for Women's Ministries) and Rosemary

Congo (Brazzaville) Territory

Makina (Africa Zonal Secretary for Women's Ministries).

When a training team from the International Projects and Development Services, IHQ, visited the territory in October 2008 they introduced the new Community Projects Management and Support System during a conference for THQ leaders.

The training confirmed to the conference delegates that, after a period of civil unrest in the country, it was time to once more take up the challenges and compassionate ministry of community development. This would need to start by discovering the possibilities and needs in various communities. To make this happen, proposals were made to train and equip officers for the task of facilitation.

As part of this project a 'Tools' seminar for divisional development officers was held in April 2009 and attended by participants from Congo Brazzaville and the Democratic Republic of Congo, with a facilitator from the International Development Section of The Netherlands and Czech Republic Territory.

STATISTICS

Officers 320 (active 264 retired 56)
  Employees 231
Corps 102 Outposts 57 Maternity Unit 2
Clinics 6 Centres 2 Schools 17
Senior Soldiers 22,569 Adherents 2,468 Junior Soldiers 6,640
Personnel serving outside territory Officers 6

STAFF
Women's Ministries: Comr Ime Akpan (TPWM) Lt-Col Eva Marseille (TSWM) Lt-Col Monique Bakemba (THLS)
Sec for Personnel: Lt-Col Prosper Bakemba
Sec for Programme: Lt-Col Alexis Sakamesso
Sec for Busness Administration: Maj Jean Pierre Sonda
Extension Training: Capt Prosper Komiena
Financial Administrator: Sgt Jean Mayandu
Health Services Coordinators: Majs Sebastien and Martine Diantezulua
Information Technology: M'Passi Loukeba Richard
Music: Wilfrid Milandou
Projects: Sgt Edy Seraphin Kanda
Property: Maj Aristide Samba
Public Relations: Maj Philippe Bonazebi
Social: Capt Blaise Kombo
Territorial Bandmaster: Sgt Sensa Malanda
Territorial Songster Leader: Wilfrid Milandou
Training: Maj Dieudonnee Louzolo
Youth and Candidates: Capt Edith Dibantsa

DIVISIONS
Brazzaville 1: c/o THQ; tel: 21 13 15; Majs Victor and Emma Nzingoula
Brazzaville 2: c/o THQ; tel: 68 95 14; Majs François and Louise Mavouna
Lekoumou: c/o THQ; tel: 58 63 92; Majs Alexandre and Madeleine Mabanza
Louingui: c/o THQ; Majs Jérôme and Jeanne Nzita
Mbanza-Ndounga: c/o THQ; Majs Gabin and Philomene Mbizi
Niari: BP 85, Dolisie; tel 5364319; Majs Urbain and Judith Loubacky
North: c/o THQ; Majs Antoine and Marianne Massiélé
Pointe Noire: BP 686, Pointe Noire; tel: 94 00 16; Majs Daniel and Angèle Taty
Yangui: BP 10, Kinkala; Majs Patrick and Clémentine Tadi

DISTRICTS
Bouenza: c/o THQ; Maj Alphonse Mayamba
Tchitondi: c/o THQ; Maj Jean-Pierre Douniama

TRAINING COLLEGE
Nzoko: c/o THQ; tel: 56 95 72

SOCIAL AND EDUCATIONAL CENTRES
Day Care Centre
Ouenze Corps, Brazzaville

Guest Houses
Pointe-Noire; Moungali (Brazzaville)

Congo (Brazzaville) Territory

Home for the Visually Impaired
Yenge, Nzoko: c/o THQ

Institute for the Blind
c/o THQ

Schools
Nursery School
Véronique Makoumbou Nursery School, Nzoko
Primary School
John Swinfen Primary School, Loua

HEALTH SERVICES
Health Clinic and Eye Treatment Centre
Moukoundji-Ngouaka: c/o THQ

Health Clinics
Moungali: BP 20, Brazzaville
Nkayi: BP 229, Nkayi
Nkouikou, Pointe Noire

Health Clinics and Maternity Units
Dolisie: BP 235, Dolisie
Loua: BP 20, Brazzaville

When more than 100 women officers from Congo (Brazzaville) Territory crossed the Congo river to visit Kinshasa, they spent several days with Women's Ministries colleagues of Democratic Republic of Congo Territory taking part in various presentations, demonstrations, discussions and worship sessions. Two of the Brazzaville contingent are pictured showing how *sakala* are used in praising God.

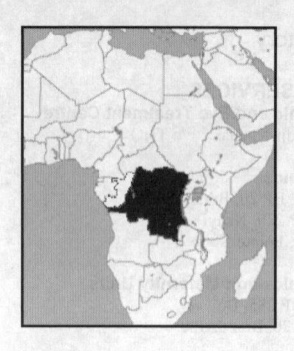

DEMOCRATIC REPUBLIC OF CONGO TERRITORY

Territorial Commander:
Colonel Madeleine Ngwanga (1 Dec 2009)

Chief Secretary:
Lieut-Colonel Barry Schwartz (1 Dec 2009)

Territorial Headquarters: Ave Ebea 23, Kinshasa-Gombe, Democratic Republic of Congo

Postal address: Armée du Salut 8636, Kinshasa 1, Democratic Republic of Congo

Tel: [243] 997-526050; email: kin_leadership@kin.salvationarmy.org

The first Salvation Army corps was established in Kinshasa in 1934 by Adjutant (later Commissioner) and Mrs Henri Becquet. By decree of Léopold III, Armée du Salut was given legal status, with powers set out in a Deed of Constitution, on 21 February 1936. Work spread to Congo in 1937 and 16 years later it became a separate command, later being elevated to territory status. Congo (Kinshasa) and Angola Territory was renamed on 1 March 2008 when Angola became a command.

Zone: Africa
Countries included in the territory: Democratic Republic of Congo
'The Salvation Army' in French: Armée du Salut; in Kikongo: Nkangu a Luvulusu; in Lingala: Basolda na Kobikisa; in Swahili: Jeshi la Wokovu; in Tshiluba: Tshiluila Tsha Luhandu
Languages in which the gospel is preached: Chokwe, French, Kikongo, Lingala, Swahili, Tshiluba, Umbundu
Periodical: *Echo d'Espoir*

SINCE 1997 the country has not experienced political stability because of rebel wars, particularly in the eastern part of the Democratic Republic of Congo, and the country has suffered the loss of more than five million people through war.

The Salvation Army has gone into these troubled areas to meet the humanitarian need of many of the survivors of this indiscriminate war. Initially with assistance given by IHQ Emergency Services, and then through funding from local donors, the territory encouraged returning refugees in Kalemie District of Katanga Province to build brick houses and supplied them with roofing zinc.

A positive result of this mission was the demand from settlers for the permanent presence of The Salvation Army in their villages, to offer a means of worship, education and health.

Worship centres – outposts – have already been opened to meet the spiritual needs of these people. Education in agriculture has also started. Lobbying the Government to

Democratic Republic of Congo Territory

establish health centres is under way.

Food relief sent from International Headquarters to assist hungry and displaced families in Kivu and Oriental Provinces in the east of the DRC led to the opening of Goma Corps and an outpost within less than six months.

As many as 135 senior soldiers were enrolled, with numerous recruits in the pipeline for soldiership. At the beginning of July 2009 a newly commissioned officer-couple was sent to take charge of Salvation Army work in Goma.

The World Bank sent a large sum of money to help the Government rebuild and erect new structures in the country. The Salvation Army won the tender to facilitate the work of repairing and constructing new schools, clinics and bridges in all the provinces. These have become the pride of both people and Government.

The Government created its own arm of service to supervise this work, namely *Fonds Sociale*. Because of the good work they see carried out by The Salvation Army, people are regarding it as a serious organisation able to help reduce suffering within their country.

The Salvation Army has started a large agricultural project in north Kivu, near Goma, in villages where relative peace has returned. The rebels have moved away to other parts of the province, making it possible for returned refugees to settle back into agriculture.

In recent months the territory has experienced a dynamic growth in soldier-making. The enrolment of senior soldiers stems from the opening of new outposts in most of the provinces. Junior soldiers are being enrolled in many of the Salvation Army schools located around the country.

STATISTICS
Officers 421 (active 336 retired 85) **Cadets** (1st Yr) 17 (2nd Yr) 17 **Employees** 4,285
Corps 178 **Outposts** 84 **Health Centres** 27 **Maternity Hospitals/Clinics** 6 **Other specialist hospitals** 1 **Other specialist clinics** (inc HIV/Aids, dental) 4 **Institutions** 5
Schools: Secondary 143 **Primary** 210 **Boarding** 2 **Maternal** 2 **University** 1
Senior Soldiers 22,244 **Adherents** 1,577 **Junior Soldiers** 11,382
Personnel serving outside territory Officers 14

STAFF
Women's Ministries: Col Madeleine Ngwanga (TPWM) Lt-Col Anja Schwartz (TSWM) Maj Bibisky Nzila (THLS and World Day of Prayer) Lt-Col Joséphine Nangi (LOM, Retired Officers) Maj Marie-Thérèse Mabwidi (Women's Development) Lt-Col Clémentine Nsumbu (Vocational Training/Literacy) Lt-Col Germaine Bueya (JHLS, Officers' Children) Maj Simone Kiboti (Widowed, Bible Studies, Gymnastics)
Sec for Business Administration: Lt-Col Joseph Bueya
Sec for Personnel: Lt-Col Henri Nangi
Sec for Programme: Lt-Col Emmanuel Nsumbu
Development and Emergency Services: Capt Dieudonné Tsilulu
Editorial/Literature: Maj Josué Leka
Extension Training: Maj Norbert Makala
Finance: Maj Barthélemy Nzila
Information Technology: Sgt Mbumu Muba Jean-Marc
Medical: Dr David Nku Imbie
Music and Creative Arts: Maj Philippe Mabwidi
  Sgt Jean-Marc Mbumu (National Bandmaster)
  Sgt Joseph Nsilulu (National Songster Leader)
  Sgt Pauline Matanu (National Timbrel Leader)
Property: Mr Claude Huguenin
Public Relations: tba

Democratic Republic of Congo Territory

Schools Coordinator: Raymond Luamba Ntolani
Social: Maj Philippe Mabwidi
  HIV/Aids Section: Miss Pauline Mavitu
  Sponsorship: Capt Philippine Tsilulu
Training: Maj Pierre Mukoko
Youth: Maj Laurent-Barnabas Ibemba
  Candidates: Maj Jeannette Ibemba

DIVISIONS

Bas-Fleuve/Océan: BP 123, Matadi; Majs Isidore and Marthe Matondo (mobile: 0990023962)
Inkisi: Armée du Salut, Kavwaya, BP 45; Majs Esaïe and Marie-José Ntembi (mobile: 0991668909)
Kasaï-Occidental: BP 1404, Kananga; Majs Jean-Jacques and Alice Nsumbu (mobile: 0997811298)
Kasangulu: BP 14, Kasangulu; Majs Norbert and Hélène Nkanu (mobile: 0815261920)
Katanga: BP 2525, Lubumbashi; Majs Denis and Modestine Mafuta (mobile: 0815102424)
Kinshasa Central: BP 8636, Kinshasa; Majs Sébastien and Godette Mbala (mobile: 0998449971)
Kinshasa East: BP 8636, Kinshasa; Majs Emmanuel and Madeleine Diakanwa (mobile: 0998336208)
Kinshasa West: Majs Graçia Victor and Isabel Matondo (mobile: 0999371303)
Luozi: Armée du Salut, Luozi; Majs Clément and Béatrice Ilunga (mobile: 0998627937)
Mbanza-Ngungu: BP 160; Majs Emmanuel and Albertine Mpanzu (mobile: 0995662729)
Orientale (Kisangani): BP 412, Kisangani; Majs Hubert and Célestine Ngoy (mobile: 0992814124)

DISTRICTS

Bandundu: Armée du Salut, Bandundu; Maj André Mobubu (mobile: 0811620092)
Isiro: BP 135 (under supervision of THQ)
Plateau: Maj Pascal Matsiona (mobile: 0998036399)
Tanganyika: (under supervision of Katanga)

SECTIONS

Bukavu: Capt André Mulenda (mobile: 0993187354)
Kwilu: Maj Pierre Masunda (mobile: 0997114730)

TRAINING COLLEGE
BP 8636, Kinshasa

UNIVERSITY
William Booth University: BP 8636, Kinshasa; Rector: Dr Mpiutu ne Mbodi Gaston

ATTACHED TO THQ
Conference Centre: Mbanza-Nzundu

MEDICAL WORK
Health Centres
Bas-Congo: Kasangulu, Boko-Mbuba, Kifuma, Kingantoko, Kingudi, Kinzambi, Kintete, Nkalama, Shefu, Kavwaya, Kimayala, Mbanza-Nsundi, Mbanza-Nzundu
Kananga: Moyo
Kinshasa: Amba (Kisenso), Bakidi (Selembao), Bomoi, Bopeto (Ndjili), Boyambi (Barumbu), Elonga, Esengo (Masina), Kimia (Kintambo), Molende (Kingasani)
Kisangani: Libota, Mokela, Dengue

Clinic
Maj Leka (Maluku/Kinshasa)

Dental Clinics
Boyambi (Barumbu), Elonga (Masuna), Kasangulu (Bas-Congo)

Diabetic Clinic
Kananga

Foot Clinic
Boyambi

Maternity Units
Bomoi Kinshasa (acc 60); Kasangulu, Bas-Congo (acc 13); Kavwaya, Bas-Congo maternity and centre (acc 14) Maluku Kinshasa (acc 12)

EDUCATION
Secondary Schools
Bandundu: Institut Elonga; Institut Kwango; Institut Mabwidi; Institut Ngampo Maku; Institut Ngobila; Institut Momwono; Institut Nsele Mpibiri; Institut Wembe; Institut Tomokoko; Institut Masamuna; Institut Ngabidjo; 11 primary schools, 11 secondary schools
Bas-Congo: Institut Boyokani (Matadi); Institut Diakanwa; Institut Kavwaya (Inkisi); Institut Beti 1; Institut Beti 2; Institut Kimbumba-Nord; Institut Bongo-Bongo; Institut Kingudi; Institut Pédagogique Kasi; Institut Dikal (Lufuku); ITP Kintete; Institut Kimayasi; Institut Kinzadi 1; Institut Kinzadi 2; CS Kimbongo;

Democratic Republic of Congo Territory

Institut Kinzambi 1 (Kasangulu);
Institut Kinzambi 2 (Luozi);
Institut Lemba Diyanika; Institut Ludiazo;
Institut Mampemba; Institut Mikalukidi;
Institut Kitundulu; Institut Kivunda;
Institut Kumba Ndilu; ITS Kumbi; ITC Lovo;
Institut Maduma; Institut Manionzi;
Institut Matanda; Institut Mateso;
Institut Nkundi (Mbanza-Ngungu);
CS Nsanga-Mamba; ITC Mbanza-Nsanda;
ITA Mbanza-Nsundi; Institut Mbanza-Nzundu;
Institut Mwala-Kinsende; ITA Nsongi-Kialelua;
Institut Ndandanga; ITC Ngongolo;
Institut Shefu; Institut Sombala; Institut Viaza;
Institut Buetesa; Institut Kimbata 1;
Institut Landulu; ITP Lukengo;
Institut Mawangu; Institut Miprosco;
Institut Odeco; Institut Sundi-Mamba;
Collège William Booth (Kasangulu);
64 primary schools, 1 kindergarden
Equateur: ITM Bukaka; Institut Obotela;
Institut Elonga; ITCA Lihau;
Institut Mambune; Institut Masobe;
Institut Mokuta; Institut Yambo;
ITA Yamwenga; Institut Yangola;
Institut Embonga; ITM Armée du Salut;
12 primary schools; 12 secondary schools,
2 kindergardens
Kasaï-Occidental (Kananga): Institut Bena-Leka 1; Institut Bena-Leka 2;
ITAV bena-Mbiye; Institut Bobumwe;
Institut Muzemba; Institut Mwanza-Ngoma;
Institut Tshibuayayi; ITC Bobumwe;
Institut Bukole, Institut Butoke;
Institut Kasende, Institut Katshimba;
Institut Kuetu, Institut Mande Muile;
ITAV Mfwamba; Institut Mpoyi;
Institut Mwanza-Ngoma, Institut Muyembe;
Institut salut; ITAV Salut; Institut Tuelekeja;
Institut Tuende; 21 primary schools,
20 secondary schools
Kinshasa: Institut Bakidi; Collège Gabriel Becquet (Selembao); Collège Bimwala;
ITC Bimwala; Institut Dianzenza; Institut Ilona; ITC Kwamouth; Institut Lukubama;
Collège John Mabwidi; Institut Mabwidi;
Lycée Matonge; Lycée Technique de Matonge; ITS Mbala; ITA Menkao; Institut Mpiutu; ITC Ndjili-Kilambu; Institut Ngizulu;
Institut Nsemi; ITC Ntolani; ITI Ntolani;
Institut Rwakadingi; Institut Wabaluku;
Institut Yanda Mayemba; Institut Yimbukulu;
24 secondary schools, 38 primary schools
Province Orientale (Kisangani): Institut Bonsomi; Institut Elikya; Institut Ilota;
Institut Ketele; Institut Wagenia;
Institut Litoka; Institut Yataka;
Institut Afutami; Institut Bagwasa;
Institut Bakota; Institut Bambunze;
Institut Kambale, Institut Lisami;
Institut Lohale; Institut Lomongo,
Institut Lotumbe; Institut Lusa;
Institut Yaengala; Institut Yalokambe;
Institut Yasaa; Institut Yasanga;
Institut Yawenda; 22 secondary schools,
42 primary schools, 2 kindergartens
Sud-Katanga (Lubumbashi): ITC Wokovu (Katuba); ITC Tujenge; Institut Flambeau;
3 secondary schools; 1 kindergardens,
5 primary schools

SOCIAL SERVICES
Children's Home and Community Child Care
Kinshasa (acc 20 and 20)

Development and Emergencies
Impini; Kasungulu; Kavwaya; Mato; Mbanza-Nzundu

Old People's Home
Kinshasa-Kintambo (acc 20)

Vocational Training Centres
Barumbu; Kinshasa (acc 114); Lubumbashi; Ndjili (acc 70); Sud-Katanga (acc 37)

Salvationists get involved in a community building project in their village

DENMARK TERRITORY

Territorial leaders:
Colonels Erling and Signe Helene Mæland

Territorial Commander:
Colonel Erling Mæland (1 Jul 2007)

Chief Secretary:
Lieut-Colonel Aino Muikku (1 Aug 2009)

**Territorial Headquarters: Frederiksberg Allé 9,
1621 Copenhagen V, Denmark**

Tel: [45] 33 31 41 92; fax: [45] 33 25 30 80; email: Frelsens@den.salvationarmy.org;
website: www.frelsens-haer.dk

The work of The Salvation Army in Denmark commenced in Copenhagen in May 1887, pioneer officers being Major (later Lieut-Colonel) and Mrs Robert Perry.

Zone: Europe
Country included in the territory: Denmark
'The Salvation Army' in Danish: Frelsens Hær
Language in which the gospel is preached: Danish
Periodicals: *Mennesker & Tro*, *Vision-Mission*

SALVATIONISTS from all over Denmark celebrated their congress in September 2008 under the theme 'Create Relationships – Upward to God, Outward to People'. Led by Commissioners Hasse and Christina Kjellgren (then zonal leaders for Europe) and Colonel Birgitte Brekke (IHQ), the congress created great excitement and brought encouragement to all who participated in the varied programme of worship, family festivals, open-air concerts and a women's brunch.

The Salvation Army's understanding of creating relationships was tested a few months later. A record number of more than 6,300 families applied for Christmas aid from the Army, but the issue of who the Movement helps was raised in the national media. The main question was: Does a Christian church give aid to Muslims even though they don't celebrate Christmas?

It led to donors indicating they would withdraw their support if the Army continued helping people of other faiths. The Army's response was a message of non-discrimination in its mission to meet human need in the name of Jesus Christ; the criteria for giving aid was that of need and poverty, not of religion.

The Army stood by this principle and as a result gained new admiration for its work. Among the many new donors who began supporting

Denmark Territory

the Movement were some who had never donated to a Christian church before but were impressed by the Army's strong message of non-discrimination.

In November the territory released its first Danish Christmas CD. Focusing on the rich traditions of Danish Christmas carols, the album met a longstanding need and consequently was well received. It immediately received airplay time on national radio.

A focus on family work and integrated mission continued. In January 2009 the territory's 'family consultants' established fellowship and advice networks within three more corps – in Esbjerg, Helsingør and Odense.

Notable growth was registered in the recycling industry, especially in new shops run by volunteers. The shops have put the Army back on the map in places where it had not operated for many years. They not only generate income for the Army but also open the way for new contacts and networks.

STATISTICS

Officers 84 (active 37 retired 47)
  Employees 260
Corps 32 **Outpost** 1 **Social Institutions** 17
  Welfare Centres 6
Senior Soldiers 960 **Adherents** 271 **Junior Soldiers** 12

STAFF

Women's Ministries: Col Signe Helene Mæland (TPWM) Maj Pia Mogensen (HL)
Sec for Field Programme: Maj Henrik Andersen
  Associate Sec for Field Programme: Maj Lisbeth Andersen
  Asst Sec for Field Programme: Maj John Wahl
Sec for Social Programme: Maj Hannelise Tvedt
Business Administrator: Mr Lars Lydholm
Communications, Public Relations and Information Technology: Mr Lars Lydholm
Editors:
  Mr Bent Dahl-Jensen (*Mennesker & Tro*)
  Maj John Wahl (*Vision-Mission*)
Finance: Mrs Annie Kristensen
Home League and Over-60s: Maj Pia Mogensen
Missing Persons: Col Jørn Lauridsen
Missionary and Child Sponsorship: Maj Ingrid Larsen
Music: Mr Erik Silfverberg
Property: Maj Terje Tvedt
Training: Maj Ingrid Larsen
Youth and Candidates: Maj Joan Munch

SOCIAL SERVICES

Head Office: Frederiksberg Allé 9, 1621 Copenhagen V; tel: 33 31 41 92

Clothing Industry (Recycling Centres)
6705 Esbjerg Ø, Ravnevej 2; tel: 75 14 24 22; fax: 75 14 00 47
5000 Odense C, Roersvej 33; tel: 66 11 25 21; fax: 66 19 05 21
9560 Hadsund, Mariagervej 3; tel: 98 57 42 48; fax: 98 57 38 72
4900 Nakskov, Narviksvej 15; tel: 54 95 12 05; fax: 54 95 12 04

Community Centres
9000 Aalborg, Skipper Clementsgade 11; tel: 98 11 50 62
1408 Copenhagen K, Wildersgade 66; tel: 32 54 44 10 (acc 80)
4900 Nakskov, Niels Nielsengade 6; tel: 54 95 30 06 (acc 60)

Day Nurseries
9900 Frederikshavn Humlebien, Knudensvej 1B; tel: 98 42 33 27 (acc 40)
2000 Frederiksberg, Melita, Mariendalsvej 4; tel: 38 87 01 48 (acc 58)
2500 Valby, Solsikken, Annexstræde 29; tel: 36 16 23 11 (acc 22)
2650 Hvidovre, Kastanjehuset, Idrætsvej 65A; tel: 36 78 40 23 (acc 33)
2650 Hvidovre, Solgården, Catherine Booths vej 22; tel: 36 78 07 71 (acc 100)
7500 Holstebro Solhøj, Skolegade 51; tel: 97 42 61 21 (acc 30)

Denmark Territory

Emergency Shelters for Families
2650 Hvidovre, Svendebjerggård, Catherine
 Booths vej 20; tel: 36 49 65 77 (acc 25)
1754 Copenhagen V, Den Åbne Dør,
 Hedebygade 30; tel: 33 24 91 03 (acc 15)
4700 Næstved, Østergade 13; tel: 55 77 22 70
 (acc 6)

Eventide Nursing Centre
2200 Copenhagen N Aftensol, Lundtoftegade 5;
 tel: 35 30 55 00 (acc 43)

Social Advice Bureau and Goodwill Centre
Grundtvigsvej 17 st, 1864 Frederiksberg C;
 tel: 33 24 56 67

Project for Long-term Unemployed
Nørholmlejren, Oldenborrevej 2, 9000 Aalborg;
 tel: 98 34 18 10 (acc 10)

Rehabilitation Centre
Hørhuset, 2300 Copenhagen S, Hørhusvej 5;
 tel: 32 55 56 22 (acc 64)

Students Residence
2100 Copenhagen Ø, Helgesengade 25;
 tel: 35 37 74 32 (acc 41)

SOCIAL SERVICES (field administered)
Community Centres
2700 Brønshøj, Ruten 14; tel: 36 17 70 06
2200 Copenhagen N, Kalejdoskop,
 Thorsgade 48 A; tel: 35 85 00 87
3000 Helsingør, Regnbuen Community Centre,
 Strandgade 60; tel: 49 21 10 06
4800 Nykøbing Falster, Jernbanegade 42,
 Community Centre and Corps activities;
 tel: 54 85 71 89
9560 Hadsund, Nørregade 10, Den Åbne Dør
 Community Centre; tel: 23 26 19 15
2500 Valby, Valby Langgade 83;
 tel: 36 45 67 67
7100 Vejle, Midtpunktet, Staldgårdsgade 4;
 tel: 75 82 78 38

Summer Camps
9000 Aalborg, Nørholmlejren, Oldenborrevej 2;
 tel: 98 34 18 10 (acc 50)
8700 Horsens, Hjarnø; tel: 75 68 32 24
 (acc 25)
5450 Otterup, Rømhildsminde, Ferievej 11-13,
 Jørgensø; tel: 64 87 13 36

UNDER THQ
Holiday Home and Conference Centre
Lillebælt, Nørre Allé 47, Strib, 5500 Middelfart;
 tel: 64 40 10 57; fax: 63 40 02 82 (acc 30)

Investigation Bureau
Frederiksberg Allé 9, 1621 Copenhagen V;
 tel: 33 31 41 92

Radio Station (Copenhagen area)
Frederiksberg Allé 9, 1621 Copenhagen V;
 tel: 33 31 41 25 (studio)

Youth and Conference Centre
Baggersminde, Fælledvej 132, 2791 Dragør;
 tel: 32 53 70 18; fax: 32 53 70 98 (acc 80)

New Project
Community Centre: 2700 Brønshøj, Ruten 14;
 tel: 36 17 70 06

EASTERN EUROPE: Salvationists distribute fresh water supplies to flood victims in Romania (*see page 104*)

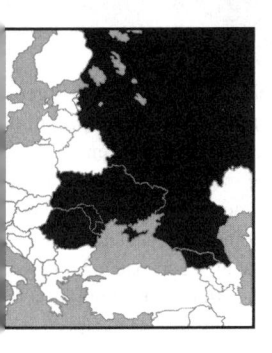

EASTERN EUROPE TERRITORY

Territorial leaders:
Commissioners Willem and Netty van der Harst

Territorial Commander:
Commissioner Willem van der Harst
(1 Jul 2007)

Chief Secretary:
Lieut-Colonel Alistair Herring (16 Sep 2006)

Territorial Headquarters: Krestiansky Tupik 16/1, Moscow

Postal address: Russian Federation, 109044 Moscow, Krestiansky Tupik 16/1

Tel: [7] (495) 911 2600/2956; fax: [7] (495) 911 2753; email: Russia@eet.salvationarmy.org; website: www.thesalvationarmy.ru

Work was initiated in Russia in 1910 by Colonel Jens Povlsen of Denmark but circumstances necessitated his withdrawal after 18 months. Army operations then recommenced in St Petersburg in 1913 as an extension to the work in Finland. After the February 1917 revolution the work flourished, Russia became a distinct command and reinforcements arrived from Sweden. As a result of the October revolution they had, however, to be withdrawn at the end of 1918, leaving 40 Russian and Finnish officers to continue the work under extreme hardship until the Army was finally proscribed in 1923.

Salvation Army activities were officially recommenced in July 1991, overseen by the Norway, Iceland and The Færoes Territory with the arrival of Lieut-Colonels John and Bjorg Bjartveit. It became a distinct command in November 1992. Work was extended to Ukraine (1993), Georgia (1993), Moldova (1994) and Romania (1999). On 1 June 2001 the command was redesignated the Eastern Europe Command. It was elevated to territory status on 1 March 2005. The final stage of registering 'the Moscow Branch of The Salvation Army' was completed in April 2009.

Zone: Europe
Countries included in territory: Georgia, Moldova, Romania, Russian Federation, Ukraine
'The Salvation Army' in Georgian: Khsnis Armia; in Moldovan/Romanian: Armata Salvarii; in Russian: Armiya Spaseniya; in Ukrainian: Armiya Spasinnya
Languages in which the gospel is preached: Georgian, Moldovan, Romanian, Russian, Ukrainian
Periodicals: *Vestnik Spaseniya* (*The War Cry*), *The Officer* (both Russian)

FOLLOWING the involvement of officers, local officers and soldiers in much discussion and preparation, the Territorial Mission Strategy Plan was launched in March 2009. It focuses on three goals: strengthening corps ministry, developing all leaders and working towards financial self-support.

The territory rejoiced as the final stage of registering the Moscow Branch of The Salvation Army was completed in April 2009. Many Salvationists had responded to the prayer request that went around the world when Russia refused to give the Army's Moscow Branch legal status, having identified it a 'militarised organisation'. But following a successful appeal in the Strasburg European Court of Human Rights in October 2006, numerous requests by the city authorities were carried through and registration was granted. This allowed Moscow Salvationists to confidently publicise and promote their activities and programmes in the city.

After four years of planning, the opening of the Moscow Homeless Programme in the Taganka Corps building is close to realisation. Extensive renovations are nearing completion and an opening celebration was scheduled for the summer of 2009.

The current separate programmes for homeless youths and adults will be brought together in the same purpose-built centre to offer meals, laundry and showering facilities, basic medical services, educational projects, life skills and Christian activities, attempting to meet the age-specific needs of each group.

The summer of 2008 became a season of emergencies for the territory as rivers flooded in parts of Romania and Moldova and a military conflict occurred between Georgia and Russia. Although many Salvationists were on holiday, they returned to assist in helping the flood victims and refugees who had lost their homes and livelihoods.

In Georgia, disused kindergartens were refitted for emergency accommodation and corps officers spent many weeks caring for refugee families. Warm shoes were specially manufactured for the children so that they could continue their schooling, as the summer clothing they had fled their homes in became inadequate when winter approached.

The people affected by both crises received immediate assistance in the form of bedding, clean water, clothing and food, plus the special love and care that comes when such work is done in Christ's name.

Although conflict occurred between two countries within the territory, the unity shared in Christ was evident as the first two people to drive together to the affected area were a Georgian and a Russian officer, both serving in Tbilisi, the capital of Georgia.

STATISTICS

Officers 136 (active) **Envoys** 6 **Cadets** (2nd Yr) 14 **Employees** 227
Corps 56 **Corps Plants** 4 **Outposts** 1 **Rehabilitation Centres** 2
Senior Soldiers 1,948 **Adherents** 834 **Junior Soldiers** 355

STAFF

Women's Ministries: Comr Netty van der Harst (TPWM)
Business Administration: Maj Richard Herivel
Audit and Asst Finance Officer: Capt Natalia Pismeniuk
Editorial: Capt Anna Kotrikadze
Education: tba
Leadership Development: tba
League of Mercy: Maj Maria Kharkova
Mission Development: Lt-Col Astrid Herring
Mission Training: Capt Alexander Sharov
Prayer Ambassador: Capt Vadim Kolesnik
Projects Cordinator: Majs Ron Cochrane
Public Relations: Maj Lyn Cochrane
Territorial Sergeant-Major: Envoy Yuri Gulanitsky
Training: Capt Svetlana Sharova

Eastern Europe Territory

DIVISIONS

Russia: 105120 Russia, Moscow, Khlebnikov Pereulok, 7 bld, 2; tel: 495 678 03 51; fax: 495 678 91 60; Capts Anthony and Patricia Kennedy

Moldova: Chisinau, 2012, Armata Salvarii, PO Box 137, Str P. Movila #19; tel: (37322) 235076; telefax: (37322) 237972; Majs Ian and Vivien Callander

Ukraine: 01023, Ukraine, Kiev, Shota Rustavely St 38, Suite 3 3; tel/fax: (380 44) 287 4598, 287 3705, 246 6689; Maj Marie Willermark

REGIONS

Georgia: 16 Ikalto St, Tbilisi 0171, Georgia; tel: (995 32) 33 37 85/86; fax: (995 32) 33 02 27; Maj Bradley Caldwell

Romania: 722212 Bucharest, Sector 2, Str Pargarilor Nr 2; tel: [10] (4037) 270 51 99; Capt Valery Lalac

MISSION TRAINING AND EDUCATION CENTRE – INSTITUTE FOR OFFICER TRAINING

Russia, Moscow, 105120 Karl Larson Centre, Khlebnikov Per 7/2; tel: (495) 678 55 14, 678 03 51

SOCIAL SERVICES
(Community outreach, HIV/Aids, alcohol, drugs, programmes for homeless)

Georgia
Children's After-school Programmes: Rustavi, Samgory, Ponichala, Central, Batumi, Lagodeki
Laundry Projects: Samgori, Rustavi, Didigomi

Moldova
Medical Clinic: Chisinau, Mesterul Manole 1; tel: (373 22) 47-2382
Mobile Medical Clinic; Rusca Women's Prison Project; 'Sally Ann' Programme; Shoe Project; Humanitarian Aid Distribution

Romania
Laundries

Russia
Moscow:
Karl Larsson Centre, Unified Homeless Services, Khlebnikov pereulok 7, bld 2; tel: (495) 678 03 51;
Feeding Programme; Food and Clothing Distribution; First Aid

Rostov-on-Don:
The Bridge Programme, Lermontovskaya St 229; tel/fax: (8632) 248-2410; email: tateosova_valery@mail.ru
HIV+ Crisis Intervention; Group Services

St Petersburg:
Liteini Prospect # 44 B, 191104; tel: (812) 273-9297
Homeless Feeding Programme; Food and Clothing Distribution; Seniors' Support Group Programme; Medical Clinic; HIV/Aids Outreach and Support Programme; Support for Orphans with HIV/Aids

Ukraine
Kirovograd Corps Social Centre (families, pensioners, invalids support, distribution of humanitarian aid): 25028 Ukraine, Kirovagrad, Volova St, #15, SPTU #8; tel: (380-522) 56-45 78

CORPS-BASED SERVICES

Feeding Programmes; After-school Programmes; Food and Clothing Distribution; Haircutting Programmes; Home Care Programmes; Homeless Children Outreach; Marriage Preparation Classes; Medical Programmes; Orphan Outreach

Commissioner van der Haarst (TC) with lawyer Anatoli Pchelintsev, who assisted in registering The Salvation Army in Moscow

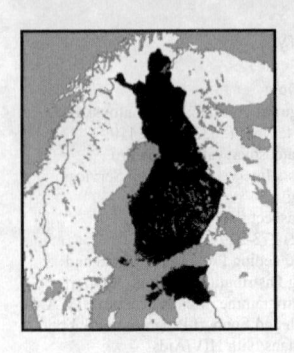

FINLAND AND ESTONIA TERRITORY

Territorial leaders:
Commissioners Dick and Vibeke Krommenhoek

Territorial Commander:
Commissioner Dick Krommenhoek
(1 Oct 2008)

Chief Secretary:
Lieut-Colonel Arja Laukkanen (1 Jun 2004)

Territorial Headquarters: Uudenmaankatu 40, 00120 Helsinki

Postal address: Post Box 161, 00121 Helsinki, Finland

Tel: [358] (09) 6812300; fax: [358] (09) 6812 3033; email: finland@pelastusarmeija.fi; website: www.pelastusarmeija.fi

Work in Finland was commenced on 8 November 1889 in Broholm's Riding School, Helsinki, by four aristocratic Finns – Captain and Mrs Constantin Boije with Lieutenants Hedvig von Haartman and Alva Forsius. Within six months Hedvig von Haartman was appointed leader of the work in the country.

Work in Estonia first commenced in 1927 and continued until 1940 when it was closed due to the Second World War. It recommenced in the autumn of 1995 when three Finnish officers were assigned to start the work in Tallinn.

Zone: Europe
Countries included in the territory: Estonia, Finland
'The Salvation Army' in Estonian: Päästearmee; in Finnish: Pelastusarmeija; in Swedish: Frälsningsarmén
Languages in which the gospel is preached: English, Estonian, Finnish, Russian, Swedish
Periodicals: *Krigsropet* (Swedish), *Nappis* (Finnish), *Sotahuuto* (Finnish)

DURING the morning of 23 September 2008 a tragedy occurred in the small Finnish town of Kauhajoki. A young man in his early 20s entered his former school, armed with guns, and within a few minutes killed nine schoolmates, a teacher and then himself. The country was later shocked to learn that the majority of its youngsters confessed to feeling deeply lonely and unable to share their problems with their parents and peers.

Moved with compassion, Captain Tero Saajoranta (the corps officer at Jyvaskyla) discussed this issue with the headmaster of the school across the street from the Salvation Army hall. The captain now spends one day a week among the pupils, offering them a listening ear and loving heart in the name of Jesus.

Finland and Estonia Territory

Having first opened its doors on 9 January 1908, the Army hostel in Helsinki has seen more than 100 years of ministry – not only serving suffering humanity but also saving souls and growing saints. With a capacity of almost 300 men and women, this fine social institution has become one of the Army's flagships in Finland.

In recognition of the centenary of Alppikatu Men's Hostel, a renowned Finnish publisher offered to publish a book about its history. The book was launched at a press conference where the author explained how many years ago he was himself homeless but found meaning and direction for his life. He had been able to build his career as an author on the life-changing experience of his own time of homelessness.

As Salvationists see the darkness, desperation and need in the world, William Booth's words, 'I'll fight', seem more challenging than ever. The territory is recognising that new generations of Salvationists are needed to respond to Christ's great commission to make people of all nations his disciples (Matthew 28:19) – doing so alongside, and in addition to, other denominations.

Developments in Estonia clearly show that this young branch of the Army is increasingly taking up the fight against sin. During the year under review 13 soldiers, nine adherents and five junior soldiers were enrolled; others are being added to the Army's forces in that country

Firmly believing that they have a gospel that matches the hour, Salvationists throughout the territory endeavour to make the Army's activities and methods relevant to today's generation. By his grace, God will continue the work that he has started (Philippians 1:6).

STATISTICS

Officers 160 (active 54 retired 106) **Cadets** 4 **Employees** 394
Corps 28 **Outposts** 8 **Goodwill Centres** 3 **Institutions** 27
Senior Soldiers 794 **Adherents** 86 **Junior Soldiers** 34

STAFF

Women's Ministries: Comr Vibeke Krommenhoek (TPWM)
Section Head for Programme: Maj Johnny Kleman
  Sec for Programme: Maj Tella Puotiniemi
  Asst Leader for Social Work: Gun-Viv Glad-Junger
  Asst for Programme Section: Sgt Kati Kivestö
  Programme Support and Youth: Capt Saga Lippo-Karvonen
  Asst for Home and Family: Maj Camilla Rahkonen
Section Head for Training and Education: Maj Petter Kornilow
  School for Officer Training: Maj Petter Kornilow
  Education: Maj Eija Kornilow
  Candidates: Maj Eija Kornilow
Section Head for Business Administration: Liisa Kaakinen
  Asst Business Administrator: Capt Rodrigo Miranda
  Finance: Liisa Kaakinen
  Property: Liisa Kaakinen
  Recycling Industry: Harri Lehti
  Information Technology: Riku Leino
Section Head for Personnel: Maj Marja Meras
Section Head for Communication: Maj Eva Kleman
  Literature and Editorial: Maj Antero Puotiniemi
  Public Relation: Maj Sirkka Paukku
  Missing Persons: Maj Kirsti Reponen
  Mission Sponsorships and Volunteers: Maj Camilla Rahkonen

Junior soldiers of Narva Corps, Estonia, sing their praises to God

SOCIAL CENTRES

Clothing Industry (Recycling Centres)
90580 Oulu, Ratamotie 22; tel: 44 757 7945
33880 Lempäälä, Rajasilta 1; tel: 44 757 7943
20300 Turku, Virusmäentie 65;
  tel: 44 757 7944
01260 Vantaa, Itäinen Valkoisenlähteentie 15;
  tel: (09) 877 0270

Homes for Alcoholics
68600 Pietarsaari, Permontie 34;
  tel: 44 757 7938 (acc 15)
33500 Tampere, Pohjolankatu 25;
  tel: 44 757 7980 (acc 36)
20500 Turku, Hämeenkatu 18;
  tel: 44 757 7897 (acc 37)

Shelters for Men
00530 Helsinki, Alppikatu 25;
  tel: (09) 7743130 (acc 234)
00550 Helsinki, Inarintie 8;
  tel: 44 757 7937 (acc 34)
28120 Pori, Veturitallinkatu 3;
  tel: 45 139 3292 (acc 25)

Shelters for Women
00530 Helsinki, Papinkuja 1; tel: (09) 77431330
  (acc 18)
00530 Helsinki, Castréninkatu 24-26 F 46
  (acc 12)

Poor Relief Distribution Centres
Alppikatu 25, 00530 Helsinki; tel: (09) 77431323
Hämeenkatu 28 B, 15140 Lahti; tel: 44 757 7910
Ratamotie 22, 90580 Oulu; tel: 44 757 7947
Pyynikintori 3, 33230 Tampere; tel: 44 757 7941
Vanha Hämeentie 29, 20540 Turku;
  tel: 44 757 7940

Service Centres
Alppikatu 25, 00530 Helsinki; tel: (09) 77431316
Permontie 34, 68600 Pietarsaari; tel: 44 757 7896
Vanha Hämeentie 29, 20540 Turku;
  tel: 44 757 7940

Children's Day Care Centres
48100 Kotka, Korkeavuorenkatu 24;
  tel: 45 635 8085 (acc 36)
15140 Lahti, Hämeenkatu 28 A 5; tel: (03) 878680
  (acc 94)
90140 Oulu, Artturintie 27; tel: 45 635 8087
  (acc 30)
06100 Porvoo, Joonaksentie 1; tel: 45 635 8089
  (acc 54)
28100 Pori, Mikonkatu 19; tel: 45 635 8088
  (acc 83)
95420 Tornio, Putaankatu 2; tel: 45 635 8090
  (acc 47)

Eventide Homes
02710 Espoo, Viherlaaksonranta 19;
  tel: (09) 84938410 (acc 60)
20740 Turku, Sigridinpolku; tel: 40 508 1291
  (acc 25)

Senior Citizens' Unit
00760 Helsinki, Puistolantie 6 (acc 75)

Summer Camp Centre
03100 Nummela, Helsinki (acc 60)

Family Support Centre (Hedvig House)
00530 Helsinki, Castréninkatu 24-26 F;
  tel: 50 400 1708

Youth Camp
Sovelontie 91, 33480 Ylöjärvi (summer use)

ESTONIA REGION

Regional Headquarters: Kopli 8-14,
  10412 Tallinn; tel: [372] 6413330;
  fax: [372] 6413331
Regional Commander: Capt Daniel Henderson

Corps 4

Hope House (Lootusemaja): Laevastiku 1a,
  10313 Tallinn; tel: [372] 6561048
Camp: Ranna 24, Loksa; tel: [372] 6031012

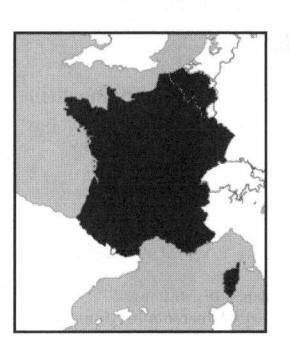

FRANCE AND BELGIUM TERRITORY

Territorial Commander:
Colonel Alain Duchêne (1 Jan 2009)

Chief Secretary:
Lieut-Colonel Massimo Paone
(1 Sep 2009)

**Territorial Headquarters: 60 rue des Frères Flavien
75976 Paris Cedex 20, France**

Tel: [33] (1) 43 62 25 00; fax: [33] (1) 43 62 25 56; website: www.armeedusalut.fr

Since 'La Maréchale' (eldest daughter of William and Catherine Booth) conducted The Salvation Army's first meeting in Paris on Sunday 13 March 1881, Salvationist influence has grown and remarkable social and spiritual results have been achieved. French officers commenced work in Algeria in 1934 and this work was maintained until 1970.

In Belgium, Salvation Army operations were pioneered on 5 May 1889 by Adjutant and Mrs Charles Rankin and Captains Velleema and Hass. Most of our work in Belgium operates within the Francophone part of the country so, from 1 January 2009, the former Belgium Command became a region linked administratively to France under the newly created France and Belgium Territory.

Zone: Europe
Countries included in the territory: Belgium, France
'The Salvation Army' in French: Armée du Salut; in Flemish: Leger des Heils
Languages in which the gospel is preached: French, Flemish
Periodicals: *Avec Vous*, *Espoir*, *Le Bulletin de la Ligue du Foyer*, *Le Fil*, *Le Magazine*, *L'Officier*, *Quand Même*

THE year 2009 began with the inauguration of the new France and Belgium Territory, the meeting being led by Commissioners Hasse and Christina Kjellgren (then Europe zonal leaders). The visiting International Secretary placed this union of the previous France Territory and Belgium Command under the sign of functional reorganisation.

It did not change the Army's mission of making Jesus known in the two countries, he said, before presenting a new territorial flag to the Territorial Commander as a symbol of the new unity. The weekend celebrations had been launched with a concert given by the Territorial Band in the Brussels Royal Chapel.

In May 2008 a number of Salvationists who originate from Africa and the Caribbean met for a cultural festival, expressing their praise to God in traditional ways. The event's theme, 'Where Is Your Neighbour?', challenged participants to look out for and, in Christ's name, look after people within their neighbourhood.

For the eighth consecutive year a series of Bible studies took place at Chambon-sur Lignon, with 30 people meeting to contemplate the Beatitudes. They spent time not only acquiring further knowledge from the Scriptures but also discovering more clearly who Jesus is – and knowing him in a deeper, personal way.

Several summer camps were held for young people. In Normandie, for example, 37 children aged from six to 14 years took part in a camp themed 'Life In The Castle'. Morning Bible studies took them through stories about the King of kings. On the last Sunday 18 children publicly accepted Jesus as Saviour; others offered prayers at the mercy seat.

Leaders of the Army's scout groups visited Portugal Command for nine days to train new scouts there. Two entertaining programmes were given in an eventide home and a Salvation Army home for children. Also, helpful times of reflection were spent in Bible study and the scouts and leaders attended a Sunday meeting at Colares.

There were echoes of the Salvation Army motto 'Soup, Soap, Salvation' when Metz Corps participated in a 'soup feast' organised by a social services centre during January 2009. Salvationists offered people bread, soap and the gospel.

The event provided many opportunities for people to come in contact with the Army and under the influence of the gospel. For example, young people met for a Bible teaching session after enjoying their soup and then left with a bar of soap.

STATISTICS
(France)
Officers 169 (active 72 retired 97) **Employees** 2,022
Corps 29 **Outposts** 2 **Institutions** 47
Senior Soldiers 919 **Adherents** 167 **Junior Soldiers** 80
Personnel serving outside territory Officers 10

THE SALVATION ARMY CONGREGATION
BOARD OF DIRECTORS
Col Alain Duchêne, Lt-Col Massimo Paone, Lt-Col Jane Paone, Maj Danièle Cesar, Maj Philippe Schmitter

STAFF
Women's Ministries: Lt-Col Jane Paone (TPWM) Maj Pascale Glories (TSWM)
Field: Maj Sylvie Arnal
Candidates: Lt-Col Jane Paone
Finance: Mr Alain Raoul
Education and Prisons: Maj Jean-Paul Thoni
Retired Officers: Majs Christian and Joëlle Exbrayat
Territorial Band: B/M Mrs Arielle Mangeard

Belgium: Maj Jacques Rouffet (RO) Maj Yvonne Rouffet (RPWM)

THE SALVATION ARMY FOUNDATION
BOARD OF DIRECTORS
President: Col Alain Duchêne
Secretary: Lt-Col Massimo Paone
Treasurer: Mr Olivier Ponsoye
Members: Mrs Marie Lottier, Mrs Irène Debu-Carbonnier, Mr Bernard Westercamp, Maj Pascale Glories

STAFF
Director General: Mr Alain Raoul
Director of Social Exclusion Programme: Mr Olivier Marguery
Director of Care, Handicap and Dependence Programme: Mr Eric Yapoudjian
Director of Youth Programme: Mr Eric Yapoudjian

France and Belgium Territory

Director of Projects and Property
  Programme: Mr Bernard Guilhou
Communications: Mr David Germain
Director of Finance: Mrs Martine Dumont
Business Manager: Mr Bruno Fontaine
Missing Persons: Maj Dominique Glories
Publications: Mr Pierre-Baptiste Cordier
Spiritual Care: Capt Jean-Claude Ngimbi
Volunteers: Maj Dominique Glories

GOODWILL CENTRES

59140 Dunkerque: 1 rue de St Pol;
  tel: (03) 28 29 09 37
75003 Paris: Centre St Martin, In front of
  31 blvd St Martin; tel: (01) 40 27 80 07
75019 Paris: Maison du Partage, 32 rue Bouret;
  tel: (01) 53 38 41 30

RETIRED PERSONS' RESIDENCES

74560 Monnetier-Mornex: Résidence Leirens,
  Chemin St Georges; tel: (04) 50 31 23 12
  (acc disabled 62)
75014 Paris: 9 bis, Villa Coeur-de-Vey;
  tel: (01) 45 43 38 75
93230 Romainville: 2 rue Vassou;
  tel: (01) 48 45 12 82

SUMMER COLONY FOR CHILDREN AND YOUTH CENTRE

30530 Chamborigaud: Chausse;
  tel/fax: (04) 66 61 47 08 (acc 100)

SOCIAL SERVICES

* These centres include workshop facilities for the unemployed

Centres for Men

27380 Radepont: Château de Radepont;
  tel: (02) 32 49 03 82 (acc 90)
*76600 Le Havre: Le Phare, 191 rue de la
  Vallée; tel: (02) 35 24 22 11 (acc 200)
*59018 Lille Cedex: Les Moulins de l'Espoir,
  48 rue de Valenciennes, BP 184;
  tel: (03) 20 52 69 09 (acc 317)
*69006 Lyon: La Cité de L'Armée du Salut,
  131 ave Thiers; tel: (04) 78 52 60 80
  (acc 147)
*13003 Marseille: 190 rue Félix Pyat;
  tel: (04) 91 02 49 37 (acc 112)
57100 Thionville: 8 place de la République;
  tel: (03) 82 83 09 60 (acc 60)
*68100 Mulhouse: Le Bon Foyer, 24 rue de
  L'Ile Napoléon; tel: (03) 89 44 43 56
  (acc 113)
*75013 Paris: La Cité de Refuge/Centre Espoir,
  12 rue Cantagrel; tel: (01) 53 61 82 00
  (acc 245)
*76005 Rouen: 26 rue de Crosne;
  tel: (02) 35 70 38 00 (acc 97)

Centre for Women

30900 Nîmes: Les Glycines (home for battered
  wives), 33 rue de la Bienfaisance;
  tel: (04) 66 62 21 90 / 66 04 99 49 (acc 52)
75011 Paris: Le Palais de la Femme, 94 rue de
  Charonne; tel: (01) 46 59 30 00 (acc 240)

Centres for Men and Women

90000 Belfort: 3 rue de l'As de Carreau
  (acc 48)
74560 Monnetier-Mornex: Holiday Home, Les
  Hutins; tel: (04) 50 36 59 52 (acc 8)
75020 Paris: Résidence Albin Peyron, 60 rue
  des Frères Flavien, tel: (01) 48 97 54 50
  (acc 332)
78100 St Germain en Laye: La Maison Verte,
  14 rue de la Maison Verte;
  tel: (01) 39 73 29 39 (acc 39)

Centres for Families

94320 Thiais: Résidence Sociale, 7 bd de
  Stalingrad; tel: (01) 48 53 57 15 (acc 57)
81200 Aussillon: 23 bd Albert Gaches;
  tel (05) 63 98 23 95 (acc 16)
74560 Monnetier-Mornex, Les Hutins;
  tel: (04) 50 36 59 52 (acc 16)

Children's Homes

35404 Saint-Malo Cedex:
  La Maison des Garçons, 35 ave Eugene
  Herpin, BP 8; tel: (02) 99 40 21 97
  (acc boys 18)
  Le Nid, 23 ave Paul Turpin, BP 21;
  tel: (02) 99 40 21 94 (acc 24)

Convalescent Centre

07800 La Voulte-sur-Rhône: Le Château de St
  Georges-les-Bains; tel: (04) 75 60 81 72
  (acc 50)

Emergency Accommodation

75013 Centre d'accueil d'urgence, 12 rue
  Cantagrel; tel: (01) 53 61 82 00 (acc 58)
75013 Paris: Palais du Peuple, 29 rue des
  Cordelières; tel: (01) 43 37 93 61 (acc 100)
75011 Paris: Résidence Catherine Booth,
  15 rue Crespin du Gast;
  tel: (01) 43 14 70 90 (acc 108)

Eventide Homes

60500 Chantilly: L'Arc-en-Ciel, 5 bd de la
  Libération; tel: (03) 44 57 00 33 (acc 52)
42028 Saint-Etienne Cedex 01 : La Sarrazinière,

France and Belgium Territory

Commissioner Hasse Kjellgren (then International Secretary for Europe) presents the new territorial flag to Colonel Alain Duchêne (TC) – a symbol of the union of the former France Territory and Belgium Command

Allée Amilcare Cipriani; tel 04 77 62 17 92 (acc 145)

47400 Tonneins: Le Soleil d'Automne, ave Blanche Peyron, Escoutet; tel: (05) 53 88 32 00 (acc 50)

Mother and Baby Home
75019 Paris: Centre Maternel des Lilas, 9 ave de la Porte des Lilas; tel: (01) 48 03 81 90 (acc 77)

Municipal Shelters (managed by The Salvation Army)
90000 Belfort: Plate-forme d'urgence sociale, 7 rue Colbert; tel (03) 84 21 05 53 (acc 104)

*51100 Reims: Le Nouvel Horizon, 10 rue Goïot; tel: (03) 26 85 23 09 (acc 184)

Rehabilitation Centre for Handicapped
45410 Artenay: Château d'Auvilliers; tel: (02) 38 80 00 14 (acc 68)

93370 Montfermeil: MAS Le Grand Saule, 2 avenue des Tilleuls; tel: (01) 41 70 30 40 (acc 52)

Training Centres for Children
67100 Strasbourg-Neudorf: Le Foyer du Jeune Homme, 42 ave Jean Jaurès; tel: (03) 88 84 16 50 (acc 50)

77270 Villeparisis: Domaine de Morfondé; tel: (01) 60 26 61 61 (acc 67)

France and Belgium Territory

34091 Montpellier Cedex: Institut Nazareth,
13 rue de Nazareth, BP 24105;
tel: (0) 4 99 58 21 21; fax: (0) 4 99 58 21 12
(acc 48)

Children's Day Care Centres
30000 Nîmes: Aire du Lycéen, 4/6 bd Victor Hugo; tel: (04) 66 21 02 88
43400 Le Chambon sur Lignon: Le Bivouac, 7 rue Neuve: tel: (04) 71 59 70 87
69007 Lyon: L'Arche de Noé, 5 rue Félissent; tel (04) 78 58 29 66

Training Centres
68200 Mulhouse: Marie-Pascale Péan,
35 ave de Colmar; tel: (03) 89 42 14 77
(acc 33)
30000 Nîmes: La Villa Blanche Peyron,
122 Impasse Calmette; tel: (04) 66 04 99 40
(acc 10)

BELGIUM REGION

Regional leaders: Maj Jacques Rouffet (RO)
Maj Yvonne Rouffet (RSWM) (1 Jan 2009)

Regional Headquarters: Place du Nouveau Marché aux Grains, 34, 1000 Brussels;
tel: [32] (02) 513 39 04;
fax: [32] (02) 513 81 49;
websites:
www.armeedusalut.be; www.legerdesheils.be

STATISTICS
(not included in statistics of France)
Officers 25 (active 13 retired 12) **Auxiliary-Captain** 1 **Employees** 86
Corps 10 **Institutions** 6 **Shops** 4 **Conference and Youth Centre** 1
Senior Soldiers 251 **Adherents** 113 **Junior Soldiers** 37

STAFF
Women's Ministries: Maj Yvonne Rouffet (RPWM)
Regional Sec: Maj Noélie Lecocq
Social and Property: Maj Noelie Lecocq
Finance: Sgt Pierre Dorthe (Financial Director) Capt Mark Dawans (Finance Officer)
Personnel: Maj Yvonne Rouffet (Officers)
Children and Youth: Sgt Anne Catherine Dorthe (Coordinator)
Editorial and Public Relations: Maj Jacques Rouffet
Missing Persons: Mrs Esther Tesch
Volunteers: Maj Yvonne Rouffet

SOCIAL SERVICES
Hostels for Men
Home Georges Motte, Bd d'Ypres 24,
1000 Brussels; tel: (02) 217 61 36
(acc 75)
'Le Foyer', Centre d'accueil, rue Bodeghem 27-29, 1000 Brussels; tel: (02) 512 17 92
(acc 70)

Family Aid (EU Food Distribution)
Bd d'Ypres 26, 1000 Brussels;
tel: (02) 223 10 44

Guidance Centre (Housing Help and Debt Counselling)
102 rue de l'Église ste Anne, 1180 Brussels;
tel: (02) 414 19 16

Refugee Centre
'Foyer Selah', Bld d'Ypres 28, 1000 Brussels;
tel: (02) 219 01 77 (acc 90)

Mothers' and Children's Home
Chaussée de Drogenbos 225, 1180 Brussels;
tel: (02) 376 17 01 (acc mothers 14, children 25)

Children's Home
'Clair Matin', rue des Trois Rois 88, 1180 Uccle-Brussels; tel: (02) 376 17 40 (acc 41)

SHOPS
Brussels: Foyer George Motte, bld d'Ypres 24, 1000 Brussels
Liège: 6 Quai Bonaparte, 4000 Liège
Quaregnon: 82A rue Monsville 7390, Quaregnon
Antwerp: Ballaerstraat 94, 2018 Antwerpen

CONFERENCE AND YOUTH CENTRE
Villa Meyerbeer, route de Barisart 256,
4900 Spa; tel: (087) 77 49 00

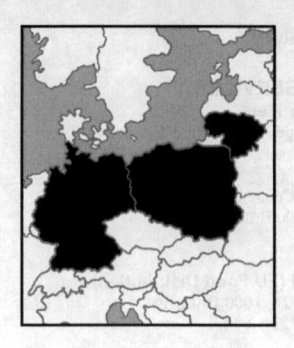

GERMANY AND LITHUANIA TERRITORY

Territorial leaders:
Commissioners Horst and Helga Charlet

Territorial Commander:
Commissioner Horst Charlet (12 Jun 2005)

Chief Secretary:
Lieut-Colonel Patrick Naud (1 May 2009)

Territorial Headquarters: 50677 Köln, Salierring 23-27, Germany

Tel: [49] (221) 20 8190; fax: [49] (221) 208 1957; email: NHQ@GER.salvationarmy.org;
website: www.heilsarmee.de

Salvation Army work in Germany began in Stuttgart on 14 November 1886 through the persistent sale of the Swiss *Kriegsruf* by Staff-Captain Fritz Schaaf who, after being converted in New York, was stationed in Switzerland and could not resist the call to bring the message over the border into his fatherland.

The Salvation Army was first registered as a limited company in Berlin in 1897 and was recognised throughout Germany as a church and public corporation on 10 October 1967 by law in Nordrhein-Westfalen. It is recognised as a religious association with public rights in the states of Berlin, Hessen, Schleswig-Holstein and Baden-Württemberg.

Salvation Army work in Lithuania having begun in 1998, the Germany Territory was redesignated the Germany and Lithuania Territory in September 2005. That same month, 'Project Warsaw' was launched to begin the Army's work in Poland (under IHQ) and on 1 July 2008 the Germany and Lithuania Territory took responsibilty for this work when a regional office for Poland was established in Dresden.

Zone: Europe
Countries included in the territory: Germany, Lithuania, Poland
'The Salvation Army' in German: Die Heilsarmee; in Lithuanian: Isganymo Armija; in Poland: Armia Zbawienia
Language in which the gospel is preached: German, Lithuanian, Polish
Periodicals: *Danke, Heilsarmee-Forum, Heilsarmee-Magazin*

THE National Congress, led by General John Larsson (Retired) and Commissioner Freda Larsson, was a marvellous occasion and the territory's biggest event of the year. Seekers at the mercy seat were among the many people who made significant spiritual decisions.

Three cadets were ordained and commissioned as officers before receiving their first appointments. The men's choir Mannssambandet from Norway, the German Staff Band and the territory's African Swing Salvation group enlivened the meetings.

As usual, every division held united meetings on Good Friday; there were good attendances of more than 200 people in each division. Several seminars for different corps sections took place in all divisions.

More than 100 women gathered for the Territorial Women's Weekend entitled 'God's Dreams For My Life'. Commissioner Helga Charlet (TPWM) led this important event.

Prayer and Repentance Day, still a public holiday in some areas, saw united meetings in all divisions. The East Division enjoyed the Ascension Day visit of Oslo 3 Band (Norway).

The Youth and Children's Department encouraged young people to take part in various corps programmes, as well as territorial youth events. As a result many young people have become Salvationists.

Decisions for Christ were made at the Territorial New Year Camp and new seekers were recorded at a children's camp. Sports events attracted children and teenagers to The Salvation Army. Many were accompanied by their parents and relatives, some attending an Army gathering for the first time.

Territorial Music Secretary Bandmaster Heinrich Schmidt led the 2008 Territorial Music Camp, with Brian Burditt (former Canadian Staff Bandmaster) as the special guest. Families and children appreciated Bible studies as well as the music.

The territorial slogan for 2009 is 'Go Deeper', placing an emphasis on spiritual motivation, prayer and quietness in God's presence as taught in Ephesians 3:16-19. Each department within THQ and the divisions prepared appropriate strategies.

STATISTICS
Officers 160 (active 88 retired 72) **Cadets** 2
Field Sergeants 13 **Employees** 730
Corps 44 **Outposts** 7 **Institutions** 40
Senior Soldiers 1,056 **Adherents** 388 **Junior Soldiers** 74

STAFF
Women's Ministries: Comr Helga Charlet (TPWM) Lt-Col Anne-Dore Naud (TSWM)
Evangelisation and Field Programme: Maj Marsha Bowles
Editor: Maj Alfred Preuß
Finance and Fund-raising: Mr Hans Joachim Bode
IT-Manager: Maj Hartmut Leisinger
Property: Mr Wilfried Otterbach
Public Relations and Internet: Maj Annette Preuß
Social: Maj Frank Honsberg
Staff Band: B/M Heinrich Schmidt
Trade: Maj Heidrun Edwards
Training and Candidates: Maj Marsha Bowles
Youth: Maj David Bowles

DIVISIONS
East: 12159 Berlin, Fregestr 13/14;
  tel: (0)30-859 8890; fax: (0)30-859 889 99;
  email: DHQ_Ost@GER.salvationarmy.org;
  Majs Beat and Annette Rieder
North: 22453 Hamburg, Borsteler Chaussee 23;
  tel: (0)40-189 89672; fax: (0)40-189 89674;
  email: DHQ_Nord@GER.salvationarmy.org;
  Maj Fernanda van Houdt
South: 70178 Stuttgart, Rotebühlstr 117;
  tel: (0)711-61 66 27; fax: (0)711-62 84 59;
  email: DHQ_Sued@GER.salvationarmy.org;
  Majs Jörg and Susann Friedl
West: 45888 Gelsenkirchen, Hohenzollernstr 83;
  tel (0)0209-14908 546; fax (0)0209-14908 545; email: DHQ_West@GER.salvationarmy.org; Majs Stephan und Andrea Weber

INVESTIGATION
Heckerstr 85, 34121 Kassel;
  tel: (0) 561 2889945; fax: (0) 561 2889946;
  email: Suchdienst@GER.salvationarmy.org;
  Lt-Col Erika Siebel

SENIOR CITIZENS' RESIDENCES
12159 Berlin, Dickhardtstr 52-53 (acc apts 42)
45127 Essen, Hoffnungsstr 23 (acc apts 25)
44623 Herne, Koppenbergshof 2 (acc apts 5 flats 9)
50858 Köln, Rosenweg 1-5;
  tel: (0)221-280 8979 (acc apts 42)
68159 Mannheim, G3, 1 + 20;
  tel: (0)621-2 5361 (acc apts 31)
68165 Mannheim, Augartenstr 43, Haus Marie Engelhardt; tel: (0)621-44 27 28 (acc apts 19)

Germany and Lithuania Territory

75175 Pforzheim, Pflügerstr 37-43;
tel: (0)7231-6 56 14 (acc apts 30)

SOCIAL SERVICES
Counselling
79106 Freiburg, Lehenerstr 115;
tel: (0)761-89 44 92; fax (0)761-500 99 98

20359 Hamburg, Counselling Centre, Talstr 11;
tel: (0)40-31 65 43

22117 Hamburg, Counselling for Alcoholics and Rehabilitation Work, Oststeinbeckerweg 2-4;
tel: (0)40-713 65 64; fax: (0)40-713 44 37

Children's Day Nursery
12159 Berlin, Fregestr 13-14; tel: (0)30-850 72920;
fax: (0)30-850 729231 (acc 30)

Drop-in Cafés
79098 Freiburg, Löwenstr 1;
tel: (0)761-38 54616; fax: (0)761-38 546 22

22453 Hamburg, Borsteler Chaussee 23;
tel: (0)40-514 314 0; fax: (0)40-514 314 14

23552 Lübeck, An der Untertrave 48-49;
tel: (0)451-73394

90443 Nürnberg, Leonhardtstr 28;
tel: (0)911-28 73 156

Hostels
60314 Frankfurt, Windeckstr 58-60;
tel: (0)69-43 22 52 (acc 38)

73033 Göppingen, Markstr 58; tel: (0)7161-7 42 17;
fax: (0)7161-7 28 10 (acc 30)

37073 Göttingen, Untere Maschstr 13b;
tel: (0)551-4 24 84; fax: (0)551-5 31 14 22
(acc 24)

23552 Lübeck, Engelsgrube 62-64;
tel: (0)451-7 33 94; fax: (0)451-7 23 86 (acc 37)

80469 München, Pestalozzistr 36;
tel: (0)89-26 71 49; fax: (0)89-26 35 26 (acc 50)

70176 Stuttgart, Silberburgstr 139;
tel: (0)711-61 09 67/68; fax: (0)711-61 33 00
(acc 52)

65189 Wiesbaden, Schwarzenbergstr 7;
tel: (0)611-70 12 68; fax: (0)0611-71 40 21
(acc 191)

Nursing Homes
14163 Berlin, Goethestr 17-21; tel: (0)30-3289000;
fax: (0)30-32890022 (acc 51)

47805 Krefeld, Voltastr 50; tel: (0)2151-93 72 60;
fax: (0)2151-93 72626 (acc 65)

Therapeutic Rehabilitation Institutions
14197 Berlin, Hanauerstr 63; tel: (0)30-8 20 08 40;
fax: (0)30-8 20 08 430 (acc 60)

22453 Hamburg, Borsteler Chaussee 23;
tel: (0)40-514 314 0; fax: (0)40-514 314 0;
email: HamburgJJH@GER.salvationarmy.org
(acc 71)

34123 Kassel, Eisenacherstr 18;
tel: (0)561-570 35 90; fax: (0)561-570 359 22
(acc 85)

50825 Köln, Marienstr 116/118;
tel: (0)221-955 6090; fax: (0)221-5595 482
(acc 80)

90443 Nürnberg, Gostenhofer Hauptstr 47-49;
tel: (0)911-28 730; fax: (0)911-28 73 1103;
email:
NuernbergSozWerk@GER.salvationarmy.org
(acc 239, including therapeutic workshops
and facilities for alcoholics and elderly men)

Therapeutic Workshops
22453 Hamburg, Borsteler Chaussee 23;
tel: (0)40-514 314 35; fax: (0) 40-514 314 14

90443 Nürnberg, Leonhardstr 17-21;
tel: (0)911 28730

Women's Hostels
34134 Kassel-Niederzwehren, Am
Donarbrunnen 32; tel: (0)561-43113 (acc 7)

90443 Nürnberg, Gostenhofer Hauptstr 65;
tel: (0)911-272 3600 (acc 12)

65197 Wiesbaden, Königsteinerstr 24;
tel: (0)611-80 67 58; fax: (0)611-981 23 03
(acc 45)

CONFERENCE AND HOLIDAY CENTRE
24306 Plön, Seehof, Steinberg 3-4;
tel: (0)4522-5088200; fax: (0)4522-5088202;
email: seehof@GER.salvationarmy.org
Conference and Holiday Home (acc 72 + 25)
Youth Camp (acc 50) Camping Ground and
3 Holiday Chalets and Flats

LITHUANIA
Isganymo Armija, Lieturvoje, Tiltu 18, LT 91246
Klaipeda; tel/fax: [370] 46-310634;
email: klaipeda@isganymo-armija.org;
Capt Susanne Kettler-Riutkenen

POLAND
Regional Officer: Maj Joseph Pawlowski
Warsaw Office: ul. Bialostocka 11 m. 21, 03-748
Warszawa, Poland; tel: (0)048 22401 7225;
email: Warszawa@GER.salvationarmy.org
Starachowice Office: ul. Nowa 10, 27-200
Starachowice, Poland; tel: (0)048 60716 5903;
email starachowice@GER.salvationarmy.org;
Maj Denise McGarvey

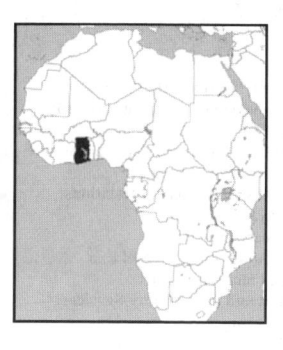

GHANA TERRITORY

Territorial leaders:
Colonels Dennis L. and Sharon Strissel

Territorial Commander:
Colonel Dennis L. Strissel (1 Feb 2007)

Chief Secretary:
Lieut-Colonel William Gyimah (1 Feb 2007)

Territorial Headquarters: PO Box CT452 Cantonments, Accra, Ghana

Tel: [233] (21) 776 971; fax: [233] (021) 772 695; email: saghana@gha.salvationarmy.org

Salvation Army operations began in Ghana in 1922 when Lieutenant King Hudson was commissioned to 'open fire' in his home town of Duakwa. Ensign and Mrs Charles Roberts were also appointed to pioneer work in Accra.

Zone: Africa
Country included in the territory: Ghana
'The Salvation Army' in Ga: Yiwalaheremo Asrafoi Le; in Fanti and Twi: Nkwagye Dom Asraafo; in Ewe: Agbexoxo Srafa Ha La
Languages in which the gospel is preached: Bassa, Builsa, Dangme, English, Ewe, Fante, Frafra, Ga, Gola, Grushia, Twi
Periodical: *Salvationist Newsletter*

A MEMORABLE event was the territorial congress, marked by the visit of General Shaw Clifton and Commissioner Helen Clifton. About 4,000 Salvationists attended the meetings, with representatives from the Republic of Togo joining their Ghanaian comrades for the first time. A march of witness saw thousands of uniformed Salvationists bringing traffic on the main Tema-Ashaiman highway virtually to a halt.

The General welcomed the 20 cadets of the Prayer Warriors Session who were commencing their training. He pointed out that it was the first time the word 'prayer' was being used in a sessional name, and said all Salvationists must be prayer warriors because there can be no army without warriors.

Because Ghana Territory was 86 years old, 86 junior soldiers were enrolled by the General and 86 junior timbrelists added colour to the occasion.

Numerical and spiritual growth was witnessed around the territory during the year under review, with 442 senior and 239 junior soldiers being enrolled. Four new outposts were opened, where 83 new converts were recorded.

The territorial leadership set a five-year strategic goal for 2009-2014, with the focus being on five areas: human resources development; serving suffering humanity; evangelism and soul-saving; education; finance.

In the field of education The Salvation Army Education Policy, which had been a longstanding concern, was approved. A copy was sent to the Director General of Education in the Ministry of Education.

The Grace Project School, generously sponsored by Salvationists from Castleford Corps (United Kingdom), was built in a community where there had previously been a leprosarium and children had been denied access to education.

Funding from Sweden Radio Help facilitated the building of a six-classroom block at Nkawkaw. A school was commissioned at Ho, in the Volta Division.

On Ghana's 48th Republic Day the territory received the National Honours Award from the then President, His Excellency John Agyekum Kufour. This was in recognition of Salvation Army services in Ghana and its contribution to national development.

STATISTICS

Officers 239 (active 189 retired 50) **Cadets** 20 **Employees** 1,423
Corps 105 **Societies** 145 **Schools** 187 **Pupils** 26,849 **Clinics** 9 **Social Centres** 8 **Day Care Centres** 66
Senior Soldiers 17,429 **Junior Soldiers** 3,817
Personnel serving outside territory Officers 12

STAFF

Women's Ministries: Col Sharon K. Strissel (TPWM) Lt-Col Mary Gyimah (TSWM) Maj Eva Kudezi (Women's Development and Training) Capt Albertha Arhin (TJHLS)
Business Administration: Maj Isaac Danso
Personnel: Lt-Col Mike Adu Manu
　Asst to Sec for Personnel: Maj Eva Danso
Programme: Lt-Col Wendy Leavey
Communications and External Relations: Mr Kofi Sakyiamah
Editor: Capt Stephen Borbor
Extension Training: Capt Michael Eku
Finance: Capt Francis Amakye
Medical, Social and Community Services: Maj Heather Craig
Projects and Child Sponsorship: Capt Margaret Amponsah
Property: Maj Modesto Kudezi
Schools: Mrs Doris Mensah
Territorial Band: B/M Emmanuel Hackman
Territorial Sec for Planned Giving: Maj Graeme Craig
Training: Maj Margaret Wickings
Youth and Candidates: Maj John Arthur

DIVISIONS

Accra: PO Box 166 Tema; tel: (022) 215 530; Majs Godfried and Felicia Oduro
Akim Central: PO Box AS 283, Asamankese; tel: (081) 23 585; Majs Peter and Grace Oduro-Amoah
Ashanti Central: PO Box 15, Kumasi; tel/fax: (051) 240 16; Majs Seth and Janet Appeateng
Ashanti North: c/o PO Box 477, Mampong, Ashanti; Majs Stephen and Cecilia Boadu
Central: PO Box 62, Agona Swedru; tel: (041) 20 285; Majs Seth and Mary Larbi
Nkawkaw: PO Box 3, Nkawkaw; tel: (0842) 22 208; Majs Edward and Mercy Addison
West Akim: PO Box 188, Akim Oda; tel: (0882) 2 305; Maj Jonas and Capt Constance Ampofo
Volta: PO Box 604, Ho, Volta Region; Majs Rockson and Emelia Oduro

DISTRICTS

Brong Ahafo: PO Box 1454, Sunyani; tel: (061) 23 513; Maj Ebenezer Danquah
East Akim: PO Box KF 1218, Koforidua E/R; tel: (081) 22 580; Maj Edward Kyei
Northern: PO Box 233, Bolgatanga; tel: (072) 22 030; Capt Prosper Adua
Western: PO Box 178, Sekondi, C/R; tel: (031) 23 763; Capt Alexander Siaw

TRAINING COLLEGE

PO Box CE 11991, Tema; tel: (022) 306 252/253

Ghana Territory

EXTENSION TRAINING CENTRE
PO Box CT 452, Cantonments, Accra;
 tel: (021) 776 971; fax: (021) 772 695

CLINICS
Accra Urban Aid: PO Box CT 452, Cantonments, Accra; tel: (021) 230 918 (acc 11, including maternity)

Accra Urban Aid Outreach: PO Box CT 452, Cantonments, Accra; tel: (021) 246 764 (mobile outreach for street children)

Adaklu-Sofa: PO Box 604, Ho, V/R (acc 4, including maternity)

Anum: PO Box 17, Senchi, E/R (acc 11, including maternity)

Ba: PO Box 8, Ba, C/R (acc 4, including maternity)

Begoro: PO Box 10, Begoro, E/R (acc 10, including maternity)

Duakwa: PO Box 2, Agona Duakwa, C/R (acc 30, including maternity)

Wenchi: PO Box 5, Wenchi, Akim Oda (acc 8, including maternity)

HEALTH CENTRE
Wiamoase: PO Box 14, Wiamoase, Ashanti; tel: (051) 32 613

EDUCATION
Sub-primary Schools 66, Primary Schools 79, Junior Secondary Schools 40, Senior Secondary Schools 2

SOCIAL WORK
Adaklu-Sofa Vocational Training Centre: PO Box 604, Ho, V/R

Anidasofie Street Girls' Training Centre: PO Box CT 452, Cantonments, Accra; tel: (021) 246 764

Begoro Rehabilitation Centre: PO Box 10, Begoro, E/R

Child Care Training Centre: PO Box 8, Ba, C/R

Community Rehabilitation Project: PO Box 2, Agona Duakwa

Malnutrition Centre: PO Box 2, Agona Duakwa, C/R

Rehabilitation Centre: PO Box 14, Wiamoase, Ashanti

Voluntary Counselling and Testing Centre: PO Box CT 452, Cantonments, Accra; tel: (021) 776 971

Below: The General gives a powerful Bible message at a Salvationists' rally during the territorial congress

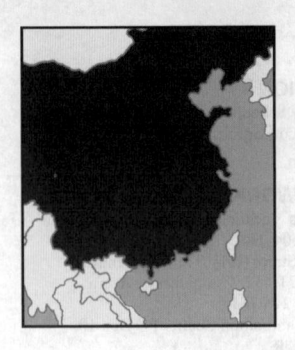

HONG KONG AND MACAU COMMAND

Command leaders:
Lieut-Colonels Samuel and Donni Pho

Officer Commanding:
Lieut-Colonel Samuel Pho (1 Jun 2009)

General Secretary:
Major Priscilla Nanlabi (1 Dec 2007)

Command Headquarters: 11 Wing Sing Lane, Yaumatei, Kowloon, Hong Kong

Postal address: PO Box 70129, Kowloon Central Post Office, Kowloon, Hong Kong

Tel: [852] 2332 4531; fax: [852] 2771 6439; email: Hongkong@hkt.salvationarmy.org; website: www.salvation.org.hk

In March 1930, at a meeting held at Government House, Hong Kong, The Salvation Army was requested to undertake women's work in the crown colony, a work pioneered by Majors Dorothy Brazier and Doris Lemon. This work was directed from Peking until, in 1935, the South China Command was established in Canton to promote wide evangelistic and welfare operations. In 1939 Hong Kong became the Army's administrative centre. Later, the inclusion of the New Territories determined that the Command Headquarters move to Kowloon. Since 1951 the General of The Salvation Army has been recognised as a Corporation Sole. From 1993, disaster relief and community development projects have been carried out in mainland China. In 1999, a pioneer officer was appointed to the Special Administrative Region of Macau and Salvation Army work began there officially on 25 March 2000. In 2001, an officer was appointed to the North/North Eastern Project Office in Beijing.

Zone: South Pacific and East Asia
Regions included in the command: Hong Kong and Macau (Special Administrative Regions of the People's Republic of China) and Mainland China
'The Salvation Army' in Cantonese: Kau Sai Kwan; in Filipino: Hukbo ng Kaligtasan; in Putonghua: Jiu Shi Jun
Languages in which the gospel is preached: Cantonese, English, Filipino, Putonghua
Periodicals: *Army Scene, The War Cry*

THE command has been totally committed to relief work following the 512 Sichuan earthquake in China in May 2008. When the preliminary stage of emergency relief was over, the command set up a permanent office in Sichuan to manage the after-quake reconstruction projects. Major Tommy Chan (DC, Hong Kong) was appointed also as Project Director.

The Blair Morison Estate-sponsored Global Chinese Ministry Training Centre, which includes the officer training college, was opened and dedicated to God's glory on 31 May 2008. The building is also utilised for lay people's training, further education

Hong Kong and Macau Command

for officers and accommodation for specialised training.

The Hong Kong Staff Band (the former Hong Kong Command Band) was established on 6 September 2008. The band carries out the role of an ambassador of music; its mission statement is: 'The pursuit of excellent sacred music interpretation; to inspire the hearts of listeners effectively; to endeavour to share the salvation of God to expand his Kingdom.'

The Hong Kong and Macau 'O! Day', held on 18 October 2008, was the command's major fund-raising activity among the business sector. Previously held in the Hong Kong area only, the event was taken for the first time across the harbour to another Special Administrative Region – Macau – where nearly 500 people helped raise 1.8 million dollars.

The command's theme in 2009 was 'Vision Possible', inspired by what William Booth wrote on his 80th birthday: 'I want you to stand up more boldly and firmly than you have ever done ... in the great business of saving the world.'

STATISTICS

Officers 52 (active 44 retired 8) **Cadets** 1 **Employees** 2,443

Corps 18 **Outposts** 2 **Institutions** 20 **Schools** 7 **Kindergartens** 7 **Nursery Schools** 17 **Social Centres and Hotels** 81

Senior Soldiers 2,179 **Adherents** 35 **Junior Soldiers** 339

Personnel serving outside command Officers 3

STAFF

Women's Ministries: Lt-Col Donni Pho (CPWM) Maj Ming-chun Connie Ip Kan (CSWM)
Asst to GS: Maj Simon Tso Kam-shing
China Development: Maj On Dieu Quang
Candidates: Capt Sara Tam Mei-shun
Community Relations: Envoy Simon Wong
Editor/Literary: Maj David Ip Kam-yuen
Educational Services: Maj Simon Tso Kam-shing
Emergency Services Coordinator: Ms Karen Ng Wai-sze
Finance: Ms Deidre Ashe
Human Resources: Ms Eva Lau
Property: Envoy Daniel Hui Wah-lun
Social: Mrs Victoria Kwok Yuen Wai-yee
Trade: Ms Karen Ng Wai-sze
Training: Maj Tony Ma Yeung-mo

DIVISION

1 Lung Chu St, Tai Hang Tung, Kowloon, HK; tel: 2195 0222; fax: 2319 0670; Maj Tommy Chan Hi-wai and Maj Helina Chan Lee Siu-king

OFFICER TRAINING COLLEGE AND GLOBAL CHINESE MINISTRY TRAINING CENTRE

1 Lung Chu St, Tai Hang Tung, Kln, PO Box 70129, Kowloon Central PO, Kln, HK; tel: 2195 0203; fax: 2319 1386; email: otc@tc.salvationarmy.org.hk

CHINA DEVELOPMENT

Hong Kong Head Office: tel: (852) 2783 2288; fax: (852) 2385 7823; China Development Secretary: Maj On Dieu Quang; tel: (852) 2783 2288; email: cdd@hkt.salvationarmy.org

North/Northeast Regional Project Office – China: D-102 Jin Mao Apartment, 2 Guang Hua Lane, Chao Yang District, Beijing 100020, China; tel: [86] (10) 6586 9331/2; fax: [86] (10) 6586 8382; email: nnerpo@hkt.salvationarmy.org

Southwest Regional Project Office – China: 6D, Unit 1, Block 8, Yin Hai Hot Spring Garden, Northern District, 173 Guan Xing Rd, Guan Shang, Kunming 650200, Yunnan, China; tel: [86] (871) 7166 111/222; fax: [86] (871) 7155 222; email: swrpo@hkt.salvationarmy.org

Xinghe Project Office – China: Rm 520, Xinghe Municipal Government Bldg, Xinghe, 013650 Inner Mongolia, China; tel/fax: (86) 474 7212 010; email: xho@hkt.salvationarmy.org

The Salvation Army Campsite and Training Centre – China: Xinhge, Inner Mongolia, China; tel: (86) 474 7212980

EDUCATIONAL SERVICES

Kindergartens

Centaline Charity Fund: G/F, under Mei Mun House, Mei Tin Estate, Tai Wai, Shatin, NT; tel: 2886 2340; fax 2886 2343 (acc 224, 2 sessions) (acc 69 full-day)

Chan Kwan Tung: G/F and 1/F, Salvation Army HQ, 11 Wing Sing Lane, Yaumatei, Kln; tel: 2384 7831; fax: 2388 5310 (acc 277, 2 sessions)

Fu Keung: Units 121-140, G/F, Fu Keung House, Tai Wo Hau Estate, NT; tel: 2614 4481; fax: 2439 0666 (acc 300, 2 sessions)

Hing Yan: G/F, Commercial Centre, Hau Tak Estate, Tseung Kwan O, Kln; tel: 2706 6222; fax: 2704 9262 (acc 378, 2 sessions) and Nursery (acc 72, 2 sessions)

Ng Kwok Wai Memorial: G/F, 22-30 Hoi Shing Rd, Clague Garden Estate, Tsuen Wan, NT; tel: 2499 7639; fax: 2414 9214 (acc 360, 2 sessions)

Ping Tin: G/F, Ping Shing House, Ping Tin Estate, Lam Tin, Kln; tel: 2775 5332; fax: 2775 5412 (acc 270; 2 sessions) plus Nursery (acc 34, 2 sessions)

Tin Ka Ping: G/F, No 15 Jat Min Chuen St, Shatin, NT; tel: 2647 4227; fax: 2645 1869 (acc 524, 2 sessions)

Crèches 1 Month-2 Years

North Point: Podium Level 2, Healthy Village, 6 Healthy St Central North Point, HK; tel: 2856 0892; fax: 2856 1398 (acc 28 full-day)

Pak Tin: G/F, Wing C, Fu Tin House, Pak Tin Estate, Pak Wan St, Shamshuipo, Kln; tel: 2778 3588; fax: 2778 9622 (acc 16 full-day)

Nursery Schools 2-6 Years

Catherine Booth: 2/F, Salvation Army HQ, 11 Wing Sing Lane, Yaumatei, Kln: tel: 2332 7963; fax: 2385 4167 (acc 110 full-day)

Hoi Fu: G/F, Wing B & C, Hoi Ning House, Hoi Fu Court, Mongkok, Kln; tel: 2148 2477; fax: 2148 1711 (acc 118 full-day)

Jat Min: 1/F, 15 Jat Min Chuen St, Jat Min Chuen, Shatin, NT; tel: 2647 4897; fax: 2646 6825 (acc 168 full-day)

Kam Tin: G/F, 103 Kam Tin Rd, Yuen Long, NT; tel: 2442 3606; fax: 2442 0523 (acc 104 full-day)

Lai Chi Kok: 1/F, Prosperity Court, 168 Lai Chi Kok Rd, Kln; tel: 2787 5788; fax: 2787 1581 (acc 100 full-day)

Lei Muk Shue: G/F, Wing B & C, Yeung Shue House, Lei Muk Shue Estate, Kwai Chung, NT; tel: 2420 2491; fax: 2619 9289 (acc 112 full-day)

Lok Man: 1/F, Block H, Lok Man Sun Chuen, Tokwawan, Kln; tel: 2365 1994; fax: 2764 8036 (acc 145 full-day)

Ming Tak: G/F, Wing B & C, Hin Ming Court, Hang Hau, Tseung Kwan O, Kln; tel: 2623 7555; fax: 2623 7551 (acc 126 full-day)

North Point: Podium Level 2, Healthy Village, 6 Healthy St, Central North Point, HK; tel: 2856 0892; fax: 2856 1398 (acc 28 full-day)

Pak Tin: G/F, Wing C, Fu Tin House, Pak Tin Estate, Pak Wan St, Shamshuipo, Kln; tel: 2778 3588; fax: 2778 9622 (acc 104 full-day)

Sam Shing: G/F, adj to Moon Yu House, Sam Shing Estate, Tuen Mun, NT; tel: 2452 0032; fax: 2541 1347 (acc 104 full-day)

Tai Wo Hau: Units 215, 217, 219 & 221-232, 2/F, Fu Keung House, Tai Wo Hau Estate, Tsuen Wan, NT; tel: 2614 7662; f ax: 2612 2571 (acc 126 full-day)

Tai Yuen: G/F, Tai Ling House, Tai Yuen Estate, Tai Po, NT; tel: 2664 9725; fax: 2666 9698 (acc 100 full-day)

Tin Ping: G/F, Units 106-110, Wing B, Tin Hor House, Tin Ping Estate, Sheung Shui, NT; tel: 2671 9972; fax: 2671 8436 (acc 112 full-day)

Tsuen Wan: 1/F, Clague Garden Estate, 22 Hoi Shing Rd, Tsuen Wan, NT; tel: 2417 1400; fax: 2411 1926 (acc 182 full-day)

Wah Fu: 1/F-2/F, Wah Sang House, Wah Fu Estate, HK; tel: 2551 6341; fax: 2538 1229 (acc 126 full-day)

Wo Che: Bays 101-114, G/F, Tak Wo House, Wo Che Estate, Shatin, NT; tel: 2604 0428; fax: 2608 0614 (acc 168 full-day)

Primary Schools

Ann Wyllie Memorial School: 100 Shing Tai Rd, Heng Fa Chuen, HK; tel: 2558 2111; fax: 2898 4377 (acc 760)

Centaline Charity Fund School: 9 Wah Ha St, Chaiwan, HK; tel: 2556 2292; fax: 2556 2722 (acc 509)

Lam Butt Chung Memorial School: 8 Yat Tung St, Yat Tung Estate, Tung Chung, Lantau, NT; tel: 2109 0328; fax: 2109 0223 (acc 950)

Sam Shing Chuen Lau Ng Ying School: Sam Shing Estate, Tuen Mun, NT; tel: 2458 8035; fax: 2618 3171 (acc 175)

Tin Ka Ping School: Pok Hong Estate, Shatin, NT; tel: 2648 9283; fax: 2649 4305 (acc 760)

Rwanda, a member of Kayenzi Home League learns a craft that could help her earn an income for her family

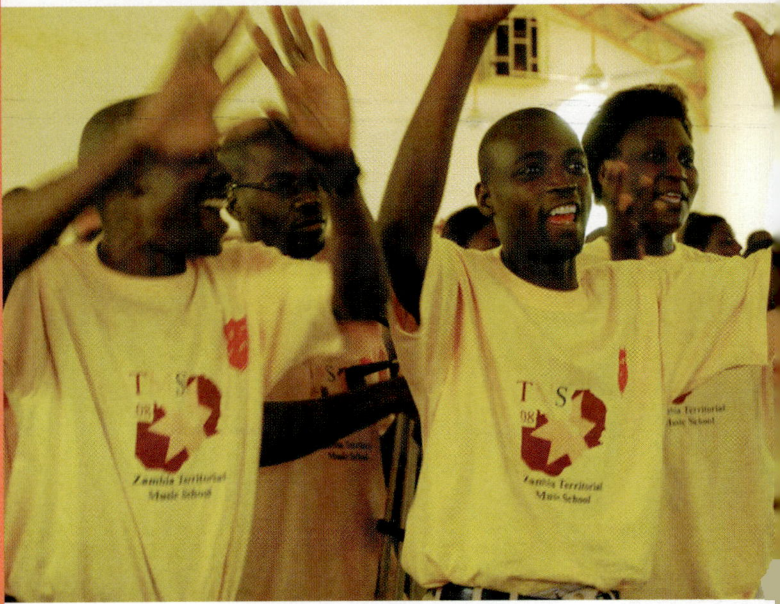
Zambia Territorial
Music School

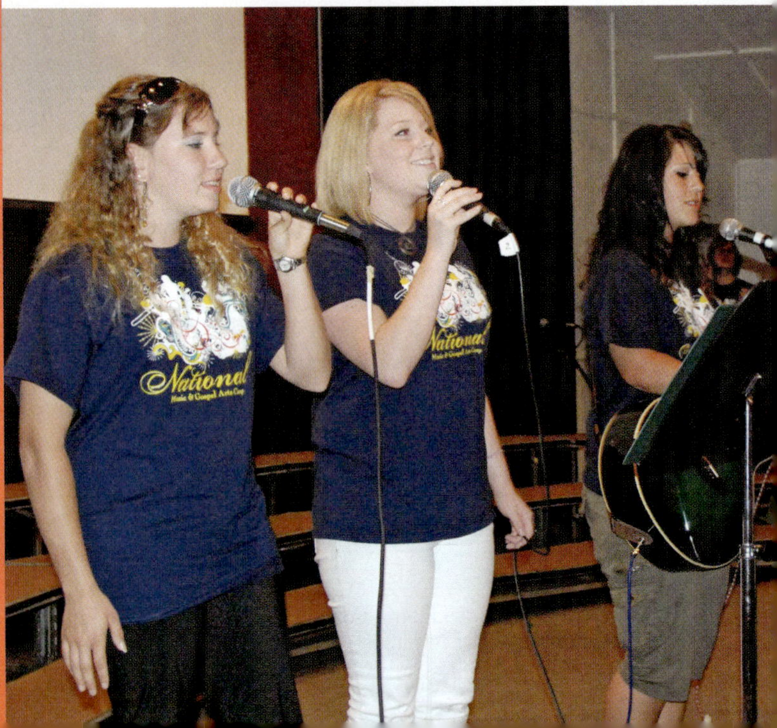
National

iving praise to God, young Salvationists are pictured (clockwise, from top ft) in Zambia, Korea, the Democratic Republic of Congo and Canada

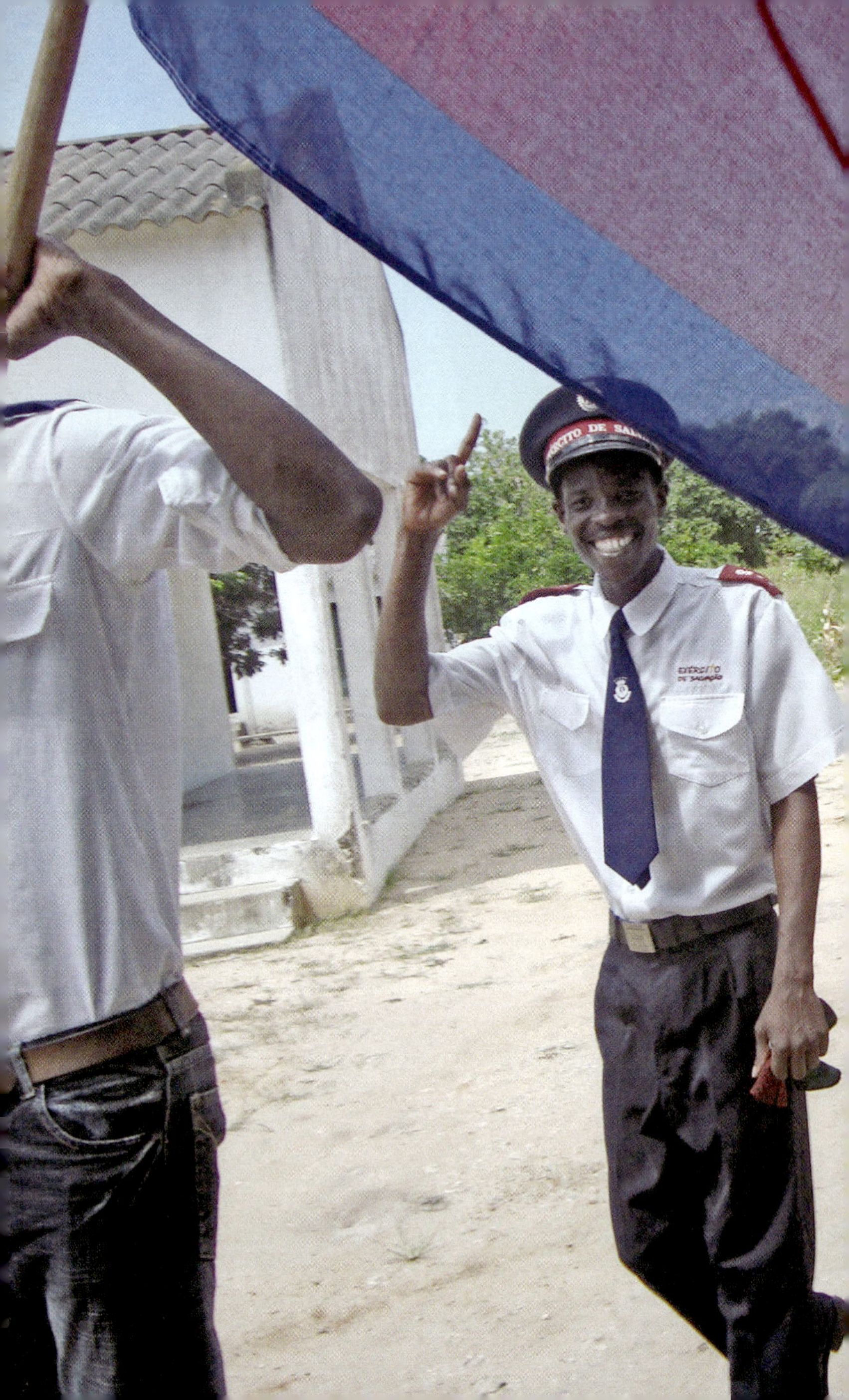

Salvationists on the march in Mozambique

Left: UK officer Major Alison Thompson, seconded to relief wo[rk] in Myanmar (Burma), makes the precarious crossing of a bamboo bridge

Below left: a victim of Australia's bushfires i[s] counselled by Major Wendy Oliver

Right: Captain M[ary] Konti-Galinou sha[res] the gospel wi[th a] woman in the red-l[ight] area of Thessalo[niki,] Gre[ece]

Below right: member[s of] the Junior Home Lea[gue] in India South Eas[tern] Territory engag[e in] passionate pra[yer]

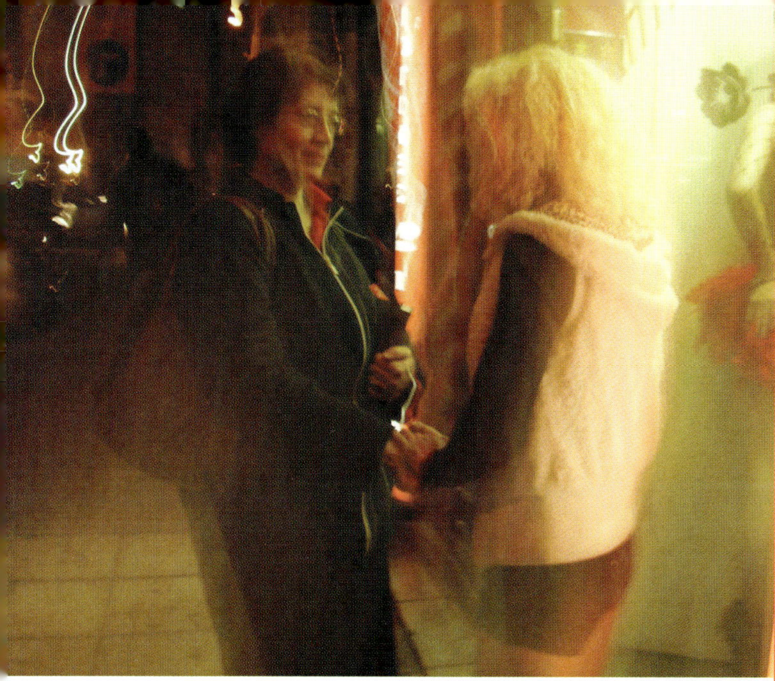

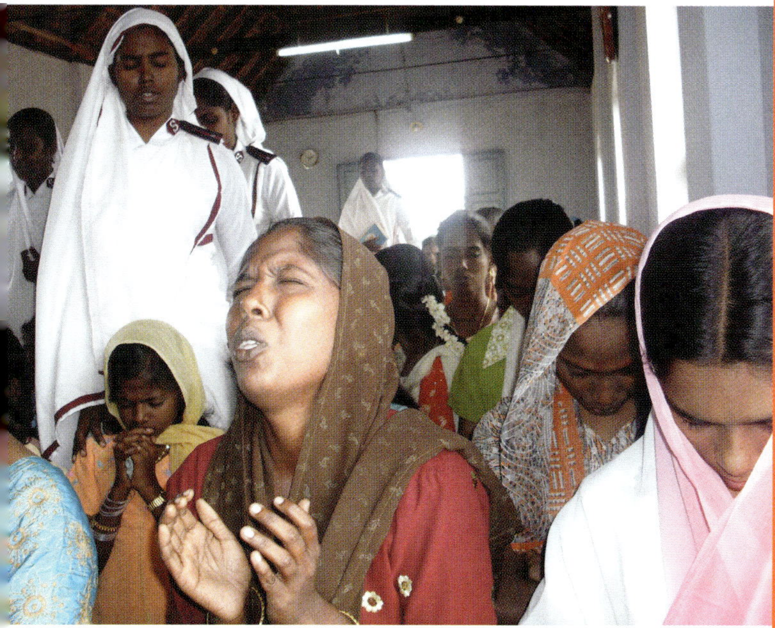

Girls from one of the seven children's homes run by The Salvation Army in Sri Lanka help celebrate the completion of a post-tsunami housing project

Hong Kong and Macau Command

Secondary School
William Booth Secondary School, 100 Yuk Wah St, Tsz Wan Shan, Kln; tel: 2326 9068; fax: 2328 0052 (acc 1,205)

Special School
Shek Wu School, Area 8 Jockey Club Rd, Sheung Shui, NT; tel: 2670 0800; fax: 2668 5353 (acc 200)

GUEST ACCOMMODATION
Booth Lodge, 7/F, 11 Wing Sing Lane, Yaumatei, Kln; tel: (852) 2771 9266; fax: (852) 2385 1140; email: boothlodge@salvationarmy.org.hk

RECYCLING PROGRAMME
Logistic Centre: 7/F Tat Ming Industrial Building, 44-52 Ta Chuen Ping St, Kwai Chung, NT; tel: 2332 4433; fax: 2332 4411; email: Recycling@hkt.salvationarmy.org

Family Stores
Chuk Yuen Store: Shop S202, 3/F, Chuk Yuen Shopping Centre, Chuk Yuen South Estate, Wong Tai Sin, Kln; tel: 2320 0050

Kowloon City Store: 1/F, HICB Building, 78-82 Tam Kung Rd, To Kwa Wan, Kln; tel: 2624 7878

Kwun Tong Store: No 237, G/F, Hay Cheuk Lau, Garden Estate, Kwun Tong, Kln; tel: 2331 2577

Macau Store: Ave Artur Tamag Barbosa, BL 9, Fl R/C, Flat CF, Ed Jardim Cidade – Man Seng Kok, Macau; tel: (853) 2843 2888

Mongkok Store: Shop 1, G/F Xing Hua Ctr, 433 Shanghai St, Mongkok, Kln; tel: 3422 3205

Nam Cheong Store: Shop 3-4, Nam Cheong West Rail Station, Kln; tel: 2387 4933

Shau Kei Wan Store: G/F, Tsang Hong Building, 139 Shau Kei Wan, Main Street East, HK; tel: 2535 8113

Shek Wai Kok Store: Shop 331, Shek Wai Kok Shopping Centre, Shek Wai Kok Estate, Tsuen Wan, NT; tel: 2499 8981

Stanley Store: G/F, 98 Stanley Main St, HK; tel: 3197 0070

Tai Hang Tung Store: G/F, 1 Lung Chu St, Tai Hang Tung, Kln; tel: 2784 0689

Tin Hau Store: G/F, 29 Wing Hing St, Tin Hau, HK; tel: 2887 5577

Wanchai Store: G/F, 31 Wood Rd, Wanchai, HK; tel: 2572 2879

Western District Store: Shop A2, G/F, Man Kwong Court, 12F-12G Smithfield Rd, Kennedy Town, Western District, HK; tel: 2974 0882

Yaumatei Store: G/F, 1A Cliff Rd, Yaumatei, Kln; tel: 2332 4448

Yue Wan Store: Shop 29-30, Yue On House, Yue Wan Estate, Chaiwan, HK; tel: 2558 8655

SOCIAL SERVICES
Camp Service
Bradbury Camp: 6 Ming Fai Rd, Cheung Chau, HK; tel: 2981 0358 (acc 108)

Ma Wan Youth Camp: Ma Wan Island, HK; tel: 2986 5244 (acc 40)

Youth Service
Children and Youth Centres
Chuk Yuen: 2-4/F, Chuk Yuen Estate Community Centre, Chuk Yuen South Estate, Kln; tel: 2351 5321

Lung Hang: G/F, Sin Sum House, Lung Hang Estate, Shatin, NT; tel: 2605 5569

Tai Wo Hau: 2-4/F, Tai Wo Hau Estate Community Centre, Tsuen Wan, NT; tel: 2428 4581

Education and Employment Service
Education and Development Centre: 6 Salvation Army St, Wanchai, HK; tel: 2572 6718

Integrated Services for Young People
Chaiwan: Podium Level Market Bldg, Wan Tsui Estate, Chaiwan, HK; tel: 2898 9750

Tai Po: 2/F, Tai Man House, Tai Yuen Estate, Tai Po, NT; tel: 2667 2913

Tuen Mun: G/F, 13-24 Hing Ping House, Tai Hing Estate, Tuen Mun, NT; tel: 2461 4741

Tuen Mun East: 5/F Ancillary Facilities Block, Fu Tai Estate, 9 Tuen Kwai Rd, Tuen Mun, NT; tel: 2467 7200

Yaumatei: 1/F, Block 4, Prosperous Garden, 3 Public Square St, Kln; tel: 2770 8933

School Social Work Services
Tuen Mun: G/F, 13-24 Hing Ping House, Tai Hing Estate, Tuen Mun, NT; tel: 2461 4741

Services for Young Night Drifters
Tuen Mun: 5/F Ancillary Facilities Block, Fu Tai Estate, 9 Tuen Kwai Rd, Tuen Mun, NT; tel: 2467 7200

Youth Special Projects
'Flying High' Child Development Project: 6 Salvation Army St, Wanchai, HK; tel: 2892 1302

Hong Kong and Macau Command

'Walk With You' Project: 6 Salvation Army St, Wanchai, HK; tel: 2834 3483

Community Service
Home Optimisation Movement for the Elderly: G/F, 145-146 Azalea Hse, So Uk Estate, Shamshuipo, Kln

Hong Kong Island Urban Renewal Social Service Team: Flat E, 20/F Tak Lee Commercial Building, 113-117 Wan Chai Rd, HK; tel: 2893 4711

Integrated Service for Street Sleepers: 1/F, GIC Bldg, 345A Shanghai St, Kln; tel: 2710 8911

Ngau Tam Mei Community Development Projects: Library, Yau Tam Mei School, Yau Tam Mei Village, Yuen Long, NT; tel: 2482 7175

Sam Mun Tsai Community Development Projects: 31 Chim Uk Village, Shuen Wan, Tai Po, NT; tel: 2660 9890

Shamshuipo Family Support Networking Team: Rm 69, 2/F Fuk Sing House, 63-69 Fuk Wing St, Shamshuipo, Kln; tel: 2390 9361

So Uk Community Service Team: G/F, 145-146 Azalea Hse, So Uk Estate, Shamshuipo, Kln; tel: 2728 3350

Sunrise House: 323 Shun Ning Rd, Cheung Sha Wan, Kln; tel: 2307 8001 (acc 310)

Urban Renewal Social Service Team: G/F, 140 Yee Kuk St, Shamshuipo, Kln; tel: 3586 3094

Yee On Hostels: Unit 111-116, 1/F, Hoi Yu House, Hoi Fu Court, Mongkok, Kln; tel: 2708 9553 (acc 40)

Day Care Centres for Senior Citizens
Bradbury: G/F, Wan Loi House, Wan Tau Tong Estate, Tai Po, NT; tel: 2638 8880 (acc 44)

Chuk Yuen: 141-150 Podium Level, Chui Yuen House, Chuk Yuen (South) Estate, Kln; tel: 2326 6683 (acc 44)

Hoi Yu: G/F, Hoi Lam House, Hoi Fu Court, 2 Hoi Ting Rd, Mongkok, Kln; tel: 2148 1480 (acc 44)

Centres for Senior Citizens
Chuk Yuen: 1/F, Chuk Yuen (South) Estate Community Centre, Kln; tel: 2320 8032

Hoi Lam: 1/F, Hoi Yu House, Hoi Fu Court, 2 Hoi Ting Rd, Mongkok, Kln; tel: 2148 1481

Nam Tai: G/F, Nam Tai House, Nam Shan Estate, Kln; tel: 2779 5983

Tai Po Multi-service: 2/F-3/F, Tai Po Community Centre, 2 Heung Sze Wui St, Tai Po Market, NT; tel: 2653 6811

Tai Wo Hau: 1/F, Tai Wo Hau Estate Community Centre, Tsuen Wan, NT; tel: 2428 8563

Wah Fu: Unit 125-129, G/F, Wah Kin House, Wah Fu Estate, Aberdeen, HK; tel: 2550 9971

Yaumatei Multi-service: 3/F, 11 Wing Sing Lane, Yaumatei, Kln; tel: 2332 0005

Community Day Activities Centre Service
Community Day Activities Centres cum Hostels
Cheung Hong: 2/F & 3/F Hong Cheung Hse, Cheung Hong Est, Tsing Yi, NT; tel: 2432 1588 (acc 40)

Lai King Home: 200-210 Lai King Hill Rd, Kwai Chung, NT; tel: 2744 1511 (acc 100)

Community Day Rehabilitation
Shaukeiwan: 456 Shaukeiwan Rd, Shaukeiwan, HK; tel: 2560 8123 (acc 40)

Tak Tin: G/F, Tak Yan House, Tak Tin Estate, Lam Tin; tel: 2177 7122

Integrated Home Care Service Teams
Kwun Tong: Unit 1-2, Wing B, G/F, Tak Lung House, Tak Tin Estate, Lam Tin, Kln; tel: 2340 0100

Sai Kung: 4/F, Po Kan House, Po Lam Estate, Tseung Kwan O, Kln; tel: 2701 5828

Tai Po (Tai Po Office):
2/F-3/F, Tai Po Community Centre, 2 Heung Sze Wui St, Tai Po Market, NT; tel: 2653 6619

Tai Po (Tai Wo Office): Unit 126-128, G/F Hang Wo House, Tai Wo Estate, Tai Po, NT; tel: 2653 3941

Yau Tsim (Kowloon Central Office): G/F & 1/F, Chee Sun Building, 161-165 Reclamation St, Yaumatei; tel: 2300 1399

Yau Tsim (Yaumatei Office): 3/F, 11 Wing Sing Lane, Yaumatei, Kln; tel: 2770 5266

Elderly Special Projects
CADENZA Community Projects
CDSMP: Rm 316, 3/F, Tai Po Community Centre, 2 Heung Sze Wui St, Tai Po Market; tel: 2651 1698

HSPTCM: Shop D, G/F, Phase 2, Prosperous Gdn, 3 Public Square St, Kln; tel: 2782 1334

Senior Citizens Talent Advancement Projects
Tung Tau Centre: Unit 1-3, G/F, Yat Tung House, Tung Tau Estate, Kln; tel: 2340 0266

Kwun Tong Centre: 1/F, Flat A, Yee On Centre, 31 Yee On St, Kwun Tong, Kln; tel: 2389 5568

Hong Kong and Macau Command

Carer Service
3/F, 11 Wing Sing Lane, Yaumatei, Kln;
tel: 2782 2229

Residential Childcare Service
Tai Wo Hau Small Group Homes: Fu Yin House,
Wing K, Tai Wo Hau Estate, Tsuen Wan, NT;
  Home of Joy: Flat 214; tel: 2615 1709
    (acc 8)
  Home of Love: Flat 314; tel: 2615 1784
    (acc 8)
  Home of Peace: Flat 112; tel: 2615 1710
    (acc 8)
Ping Tin Small Group Homes: Ping Wong House,
Ping Tin Estates, Lam Tin, Kln;
  Home of Faithfulness: Flat 103;
    tel: 2952 3691 (acc 8)
  Home of Goodness: Flat 203;
    tel: 2952 3692 (acc 8)
  Home of Kindness: Flat 303;
    tel: 2775 3542 (acc 8)
Wan Tsui Home for Boys: 115-128 G/F, Chak
Tsui House, Wan Tsui Estate, Chai Wan, HK;
tel: 2557 3290 (acc 48)
Yue Wan Boys' Hostel: 3-8 Yue Tai House,
Yue Wan Estate, Chaiwan, HK; tel: 2558 4048
(acc 15)

Residences for Senior Citizens
Bradbury Home of Loving Kindness: 16 Tung
Lo Wan Hill Rd, Tai Wai, Shatin, NT;
tel: 2601 5000 (acc 136)
Hoi Tai: 2/F, Hoi Tai House, Hoi Fu Court,
2 Hoi Ting Rd, Mongkok, Kln; tel: 2148 2000
(acc 98)
Lung Hang: 3&4/F, Wing Sam House, Lung
Hang Estate, Shatin, NT; tel: 2602 3696
(acc 155)
Nam Ming Haven for Women: G/F, Nam Ming
House, Nam Shan Estate, Shek Kip Mei, Kln;
tel: 2777 5484 (acc 38)
Nam Shan: 1&2/F, Nam Ming House, Nam Shan
Estate, Shek Kip Mei, Kln; tel: 2777 5102
(acc 150)
Po Lam: 4/F, Po Kan House, Po Lam Estate,
Tseung Kwan O, Kln; tel: 2701 5828
(acc 141)
Tak Tin: 2/F, Tak King House, Tak Tin Estate,
Lam Tin, Kln; tel: 2347 8183 (acc 81)
Kam Tin: 103 Kam Tin Rd, Yuen Long, NT;
tel: 2944 1369 (acc 150)

Sheltered Housing
Grace Apartments: Flat 3-95, Lotus Tower 4,
297 Ngau Tau Kok Rd, Kln; tel: 2763 6367
Kei Lok Apartments: Rm 225, Block 5,
Prosperous Garden, Public Square St,
Yaumatei, Kln; tel: 2782 6655

Integrated Vocational and Rehabilitation Service
Heng On Integrated Vocational Rehabilitation
Service: G/F, Heng Kong House, Heng On
Estate, Ma On Shan, NT; tel: 2640 0656
(acc 285)
On the Job Training Programme for People
with Disabilities: G/F, Heng Kong Hse, Heng
On Est, Ma On Shan, NT; tel: 2640 0656
(acc 18)
Sunnyway – On the Job Training Programme for
Young People with Disabilities: G/F, Heng
Kong Hse, Heng On Est, Ma On Shan, NT;
tel: 2640 0656 (acc 30)

Community Living with Support Services
Heng On Hostel: G/F, Heng Shan House, Heng
On Estate, Ma On Shan, NT; tel: 2640 0581
(acc 62)
Talent Shop: G/F, Heng Sing House, Heng On
Estate, Ma On Shan, Shatin, NT;
tel: 2633 7116

Rehabilitation Special Projects
Share-Care New Scope Project: 200-210 Lai King
Hill Rd, Kwai Chung, NT; tel: 2744 1511
Family Support Service for Persons with Autism:
6 Salvation Army St, Wanchai, HK;
tel: 2893 2537

Social Enterprise
Digital Plus: Unit D, 5/F Kwun Tong Industrial
Ctr, Phase 1, 472-484 Kwun Tong Rd, Kln;
tel: 3595 2320
Shatin Family Store: Shop no 70-72, G/F Ming
Yiu Lau, Jat Min Chuen, Shatin, NT;
tel: 2636 6113
Shatin Park Food Kiosk: Kiosk no 4, Shatin Park,
2 Yuen Wo Rd, Shatink, NT
The WARM Project (Wheelchair & Assistive
Device Re-engagement Movement): 1/F,
Flat A, Yee On Centre, 31 Yee On St, Kwun
Tong, Kln; tel: 2389 5568
Tuen Mun Family Store: Shop no 41-42, Chik
Lok Garden, Tuen Mun, NT; tel: 2618 2241

INDIA NATIONAL SECRETARIAT

Postal address: 37 Lenin Sarani (1st Floor), Dharamtala St, PO Box 8994,
Kolkatta – 700 013, West Bengal, India

Tel: [91] (0) 33 2227 5780 ®/2249 7210 (O); email:IND_Secretariat@ind.salvationarmy.org;
website: www.salvationarmy.org/ind

India is The Salvation Army's oldest mission field. Frederick St George de Latour Tucker, of the Indian Civil Service, read a copy of *The War Cry*, became a Salvationist and, as Major Tucker (later Commissioner Booth-Tucker), took the Indian name of Fakir Singh and commenced The Salvation Army's work in Bombay on 19 September 1882. The adoption of Indian food, dress, names and customs gave the pioneers ready access to the people, especially in the villages.

In addition to evangelistic work, various social programmes were inaugurated for the relief of distress from famine, flood and epidemic. Educational facilities such as elementary, secondary, higher secondary and industrial schools, cottage industries and settlements were provided for the depressed classes. Medical work originated in Nagercoil in 1893 when Captain (Dr) Harry Andrews set up a dispensary at the headquarters there. The medical work has grown from this. Work among the then Criminal Tribes began in 1908 at government invitation.

The Salvation Army is registered as a Guarantee Company under the Indian Companies Act 1913.

Publication: *The War Cry* (English)

THE National Secretariat for India serves the country's six territories. The Conference of Indian Leaders (COIL), established in 1989, meets annually to coordinate national Salvation Army affairs and give direction to the National Secretariat.

Several national offices had been established in earlier years, including the Editorial and Literary Office and the Audit Office.

Since the establishment of The Salvation Army Health Services Advisory Council (SAHSAC) in 1986 a regionally based National Secretariat evolved to provide support to many aspects of Salvation Army work in India.

An administrative reorganisation took place in 2008. This led to all the Secretariat departments being brought together in one building under the leadership of a National Secretary with the result that, for the first time, the National Secretariat can function as a whole and not as separate departments.

THE SALVATION ARMY ASSOCIATION

Chairman: Comr M. C. James
National Sec: Lt-Col K. C. David

Office Manager: Maj Sebagnanam Murial Joice
Business Administration: Maj Swinder Masih
Communications: Maj Ashok K. Dushing
Editorial and Publications: Maj Sanjivani Dushing (Editor)
Human Resources Development and Education: Capt Lalramliana Hnmte
Social, Health and Emergencies: Maj Jeevaratnam Darse
Women's Advisory Council: Capt C. Lalhriatpuii

THE SALVATION ARMY CHRISTIAN RETREAT CONFERENCE CENTRE

'Surrenden', 15-18 Orange Grove Rd, Coonoor – 643 101, Nilgiris Dt, Tamil Nadu, S India; tel: (0423) 2230242

Left: new motor cycles for officers engaged in extension work in **INDIA CENTRAL**

Below: praise at an **INDIA EASTERN** SAY (Salvation Army Youth) Congress

Below: prayer and Bible study at **INDIA SOUTH WESTERN**'s new Prayer Centre for Spiritual Empowerment

Below: the dedication of the Home League Centenary Retreat Centre in **INDIA SOUTH EASTERN**

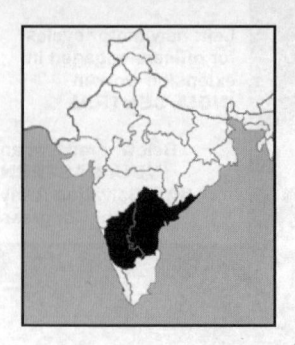

INDIA CENTRAL TERRITORY

Territorial leaders:
Commissioners M. Y. Emmanuel and T. Regina Chandra Bai

Territorial Commander:
Commissioner M. Y. Emmanuel (1 Dec 2006)

Chief Secretary:
Lieut-Colonel P. T. Abraham (1 Mar 2007)

Territorial Headquarters: 31 (15) Ritherdon Road, Vepery, Chennai 600 007

Postal address: PO Box 453, Vepery, Chennai 600 007, India
Tel: [91] (044) 2532 3148; fax: [91] (044) 2532 5987; email: ICT_mail@ICT.salvationarmy.org;
website: www.salvationarmy.org/ind

The India Central Territory comprises three regions – North Tamil Nadu (Madras-Chennai), Karnataka and Andhra Pradesh. Salvation Army work commenced at Vijayawada in Andhra Pradesh in 1895 by Staff Captain Abdul Aziz, a person of Muslim background, with his friend Mahanada. Captain Abdul attended a revival meeting led by Captain Henry Bullard in 1884 at Bangalore and subsequently dedicated himself to be a Salvation Army officer. The territory was named the India Central Territory in 1992, with its headquarters at Madras (Chennai).

Zone: South Asia
States included in the territory: Andhra Pradesh, Karnataka, Tamil Nadu
'The Salvation Army' in Tamil: Ratchania Senai; in Telugu: Rakshana Sinyamu
Languages in which the gospel is preached: English, Tamil, Telugu
Periodicals: *Home League Magazine*, *Udyogasthudu*, *Yovana Veerudu*, *Yudha Dwani*

WITH the theme 'Lift Up The Cup Of Salvation', outreach evangelism was given priority during the year and by the grace of God six new corps were opened. In Andhra Pradesh, which consists of 25 revenue districts, The Salvation Army had operated in only nine districts but extension work was started in a further eight. Salvationists are striving hard to now infiltrate the unreached areas.

One of the territory's visions had been to open a youth centre for the underprivileged and poor. Hopes were realised when, at Bapatla William Booth Junior College Campus, such a centre was constructed and opened by the Territorial Commander on 11 July 2008.

Training courses will be given in computer skills, spoken English, sewing and fashion design. For students who cannot bear the cost of further studies, some technical and vocational courses are taught which will help them find jobs. Only a

India Central Territory

nominal fee is taken from the students for these diploma courses.

A community college was opened at Virugambakkam, with financial support from Mr Jochen Tewes, the founder and General Secretary of Inter-mission Industrial Development Association (IIDA). This centre will enable poor and underprivileged young people to continue their higher education.

Two new hostels for girls were established at Tenali and Mandavalli. The children are sponsored by Salvationists and friends in the territory. An English medium school was started at Brahmanandapuram Corps.

In Stuartpuram a longstanding problem concerning encroachment of 43 acres of land has been resolved with the forming of a property affairs committee and the construction of a compound wall.

Self-help groups are progressing in the territory; there is a membership of 3,067 within 277 groups. The number of Salvation Army Medical Fellowship members increased from 222 to 328. During the year, 26 hospitals were visited by League of Mercy members. Home League Helping-Hand gifts realised a 10 per cent increase on the 2007-08 total.

The territory's officers regarded it a great privilege to have councils after a gap of three years and were re-energised by the theme 'He Makes His Ministers A Flame Of Fire'. It was a joyful opportunity for them – 495 active and 32 retired officers – to meet together to remember their covenant with God and have their spiritual lives strengthened.

Cadets of the Prayer Warriors Session participated in the councils on the last day.

STATISTICS
Officers 712 (active 528 retired 179) **Cadets** 31 **Employees** 510
Corps 270 **Outposts** 158 **Societies** 141 **Institutions** 14 **Schools and Colleges** 71 **Day Care Centres** 3 **Clinic** 1 **Homes and Hostels** 20
Senior Soldiers 6,9753 **Adherents** 8,268 **Junior Soldiers** 9,548

STAFF
Women's Ministries: Comr T. Regina Chandra Bai (TPWM) Lt-Col C. Mariamma Abraham (TSWM) Maj S. Vimalakumari (THLS) Maj Yesuamma (TLOMS) Maj Rajeswari (S&GSS) Maj D. Mani Kumari (TWDO)
Editor: Maj B. Annamani
Education: Maj A. Nathaniel
Emergencies: Maj O. Philip Raju
Field: Maj S. P. Abbulu
Finance: Maj John Kumar Dasari
Human Resources Development: Maj K. Yesudas
Music and Creative Arts: Capt Prabathkumar
Evangelism and Outreach: Maj M. Prakasha Rao
Property and Projects: Maj B. G. Prakash Rao
Social: Maj K. Yesu Dhana Kumar
Sponsorship: Capt I.D. Ebenezer
Trade: Maj Yesamma (O-i-C)
Training: Maj John Williams
Youth: Maj B. Joseph

DIVISIONS
Bapatla: Bapatla, Guntur District, 522 101; tel: (086432) 23931; Majs D. Joshi and Leela Mani
Chennai: 109 Gangadeeswara Koil St, Chennai 600 084; tel: (044) 2641 5021; Majs K. Suvarna Raju and K. Jhansi Bai
Eluru: Adivarapupet, Eluru, West Godavari District, 534 005; tel: (08812) 237484; Majs S. Jayananda Rao and Christiansen
Gudivada: Krishna District, 521 301; tel: (08764) 243524; Majs M. Daniel and M. Rachel Raju
Hyderabad: 6d Walker Town, Padmarao Nagar, Secunderabad, 500 025; tel: (040) 27502610; Majs G. V. Ratnam and Rajakumari

India Central Territory

Nellore: Dargamitta, Nellore, 524 003;
tel: (0861) 2322 589; Majs P. Samuel Rathan and P. Ananda Kumari

Rajahmundry: Mallayapet, East Godavari District, 533 105; tel: (0883) 5579200; Majs K. Y. Raj Kumar Babu and K. Y. Krupa Bai

Tanuku: West Godavari District, 534 211; tel: (08819) 225366; Majs K. Sundar Rao and K. Dasaratna Kumari

Tenali: Ithanagar, Tenali, Guntur District, 522 201; tel: (08644) 225949; Majs M.P.C.H. Prasad and Krupamma

Vijayawada: nr Gymkhana Club Eastside H. No 26-191/2, Ghandi Nagar, Vijayawada, 521 003; tel: (0866) 2575 168; Majs K. Samuel Raju and K. Raja Kumari

DISTRICTS

Bangalore: Karnataka Main Rd, J. P. Nagar, Bangalore 560 078, Karnataka State; Maj P. Rajan

Divi: PO Nagayalanka, Krishna District, 521 120; tel: (08671) 274991; Maj N. Jeeva Ratnam

Machilipatnam: The Salvation Army, Edepalli, Door No 15/344, Machilipatnam; Maj Chella Wycliff

Mandavalli: Station Rd, Mandavalli, Krishna District, 521 345; tel: (08677) 280503; Maj Chella Solomon Raju

Prakasam: Stuartpuram, Guntur District, 522 317; tel: (086432) 271131; Maj Valley Prabhadus

NEW EXTENSION AREAS
(under THQ)

Chittor: Extension Officer, The Salvation Army, c/o Kamalamma Samuel, D No 4 – 84, Balaji Nagar, Greamspet, Chittor

Kadapa: Extension Officer, The Salvation Army, c/o Mr M. Ajay Kumar, D No 2/147 – 3, Balaji Nagar, Kadapa – 515 003; tel: 09866077318

Khammam: Extension Officer, The Salvation Army, c/o Ch. Prabhakara Rao, D No 4-2-119, Sreenagar Colony, nr Mamatha Medical College, Khammam

Kurnool: Extension Officer, The Salvation Army, c/o Y. A. Evangeline, D No 40 – 448, A1A, Gipson Colony, Kurnool; tel: 09391107852

Mahabub Nagar: Extension Officer, The Salvation Army, Venkateswara Colony, behind Jagadhamba Temple, Laxmi Nager Colony, Mahabub Nagar District

Nalgonda: Extension Officer, The Salvation Army, H No 7-1-155/D/19/4, Aruna Nilayam, Srinagar Colony, Panagal Rd, Nalgonda PO and District

Rangareddy: Extension Officer, The Salvation Army, H No 20 – 45, Madhuranagar, Shamshebad, Rangareddy District

Warangal: Extension Officer, The Salvation Army, H No 7 – 91, Gorry Kunta Crossroad, Labour Colony, Warangal

TRAINING COLLEGE
Dargamitta, Nellore, 524 003; tel: (0861) 2322687

CONFERENCE AND TRAINING CENTRE
Vadarevu: Nr Chirala, Prakasam District

HUMAN RESOURCES DEVELOPMENT
PB9, Nidubrolu, Guntur District 522 123; tel: (08643) 243447

EDUCATION
College (with hostel for boys and girls)
William Booth Junior College, Bapatla, Guntur District, 522 101; tel: (086432) 24259

Community College
Virugambakkam, Chennai

High Schools (with hostels for boys and girls)
Bapatla: Guntur District, 522 101; tel: (086432) 24282 (acc 300)

Stuartpuram: Prakasham District, 522 317; tel: (086432) 271131 (acc 150)

Upper Primary School
Dargamitta, Nellore, Nellore District

Elementary Schools (Telugu Medium)
Bapatla Division: Bethapudi, Chintayapalem, Gudipudi, Kattivaripalem, Mallolapalem, MR Nagar, Murukondapadu, Valluvaripalem, Perlipadu, Pasumarthivaripalem, Pedapalli, Parli Vadapalem, Yaramvaripalem, Yazali

Eluru Division: Bhogapuram, Dendulur, Gopavaram, Gandivarigudem, Kovvali, Musunur, Pathamupparru, Surappagudem, Velpucharla

Gudivada Division: Chinaparupudi, Edulamadalli, Guraza, Gajulapadu, Gudivada, Kodur, Kancharlapalem, Kornipadu, Mandavalli, Narasannapalem, Pedaparupudi, Ramapuram

Nellore Division: Alluru, Buchireddipalem, Chowkacherla, Iskapalli, Kakupalli,

India Central Territory

Kanapartipadu, Mudivarthi, Modegunta, North Mopur, Pallaprolu, Rebala
Tenali Division: Annavaram, Burripalem, Chukkapallivaripalem, Duggirala, Danthuluru, Emani, Ithanagar, Kollipara, Kattivaram, Nambur, Nelapadu
Prakasam District: Cherukuru, Stuartpuram

Primary Schools (English Medium)
The Haven, 21 Thiru Narayanaguru Rd, Choolai, Chennai 600 112; tel: (044) 2661 2784
Teachers' Colony, Vijayawada 500 008, Krishna District; tel: (0866) 2479854
Hyderabad, 6D Walker Town, Padmarao Nagar PO, Secunderabad 500 025 (with day care centre)
Nidubrolu; Villivakkam and Chennai; Hosur-Karnataka

English Medium High School
Teachers' Colony, Vijayawada 500 008; tel: (0866) 2479854

English Medium Matriculation School
The Haven, 21 Tiru Narayanaguru Rd, Choolai, Chennai 600 112; tel: (044) 2661 2784

English Medium Upper Primary School
B. H. Puram, Mangalagir Post, Vijayawada

Residential School
Tissot Sunrise School, PB9 Bapatla, 522 101; tel: (086432) 23336 (acc 125)

Vocational Training Centre
Adivarpet, Eluru, West Godivari District, 534 005 (with boys' hostel); tel: (08812) 550070

MEDICAL WORK
Evangeline Booth Hospital: Nidubrolu, Guntur District, 522 123; tel: (08643) 2522124 (acc 100)
Evangeline Booth Hospital (with home for the aged), Bapatla, Guntur District, 522 101; tel: (086432) 24134 (acc 75)
Clinic: Dindi, Nagayalanka PO, Nagayalanka Mandal, Krishna District, 521 120

HIV/Aids Programme
The Salvation Army, H. No 7-1-155/D/19/4, Aruna Nilayam, Srinagr Colony, Panagal Rd, Nalagonda PO

SOCIAL WORK
Children's Homes and Hostels
Boys' Hostel, Mallayyapet, Rajahmundry; tel: (0883) 2427926 (acc 40)
Boys' and Girls' Hostel: Stuartpuram, Bapatla Mandal; tel: (08643) 71307 (acc 80, 8 girls)
Boys' Hostel: Virugambakkam, Chennai; tel: (044) 23772723 (acc 80)
Boys' and Girls' Hostel: Nellore; tel: (0861) 2340202 (acc 120)
Girls' Home and Old Age Home: Virugambakkam, Chennai; tel: (044) 23770400 (acc 70)
Girls' Hostel: Adivarpet, Eluru; tel: (08812) 226048 (acc 60)
Girls' Hostel: Nagayalanka; tel: (08671) 274512 (acc 24)
Girls' Hostel: Gudivada, Krishna District; tel: (08674) 240739 (acc 25)
Girls' Hostel: 'Home of Peace', Tanuku; tel: (08819) 229163 (acc 30)
Girls' Hostel: Catherine Booth Girls' Hostel, Tenali (acc 30)
Girls' Hostel: Miriam Girls' Hostel. Kaikaluru, Mandavalli (acc 30)
Hostel for Boys and Girls: c/o William Booth Junior College, Bapatla, Guntur District, 522 101; tel: (086432) 24259

Emergency Disaster Relief
c/o THQ, Chennai; tel: (044) 2665 0648

Working Women's Hostel
The Haven, 21 Thiru Narayanaguru Rd, Choolai, Chennai 600 112; tel: (044) 2532 1789

Day Care Centre
21 Thiru Narayanaguru Rd, Choolai, Chennai 600 112; tel: (044) 2532 1789

Red Shield Guest House
15/31 Ritherdon Rd, Vepery, Chennai 600 007; tel: (044) 2532 1821 (acc 60)

Waste Paper and Free Feeding Programmes
6D Walker Town, Secunderabad 500 025, AP
8 Perianna Maistry St, Periamet, Chennai-3

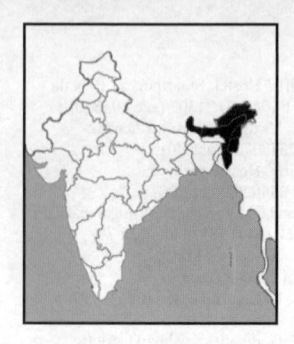

INDIA EASTERN TERRITORY

Territorial leaders:
Colonels Samuel and Bimla Charan

Territorial Commander:
Colonel Samuel Charan (1 Jul 2008)

Chief Secretary:
Lieut-Colonel Lalngaihawmi (1 Mar 2007)

Territorial Headquarters: PO Box 5, Aizawl 796001, Mizoram, India

Tel: [91] 389 2322290 (EPABX)/321864; fax: [91] 389 2326123;
email: IET_mail@IET.salvationarmy.org; website: www.salvationarmy.org/ind

Work in the region commenced on 26 April 1917 when Lieutenant Kawlkhuma, the first Mizo officer commissioned in India, returned to start the Army work. He was then joined by a group of earnest believers who shared his vision of an 'Army like a church, very much in line with The Salvation Army'. India Eastern became a separate command on 1 June 1991 and became a territory in 1993. Work was officially opened in Nepal on 26 April 2009

Zone: South Asia
States included in the territory: Arunachal Pradesh, Assam, Manipur, Meghalaya, Mizoram, Nagaland, Sikkim, Tripura, West Bengal; also the Federal Democratic Republic of Nepal (part)
'The Salvation Army' in Mizo: Chhandamna Sipai Pawl
Languages in which the gospel is preached: Adhibasi, Bengali, Bru, English, Hindi, Hmar, Manipuri (Meitei), Mizo, Nagamese, Nepali, Paite, Pali, Simte, Thadou, Vaiphai
Periodicals: *Sipai Tlangau* (Mizo *War Cry*), *The Officer* (Mizo), *Young Salvationist* (Mizo), *Chunnunpar* (Mizo Women's Ministries magazine)

THE General having given full approval to the commencement of Salvation Army ministry in Nepal, work in that country was officially opened by the Territorial Commander on 26 April 2009. Since 2005, several exploratory and support visits had been carried out by a group of officers and lay Salvationists. In 2007 an officer-couple was appointed to carry out further exploration and remained in the country for one year.

A Salvation Army fellowship, comprising around 20 members, is now meeting regularly under the Army flag. Majors Lalsangliana and Lalnunsangi have been appointed Extension Officer and Associate Extension Officer, stationed in Nepal's capital, Khatmandu.

As part of a reorganisation at divisional level, the creation of the Himalayan Division will ultimately strengthen the Army's witness in a non-Christian region.

Also to help meet the territorial leaders' aspirations of future growth, a youth campaign was launched

India Eastern Territory

throughout the territory whereby greater emphasis was given to the ministry among young people.

Nearly 3,500 delegates were attracted to the Territorial Youth Congress (31 October - 2 November 2008), with a large number attending from outreach areas where many unbelievers have come to faith. During this three-day event a mission night was observed and 73 young people dedicated their lives for mission work.

An early morning Bible study held at Chaltlang Corps was very much appreciated by the delegates. The Territorial SAY Songsters released their first CD album at the congress.

South Asia zonal leaders Commissioners Lalkiamlova and Lalhlimpuii were the main speakers at the Territorial Corps Cadet Congress (20-22 March 2009). This was another of the territory's significant events, with 1,368 delegates attending and 136 of them dedicating their lives to become officers. A march of witness through Lunglei preceded open-air meetings at two of the town's main locations.

Nine enthusiastic cadets of the Witnesses For Christ Session were ordained and commissioned as officers during Easter Sunday meetings led by Commissioner Lalkiamlova.

The territorial leaders declared 'Keep Yourself Pure' (1 Timothy 5:22 *New International Version*) as a slogan for 2009. It was a continuation of the previous territorial theme, 'Sanctify Yourselves'.

STATISTICS
Officers 288 (active 222 retired 66) **Cadets** 18 **Employees** 371
Corps 224 **Societies/Outposts** 120 **Social Institutions** 12 **Schools** 17
Senior Soldiers 35,002 **Adherents** 862 **Junior Soldiers** 9,641

STAFF
Women's Ministries: Col Bimla Charan (TPWM) Lt-Col Lalngaihawmi (TSWM) Maj Thantluangi (THLS) Maj Lalbiaktluangi (Dir, Special Services) Maj Thanzuali (LOMS) Maj K. C. Ropari (SAMF) Maj Vanlalnungi (WDO) Maj K. Lalchhuanmawii (OSS) Maj Biaksailovi (Prayer Fellowship Sec) Maj Lalchhuanmawii (Fund-raising Sec) Maj Hoihniang (Retired and Pensioned Fellowship Sec) Maj Zoawii (Literature Sec) Maj Ramthanmawii (Officers' Children Sec) Maj Maj. Lalfakzuali (FLC Sec) Lt Lalnunmawii (Asst to TPWM) Maj Zorammuani (i/c Provision Store) Maj Lalduhsangi (i/c Tailoring Centre)
Editor: Maj Vanlalfela
Property and Legal: Maj Jonathan Thanruma
Personnel: Maj Thanhlira
Community Health Action Network (CHAN): under THQ
Education: Maj Lalhriatpuia
Finance: Maj Shamu Meitei
Human Resources and Development: Maj Khaizadinga
Music and Creative Arts: Maj Chawnghluna
Outreach: Maj Hrangngura
Projects: Maj Shamu Meitei
Public Relations and Communications: Maj Khaizadinga
Social: Maj Lianhlira
Sponsorship: Maj Vanlalnungi
Territorial Bandmaster: B/M P.C. Lalchhandama
Territorial Songster Leader: S/L K. Zohmingthanga
Trade: Maj K. Lalrinawma
Training: Maj Laithanmawia
Youth and Candidates: Maj Zothanmawia

DIVISIONS
Central North: PO Aizawl, 796 001, Mizoram; tel: (0389) 2317097; Majs Sangchhunga and Vanlalauvi
Central South: PO Kulikawn 796005 Aizawl – Mizoram; tel: (0389) 2300246; Majs Lalhmingliana and Lalhlimpuii
Himalayan: 8 Bylane Zoo Narengi Rd, nr SBI

India Eastern Territory

Geeta Nagar Branch, PO Box 65, Guwahati –
781021 Assam; tel and fax: (0361) 2413405;
Majs S. T. Dula and Malsawmi
Manipur: Salvation Rd, PO Churachanpur,
795 128, Manipur; tel: (3874) 233188;
Majs Lianthanga and Ringliani
Southern: PO Lunglei, 796 701, Mizoram;
tel: (95372) 2324027; Majs C. Dawngliana
and H. Manthangi
Western: PO Kolasib, 796 081, Mizoram;
tel: (3837) 220037; Majs S. Biakliana and
Biakmawii

UNDER THQ
Nepal: PO Box 8975, EPC-1677, Kathmandu,
Nepal; tel: 00977-1-5537552;
mobile: 00977-9851093256;
email: sangliana@sify.com; Majs Lalsangliana
and Lalunsangi (Extension Officers)

TRAINING COLLEGE
Kolasib Vengthar, PO Kolasib, 796 081,
Mizoram; tel: (3837) 220466

EDUCATION
Special Residential Schools for the Physically Challenged
Mary Scott Home for the Blind: Kalimpong,
West Bengal; tel: (3552) 255252;
email: sa_msh_kpg@yahoo.co.in (acc 80)
School for Deaf and Dumb Children: Darjeeling,
West Bengal; tel: (354) 2252332/2257645
email: sadeaf@sify.com (acc 50)

Higher Secondary Schools
Children's Training Higher Secondary School:
Churachandpur, Manipur; tel: (3874) 235097
Modern English Higher Secondary School:
Aizawl, Mizoram; tel: (389) 2323248

High Schools
Blue Mount: Behliangchhip, Zampui, Tripura
Booth Tucker Memorial School: Gahrodpunjee,
Cachar
Hermon Junior: Moreh, Manipur
School for the Blind (Junior High School):
Kalimpong

Middle Schools
Children's Education School: Zezaw, Manipur
Children's Training School: Singngat, Manipur
Booth Tucker: Thingkangphai, Manipur
Hermon Junior: Moreh, Manipur
SA Middle School: Saikawt, Manipur
School for the Deaf: Darjeeling
Willow Mount: Durtlang, Mizoram

Primary School
Integrated Primary School: Kolasib

Outreach Schools: 27

SOCIAL WORK
Home for Boys and Girls
Mary Scott Home for the Blind: Kalimpong,
West Bengal
Hostel for the Deaf and Dumb: Darjeeling, West
Bengal

Homes for Boys
Hostel for the Blind: Kolasib, Mizoram;
tel: (3837) 220236 (acc 25)
Enna In: Kolasib; tel: (3837) 221419 (acc 30)
Kawlkhuma Home: Lunglei; tel: (372) 224420
(acc 25)
Muanna In: Mualpui, Aizawl; tel: (389) 2320426
(acc 30)
Manipur Boys' Home: Mualvaiphei,
Churachandpur; tel: (3874) 235469 (acc 25)
Orphanage, Saiha: tel: (3835) 226140 (acc 15)
Silchar Home (acc 20)

Home for Girls
Hlimna In: Keifang, Mizoram; tel: (389) 2862278
(acc 65)

Motherless Babies' Homes
Aizawl: Tuikal 'A', Aizawl, Mizoram;
tel: (389) 2329868 (acc 35)
Manipur: Mualvaiphei, Churachandpur,
Manipur; tel: (3874) 235469 (acc 10)

Community Caring Programme
Churachandpur, Manipur; tel: (3874) 235469

Deafness Reduction Programme
Darjeeling, West Bengal

HIV/AIDS PROGRAMME
Community Health Action Network (CHAN)
Kawlkhuma Bldg, Tuikal 'A', PO Box 5,
Aizawl 796001; tel: (389) 2320202/2327609;
fax: (389) 2326106;
email: chanaizawl@sancharnet.in

CENTENARY PRESS
PO Box 5, Tuikal 'A', Aizawl, Mizoram;
tel: (389) 2329626

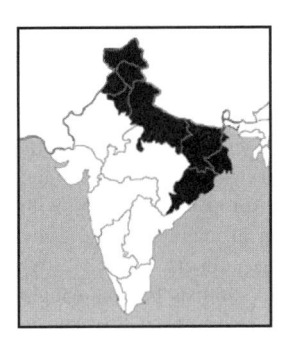

INDIA NORTHERN TERRITORY

Territorial leaders:
Commissioners Kashinath and Kusum Lahase

Territorial Commander:
Commissioner Kashinath Lahase
(1 Jan 2006)

Chief Secretary:
Lieut-Colonel Paul Christian
(1 Dec 2006)

Territorial Headquarters: Flat No 103, Aashirwad Complex, D-1, Green Park, New Delhi 110 016, India

Tel: [91] (11) 2651 2394; fax: [91] (11) 2651 6912; email: INT_mail@INT.salvationarmy.org;

website: www.salvationarmy.org/ind

Shortly after arriving in India in 1882, Booth-Tucker visited major cities in northern India, including Allahabad, Delhi, Lucknow, Benares and Kolkata (Calcutta). Rural work was established later and operations were extended to Bihar and Orissa. The boundaries of the India Northern Territory have changed over the years; there have been headquarters in Gurdaspur, Bareilly, Lucknow, Benares and Kolkata and more recently Delhi. In 1947, part of the territory became Pakistan. The present territory was established on 1 June 1991.

Zone: South Asia
The territory is comprised of: the States of Bihar, Chattisgarh, Haryana, Himachal Pradesh, Jammu and Kashmir, Orissa, Punjab, Uttar Anchal, Uttar Pradesh, West Bengal; the Union Territories of Delhi, Chandigarh, and the Andaman and Nicobar Islands
'The Salvation Army' in Hindi, Punjabi and Urdu: Mukti Fauj
Languages in which the gospel is preached: Bengali, English, Hindi, Kui, Nepali, Oriya, Punjabi, Santhali, Tamil, Urdu
Periodicals: *Home League Yearly* (Hindi and English), *Mukti Samachar* (Hindi and Punjabi), *The Officer* (Hindi), *Yuva Sipai* (Hindi)

TWENTY-SEVEN new soldiers were enrolled at Chandigarh during the visit of South Asia zonal leaders Commissioners Lalkiamlova and Lalhlimpuii. Fifteen soldiers were enrolled at Nawan Pind Corps by the Territorial Commander, and at Tilak Nagar a whole family was enrolled.

Three new corps were opened – at Hoshiarpur (Mukerian District), Fathehgarh (Dera Baba Nanak Division) and Sonarpur (West Bengal Division) – and three extension areas are being pioneered in Patiala (Punjab), Shahjahanpur (Utter Pradesh) and Bajpur (Utter Anchal).

The territory also praises God for the 47 cadets who entered the train-

India Northern Territory

ing college for the Prayer Warriors Session (2008-10).

Salvation Army relief teams distributed supplies to flood victims in Midnapur and other districts in West Bengal where the properties and lives of poverty-stricken people had been devastated.

In Bihar the relief team, assisted by Major William Berthau (from the Canada and Bermuda THQ Social Services Department), provided winter kits to flood victims. The kits (made up of tarpaulin for making a temporary shelter; sheets, blankets and a plastic or jute mat for bedding; shawls; woollen clothing for children) were distributed to more than 4,000 people in 750 families.

People receiving daily meals at the free feeding programme in Kolkata and New Delhi are being influenced to attend Sunday meetings on a regular basis. Many are from non-Christian backgrounds but seeds of faith are being sown in their lives.

Also in New Delhi and Kolkata, many street children who find their livelihood from the garbage and waste tips are being taken care of by The Salvation Army and their lives are being transformed.

Nearly 300 women's self-help groups are functioning successfully in the territory, among them 20 formed in Andaman as part of the Indian Ocean Tsunami Project. Staff visit the groups to conduct weekly meetings with members, encouraging them to save small amounts of money, start small businesses with their savings, and combat diseases through health and sanitation education.

Women's Ministries staff at THQ have begun teaching tailoring and embroidery to women officers with the intention of manufacturing 'Sally Ann' trading products.

When Salvationists became caught up in violence against Christians in the state of Orissa two prayer halls, an officers' quarters and the boys' home in Paburia were destroyed. The home housed nearly 40 boys, aged six to 15 years, who studied in a nearby government school.

As the anti-Christian mob destroyed the home, the officer-in-charge took his wife and family, gathered the boys together and fled for their lives. For three days they hid in the jungle, without food or shelter and in heavy rain.

On the fourth day, hungry and exhausted, they sought help from the leaders of a Hindu community. Following contact with the district magistrate, the group was taken to a relief camp which had been established by the Government. There the children were soon reunited with their parents.

STATISTICS
Officers 446 (active 356 retired 90) **Cadets** 47 **Employees** 265
Corps 146 **Outposts** 384 **Societies** 859 **Institutions** 33 **Schools** 9 **College** 1
Senior Soldiers 60,094 **Adherents** 2,933 **Junior Soldiers** 8,187

STAFF
Women's Ministries: Comr Kusum K. Lahase (TPWM) Lt-Col Anandi Christian (TSWM) Maj Mariam Parkash (THLS)

India Northern Territory

Church Growth: Maj Robin Kumar Sahu
Editor: Maj Yaqoob Masih
Education and Disaster: Maj Tarsem Masih
Field: Maj Parkash Masih
Finance: Maj Thomas Gera
Human Resources: Maj Dilip Singh
Legal and Community Development:
  Maj Samir Patra
Music Ministry: Maj Salamat Masih
Property and Projects: Maj Kashmir Masih
Public Relations and Fund-raising:
  Capt Robin
Social: Maj Joginder Masih
Sponsorship: Maj Simon Peter
Training: Maj Raj Kumar
Youth/Candidates: Maj Philip Nayak

DIVISIONS

Amritsar: 25 Krishna Nagar, Lawrence Rd, Amritsar 143 001, Punjab; Majs Makhan and Sunila Masih

Angul: Angul 759 122, Orissa; tel: 06764-232829; Maj Sabita Das

Bareilly: 220 Civil Lines, Bareilly 243 001, UP; tel: 0581-2427081; Majs Lazar and Sharbati Masih

Batala: Dera Baba Nanak Rd, Batala 143 505, Dist Gurdaspur, Punjab; tel: 01871-243038; Majs Gurnam and Razia Masih

Beas: Ajeet Nagar, Beas, Amritsar 143 201, Punjab; tel: 01853-273834; Majs Gian and Salima Masih

Chandigarh: Surajpur Rd, Firojpur, PO Dhamala Via Pinjore, Dist Panchkula, Haryana 134 102; tel: 01733-654946; Majs Vijayapal and Roseleen Singh

Dera Baba Nanak: Dist Gurdaspur, PO Dera Baba Nanak 143 604, Punjab; tel: 01871-247262; Majs Daniel and Parveen Gill

Gurdaspur: Jail Rd, Dist Gurdaspur 143 521, Punjab; tel: 01874-220622; Majs Piara and Grace Masih

Kolkata: 37 Lenin Saranee, Kolkata 700 013; tel: 033-55101 591; fax: 033-22493910; Majs Manuel and Anita Masih

Moradabad: Kanth Rd, near Gandhi Ashram PAC, Moradabad 244 001; Majs Manga and Roseleen Masih

DISTRICTS

Jasidih: Deoghar Rd, Ramchanderpur, Jasidih, Jharkand – 814 142; Maj Chotka Hembrom
Mukerian: Rikhipura Mohalla, Dist Hoshiyarpur, Mukerian – 144 211, Punjab; tel: 01883-248733; Maj Peter Masih

EXTENSION WORK

Pathankot: Daulatpur Rd Prem Nagar, nr FCI Godwan, Pathankot, Punjab; tel: 09815-358238; Maj Samuel Masih

Patiala: c/o Davinder Singh, House 346, Street 7, Bajwa Colony, Patiala – 147001, Punjab; Maj Gurcharan Masih

Port Blair: near Income Tax Office, Shadi Pur, Port Blair – 744101, Andaman Nicobar Islands; Capt Arun Biswas

Shahjahanpur: c/o Mr. Sarvesh Singh, House 19, Shri Malaram Enclave, Vill Chinour, Post Paina Buzurg, Dist Shahjahanpur, UP – 242001; Capt Sanjay Robinson

Taran Taran: Sandhu Ave, nr Shota Kazi Kot Rd, Ward 11, Taran Taran, Dist Amritsar, Punjab; Maj Piara Lal

Uttar Anchal – Bajpur: c/o Mr Matloob Masih, Indira Colony, Baria Rd, Bajpur Udham Singh Nagar – 261 401, Uttara Khand; mobile: 91-9758635462; Maj Masih Dayal

TRAINING COLLEGE

Bareilly: 220 Civil Lines, Bareilly 243 001, UP; tel: 0581-2423304

MEDICAL WORK

Hospital

MacRobert Hospital: Dhariwal, Dist Gurdaspur 143 519, Punjab; tel: 01874-275152/275274 (acc 50)

Clinics

Social Service Centre: 172 Acharya Jagdish Chandra Bose Rd, Kolkata 700 014; tel: 033-22840441

Community Health Centre: 192-A, Arjun Nager, New Delhi 110 029; tel: 011-26168895

Eye Hospital: Surajpur Rd, Firojpur, PO Dhamala via Pinjore, Dist Panchkula, Haryana 134 102; tel: 01733-654946

EDUCATION

Senior Secondary School

Aliwal Rd, Batala 143 505, Dist Gurdaspur, Punjab; tel: 01871-242593 (acc 900)

Extension Branch

Gurdaspur School: The Salvation Army DHQ Compound, Jail Rd, Dist Gurdaspur, Punjab; tel: 01874-20622

English Medium Schools

Behala: 671 D. H. Rd, Hindustan Park, Behala, Kolkata 700034; tel: 033-23972692
Moradabad: Kanth Rd, opp Gandhi Ashram

India Northern Territory

PAC, Moradabad 244 001, UP;
tel: 0591-2417351/2429184; (acc 400)
William Booth Memorial School: 220 Civil Lines,
Bareilly 243001, UP; tel: 0581-2420007;
(acc 200)

College
Catherine Booth College for Girls: Aliwal Rd,
Batala 143 505, Dist Gurdaspur, Punjab;
tel: 01871-242593 (acc 300)

Non-residential Tailoring Units
Dera Baba Nanak: Dist Gurdaspur, Punjab
Kancharapada: West Bengal
New Delhi: H-15, Green Park Extn, New Delhi – 110 016

SOCIAL WORK
Free Feeding Programme
Kolkata: 172 Acharya Jagadish Chandra Rd,
Kolkata 700 014; (beneficiaries 250)
New Delhi: 6 Malik Bldg, Chunamundi,
Paharganj, New Delhi 110 055;
tel: 011-23588433; (beneficiaries 150)

Homes for the Aged
Bareilly: 220 Civil Lines, Bareilly 243 001, UP;
tel: 0581-2421432 (acc 20)
Dhariwal: MacRobert Hospital, Dhariwal,
Dist Gurdaspur 143 519, Punjab;
tel: 01874-275152/275274 (acc 20)
Kolkata: 172 Acharya Jagadish Chandra Rd,
Kolkata 700 014 (acc 15)

Homes for Boys
Angul: Angul 759 122, Orissa;
tel: 06764-232829 (acc 10)
Batala: Aliwal Rd, Batala 143 505, Dist Gurdaspur (acc 60)
Kolkata: 37 Lenin Saranee, Kolkata 700 013; tel: 033-55124567 (acc 30)
Moradabad: Kanth Rd, Moradabad 244 001, UP; tel: 0591-2417351 (acc 40)
Paburia: At/PO-Paburia, Dist Kandhamal, 762 112 (Orissa); tel: 06847-264063 (acc 30)
Simultala: Simultala 811 316, Dist Jamui, Bihar (acc 43)

Homes for Girls
Angul: Angul 759 122, Orissa;
tel: 06764-232829 (acc 40)
Bareilly: 220 Civil Lines, Bareilly 243 001, UP; tel: 0581-2421432 (acc 40)
Batala: Aliwal Rd, Batala 143505, Dist Gurdaspur (acc 60)
Behala: 671 D. H. Rd, Hindustan Park, Behala, Kolkata 700034; tel: 033-23972692 (acc 120)
Gurdaspur: Jail Rd, Dist Gurdaspur 143 521, Punjab (acc 100)

Hostels
Blind (Men)
172 Acharya Jagdish Chandra Rd, Kolkata 700 014 (acc 30)

Working Men and Students
172 Acharya Jagdish Chandra Rd, Kolkata 700 014; tel: 033-22840441 (acc 200)

Young Women
Bareilly: 220 Civil Lines, Bareilly 243 001, UP; tel: 0581-2421432
Kolkata: 38 Lenin Saranee, Kolkata 700 013; tel: 033-22274281 (acc 50)
Ludhiana: 2230, ISA Nagari, Ludhiana – 141 008, Punjab

RED SHIELD GUEST HOUSE
Kolkata: 2 Saddar St, Kolkata 700 016; tel: 033-22861659 (acc 80)

TRANSIT HOUSE
New Delhi: P-2 S Extension, Part II, New Delhi 110 049; tel: 011-2625 7310

WASTE PAPER DEPARTMENT
6 Malik Bldg, Chunamundi, Paharganj, New Delhi 110 055; tel: 011-2358 8433

Below: A village head oversees the distribution of cyclone relief supplies in West Bengal

INDIA SOUTH EASTERN TERRITORY

Territorial leaders:
Commissioners M. C. and Susamma James

Territorial Commander:
Commissioner M. C. James (1 Dec 2006)

Chief Secretary:
Lieut-Colonel Thumati Vijayakumar (1 May 2008)

Territorial Headquarters: High Ground Road, Maharajanagar PO, Tirunelveli – 627 011, Tamil Nadu, India
Tel: [91] (462) 2574331/2574313; fax: [91] (462) 2577152;
email: ISE_mail@ISE.salvationarmy.org; website: www.salvationarmy.org/ind

The Salvation Army commenced operations in south-east India on 27 May 1892 as a result of the vision received by Major Deva Sundaram at Medicine Hill, while praying and fasting with three officers when the persecution in Southern Tamil Nadu was at its height. On 1 October 1970 the Tamil-speaking part of the Southern India Territory became a separate entity as the Army experienced rapid growth.

Zone: South Asia
States included in the territory: Pondicherry, Tamil Nadu
'The Salvation Army' in Tamil: Ratchaniya Senai; in Malayalam: Raksha Sainyam
Languages in which the gospel is preached: English, Malayalam, Tamil
Periodicals: *Chiruveeran* (Tamil), *Home League Quarterly*, *Poresatham* (Tamil), *The Officer* (Tamil)

A PROCESSION and rally in Nagercoil, bringing the entire Salvationist community into a mammoth gathering on 27 February 2009, demonstrated the strength of The Salvation Army in Tamil Nadu State and made a significant impact on the Government. The purpose of this peaceful demonstration was to claim the status as other Christians and to ask the Government to include Dalit Christians in the scheduled caste list and not discriminate on the basis of religion.

Another vital issue has been to empower Salvationists who are economically underprivileged to obtain Government approval to undertake Bachelor of Science nursing courses so that more Salvationist nurses could be trained and subsequently earn a decent living. The Territorial Commander took various initiatives in order to receive the Tamil Nadu Government's approval.

Salvation Army ministries are carried out predominantly among the oppressed and those people who have no access to formal education. Two committed Salvationist teachers who served for many years were honoured when retiring from

India South Eastern Territory

Government service. In response they decided to continue their service by helping in the field of education and engaging in corps ministry.

Officers councils, held soon after the introduction of the territorial theme, 'Walking With Christ', enriched the fellowship of officers who serve in areas many miles from each other. A half-night of prayer and opportunities to share concerns enhanced their spiritual bonding.

During the Territorial Youth Camp hundreds of young people responded to the call to holy living and many of them considered officer training after they complete their schooling. Youth Mission Teams and Sports Ministries programmes were organised in all divisions.

The territory was blessed by several visitors from overseas, especially Lieut-Colonel Wayne Pritchett (Secretary for International Training and Leader Development, IHQ) who advised on training methodology and was a great source of help to training college staff.

On Commissioning Day 24 cadets signed their covenants at the training college as they made their lifelong commitment to God's service. In the evening they were ordained and commissioned as officers by the TC. The new forces would strengthen existing corps and be used in planting new openings within the territory.

STATISTICS
Officers 620 (active 454 retired 166)
  Employees 811
Corps 273 **Outposts** 124 **Societies** 75
Schools 19 **Institutions** 45
Senior Soldiers 47,470 **Adherents** 17,228
  Junior Soldiers 4,939
Personnel serving outside territory Officers 16

STAFF
Women's Ministries: Comr L. Susamma James (TPWM) Lt-Col Keraham Manikyam (TSWM) Maj Retnam (THLS)
Community Health Development: Mr Benjamin Dhaya
Editor: Maj Yesudian Ponnappan
Education and Social: Maj Chelliah Mony
Field: Maj Arulappan Paramadhas
Finance: Maj Jebamony Jayaseelan
Human Resources: Maj Chellian Anbayan
Projects: Maj Ponniah Ashok Sundar
Property and Legal: Maj Appavoo Sam Devaraj
Public Relations: Maj Abraham Jeyasekhar
Supplies: Maj Subanantharaj Appaji (in charge)
Training: Maj Jeyaraj Daniel Jebasingh Raj
Youth and Candidates: Maj Yacob Selvam

DIVISIONS
Azhagiapandipuram: KK Dist PO, 629 852; tel: (04652) 281952; Lt-Cols Appavoo William and Thavamony
Kanyakumari: Kadaigramam, Suchindram PO, KK Dist 629 704; tel: (04652) 243955); Majs Sundaram Motchakan and Selvabai
Kulasekharam: Kulasekharam PO, 629 161 KK Dist; tel: (04651) 279446; Majs Chelliah Swamidhas and Joicebai
Marthandam: Pammam, Marthandam PO, 629 165; tel: (04651) 272492; Majs Perinbanayagam Suthananthadhas and Esther Evangelin
Nagercoil: Vetturnimadam PO, Nagercoil 629 003; tel: (04652) 272787; Majs Tharmar Alfred and Rajabai
Palayamcottai: 28 Bell Amorses Colony, Palayamcottai 627 002; tel: (0462) 2580093; Majs Job William and Daisybai
Radhapuram: Radhapuram PO, 627 111; tel: (04637) 254318; Majs Asirvatham Devadhas and Jothi Vasanthakumari
Tenkasi: Tenkasi PO, 627 811; tel: (04633) 280774; Majs Nallathambi Edwin Sathyadhas and Gnana Jessi Bell
Thuckalay: Mettukadai, Thuckalay PO, 629 175; tel: (04651) 252443; Majs Devasundaram Samuel Raj and Kanagamony
Valliyoor: Valliyoor PO, 627 117; tel: (04637) 221454; Majs Jeyaraj Samraj and Jessie

India South Eastern Territory

DISTRICTS
Coimbatore: Daniel Ngr, K. Vadamaduai PO, 641 017; tel: (0422) 2461277; Maj Daniel Dhason

Erode: 155 Amman Nager, Erode 638 002; tel: (0424) 2283909; Maj S. Yesuretinam

Madurai: TPK Rd, Palanganatham PO, 625 003; tel: (0452) 2370169; Maj Geevanantham Kumaradhas

Trichy: New Town, Malakovil, Thiruvarumbur 620 013; tel: (0431) 2510464; Maj Yovan Dhason

Tuticorin: 5/254 G, Caldwell Colony, Tuticorin 628 008; tel: (0461) 2376841; Maj Sebagnanam James

Pondicherry Extension Area: opp Mahatma Dental College, Kamaraj Ngr, Goremedu Check Post, Pondicherry 605 006; tel: (0413) 2271933; Maj Masilamony Yesudhason

TRAINING COLLEGE
WCC Rd, Nagercoil 629 001; tel: (04652) 231471

RED SHIELD HOUSE AND RETREAT CENTRE
Muttom, via Nagercoil 629 202; tel: (04651) 238321

MEDICAL WORK
Catherine Booth Hospital: Nagercoil 629 001; tel: (04652) 275516/7; fax: (04652) 275489; Administrator: Maj S. P. Simon

COMMUNITY HEALTH AND DEVELOPMENT PROGRAMMES
Catherine Booth Hospital, Nagercoil 629 001; tel: (04652) 272068
Women's Micro-credit and Health Programme; Community-based HIV/Aids Care and Support Programmes; Reproductive and Child Health Programme Community Health Centre; Voluntary Counselling and Testing Centre cum STD Clinic Programme; Community Eye Health Programme

EDUCATION
Higher Secondary School (mixed)
Nagercoil 629003; tel: (04652) 272647; Headmaster: Mr M. Kingsly

Matriculation Higher Secondary School (mixed)
Nagercoil; tel: (04652) 272534; Principal: Mr Monickadhas

Middle School (mixed)
Nambithoppu Middle School; Headmaster: Mr Vethamuthu

Noble Memorial High School
Valliyoor; tel: (04637) 220380; Headmaster: Mr A. Benjamin

Village Primary Schools: 9

Nursery and English Medium Primary Schools: 6

SOCIAL SERVICES
Hostels
Boys' Hostel: Nagercoil; tel: (04652) 272953 (acc 72)
Noble Memorial Boys' Hostel: Valliyoor; tel: (04637) 221289 (acc 70)
Tucker Girls' Hostel: Nagercoil; tel: (04652) 231293 (acc 135)
Girls' Hostel: Thuckalay; tel: (04651) 252764 (acc 100)

Motherless Babies' Home
Palayamcottai 627 002; tel (0462) 2584441

Child Development Centres
Chemparuthivilai, Chemponvilai, Kadaigramam, Madurai, Nagercoil, Pondicherry, Thuckalay, Valliyoor

Vocational Training Centre for the Physically Handicapped (Men and Boys)
Aramboly 629 003; tel: (04652) 263133

Vocational Training Centre for Women and Home League Retreat Centre
Nagercoil 629 003; tel: (04652) 232348

Rural Development and Vocational Training Centre
Chemparuthivilai 629 166; tel: (04651) 253292

Vocational Training Institute
Kilkothagiri Junction, 643 216 Nilgris

Industrial Training School
Aramboly; tel: (04652) 262198

RETIRED OFFICERS' HOME
Catherine Booth Hospital, Nagercoil 629 001

INDIA SOUTH WESTERN TERRITORY

Territorial leaders:
Colonels Jayapaul and Yesudayamma Devarapalli

Territorial Commander:
Colonel Jayapaul Devarapalli (1 Jul 2008)

Chief Secretary:
Lieut-Colonel Masilamony Ponniah (1 Jul 2008)

Territorial Headquarters: The Salvation Army, Kowdiar, Thiruvananthapuram, Kerala

Postal address: PO Box 802, Kowdiar, Thiruvananthapuram 695 003, Kerala State, India
Tel: [91] (471) 2314626/2723238; fax: [91] (471) 2318790;
email: ISW_mail@ISW.salvationarmy.org; website: www.salvationarmy.org/ind

Salvation Army work commenced in the old Travancore State on 18 March 1894 by Captain Yesudasen Sanjivi, who was a high-caste Brahmin before his conversion. His son, Colonel Donald A. Sanjivi, became the first territorial commander from Kerala. The work spread to other parts of the state through the dedication of pioneer officers, including Commissioner P. E. George. The India South Western Territory came into being on 1 October 1970 when the Southern India Territory divided into two. The territory has its headquarters at Thiruvananthapuram and comprises the entire Malayalam-speaking area known as Kerala State.

Zone: South Asia
State included in the territory: Kerala
'The Salvation Army' in Malayalam: Raksha Sainyam; in Tamil: Ratchania Senai
Languages in which the gospel is preached: English, Malayalam, Tamil
Periodicals: *Home League Quarterly* (Malayalam/English), *The Officer* (Malayalam), *Youdha Shabdam* (Malayalam), *Yuva Veeran* (Malayalam)

A PRAYER Centre for Spiritual Empowerment, opened by the Territorial Commander, is being seen as the realisation of the territory's vision for a centre to provide Salvationists with spiritual nourishment and church growth training. For 31 days after the opening, powerful messages blended with miracles and wonders as round-the-clock prayer ascended to Heaven from the centre.

Bible studies for officers, local officers and soldiers were organised at territorial headquarters and in divisional forums, instilling into people a greater desire to know more of God's Word.

Special evangelistic campaigns during vacation and festival seasons were a thrilling experience. Open-air meetings were held in towns and remote villages, and the gospel was shared during house-to-house visitation and at gatherings in corps halls. Revival meetings renewed the souls and minds of people throughout the territory.

Divisional rallies for women highlighted a healthy competition among home leagues in the various corps as they sought to win the divisional shield through members' Bible knowledge, recruitment successes and their contributions towards Helping-Hand Scheme projects.

The Women's Ministries Department conducted skill-training programmes and organised weekly prayer meetings to petition God's blessing on The Salvation Army and pray for people's well-being.

Mission support and community projects helped to raise the status of women and children in society, promoted savings and income-generating programmes in poorer communities through women-empowerment and self-help programmes, and addressed various health issues.

There has been a spiritual awakening among young people. During the year under review there were 43 applications for officership. The involvement of youth in corps activities increased; for example, junior soldiers at Trivnadrum Central formed a prayer cell as an outcome of the inspiration they gained from their corps Brengle Institute.

Salvation Army children's homes maintain an excellent reputation among the communities in which they are located. There have been more applications for places than could be accommodated as children from impoverished, orphaned and broken families continued looking for admission into Army homes.

STATISTICS
Officers 693 (active 449 retired 244) **Cadets** 24 **Employees** 174
Corps 333 **Societies and Outposts** 460 **Schools** 16 **Institutions** 20
Senior Soldiers 41,568 **Adherents** 15,374 **Junior Soldiers** 3,879
Personnel serving outside territory Officers 12

STAFF
Women's Ministries: Col Yesudayamma Devarapalli (TPWM) Lt-Col Sathiabama Ponniah (TSWM) Maj Lillybai Samuelkutty (TLOMS) Maj Elizabeth Solomon (SSFS)
Business Administration: tba
Editor: Maj Charles V. John
Education: Maj Simson Samuelkutty
Field: tba
Finance: Maj K. M. Gabriel
Human Resources Development: Maj N. S. George
Projects: Maj C. J. Bennymon
Property: Major P. S. Johnson
Social and Legal: Maj John Suseelkumar
Territorial Evangelist and Church Growth Sec: Maj K. M. Solomon
Training: Maj John Samuel
Youth and Candidates: Maj O. P. John

DIVISIONS
Adoor: Adoor 691 523; tel: 0473-4229648; Majs P. V. Stanly Babu and Nirmala Stanly Babu
Cochin: Erumathala PO, Alwaye 683 105; tel: 0484-2638429; Majs C. S. Yohannan and L. Rachel Yohannan
Kangazha: Edayirikapuzha PO, Kangazha 686 541; tel: 0481-2494773; Majs P. J. Yohannan and Annamma Yohannan
Kattakada: Kattakada 695 572; tel: 0471-2290484; Majs Sam Immanuel and Rachel Immanuel
Kottarakara: Kottarakara 691 506; tel: 452650; Majs Rajan K. John and Susamma Rajan
Malabar: Veliyamthode, Chandakunnu PO, Nilambur 679 342; tel: 2222824; Majs D. Sathiyaseelan and Aleyamma Sathiaseelan

India South Western Territory

Mavelikara: Thazhakara, Mavelikara 690 102; tel: 2303284; Majs N. J. George and M. C. Ruth George

Nedumangadu: Nedumangadu 695 541; tel: 2800352; Majs T. J. Simon and Ammini Simon

Neyyattinkara: Neyyattinkara 695 121; tel: 2222916; Majs P. K. Philip and Rachel Phillip

Peermade: Kuttikanam PO, Peermade 685 501; tel: 232816; Majs Rajamani Christuraj and Mary Christuraj

Tiruvella: Tiruvella 689 101; tel: 2602657; Majs Davidson Daniel and M. V. Estherbai Davidson

Thiruvananthapuram: Parambuconam, Kowdiar PO, Thiruvananthapuram 695 003; tel: 2433215; Majs M. Samuel and K. Thankamma Samuel

DISTRICTS

Kottayam: Manganam PO, Kottayam 686 018; tel: 0481-2577481; Maj D. Gnanadasan

Punalur: The Salvation Army, PPM PO, Punalur; tel: 0475-2229218; Maj V. D. Samuel

TRAINING COLLEGE

Kowdiar, Thiruvananthapuram 695 003; tel: 2315313

TERRITORIAL PRAYER CENTRE FOR SPIRITUAL EMPOWERMENT

Kowdiar PO, Thiruvanathapuram 695 003; tel: 0471-2723237

MEDICAL WORK

Evangeline Booth Community Hospital: Puthencruz 682 308; tel: Ernakulam 2731056

Evangeline Booth Leprosarium: Puthencruz 682 308; tel: Ernakulam 2730054 (acc 200)

General Hospital: Kulathummel, Kattakada 695 572 Thiruvananthapuram Dist; tel: Kattakada 2290485 (acc 60)

Medical Centres: Kanghaza 686 541, Edayappara; tel: Kangazha 2494273 (acc 12)

EDUCATION

Higher Secondary School (mixed)
Thiruvananthapuram 695 003; tel: 2315488 (acc 1,371)

Primary Schools: 15 (acc 2,640)

SOCIAL WORK

Boys' Homes
Kangazha 686 541 (acc 30)
Kottarakara 691 506 (acc 30)
Kowdiar, Thiruvananthapuram 695 003 (acc 20)
Mavelikara 690 102 (acc 25)

Community Development Centres
North: Trikkakara – Cochin 682 021
South: Konchira, Thiruvananthapuram 695 607; tel: 0472-2831540

Girls' Homes
Adoor 691 523 (acc 25)
Kowdiar, Thiruvananthapuram 695 003 (acc 24)
Nedumangad 695 541 (acc 30)
Peermade, Kuttikanam 685 501 (acc 30)
Thiruvalla 689 101; tel: 0469-2831540 (acc 25)

Vocational Training Centre for Women
Nedumangad 695 541 (acc 25)

Young Men's Training Centres
Thazhakara, Mavelikara 690 102
Thiruvananthapuram 695 003

Printing Press
Kowdiar, Thiruvananthapuram 695 003; tel: 0471 2725358

ITI and Computer Training Centre
Kowdiar, Thiruvananthapuram; tel: 2318524

Tailoring Centres
Adoor, Cochin, Kangazha, Kattakada, Kottarakara, Malabar, Neyyattinkara, Peermade

Young Women's Hostel (Goodwill Hostel)
Thiruvananthapuram 695 003; tel: 2319917 (acc 20)

Working Women's Hostel
Thrikkakara, B. M. C. PO, Ernakulam

Youth Centre
Kowdiar, Thiruvananthapuram 695 003

RED SHIELD GUEST HOUSES

Kowdiar, Thiruvananthapuram 695 003; tel: 0471-2319926
Kovalam, Thiruvananthapuram; tel: 0471 2485895

RETIREMENT COTTAGES FOR OFFICERS

Thiruvananthapuram (cottages 4)

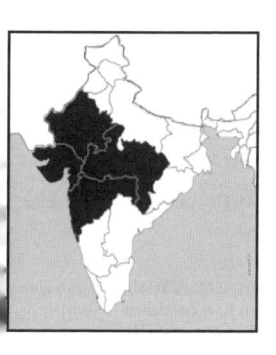

INDIA WESTERN TERRITORY

Territorial Commander:
Commissioner P. Mary Rajakumari
(1 Aug 2007)

Chief Secretary:
Lieut-Colonel Lalramhluna (1 May 2007)

Territorial Headquarters: Sheikh Hafizuddin Marg, Byculla, Mumbai 400 008

Postal address: PO Box 4510, Mumbai 400 008, India
Tel: [91] (022) 2308 4705/2307 1140; fax: [91] (022) 2309 9245;
email: IWT_mail@iwt.salvationarmy.org; website: www.salvationarmy.org/ind

The Salvation Army began its work in Bombay (later Mumbai) in 1882 as a pioneer party led by Major Frederick Tucker and including Veerasoriya, a Sri Lankan convert, invaded India with the love and compassion of Jesus. Bombay (Mumbai) was the capital of Bombay Province, which included Gujarat and Maharashtra, and the first headquarters in India was in a rented building at Khatwadi. From these beginnings the work of God grew in Bombay Province. Various models of administration were tried for the work in Gujarat and Maharashtra until the India Western Territory was established in 1921.

Zone: South Asia
States included in the territory: Gujarat, Maharashtra, Madhya Pradesh, Rajasthan
'The Salvation Army' in Gujarati and Marathi: Muktifauj
Languages in which the gospel is preached: English, Gujarati, Hindi, Marathi, Tamil
Periodicals: *Home League Quarterly* (Gujarati and Marathi), *The Officer* (Gujarati and Marathi), *The War Cry* (Gujarati and Marathi), *The Young Soldier* (Gujarati and Marathi)

DISCOVERING and targeting new openings was the territory's aim during the year under review and, by God's grace, it led to The Salvation Army making inroads into many areas. Shouts of 'Hallelujah!' echoed around the hills of South Gujarat, where nearly 30 new corps were opened. Two started in Rajasthan and three in Madhya Pradesh – new extension areas that will be elevated to the status of districts.

A Salvationist in India Eastern Territory has taken a keen interest in work in the Sangli Extension and is generously sponsoring six corps helpers.

'Non-stop' campaigns were conducted in Dharampur, the biggest tribal town of South Gujarat, where three non-Christian families were converted and joined the Army. Many non-Christians evidenced a great change in these families' lives.

More than 500 people attended an open-air meeting and a number of people of other faiths who were suffering from various illnesses received God's healing power.

As part of the youth programme

in Maharashtra and Gujarat a Bible oratory challenge attracted 2,877 participants. A further 1,866 young people from both regions attended the territory's Bible quiz, an event at which they were encouraged to study God's Word and get to know more about Jesus.

As part of the anti-sex trafficking ministry in five areas of Maharashtra, a children's drop-in centre was opened at Sangli. The issue of sex trafficking is already being addressed in Mumbai. Contact has been made with more than 1,300 women involved in prostitution, and of the 16 rescued from the sex trade eight were minors.

Through the Army's CARE programme and support project nearly 1,300 people living with HIV/Aids were reached and 528 families given training on home-based preventative care. Nearly 100 self-help groups were established, with 1,215 members as beneficiaries.

The Social Foundation Trust presented Captains Sunil and Jaymala Salve with the Sujan Sunman Award for their work with the Army's HIV/Aids awareness programme and their coordinating of a blood and eye donors scheme.

Twenty churches in Mumbai participated in a singing competition and the choir from the Army's hostel for blind working men was awarded first prize. For the third consecutive year the English Medium School in Gujarat had excellent results of 100 per cent.

STATISTICS
Officers 596 (active 376 retired 220) **Cadets** 24 **Employees** 260
Corps 250 **Outposts** 342 **Institutions** 20 **Day Schools** 11
Senior Soldiers 35,776 **Adherents** 3,755 **Junior Soldiers** 9,006

STAFF
Women's Ministries: Comr P. Mary Rajakumari (TPWM) Lt-Col Kawlramthangi (TSWM) Maj Indumati G. Christian (THLS - Gujarati) Maj Sudina Gaikwad (THLS - Marathi); Maj Sophia Macwan (LOMS - G) Maj Kusum Tribhuvan (LOMS - M) Maj S. Retnabai (SAMF - G) Maj Shobha Jadhav (SAMF - M) Maj Sheila Mandgule (SSM - M) Maj Margaret Macwan (SSM - G) Maj Ruth Mahida (ROS - G) Maj Ratnamala Randive (ROS - M)
Editor: Lt Jaishri Pawar (Marathi) (pro tem) Maj Ruth Macwan (Gujarati)
Education: Maj Punjalal U. Macwan (Gujarati)
Field: Maj Gabriel I. Christian (Gujarat) Maj Benjamin Gaikwad (Maharashtra)
Finance: Maj Jashwant D. Mahida
Human Resources: Maj Phulen Macwan (Gujarat) Maj J. P. Salve (Maharashtra)
Property and Development: Maj Vijay Dalvi (Maharashtra)
Property: Maj Jashwant Mahida (Gujarat)
Public Relations: Maj Benjamin Randive
Social: Maj Punjalal U. Macwan (Gujarat) Maj B. P. Jadhav (Maharashtra)
Training: Maj Nicolas Damor (Gujarat); Maj Ratnakar D. Kale (Maharashtra)
Youth: Maj Yakub G. Macwan (Gujarat) Maj Ashok Mandgule (Maharashtra)

DIVISIONS
Gujarat
Ahmedabad: Behrampura, Ahmedabad 380 022; tel: (079) 2539 4258; Majs Jashwant and Sunita Macwan
Anand: Amul Dairy Rd, Anand 388 001; tel: (02692) 240638; Majs David K. and Vimlaben Sevak
Matar: Behind Civil Court, Matar District Kheda 387 530; tel: (02694) 285482; Majs Paul and Febiben Maganlal
Nadiad: Nadiad, District Kheda, 387 002; tel: (0268) 2558856; Majs Jashwant S. and Indiraben Chauhan
Panchmahal: Dohad, Panchmahal, 389 151; tel: (02673) 221771; Majs Rasik P. and Ramilaben Christian

India Western Territory

Petlad: Sunav Rd, Post Petlad, District Anand, 388 450; tel: (02679) 221527; Majs Prabhudas J. and Persis Christian

South Gujarat: Khambla Zampa, PO Vansda, 396 580District Navsari; Majs Kantilal K. and Eunice K. Parmar

Maharashtra

Ahmednagar: Fariabagh, Sholapur Rd, 414 001; tel: (95241) 358194; Capts Sanjay and Sunita Wanjare

Mumbai: Sankli St, Byculla, Mumbai 400 008; tel: (022) 2300 3990; Majs Suresh and Martha Pawar

Pathardi: Pathardi, District Ahmednagar, 414 102; tel: (952428) 223116; Majs Devdan L. and Mariyabai Kasbe

Pune: 19 Napier Rd, 411 040; tel: (9520) 2636 3198; Majs Surendra and Helenabai Chopde

Satara: Satara, District Satara 415 001; tel: (952162) 234006; Majs Pramod and Shanta Kamble

Shevgaon: Shevgaon, District Ahmednagar, 414 502; tel: (952429) 223191; Majs Bhausaheb and Pushpa Magar

Shrirampur: District Ahmednagar, 413 709, Tal Shrirampur; Majs Philip B. and Rebecca Jadhav

EXTENSION

Sangli: Majs Sunil and Sunita Waghmare

TRAINING COLLEGES

Gujarat: Anand 388 001, District Anand, Amul Dairy Rd; tel: (02692) 254801

Maharashtra: Fariabagh, Ahmednagar 414 001; tel: (95241) 2355950

EDUCATION

Boarding Schools (Boys and Girls)

William Booth Memorial Children's Home and Hostel: Anand 388 001, District Anand, Gujarat; tel: (2692) 255580 (acc 226)

William Booth Memorial Primary and High Schools: Farlabagh, District Ahmednagar, 414 001, Maharashtra; tel: (022) 95241 2324267 (acc 513)

Day Schools

Anand:
William Booth Memorial High School, Amul Dairy Rd; tel: (2692) 254901 (acc 276)
English Medium Primary School (acc 260)
William Booth Primary School (acc 476)

Ashakiran: Primary School, Satara; under DHQ (acc 130)

Dahod: English Medium School (acc 210)

Dynanjot: English Medium School, Vishrantwadi, 411 015; tel: (9520) 2669 2761 (acc 25)

Muktipur: PO Bareja 382 425, District Ahmednabad; tel: 02718 233318 (acc 93)

Mumbai: Tucker English Medium School, Sankli St, Byculla, Mumbai 400 008; tel: (022) 307 7062 (acc 652)

Vadodara: English Medium School: Chhani Rd, Vadodra; tel: (0265) 277 5361 (acc 150)

MEDICAL WORK

Emery Hospital: Anand, District Anand, Gujarat; address: Amul Dairy Rd, 388 001; tel: (2692) 253737 (acc 160)

Evangeline Booth Hospital: Ahmednagar 414 001, Maharashtra; tel: (022) 95241 2325976 (acc 172)

Community-Based Aids Programme and Confidential Aids Counselling Clinic: Byculla, Mumbai; tel: (022) 2309 3566

HUMAN RESOURCES DEVELOPMENT CENTRES

Anand (Gujarat): Faujabad Comp, Ananda 388 001

Ahmednagar (Maharashtra): tel: (022) 95241 2358489

SOCIAL WORK

CARE Programme Centre

Byculla, Mumbai; tel: (022) 309 3566; Community Based Aids Programme, Confidential Aids Counselling Clinic, Aruna Children's Programme, Asha Deep Tailoring Programme

Farm Colony

Muktipur 382 425, Post Bareja, District Ahmedabad; tel: (02718) 33318

Feeding Programme

Mumbai (under King Edward Home); tel: (022) 23071346

Homes
Children

Mumbai: Sion Rd, IOB Bldg, Sion (E) 400 022; tel: (022) 2409 4405 (acc 170)

Hope House, Pune: Gidney Park, Salisbury Park Plot 41 No 554/2 Pune 411 037; tel: 9529 24271728 (acc 50)

India Western Territory

Elderly Men
Mumbai 400 008: 122 Maulana Azad Rd, Byculla; tel: (022) 23071346; (acc 50)

Industrial
King Edward Home: 122 Maulana Azad Rd, Byculla, Mumbai 400 008; tel: (022) 2307 1346

Physically Handicapped Children
Joyland, Anand 388 001, District Anand, Gujarat; tel: (02692) 251891 (acc 60)

Ray of Hope Home
Vansda (under DHQ) (acc 60)

Hostels
Blind Working Men
Ahmedabad: Locoshed, Rajpur-Hirpur, Ahmedabad, Gujarat; tel: (079) 2294 1217; (acc 40)

Mumbai 400 008: Sankli St, Byculla; tel: (022) 2305 1573 (acc 70)

Young Men
Satara: c/o DHQ; tel: (952162) 234006 (acc 30)

Young Women
Anand: District Kheda, Gujarat; tel: (02692) 254499 (acc 50)
Baroda: Nava Yard, Chhani Rd, Vadodara; tel: (0265) 2775361
Mumbai 400 008: Concord House, Morland Rd, Byculla; tel: (022) 2301 4219 (acc 63)
Pune: c/o DHQ, 19 Napier Rd, Pune 411 040 (acc 16)

RED SHIELD HOTEL
30 Mereweather Rd, Fort, Mumbai 400 039; tel: (022) 2284 1824; fax: (022) 2282 4613 (acc 450)

ITALY: Having just enrolled them as soldiers of Rome Corps, the General prays for the command's newest reinforcements – three Italians and three from Kenya, representing the increasingly international corps family (*see pages 153-154*)

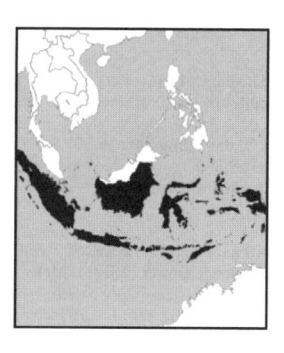

INDONESIA TERRITORY

Territorial leaders:
Commissioners Basuki and Marie Kartodarsono

Territorial Commander:
Commissioner Basuki Kartodarsono
(1 Oct 2006)

Chief Secretary:
Colonel Ross Gower (1 Feb 2009)

Territorial Headquarters: Jalan Jawa 20, Bandung 40117
Postal address: Post Box 1640, Bandung 40016, Indonesia
Tel: [62] (22) 4207029/4205056; fax: [62] (22) 423 6754;
website: www.salvationarmy.or.id

The Salvation Army commenced in Indonesia (Java) in 1894. Operations were extended to Ambon, Bali, East Kalimantan, Sulawesi (Central, North and South), Sumatra (North and South) and East Nusa Tenggara, Aceh and Papua. A network of educational, medical and social services began.

Zone: South Pacific and East Asia
Country included in the territory: Indonesia
'The Salvation Army' in all Indonesian languages: Bala Keselamatan
Languages in which the gospel is preached: Indonesian with various dialects such as Batak, Daa, Dayak, Javanese, Ledo, Makassarese, Moma, Niasnese, Tado and Uma

THE highlight of 2008 was the visit of then South Pacific and East Asia zonal leaders Commissioners Barry and Raemor Pobjie for a territorial review and the ordination and commissioning of 20 officers of the God's Fellow-Workers Session. The commissioners then attended the annual Territorial Leadership Conference in Salatiga, Central Java, in which the territorial leaders introduced the theme for 2009 – 'Jesus Christ Is Our Great Shepherd'.

In addition, a workshop was held for the first time for corps leader sergeants from East and West Palu Divisions and Java-Bali Division. Their faithfulness and dedication is greatly appreciated because of their deep concern for congregations in areas where there is an insufficient number of corps officers.

God answered prayers when local government permission was given to open an outpost on Batam Island, south of Singapore, and the building was dedicated to God's glory on 20 December 2008.

The outpost's opening means The Salvation Army is now ministering in 20 of Indonesia's 33 regions. Also, several new corps buildings were opened and two outposts – Padena (East Palu Division) and Eben Haezer (Central Sulawesi) – were elevated to corps status.

Lieut-Colonels Graham and Rhondda Durston (then CS and TSWM, The Philippines) conducted a Brengle Institute in two areas.

Salvostore, a two-storey building located in the THQ compound, was opened on 10 December 2008. It will supply the territory with Salvation Army resources and other Christian material such as books and CDs.

February 2009 saw a further significant event when, in the predominantly Muslim area of Nangroe Aceh Darusallam, God's name was honoured as the territory handed over 500 newly built houses to people who had been made homeless by the 2004 tsunami in Meulaboh, West Aceh.

Following the dedication ceremony the Territorial Commander signed over the plaque attesting the presence of The Salvation Army in Leuhan Subdivision. The plaque was countersigned by the Regent of West Aceh.

Prior to the territory's National Congress in July 2009, several social services projects were implemented. They included harelip surgery to 67 patients (in collaboration with the Obor Berkat Foundation), cataract surgery to 177 patients, groceries distribution and an HIV/Aids seminar.

STATISTICS

Officers 700 (active 561 retired 139) **Cadets** (1st Yr) 19 (2nd Yr) 18 **Employees** 1,671
Corps 274 **Outposts** 119 **Kindergartens** 7 **Primary Schools** 64 **Secondary Schools** 18 **High Schools** 5 **Technical High School** 1 **Hospitals** 6 **Theological University** 1 **Clinics** 20 **Academies for Nurses** 2 **Social Institutions** 20
Senior Soldiers 27,056 **Adherents** 16,524 **Junior Soldiers** 7,880
Officers serving outside Territory 4

STAFF

Women's Ministries: Comr Marie Kartodarsono (TPWM), Col Annette Gower (TSWM) Maj Anastasia Poa (HL)
Sec for Business Administration: Lt-Col Pieter Siagian
  Asst Business Sec: Maj Yusak Tampai
  Finance: Maj Yusak Tampai
  Audit: Maj Yohanes Sayuti
  Property: Maj Sutrisno Suherman
  Information Technology: Kadek White
Sec for Programme: Lt-Col Selly Poa
  Social Services: Maj Widiawati Tampai
  Corps Growth and Education: Maj Made Petrus
  Legal and Parliament: Maj Sasmoko Hertjahjo
  Youth and Children's Ministries: Capt Alberth Sarimin
Sec for Personnel: Lt-Col Yohannes Sayuti
  Officers' Training and Development: Maj Margaretha Petrus
  Candidates: Maj Risma Manurung

Literature and Editorial: Maj Sasmoko Hertjahjo
Projects: Capt Nyoman Timonuli
Public Relations: Maj Spener Tetenaung Jl. Kramat Raya 55, Jakarta Pusat; tel: (021) 391 4518; fax: (021) 392 8636
Training: Maj Gidion Rangi

DIVISIONS

East Regional Indonesia: Jl Dr Sutomo No 10, Makasar; tel/fax: (0411) 312 919; Majs Made Sadia and Syastiel Lempid
Jawa and Bali: Jalan Dr Cipto 64b, Kelurahan Bugangan, Semarang 50126, Jateng; tel: (024) 355 1361; Maj Mulyati Mitra Sumarta
Kulawi: Bala Kesalamatan Post Office, Kulawi 94363, Sulteng; tel/fax: (0451) 811 017; Majs Indra and Helly Mangiwa
Manggala (Mamuju Manggala – Central Sulawesi): c/o Jalan Miangas 1-3, Palu 94112; Majs Sadrackh and Patricia Lanto
Palu Timur (East Palu): Jalan Miangas 1, Kantor Pos Palu 94112; tel: (0451) 426 821; fax: (0451) 425 846; Lt-Cols Mesak and Mona Losso

Indonesia Territory

Palu Barat (West Palu): Jalan Miangas 1-3, Palu 94112, Sulteng; mobile: 0816 4304498; Majs Wayan and Herlina Widyanoadi

Sulawesi Utara (North Sulawesi): Jalan A. Yani 15, Manado 95114; tel/fax: (0431) 864 052; Majs Jones and Mariyam Kasaedja

Sumatera Utara: Jl. Sei Kera 186 Medan 20232, Sumatera Utara; tel: (061) 4510284; Maj Marthen Pandorante

DISTRICTS
Under Jawa and Bali Division
  East Kalimantan: Maj Ezra Mangela
Under East Palu Division
  Kamarora: Capt Yonas Parese
  Maranatha: Maj Jantje Kasumba
  Palolo: Capt Yahya Benyamin
Under West Palu Division
  Dombu: Maj Elias Sale
  Pakawa: Capt Bambang Tadewatu
  Porame: Maj Pifser Sango
  Rowiga:
  Wawugaga: Capt Yusdimer Momi
Under Manggala Division
  Bunggu I: Capt Aser Yupa
  Bunggu II: Capt Gunawan Mantaely
  Dombu: Maj Gidion Rikko
  Malino:
Under Kulawi Division
  Gimpu: Maj I. Ketut Putrayasa
  Kantewu:
  Karangana: Capt Janji Rusanto
  Lindu: Capt Victor R. Tahadi
  Tobaku: Capt Hendry Simanjuntak
Under North Sumatera Division
  Nias: Capt Arifin Pasaua

OFFICER TRAINING COLLEGE
Jalan Kramat Raya 55, Jakarta 10450, PO Box 3203, Jakarta 10002; tel: (021) 310 8148; fax: (021) 391 0410

EDUCATION
Central Sulawesi: 79 schools (acc 6,539), 1 theological university (acc 60)
East Kalimantan: 1 school (acc 42)
Jawa: 8 schools (acc 777)
Kalawara: 4 schools (acc 400)
North Sumatra: 2 schools (acc 303)
South Sulawesi: 3 schools (acc 257)

MEDICAL WORK
General Hospitals (Jawa)
Bandung: Bungsu Hospital, Jalan Veteran 6; tel: (022) 423 1550/1695; fax: (022) 423 1582 (acc 49) (poli-clinic attached)

Semarang: William Booth Hospital, Jalan Let Jen S. Parman 5 Semarang, 50232; tel: (024) 841 1800/844 8773; fax: (024) 844 8773 (acc 100) (eye and general clinic attached)

Surabaya: William Booth Hospital, Jalan Diponegoro 34; tel: (031) 561 4615/4616/5349; fax: (031) 567 1380 (acc 200) (maternity hospital and 3 poli-clinics attached)

Turen: Bokor Hospital, Jalan Jen A. Yani 89, Turen near Malang; tel: (0341) 824 453/002; fax: (0341) 823 878 (acc 150) (poli-clinic and outpost clinic attached)

General Hospitals and Clinics (Sulawesi)
Palu: Woodward Hospital, Jalan L. H. Woodward 1, Kantor Pos Palu, Sulawesi Tengah; tel: (0451) 421 769/482 914/426 361; fax: (0451) 423 744 (acc 110)

Branch Hospitals
Ampera: under Woodward Hospital
Kulawi: Bethesda Hou Popakauria

Clinics
Ambon, East Kalimantan, Gimpu, Kamarora, Kantewu, Lembah Tongoa, Towulu
Sulawesi Utara: Kantor Pos Amurang, Kumelembuai, Makasili, Sulut

Maternity Hospital
Makassar, Sulawesi Selatan: Catherine Booth Mother and Child Hospital, Jalan Arif, Rate 15 or Post Box 33; tel: (0411) 873 803/852 344; fax: (0411) 873 803 (acc 53, poli-clinic attached)

Academies for Nurses' Training
Palu: under Woodward Hospital (acc 200)
Surabaya: under William Booth Hospital (acc 200)

SOCIAL WORK
Babies' and Toddlers' Home
Surabaya: Matahari Terbit, Jalan Kombes Pol Durjat 10-12, Surabaya 60262; tel: (031) 534 1132; fax: (031) 532 2118 (acc 60)

Boys' Homes
Bandung: Maranatha, Jalan Dr Cipto 7; tel: (022) 423 0480 (acc 80)
Denpasar, Bali: William Booth Home, Jalan Kebo Iwa No 29, Banjar Liligundi, Ubung Kaja, Denpasar, Bali (acc 200)
Kalawara: Bahagia, Kantor Pos Palu, Sul Teng (acc 60)

On a visit to Indonesia to inspect Salvation Army ministries in that territory, Commissioner Raemor Pobjie (IHQ) pauses to play with children who are in the Army's care

Medan: William Booth Home, Jalan K. L. Yos Sudarso 10, Lorong 1A; tel: (061) 661 3840 (acc 90)

Semarang: Betlehem, Jalan Musi Raya 2, Kel Rejosari, Semarang 50125; tel: (024) 355 3287 (acc 80)

Surabaya: Imanuel, Jalan Gatotan 36; tel: (031) 352 2932 (acc 60)

Tompaso: Wisma Anugerah, Post Box 1100, Manado/Desa Liba, Kecamatan Tompaso 95693, Kab Minahasa; tel: (0431) 371 524 (acc 80)

Yogyakarta: Tunas Harapan, Jalan Kenari 7, Miliran Post Box 1095; tel: (0274) 563598 (acc 32)

Children's Homes

Bandung: William Booth Home, Jalan Jawa 18; tel: (022) 420 5549 (acc 90)

Denpasar: Anugerah, Jalan Hos Cokroaminoto 34; tel/fax: (0361) 426 484 (acc 60)

Jakarta: Catherine Booth Home, Pondok Cabe (acc 100)

Malang: Elim, Jalan Panglima Sudirman 97; tel: (0341) 362 905 (acc 80)

Manado: Bukit Harapan, Jalan Arnold Manonutu 501, Post Box 118; tel: (0431) 863 394 (acc 60)

Medan: Evangeline Booth Home, Jalan Samanhudi 27; tel: (061) 414 2148 (acc 80)

Palu: Sejahtera, Jalan Maluku 18, Palu 94112; tel: (0451) 424 586 (acc 80)

Centre for Homeless People

Semarang: Eben Haezer, Jalan Dr Cipto 64a, Kelurahan Bugangan, Semarang 50126, Jateng; tel: (024) 771 0501/354 2536 (acc 100) (dairy farm attached)

Eventide Homes

Bandung: Senjarawi, Jalan Jeruk 7; tel: (022) 727 1369 (acc 100)

Semarang: Bethany, Jalan Musi Raya 4-6; tel: (024) 354 4855 (acc 60)

Turen: Tresno Mukti, Jalan Achmad Yani 180; tel: (0341) 825 290 (acc 50)

Students' Hostels

Bandung: Jalan Dr Cipto 7; tel: (022) 423 0480 (acc 32)

Bandung: Jalan Jawa 18; tel: (022) 420 5549 (acc 32)

Medan: Jalan Samanhudi 27; tel: (061) 414 2148 (acc 30)

Surabaya: Jalan Gatotan 36; tel: (031) 352 2932 (acc 24)

Yogyakarta: Jalan Kenari 7, Miliran; tel: (0274) 563 598 (acc 8)

Transient House

Jalan Kramat Raya 55; tel: (021) 391 4518 (acc 18)

THQ GUEST HOUSE

Jalan Jawa 20; tel: (022) 420 7029 (acc 10)

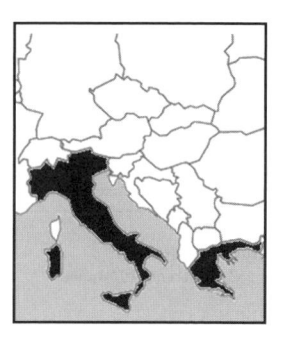

ITALY COMMAND

Command leaders:
Lieut-Colonels Daniel and Eliane Naud

Officer Commanding:
Lieut-Colonel Daniel Naud (1 Sep 2009)

General Secretary:
Major Massimo Tursi (1 Aug 2007)

Command Headquarters: Via degli Apuli 39, 00185 Rome, Italy

Tel: [39] 06 4462614/06 4941089; fax: [39] 06 490078;
email: Italy_Command@ity.salvationarmy.org; website: www.esercitodellasalvezza.org

The Salvation Army flag was unfurled in Italy on 20 February 1887 by Major and Mrs James Vint and Lieutenant Fanny Hack, though subsequent difficulties necessitated withdrawal. In 1890 Fritz Malan (later lieut-colonel) began meetings in his native village in the Waldensian Valleys. In 1893 Army work was re-established. In a decree of the President on 1 April 1965, The Salvation Army was recognised as a philanthropic organisation competent to acquire and hold properties and to receive donations and legacies. It received legal status as a religious body/church on 20 March 2009.

On 8 October 2007 The Salvation Army began operations in Greece, the work being linked to the Italy Command with the command leadership giving guidance and support to future development. Thessaloniki was identified as the centre of the new undertaking and Captains Polis Pantelidis and Maria Konti-Galinou, UK officers of Greek nationality, were entrusted with the task of launching the Army's mission in their home country.

Zone: Europe
Countries included in the command: Greece, Italy
'The Salvation Army' in Italian: Esercito della Salvezza; in Greek: O Stratos Tis Sotirias
Languages in which the gospel is preached: Greek, Italian
Periodicals: *Il Bollettino dell' Unione Femminile, Il Grido di Guerra*

WITH the President of the Republic's decree of 20 March 2009, the legal status of the religious body/church *Esercito della Salvezza in Italia* (The Salvation Army in Italy) with headquarters in Rome was recognised and approved, as well as the Constitution composed of 21 articles. Salvationists are grateful to God for this State recognition, which gives a firm legal foundation on which the Army in Italy can build.

The Army continues to reach out to people in Christ's name in both Italy and Greece. Converts have been won and soldiers recruited. Much encouragement was received when a married couple became the first soldiers to be enrolled in Greece. They are now training for officership in the UK, along with an Italian cadet.

Six soldiers of Rome Corps – three Italians and three from Kenya, representing the increasingly international corps family – were enrolled by General Shaw Clifton on Palm

Italy Command

Sunday 2009 when he and Commissioner Helen Clifton led weekend meetings during what he termed 'a tour of encouragement'.

During Pentecost weekend 2008, then Europe zonal leaders Commissioners Hasse and Christina Kjellgren presided over the opening of newly refurbished worship and community halls in Turin.

The musical *The Witness* was translated into Italian and presented by young people from different parts of the country. Performances were given in the north and south of Italy.

In the summer the Ministry of Internal Affairs contacted The Salvation Army for assistance in dealing with large numbers of refugees arriving in the country. From October 2008 until March 2009 accommodation in the Army's premises in Atena Lucana (Salerno) was given to 50 asylum seekers from eight different countries. Many people commented on the meaningful spiritual ministry carried out by Salvationists.

In Greece, Captains Polis Pantelidis and Maria Konti-Galinou continue contacting many people in need on the streets of Thessaloniki. A number of women have found the Lord and left the sex industry thanks to weekly visits of the 'Open Doors' team in the red light district. Weekly Bible study and soldiership preparation classes are taking place.

Salvationists in Italy give strong support to the work in Greece through prayer and practical means. The Helping-Hand Scheme contributes to a 'safe house' project and the purchase of Bibles.

STATISTICS
Officers 51 (active 27 retired 24) **Auxiliary-Captains** 4 **Auxiliary-Lieutenants** 2 **Employees** 10
Corps 17 **Outposts** 15 **Institutions** 7
Senior Soldiers 263 **Adherents** 102 **Junior Soldiers** 37

STAFF
General's Personal Representative to the Vatican: Lt-Col Daniel Naud
Women's Ministries (and Resources): Lt-Col Eliane Naud (CPWM) Maj Anne-Florence Tursi (CSWM)
Finance: Capt Patricia Pavoni
Family Tracing: Maj Angela Dentico
Youth: Capt Adriana De Nicola
Candidates: Maj Lidia Bruno

SOCIAL WORK
Centre for the Homeless
Centro Virgilio Paglieri, Via degli Apuli 41, 00185 Roma; tel: 06 4451351; fax: 06 4456306 (acc 225)

Workers' Lodge
Villa Speranza, Contrada Serra 57a, 85100 Potenza; tel/fax: (0971) 51245 (acc 15)

Holiday Centres
Le Casermette, Via Pellice 4, 10060 Bobbio Pellice (To); tel/fax: (0121) 957728; email: direzione@centrovacanzebobbio.it (acc 120)
Concordia, Via Casa di Majo 32-36, 80075 Forio d'Ischia (Na); tel/fax: (081) 997324; email: concordia@esercitodellasalvezza.org (acc 65)
L'Uliveto, Via Stretta della Croce 20, 84030 Atena Lucana (Sa); tel/fax: (0975) 76321 (acc 70)

Guest Houses
Florence: Villa delle Rose, Via Aretina 91, 50136 Firenze; tel/fax: (055) 660445 email: davidcavanagh@esercitodellasalvezza.org (acc 13)
Rome: Foresteria, Via degli Apuli 41, 00185 Roma; tel/fax: 06 44 51 351; email: foresteriaroma@esercitodellasalvezza.org (acc 70)

GREECE
1A Notara la Pylaia, GR 555 35, Thessaloniki, Greece; tel: 00 30 2310 315027; email: polis@salvationarmy.gr; Capts Polis Pantelidis and Maria Konti-Galinou

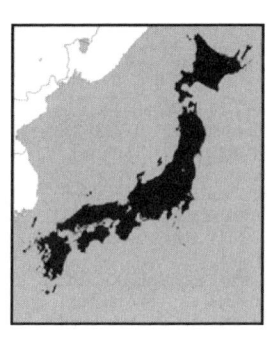

JAPAN TERRITORY

Territorial leaders:
Commissioners Makoto and Kaoru Yoshida

Territorial Commander:
Commissioner Makoto Yoshida (1 Jun 2006)

Chief Secretary:
Lieut-Colonel Naoshi Hiramoto (1 Mar 2004)

Territorial Headquarters: 17, 2-chome, Kanda Jimbocho, Chiyoda-ku, Tokyo 101-0051, Japan

Tel: [81] (03) 3237 0881; fax: [81] (03) 3237 7676; website: www.salvationarmy.or.jp

In 1895 a small group of pioneer officers from Britain arrived in Japan at Yokohama to start operations. In spite of great difficulties, work was soon established. Of several outstanding Japanese who were attracted to The Salvation Army, the most distinguished was Commissioner Gunpei Yamamuro OF, prominent evangelist and author, whose book *The Common People's Gospel* has been reprinted more than 500 times.

Zone: South Pacific and East Asia
Country included in the territory: Japan
Language in which the gospel is preached: Japanese
Periodicals: *Home League Quarterly, The Officer, The Sunday School Guide, Toki-no-Koe, Toki-no-Koe Junior*

THE territory's different themes for the past three years have focused on sharing the gospel, relying on the growth God gives and claiming his promise of hope. Linked with those has been an ongoing focus on integrated mission. The territory is now intentionally working on bringing together each department's area of work as far as possible.

For the first time in the territory's history Salvationist and non-Salvationist employees were brought together to focus purely on the Movement's mission. A Salvation Army seminar sought to help them see the need for integrated mission. Seminars for staff at medical and social institutions also provided a better understanding of the Army's ethos.

March 2009 saw the conclusion of a three-year community development project in Papua New Guinea, carried out in partnership with JICA (Japan International Cooperation Agency) and with the support of PNG Territory. It included the installation of a clean drinking water supply, improvement of hygiene and sanitary conditions, and capacity-building of the community to properly manage and maintain the new water supply. These have contributed to bringing

Japan Territory

sustainable self-development to the community.

As part of Youth Capacity Development, a group of young people made a study visit to the PNG project site in September 2008. It was an excellent opportunity for them to be exposed to needs outside their own country, also making the young people aware of the Army's internationalism.

A shortage of officers has been a challenge to the territory; however, God is to be praised for three first-year cadets being accepted for the Ambassadors Of Holiness Session that opened in April 2009. This took the total of cadets in training to six.

In spite of challenges within the territory, God is showing Japan's Salvationists a future with much hope and promise.

STATISTICS
Officers 178 (active 83 retired 95) **Cadets** (1st Yr) 3 (2nd Yr) 3 **Employees** 908
Corps 49 **Outposts** 11 **Institutions** 20 **Hospitals** 2
Senior Soldiers 2,862 **Adherents** 41 **Junior Soldiers** 88

STAFF
Women's Ministries: Comr Kaoru Yoshida (TPWM) Lt-Col Seiko Hiramoto (TSWM)
Business Administration: Maj Jiro Katsuchi
Candidates: Maj Kyoko Yoshida
Editor: Sis Keiko Saito
Literary: Maj Kazumitsu Higuchi
Medical: Maj Naoko Harita
Music: B/M Hajime Suzuki
Personnel: Maj Haruhisa Ota
Programme: Maj Kazumitsu Higuchi
Social: Maj Naoko Harita
Staff Band: B/M Hajime Suzuki
Staff Songsters: S/L Mikako Ebara
Training: Maj Tsukasa Yoshida
Youth: Maj Hiromi Ota

DIVISIONS
Hokkaido: Nishi 1-13-1, Minami-4-jo, Chuo-ku, Sapporo-shi 064-0804; tel: (011) 231 2805; fax: (011) 231 2825; Majs Kiyoshi and Fumiko Namai

Kanto-Tohoku: 5 Yoriai-cho, Takasaki-shi, Gunma Ken 370-0822; tel: (027) 323 1337; fax: (027) 323 1334; Majs Masaru and Machiko Yamanaka

Nishi Nihon: 3-6-20 Tenjinbashi, Kita-ku, Osaka-shi 530-0041; tel: (06) 6351 0084; fax: (06) 6351 0093; Majs Nobuhiro and Yasuko Hiramoto

Tokyo-Tokaido: 4-11-3 Taihei, Sumida-ku, Tokyo 130-0012; tel: (03) 5819 1460; fax: (03) 5819 1461; Maj Chieko Tanaka

TRAINING COLLEGE
1-39-5 Wada Suginami-ku, Tokyo 166-0012; tel: (03) 3381 9837

MEDICAL WORK
Booth Memorial Hospital: 1-40-5 Wada, Suginami-ku, Tokyo 166-0012; tel: (03) 3381 7236; fax: (03) 5385 0734 (acc hospital 179 hospice 20)

Kiyose Hospital: 1-17-9 Takeoka, Kiyose-shi, Tokyo, 204-0023; tel: (042) 491 1411/3; fax: (042) 491 3900 (acc hospital 117 hospice 25)

SOCIAL WORK
Alcoholic Rehabilitation Centre
Jiseikan, 1-17-60 Takeoka, Kiyose-shi, Tokyo 204-0023; tel: (042) 493 5374 (acc 50)

Rehabilitation Centre (Men)
2-21-2 Wada Suginami-ku, Tokyo 166-0012 tel: (03) 3384-9114 (acc 15)

Social Service Centre (Men) (Bazaar)
2-21-2 Wada Suginami-ku, Tokyo 166-0012; tel: (03) 3384 3769

Working Men's Homes
Jijokan, 2-17-10 Tsukishima, Chuo-ku, Tokyo 104-0052; tel: (03) 3531 3516 (acc 35)

Shinkokan, 87 Akagishita-machi, Shinjuku-ku, Tokyo 162-0803; tel: (03) 3269 4901 (acc 40)

Women's Homes
Fujinryo: 1-43-11 Wada Suginami-ku, Tokyo 166-0012; tel: (03) 3381 0992 (acc 40)

Making a study visit to Papua New Guinea, a group of young Japanese Salvationists inspect a clean drinking water supply that had been installed as part of a three-year community development project

Shinseiryo: 4-11-14 Shibazaki-cho, Tachikawa-shi, Tokyo 190-0023; tel: (042) 522 2306 (acc 70)

Children's Homes
Aikoen: 1-3 Aoyama-cho, Kure-shi, Hiroshima 737-0023; tel: (0823) 21 6374 (acc 30)
Kibokan: 2-16-11, Nakahodzumi, Ibaraki-shi, Osaka 567-0034; tel: (0726) 23 3758 (acc 65)
Kiekoryo: 4-12-10 Kami Ikedai, Ota-ku, Tokyo 145-0064; tel: (03) 3729 0357 (acc 35)
Sekoryo: 2-21-1 Wada, Suginami-ku, Tokyo 166-0012; tel: (03) 3381 0545 (acc 50)
Toyohama-Gakuryo: 3082-5 Toyoshima, Toyohama-cho, Kure-shi, Hiroshima 734-0101; tel: (08466) 8 2029 (acc 60)

Day Nurseries
Kikusui Kamimachi Hoikuen: 2-52 Kikusui Kamimachi 3-jo, Shiroishi-ku, Sapporo-shi 003-0813; tel: (011) 821 2879 (acc 90)
Kure Hoikusho: 1-4 Aoyama-cho, Kure-shi 737-0023; tel: (0823) 21 4711 (acc 60)
Sano Hoikuen: 182 Asanuma-cho, Sano-shi 327-0831; tel: (0283) 22 4081 (acc 126)
Shiseikan Hoikuen: Nishi 7, Minami 3-jo, Chuo-ku, Sapporo-shi 060-0063; tel: (011) 204 9560 (acc 120)

Soen Hoikusho: Nishi 14-1, Kita 5-jo, Chuo-ku, Sapporo-shi 060-0005; tel: (011) 221 6630 (acc 60)

Home for the Aged
Keisen Home: 1-17-61 Takeoka, Kiyose-shi, Tokyo 204-0023; tel: (042) 493 5161/2 (acc 50)

Hostel
Kyoto Hostel: 37 Tokushoji-machi, Tominokoji-dori 4-jo Sagaru, Shimogyo-ku, Kyoto-shi 600-8051; tel: (075) 363 3926 (acc 16)

Senior Citizens' Housing and Care Centre
Grace: 1-40-15 Wada, Suginami-ku, Tokyo 166-0012; tel: (03) 3380 1248; fax: (03) 3380 1206 (acc 100)

Care House
Izumi: 1-17-24 Takeoka, Kiyose-shi, Tokyo 204-0023; tel: (042) 496 7575 (acc 32)

RETIRED OFFICERS' APARTMENTS
Olive House: 1-39-12 Wada, Suginami-ku, Tokyo 166-0012
Osaka Central Hall 5F: 3-6-20 Tenjinbashi, Kita-ku, Osaka 530-0041
Tokiwa House: 1-17-12 Takeoka, Kiyose-shi, Tokyo 204-0023

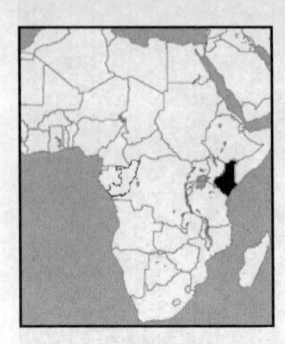

KENYA EAST TERRITORY

Territorial Commander:
Commissioner Hezekiel Anzeze
(1 Mar 2008)

Chief Secretary:
Colonel Steven Howard (1 Jun 2009)

Territorial Headquarters: Marist Lane, Karen, Nairobi, Kenya

Postal address: Box 24927, Karen 00502, Nairobi, Kenya
Tel: [254] (020) 240-3260; fax: [254] (020) 240-3263

In 1896 three Salvationists went to Kenya to work on the building of a new railway and made their witness while based at the Taru Camp. The first official meetings were held in Nairobi in April 1921, led by Lieut-Colonel and Mrs James Allister Smith. The first cadets were trained in 1923. On 1 March 2008, Kenya Territory was divided into two and the Kenya East Territory and Kenya West Territory were created.

Zone: Africa
Country included in the territory: Kenya
'The Salvation Army' in Kiswahili: Jeshi La Wokovu
Languages in which the gospel is preached: English, Kiswahili and a number of tribal languages
Periodicals: *Sauti ya Vita* (English and Kiswahili)

WITH 'Moving Forward' as its theme, the territory saw continued growth during its first full year of operations. The number of senior soldiers grew by more than five per cent within eight months of the territory's inauguration, and there have been increases in almost every category of activity and membership. A new corps was established approximately every two weeks. Five new districts were created and two districts upgraded to divisional status.

The territory increased its giving to the International Self-Denial Fund by more than 27 per cent over 2008, and as new divisions and districts are created, local commitment to tithing and good stewardship increases correspondingly. The territory has identified financial self-sufficiency as among its top strategic goals, and its soldiers and officers are working hard towards that end.

November 2008 saw the first joint commissioning activities for the Kenya East and West Territories, held in Nairobi. The territory is also witnessing a growing number of candidates for training. The places for the next two sessions at the National Officers Training College are full and applications are already being processed for 2012.

Education is highly valued in Kenya, and a good nursery school education offers children the best chance of being accepted into primary

Kenya East Territory

school and going on to employment. But it is not always easy to provide the start parents would wish for their children.

Deep within the Kibera slums – considered the largest in Africa, after Soweto in South Africa – the Salvation Army corps at Laini Saba and Mashimoni are responding to local needs for nursery care and schooling. Conditions, however, are desperate. Nothing looks like a nursery: there are no bright colours, no toys, no equipment, no children's furniture. The walls are made of mud and cardboard.

Parents leave their children, often from 6.30 am, for up to 12 hours. They always arrive hungry – few families have regular income since there is no consistent employment, and the parents spend the day looking for casual work or selling vegetables or bananas on the roadside. Many families live on less than US$1 a day. Although the corps officers attempt to feed the children, they often do not have sufficient funds to do so.

In spite of such poor conditions, the officers work hard in caring for the children and providing early education. Their work at these two nursery schools epitomises Christian love in action.

STATISTICS

Officers 499 (active 422 retired 77) **Cadets** 108 (51 Kenya East, 57 Kenya West) **Envoys in training** 2 **Employees** 45

Corps 340 **Outposts** 409 **Pre-primary Schools** 3 **Primary Schools** 159 **Secondary Schools** 26 **Institutions** 13

Senior Soldiers 69,554 **Junior Soldiers** 58,126

STAFF

Women's Ministries: Col Janice Howard (TLWM)
Business Administration: Lt-Col Gabriel Kathuri
Personnel: Lt-Col Jackson Muasa
Programme: Lt-Col Sarah Wanyama
Audit: Maj Jonathan Kipnusu
Finance: Maj Lalbulliana
Projects: Marshall Currie
Property: Maj Samuel Muli
Social and Education: Capt Armida LaMarr
Territorial Band: B/M Samuel Odiara
Territorial Songsters: S/L Lucas Nandwa
Trade: Mr Piet Evert van Altena
Training (National): Maj Enock Lufumbu
Youth: Capt Luke Khayumbi
  Candidates: Capt Rasoah Khayumbi

DIVISIONS

Coast: PO Box 98277, Mombasa; tel: 041-490629; Majs Boniface and Esther Munyekhe
Embu: PO Box 74, Embu; tel: 068-20107; Majs Frederick and Jescah Khamalishi
Kangundo: PO Box 324, Kangundo; tel: 044-21049; Majs Francis and Lucy Nganda
Kibwezi: PO Box 428, Sultan Hamud; tel: 044-52200; Majs Johnstone and Nancy Kathendu
Machakos: PO Box 160, Machakos; tel: 044-21660; Lt-Cols Julius and Phyllis Mukonga
Nairobi: PO Box 31205, Nairobi; tel: 020-767208; Majs John and Mary Olewa
Yatta: PO Box 29 Kithimani; Majs Lucas and Agnes Kithome

DISTRICTS

Kathiani: PO Box 2, Kathiani; Maj Nathan Musieni
Kilome: PO Box 85, Nunguni; Capt Samwel Opuka
Kirinyaga: PO Box 21, Kerugoya; Capt Ernest Njagi
Makueni: PO Box 40, Wote; tel: 044-77 Makueni; Capt Samuel Kang'ara
Matungulu: PO Box 422, Tala; Capt Joseph Muindi
Meru: PO Box 465, Nkubu, Meru; tel: 064-51207; Capt Ibrahim Lorot
Mwala: PO Box 19, Mwala; Maj Matthew Wangubo
Nakuru: PO Box 672, Nakuru; tel: 051-212455; Maj Joseph Mwanga

Kenya East Territory

Thika: PO Box 809, Thika; tel: 067-22056; Capt Jonathan Barasa
West Nairobi: PO Box 25240, Nairobi; Capt Thomas Musyoki

NATIONAL TRAINING COLLEGE
PO Box 4467, Thika; tel: 0733-629411

FARM
Avontour Estate, PO Box 274, Thika

EDUCATIONAL WORK
SA Sponsored Primary Schools: 159

SA Sponsored and Managed Secondary Schools: 26

Special Schools
Visually Handicapped
High School
Thika: PO Box 704, Thika; tel: 067-22092 (acc 163)
Primary Schools
Likoni: PO Box 96089, Mombasa; tel: 041-451101 (acc 120)
Thika: PO Box 80, Thika; tel: 067-21691 (acc 297)

Physically Disabled
Primary Schools
Joytown: PO Box 326, Thika; tel: 067-21291 (acc 215)

Secondary School
Joytown: PO Box 1370, Thika; tel: 067-30588 (acc 110)

Multi-Handicapped Special Units
Joytown: PO Box 326, Thika; tel: 067-21291 (acc 22)
Njoro Special School: PO Box 359, Njoro
Thika Primary School: PO Box 80, Thika; tel: 067-21691

SOCIAL SERVICES
Children's Homes
Kabete: PO Box 210-00606 Sarit Centre, Nairobi; tel: 020-442766 (acc 114)
Mombasa: PO Box 90531, Mombasa; tel: 041-224387 (acc 40)
Thika: Karibu Children's Centre, PO Box 1625, Thika 01000

Community Centre
Kibera: PO Box 21608, Nairobi; tel: 020-567064

Girls' Hostel
Nairobi: PO Box 31354, Nairobi; tel: 020-765750

Vocational Training Centres
Variety Village: PO Box 1472, Thika; tel: 020-2106603
Nairobi Girls' Centre: PO Box 31304, Nairobi; tel: 020-766375 (acc 60)

Cadets of the Witnesses For Christ Session who were commissioned as officers at the first joint commissioning activities for the Kenya East and Kenya West Territories, held in Nairobi

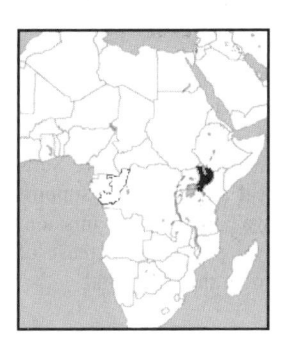

KENYA WEST TERRITORY

Territorial leaders:
Commissioners William and Nancy Roberts

Territorial Commander:
Commissioner William Roberts (1 Mar 2008)

Chief Secretary:
Colonel Henry Nyagah (1 Mar 2008)

Territorial Headquarters: Mumia Highway Rd, Kakamega, Kenya

Postal address: PO Box 660, Kakamega 50100, Kenya

In 1896 three Salvationists went to Kenya to work on the building of a new railway and made their witness while based at the Taru Camp. The first official meetings were held in Nairobi in April 1921, led by Lieut-Colonel and Mrs James Allister Smith. The first cadets were trained in 1923. On 1 March 2008, Kenya Territory was divided into two and the Kenya East Territory and Kenya West Territory were created.

Zone: Africa
Country included in the territory: Kenya
'The Salvation Army' in Kiswahili: Jeshi La Wokuvu
Languages in which the gospel is preached: English, Kiswahili and a number of tribal languages
Periodicals: *Sauti ya Vita* (English and Kiswahili)

FOLLOWING the euphoria of the opening of Kenya West Territory in the first quarter of 2008, Salvationists gave their attention to 'New Beginnings', the territorial theme for its first year. All that was attempted and accomplished in Jesus' name was accompanied by enthusiasm and anticipation of what might lie ahead. This was indeed a season of great joy.

The first year of the territory's life saw the enrolment of 3,832 senior soldiers and 2,012 junior soldiers, and the opening of 14 corps and 268 outposts. Nearly 3,000 people were brought to faith in Christ.

The first Territorial School of Music was conducted in August 2008, led and supported by Salvationists from Golden State Division (USA Western). Some 120 musicians gathered in Kakamega for seven days of concentrated instruction and spiritual development.

While one team of the visiting American Salvationists directed the school, another conducted leadership seminars in several divisions and districts as a third engaged in much-needed manual labour at the two Kibos schools for the visually impaired in Kisumu.

In this year of 'firsts', November saw 15 cadets of the Witnesses For Christ Session from Kenya West ordained and commissioned as officers and receiving their appointments at the first-ever joint commissioning activities for the Kenya East and West Territories, held in Nairobi. Twenty-three Kenya West cadets are part of the Prayer Warriors Session and, in January 2009, another 25 joined them as members of the Ambassadors Of Holiness Session.

Appreciation is expressed for the opportunities for growth and development provided by the Partners In Mission programme. In 2009, Texas Division (USA Southern) began its partner relationship with Kenya West. In January the territorial leaders had the privilege of visiting Texas to tell the story of the new territory.

Shortly afterwards, Major Mark Brown (USA Southern) travelled to Kenya West to shoot video, take photographs and interview Salvationists. One of the highlights of his visit was an appointment with the Western Provincial Commissioner, who stated: 'The Salvation Army has brought value to Kakamega.'

Ministry and service to women of the territory is strong, and getting stronger, through expressions such as the WORTH empowerment programme, continuing emphasis on HIV/Aids education, prevention and care, and giving valuable support to anti-sex trafficking efforts.

On 1 March 2009, the first anniversary of the birth of the territory, celebrations and thanksgiving services were held in every corps and centre. With singing and dancing, enthusiastic praise was offered to God and thanks were given for his blessings on the territory.

The following month saw the Self-Denial Appeal ingathering in support of the Army's worldwide mission. The territory reported an increase of 64 per cent over the 2008 total.

STATISTICS
Officers 665 (active 446 retired 219) **Cadets** (1st Yr) 25 (2nd Yr) 23 **Envoys in training** 9 **Employees** 8
Corps 331 **Outposts** 914 **Pre-primary Schools** 131 **Primary Schools** 280 **Secondary Schools** 30 **Institutions** 3
Senior Soldiers 113,030 **Junior Soldiers** 122,697

STAFF
Women's Ministries: Comr Nancy Roberts (TLWM) Col Catherine Nyagah (TSWM) Lt-Col Mebo Mbaja (THLS) Lt-Col Zipporah Njiru (TDCM) Capt Gaudencia Omukonyi (TJHLS)
Business Administration: Lt-Col Nahashon Njiru
Personnel: Lt-Col Tiras Mbaja
Programme and Spiritual Life Development: Lt-Col Christopher Mabuto
Audit: Maj Jacob Olubwayo
Editor: Capt Julius Omukonyi
Education/ETO: Capt Hassan Masika
Finance: Maj William Mutungi
Information Technology: Capt Brown Musasia
Projects: Capt Isaac Siundu
Property: Mr Moses Maruti
Public Relations: Capt Julius Omukonyi
Social: Maj Jacoba de Ligt
Sponsorships: Maj Miriam Wekesa
Statistics: Maj Richard Wekesa
Youth: Capt Newton Madegwa
  Candidates: Capt Felisters Madegwa

DIVISIONS
Bungoma: PO Box 1106, Bungoma; tel: 055-30589; Majs James and Grace Mukubwa
Eldoret: PO Box 125, Eldoret; tel: 053-22266; Majs Peter and Ann Mutuku
Kakamega: PO Box 660, Kakamega; tel: 331-20344; Capts Harun and Beatrice Chepsiri
Mbale: PO Box 80, Maragoli; tel: 056-51076; Majs Daniel and Nolega Imbiakha

Kenya West Territory

Musudzuu: PO Box 278, Seremi; tel: 056-45055; Majs Isaac and Naomi Kivindyo
Shigomere: PO Box 125, Khwisero; tel: 056-20260; Majs Herman and Lucia Mbakaya
Tongaren: PO Box 127, Tongaren; Majs Moses and Gladys Shavanga

DISTRICTS

Bunyore: PO Box 81, Bunyore; Maj Simon Mbuthu
Elgon: PO Box 274, Malakisi; tel: 055-20443; Capt Edward Mbogo
Kapsabet: PO Box 409, Kapsabet; Maj Sarah M'tetu
Kimilili: PO Box 220, Kimilili; Capt Frederick Omuzee
Kisumu: PO Box 288, Kisumu; tel: 057-2025632; Maj Isaac Liviala
Kitale: PO Box 548, Kitale; tel: 054-30259; Maj Johnstone Wolayo
Migori: PO Box 59, Suna, Migori; Capt Cleopas Gilkau
Turkana: PO Box 118-30500, Lodwar; tel: 054-21010; Maj Joshua Kitonyi
Webuye: PO Box 484, Webuye; Capt Meshack Wanjia

EDUCATIONAL WORK

SA Sponsored Kindergarten: 130
SA Sponsored Primary Schools: 280
SA Sponsored and Managed Secondary Schools: 25

Special Schools
Schools for Visually Impaired
Kibos Primary School: PO Box 477-40123, Kisumu (130 pupils)
Kibos Secondary School: PO Box 77-40123, Kisumu (18 pupils)

Schools for Physically Impaired
Joyland Primary School: PO Box 1790-40123, Kisumu (235 pupils)
Joyland Secondary School: PO Box 19494-40123, Kisumu (174 students)

School for Hearing Impaired
Chekombero Primary School: PO Box 93, Wodanga via Maragoli (60 pupils)

School for Mentally Challenged
Madegwa Primary School: PO Box 52, Maragoli (55 pupils)

Inclusive School
Joy Valley Primary School – Kimatuni: PO Box 1293, Bungoma (236 pupils)

SOCIAL SERVICES
Feeding Programmes for Destitutes
Kisumu: PO Box 288, Kisumu; tel: 057-4151 Shinoyi Community Centre

Health Centre
Kolanya: PO Box 88, Malakisi via Bungoma

Below: Delegates of the Territorial School of Music hold an open-air meeting. Some 120 musicians gathered in Kakamega for seven days of concentrated instruction and spiritual development.

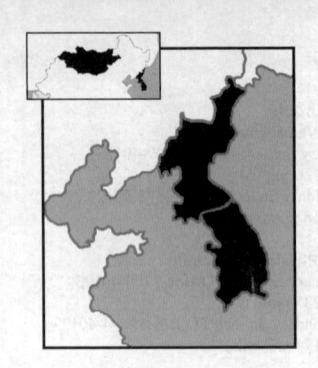

KOREA TERRITORY

Territorial leaders:
Commissioner Chun, Kwang-pyo and Commissioner Yoo, Sung-ja

Territorial Commander:
Commissioner Chun, Kwang-pyo
(1 Jan 2005)

Chief Secretary:
Colonel Park, Man-hee (1 Jan 2005)

Territorial Headquarters: The Salvation Army Central Hall, 1-23 Chung dong, Choong Ku, Seoul 100-120

Postal address: The Salvation Army, Central PO Box 1192, Seoul 100-709, Republic of Korea
Tel: [82] (2) 720 9494 (Korean); [82] (2) 720 9403 (English);
email: korea@kor.salvationarmy.org; website: www.salvationarmy.or.kr

Responding to a request while visiting Japan in 1907, the Founder despatched Commissioner George Scott Railton to survey prospects on the Korean peninsula. As a result, in October 1908 Colonel and Mrs Robert Hoggard (née Annie Johns) arrived with a group of officers to 'open fire' in Seoul. During the Korean conflict, which took place from 1950 to 1953, one Korean officer was martyred, one killed and two have been listed as missing.

Outreach work in Mongolia was officially commenced in October 2008.

Zone: South Pacific and East Asia
Countries included in the territory: Republic of Korea (South Korea), Democratic People's Republic of Korea (North Korea), Mongolia
'The Salvation Army' in Korean: (pronounced) 'Koo Sei Goon'
Language in which the gospel is preached: Korean
Periodicals: *Home League Programme Helps*, *Loving Hands* (sponsorship magazine), *The Officer*, *The War Cry*

UNDER the 2008 territorial theme 'Filling The Land With God's Hope' various memorable centenary events took place throughout the year, the main focus being the Territorial Centenary Congress conducted by General Shaw Clifton and Commissioner Helen Clifton (29 September - 5 October).

During the Sunday morning Centenary Thanksgiving Worship, held in Changchoong Stadium, the General entreated a congregation of 9,000 to march forward with holy courage. He gave the official charge to Captain Lee, Min-ho and Captain Chang, Mi-hyun to begin the Army's ministry in Mongolia, an outreach solely sponsored by Korea Territory.

Having already been to Mongolia for research and preparation, the captains enthusiastically accepted their challenge before departing for Ulaanbaatar on 13 October. The first holiness meeting was held the next Sunday, with eight people present. The territory has arranged a fundraising and prayer appeal for this missionary endeavour.

A sacred occasion was the Friday afternoon World Mission Rally when all the Salvationists, including overseas delegates representing 14 territories, gave praise and thanks to God for the 167 support officers who had served in the country over the years, recognising the dedicated and sacrificial service they had given.

A highlight of the gathering was the awarding of medals to 24 officers who had previously served in Korea and were present for the centenary celebrations. One guest, Mrs Lieut-Colonel Joan Perry from the UK, presented the Territorial Commander with a *taegukki* (Korean flag) almost 100 years old. It belonged to her parents, early-day missionary officers Colonel and Mrs Charles Sylvester, who had kept it from their ministry in Korea. The flag is now displayed in the Territorial Heritage Centre.

The official release of the Korean language history book was included in the Centenary Celebration Banquet attended by 170 specially invited guests.

On Congress Sunday afternoon 2,000 uniformed Salvationists took part in a march of witness around downtown Seoul. An evening Peace Concert on Seoul Plaza concluded the celebrations, throughout which the Melbourne Staff Band provided music.

The General and Commissioner Clifton were warmly greeted by President Lee, Myung-bak and First Lady Kim, Yoon-ok at Chong Wa Dae (The Blue House). They also visited Army facilities, including the Bridge Centre for homeless people and Seoul Broadview Children's Home, and inspected The Salvation Army Centennial Building construction site at Choong Chung Ro.

Two projects for ministry to North Korea were accomplished in conjunction with the territory's centenary celebrations. The 'Planting Trees Of Peace' initiative resulted in 12,000 chestnut trees being planted to help restore denuded hills on a 30-hectare site in Kangwon Province. The other project was the renovation of Wahwoo-doh Hospital in Nampo.

Jointly hosted by The Salvation Army and CTS (Christian Television System), the Territorial Corps Growth Seminar was held in February 2009. The 670 officers and clergy in attendance learned how to make healthy growth and revival happen in corps and churches nationwide.

STATISTICS
Officers 725 (active 582 retired 143) **Cadets** (1st Yr) 30 (2nd Yr) 29 **Employees** 800
Corps 247 **Outposts and Societies** 16 **Institutions** 37 **School** 1 **Conference Centres** 4 **Corps Child Day Care Centres** 22 **Students' Study Centres (and after-school programmes)** 35 **Counselling Centres** 6 **Food Banks** 15 **Sarangbang Centres** 4 **Special Service Vehicle Units** 4 **HIV/Aids Care and Prevention Team Units** 2 **Bridge Centre for the Homeless** 1 **Community Centres** 20 **Day Centres for the Elderly** 10
Senior Soldiers 41,723 **Adherents** 10,561 **Junior Soldiers** 6,411
Personnel serving outside territory Officers 15

Korea Territory

STAFF
Women's Ministries: Comr Yoo, Sung-ja (TPWM) Col Kim, Keum-nyeo (TSWM) Lt-Col Yeo, Keum-soo (THLS) Lt-Col Chun, Soon-ja (TLMS) Lt-Col Lee, Ok-kyung (TSAMFS) Maj Pyo, Choon-yun (TSSS)
Sec for Personnel: Lt-Col Lim, Hun-taek
   Editor and Education: Capt Kim, Jong-sun
   Literary: Capt Lee, Bo-tak
   Development Ministry: Capt Park, Sung-ha
   Overseas Service Bureau: Capt Lee, Bo-tak
Sec for Programme: Lt-Col Lim, Young-sik
   Church Growth: Capt Chung, In-ok
   Social: Maj Yang, Shin-kyong
   Youth: Maj Kim, Hyung-kwang
   Music: Capt Kim, Hai-du
Sec for Business: Lt-Col Kim, Un-ho
   Finance and Audit: Maj Kim, Young-tae
   Information Technology: Capt Lee, Hyun-hee
   Property: Maj Lee, Ki-yong
   Public Relations: Maj Ahn, Guhn-shik
   Child Sponsorship: Maj Yang, Shin-kyong
   Trade: Capt Kim, Sook-yung
Territorial Archivist: Lt-Col Kim, Joon-chul
Training: Maj Hwang, Sun-yup

DIVISIONS
Choong Buk: 704 Doosan Hansol 1 cha Apartments 101 dong, 447-15 Kaeshin Dong, Heungduk Ku, Chung Ju, Choong Book 361-746; tel: (043) 276 1634; fax: (043) 263 6387; Maj Chun, Joon-hong and Maj Shin, Myung-ja

Choong Chung: 603 Oosung Apartments 126 dong, 640 Chunglim dong, Suh ku, Taejon, Choong Nam Do 302-795; tel: (042) 584 2891; fax: (042) 584 2892; Maj Park, Nai-hoon and Maj Kil, Soon-boon

Choong Saw: 401 Hyundai Apartments 3-cha 302 dong, 388-2 Ssangyong dong, Suh Buk Ku, Chonan, Choong Nam Do 330-091; tel: (041) 572 0855; fax: (041) 578 0855; Maj Pang, Kie-chang and Maj Park, Keum-ja

Chulla: 375-21 Song San Dong, Chung Eup, Chun Buk 580-200; tel: (063) 536 1190; fax: (063) 536 1191; Maj Kim, Nam-sun

Kyung Buk: 901 Doosan We've Apartments 102 dong, Sung Dang 2 dong 728-1, Dahl suh ku, Taegu 704-980; tel: (053) 322 3695; fax: (053) 322 3694; Maj Choo, Seung-chan and Maj Lee, Ok-hee

Kyung Nam: 1306 Green Core Apartments 301 dong, 216 7 Manduk 3 dong, Buk ku, Pusan, Kyung Sang Nam Do 616-782; tel: (051) 337 0789; fax: (051) 337 2292; Maj Kang, Jik-koo and Maj Kim, Chung-sook

Seoul: The Salvation Army Office Building, #705, 58-1 Shinmoonro 1-ga, Chongno gu, Seoul 110-061; tel: (02) 720 9543; fax: (02) 720 9546; Lt-Col Park, Chong-duk and Lt-Col Yoon, Eun-sook

Seoul South: 602, Soojung Hanyang Apartments 235-dong, 1086 Sunboo 3-dong, Danwon Ku, Ansan, Kyunggi-do 425-765; tel: (031) 413 7811; fax: (031) 413 7812; Lt-Col Yang, Tae-soo and Lt-Col Chun, Ok-kyung

Suh Hae: 301 Dongshin Apartments 204 dong, Eupnae Dong 624-1, Sosan, Choong Nam 356-758; tel: (041) 667 2580; fax: (041) 667 2576; Maj Kwon, Sung-dal and Maj Kim, Moon-ok

CONFERENCE CENTRES
Territorial Retreat and Conference Centre: Paekhwasan (Mount Paekhwa) (acc 1,000)
Choong Chung Div: Taejon Central Corps, Taejon (acc 400)
Seoul Div: Ah Hyun Corps, Kangwondo (acc 300)
Seoul Div: Youngwol Corps (acc 50)

OFFICER TRAINING COLLEGE
83-2 Chungang-dong, Kwachun, Kyunggi-do 427-010; tel: (02) 502 9505/2927; fax: (02) 502 7160

RETIRED OFFICERS' RESIDENCE
'Victory Lodge' Silver Nursing Home (acc 50)

SCHOOL
Inpyung Technical High School (acc 1,340)

TERRITORIAL HERITAGE CENTRE
1st floor, The Salvation Army Central Hall, 1-23 Chung dong, Choong Ku, Seoul 100-120

THE SALVATION ARMY OFFICE BUILDING (THE SAOB)
58-1 Shinmoon ro 1-ga, Chongno Ku, Seoul 110-061

THE SALVATION ARMY CENTENNIAL BUILDING
58-1 Choong Chung Ro 3-ga, Sudaemun Gu, Seoul 120-837 (to be completed mid-2010)

SOCIAL MINISTRIES
Adult Rehabilitation Centre (ARC)
Iljook

Korea Territory

Bridge Centres (drop-in centres)
Seoul (acc 31,218)

Centres for the Handicapped
Kunsan: Catherine Centre for the Handicapped (acc 54); Day Care Centre for the Handicapped (acc 25)
Suwon: Support Centre for the Handicapped (acc 6); Rehabilitation Centre for the Handicapped (acc 15); Day Care Centre for the Handicapped (acc 15)

Children's Homes
Kunsan (acc 75), Sarangsaem (acc 7), Seoul Broadview (acc 160), Taegu (acc 61), Taejon No 1 (acc 50), Taejon No 2 (acc 75)

Community Centres
Community Centres: Hapchong, Hongeun, Kang Buk, Myung Chun, Suh San Suklim, Youngwol
Corps Welfare Centres: An Sung Gongdo, Booyuh, Cheju, Mosan, Najoo, Seogwipo, Taegu, Taegu Chil Kok Centre for the Elderly, Yoju
Self-Support Training Centres: Asan, Bohryung, Nonsan, Sosan, Tai An,

Corps Day Care Centres
Bahnyawol, Boo Nam, Chin Chang, Chun Kok, Hap Duk, Kang Buk, Kim Chon, Kwachun, Masan (Moonwha), Mindalae, Mosan, Myung Chun, Osan Saetbyeol (Star), San Kok, Sharon, Sok Cho,Suhdaemun, Suh Taegu, Suh San Suk Lim, Taegu, Wonju, Yul Mok

Counselling and Friendship Centres
Chonan Counselling Centre for Women, Tong Taegu, Taegu, Suh Taejon, Tong Taejon, Taejon

Food Banks and Distribution Centres
Asan, Bohryung, Cheju, Chun An, Kwachun, Mapo, Nonsan, Seogwipo, Song Dong, Sosan, Suh Chung Ju, Taejon, Taian, Yea San, Yeoju

HIV/Aids Care and Prevention Programme Units
Pusan Shelter; Red Ribbon Centre, Seoul

Oori Jip (transitional housing for those leaving children's homes)
Ah Hyun (acc 6), Choongdong (Seoul Broadview Children's Home) (acc 2), Chun Yun (acc 3), Yung Chun (acc 4)

Sarangbang Centres (hostels for the homeless)
Buk Ah Hyun Dong (acc 30), Iljook (acc 59), Mangu Dong (acc 75), Sudaemun (acc 50)

Self-Support Training Centres
Boryung, Nonsan, Taian

Senior Citizens' Services
Residential
Ansung Nursing Home (acc 60)
Ansung Peace Village Nursing Home (acc 71)
Kwachun Home for the Elderly (acc 30)
Kwachun Nursing Home (acc 50)
Namdong Peace Village (acc 60)
Pusan Home for the Elderly (acc 71)
'Victory Lodge' Silver Nursing Home, Kwachun (acc 50)

Day Centres
Hapjung Day Centre for the Elderly (acc 14)
Hongjae Dong Day Centre for the Elderly (acc 20)
Mooan for the Elderly (acc 5)
Najoo Day Centre for the Elderly (acc 10)
Namdong Day Centre for the Elderly (acc 71)
Suhsansung Day Centre for the Elderly (acc 20)
Suwon Day Care Centre for the Elderly (acc 15)
Wolsung Day Care Centre for the Elderly (acc 18)

Welfare Centres for Seniors
Ansung, Taian

Special Service and Relief Services
4 vehicles

Students' Study Centres (and after-school programmes)
1318 Happy Zone (Cheju), 1318 Happy Zone (Onyang), Asan, Baesan, Boo Nam, Buk Choon Chun, Buk Gumi, Cheju, Chew Kok, Chin Hae, Chisan, Chun An, Daniel (Eonyak), Doriwon, Eden, Haram (Nonsan), Hongjae, Keumsan, Mil Yang, Oh Ka, Sae Chung Ju, Sae Sungnam, Seogwipo, Seoul Broadview, Shim Chon, Shinchang, Suh Taegu Pisan 4-dong, Taegu, Taegu Chil Kok, Wadong, Yea San, Yong Dong, Yoju, Youngwol

Korea Territory

Student Accommodation
Taejon (university students, acc 23)

Thrift Stores
Sudaemun, Seoul; Yun Hie, Seoul

Thrift Stores and Sally's Coffee
Seoul: Ah Hyun, Daehangno, Namdaemun Market

Food Markets, Thrift Stores and Sally's Coffee
Seoul: Seon Dong, Buk Ah Hyung Dong, Mapo #1 (no Sally's Coffee), Mapo #2

Vocational Training and Support Centres
Chung Daoon House, Taejon (acc 30); Sally Home, Pusan (acc 22)

Women's Homes
Chonan House of Hope (acc 10); Doori Home, Seoul (acc 35); Taejon Women's Refuge Shelter (acc 55)

MONGOLIA

The Salvation Army, Apartment No 9, 145th Narliizam, Bayanzurkh District 13th Mini District 6, Ulaanbaatar, Mongolia; Capt Lee, Min-ho and Capt Chang, Mi-hyun

The General, waving the flag of Mongolia, leads a time of joyous praise during Korea's Centenary Congress, having given his official charge to Captain Lee, Min-ho and Captain Chang, Mi-hyun (right) to commence Salvation Army ministry in that country. The captains departed for Ulaanbaatar encouraged by the news that their territory had arranged a special fundraising and prayer appeal for this missionary endeavour.

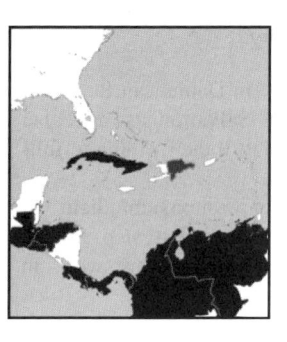

LATIN AMERICA NORTH TERRITORY

Territorial leaders:
Colonels Oscar and Ana Rosa Sánchez

Territorial Commander:
Colonel Oscar Sánchez (1 Feb 2007)

Chief Secretary:
Lieut-Colonel Zoilo Pardo (1 Jul 2006)

Territorial Headquarters: Avenida 11, Calle 20, San José, Costa Rica

Postal address: Apartado Postal 125-1005, Barrio México, San José, Costa Rica
Tel: [506] 2257-7535; fax: [506] 2257-5291; email: sallan@sol.racsa.co.cr;

The Salvation Army's work commenced in the Isthmus of Panama (1904), Costa Rica (1907), Cuba (1918), Venezuela (1972), Guatemala (1976), Colombia (1985), El Salvador (1989), Dominican Republic (1995) and Honduras (2000).
    Legal recognition was given to El Ejército de Salvación by the Republic of Panama (1946), Costa Rica (1975), Guatemala (1978), Colombia (1988), The Dominican Republic (1995), El Salvador (1996) and Honduras (2001). The territory was formed on 1 October 1976, then reformed on 1 September 1998, when Mexico became a command.

Zone: Americas and Caribbean
Countries included in the territory: Colombia, Costa Rica, Cuba, Dominican Republic, El Salvador, Guatemala, Honduras, Panama, Venezuela
'The Salvation Army' in Spanish: Ejército de Salvación
Languages in which the gospel is preached: English, Kacchikel, Spanish
Publications: *Voz de Salvación (Salvation Voice), Arco Iris de Ideas (Rainbow of Ideas)*

AT various zonal symposiums during 2008, training was given to all the territory's officers to help them analyse their local situations and set faith goals. The challenge was to increase the number of soldiers and improve the social services offered by The Salvation Army.

In spite of a delicate political situation in Cuba, this is the division that is reporting increased activities and significant growth. The project to build a new corps hall, community centre and officers' quarters in San Francisco de Paula was completed and the decision taken to move the Extension Training College to these premises to reduce costs and bring the cadets closer to the divisional centre in Havana.

A rehabilitation programme for alcoholics continues in Cuba with support from the British Embassy. There has already been success with four clients.

The new school for the blind in Panama was opened in February 2009, with a computer classroom specially designed for blind people. There is a great need for such a ministry in this country.

In Guatemala, the Tierra Nueva Corps held an evangelistic campaign with support from the USA Southern Territory Mission Team. Cadets from the training college in Costa Rica travelled north to campaign in the Guanacaste area.

There has been a strong emphasis on youth work throughout the territory. Several youth camps were held, while a Sports Ministries programme in Columbia and Cuba included basketball and soccer competitions to attract more youth.

Corps cadet brigades continue to operate effectively in Cuba and Columbia, while Guatemala has seen the recommencement of these sections. Cuba and El Salvador organised Bible rallies to increase young people's knowledge of Scripture. Young people in Columbia carried out a prayer walk, asking God's help to build up his Kingdom in this country.

Guatemala reactivated the Divisional Youth Leadership Support Team, which met regularly with corps youth leaders to help train them in aspects of leadership. Training has also been given to youth leaders and YP local officers in Columbia, Costa Rica and Cuba.

During Candidates and Future Officers Fellowship Sunday in Cuba, 23 people responded publicly to the call to officership. They are being trained twice a month to develop their service in their corps and to confirm their calling. In Dominican Republic, five young Salvationists are also working to fulfill their calling to full-time service.

A leaders symposium held in Nicaragua was a first step toward restarting Salvation Army work in that country.

STATISTICS
Officers 142 (active 124 retired 18) **Cadets** (2nd Yr) 14 **Employees** 175

Corps 55 **Outposts** 20 **Institutions** 10 **Schools** 21 **Day Care Centres** 10 **Children's Development Centres** 8 **Vocational Training Centres** 7 **Feeding Centres** 14 **Camps** 2

Senior Soldiers 2,734 **Adherents** 1,021 **Junior Soldiers** 1,276

STAFF
Women's Ministries: Col Ana Rosa Sánchez (TPWM) Lt-Col Magali Pardo (TSWM)
Business Administration: Maj Esteban Calvo
Personnel: tba
Programme: Maj María Eugenia Obando
Candidates: Maj Ileana Calvo
Editorial: Maj Ileana Calvo
Education: Maj Javier Obando
Finance: Maj Esteban Calvo
Projects and Sponsorship: Maj Esteban Calvo
Social: Maj Max Mayorga
Training: Maj Eduardo Almendras

DIVISIONS
Colombia: Apartado Aéreo 17756 Santa Fe de Bogotá, Colombia; tel: (571) 263 2633; fax: (571) 295 2921; email: coldiv_leadership@lan.salvatonarmy.org; Majs José and Hilda Santiago

Costa Rica: Apartado Postal 6227-1000, San José, Costa Rica; tel: (506) 2221 8266; fax: (506) 2223 0250; email: crdiv_leadership@lan.salvationarmy.org; Majs Jorge and Idali Méndez

Cuba: Calle 96 Nª 5513 entre 55 Y 57, Marianao CP 11400, Ciudad de la Habana, Cuba; tel: (53) 7260-2171; fax: (53) 7267-2537; email: ejdivcuba@enet.cu; Capts Orestes and Sandra Linares

Guatemala: Apartado Postal 1881, Guatemala CA; 2a Avenida 3-10, Sector A4 San Cristóbal 1, Zona 8 de Mixco, Guatemala; tel/fax: (502) 2478-4112/2443-2484; email:

Latin America North Territory

guadiv_leadership@lan.salvationarmy.org
Majs Manuel and Nancy Muñoz;
Panama: Apartado Postal 0843-01134 Balboa, Ancón Panamá, República de Panamá, Balboa Calle La Boca, Calle Julio Linares Edificio 0792, República de Panamá; tel: (507) 228-0148; Maj Deisy Costas

REGIONS

Dominican Republic: Ejército de Salvación, Apartado Postal M215, Oficina Postal Los Mameyes, Calle 4ta, Esquina 26 De Enero, Santo Domingo Este, Dominican Republic; tel: 1(809) 335 2678; fax: 1(809) 335 2678; email: armyregion@gmail.com; Maj Gerardo Góchez

El Salvador: Apartado Postal No 7, Centro de Gobierno, Calle 15 de Septiembre N° 119 y N° 121 Barrio Candelaria, San Salvador; tel: (503) 2280-1805; fax: (503) 2280-3293; email: ejercito-salvacion@salnet.net; Maj Donald Wilson

Honduras Project: (under THQ) Colonia El Hogar Bloque B Casa N°11 Tegucigalpa Apartado Postal 6590, Honduras; tel/fax: (504) 232-4927/235-9855; email: ejercitodesalvacionhn@gmail.com; Maj Noé Flores

Venezuela: Calle San Juan de Dios Melián, Entre calle san Rafael y la Segunda de Cabudare Riviera Departamento 1, Cabudare-Barquisimento, Venezuela; tel: (058) 251 261-6318; email: ejercitodes.venz@yahoo.es; Maj Pedro López

TRAINING COLLEGE

Calle Puente de Piedra, 1 km norte del Puente de Piedra, Barrio Los Angeles, San Rafael de Heredia, Costa Rica; Postal address: Apartado 173-3015 San Rafael de Heredia, Costa Rica; tel: (506) 2262 0061; fax: (506) 2262 0733

EXTENSION TRAINING COLLEGE IN CUBA

Calle Angeles #163 altos/Montes y Corrales, Centro Habana CP 10200, Ciudad de la Habana – Cuba; tel: (53) 7866 6572

SOCIAL SERVICES
Institutions
Centre for Homeless
Costa Rica: Refugio de Esperanza: Avenida 9 Zona Roja, San José; tel: (506) 2233-2059 (acc 30)

Disabled Centre
Costa Rica: Hogar Sustituto 'Tierra Prometida', Carretera Interamericana 100 metros sur de Autos Mundiales, Pérez Zeledón; tel: (506) 2771-2517 (acc13)

Residential Homes for the Elderly
Cuba: William Booth Home, Calle 84 No 5525 e/55 y Lindero, Mariano, CP 11400, Ciudad de la Habana; tel: (537) 260-1118

Panama: Hogar Jackson Home, Avenida Amador Guerrero y Calle 3 No 2014, Colón; tel: (507) 441-3371 (acc 30)

Residential Homes for Children
El Salvador: Hogar de Niños 'El Alba', Canton de Gualache, Colonia Joselly, Departamento de Usulután.

Panama: Hogar Dr Eno (Girls), Transísmica, Sabanitas, Colón; tel: (507) 442-0371 (acc 20)

Venezuela: Hogar Nido Alegre, Calle 71 # 14 A63, Juana de Avila, Apdo Postal 1464 Maracaibo 4001; Estado de Zulia, Venezuela; tel: (58-261) 798-3761 (acc 50)

Adult Rehabilitation Centres
Costa Rica:
Centro Modelo: Calle Naranjo, Concepción de Tres Ríos, Cartago; tel: (506) 2273-6307
Refugio de Esperanza Liberia: Frente a la Estación de Bomberos, Guanacaste; tel: (506) 2666-5567/2666-4691

Cuba: Centro de Rehabilitación de Alcoholicos: Carretera de Vertienes Km 3 #335, Reparto Río Verde Camagüey CP 71200; tel: (53) 3225-8230

Schools
Kindergartens
Dominican Republic: Moca: Moca Republica Dominicana; tel: (1809) 578-4792 (acc 20)

El Salvador: Merliot Corps: Jardines del Volcán, Calle El Jabali # 36, Ciudad Merliot, La Libertad; tel: (503) 2278-4982 (acc 60)

Panama: Panamá Templo: Calle 25 y Avenida Cuba-Este; tel: (507) 262-2545 (acc 30)

Kindergartens and Schools
Dominican Republic:
Cotui: 16 de Agosto N° 98, Cotui, Sánchez Ramírez; tel: (809) 585-3393 (acc 40)
Tres Brazos: Calle Matadero N° 70 (acc 20)

Guatemala:
Chimaltenango: 7a Avenida y 1a Calle, Zona 1, Villas del Pilar; tel: (502) 7839-6585 (acc 150)

Latin America North Territory

Maya: Manzana #2, Lote 262, Zona 18, Conia Maya; tel: (502) 2260 1519

Mezquital: 4a Calle 3-99, Zona 12, Colonia Mezquital; tel: (502) 2479-8443 (acc 150)

Satelite: Lote 5, Manzana 27, Proyecto 2, Ciudad Satelite, Mixto; tel: (502) 484-3052 (acc 30)

Tierra Nueva: Sector B-1, Manzana D, Lote 3, Colonia Tierra Nueva 11, Chinautla; tel: (502) 2484-1255 (acc 150)

Honduras: San Pedro Sula: Colonia Trejos – IV Etapa, Calle 22E, 21-23 Avenida, Town House No 1, San Pedro Sula, Honduras; Apartado Postal No 2270, San Pedro Sula, Honduras; tel/fax: (504) 556 7238

Panama: Calle 11y1/2, La Pulida, Río Abajo; tel: (507) 224-7480 (acc 40)

Kindergarten, Primary and Secondary School

Guatemala: Limón: Colegio William Booth, Centro Communal 'El Limón' Costado Derecho, Zona 18; tel: (502) 2260-0723 (acc 395)

School for the Blind

Panama: contact Panama DHQ

Health-Education in Hospitals

Honduras:
Avanzada de Tegucigalpa: Hospital Materno Infantil (4 classrooms); tel: (504) 232-4927

Avanzada San Pedro Sula: Hospital Mario Catarino Rivas (2 classrooms); tel: (504) 556-7238

Day Care Centres

Colombia: San Cristóbal Sur, Bogotá: Calle 12 Sur # 11-71 Este, Barrio San Cristóbal Sur, Santa Fe de Bogotá; tel: (571) 333-0606/289-2672

Costa Rica:
Central Corps: Avenida 16, Entre Calle 5 y 7 San José; tel: (506) 2233-6850 (acc 35)

León XIII: Ciudadela León XIII, Detrás de la Escuela de León XIII, San José; tel: (506) 2231-1786 (acc 80)

Limón Central: Av 4 entre Calles 7 y 9; tel: (506) 2758-0657 (acc 75)

Pavas: Villa Esperanza de Pravas, Contiguo Al Instituto Nacional de Aprendizaje, San José; tel: (506) 2231-1786 (acc 80)

El Salvador:
Gualache: Colonia Joselyn, Canton de Gualache, Departamento de Usulután

Merliot Corps: Jardines del Volcán, Calle El Jabali # 36, Ciudad Merliot, La Libertad; tel: (503) 2278-8249 (acc 60)

Guatemala: Satelite: Lote 5, Manzana 27, Proyecto 2, Ciudad Satelite, Mixco; tel: (502) 484-3052 (acc 30)

Panama:
Panamá Templo: Calle 25 Avenida Cuba-Este; tel: (507) 262-2545 (acc 20)

Río Abajo: Calle 11y1/2 La Pulida; tel: (507) 224-7480 (acc 25)

Children's Development Centres

Colombia:
Armenia Outpost: Carrera 11 # 14-19 Barrio Guayaquil; tel: (576) 746-8591

Nuevo Kennedy: Avda Calle 43 Sur #79 B47, Barrio Nuevo Kennedy, Santa Fe de Bogotá, Colombia; tel: (57) 1 264 9161

Ibague, Tolima: Carrera 4ta Sur # 20A-34, Barrio Yuldaima, Apartado Aéreo 792; tel: (578) 260-8032

Robledo, Medellín: Carrera 84B # 63-73, Barrio Robledo, Medellín, Antioquía; tel: (094) 234-8250

San Cristóbal Sur, Bogotá: Calle 12 Sur # 11-71 Este, Barrio San Cristóbal Sur, Santa Fe de Bogotá; tel: (571) 333-0606/289-2672

El Salvador:
Cuerpo Central: Calle 15 de Septiembre # 199 y # 121, Barrio Candelaria, San Salvador; tel: (503) 270-5273 (acc 246)

Usulután: 6a Avenida y 7a, Calle Oriente # 31, Barrio El Calvario, Departamento de Usulután; tel: (503) 662-4428 (acc120)

Venezuela: Maracaibo: Calle 10 (99E) #62-09, Barrio Simón Bolivar, Apartado postal 322, Maracaibo 4001, Estado Zulia

Vocational Training Centres

Costa Rica:
Computer Centre: Villa Esperanza de Pavas, Contiguo al Instituto Nacional de Aprendizaje (acc 15)

Cuba:
Cuerpo Central: Computer Centre, Calle 96 Nª 5513 entre 55 y 57, Marianao 11400, La Habana; tel: (53) 260-2171

Diezmero: Dressmaking, Calle 3ra Nª 25304 entre 2da y Martí Diezmero San Miguel del Padrón, CP 130000 Guevara, La Habana

El Salvador:
Computer Centres:
Cuerpo Central: Calle 15 de Septiembre # 199 y # 121, Barrio Candelaria, San Salvador; tel: (503) 270-5273 (acc 246)

Merliot: Jardines del Volcán, Calle El Jabali

Latin America North Territory

Above: Junior soldiers are enrolled at San Salvador Central Corps in El Salvador

Right: Children are taught Bible stories during a Sunday school class at Cotui Corps in Dominican Republic

36, Ciudad Merliot, La Libertad; tel: (503) 2278-8249 (acc 60)
Guatemala: Mecanografia: Satelite Lote 5, Manzana 27, Proyecto 2, Ciudad Satelite, Mixto; tel: (502) 484-3052 (acc 30)
Venezuela: Computer, Carpentry and Dressmaking Classes: Calle 71 # 14 A63, Juana de Avila, Apdo Postal 1464, Maracaibo 4001; Estado de Zulia, Venezuela; tel: (0261) 798-3761 (acc 50)

Feeding Centres

Colombia: Ibague, Tolima: Carrera 4ta Sur # 20A-34, Barrio Yuldaima, Apartado Aéreo 792; tel: (578) 260-8032

Costa Rica:
Liberia: 500 mts Norte Estación de Bomberos 100 Este y 50 Norte, Barrio San Roque; tel: (506) 2666-3603 (acc 100)
Limón 2000: Barrio Limón 2000 frente al Predio El Aragón, Alameda # 4; tel: (506) 2797-1602 (acc 30)
Nicoya: Escuela de San Martín 900 al Oeste, Barrio San Martín; tel: (506) 2685-5531 (acc 100)
Salitrillos: Salitrillos de Aserri, de las Prestaciones, 300 metros al sur; tel: (506) 2230-4668 (acc 80)
San Isidro del General: Barrio Los Angeles, Apartado Postal 7-8000; tel: (506) 2770-6756 (acc 150)
Santa Cruz: Barrio Tulita Sandino, 300 este del IDA Guanacaste; tel: (506) 2680-0724 (acc 100)
San Ramón de Alajuela: Barrio San Juan, 150 metros oeste del Aserradero San Juan

Cuba:
Bejucal: Calle 8 Nª 1911 entre 19 y 21 Bejucal CP 32600, Habana
Comedor William Booth: Calle 96 No 5513 entre 55 y 57

Panama:
Colon: Avenida Amador Guerrero 14201, Apartado 1163; tel: (507) 441-4570 (acc 75)
Chilibre: Transistmica, Lote No 175 Chilibre; tel: (507) 216-2501 (acc 100)
Panamá Templo: Calle 25 y Avenida Cuba Este, Panamá; tel: (507) 262 2545

Venezuela: Simón Bolívar, Calle 10 (99E) #62-09, Barrio Simón Bolivar, Apartado postal 322, Maracaibo 4001, Estado Zulia

Camps

El Salvador: Km 50, Carretera a la Herradura, Caserio los Novios, Hacienda del Cauca; tel: (503) 2354-4530 (acc 150)
Guatemala: Tecpán: Calle Tte Coronel Jack Waters, Barrio Poromá, Colonia Iximché; tel: (502) 7840-3998 (acc 100)

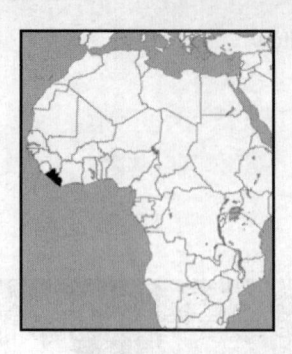

LIBERIA COMMAND

Command leaders:
Lieut-Colonels Peter and Jessica Dali

Officer Commanding:
Lieut-Colonel Peter Dali (1 May 2008)

General Secretary:
Major Charles Swansbury (1 Feb 2009)

Command Headquarters: 17th Street, Sinkor, Monrovia
Postal address: PO Box 20/5792, Monrovia, Liberia

The Salvation Army opened fire in Liberia in May 1988 as part of the Ghana and Liberia Territory, with Major and Mrs Leonard Millar as pioneer officers. Progress was monitored by Ghana during the civil war, from May 1990. Liberia became a separate command on 1 January 1997.

Zone: Africa
Country included in the command: Liberia
Languages in which the gospel is preached: Bassa, English, Gola, Krahn, Pele

DESPITE a heavy downpour of rain, Liberia's Salvationists welcomed Lieut-Colonels Peter and Jessica Dali as they commenced their appointment as command leaders. They were installed by Colonels Dennis and Sharon Strissel (territorial leaders, Ghana) during a meeting held at Paynesville Corps.

In line with a vision to strengthen the command and equip Salvationists to face future challenges, the Officer Commanding has established 11 sections, grouping together corps, outposts and societies across the command. The new leaders were not only appointed to oversee work within the area of their responsibility but also given the prerogative of expanding the Army into neighbouring areas.

The new Vocational Training Centre building was opened and dedicated to God in September 2008. One-year training courses in six disciplines were commenced, with an initial enrolment of 111 students.

For the first time in the history of the command and Africa in general, an Education Secretariat was established. Operating from command headquarters, the secretariat manages the Army's schools system, providing oversight and supervision of all registered schools.

Girls from the Evangeline Booth Girls' Hostel have been rehoused with family, relatives or close friends following the introduction of a foster parents programme.

FAAST (Faith Alliance Against Slavery and Human Trafficking), a programme funded by SAWSO and

Liberia Command

a collaboration between The Salvation Army in Liberia and World Hope International, established two apartments within the CHQ building to house victims referred by World Hope International.

Cadets of the Prayer Warriors Session visited the Mercy Ship *Africa Mercy* docked at Monrovia Free Port. Mercy ships are ocean vessels providing health care to the poor in port areas around the world. The visit was arranged with the help of a crew member who is a Canadian Salvationist. The cadets joined in the evening evangelistic service.

Major Pamela McKee (USA Southern) provided support as interim command administrator prior to Majors Charles and Denise Swansbury taking up their posts as General Secretary and Command Secretary for Women's Ministries. Major McKee also conducted a series of courses for the newly-appointed sectional leaders and selected headquarters' officers in leadership.

STATISTICS
Officers 52 **Auxiliary-Captains** 8 **Envoys** 5 **Corps Leaders** 5 **Cadets** 9 **Employees** 206
Corps 19 **Outposts** 18 **Schools** 12 (pupils 2,992) **Child Day Care Centres** 8 **Clinic** 1 **Mobile Clinic** 1
Senior Soldiers 2,028 **Adherents** 54 **Junior Soldiers** 424

STAFF
Women's Ministries: Lt-Col Jessica Dali (CPWM) Maj Denise Swansbury (CSWM) Maj Etta Gaymo (LOMS)
Education Secretariat: Mr Albert Benson Sesay (Dir Education) Mr David Massaquoi Mr Elijah Sowen (Education Officers)
Extension Training: Capt John Bundu
Field: Maj Ben Gaymo
Finance: Capt Kwadwo Amoah Bimpong
High School Coordinator: Maj Denise Swansbury
Programme Coordinator – VTTC: Mr Tweh Wesseh
Projects: Maj Denise Swansbury
Social Welfare Coordinator: Capt Monica Amoah Bimpong
Trade: Miss Joanna Teah
Training: Maj James Oduro
Youth and Candidates: Capt Morris Mckay

DISTRICT
Grand Bassa: c/o CHQ, PO Box 20/5792, Monrovia; Capt Anthony Sio

SECTIONS
(c/o CHQ, PO Box 20/5792, Monrovia)
Bomi: Capt Abraham Colins
Bong: Capt Amos Barnard
Buchanan City: Capt Jerry Duwah
Bushrod Island: Capt Shad Joloe
Compound Three: Capt Jonah Edna Roberts
Grand Gedeh: Maj William Zogar
Margibi: Capt Amos Diah
Monrovia City: Capt Phillip Boweh
Mount Coffee: Maj Hilton Youngar
Paynesville: Capt Samson Kanmoe
Sinoe: Capt Broton Weah

SCHOOLS AND COLLEGES
(c/o CHQ, PO Box 20/5792, Monrovia)
Salvation Army Vocational Technical and Training College; Programme Coordinator: contact Mr Tweh Wesseh; Programme Consultant: Mr Taweh Johnson MSc
William Booth High School; Principal: Mr Brima Dennis MA
William Booth Primary & Elementary School; Principal: Mrs Catherine Sesay (BSc)
Len Millar High School; Principal: Mr Melville V. Edmond MA
Len Millar Primary and Elementary School; Mr Egbinda Brima BSc
Bill Norris Primary, Elementary and Junior High School; Principal: Capt John Bundu

COLLEGE
William Booth Clinic: c/o CHQ, PO Box 20/5792, Monrovia;
Administrator: Mrs Korlu E. Smoke Geh;
Physcian Asst: Mr Johannson L. David

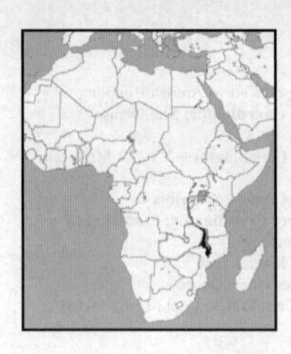

MALAWI COMMAND

Command leaders:
Lieut-Colonels Godfrey and Diane Payne

Officer Commanding:
Lieut-Colonel Godfrey Payne
(1 Jul 2007)

General Secretary:
Major Francis Nyambalo (1 Feb 2007)

Command Headquarters: PO Box 51140, Limbe, Malawi

Tel: [265] 1 917073 / 917545

The Salvation Army began operations in Malawi on 13 November 1967 and was granted official government recognition on 2 October 1973. The Malawi Division was part of the Zimbabwe Territory until 1988, when it was integrated into the Zambia Command, which was given territorial status and became known as the Zambia and Malawi Territory. The Army's work in Malawi has grown and developed and on 1 October 2002 it became a separate region. Further growth and expansion of the work in Malawi resulted in the region being elevated to command status on 1 February 2004.

Zone: Africa
Country included in the command: Malawi
'The Salvation Army' in Chichewa: Nkhondo ya Chipulumutso
Languages in which the gospel is preached: Chichewa, English, Lomwe, Sena, Tumbuka

ONE of the factors that mark out the command is the number of community-based projects in operation. For many years the policy has been to involve corps as much as possible in community programmes rather than using social centres. This makes social and community work much more integrated with corps life.

The programme that has probably had the largest impact is the integrated livelihood programme for food security (I-Life) funded by USAID, which has worked for five years in Phalombe, an area in the south.

The command's work among children who are being either trafficked or sold for cheap labour continues. A building programme at its centre in Mchinji is a sure sign of this ministry's development; the new extension means the centre can now provide accommodation for 40 children.

The training college, opened in March 2008, continues to deliver its vital ministry to 14 cadets of the Prayer Warriors Session. Apart from the first and last three-month periods of their training, cadets are only resident in college for one month at a time while they alternate with periods in field appointments. This ensures the cadets' training is well 'earthed' to corps work and gives them opportunity to put into practice

Malawi Command

what they learn at their desks and in fellowship with college staff.

More than 20 candidates have been preparing for entry into the training college in early 2010, but the premises has only eight double bedrooms and there are insufficient funds to build any extra.

The construction of several new halls began during 2008-09. Local Salvationists worked hard to mould thousands of bricks, and to collect or buy firewood with which to bake them. Contributions from many supporters in various other countries were used to purchase cement for some of these centres.

Senior officers met three times in the year to establish ongoing strategic planning. This proved to be a most helpful undertaking, and reports of their deliberations were enthusiastically received by officers and local officers throughout the command.

STATISTICS
Officers 61 (active 55 retired 6) **Envoy** 1 **Cadets** (2nd year 14) **Employees** 70
Corps 35 **Outposts** 13 **Outreach Units and New Openings** 57
Senior Soldiers 5,472 **Junior Soldiers** 1,296
Personnel serving outside command Officers 2

STAFF
Women's Ministries: Lt-Col Diane Payne (CPWM) Maj Jamiya Nyambalo (CSWM)
Business: Mr Lameck Adam
Development Services: Karen Smith
Extension Training and Candidates: Capt Robert Mtengowalira
Property: Capt Godfrey Chagwa
Training: Maj Samuel Oklah
Youth: Capt Luke Msikita

DIVISIONS
Blantyre: PO Box 51749, Limbe; tel: 01 655 901; Maj Effort and Capt Annet Paswera

Central: PO Box 40058, Kanengo, Lilongwe; tel: 01 716 869; Capts Alfred and Pamela Banda
Phalombe: PO Box 99, Migowi; tel: 01 481 216; Majs Gerald and Ellen Chimimba
Shire Valley: PO Box 48, Chiromo; Capts Paul and Doreen Kholowa

DISTRICTS
Northern: PO Box 1129, Mzuzu: Capt Dickson Mpakula
Upper Shire: P/Bag 8, Ntcheu CDSS, Ntcheu; Capt Dyson Chifudzeni

OFFICER TRAINING COLLEGE AND EXTENSION TRAINING CENTRE
Ndirande Ring Rd, Chinseu, Blantyre; PO Box 51140, Limbe

COMMUNITY DEVELOPMENT PROGRAMMES
Adult Literacy
Blantyre, Central, Phalombe and Shire Valley Divisions, Northern District

Agriculture, Irrigation, Food Security Programme
Shire Valley Division

Child Advocacy
Central Division

Feeding/Food for Work
Chikwawa, Migowi, Nguludi, Nsanje

HIV/Aids Home-based Care
Bangwe, Migowi, Nguludi, Nsanje

Micro-credit Schemes
All divisions and districts

Orphans and Vulnerable Children
All divisions and districts

Rural Women Empowerment (inc boreholes)
Blantyre, Central and Shire Valley Divisions

SOCIAL SERVICES
Hans Andersen Memorial Youth Centre for Child Anti-Trafficking: PO Box 167, Mchinji

MEXICO TERRITORY

Territorial leaders:
Commissioners David and Grace Bringans

Territorial Commander:
Commissioner David Bringans
(1 Jul 2009)

Chief Secretary:
Lieut-Colonel Josué Cerezo (1 Apr 2004)

Territorial Headquarters: San Borja #1456, Colonia Vértiz Narvarte, Delegación Benito Juárez, México 03600, DF

Postal address: Apartado Postal 12-668, México 03020, DF

Tel: [525] 55575-1042; 55559-5244/9625; fax: [525] 55575-3266; email: mexico@salvationarmy.org; website: www.ejercitodesalvacionmx.org

In 1934, a group known as the Salvation Patrol was commenced in Mexico by Alejandro Guzmán. In October 1937, he was presented with a flag by General Evangeline Booth at the USA Southern Territory Congress in Atlanta, Georgia. The Salvation Patrol then became absorbed into the international Salvation Army, operating under the supervision of DHQ in Dallas, Texas, later becoming part of Latin America North Territory. On 1 September 1998 it was made a command and, on 1 October 2001, it became a territory.

Zone: Americas and Caribbean
Country included in the territory: Mexico
'The Salvation Army' in Spanish: Ejército de Salvación
Language in which the gospel is preached: Spanish
Publications: *El Grito de Guerra (The War Cry), El Eslabon (The Link)*

A VAST, heavily populated country with diverse geography – from sun-baked beaches and deserts to rugged mountain ranges and fertile plains – Mexico is blessed with beauty. But just as attractive is the spiritual beauty seen within the lives of the country's Salvationists who are 'Celebrating His Glory' (the 2009 territorial theme) by their witness in open-air meetings, their ministry within Salvation Army facilities and through their community programmes.

Every day thousands of young people are being given a better life and future in 20 children's homes and through the Army's educational and day-care programmes. Officers and centre staff are undertaking special training in the care and rights of children. The many feeding centres give physical nourishment, some protection from trafficking and spiritual counsel to countless street children.

The territory's youth programme included music camps, youth councils in various locations and a retreat for youth and adults contemplating officership. Consequently, there are signs of spiritual maturity as many

Mexico Territory

prospective candidates offer their lives to God for full-time service.

In May 2008 five cadets of the God's Fellow Workers Session were ordained and commissioned as lieutenants. Commissioners Phil and Patricia Swyers (territorial leaders, USA Western) challenged the new officers to faithfully proclaim the gospel. The commissioners also participated in a dedication ceremony at the newly purchased property in Xochimilco, Mexico City, where a territorial headquarters, school for officer training and accommodation are to be built, funded by their territory.

Six cadets of the Prayer Warriors Session were welcomed into training in September.

Emergency services training having been given to selected personnel, 10 Mexican officers supported emergency work following flooding in Texas towards the end of 2008. New and used fully equipped emergency vehicles have been donated to the territory and strategically located in the country to meet future disasters.

In April 2009 Commissioners Max and Lenora Feener (territorial leaders, USA Southern) were guests at the opening of facilities for students at Puerto Vallarta and a new children's home at Culiacán (the previous one was burnt down). Both are funded by USA Southern.

STATISTICS

Officers 150 (active 123 retired 27) **Auxiliary-Captains** 4 **Envoys** 4 **Cadets** (1st Yr) 6 (2nd Yr) 4 **Employees** 42

Corps 48 **Outposts** 9 **Institutions** 51
Senior Soldiers 1,949 **Adherents** 364 **Junior Soldiers** 1,139

STAFF
Women's Ministries: Comr Grace Bringans (TPWM) Lt-Col Ruth Cerezo (TSWM)
Personnel: Maj José Sánchez
Programme: Captain Luis Camarillo
Education: Maj Leticia García
Finance: Maj Shirley Adams
Legal: Maj Humberto García
Property: Maj James Hood
Social: Maj Sallyann Hood
Training: Maj Humberto García
Youth and Candidates: Capt Nohemí Camarillo

DIVISIONS
Capital: Alicante No 88, Colonia Álamos Delegación Benito Juárez, 03400 México, DF; Apartado Postal 13-013, México, DF 03501; tel: 5590-9220; fax: 5590-9603; Maj Guadalupe Galván
Noroeste: Tamborel No. 601, Colonia Santa Rosa, Chihuahua, Chihuahua CP31050; tel: (614) 435-5968; tel/fax: (614) 420-4002; Majs César and Guadalupe Centeno
Río Bravo: Lombardo Toledano No 2709, Colonia Alta Vista Sur, 64740 Monterrey, Nuevo León; Apartado Postal # 1097, 64000 Monterrey, Nuevo León, México; tel: (81) 8359-5711; fax: (81) 8359-9115; Majs Manuel and Ana Campos

REGION
Sureste: Calle 19 No 116 x 22 y 24, Colonia México, Mérida, Yucatán 97128; tel: (999) 944-6415; Maj Jorge Martínez

TRAINING COLLEGE
Calle Monte Albán No 510, Colonia Independencia, México 03630, DF; tel: (55) 5672-7986; fax: (55) 5672-0608

SOCIAL SERVICES
Centre for Care of Persons in Transition
La Esperanza Centre: Labradores No 85 Esquina con Imprenta, Colonia Morelos, México 15270, DF; tel: (55) 5789-1511; fax: 5702-8033

Children's Care Centres
Ciudad Juárez, Chihuahua: Ulises Irigoyen #1674 Colonia Chaveña, CP 32060; tel: (656) 1614-2828 (acc 50)

Mexico Territory

Chihuahua, Chihuahua: Tamborel 601, Colonia Santa Rosa, CP 31050; tel: (614) 1420-4002 (acc 70)

Culiacán, Sinaloa: Cuauhtémoc #40 Sur, Colonia Las Vegas, Esquina Alba de Acosta, Cerca de KZ4, CP 80090; tel: (667) 715-1043 (acc 27)

Matamoros, Tamaulipas: Calle Sonora #15 Esquina San Pedro, Colonia Esperanza, CP 87310; tel: (868) 810-1369 (acc 45)

Mexicali, Baja California: Avenida Aguascalientes #2300, Colonia Santa Clara; tel: (686) 553-1194 (acc 30)

México, DF: Imprenta #225, Colonia Morelos, CP 15270; tel: (55) 5789-0554; fax: (55) 5702-3666 (acc 30)

Nuevo Laredo, Tamaulipas: Avenida Santos Degollado #1217, Sector Centro, CP 8800; tel: (867) 712-1455 (acc 30)

Reynosa, Tamaulipas: Allende #465 Poniente, Colonia Centro, CP 88500; tel: (899) 922-5463 (acc 75)

San Luis Potosí, San Luís Potosí: Bolívar #1426 Barrio San Miguelito, CP 78339; tel: (444) 815-4530 (acc 30)

Tampico, Tamaulipas: Avenida Central #501, Colonia Moctezuma, CP 89250; tel: (833) 212-0365 (acc 55)

Tapachula, Chiapas: Avenida 11 Sur #44, Colonia 16 de Septiembre, entre la 18y20, Oriente; tel: (962) 625-6733 (acc 50)

Tijuana, Baja California: Calle Aquiles Serdán #11585, Colonia Libertad, Parte Baja, CP 22300; tel: (664) 683-2694 (acc 85)

Torreón, Coahuila: Calle 21, #373 Nte, CP 27000; tel: (871) 7136-023 (acc 65)

Villahermosa, Tabasco: Calle Fco Sarabia #304, Colonia Segunda del Águila, CP 86080; tel: (993) 315-2694 (acc 30)

Children's Homes

Acapulco, Guerrero: Avenida de los Cantiles #16, Fraccionamiento Mozimba, CP 39460; tel: (744) 446-0359 (acc 90)

Chihuahua, Chihuahua: Tamborel #601, Colonia Santa Rosa, CP 31050; tel: (614) 420-4002 (acc 70)

Coatzacoalcos, Veracruz: Gutiérrez Zamora #1120 Colonia Centro, CP 96400; tel: (921) 214-5923 (acc 50)

Cuernavaca, Morelos: Avenida Atlacomúlco #124, Colonia Acapantzingo, CP 62440; tel: (777) 312-8207/ 8238 (acc 45)

Culiacán, Sinaloa: Chauhutémoc #40 Sur, Colonia Las Vegas, Esquina Alba de Acosta, Cerca de KZ4, CP 80090; tel: (667) 715-1043 (acc 27)

Guadalajara, Jalisco: Calzada Revolución #2011, Sector Reforma, CP 44800; tel: (33) 3635-4192 (acc 100)

Matamoros, Tamaulipas: Calle Sonora #15, Esquina San Pedro, Colonia Esperanza, CP 87310; tel: (868) 810-1369 (acc 30)

Mazatlán, Sinaloa: Calle Ángel Flores s/n, Colonia El Venadillo CP 82129; tel: (669) 980-7609 (acc 30)

Mérida, Yucatán: Calle 103, #506 Ax 62, Colonia Delio Moreno Cantón, CP 97268; tel: (999) 928-5153 (acc 30)

México, DF: Avenida Encino Grande #550, Tetelpán, VAO, CP 17000; tel: (55) 5585-0144 (acc 120)

Nuevo Laredo, Tamaulipas: Avenida Santos Degollado 1217, CP 88000; tel: (867) 712-1455 (acc 30)

Puebla, Puebla: Calle 16 Sur #704 Colonia Analco Centro, CP 72000; tel: (222) 242-6047 (acc 35)

Puerto Vallarta, Jalisco: Sonora No 232, Colonia Mjoneras, Apartado Postal 75-C Terminal Marítima, CP 48321; tel: (322) 290-1587 (acc 30)

Reynosa, Tamaulipas: Allende #465 Poniente, Colonia Centro, CP 88500; tel: (899) 922-5463; fax: (899) 930-9028 (acc 25)

Saltillo, Coahuila: Durazno #354, Colonia del Valle, CP 25000; tel: (844) 436-2005 (acc 40)

San Luis Potosí, San Luis Potosí: Bolívar #1426, Barrio San Miguelito, CP 78339; tel: (444) 815-4530 (acc 30)

Tampico, Tamaulipas: Avenida Central #501 Colonia Moctezuma, CP 89250; tel: (833) 212-0365 (acc 55)

Torreón, Coahuila: Calle 21, #373 Nte, CP 27000; tel: (871) 7136-023 (acc 50)

Veracruz, Veracruz: Revillagigedo #1507, Colonia México, CP 91756; tel: (229) 934-1927 (acc 50)

Villahermosa, Tabasco: Calle Fco Sarabia #304, Colonia Segunda del Águila, CP 86080; tel: (993) 315-2694 (acc 30)

Clinic and Dispensary

México DF: Clínica de Salud Mental, Calle Imprenta No 221 Colonia Morelos, CP 15270; tel: (55) 5794-1994

Day Care Centres

México, DF (Corps #1) (acc 25)
Ciudad Juárez: (acc 150)
Matamoros, Tamaulipas (acc 15)
Mexicali (acc 20)
Torreón (acc 15)

Mexico Territory

Feeding Centres
(Senior Citizens and Children)

Alvarado, Veracruz: Ignacio Ramírez #87, CP 95250, Apartado Postal 1; tel: (297) 973-2191 (acc 160)

Can Cún, Quintana Roo: Avenida Talleres entre 109 y 111 región 94, Manzana 80 Lote 28, Can Cún, Quintana Roo; tel/fax: (998) 840-1074 (acc 30)

Ciudad Juárez: Ulises Irigoyen No 1674, Colonia Chaveta, CP 32060, Apartado Postal 807; tel/fax: (656) 614-2828/632-0068 (acc 60)

Ciudad Madero, Tamaulipas: Calle Elena Alanís No 510 Norte, Esquinta Río Verde, Colonia Ampliación, Candaleario Garza, Diudad Madero, Tamaulipas, Apartado Postal 103, Cd Madero, Tamaulipas; tel: (833) 211-7661 (acc 25)

Cocotitlán, Estado de México: Acercamiento Nacional No 31, Esq con Abasolo, Colonia Centro, Cocotitlán, Estado de México 56680 (acc 25)

Culiacán, Sinaloa: Chuahutémoc #40 Sur, Colonia Las Vegas, Esquina Epitacio Alba de Acosta, Cerca de KZ4, CP 80090; tel: (667) 715-1043 (acc 33)

El Paso Texas, Mérida, Yucatán: Calle 159 #251, Colonia Emiliano Zapata III, Mérida, Yucatán 9720 (acc 50)

Genaro Vázquez, Nuevo León: Manzana Heroica Lote 13, Colonia Genaro Vázquez, Monterrey, Nuevo Léon (acc 100)

Hermosillo, Sonora: Calle Ignacio M. Altamirano No 574, Colonia Benito Juárez, Hermosillo, Sonora 83110; tel: (622) 118-6709

La Gloria, Tijuana, Baja California: Avenida Benito Juárea No 26, Poblado 'La Gloria', Colonia La Joya, Tijuana, BC 22674

Mexicali, Baja California: Avenida Aguascalientes #2300, Colonia Santa Clara, CP 21110; tel: (686) 553-1194 (acc 30)

México, DF (Corps #3): Norte 68 #3742, Colonia M. de Río Blanco, CP 07880; tel: (55) 5751-3598 (acc 60)

México, DF (Corps #6): Calle 12 #68 Esquina Avenida Pantitlán, Colonia Provenir, CP 57430, Netzahualcoyotl, Estado de México; tel/fax: (55) 5200-1839 (acc 30)

Monclova, Coahuila: Benjamín Garza #1221, Colonia Primero de Mayo, CP 25760; tel: (866) 631-3502 (acc 50)

Nogales, Sonora: Calle San Juan #191, Colonia Benit Juárez, CP 84015; tel/fax: (631) 312-4647 (acc 45)

Piedras Negras: Victoria No 805 Nte, Colonia Centro, CP 26030; tel/fax: (878) 782-2707 (acc 30)

Puerto Vallarta, Jalisco: Sonora 232 Colonia Mojoneras, Puerto Vallarta, Jalisco 48300; tel: (322) 290-1587 (acc 50)

Querétaro, Querétaro: Heriberto Jara No 211, Colonia Lázaro Cárdenas, Querétaro, Querétaro 76087; tel: (442) 222-9623 (acc 25)

Sabinitas, Nuevo León: Calle Plutarco Elías Calles #401, Colonia 6 de Marzo, Guadalupe, NL 67160; tel: (81) 8299-5981 (acc 75)

Saltillo, Coahuila: Sosténes Rocha 170, Colonia Chamizal, CP 25180; tel: (844) 135-3458 (acc 35)

San Juan Ixhuatepec, Estado de México: Tenochtitlan #10, Administración San Juan Ixhuatepec, Tlanepantla, Edo de México, CP 54180; tel: (55) 5715-0649 (acc 30)

Tijuana, Baja California: Calle Aquiles Serdán #11585, Colonia Libertad, CP 22300, Apartado Postal 5-G; tel: (664) 683-2694 (acc 45)

Toluca, Estado de México: Calle Pangue Iztaccihuati #3, Colonia Parques Nacionales, Toluca, Estado de México 50100; tel: (722) 278-7335 (acc 25)

Xochitepec, Morelos: Calle Hidalgo S/N esquina Jalisco, Colonia Lázaro Cárdenas, Xochitepec, Morelos 6279o; tel/fax: (777) 361-3628 (acc 40)

(Men)

Mexicali, Baja California: Avenida Aguascalientes #2300, Colonia Santa Clara, CP 21110; tel: (686) 553-1194 (acc 50)

Night Shelters (Men)

Mexicali, Baja California: Avenida Aguascalientes #2300, Colonia Santa Clara, CP 21110; tel: (686) 553-1194 (acc 50)

México, DF: La Esperanza, Labradores #85, Esquina con Imprenta, Colonia Morelos, México 15270 DF; tel: (55) 5789-1511 (acc 125)

Monterrey, Nuevo León: Carvajal y de la Cueva #1716 Nte, Colonia Primero de Mayo, CP 64580; tel: (81) 8375-0379 (acc 80)

Piedras Negras, Coahuila: Victoria #805 Nte, Colonia Centro CP 26030; tel: (878) 782-2707 (acc 50)

Tijuana, Baja California: Calle Aquiles Serdán #11585, Colonia Libertad, Porte Baja, CP 22300; tel: (664) 683-2694 (acc 45)

Vocational Training Centre

México DF: Labradores #85 Esquina con Imprenta, Colonia Morelos, CP 15270; tel: (55) 5789-1511

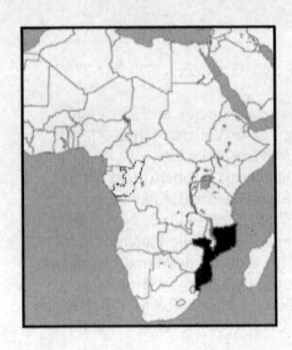

MOZAMBIQUE COMMAND

Command leaders:
Lieut-Colonels Torben and Deise Eliasen

Officer Commanding:
Lieut-Colonel Torben Eliasen
(1 Mar 2008)

General Secretary:
Major Celestino Pepe Pululu (1 Mar 2008)

Command Headquarters: Avenue Filipe Samuel Magaia, 860, Maputo, Mozambique

Postal address: PO Box 4099, Maputo, Mozambique

Tel: [258] 2132 8145; fax: [258] 2132 8146

The Salvation Army's evangelistic endeavours in Mozambique were pioneered in 1916 by Mozambican converts returning from South Africa. The work was recognised by the Mozambique government in 1986 and officially registered in June 2005. Previously part of the Southern Africa Territory, Mozambique became a separate command on 1 March 2008.

Zone: Africa
Country included in the command: Mozambique
'The Salvation Army' in Portuguese (the official language): Exército de Salvação
Languages in which the gospel is preached: Portuguese, Chopi, Gitonga, Makhuwa, Ndau, Sena, Tsonga, Tswa.
Periodicals: *Devocionias para Encontros da Liga do Lar* (Home League resource manual)

ONE of the characteristics of The Salvation Army in Mozambique is that it is corps-based; there are no social services centres. That does not, however, diminish the social impact within those communities where the Army is at work.

Corps throughout the command are displaying a passion for community development, and the Community Care Ministries facilitation teams are very eager to engage in community conversation, cooperation and commitment. In this way they support and help communities to overcome challenges and find possibilities of future progress.

Building on this strength, during 2009 the command held several seminars for its officers, soldiers and home league members to help them sharpen their knowledge and skills about community development. The subject was included in the training college curriculum for future cadets to learn in a systematic way.

One of the main challenges continues to be overseeing the growing work across the country. There are only seven administrative officers and 32 corps officers to take care of 100 congregations (40 corps and 60 outposts), so the command eagerly awaited the commissioning of eight cadets of the Prayer Warriors Session in December 2009.

The command is creating its first division in the central north of the country, with a new divisional headquarters being built in the city of Beira. The appointment of divisional leaders is expected at the beginning of 2010.

Another development has been the signing of memorandums of understanding between the Army and other strategic partners (such as Tear Fund and the Mozambique Human Rights League), enabling good networking and more-effective ministry.

STATISTICS
Officers 39 **Cadets** 8 **Employees** 20
Corps 40 **Outposts** 60 **Day Care Centres** 4
   HIV Home-based Care and OVC Projects 4
   Adult Literacy Projects 50
Senior Soldiers 3,559 **Junior Soldiers** 1,267

STAFF
Women's Ministries: Lt-Col Deise Eliasen
   (TPWM) Maj Veronica Pululu (TSWM)
Finance: Capt Dini Varte
Projects: Mr Virgilio Suande
Property: Capt Felix Nhaduate
Sponsorship: Lt-Col Deise Eliasen
Training and Education: Capt Mario Nhacumba
Youth and Candidates: Capt Jose Nharugue

NEW ZEALAND, FIJI AND TONGA: Some of the 500 Salvation Army young people who met at a combined Easter camp for the North Island, **New Zealand** (Photo: Cara Wood)

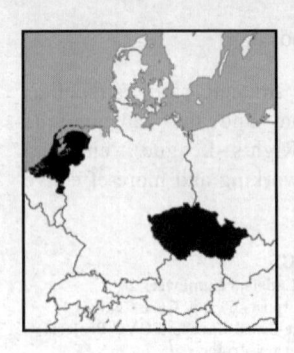

THE NETHERLANDS AND CZECH REPUBLIC TERRITORY

Territorial leaders:
Commissioners Roy and Arda Frans

Territorial Commander:
Commissioner Roy Frans (1 Jul 2007)

Chief Secretary:
Colonel Pieter Dijkstra (25 Mar 2008)

Territorial Headquarters: Spoordreef 10, 1315 GN Almere, The Netherlands

Tel: [31] (36) 5398111; fax: [31] (36) 5331458; email: ldhnl@legerdesheils.nl;
websites: www.legerdesheils.nl; www.armadaspasy.cz

Captain and Mrs Joseph K. Tyler, English officers, and Lieutenant Gerrit J. Govaars, a gifted Dutch teacher, commenced Salvation Army work in the Gerard Doustraat, Amsterdam, on 8 May 1887. Operations soon spread throughout the country and reached Indonesia (then The Netherlands East Indies) in 1894. Further advances were made in 1926 in Surinam and in 1927 in Curaçao.

Salvation Army operations in Czechoslovakia commenced in 1919, the pioneer being Colonel Karl Larsson. Evangelistic and social activities were maintained until suppressed in June 1950. After the opening of the central European borders, The Salvation Army's work was re-established and The Netherlands Territory was asked to take charge of the redevelopment. By the end of 1990 centres were reopened in Havirov, Prague, Brno and Ostrava and the work has grown steadily since then.

On 1 February 2002 the territory was renamed The Netherlands and Czech Republic Territory.

Zone: Europe
Countries included in the territory: Czech Republic, The Netherlands
'The Salvation Army' in Dutch and Flemish: Leger des Heils; in Czech: Armáda Spásy
Languages in which the gospel is preached: Czech, Dutch, Flemish
Periodicals: *Dag In Dag Uit*, *Heils-en Strijdzangen*, *InterCom*, *Strijdkreet*, (all Dutch), *Prapor Spásy* (Czech)

THE territory is committed to move forward under the slogan 'As One Army – Unity In Mission and Diversity In Organisation'. An advisory group has been established with its main task of making recommendations to the territorial leadership on new avenues that would increase mission effectiveness and efficiency.

The Territorial Youth Commission has already taken some significant steps to develop a strategy for youth ministries aimed at spiritual awakening and numerical growth.

'New-Style Spring Festival', attended by many Salvationists, friends and their families from around The Netherlands, was a day of worship, gatherings, prayer, evangelistic outreach through open-air witness, seminars, workshops and exhibitions of various aspects of Salvation Army work.

The day was crowned with a very successful music festival featuring Vasa Gospel Choir from Sweden and Bandsman Andrew Poirier (trombone soloist, Canada) as special guests.

'Work For All' was one of William Booth's many visionary concepts recorded in his book *In Darkest England and The Way Out*, so the territory is aiming to provide job training and work opportunities. New initiatives have been developed with the business community and the Army's own operational units.

Research has shown that 30 per cent of the Dutch population are lonely. The Army is doing as much as possible to combat this issue and help reduce the number of lonely people to 25 per cent by 2011.

The year's Bosshardt Award was presented to Mrs Hannie van Leeuwen and Frans Derks from the More Than Football Foundation. The award ceremony took place in the Carré Theatre, Amsterdam, during a Gala Night when Salvationists joined popular artists and musicians to perform music and drama items. Government dignitaries, the Mayor of Amsterdam, notable politicians and leading businessmen were among the specially invited guests.

Proposals for education, income-generation and health projects that could be funded by the Dutch Government were discussed at a consultation on partnership held in Lunteren and attended by Salvation Army leaders and project officers from Latin America North, Democratic Republic of Congo, Congo Brazzaville, Mozambique and International Headquarters.

In the Czech Republic, Armáda Spásy has shown notable growth and progress. A new mothers and children centre opened in Prerov and an alcohol and drug rehabilitation project was launched in Havirov. A former sex worker gave a powerful testimony during a spiritually uplifting weekend attended by soldiers, adherents and friends.

STATISTICS
Officers 329 (active 126 retired 203) **Cadets** (1st Yr) 6 (2nd Yr) 1 **Employees** 4,871
Corps 72 (99 local service centres) **Business Units** 17 (187 local service centres)
Senior Soldiers 4,618 **Adherents** 1,218 **Junior Soldiers** 525

STAFF
The Salvation Army Church
Women's Ministries: Comr Arda Frans (TPWM) Col Alida Dijkstra (TSWM)
Adult Ministries: see Field Programme Support
Field: Col Alida Dijkstra (pro-tem)
Field Programme Support (inc Youth and Adult Ministries):
Candidates: Maj Tineke van de Wetering
Editor-in-Chief: Mr Rudi Tinga
Education and Training: Maj Hendrika Scholtens
Finance and International Projects: Envoy Harm Slomp
Finance, Accommodation and Dataprocessing: Mr Bert Barink
Literary: Maj Simon M. van der Vlugt
Music: Mr Roel van Kesteren

DIVISIONS
Central: Piccolostraat 13, 1312 RC Almere; tel: (36) 536 51 06; Maj Elsje Klarenbeek

The Netherlands and Czech Republic Territory

North/East: Gein 27, 8032 BB Zwolle;
tel: (38) 452 67 13; fax: (38) 452 67 19;
Majs Teunis and Hendrika Scholtens
South: Wittebrem 22, 3068 TM Rotterdam;
tel: (10) 4557921; Majs Johannes and
Annetje den Hollander

THE SALVATION ARMY MAIN FOUNDATION
Board of Administration
Chairman: Comr Roy Frans (TC)

Staff
Secretary: Col Pieter Dijkstra (CS)
Financial Sec and Managing Director: Envoy Harm Slomp

THE SALVATION ARMY SERVICES FOUNDATION
Board of Administration
Chairman: Comr Roy Frans (TC)
Vice-Chairman: Col Pieter Dijkstra (CS)
Official (non-voting) Sec: Envoy Harm Slomp RA
Members: Mr G. L. Telling, Mrs L. M. Welschen-van der Hoek, Mr P. Visser

Staff
Managing Director: Envoy Ed Bosma
Communications: Mrs Hella van der Schoot
Domestic Affairs Staff/Personnel: Mr Arie M. Rietveld
Family Tracing: Maj Jaap de Ruiter
Fund-Raising and Marketing: Mr Will van Heugten
Finance and Information Technology: Mr Joop Rozema
Sales and Supplies: Maj Henk van Essen (pro tem)

ReSHARE BV (Recycling Services)
Koopvaardijweg 15, 4906 CV Oosterhout;
tel: (0900) 9900099
Depot: Hattem
Director Operations: Capt Robert Paul Fennema

THE SALVATION ARMY FUND-RAISING FOUNDATION
Board of Administration
Chairman: Comr Roy Frans (TC)
Vice-Chairman: Col Pieter Dijkstra (CS)
Official Sec: Envoy Harm Slomp RA
Members: Mrs F. H. van Ham-Laning, Mr C. Hendriks, Mr J. de Widt, Mr F. B. A. M. van Oss

Staff
Managing Director: Envoy Ed Bosma
All activities of the Foundation are to be executed by The Salvation Army Services Foundation.

THE SALVATION ARMY FOUNDATION FOR WELFARE AND HEALTH CARE
Care for the Homeless (total acc 3,313): night shelter (417); day care (acc 668); 24-hour shelter (acc 1,478); care for vulnerable people (646); young people (acc 218); supervised living (acc 532); preventative homelessness projects, ambulatory programs (57 FTE)
Substance Misuse Services (total acc 63): residential (acc 20); supervised living (acc 43); ambulatory programs (3 FTE)
Probation Services: ambulatory programmes (134 FTE); day training centres (acc 40)
Health Care and Care for the Elderly (total capacity 1,395): permanent stay (acc 355); hospice care (acc 19); temporary stay (inc medical care of homeless) (acc 175); day care (acc 20); ambulatory programmes (inc home care) (94 FTE); supervised living (acc 237); psychiatric clinic (acc 57)
Custody Care (total pupils 2,351): ambulatory programmes (156 FTE)
Care for Children and Young People (total acc 383): residential care (acc 379); day care (acc 4)
Prevention and Social Rehabilitation Services (total acc 152): community centres (6); ambulatory programmes (acc 122 FTE); work coaching (acc 152)

Board of Administration
Chairman: Comr Roy Frans (TC)
Vice-Chairman: Col Pieter Dijkstra (CS)
Sec/Treasurer: Envoy Harm Slomp
Members: Mr L. H. van den Heuvel, Mr F. van der Meulen, Mrs G.W. van Montfrans-Hartman, Mrs M. Trompetter

Staff
Managing Director: Lt-Col Christina A. Voorham
Deputy Director: Mr Hermanus M. van Teijlingen
Finance, Property, HRM and ICT: Mr Ruud de Vries
Issue Managers: Mr Marinus A. J. Timmer, Mr Josephus J. Sesink, Mr Jeroen Hoogteijling, Rev Johannes J. Blom, Envoy Johannes W. Kanis
Controller: Mr Piet van Keulen

A march of witness in the afternoon of the 'New-Style Spring Festival' is led by THQ officers and the Amsterdam Staff Band and Staff Songsters

Main Office: Spoordreef 10, 1315 GN Almere; tel: (36) 539 82 50; fax: (36) 534 07 10

CENTRES FOR LIVING, CARE AND WELFARE

Central Region
Information: Aïdadreef 8, 3561 GE Utrecht; tel: (30) 274 91 21

Northern Region
Information: Kwinkenplein 10-A, 9712 GZ Groningen; tel: (50) 317 26 70

South-Western Region
Information: Kromhout 110, 3311 RH Dordrecht; tel: (78) 632 07 00

Flevoland
Information: Spoordreef 12, 1315 GN Almere; tel: (36) 549 68 00

Gelderland
Information: Hoenderloseweg 108, 7339 GK Ugchelen; tel: (55) 538 03 33

Limburg/Brabant
Information: Mariastraat 13, 6211 EP Maastricht; tel: (43) 350 33 84

Northern Holland
Information: Mariettahof 25, 2033 WS Haarlem; tel: (23) 553 39 33

Overijssel
Information: Eiffelstraat 1 – 117, 8013 RT Zwolle; tel: (38) 467 19 40

Amsterdam Goodwill Centres
Information: Rode Kruisstraat 24b, 1025 KN Amsterdam; tel: (20) 630 11 11

The Hague Goodwill Work
Information: St Barbaraweg 4, 2516 BT Den Haag; tel: (70) 311 55 40

Rotterdam Centres for Social Services
Information: Kooikerweg 28, 3069 WP Rotterdam; tel: (10) 222 98 88

Probation Services Leger des Heils Jeugdzorg and Reclassering
Central Office: Zeehaenkade 30, 3526 LC Utrecht; tel: (88) 090 10 00

HOTEL AND CONFERENCE CENTRE

'Belmont', Goorsteeg 66, 6718 TB Ede; tel: (31) 848 23 65 (50 twin-bedded rooms; 14 conference rooms acc varying 12-375; during summer 96 extra beds available, in tents acc 160)

CZECH REPUBLIC

Officer-in-charge: Maj Mike Stannett (1 May 2008)

National Headquarters: Petrzilkova 2565/23, 158 00 Praha 5; tel/fax: (00420) 251 106 424; email: info@armadaspasy.cz; website: www.armadaspasy.cz

STATISTICS

(not included in statistics of The Netherlands)
Officers 17 **Cadets** (2nd Yr) 2 **Employees** 300
Corps 8 **Community Centres** 15 **Institutions** 20
Senior Soldiers 61 **Adherents** 44 **Junior Soldiers** 10

STAFF

Asst Officer-in-charge: Maj Ruth Stannett
Personal Assistant: Pavla Vopeláková

The Netherlands and Czech Republic Territory

Training: Capt Aleš Malach
Finance: Mrs Hana Kosová

CENTRES

Hostels for Men and Women and Night Shelters
Brno: Mlýnská 25, 602 00 Brno;
  tel: 543 212 530 (acc 136)
Krnov: Csl armády 837 bcd, 794 01 Krnov;
  tel: 554 612 296 (acc 85, includes mothers and children)
Opava: Nákladní 24, 746 01 Opava;
  tel: 553 712 984 (acc 48)
Prague: Tusarova 60, 170 00 Praha 7;
  tel: 220 184 000 (acc 220)

Hostels for Men and Night Shelters
Havírov:
  Hostel, Na spojce 2, 736 01 Havírov;
    tel: 596 810 197 (acc 53)
  Night Shelter, Pod Svahem 1, Havírov-Šubark;
    tel: 596 881 007 (acc 24)
Karlovy Vary: Nákladní 7, 360 05 Karlovy Vary;
  tel: 353 569 267 (acc 45)
Opava: Nákladní 24, 746 01 Opava;
  tel: 553 712 984 (acc 48)
Ostrava: U Novych Válcoven 9,
  709 00 Ostrava-Mariánské Hory;
  tel: 596 620 650 (acc 114)
Šumperk: Vikyrovicka 1495, Šumperk-Luže;
  tel: 583 224 634 (acc 35)

Homes for Mothers and Children
Havírov: Dvorákova 21/235, 736 01 Havírov;
  tel: 596 810 221 (acc 18 mothers plus children)
Krnov: Csl armády 837 bcd, 794 01 Krnov;
  tel: 554 612 296 (acc 85, includes hostel for men and women)
Ostrava: Gen Píky 25, Ostrava-Fifejdy 702 00;
  tel: 596 611 962 (acc women 30, mothers 10, children 15-20)
Opava: Rybárská 86, 746 01 Opava;
  tel: 553 712 984 (acc mothers 11, children 33)
Přerov: 9 kvetna 2481/107, 750 02 Přerov;
  tel: 581 210 769 (acc 45)

Alternative Punishment Programme
Opava: Nákladní 24, 746 01 Opava;
  tel: 553 712 984

Elderly Persons Project
Ostrava-Kuncicky: Holvekova 38, 710 00
  Ostrava-Kuncicky; tel: 596 237 151 (acc 40)

Farm Rehabilitation Project
747 24 Strahovice 1; mobile: 737 215 396 (acc 4)

Prison Work
Prague: Petržilkova 2565/23, 158 00 Praha 5;
  tel/fax: (00420) 737 215 427

Youth Centre
Brno-Bystrc: Kubickova 23, 635 00 Brno-Bystrc;
  tel: 546 221 756

Salvationists of the Czech Republic carry out evangelism among the Roma (Gypsy) community at Privov, in Northern Moravia

NEW ZEALAND, FIJI AND TONGA TERRITORY

Territorial leaders:
Commissioners Donald C. and Debra K. Bell

Territorial Commander:
Commissioner Donald C. Bell (1 Mar 2009)

Chief Secretary:
Colonel Graeme Reddish (1 Mar 2009)

Territorial Headquarters: 204 Cuba Street, Wellington, New Zealand

Postal address: PO Box 6015, Wellington 6141, New Zealand

Tel: [64] (04) 384 5649; fax: [64] (04) 802 6258; website: www.salvationarmy.org.nz

On 1 April 1883 Salvation Army activities were commenced at Dunedin by Captain George Pollard and Lieutenant Edward Wright. Social work began in 1884 with a home for ex-prisoners. Work was begun officially in Fiji on 14 November 1973 by Captain Brian and Mrs Beverley McStay, and in Tonga on 9 January 1986 by Captain Tifare and Mrs Rebecca Inia.

Zone: South Pacific and East Asia
Countries included in the territory: Fiji, New Zealand, Tonga
'The Salvation Army' in Maori: Te Ope Whakaora
Languages in which the gospel is preached: English, Fijian, Hindi, Korean, Maori, Rotuman, Samoan, Tongan and Vietnamese
Periodical: *War Cry*

THE territory is in the final year of its five-year strategic plan to support its mission of 'caring for people, transforming lives and reforming society by God's power'. Salvationists are focused on four specific goals:

To grow all Salvationists as dynamic disciples; to increase the number of new soldiers; to take significant steps towards the eradication of poverty; to be a connected, streamlined and mission-focused Army.

Enthusiasm for soldiership continues to grow, including among young people. Tonga enrolled its hundredth soldier in June 2008. Twenty cadets of the Ambassadors Of Holiness Session are in training, the largest session since 1986.

The global economic crisis is a challenge and an opportunity. In the first half of 2009, Salvation Army food banks experienced a 30 to 40 per cent increase in demand. In mid-2008 the territory said it would no longer accept grants of money directly raised through gambling.

The general public continues to respond enthusiastically to Salvation Army fundraising campaigns, showing solidarity with people in need.

New Zealand, Fiji and Tonga Territory

Social programmes refer clients between services in a total package of Salvation Army care, with corps and centres exploring new ways to welcome people into their premises.

In March 2009, 230 Salvation Army social work practitioners met for an inaugural social services conference. Reciprocity was a theme, shifting from a 'hand-out' or even 'hand-up' approach to one of 'sharing the workload together'. A pilot scheme of practical support and friendship for seniors was launched.

Fiji has experienced political uncertainty since a bloodless coup in late 2006 put increasing pressure on its poor. When floods struck in January 2009, described as Fiji's 'worst ever natural disaster', The Salvation Army responded with food and safe premises for evacuees.

The Army's work is highly respected in Fiji – as also in Tonga, where health and addiction education are strong aspects of outreach programmes. Some children and families supported through child sponsorship in Fiji and Tonga have become soldiers and junior soldiers, in part because of the pastoral care received from Salvationists.

In March 2009 more than 1,500 Salvationists were in Wellington for the 'New Zeal 09' weekend, its theme being 'Heaven Invading Earth'. Dr Tony Campolo, American pastor and author internationally renowned among evangelical Christians, was a guest speaker.

The event was a call to total consecration and radical discipleship; a first-time salvation encounter with God for some, but for most an encounter with the truth of the gospel – that taking God's love into communities remains the only way to bring Heaven to Earth.

Zeal for The Salvation Army's mission remains strong in New Zealand, Fiji and Tonga.

STATISTICS
Officers 538 (active 316 retired 222) **Cadets** (1st Yr) 20 (2nd Yr) 8 **Employees** 2,788
Corps 94 **Plants** 5 **Outposts** 5 **Recovery Churches** 10 **Institutions** 82
Senior Soldiers 5,565 **Adherents** 1,456 **Junior Soldiers** 718
Personnel serving outside territory Officers 19

STAFF
Women's Ministries: Comr Debora K. Bell (TPWM) Col Wynne Reddish (TSWM)
Business Administration: Maj Bruce Vyle
  Audit: Mr Graeme Tongs
  Finance: Maj David Bateman
  Information Technology: Mr Mark Bennett
  Property: Mr Ian McLaren
  Public Relations: Maj Robbie Ross
  Trade: Mr George Borthwick
  Communications: Maj Christina Tyson
Personnel: Lt-Col Wilfred Arnold
  Asst (Officer Resources and Overseas Service): Maj Tanya Dunn
  Asst (Pastoral Care): Lt-Col Margaret Arnold
  Human Resources: Mr Paul Geoghegan
  Booth College of Mission:
    Principal: Maj David Noakes
    School for Bible and Mission: Maj Garth Stevenson
    Centre for Leadership Development: Caroline Jewkes
    Education Consultant and Registrar: Alison Mawson
    Candidates: Maj Yvonne Westrupp
Programme: Maj Lyndon Buckingham
  Asst: Maj Bronwyn Buckingham
  Social Programme: Maj Campbell Roberts
  Creative Ministries: Matthew Pethybridge
  National Youth Bandmaster: Grant Pitcher
  Youth: Capt Rebecca Gane

New Zealand, Fiji and Tonga Territory

Planned Giving: Maj Sandra Mellsop
SpiritSong: Vocal Leader Denise Hewitt
Children's Ministries: Capt Brenda Luscombe
Book Production: Maj Christina Tyson
Moral and Social Issues Council: Maj Ian Hutson
Overseas Development Consultant: Maj Vyvyenne Noakes
Social Policy and Parliamentary Unit: Maj Ian Kilgour
Territorial Events Co-Ordinator: Joanne Poole

DIVISIONS

Central: 204 Cuba St, Wellington 6011, PO Box 6421, Wellington 6141; tel: (04) 384 4713; fax: (04) 802 6267; email: cdhq@nzf.salvationarmy.org; Majs Rod and Jenny Carey

Midland: 12 Vialou St, PO Box 500, Hamilton 3240; tel: (07) 839 2242; fax: (07) 839 2282; email: Midland_dhq@nzf.salvationarmy.org; Majs Andrew and Yvonne Westrupp

Northern: 369 Queen St, PO Box 5035, Auckland 1001; tel: (09) 337 1318; fax: (09) 379 4152; email: ndhq@nzf.salvationarmy.org; Maj Heather Rodwell

Southern: 71 Peterborough St, Christchurch 8013, PO Box 25-207, Christchurch 8144; tel: (03) 377 0799; fax: (03) 377 3575; email: southern@nzf.salvationarmy.org; Majs Clive and Lesley Nicolson

FIJI DIVISION

Headquarters: PO Box 14412, Suva, Fiji; tel: [679] 331 5177; fax: [679] 330 3112
Divisional leader: Capts Iliesa and Litiana Cola; email: dhq_fiji@nzf.salvationarmy.org
Corps 11 Corps Plant 1 Outposts 4

School for Officer Training and Leadership Training
tel: (679) 330 7749; fax: (679) 330 7010; email: SFOT_FIJI@nzf.salvationarmy.org

Community Ministries Offices
Eastern: Grantham Rd, Raiwai, Suva; tel: (679) 337 2122
Western: 38 Sukanaivalu Rd, Waiyavi Lautoka; tel: (679) 664 5471

Family Care Centres
Labasa: Sarwan Singh St, Nasea, Labasa; tel: (679) 881 1898 (acc 12)
Lautoka: 160 VM Pillai Rd, Drasa-Vitogo, Lautoka; tel: (679) 665 0952 (acc 16)
Suva: 21 Spring St, Toorak, Suva; tel: (679) 330 5518 (acc 18)

Court and Prison Officers
Lautoka; tel: (679) 665 0952/664 5471
Suva; tel: (679) 331 5440

Farm Project
Farm 80, Lomaivuna; tel: (679) 368 0771 (acc 10)

Girls' Home
Mahaffy Dr, Suva; tel: (679) 331 3318 (acc 20)

Raiwai Hostel
Hostel for young male tertiary students, Grantham Rd, Suva; tel: (679) 338 7438 (acc 20)

Red Shield House
Hostel for young females, 37 Moala St, Samabula, Suva; tel: (679) 338 1347 (acc 9)

Sewing Skills Programmes
Labasa: Lot 2 Batinikama, Siberia Rd; tel: (679) 881 4822
Lautoka: 38 Sukanaivalu Rd, Waiyavi; tel: (679) 666 3712
Sigatoka: Kulukulu Subdiv'n; tel: (679) 650 0782
Suva: 50 MacGregor Rd; tel: (679) 3307 746

Tiny Tots Kindergartens
Ba: 6 Old Kings Rd, Yalalevu; tel: (679) 667 0155 (acc 15)
Labasa: Lot 2 Batinikama, Siberia Rd, Labasa; tel: (679) 881 4822 (acc 15)
Lautoka: 38 Sukanaivalu Rd, Waiyavi Lautoka; tel: (679) 666 3712 (acc 15)
Lomaivuna: Farm 80, Lomaivuna; tel: (679) 360 1238 (acc 15)
Nadi: Lot 30-32, Goundar St, Namaka, Nadi; tel: (679) 670 0405 (acc 15)
Nasinu: Yaka Place, Valelevu, Nasinu; tel: (679) 339 3744 (acc 30)
Suva Central: 50 MacGregor Rd, Suva; tel: (679) 3307 746 (acc 30)

TONGA REGION

Regional Headquarters: Mosimani Building, cnr Hala Fatafehi and Mateialona, Nuku'alofa, PO Box 1035, Nuku'alofa, Tonga; tel: (676) 23-760; fax (676) 28-731; email: rhq_tga@nzf.salvationarmy.org
Regional leaders: Majs Rex and Geraldine Johnson
Corps 4 Corps Plant 1

New Zealand, Fiji and Tonga Territory

Community Ministries: Mosimani Building, cnr Hala Fatafehi and Mateialonga, Nuku'alofa, Tonga
Court and Prison Work: Nuku'alofa
Addiction Programme: Mosimani Building, cnr Hala Fatafehi and Mateialonga, Nuku'alofa, Tonga tel: (676) 23760;
email: rhq_tga@nzf.salvationarmy.org
Kindergartens:
Sopu, Nuku'alofa; tel: (676) 26370 (acc 30)
Kolovai; tel: (676) 11737 (acc 25)
Mobile Health Clinic: Popua and Patangata Community

BOOTH COLLEGE OF MISSION (BCM)

School for Officer Training (SFOT); Centre for Leadership Development; School of Bible and Mission: 20 William Booth Grove, Upper Hutt 5018; PO Box 40-542, Upper Hutt, 5140; tel: (04) 528 8628; fax: (04) 527 6900
Principal, BCM and SFOT: Maj David Noakes

FAMILY TRACING SERVICE

PO Box 6015, Wellington 6015;
tel: (04) 382 0710; fax: (04) 802 6257;
email: familytracing@nzf.salvationarmy.org

ARCHIVES AND MUSEUM

202-204 Cuba St, PO Box 6015, Wellington 6141;
tel: (04) 382 0732; fax(04) 802 6259;
email: archives@nzf.salvationarmy.org;
Maj Garry Mellsop

FARM

Jeff Memorial Farm, Kaiwera RD 2, Gore;
tel: (03) 205 3572

INDEPENDENT LIVING UNITS

Ashburton: Wilson Court, 251-255 Tancred St (units 3)
Auckland: 353 Blockhouse Bay Rd (units 20)
New Plymouth: Bingham Court, 46 Murray St, Bell Block (units 10)
Blenheim: 35 George St (units 7)
Carterton: 204 High St South (units 8)
Christchurch: 794 Main North Rd, Belfast (units 10)
Gisborne: Edward Murphy Village, 481 Aberdeen Rd (units 30)
Hamilton: Nawton Village, 57 Enfield St (units 40)
Kapiti: 41 Bluegum Rd, Paraparaumu Beach (units 18)
Mosgiel: Elmwood Retirement Village, 22 Elmwood Dr (units 30); 17 Cedar Cres (units 30)
Oamaru: Glenside, 9 Arthur St (units 12)
Papakura: 91 Clevedon Rd (units 6)
Wellington: Summerset Units, Newtown: 182a Owen St (units 11); 210, 212, 214 Owen St (units 3); 226 Owen St (units 9)

RETIRED OFFICERS' ACCOMMODATION (under THQ)

Auckland: Lang Court, 9 Willcott St (units 6);
6D Liston St, Northcote (unit 1);
19 Splendour Cl, Henderson (unit 1)
Wellington: 176, 176a, 178, 178a Queens Dr, Lyall Bay (units 4)

YOUTH CAMPS AND CONFERENCE CENTRES

Blue Mountain Adventure Centre: RD 1, Owhango 3989; tel: (07) 892 2630;
website: www.bluemountainadventure.co.nz

SOCIAL SERVICES (under THQ)
Addiction and Supportive Accommodation Services

National Office: Level 2, 369 Queen St, PO Box 7342, Wellesley St, Auckland 1141;
tel: (09) 337 1351; fax: (09) 377 1249;
National Manager: Maj Lynette Hutson
email: lynette_hutson@nzf.salvationarmy.org

Bridge Programme: Community and Residential Programmes (Treatment of Alcohol and Drug Dependency)

Auckland: Bridge Centre, PO Box 56-442, 7-15 Ewington Ave, Mt Eden, Auckland 1024;
tel: (09) 630 1491; fax: (09) 630 8395;
email: akbridge@xtra.co.nz (acc assessment 21, treatment 16, day clients 7)
Christchurch: The Bridge Programme, PO Box 9070, Tower Junction, Christchurch 8149;
Addington, 35 Collins St, Christchurch 8324;
tel: (03) 338 4436; fax: (03) 338 4312; email: christchurch_bridge@nzf.salvationarmy.org (acc 26)
Dunedin: PO Box 934, Dunedin 9054, 160 Crawford St, Dunedin 9016;
tel: (03) 477 9852; fax: (03) 477 1493; email: Dunedin_bridge@nzf.salvationarmy.org (acc 7)
Hamilton: Midland Regional Residential and Detox Centre, 227 Baverstock Rd, Hamilton 3200, PO Box 15 673, Hamilton 3204;
tel: (07) 839 6871; fax: (07) 839 6872
Invercargill: 110 Leven St, PO Box 74, Invercargill 9840; tel: (03) 218 3094;
fax: (03) 218 7934; email: Invercargill_bridge@nzf.salvationarmy.org
Manukau: Bridge Centre, 16b Bakerfield Place, PO Box 76075, Manukau City 2241;

New Zealand, Fiji and Tonga Territory

tel: (09) 261 0887; fax: (09) 263 9325;
email: mkbridge@xtra.co.nz
Waikato: The Bridge Programme, 25 Thackeray St, Hamilton 3204; tel: (07) 839 6871; fax: (07) 839 6872
Waitakere: Bridge Centre, 17 James Laurie St, PO Box 69 005, Glendene, Waitakere City 0645; tel: (09) 835 4069; fax: (09) 835 4690; email: wkbridge@xtra.co.nz
Wellington: 22-26 Riddiford St, PO Box 6033, Wellington 6141; tel: (04) 389 6566; fax: (04) 389 7110; email: wbridge@nzf.salvationarmy.org (acc 24)
Whangarei: Northland Bridge, PO Box 1746, Whangarei 0140, 6 Alexander St, Whangarei 0110; tel: (09) 430 7500; fax: (09) 430 7501

Oasis Centres: Treatment Centres for Gambling
Auckland: PO Box 41-309, St Lukes, Auckland 1346; 726 New North Rd, Auckland 1025; tel: (09) 846 0660; fax: (09) 846 0440
Christchurch: PO Box 9070, Addington, Tower Junction, Christchurch 8149; 126 Bealey Ave; tel: (03) 365 9659; fax: (03) 365 7585; email: oasisch@xtra.co.nz
Dunedin: PO Box 934, Dunedin 9054, 160 Crawford St, Dunedin 9016 ; tel: (03) 477 9852; fax: (03) 477 1493; email: Dunedin_oasis@nzf.salvationarmy.org
Hamilton: 2nd Floor, Cecil House, Garden Pl; Postal address: 25 Thackeray St, Hamilton 3204; tel: (07) 839 7053; fax: (07) 839 4428
Queenstown: 29 Camp St, PO Box 887, Queenstown 9348; tel: (03) 442 5103; fax: (03) 442 9644
Wellington: 22 Riddiford St, PO Box 6033, Wellington 6141; tel: (04) 389 6566; fax: (04) 389 7110

Community Addictions Programme
Invercargill: Social Service Centre, PO Box 74, Invercargill 9840, cnr Gala and Leven Sts; tel: (03) 218 3094; fax: (03) 218 7934
Kaitaia: PO Box 495, Kaitaia 0441, 40 Commerce St; tel: (09) 408 6180; fax: (09) 408 3365
Kaikohe: PO Box 748, Kaikohe 0440, 2 Station Rd, Kaikohe 0405; tel: (09) 401 2865
Tauranga: PO Box 164, Tauranga 3140, 375 Cameron Rd; tel: (07) 578 4264; fax: (07) 578 4536

Supportive Accommodation Services
Auckland: Epsom Lodge: PO Box 26-098, Auckland 1344; 18 Margot St, Epsom, Auckland 1344; tel: (09) 524 0252; fax: (09) 524 9604 (acc men 90)
Christchurch: Addington Supportive Accommodation Services Social Services Centre, PO Box 9057, Tower Junction, Christchurch 8149; 62 Poulson St, Addington, Christchurch 8024; tel: (03) 338 5154; fax: (03) 338 4390 (acc 70)
Invercargill: PO Box 74, Invercargill 9840; cnr Gala and Leven Sts; tel: (03) 218 3094; fax: (03) 218 7934 (acc 35)
Temuka: Bramwell Booth House (Intellectual Disability): PO Box 57, Temuka 7948, Milford Rd; tel: (03) 615 9570; fax: (03) 615 9571 (acc 18)
Wellington: (Intellectual Disability) PO Box 6033, 26 Riddiford St; tel: (04) 389 0594; fax: (04) 389 1130 (acc 12)

Reintegration Services
Christchurch: 62 Poulson St, PO Box 9057, Temuka 7948, Christchurch 8024; tel: (03) 338 2643; fax: (03) 338 4390
Wellington: PO Box 40328, Upper Hutt 5140; tel: (04) 527 7462; fax: (04) 528 9445

Mothercraft Centre
Bethany: 35 Dryden St, Grey Lynn, Auckland 1021; tel: (09) 376 1324; fax: (09) 376 1307; website: www.bethanycentre.org.nz
(acc antenatal 14, mothers and babies 7)

Employment Plus
National Office: 204 Cuba St, PO Box 6015, Wellington 6141; tel: (04) 382 0714; fax: (04) 382 0711; toll free: 0800 437 587
National Manager: Mr Mark Pickering; email: m.pickering@eplus.salvationarmy.org.nz
National Mission Directors: Majs Wayne and Joanne Jellyman; email:
wayne_jellyman@nzf.salvationarmy.org
joanne_jellyman@nzf.salvationarmy.org
Finance Service Bureau: 12 Vialou St, PO Box 5347, Frankton, Hamilton; tel: (07) 834 3195; fax: (07) 834 3198

Regions
Auckland: 16b Bakerfield Pl, PO Box 76 075, Manukau City 2241; tel: (09) 261 1063; fax: (09) 262 4103; email: t.huri@eplus-salvationarmy.org.nz
Bay of Plenty: 21 Mill Rd, PO Box 2046, Kopeopeo, Whakatane 3159; tel: (07) 308 7448; fax: (07) 307 0297; email: p.rodgers@eplus-salvationarmy.org.nz
Central: 148 Manchester St, PO Box 569,

New Zealand, Fiji and Tonga Territory

Feilding 4740; tel: (06) 323 9017;
fax: (06) 323 9620; email:
a.adams@eplus-salvationarmy.org.nz

Lower South: 160 Crawford St, Dunedin; PO Box 784, Dunedin 9054; tel: (03) 476 7111;
fax: (03) 476 7188; email:
b.lee@eplus-salvationarmy.org.nz

Northern: 12 Kaka St, PO Box 1524, Whangarei 0140; tel: (09) 438 4470; fax: (09) 438 6500;
email: g.eilering@eplus-salvationarmy.org.nz

Upper South: Level 2, Science Alive Building, Moorhouse Ave, PO Box 7198, Christchurch 8240; tel: (03) 379 4736; fax: (03) 377 2989;
email: d.dixon@eplus-salvationarmy.org.nz

Waikato: 182 Grandview Rd, Grandview, PO Box 5347, Hamilton 3200; tel: (07) 846 5216;
fax: (07) 846 5217; email:
a.murphy@eplus-salvationarmy.org.nz

Home Care Services

National Office: 71 Seddon Rd, Hamilton 3204; PO Box 9417, Hamilton 3240;
tel: (07) 848 2157; fax: (07) 846 1026;
email: homecare.hamilton@xtra.co.nz

Service Centres: Auckland, Hamilton, Paeroa, Rotorua, Tauranga

SOCIAL SERVICES (under DHQ)
Community Ministries

Aranui: 34 Portsmouth St, Christchurch 8061;
tel/fax: (03) 388 1072

Auckland City: PO Box 27-153, 691 Mt Albert Rd, Royal Oak; tel: (09) 625 7940;
fax: (09) 625 6045

Blenheim: Cnrs George and Henry Sts, PO Box 417 Blenheim 7240; tel: (03) 578 0862;
fax: (03) 578 0990

Carterton: PO Box 145, Carterton 5743; 204-210 High St South, Carterton 5713;
tel: (06) 379 7176; fax: (06) 379 6109;
email: carterton_corps@nzf.salvationarmy.org

Christchurch: PO Box 1015, Christchurch 8140; 32 Lichfield St, Christchurch 8011;
tel: (03) 366 8128; fax: (03) 366 8295

Dunedin: 160 Crawford St, P O Box 934, Dunedin 9016 tel: (03) 477 9852;
fax: (03) 477 1493

Feilding: 124 Manchester St, Feilding;
tel: (06) 323 4718; email:
feilding_corps@nzf.salvationarmy.org

Foxton: Avenue Rd, Foxton 4814; PO Box 51, Foxton 4848; tel: (06) 363 8669;
email: foxton_corps@nzf.salvationarmy.org

Gisborne: PO Box 1086, 389 Gladstone Rd;
tel: (06) 868 9468; fax: (06) 868 1395;
email: Gisborne_corps@nzf.salvationarmy.org

Gore: 21 Irwell St; tel: (03) 208 4443

Hamilton: The Nest, PO Box 8020, Kahikatea Dr;
tel: (07) 843 4509; fax: (07) 843 3865;
incl Mary Bryant Family Home, 24 Ohaupo Rd;
tel: (07) 843 4509; email:
the_nest@nzf.salvationarmy.org (acc 8)

Hastings: PO Box 999, cnr Warren St and Ave Rd; tel: (06) 876 5771; fax (06)870 9331;
email: hastings_corps@nzf.salvationarmy.org

Hornby: 23 Manurere St, Hei Hei, Christchurch 8042; PO Box 16 967, Christchurch 8441;
tel: (03) 349 6268; fax: (03) 344 5376

Hutt City: cnr Kings Cres and Cornwall St, Lower Hutt 5010; PO Box 30745, Lower Hutt;
tel: (04) 570 0273; fax: (04) 570 0274;
email: huttcity_corps@nzf.salvationarmy.org

Invercargill: PO Box 252, Invercargill 9840; 105 Tay St, Invercargill 9810;
tel/fax: (03) 214 0223

Linwood: 177 Linwood Ave, Christchurch 8067;
tel: (03) 389 3723

Manukau City: PO Box 76-075, 16b Bakerfield Pl, Manukau City; tel: (09) 262 2332;
fax: (09) 262 4103

Motueka: PO Box 85, Motueka 7143;
tel: (03) 528 9338; fax: (03) 528 5109

Napier: PO Box 3086, 36 Faraday St;
tel: (06) 834 0759; fax: (06) 834 0759;
email: napier_cfs@nzf.salvationarmy.org

Nelson: 57 Rutherford St, Nelson 7010;
PO Box 22, Nelson 7040; tel: (03) 548 4807;
fax: (03) 548 4810

North Shore City: 407 Glenfield Rd, Glenfield, Auckland, PO Box 40555, Glenfield;
tel: (09) 441 2554; fax: (09) 441 7599

North Taranaki: PO Box 384, cnr Powderham and Dawson Sts, New Plymouth;
tel: (06) 758 9338; fax (06) 758 2325;
email:
northtaranaki_corps@nzf.salvationarmy.org

Palmerston North: 431 Church St, Palmerston North 4410; PO Box 869, Palmerston North 4440; tel: (06) 358 7455; fax: (06) 358 2314;
email:
palmerstonnorth_cfs@nzf.salvationarmy.org

Porirua: PO Box 53-025, Cannons Creek 5243; cnr Warspite Ave and Fantame St, Porirua East 5024; tel: (04) 235 6266; fax: (04) 235 6482;
email: porirua_cm@nzf.salvationarmy.org

Queenstown: PO Box 887, Queenstown 9348; Camp St, Queenstown 9300; tel: (03) 442 5103;
fax: (03) 442 9644

Rotorua: 1115 Haupapa St; tel: (07) 346 8113;
fax: (07) 346 8075; email:
rotorua_cfs@nzf.salvationarmy.org

New Zealand, Fiji and Tonga Territory

Sydenham: 17 Southampton St; Christchurch 8023; tel: (03) 331 7483; fax: (03) 332 8395

Tauranga: PO Box 164, 375 Cameron Rd; tel: (07) 578 5505; fax: (07) 578 4536; email: tauranga_corps@nzf.salvationarmy.org

Timaru: 206 Wai-iti Rd, Timaru 7910; tel/fax: (03) 684 7139

Tokoroa: PO Box 567; tel: (07) 886 9812; fax 886 9051; email: tokoroa_cfs@nzf.salvationarmy.org

Upper Hutt: 695 Fergusson Dr, Upper Hutt 5018; tel: (04) 528 6745; fax: (04) 528 6748; email: upper_hutt_corps@nzf.salvationarmy.org

Waitakere City: PO Box 21-708 Henderson, 7-9 View Rd; tel: (09) 837 4471; fax: (09) 837 1246

Wellington: 26 Riddiford St, Newtown, Wellington 6021; tel: (04) 389 0594; fax: (04) 389 1130;

Counselling Service: 26 Riddiford St, Newtown, Wellington 6021; tel: (04) 389 0594; fax: (04) 389 1130; email: wellingtoncfs@nzf.salvationarmy.org

614 Youth Services: 1 Ghuznee St, Wellington 6011; PO Box 27459, Wellington 6141; tel: (04) 384 6119; fax: (04) 384 6115

Early Childhood Education Centres

Gisborne: 'Noah's Young Ones': PO Box 1086, 389 Gladstone Rd, Gisborne; tel: (06) 868 9468; fax: (06) 868 1395 (roll 24)

Hamilton: The Nest Educare: PO Box 8020, Kahikatea Dr; tel: (07) 843 4066; fax: (07) 843 3865 (roll 50)

Masterton: Cecilia Whatman Early Childhood Education Centre: 132-140 Ngaumutawa Rd, Masterton 5810; tel: (06) 378 7316 (roll 38)

Upper Hutt: William Booth Educare: PO Box 40-542 Upper Hutt; tel: (04) 528 8628 527 6929 (roll 25)

Waitakere: Kidz Matter 2US: PO Box 21-708, Henderson; tel: (09) 837 4471; fax: (09) 837 1246 (roll 25)

Wellington:
Britomart ECEC: 126 Britomart St, Berhampore, Wellington 6002; tel: (04) 389 9781 (roll 28)

Wellington Bridge – Te Matua Tamariki Home-based ECE Service: PO Box 6033, Wellington 6002

COURT AND PRISON SERVICE

National Consultant: PO Box 7342, Auckland; tel: (09) 337 1351; fax: (09) 337 1249; mobile: 027 478 9758

Auckland: PO Box 7342, Wellesley St, Auckland; tel: (09) 916 9267; fax: (09) 309 9751; cellphone: 027 478 4457

Alexandra: 21 Aronui Rd; tel: (03) 448 9436; cellphone: 021 264 4765

Ashburton: PO Box 248; tel: 03 308 7610, cellphone 027 227 7029

Blenheim: PO Box 417; tel: (03) 578 0862; fax: (03) 578 0990

Christchurch: PO Box 25 207; tel: (03) 377 0799; fax: (03) 377 3575; mobile: 027 435 7915

Dunedin: 44a Filleul St; tel: (03) 477 9852; fax: (03) 477 1493; mobile: 027 496 7194

Gore: 21 Irwell St; tel/fax: (03) 208 4443

Hamilton: tel: (07) 843 4509; fax: (07) 843 3865; mobile: 027 280 9673

Invercargill: 14 Trent St; tel/fax: (03) 217 1131; mobile: 027 436 9796

North Shore: PO Box 40 034, Glenfield; tel: (09) 337 1351

Manukau: PO Box 76 075; tel/fax: (09) 525 2473; mobile: 027 478 4429

Kaitaia: PO Box 391; tel: (09) 408 3362; fax (09) 408 3362

Lower Hutt/Upper Hutt: PO Box 31 363, Lower Hutt; tel: (04) 389 0594; fax: (04) 389 1130

Palmerston North: PO Box 869; tel/fax: (06) 353 3459

Porirua: PO Box 53 025, Porirua East; tel: (04) 914 3260; mobile: 027 482 7437; fax: (04) 914 3262

Tauranga: PO Box 164, Tauranga; tel: (07) 578 5505; mobile: 027 6764 155

Thames: PO Box 142, Thames; tel: (07) 868 5495

Timaru: 206 Wai-iti Rd; tel/fax: (03) 684 7139

Waitakere: mobile: 027 243 0586

Wellington: PO Box 5094; tel: (04) 918 8063; fax: (04) 918 8098

Westport: tel: (03) 789 8085; fax: (03) 789 8058

Whangarei: tel: (09) 983 5460

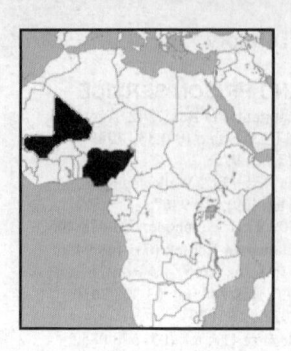

NIGERIA TERRITORY

Territorial leaders:
Commissioners Jean B. and Véronique Ludiazo

Territorial Commander:
Commissioner Jean B. Ludiazo
(1 Feb 2007)

Chief Secretary:
Lieut-Colonel Festus Oloruntoba (1 Sep 2007)

Territorial Headquarters: 6 Shipeolu St, Igbobi, Shomolu, Lagos

Postal address: Box 3025, Shomolu, Lagos, Nigeria

Tel/fax: [234] (1) 774 9125; email: Nigeria@NIG.salvationarmy.org

Salvation Army operations began in Nigeria in 1920 when Lieut-Colonel and Mrs George H. Souter landed in Lagos, to be followed later by Staff-Captain and Mrs Charles Smith with 10 West Indian officers. Following an invitation for the Army to establish a presence in Mali, with registration being given on 29 November 2007, a response was undertaken under local leadership until work in the country became official in February 2008 with the appointment of officers.

Zone: Africa

Countries included in the territory: Mali, Nigeria

'The Salvation Army' in Yoruba: Ogun Igbala Na; in Ibo: Igwe Agha Nzoputa; in Efik: Nka Erinyana; in Edo: Iyo Kuo Imienfan; in Urhobo: Ofovwi re Arhc Na; in Hausa: Soldiogi Cheta

Languages in which the gospel is preached: Calabari, Edo, Efik/Ibibio, English, French, Hausa, Ibo, Ijaw, Tiv, Urhobo, Yoruba

Periodicals: *Salvationist, The Shepherd, The War Cry*

THE 2008 theme 'Rooted And Built Up In Jesus For The Mission' brought a good response from Salvationists. The territory then entered 2009 with the slogan 'Leading Through Change' and saw more than 100 of its officers meeting for 10-day refresher courses (in February and May) to be spiritually renewed.

THQ staff and all the territory's corps, societies and outposts organised Holy Week events to meditate on the passion of Christ before ushering in Easter Sunday.

The Self-Denial Fasting Week (27 April - 2 May) preceded Self-Denial Appeal altar services in all corps and societies. The Territorial Self-Denial Ingathering, held at Lagos Central in early June, was attended by more than 300 Salvationists.

Thirty-one seekers were recorded during Decision Sunday meetings as young people knelt at mercy seats around the territory.

Akwa Ibom State Government officials and other local dignitaries were specially invited guests when

Nigeria Territory

their state hosted territorial officers councils at The Salvation Army Secondary School in Akai Ubium (Akwa Ibom East Division).

Under their 2008 theme 'Rooted In Christ To Bear Fruit', staff of the Women's Ministries Department gathered all women officers and local officers together in three zones – Western, Eastern and Northern – for teaching on various topics. These included 'My Call and Responsibilities as a Woman Officer', 'Women and Family Health', 'Fidelity Within Marriage' and 'Generation Next'.

After launching the 2009 theme – 'Strength For Today and Hope For Tomorrow' – the Women's Ministries Department organised workshops and rallies in the Western and Eastern Zones. Topics discussed included 'The Importance of Discretion in Our Ministry', 'Relationships With Our Family and Our Calling', 'My Ministry and My Community' and 'Domestic Violence'. The women also learned various crafts.

The Catherine Booth Nursery and Primary School in Lagos now has accommodation for 135 pupils.

STATISTICS
Officers 375 (active 315 retired 60) **Cadets** 15 **Employees** 398
Corps 181 **Societies and Outposts** 173 **Institutions** 19 **Schools** 41 **Clinics** 19
Senior Soldiers 29,323 **Adherents** 3,033 **Junior Soldiers** 9,678
Personnel serving outside territory Officers 4

STAFF
Women's Ministries: Comr Véronique Ludiazo (TPWM) Lt-Col Patience Akpan (THLS) Maj Mary Adejoro (TLOM), Lt-Col Theresa Baah (Junior Miss and Young Women's Sec) Lt-Col Norma Kwenda (Development and Ret Officers' Sec)
Business Administration: Lt-Col Peter Kwenda
Editor/Literary: Capt Ifeayinwa Olebunne
Extension Training: Capt Michael Olatunde
Field Programme: Lt-Col Samuel Baah
Finance: Joseph Vaihkuma
Personnel: Lt-Col Joseph U. Akpan
Prison Chaplain: Maj Benson Erhuwumnsee
Projects: Helen Vaihkuma
Property: Lazarus Akpadiaha
Public Relations: Maj Obed Mgbebuihe
Social: Maj Ebenezer O. Abayomi
HIV/Aids: Maj G. Omokaro
Sponsorship: Maj Comfort Abayomi
Training: Maj Gabriel O. Adepoju
Youth and Candidates: Capt Gabriel Ogungbenle

DIVISIONS
Akwa Ibom Central: c/o Afia Nisit PA, via Uyo; Majs Udoh and Esther Uwak
Akwa Ibom East: PO Box 20, Ikot Ubo, via Eket; Majs Paul and Edina Onyekwere
Akwa Ibom South West: c/o Abak PO Box 23, Abak; Majs Michael and Roseline Oyesanya
Akwa Ibom West: PO Box 47, Etinan; Majs Michael and Comfort Sijuade
Anambra East: Umuchu; Majs Edwin and Agnes Okorougo
Anambra West: 5 Urenebo St, Housing Estate, PO Box 1168, Onitsha, Anambra State; Majs Stephen and Edith Uzoho
Ibadan: PO Box 261, Ibadan, Oyo State; Majs Patrick and Blessing Orasibe
Imo Central: based at Orogwe, Owerri; Majs Chika B. and Virginia Ezekwere
Lagos: PO Box 2640, Surulere, Lagos State; Majs Benson and Celine Mgbebuihe
Ondo/Ekiti: PO Box 51, Akure, Ondo State; Majs Raphael and Esther Ogundahunsi

DISTRICTS
Abia: 2-8 Market Rd, PO Box 812, Aba, Abia State; Maj Simon Ekpendu
Badagry: PO Badagry, Lagos State; Maj Etim A. Udoh
Cross River: PO Box 11, Calabar, Cross River State; tel: (087) 220284; Maj Samuel Edung
Edo/Delta: PO Box 108, Benin City, Edo State; Maj Joseph Ogunde
Egba: PO Box 46, Ado Odo, Ogun State; Maj Bramwell Chukwunwem
Imo North: PO Box 512, Akokwa; Maj Godspower Sampson

Nigeria Territory

Northern: PO Box 512, Jos, Plateau State;
Maj Edet Essien
Rivers: PO Box 1161, Port Harcourt, Rivers
State; Capt Joseph Mbagwu

SECTIONS
Akwa Ibom South East: PO Box 25 Ikot Abasi;
Maj Maurice Akpabio
Enugu/Ebonyi: Enugu, PO Box 1454,
4 Moorehouse St, Ogui, Enugu State;
Maj Kennedy Inyang

TRAINING COLLEGE
4 Shipeolu St, PO Box 17, Shomolu, Igbobi,
Lagos; tel: (01) 774 9125

SOCIAL SERVICES
Corps-based Prison Ministry
Afaha Eket Corps Prison Work, Agbor Corps,
Badagry Prison Work, Benin Central Prison
Work, Ibadan Central Corps, Port Harcourt
Corps Prison Team

THQ-based Prison Ministry
Badagry Prison, Ikoyi Prison, Kirikiri Maximum
Security, Kirikiri Minimum Security, Kirikiri
Women's Prison

HIV/Aids Action Centre and Voluntary Counselling and Testing Centre
11 Odunlami St, PO Box 125, Lagos

Medical Centres
Ado Odo Medical Centre: Ado Odo Corps,
PO Box 46, Ado Odo, Ogun State (acc 2)
Gbethromy Training and Medical Centre:
c/o Badagry PO, Badagry, Lagos State (acc 8)
Iyara Health Centre: c/o Ado Irele, Ondo State
(acc 3)
Lagos Central Corps Clinic: 11 Odunlami St,
PO Box 125, Lagos State (acc 2)
Nda Nsit Clinic/Maternity: Nda Nsit Corps,
via Uyo, Akwa Idom State (acc 2)
Nkoro Corps Mobile Clinic: Nkoro Corps,
via Boni PO Box, Rivers State (acc 4)
Ubrama Health Centre/Clinic: Ubrama PO Box
Ahoada Alaga, Rivers State
Umucheke Corps Clinic: via Uruala PO, Ideato
L/G. A., Imo State (acc 4)

Social Centres/Institutions/Programmes
Akai Children's Home: PO Box 1009, Eket,
Akwa Ibom State (acc 35)
Benin Rehabilitation Centre: 20A First East
Circular Rd, PO Box 108, Benin City,
Edo State (acc 17)
Oji River Rehabilitation Centre: Oji River PO,
via Enugu, Enugu State (acc 64)
Orphans/Vulnerable Children Centre/Orphans
Psycho-Social Centre – Akai: PO Box 1009,
Eket Akwa Ibom State

SCHOOLS
Nursery
Aba Corps, Agbor Corps, Akai Corps, Akokwa
Corps, Amauzari Corps, Benin Corps,
Ibughubu Corps, Ikot Inyang Eti, Ile Ife
Corps, Ivue Corps, Jos Corps, Mpape Corps,
Onitsha Corps, Osumenyi Corps, Somorika
Corps, Suleja, Umucheke Corps, Umuchu
Corps, Umudike Corps

Primary
Aba Corps, Akai, Amauzari Corps, Benin Corps,
Ile Ife, Ikot Inyang Eti, Ivue Corps, Jos Corps,
Mpape Corps, Onitsha Corps, Somorika Corps,
Suleja

VOCATIONAL TRAINING CENTRES
Afia Nsit-Nsit VTC: Afia Nsit-Nsit Corps,
PO Box 8, Afia Nsit Urua Nko, Akwa Ibom
State (acc 8)
Abak Training Centre: Abak Corps, PO Box 23,
Abak, Akwa Ibom State (acc 4)
Amauzari VTC: Amauzari Corps, via Owerri PO,
Imo State (acc 4)
Enugu VTC: Enugu Corps, 4 Moorhouse St,
PO Box 1454, Ogui, Enugu State (acc 6)
Ibesit Training Centre: Ibesit Corps, Anang PA,
Ukanafun LGA, Akwa Ibom State (acc 3)
Ikot Okobo Training Centre: PO Box 493, Eket,
Akwa Ibom State (acc 156)
Ilesha VTC: Ilesha Corps, PO Box 91, Ilesha,
Oyo State (acc 30)
Ile-Ife VTC: Ile-Ife Corps, PO Box 113, Ile-Ife,
Oyo State
Orogwe VTC: Orogwe Corps, via Owerri PO,
Imo State (acc 235)
Supare VTC: Supare Corps, PMB 257,
via Ikare Akoko, Ondo State (acc 30)
Umuogo VTC: Umuogo Corps, c/o Amuzu PA,
via Owerri, Imo State (acc 8)

MALI (under THQ)
Officer-in-charge: Maj Eugene Dikalembolovanga
Armée du Salut/The Salvation Army,
Rue N° 477, Porte N° 39, Immeuble Drissa,
Dissa, Hamdallaye-ACI 2000; Bamako
tel: (223) 7465 30 76/2023 83 15

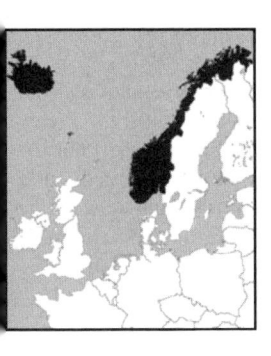

NORWAY, ICELAND AND THE FÆROES TERRITORY

Territorial leaders:
Commissioners Carl and Gudrun Lydholm

Territorial Commander:
Commissioner Carl Lydholm (11 Jul 2005)

Chief Secretary:
Colonel Clive Adams (1 Jul 2007)

Territorial Headquarters: Kommandør T I Øgrims plass 4, 0165 Oslo, Norway

Postal address: Box 6866, St Olavs Plass, 0130 Oslo, Norway
Tel: [47] 22 99 85 00; fax: [47] 22 20 84 49; email: nor.leadership@frelsesarmeen.no;
website: www.frelsesarmeen.no

Commissioners Hanna Ouchterlony and George Scott Railton with Staff-Captain and Mrs Albert Orsborn 'opened fire' in Oslo (Kristiania) on 22 January 1888. Work began in Iceland on 12 May 1895, pioneered by Adjutant Christian Eriksen, Captain Thorstein Davidsson and Lieutenant Lange, and spread to The Færoes in 1924.

Zone: Europe
Countries included in the territory: Iceland, Norway, The Færoes
'The Salvation Army' in Norwegian: Frelsesarmeen; in Icelandic: Hjälpraedisherinn; in Færoese: Frelsunarherurin
Languages in which the gospel is preached: Færoese, Icelandic, Norwegian
Periodicals: *FAbU nytt, Krigsropet, Uni-Form* (all Norwegian), *Herópid* (Icelandic)

PEOPLE were saved, while many others were spiritually renewed and recommitted their lives to God during the annual five-day congress at which Retired General Eva Burrows was guest speaker. Meeting after meeting, people responded to her direct Bible preaching.

For the second year running, youth had a separate event, joining the adult congress for the last meeting. Many of the young people made life-transforming decisions.

Fifty Salvationists from The Færoes made the long and costly journey to attend the congress, no doubt inspired by the fact that four of their comrades were among the new officers being ordained and commissioned during the weekend.

The first edition of *Uni-Form* – the territory's new internal publication – was distributed at the congress with a generally positive response. Also, two new CDs went on sale. These are albums by Tehilla, a gospel choir based in Tønsberg Corps, and Mannsambandet, a male-voice group that has produced several CDs since being formed in 1994.

Krigsropet (The War Cry) has been redesigned with the aim to make the publication more appealing to a younger readership. The territorial website has been revamped and can be viewed at http://www.frelsesarmeen.no

The Nordic Leaders Development Institute held its inaugural officers' session, with Retired General Paul Rader and Commissioner Kay Rader as guest lecturers. Delegates speak highly of the impact the ongoing course is having on their leadership and personal development.

'A Relevant Army – A Meaningful Ministry' was the overall theme for the Teritorial Leaders Conference, at which Commissioner Christine MacMillan (International Director for Social Justice, IHQ) was a guest speaker.

Dutch and Finnish scouts were among 560 participants at a combined scout camp and youth festival in Røros. Encouragingly, three young people were saved; two are quite new to the Army, coming from the blossoming work in Akureyri, Iceland.

In addition to many other events – at territorial, divisional and local level – the territory was privileged to enjoy a visit by the USA Southern Territory's National Songsters as part of their Scandinavian tour.

Fretex – the territory's recycling and vocational rehabilitation company – conducted a survey among its 1,500-plus employees with very satisfactory results. A Fretex advertisement campaign – 'Look At My Dress', which is based on a popular children's song – won the bronze prize in the advertisement category at Cannes Film Festival.

STATISTICS
Officers 400 (active 182 retired 218) **Cadets** (1st year) 8 **Employees** 1,380
Corps 111 **Outposts** 327 **Institutions** 34 (incl slum posts) **Industrial Centres/Second-hand Shops** 45
Senior Soldiers 5,515 **Adherents** 1,339 **Junior Soldiers** 43
Personnel serving outside territory Officers 23

STAFF
Women's Ministries: Comr Gudrun Lydholm (TPWM) Col Marianne Adams (TSWM) Maj Brit Knedal (Home and Family)
Asst CS: Maj Arne Undersrud
Sec for Business Administration: Maj Jan Peder Fosen
   Financial Sec: Maj Knud David Welander
   Chief Accountant: Egil Hognerud
   Missionary Projects: Maj Eli Nodland Hagen
   Property: Dag Tellefsen
   'Sally Ann' – Trading Programme: Sally Ann Norway Ltd; Manager: Sissel Skogly; Shop: Kirkeveien 62, 0330 Oslo
Sec for Communication: Maj Inger Marit Nygård
   Section for Communicaton: Andrew Hannevik
   Editor: Hilde Dagfinrud Valen
Sec for Personnel: Maj Lise O. Luther
Sec for Field and Programme: Maj Jan Øystein Knedal
   Asst Sec for Field and Programme: Maj Anne-Lise Undersrud
   Community: Maj Birgit T. Fosen
   Music: Maj Jan Harald Hagen
   Over 60s: Maj Leif-Erling Fagermo
   Territorial Band: B/M John Philip Hannevik
   Youth: Maj Lisbeth Welander
Sec for Social Services: Maj Elisabeth Henne
   Asst Sec for Social Services: Maj Thorgeir Nybo
   Alcohol and Drug Rehabilitation: Frode Woldsund (acting)
   Children and Family Homes: Lindis Evja
   Day Care Centres for Children: Anne-Dorthe Nodland Aasen

Norway, Iceland and The Færoes Territory

Investigation: Maj Erling Levang
Welfare and Development: Elin Herikstad
Work Rehabilitation and Recycling:
Thor Fjellvang
THQ
Training: Maj Gro Merete Berg

DIVISIONS
Central: Heimdalsgt 14, PO Box 2869, Tøyen, 0608 Oslo; tel: 23 24 49 20; fax: 23 24 49 21; Majs Frank and Tone Gjeruldsen
Eastern: Kneika 11, PO Box 40, 3056 Solbergelva; tel: 32 87 12 90; fax: 32 87 12 01; Majs Per Arne and Lillian Pettersen
Midland: Knausv 12, Smeby, PO Box 3002, 2318 Hamar; tel: 62 52 21 83; fax: 62 54 91 08; Maj Brith-Mari Heggelund
Northern: Bjørkvn 12, PO Box 8255 Jakobsli, 7458 Trondheim; tel: 73 57 14 20; fax: 73 57 16 93; Majs Bernt Olaf and Hildegard Ørsnes
North Norway: Skolegt 6, PO Box 177, 9252 Tromsø; tel: 77 68 83 70; fax: 77 68 81 51; Majs Paul-William and Margaret Marti
Western: Kongsgt 50, PO Box 553, 4003 Stavanger; tel: 51 56 41 60; fax: 51 56 41 61; Lt-Cols Odd and Grethe Berg

ICELAND REGION
Kirkjurstræti 2, IS 121 Reykjavik; tel: (00354) 552 0788, fax: (00354) 562 0780; Maj Anne Marie Reinholdtsen
Convalescent Home: Skólabraut 10, PO Box 115, IS-172 Seltjarnarnes; tel: [354] 561 2090; fax: [354] 561 2089
Guest Home: PO Box 866, IS-121 Reykjavik; tel: [354] 561 3203; fax: [354] 561 3315

THE FÆROES DISTRICT
(under THQ)
Torsgøta 19, PO Box 352, FO-110 Torshavn, Færøyene; tel/fax: (00298) 31 21 89; Maj Samuel Jakob Joensen
Hostel: FO-100 Torshavn, N Winthersgt 3; tel: (00298) 31 73 93

TRAINING COLLEGE
1385 Asker, Brendsrudtoppen 40; tel: 66 76 49 70; fax: 66 76 49 71

UNDER THQ
Jeløy Folk High School
1516 Moss, Nokiavn 30b, Folk High School; tel: 69 91 10 70; fax: 69 91 10 80

SOCIAL SERVICES
Head Office: 0165 Oslo, Kommandør T. I. Øgrims plass 4 ; tel: 22 99 85 00; fax: 22 99 85 84

Children's and Youths' Homes
3018 Drammen, Hotvedtveien 57; tel: 23 69 19 90
3028 Drammen, Bolstadhagen 61; tel: 32 20 45 80; fax: 32 20 45 81
1441 Drøbak, Nils Carlsensgt 31; tel: 64 90 51 30; fax: 64 91 51 31
1112 Oslo, Nordstrandsvn 7; tel: 23 16 89 10; fax: 23 16 89 19
2021 Skedsmokorset, Flesvigs vei 4; tel: 63 87 44 19; fax: 63 87 41 77
4011 Stavanger, Vidarsgt 4; tel: 51 52 11 49; fax: 51 52 66 31
7037 Trondheim, Øystein Møylas veg 20 B; tel: 73 95 44 33, fax: 73 95 44 39
1540 Vestby, Soldammen, Gjølstadveien 73; tel: 64 98 04 70; fax: 64 98 04 71

Day Care Centres for Children
1385 Asker, Brendsrudtoppen 60; tel: 66 78 74 86; fax: 66 79 02 64
5011 Bergen, Skottegt 16; tel: 55 23 08 83; fax: 55 23 47 45
1441 Drøbak, Nils Carlsensgt 31; tel: 64 93 15 09; fax: 64 93 15 73
0664 Oslo, Regnbuevn 2C; tel: 23 03 93 30, fax: 23 03 93 39
4017 Stavanger, Auglendsdalen 62; tel: 51 82 87 30

Family Centre
0487 Oslo, Kapellvn 61; tel: 22 09 86 20, fax: 22 09 86 21

Home-Start Family Contact
0686 Oslo, Vetlandsveien 99/100; tel: 23 43 89 10
3007 Drammen, Rådhusgt 19; tel: 478 93 800
Nedre Eiker, adr 3007 Drammen, Rådhusgt 19

Old People's Welfare Centre
0661 Oslo, Malerhaugvn 10b; tel: 22 57 66 30; fax: 22 67 09 34

Slum and Goodwill Centres
6005 Ålesund, Giskegt 27; tel: 70 12 18 05; fax: 70 12 18 05
5808 Bergen, Ladegårdsgt 21; tel: 55 56 34 70; fax: 55 56 34 71
0656 Oslo, Borggt 2; tel: 23 03 74 494004

Hostels
5812 Bergen, Bakkegt 7; tel: 55 30 22 85, fax: 55 30 22 90

Norway, Iceland and The Færoes Territory

8001 Bodø, Kongensgt 16; tel: 75 52 23 38;
 fax: 75 52 23 39
5501 Haugesund, Sørhauggt 215; tel: 52 72 77 01;
 fax: 52 72 35 30
0561 Oslo, Heimen, Heimdalsgt 27 A;
 tel: 23 21 09 60; fax: 22 68 00 98
0656 Oslo, Schweigaardsgt 70; tel: 23 24 39 00;
 fax: 23 24 39 09
0354 Oslo, Sporveisgt 33; tel: 22 95 73 50;
 fax: 22 95 73 51
3111 Tønsberg, Farmannsvn 26; tel: 33 31 54 09;
 fax: 33 31 07 74
7041 Trondheim, Furulund, Lade Allè 84;
 tel: 73 90 70 30; fax: 73 90 70 40

Self-catering Accommodation for Female Drug Addicts
8000 Bodø, Prinsensgate 151B; tel: 75 52 39 90;
 fax 75 52 23 39

Work-rehabilitation Programme among Alcohol and Drug Addicts (The Job)
0650 Oslo, Schweigaardsgt 68;
 tel: 61 60 06 84
2609 Lillehammer, Morterudveien 15;
 tel: 61 60 06 84
6400 Molde, Spolertbakken 3

Rehabilitation Homes for Alcohol and Drug Addicts
4017 Stavanger, Auglendsdalen 64;
 tel: 51 82 87 00; fax: 51 82 87 82
4463 Ualand, Heskestad; tel: 51 40 50 13;
 fax 41 40 50 11

Day Care Centres (Alcohol and Drug Addicts)
0187 Oslo, Urtegaten 16 A/C; tel: 23 03 66 80;
 fax: 23 03 66 81
4379 Egersund, Bedehusgaten 3; tel: 51 46 70 00
1301 Sandvika, Kinoveien 4; mobile: 40 48 63 70
7012 Trondheim, Hvedingsveita 3;
 tel: 73 52 09 00; fax: 73 51 03 97
8001 Bodø, Kongensgt 16

Supervisons of Residence (Alcohol and Drug Addicts)
0561 Oslo, Heimdalsgt 27A; tel: 23 121 09 73

Health Clinics for Drug Addicts
0650 Oslo, Borggt 2, tel: 22 08 36 70
0187 Oslo, Urtegt 16 A/C; tel: 22 67 43 45

Prison Work
5032 Bergen, Bakkegt 7

0666 Oslo, Ole Deviksv 20; tel: 23 06 92 35,
 fax: 22 65 57 74
0650 Oslo, Borggt 2
4002 Stavanger, Kongensgt 50

Home for Prisoners
0666 Oslo, Ole Deviksv 20; tel: 23 06 92 35;
 fax: 22 65 57 74

Work Rehabilitation and Recycling Centres (FRETEX)
(including 44 second-hand shops)
6002 Ålesund, Korsegt 6; tel: 70 12 71 75;
 fax: 70 12 71 75
813 Bodø, Notveien 17; tel: 75 21 03 505852
Bergen, Sandalsringen 3; tel: 55 92 59 00; fax:
 55 92 59 10
3036 Drammen, Kobbevikdalen 71;
 tel: 32 20 83 50; fax: 32 20 83 51
4110 Forsand, Myra Industriområde;
 tel: 51 70 39 07
3550 Gol, Sentrumsvn. 63; tel: 32 07 98 80;
 fax: 32 07 98 81
9406 Harstad, Storgt 34; tel: 77 00 24 77;
 fax: 77 00 24 71
7080 Heimdal, Heggstadmyra 2; tel: 72 59 59 15;
 fax: 72 59 59 19
9900 Kirkenes, Pasvikvn 2; tel: 78 97 02 40;
 fax: 78 97 02 41
2615 Lillehammer, Storgt 91; tel: 61 24 65 50;
 fax: 61 24 65 51
0668 Oslo, Ole Deviksvei 20; tel: 23 06 92 00;
 fax: 23 06 92 01
3735 Skien, Bedriftsvn 58; tel: 35 59 89 44;
 fax: 35 59 57 44
4315 Sandnes, Tornerosevn 7; tel: 51 95 13 00
9018 Tromsø, Skattøravn 39; tel: 77 67 22 88;
 fax: 77 67 22 87
6002 Ålesund, Korsegt 6; tel: 70 12 71 75;
 fax: 70 12 71 75
813 Bodø, Notveien 17; tel: 75 21 03 50
Second-hand Shops:
 Bergen (5), Bodø, Bryne, Drammen,
 Fredrikstad, Gol, Harstad, Haugesund,
 Jessheim, Jørpeland, Kirkenes, Kristiansand,
 Lillehammer, Lillestrøm, Lyngdal, Mandal,
 Molde, Moss, Oslo (5), Sandnes (2), Sandvika,
 Skien, Stavanger (3), Stjørdal, Tromsø,
 Trondheim (5), Tønsberg, Voss, Ålesund (2)
Art Galleri:
 Bergen

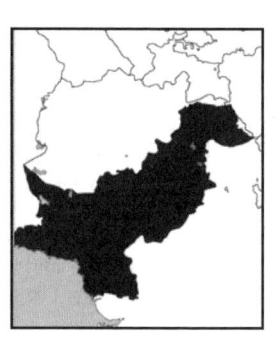

PAKISTAN TERRITORY

Territorial leaders:
Colonels Robert and Marguerite Ward

Territorial Commander:
Colonel Robert Ward (1 Feb 2008)

Chief Secretary:
Lieut-Colonel Yousaf Ghulam (1 Oct 2007)

Territorial Headquarters: 35 Shahrah-e-Fatima Jinnah, Lahore

Postal address: PO Box 242, Lahore 54000, Pakistan

Tel: [92] (42) 758 1644/756 9940; fax: [92] (42) 757 2699;

website:www.salvationarmy.org/pakistan

The Salvation Army began work in Lahore in 1883 and was eventually incorporated under the Companies Act of 1913 on 9 October 1968.

Zone: South Asia
Country included in the territory: Pakistan
Languages in which the gospel is preached: English, Punjabi, Pashto, Urdu
Periodicals: *Home League Quarterly, The War Cry* (in Urdu)

THE territory concluded its 125th anniversary celebrations with a visit from General Shaw Clifton and Commissioner Helen Clifton (28 November - 3 December 2008). An enthusiastic welcome reflected the joy of their return to the territory where they had been leaders (1997 - 2002).

Gatherings featured music, dance and the sharing of God's Word as Salvationists remembered those who had gone before and, with a renewed sense of optimism, considered the future that God has in mind for the territory. There was a steady flow of people making public commitments to Christ in response to the General's clear Bible message.

Celebrations also took place during Home League rallies and events in divisions and social services centres.

Four new buildings for worship – at Amritnagar, Bahooman, Muslim League Village and Sikanderabad – were dedicated to God's glory. The Bahooman building was funded by the Women's Ministries Helping-Hand Scheme. In addition, a new corps was opened in Korangi 2 1/2 (Karachi).

The cabinet system of senior management was introduced, with territorial departments now aligned alongside Personnel, Programme and Business Services.

Three successful sets of executive officers councils were held, bringing together leaders from across the territory to consult on strategic and policy matters. As part of their deliberations, the territorial theme was chosen – 'Mission Together' – which calls for a renewed sense of the Army's mission and what it means for Pakistan. The theme also highlights the need for a united effort to accomplish the territory's goals.

The Sustainable Livelihood Development project commenced in four divisions. Funded by Switzerland, Austria and Hungary Territory, the three-year project is intended to provide employable skills for needy families.

At the same time, a manager was hired for the 'Sally Ann' trading project – a vision of the previous territorial administration. The purpose of 'Sally Ann' is to link markets with products made by local people in order to provide them with income. The Women's Ministries are providing support for this initiative.

The territory aided 1,000 families devastated by an earthquake in Baluchistan. Emergency relief was also given to families affected by military action in the Northwest Frontier province. In both situations support was gratefully received from the international Salvation Army community through IHQ.

In addition to two Brengle Institutes for officers, a Holiness Trek was held in every division and at THQ. Officers and soldiers alike demonstrated a thirst for the teaching and experience of holiness.

A Peace Award was accepted by the Territorial Commander on behalf of the territory. Presented by the Speaker of the Punjab Provincial Assembly, the award is sponsored by the Peace and Justice Council of Pakistan, an interfaith initiative.

Thirty cadets of the Witnesses For Jesus Session were ordained and commissioned as lieutenants. UK territorial leaders Commissioners John and Betty Matear presided, their visit substantially strengthening relationships with a Partners In Mission territory.

STATISTICS
Officers 381 (active 300 retired 81) **Cadets** (1st Yr) 39 **Employees** 174
Corps 133 **Societies** 568 **Institutions** 7 **Schools** 3
Senior Soldiers 62,280 **Adherents** 11,926 **Junior Soldiers** 15,139

STAFF
Women's Ministries: Col Marguerite Ward (TPWM) Lt-Col Rebecca Yousaf (TSWM)
Projects: Capt MacDonald Chandi
'Sally Ann': Faisal Yacoob
Secretary for Business: tba
Chief Accountant: Andrew Lee
Editor: Capt Raja Azeem Zia
Finance: tba
Property: tba
Secretary for Personnel: Lt-Col Morris John
Candidates: Capt Rebecca Samuel
Mission Training and Education Coordinator: Maj Lynn Gensler
Training: tba
Secretary for Programme: Maj Samuel Tari
Prayer Coordinator: Maj Victoria Samuel
Social Services and Sponsorship: Capt Diana MacDonald
Youth: Capt Samuel John

DIVISIONS
Faisalabad: Jamilabad Jamia Salfia Rd, Faisalabad; tel: (411) 753586; Majs Shafqat Masih and Perveen Shafqat
Islamabad: William Booth Village, Khana Kak (Majaraj Plaza) Iqbal Town, Islamabad; mobile: 0300 5244618; Capts Washington Daniel and Azra Washington

League of Mercy members donate gifts ready for distribution among needy families

Jaranwala: Water Works Rd, nr Telephone Exchange, Jaranwala; tel: (468) 312423; Majs Salamat Masih and Grace Salamat
Jhang: Yousaf Shah Rd, Jhang Saddar; tel: (471) 611589; Capts Michael Gabriel and Shamim Gabriel
Karachi: 78 NI Lines, Frere St, Saddar, Karachi 74400; tel: (21) 225 4260; Lt-Col Zarina Viru
Khanewal: Chak Shahana Rd, Khanewal 58150; tel: (692) 53860; Majs Walter Emmanuel and Mussaraf Walter
Lahore: The Salvation Army, Bahar Colony, Kot Lakhpat, Lahore; tel: (42) 583 4568; Majs Samuel Barkat and Margaret Samuel
Sahiwal: Karbala Rd, Sahiwal; tel: (441) 66383; Capts Haroon Ghulam and Jennifer Haroon
Sheikhupura: 16 Civil Lines Rd, Qila, Sheikhupura; tel: (4931) 56521; Majs Javed Yousaf and Surriya Javed

DISTRICT
Hyderabad: Bungalow No 9, 'E' Block, Unit No 11, Latifabad 11, Hyderabad; tel: (221) 813445; Maj Khuram Shahzada

TRAINING COLLEGE
Ali Bridge, Canal Bank Rd North, Tulspura, Lahore; tel: (42) 658 2450; email: sacollege@cyber.net.pk

CONFERENCE CENTRE
Lahore: 35 Shahrah-e-Fatima Jinnah, PO Box 242, Lahore 54000; tel: (42) 758 1644 ext 338

MISSION TRAINING AND EDUCATION CENTRE
35 Shahrah-e-Fatima Jinnah, PO Box 242, Lahore 54000; tel: (42) 758 1644

SOCIAL SERVICES
Boarding Hostels
Boys
Jhang: Yousaf Shah Rd, Jhang Saddar; tel: (471) 624763 (acc 70)
Girls
Lahore: 35 Shahrah-e-Fatima Jinnah, PO Box 242, Lahore 54000; tel: (42) 756 9940 (acc 60)

Children's Homes
Karachi Boys' Home: Site Metroville, PO Box 10682, Karachi 75700; tel: (21) 665 0513 (acc 50)
Joyland Girls' Home: 90-B Block, Model Town, Lahore; tel: (42) 585 0190 (acc 60)
Sheikhupura Children's Home: 16 Civil Lines, Qilla, Sheikhupura; tel: (56) 378 4378 (acc 50)

EDUCATION
Schools
Azam Town Secondary School, Street 6, 100 Foot Rd, Azam Town, Karachi 75460; tel: (21) 538 4223
Shantinagar Educational Institute: Chak No 72/10-R, Shantinagar, Khanewal; tel: (692) 52985
Tibba Coaching Centre: Chak No 72/10-R, Tibba, Shantinagar, Khanewal; tel: (692) 52985

REHABILITATION CENTRES FOR DISABLED
Karachi: Manzil-e-Umead, PO Box 10735, Site Metroville, Karachi 75700; tel: (21) 665 0434
Lahore: Manzil-e-Shifa, 35 Shahrah-e-Fatima Jinnah, PO Box 242, Lahore 54000; tel: (42) 758 2391

PAPUA NEW GUINEA TERRITORY

Territorial Commander:
Commissioner Andrew Kalai (1 Jun 2005)

Chief Secretary:
Lieut-Colonel Hans van Vliet (1 Mar 2008)

Territorial Headquarters: Angau Dr, Boroko, National Capital District
Postal address: PO Box 1323, Boroko, NCD, Papua New Guinea
Tel: [675] 325-5522/5507; fax: [675] 323 3282; website: www.png.salvationarmy.org

The Salvation Army officially commenced in Papua New Guinea on 31 August 1956 and the first meeting was conducted on Sunday 21 October at the Royal Police Constabulary Barracks in Port Moresby. The first officers appointed to the work there were Major Keith Baker, Mrs Major Edna Baker and Lieutenant Ian Cutmore. On 4 July 1994, after 38 years as part of the Australia Eastern Territory, Papua New Guinea became an independent command and on 9 December 2000 was elevated to territory status.

Zone: South Pacific and East Asia
Country included in the territory: Papua New Guinea
Languages in which the gospel is preached: English, Hiri Motu, Pidgin and many local languages
Periodicals: *Tokaut*

'GOD First – Look Beyond' was the theme of celebrations for 50 years of The Salvation Army's work in the Highlands region. Music, dancing, colourful costumes and commitments to Christ marked the anniversary congress held during August 2008.

Thousands of soldiers, friends and officers gathered from all over PNG under the leadership of Chief of the Staff Commissioner Robin Dunster to praise God and thank him for his faithfulness.

During the year under review, 31 officers were commissioned – cadets from the training college and others who had completed their training by distance education. Seven new fellowships were created, mainly by people who joined the Army while living in urban centres and later commenced outposts when returning to their villages.

Plans are well advanced for the introduction of a new songbook, with songs in the three national languages of Tok Pisin, Motu and English. A website has been launched at www.png.salvationarmy.org

Education remains a major focus. Koki Secondary School relocated to refurbished accommodation, Lae Primary School opened new classrooms and Boroko Primary School had record enrolments.

Many corps have commenced elementary schools wherever there

Papua New Guinea Territory

has been room. At Lae, two young Salvationists are teaching nearly 200 five- to 16-year-old street kids in two rooms. In all the Army's schools, the love of God is at the centre.

Innovation is seen at a computer school in Kimbe, where technology has been introduced into isolated areas. The Flexible Open Distance Education programme is enabling young and mature students, including officers, to complete their secondary education.

Funds from overseas sources have assisted with the development of primary health care services such as sanitation and hygiene workshops, construction of pit latrines, distribution of treated mosquito bed nets and village health volunteer training.

These projects scattered around the rural areas have helped provide safe drinking water through the installation of water tanks with catchment shelters, water wells with hand pumps, and simple gravity-fed water systems.

In March 2009 the territory was privileged to be the global focus for World Day of Prayer. Also, the two Australian territories' Self-Denial Appeal concentrated on PNG. The prayers of fellow Salvationists are greatly valued.

The territory has sent its first 'overseas missionaries' to Australia Eastern. An officer couple is working with minority islander ethnic groups, including PNG expatriates who are living in the Cairns area.

STATISTICS
Officers 224 (active 195 retired 29) **Cadets** (1st Yr) 12 (2nd Yr) 6 **Employees** 393
Corps 54 **Outposts** 78 **Institutions** 1 **Motels** 2 **Schools** 8 **Health Centre and Sub-Centres** 6 **Community Health Posts** 19 **Counselling Centres** 3 **Staff Clinic** 1
Senior Soldiers 6,585 **Adherents** 4,731 **Junior Soldiers** 1,722

STAFF
Women's Ministries: Lt-Col Marja van Vliet (TSWM)
Business Administration: Maj Ritchie Watson
Personnel: Maj James Cocker
Programme: Maj Kelvin Alley
Leadership Development: tba
Editorial/Literature: Dawn Beeson
Property: Malcolm Beeson
Projects: Dawn Beeson
Public Relations: Maj Soddy Maraga
SALT: Maj Borley Yanderave
Training: Maj Marcia Cocker
Youth Resources Co-ordinator: Capt Kila Apa

DIVISIONS
North Coastal: PO Box 667, Lae, Morobe Province; tel: 472 0905, fax: 472 0897; Capts David and Rita Vele
North Eastern: PO Box 343, Kainantu, Eastern Highlands Province; tel: 737 1482; tel/fax: 737 1220; Maj Borley Yanderave (acting DC)
North Western: PO Box 365, Goroka, Eastern Highlands Province; tel: 732 1382; fax/ph: 732 1218, Maj David and Capt Doreen Temine
South Eastern: PO Box 49, Kwikila, Central Province; 2-way Radio Cell call no: 8564; mobile: 698 5966; Majs Kabona and Margaret Rotona
South Western: PO Box 4227, Boroko, National Capital District; tel: 321 6000/321 6006; fax: 321 6008, Capts Christian and Tilitah Goa
Gulf Regional Office: PO Box 132, Kerema, Gulf Province; tel/fax: 648 1384; Capts Paul and Gaba Bina
Sepik Regional Office: PO Box 184, Wewak, East Sepik Province; tel/fax: 856 1642; Capts Michael and Giam Dengi

OFFICER TRAINING COLLEGE
PO Box 5355, Boroko, National Capital District; tel: 323 0553; fax: 325 6668

Papua New Guinea Territory

SALT COLLEGE
PO Box 343, Kainantu, Eastern Highlands
Province; tel: 737 1125; fax: 737 1220

EDUCATION SERVICES
Mary and Martha Child Care Centre, Koki
(acc 25)
Boroko Primary School (acc 750)
Lae Primary School (acc 650)
Koki Secondary School (acc 250 Grades 9, 10, 11, 12)
Goroka Elementary School (acc 80)
Kainantu Elementary School (acc 260)
Kerowagi Elementary School (acc 200)
Tamba Elementary School (acc 260)
Boroko FODE Centre (acc 494)
Boroko Driving School
Kimbe Computer School (acc 30)

Community Health Workers Training School
Private Mail Bag 3, Kainantu, Eastern Highlands
Province; tel: 737 1404 (acc 50)

SOCIAL PROGRAMME
Community Services and HIV/Aids
Courts and Prison Ministry, Missing Persons,
Welfare Feeding Projects
Jim Jacobsen Centre: PO Box 901, Lae, Morobe
Province; tel/fax: 472 1117
House of Hope (Ela Beach Care and Counselling
Centre); tel: 320 0389

DEVELOPMENT SERVICES
Onamuga Development Project: Private Mail
Bag 3, Kainantu, Eastern Highlands Province
Literacy Programmes: each division

HEALTH SERVICES PROGRAMMES
North Coastal: PO Box 667 Lae, Morobe
Province; tel: 472 0905, fax 472 0897
Community Health Posts: Pongani, Waru
North Eastern: Private Mail Bag 3, Kainantu,
Eastern Highlands Province; tel/fax: 737 1279
Onamuga Health Centre (acc 35)
Community Health Posts: Barokira, Kokopi,
Norikori, Pitanka, Yauna
North Western: PO Box 365, Goroka, Eastern
Highlands Province; tel: 732 1382;
fax: 732 1218
Health Sub Centre: Misapi
Community Health Posts: Kamila, Kwongi
South Eastern: PO Box 49, Kwikila, Central
Province
Health Sub Centre: Boregaina (acc 10)
Community Health Posts: Dirinomu,
Kokorogoro, Kwaipo, Matairuka, Meirobu
South Western: PO Box 4227, Boroko, National
Capital District; tel: 321 6000; fax: 321 6008
Community Health Posts: Ilavapari, Lapari,
Papa, Sogeri

MOTELS
Goroka Motel: PO Box 365, Goroka, Eastern
Highlands Province; tel: 732 1382;
fax: 732 1218 (family units 2, double units 4, house 1)
The Elphick Motel: PO Box 637, Lae, Morobe
Province; tel: 472 2487; fax: 472 7487
(double rooms 8)

A student is congratulated on completing a driving course at the Salvation Army Driving School attached to the Flexible Optional Distance Education Centre in Port Moresby

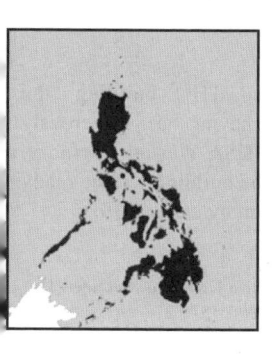

THE PHILIPPINES TERRITORY

Territorial leaders:
Colonels Malcolm and Irene Induruwage

Territorial Commander:
Colonel Malcolm Induruwage (2 Apr 2006)

Chief Secretary:
Lieut-Colonel Ronald Clinch (1 May 2009)

Territorial Headquarters: 1414 Leon Guinto Sr St, Ermita, Manila 1000

Postal address: PO Box 3830, Manila 1099, The Philippines

Tel: [63] (2) 524 0086/88; fax: [63] (2) 521 6912; PR Dept: [63] (2) 536 3068;
email: saphl1@phl.salvationarmy.org

The first Protestant preaching of the gospel in The Philippines was done by Major John Milsaps, a chaplain appointed to accompany US troops from San Francisco to Manila in July 1898. Major Milsaps conducted open-air and regular meetings and led many into a saving knowledge of Jesus Christ.

The advance of The Salvation Army in The Philippines came at the initiative of Filipinos who had been converted through contact with The Salvation Army in Hawaii, returned to their homeland and commenced meetings in Panay, Luzon, Cebu and Mindanao Islands during the period 1933-37. On 6 June 1937 Colonel and Mrs Alfred Lindvall officially inaugurated this widespread work.

The Salvation Army Philippines was incorporated in 1963 as a religious and charitable corporation under Company Registration No 24211. The Salvation Army Social Services was incorporated in 1977 as a social welfare and development corporation under Company Registration No 73979 and The Salvation Army Educational Services was incorporated in 2001 as an educational corporation under Company Registration No A200009937.

Zone: South Pacific and East Asia
Country included in the territory: The Philippines
'The Salvation Army' in Filipino: Hukbo ng Kaligtasan; in Ilocano: Buyot ti Salakan
Languages in which the gospel is preached: Antiqueño (Kinaray-a), Bagobo, Bicolano, Cebuano, English, Filipino (Tagalog), Hiligaynon (Ilonggo), Ilocano, Korean, Pangasinan, T'boli, Waray
Periodical: *The War Cry*

THE period under review can be best described as a year of partnerships – primarily, partnership with God as at a new year rally the territory's theme, 'Keep In Step With The Spirit', was launched; and secondly, partnership with the worldwide Salvation Army.

Commissioners Robert and Janet Street (then IS to the Chief of the Staff and World Secretary for Women's Ministries, IHQ) conducted the Brengle Institute, held for the first time in many years. Attended by officers from across the many islands that comprise the territory, it was a significant time of learning and development for all participants.

Later, Commissioner Janet Street conducted a territorial women's leadership training event before the commissioners conducted the final meeting, a holiness celebration, with a large crowd in attendance.

One of the territory's enthusiastic supporters is USA Western, so it was significant to have its Territorial Commander, Commissioner Philip Swyers, as special guest for the commissioning weekend – described as being 'one of the most exciting occasions in memory'.

Events began with officers councils at Manila Korean Corps. A full-day music workshop and a concert were held at Manila Tondo Corps, a brass ensemble from USA Western (under the leadership of Bandmaster Kevin Larsson) conducting the workshop and augmenting the music support for the commissioning meetings.

More than 1,000 people gathered at the Aguinaldo Theatre, Quezon City, to witness the ordination and commissioning of 12 officers of the Witnesses For Christ Session. This was an occasion of much enthusiasm and deep commitment, especially when many people went forward for prayer and to commit their lives to serve in The Salvation Army.

A 'triple wedding' of six of the new lieutenants took place immediately after the commissioning.

It was fitting that Commissioner Swyers was present to participate in the turning of the soil at the site of the proposed THQ building, the new facility having been generously provided by USA Western Territory. It is hoped the building will be ready for occupation by early 2010.

STATISTICS
Officers 226 (active 178 retired 48) **Cadets** 11 **Envoys** 2 **Employees** 50
Corps 78 **Societies, Outposts and Outreaches** 75 **Institutions** 2 **Social Programmes** 23
Senior Soldiers 6,326 **Recruits** 2,922 **Adherents** 1,628 **Junior Soldiers** 1,110
Personnel serving outside territory Officers 11 Layworkers 1

STAFF
Women's Ministries: Col Irene Induruwage (TPWM) Lt-Col Robyn Clinch (TSWM)
Sec for Business Administration: tba
  Finance: Maj Estelita Bautista
  Christian Bookstore: tba
  Information Technology: Mr Victor Benganan Jr
  Property: Mr Alfredo Agpaoa Jr
Sec for Personnel Administration: Lt-Col Elnora Urbien
  Candidates: Maj Quintin Casidsid
  Training and Development: Capt Ruby Casimero
Sec for Programme Administration: tba
  Social Programme: Maj Susan Tandayag
  Corps Programme: Capt David Casimero
  Training: Capt David Oalang
  Training and Development/Education Services: Capt Ruby Casimero
  Editor: Maj Aida Selma
  Gospel Arts Coordinator: Mr Nicanor Bagasol
  Legal Consultant: Mr Paul Stephen Salegumba
  Public Relations Coordinator: Mr Efren Bargan

DIVISIONS
Central Philippines: 20 Senatorial Dr, Congressional Village, Project 8, Quezon City; tel: (02) 453 8208/929 6312; email: Central@phl.salvationarmy.org; Majs Virgilio and Ma Luisa Menia
Mindanao Island: 344 NLSA Rd, Purok Bayanihan, San Isidro, Lagao 9500 General Santos City; tel: (083) 553 5956/(083) 302 3798; email: Mid@phl.salvationarmy.org; Majs Joel and Susan Ceneciro

The Philippines Territory

Northern Luzon: Doña Loleng Subd., Nancayasan 2428 Urdaneta Pangasinan City; tel: (075) 656 2383/(075) 568 3037; email: Northern@phl.salvationarmy.org; Majs Alexander and Jocelyn Genabe

Visayas Islands: 731 M. J. Cuenco Ave, Cebu City; tel: (032) 416 7126; tel/fax: (032) 416 7346; email: Vid@phl.salvationarmy.org; Maj Myline Joy Flores

TRAINING COLLEGE
Pantay Rd, Sitio Bukal Brgy, Tandang Kutyo, Tanay, Rizal; tel: (02) 654 2909; fax: (02) 654 2895

UNDER THQ
Sponsorship/Scholarship Programme, Missing Persons/Family Tracing Service, Emergency Disaster Relief

SOCIAL SERVICES
Residential Social Centres
(Abused girls/children)
Bethany Home: 20 Senatorial Dr, Congressional Village, Project 8, Quezon City (acc 40)

(Street children)
Joyville Home: Pantay Rd, Sitio Bukal, Tanay, Rizal (acc 25)

Learning Centres
Asingan Educational Services Inc: Bautista St, Poblacion, 2439 Asingan, Pangasinan
Iloilo: Arroyo St, 5000 La Paz, Iloilo City

Child Care Centres
Bagong Silang: Phase 7 B-Blk 6, Lot 3A, Package 3, Bagong Silang Tala, Caloocan City
Bulalacao: Bulalacao, 5214 Oriental Mindoro
Caloocan: Cor Langaray, Dagat-dagatan Ave, Caloocan City
Cebu: 731 M. J. Cuenco Ave, 6000 Cebu City
Dagupan: Puelay District, 2400 Dagupan City
Davao: Blk 14, Lot 10, Kingfisher St, RPJ Village II, Seaside Subd, Matina Aplaya, Matina, 8000 Davao City
General Santos: 344 NLSA Rd, Purok Bayanihan, San Isidro, Lagao, 9500 General Santos City
Laoag: 50 Buttong, 2900 Laoag City, Ilocos Norte
Legazpi: 332 San Roque, Governor St, San Roque, Legazpi City
Mariveles: Porto del Sur, National Rd, 2105 Mariveles, Bataan
Olongapo: Camia St, Sta Rita, 2200 Olongapo City
Quezon City 2: 20 Senatorial Dr, Congressional Village, Project 8, Quezon City
Signal Village: Daisy St, Zone 6, Signal Village, Taguig, Metro Manila
Sta Barbara: 20 Poblacion Norte, 2419 Sta Barbara, Pangasinan
Tondo: 18215 Velasquez St, 1012 Tondo, Manila

Nutrition, Feeding and Day Care Centres
Dasmarinas: Blk 11, Lot 6, San Antonio de Padua II Area E, DBB, Dasmarinas, Cavite
Makati: 3493 Honda St, Pinagkaisahan, 1200 Makati City
Signal Village: Daisy St, Zone 6, Signal Village, Taguig, Metro Manila

Dormitories for Students and Working Women
Baguio: 35-37 P. Guevarra St, Aurora Hill, 2600 Baguio City (acc 50)
Lapu-Lapu: Gun-ob, Lapu-lapu City (acc 12)
Makati: 3493 Honda St, Pinagkaishan, 1200 Makati City (acc 12)
Quezon City 1: 67 Batanes St, Galas, Quezon City (acc 12)
San Jose Mindoro: 3090 Roxas St, Doña Consuelo Subd, 5100 San Jose, Occidental Mindoro (acc 12)

Programmes for Minorities
Bamban: c/o San Jose Corps, 3090 Roxas St, Doña Consuelo Subd, Occidental Mindoro
Bulalacao: Bulalacao, 5214 Oriental Mindoro
Lake Sebu: T'boli Village, Lake Sebu
Wali: Bo Wali, Maitum, Saranggani Province

Skills Training
Lapu-lapu: Vincent Drive, Gun-ob 6015, Lapu-lapu City

Livelihood Support
Ansiray Fishcages: Ansiray, 5100 San Jose, Occidental Mindoro
Bamban Carabao Raising: 3090 Roxas St, Doña Consuelo Subd, 511 San Jose, Occidental Mindoro
Bella Luz Cooperative Store: Brgy Bella Luz, 3318 San Mateo, Isabela

The Philippines Territory

Cabayaoasan Agricultural Cooperative: Cabayaoasan, 2413 Mangatarem, Pangasinon

Camangaan Agricultural Cooperative: Bo Camangaan, Rosales, 2442 Pangasinon

Lake Sebu Tinalak Weaving: 9512 Poblacion, Lake Sebu, South Cotabuto

Lopez Quezon Carabao Raising: Abines St, Talolong Lopez, Quezon

Lourdes Carabao Raising: Barangay Lourdes, Lopez, Quezon

Merville: 128 Sitio Malaya, Brgy Merville, Paranaque City

Nasukob: Nasukob, 5214 Bulalacao, Oriental Mindoro

Pahanocoy Tricycad: Florence Ville Subd, Pahanocoy, 6100 Bacolod City

Agricultural Assistance

Bella Luz: Barangay Bella Luz, 3318 San Mateo, Isabela

Nasukob Agricultural Loan: Nasukob, 5214 Bulalacao

Santa Agricultural Loan: Mabibila Sur, Santa, Ilocos Sur

Wali: Bo Wali, Maitum, Saranggani Province

Micro-Credit Enterprise Projects

Ansiray: 5100 San Jose, Occidental Mindoro

Badipa: Bayaoas, Urdaneta, Pangasinan

Cacutud: 34-B Misael St, Diamond Subd, Balibago, Angeles City

Cebu Central: 731 M. J. Cuenco Ave, Cebon City 6000

Dagupan: Puelay District, 2400 Dagupan City

A 'triple wedding' involving four of the new lieutenants of the Witnesses For Christ Session takes place immediately after their ordination and commissioning as officers. They are pictured with (back row, right to left) Colonel Malcolm Induruwage (TC), Lieut-Colonel Graham Durston (then CS), Commissioner Philip Swyers, who was special guest for the commissioning, and Captain David Oalang (then Training Principal).

Prayers at the site of the new THQ building

Davao: Block 14 Lot 10, Kingfisher St, RPJ Village II, Seaside Subdivision Matina Aplaya, Matina 8000, Davao City
General Santos: 344 NLSA Rd, Purok Bayanihan, San Isidoro, Lagao 9500 General Santos City
Iligan: Purok 5A Tambo, 9200 Iligan City, Lanao del Norte
Lake Sebu: 4512 Poblacion, Lake Sebu, South Cotabato
Legaspi: Governor St, 332 San Roque Legaspi City
Liloan: Catherine Booth Development Center, Tayud, Liloan, 6002 Cebu City
Magsaysay: Burgos St, Magsaysay, Occidental Mindoro
Malingao: Bo Malingao, Tubod, 9202 Lanao del Norte
Manila Central: 1414 Leon Guinto Sr, St 1000 Ermita, Manila
Mariveles: Porto del Sur, National Rd, 2105 Mariveles, Bataan
Merville: 128 Sitio Malaya, Brgy Merville, Paranaque City
Nasukob: Nasukob 5214 Bulalacao, Oriental Mindoro
Orani: 163 Calero St, Orani, 2112 Bataan
Ozamis: Carmen Annex, 7200 Ozamis City
San Jose Mindoro: 3090 Roxas St, Doña Consuelo Subd, 511 San Jose, Occidental Mindoro
Signal Village: Daisy St, Zone 6, Signal Village, Taguig, Metro Manila
Sta Ana: 2439 Asingan, Pangasinan
Wali: Wali, Maiturn, 9515 Saranggani Province

Water Systems
Bulalacao: Bulalacao, 5214 Oriental Mindoro
Camangaan: Bo Carmangaan, Rosales 2442, Pangasinon
Lopez: San Vicente St, Barangay Magsaysay, Lopez, Quezon
Lourdes: Barangay Lourdes, Lopez, Quezon
Mariveles: Porto del Sur, National Rd, 2105 Mariveles, Bataan
Nasukob: Nasukob, 5214 Bulalacao, Oriental Mindoro
Palili: c/o The Salvation Army, 163 Calero St, Orani 2112, Bataan
Sampaloc: Sitio, Hinadiongan Sampalac Tanay, Rizal 1080
Upper Katalicanan: c/o Midsayap Corps, Poblacion 8, Midsayap 9410, North Cotabato

Housing Project
Lopez, Quezon: Abines St, Talolong, Lopez, Quezo

Anti-Human Trafficking Projects
Bacolod; Cebu; Darapuay; Dasmarinas; Davao; Diamond/Cacutud; General Santos; Iligan; Laoag; Lapu-Lapu; Mariveles Corps; Olongapo; Orani; Pasay; Quezon City 2; Sinamar; San Jose Mindoro

HEALTH
Barangay Health Workers in Rural Corps
Botica sa Barangay
Cabayaosan Corps: Cabayaosan, Mangatarem Pangasinan
San Jose Occidental Mindoro: 3090 Roxas St, Doña Consuelo Subd, San Jose Occidental Mindoro

HIV/Aids Programmes
Ansiray; Bacolod; Bella Luz; Bulalacao; Cantamuak; Cebu; Dagupan; Darapuay; Dasmarinas; Davao; Diamond/Cacutud; Diffun; General Santos; Iligan; Lake Sebu; Laoag; La Paz; Lapu-Lapu; Lebe; Legaspi; Mariveles Nasukob; Olongapo; Orani; Pandanan; San Jose Antique; San Jose Mindoro; Santiago; Sinamar; Tacloban; Tondo; Urdaneta; Villa Ros; Wali

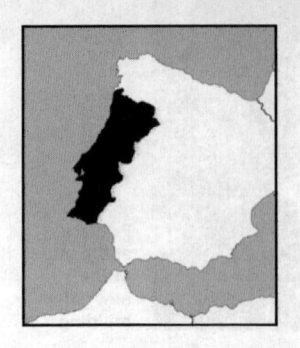

PORTUGAL COMMAND

Command leaders:
Majors Alberto and Maria José Serém

Officer Commanding:
Major Alberto Serém (1 Sep 2006)

Command Headquarters: Rua Dr Silva Teles, 16, 1050-080 Lisboa
Postal address: Apartado 14109, 1064-002 Lisboa, Portugal
Tel: [351] (21) 780 2930; fax: [351] (21) 780 2940;
email:Portugal_Command@POR.salvationarmy.org; website: www.exercitodesalvacao.pt

On 25 July 1971, official recognition was given to the first corps established in Portugal. The work was started in the northern city of Porto by a group of evangelical Christians. On 28 January 1972, Major and Mrs Carl S. Eliasen arrived in Lisbon to start work there and to supervise the existing activities.

On 4 July 1974 The Salvation Army was recognised by the Ministry of Justice as a religious and philanthropic organisation. All social activities are incorporated in Centro Social do Exército de Salvação which was constituted in Portugal on 26 March 1981 (Public Utility Register 16/82 dated 10 March 1982). On 8 March 2007 The Salvation Army was registered as a Collective Religious Person (the legal term for a church).

Zone: Europe
Country included in the command: Portugal
'The Salvation Army' in Portuguese: Exército de Salvação
Language in which the gospel is preached: Portuguese
Periodicals: *O Salvacionista*, *Ideias & Recursos* (for Women's Ministries)

A KEEN interest in the work of The Salvation Army was awakened by Portugal's First Lady, Dr Maria Cavaco Silva, at an hour-long audience given to the command's leaders at the presidential palace in January 2009.

Two months later she visited the Army's shelter for the homeless in Lisbon, marking the centre's 12th anniversary. The First Lady (pictured on facing page) praised the Army's ministry and encouraged its continued work battling poverty and social exclusion.

During the weekend of 31 May-1 June 2008 the command celebrated its National Congress, led by Chief of the Staff Commissioner Robin Dunster. The event was well covered on television, which included an interview with the Chief. The meetings, full of joy and enthusiasm, had moments of deep spiritual challenge when many people knelt at the mercy seat to register decisions for Christ.

EuroMusic 2008 took place in the Algarve (9-16 August) with 52 enthusiastic students coming from several parts of Europe to develop not only as musicians but as Christians too. Most of them rededicated their

Portugal Command

lives to Christ as they stood round a wooden cross. In the school's final days there were three public concerts – in a church, in the open air and in a theatre.

January 2009 saw the first edition of *O Salvacionista*, a new publication for Salvationists and the public.

An intensive Baby Song seminar (9-10 March) was led by Major Ruth Walz (Germany and Lithuania). All participants were positive that this new opportunity of ministry, full of possibilities, will begin soon in Portugal.

STATISTICS
Officers (active) 16 **Employees** 119
Mission Areas with Corps 5 **Institutions** 7
Senior Soldiers 89 **Adherents** 72 **Junior Soldiers** 26
Personnel serving outside command Officers 3

STAFF
Women's Ministries: Maj Maria José Serém (CPWM)
Finance: Maj Arlette Reichenbach
Projects: Maj Mendes Reichenbach
Social: Dra Sandra Martins Lopes

SOCIAL SERVICES
Children's Home
Centro de Acolhimento Novo Mundo,
 Ave Desidério Cambournac, 14,
 2710-553 Sintra; tel: 219 244 239;
 fax: 219 249 688 (acc 14)

Clothing and Food Distribution Centre
Rua Escola do Exército, 11-B, 1150-143 Lisboa; tel: 213 528 137; fax: 213 160 732

Thrift Shop
Chelas: Rua Rui de Sousa, Lote 65 A-Loja C, 1900-802 Lisboa

Day Centres for the Elderly and Home Help Services
Colares: Av dos Bombeiros Voluntários, Várzea de Colares, 2705-180 Sintra; tel: 219 288 450; fax: 219 288 458
Lisboa: Rua Capitão Roby, 19 (Picheleira), 1900-111 Lisboa; tel: 218 409 108; fax: 218 409 112
Porto: Av Vasco da Gama, 645, Lojas 1 e 2, Ramalde, 4100-491 Porto; tel: 226 172 769; fax: 226 171 120

Eventide Homes
Nosso Lar: Av dos Bombeiros Voluntários, Várzea de Colares, 2705-180 Colares;
 tel: 219 288 450; fax: 219 288 458 (acc 30)
Marinel: Rua das Marinhas, 13, Tomadia, Praia das Maçãs, 2705-313 Colares;
 tel: 219 288 480; fax: 219 288 481 (acc 50)

Night Shelter for the Homeless
Rua da Manutenção, 7 (Xabregas) – 1900-318 Lisboa; tel: 218 680 908; fax: 218 680 913 (acc 75)

HOLIDAY AND CONFERENCE CENTRES
Casa Marinel, Av José Félix da Costa, 9, Praia das Maçãs – 2705-312 Colares (information from CHQ)
Vivenda Boa Nova, Rua do Vinagre, 9, 2705-354 Colares; tel: 219 291 718 (holiday bookings to CHQ)

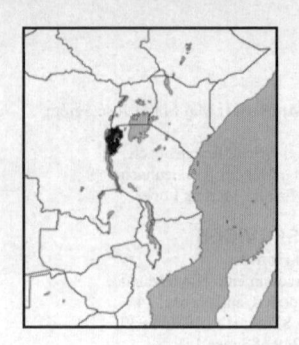

RWANDA AND BURUNDI REGION

Regional leaders:
Majors Stephen and Grace Chepkurui

Regional Commander:
Major Stephen Chepkurui (1 Feb 2007)

Regional Headquarters: Plot 11737, Kibagabaga Road, Kimironko, Kimironko Sector, Kigali

Postal address: PO Box 812, Kigali, Rwanda

Tel: [250] 587639; fax: [250] 511812; email: Rwanda@rwa.salvationarmy.org

As a result of civil war and genocide in Rwanda, The Salvation Army became actively involved in relief work in September 1994. Operations were concentrated in Kayenzi Commune, part of the Gitarama Prefecture. Following mission work by officers from Zaïre, Uganda and Tanzania in 1995, officers were appointed from Congo (Brazzaville) to develop corps and mission work in Kayenzi Commune. Kayenzi Corps officially began its ministry on 5 November 1995. The Salvation Army was officially registered as a church in Rwanda on 15 September 2008.

In 1983, Justin Lusombo-Musese (a Congolese born in Burundi) was introduced by a friend to some of William Booth's writings and learned about The Salvation Army's early history. Justin and the friend were so enthused they decided to become members of the Army. Over the ensuing years they persistently requested International Headquarters to start Army operations in Burundi, and on 5 August 2007 the work was officially recognised with the warranting of Justin Lusombo-Musese and his wife Justine Fatouma as auxiliary-captains. The Rwanda Region was redesignated Rwanda and Burundi Region in October 2008.

Zone: Africa
Countries included in the region: Burundi, Rwanda
The Salvation Army in Kinyarwanda: Ingabo Z'Agakiza
Languages in which the gospel is preached: English, French, Kinyarwanda, Kirundi, Kiswahili
Periodical: *Salvationist News*

THE theme 'New Beginnings' took hold in the region as many new events were held during 2008-09. On 15 September 2008 The Salvation Army was officially recognised as a church in Rwanda and is now registered as such.

Officers' reviews took place for the first time (4-6 February 2009), with eight officers from the Bridgebuilders Session participating in a five-year officership review.

All officers attended the region's first-ever Brengle Institute (16-20 February 2009), conducted by Commissioners Stuart and Hope Mungate (territorial leaders, Democratic Republic of Congo).

The new regional headquarters building was opened (27 February 2009) and dedicated to God by Lieut-Colonels Kenneth and Paula Johnson (USA Southern), whose territory supported the project.

Rwanda and Burundi Region

The first publication of a monthly regional newsletter, *Salvationist News*, was published in March 2009. This will endeavour to link regional headquarters with corps and outposts throughout both Rwanda and Burundi as it provides news, features on evangelism, and pastoral articles to encourage and support Salvationists.

The Africa HIV/Aids Facilitation Team visited (10-25 March 2009) and carried out workshops and training to enable a strategic plan to be put into practice.

The new beginnings are seen as an encouraging way forward for further development, evangelism and ministry to the people of Rwanda and Burundi. The region is aiming to increase its number of senior soldiers by 1,000.

STATISTICS
Officers 19 **Auxiliary-Captains** 2 **Corps Leaders** 14 **Employees** 30
Corps 11 **Outreach Unit** 1 **Outposts** 11 **Pre-School Facility** 2 (acc 170)
Senior Soldiers 1,413 **Adherents** 548 **Junior Soldiers** 857

STAFF
Women's Ministries: Maj Grace Chepkurui (RPWM) Maj Brigitte Bamanabio (RSWM)
Regional Sec: Maj Eugene Bamanabio
Education: Capt Dancille Ndagijimana
Emergency Response: Capt Brian Martin
Extension Training: Capt Dancille Ndagijimana
Finance: tba
HIV/Aids Coordinator: Capt Beatrice Ayabagabo
Information Technology: Mr Pascal Igiraneza
Projects: Capt Brian Martin
Public Relations: Capt Emmanuel Ndagijimana
Social: tba
Sponsorship: Capt Amanda Martin
Youth and Candidates: Capt Emmanuel Ndagijimana

DISTRICT
Kayenzi: PO Box 812, Kigali; Capt Celestin Ayabagabo; mobile: 250 08587988

SECTIONS
Kigali: c/o PO Box 812, Kigali
Muhanga: c/o PO Box 812, Kigali

BURUNDI
Ruhero II, Boulevard de l'Independence, Parcelle No 1416, Bujumbura, Burundi; Aux-Capts Justin and Justine Lusombo-Musese; mobile: 257 79996148; email: lusombo@yahoo.com

A class of children learn happily at the Army's pre-school in Kayenzi, Rwanda

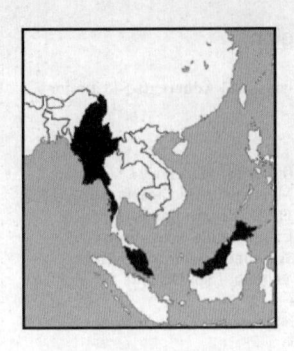

SINGAPORE, MALAYSIA AND MYANMAR TERRITORY

Territorial leaders:
Colonels Keith and Beryl Burridge

Territorial Commander:
Colonel Keith Burridge (1 May 2009)

Chief Secretary:
Lieut-Colonel Bob Lee (1 May 2009)

Territorial Headquarters: 20 Bishan St 22, Singapore 579768

Postal address: Ang Mo Kio Central, PO Box 640, Singapore 915605

Tel: [65] 6555 0188; fax: [65] 6552 8542; website: www.salvationarmy.org.sg

In May 1935 Salvation Army work began in Singapore. It spread to Penang (1938), Melaka and Ipoh (1940), Kuching (Sarawak) (1950), Kuala Lumpur (1966) and Kota Kinabalu (Sabah) (1996).

'The General of The Salvation Army' is a 'corporation sole' by The Salvation Army Ordinance 1939 in the Straits Settlements; by The Salvation Army (Incorporation) Ordinance 1956 in the Federation of Malaya; and by the Missionary Societies Order 1957 in the Colony of Sarawak.

Adjutant Taran Das (Reuben Moss), who was attached to the Lahore headquarters in India, was appointed to open the work in Burma (now Myanmar) by Commissioner Booth Tucker in January 1915. Myanmar Salvationists have, since 1966, developed their witness and service despite the restriction on reinforcements from overseas. In 1994 Myanmar was joined to the Singapore and Malaysia Command. The command was elevated to territory status on 1 March 2005.

Zone: South Pacific and East Asia
Countries included in the territory: Malaysia, Myanmar, Singapore
'The Salvation Army' in Chinese: (Mandarin) Chiu Shi Chen, (Cantonese) Kau Shai Kwan, (Amoy, Hokkien) Kiu Se Kun; Bahasa: Bala Keselamatan; Myanmar: Kae Tin Chin Tat; Tamil: Retchania Senai
Languages in which the gospel is preached: Burmese, Chin (Mizo, Zahau, Dai), Chinese (Amoy, Cantonese, Hokkien, Mandarin), English, Bahasa, Malay, Tamil, Telegu
Periodical: *The War Cry*

CYCLONE Nargis tore through the Irrawaddy Delta and Yangon (Myanmar) on 4 May 2008, leaving extensive devastation and loss of life in its wake. In the days before international aid and relief workers became available, five teams of officers and soldiers worked almost non-stop distributing rice, water, medicines and clothing to people in the surrounding areas. Reconstruction work is well under way.

Malaysia's 70th anniversary celebrations (30 May - 1 June) were rich in blessing for the hundreds of Salvationists who attended. The 21

Singapore, Malaysia and Myanmar Territory

delegates from Myanmar received a special welcome. Commissioners Ivan and Heather Lang (Australia Southern), who had served in Singapore, were guest leaders and with them came Perth Fortress Band to give music support.

On 29 October approval to register The Salvation Army in the state of Sabah, East Malaysia, was finally given. This means the territory can proceed to develop work there.

The Myanmar Region is developing a further two corps plants: in Tacheleik, a cross-border town in Shan State, and in Mandalay. Both plants report growing attendances; outreach into outlying villages is being investigated.

The then territorial leaders, Commissioners David and Grace Bringans, visited Myanmar for the opening of the new district office and Tahan Corps building. They also led an officers' fellowship session in Mandalay, with every officer contributing ideas toward visionary planning. All corps and corps plants are working towards growing spiritually and numerically.

The Norwegian Government in partnership with Norway, Iceland and The Færoes Territory is funding a large HIV/Aids project, mostly in Upper Myanmar where the need is greatest. On a monitoring visit to this area they found Salvationists and volunteers willingly and tirelessly connecting with the needy.

Vision became reality in Malaysia when Lovehaven Children's Home and Day Care Centre in Bintulu was opened. A new wing was also opened at Ipoh Children's Home, offering specialised facilities for older girls to learn independent living skills.

In Singapore, Hope Centre – a residents' living area for people with early dementia – was opened at Peacehaven Elderly People's Nursing Home. The launch of an Integrated Care In Place programme at Bedok Multiservice and Rehabilitation Centre also took place.

Cadets of the Ambassadors Of Holiness Session commenced training at the schools for officer training in Singapore and Yangon.

When delegates from the Singapore Youth Camp travelled to Taiwan to engage in ministry at Puli Corps, the visit left a deep impression on them. The Malaysian Youth and Children's Camp at Ipoh resulted in many delegates making new commitments of service to God.

STATISTICS
Officers 131 (active 119 retired 12) Cadets 17 Employees 700
Corps 48 Outposts 21 Institutions 16 Kindergarten 2 Day Care Centres 17
Senior Soldiers 2,485 Adherents 412 Junior Soldiers 356

STAFF
Women's Ministries: Col Beryl Burridge (TPWM) Lt-Col Wendy Lee (TSWM)
Editor: Maj Katrina Thomas
Finance: Mdm Koh Guek Eng
Human Resources: Mrs Toh-Chia Lai Ying
Programme: Maj Darrell Thomas
Property: Mr John Ng
Public Relations: Mr Gregory Lee
Projects: Lt-Col Bob Lee
Training: Lt-Col Bob Lee
Youth and Candidates: Capt Hary Haran

Singapore, Malaysia and Myanmar Territory

SCHOOL FOR OFFICER TRAINING (SINGAPORE AND MALAYSIA)
500 Upper Bukit Timah Rd, Singapore 678106; tel: 6349 5333

SINGAPORE

Children's Homes
Gracehaven: 3 Lorong Napiri (off Yio Chu Kang Rd), Singapore 547528; tel: 6488 1510 (acc 160)
The Haven: 350 Pasir Panjang Rd, Singapore 118692; tel: 6774 9588/9 (acc 50)

Day Care Centres for Children
Ang Mo Kio Child Care Centre: Blk 610 Ang Mo Kio Ave 4, #01-1227 Singapore 560610; tel: 6452 4862 (acc 89)
Bukit Batok East Child Care Centre: Blk 247 Bukit Batok East Ave 5, #01-86 Singapore 650247; tel: 6562 4976 (acc 73)
Bukit Panjang Child Care Centre: Blk 402 Fajar Rd, #01-217 Singapore 670402; tel: 6760 2624 (acc 82)
Pasir Ris Child Care Centre: Blk 427 Pasir Ris Dr 6, #01-43 Singapore 510427; tel: 6582 0286 (acc 76)
Tampines Child Care Centre: Blk 159 Tampines St 12, #01-95 Singapore 521159; tel: 6785 2976 (acc 90)

Day Care Centres for the Elderly
Bedok Multiservice Centre for the Elderly: Blk 121, #01-161 Bedok North Rd, Singapore 460121; tel: 6445 1630 (acc 65)
Bedok Rehabilitation Centre: Blk 121, #01-163 Bedok North Rd, Singapore 460121; tel: 6445 1630 (acc 35)

Family Support Services
Blk 42, Beo Cresc, #01-95 Singapore 160042; tel: 6273 7207
Bukit Panjang Family Service Centre: Blk 404 Fajar Rd, #01-267 Singapore 670404; tel: 6763 0837 (acc 98)

Hostels
Peacehaven Nurses' Hostel: 9 Upper Changi Rd North, Singapore 507706; tel: 6546 5678 (acc 100)
Young Women's Hostel: The Haven, 350 Pasir Panjang Rd, Singapore 118692; tel: 6774 9588/9 (acc 10)

Retreat Centre
Praisehaven, 500 Upp Bukit Timah Rd, Singapore 678106; tel: 6349 5302 (acc 191)

Nursing Home
Peacehaven, 9 Upper Changi Rd North, Singapore 507706; tel: 6546 5678 (acc 374)

Prison Support Services – Kids In Play
9 Upper Changi Rd North, Singapore 507706; tel 6546 5868

Red Shield Industries
309 Upper Serangoon Rd, Singapore 347693; tel: 6288 5438

Youth Development Centres
Youth Development Centre: Blk 65 Kallang Bahru, #01-305 Singapore 330065; tel: 6291 6303; under Territorial Youth Dept
Kallang Bahru Community Centre: Blk 66 Kallang Bahru, #01-507 Singapore 330066; tel: 62916303

EAST MALAYSIA

Boys' Home
Kuching Boys' Home: Jalan Ban Hock, 93100, Kuching; PO Box 547, 93700 Kuching, Sarawak, Malaysia; tel: (082) 24 2623 (acc 35)

Children's Home
Kuching Children's Home: 138 Jalan Upland, 93200 Kuching; PO Box 106, 93700 Kuching, Sarawak, Malaysia; tel: (082) 24 8234 (acc 60)

Day Care Centres for Children
Kuching Kindergarten: Sekama Rd, 93300, Kuching, Sarawak, Malaysia; PO Box 44, 93700 Kuching Sarawak, Malaysia; tel: (082) 333981 (acc 120)
Lovehaven: 479 Taman Seaview, Bintulu, Sarawak, Malaysia; tel: (086) 315843

Corps Community Services
Bintulu Corps and Community Services: Lot 216, 2nd Floor BDA Shophouse, 16 Jalan Tanjong Batu, 97000 Bintulu, Malaysia; tel: (086) 315 843
Kota Kinabalu Corps and Community Services: Lot 1, Taman Seri Kiansom Lorong Seri Kiansom, Inanam, Kota Kinabalu, Malaysia; tel: (088) 433766
Kuching Corps and Community Services: Jalan Ban Hock, 93100 Kuching, Sarawak, Malaysia; tel: (082) 242623

Singapore, Malaysia and Myanmar Territory

Youth Development Centre
Bintulu: S/Lot 16, Lot 1362, 1st Flr Tanjung Batu Commercial Centre, Jalan Tun razak, 97000 Bintulu; tel: (086) 315843

Red Shield Industries
Ground – 1st Flr, 1 Jalan Ang Cheng Ho, 93100 Kuching; tel: 082 410564

WEST MALAYSIA
Liaison and Public Relations Office: 26-1 Jalan Puteri, 4/2 Bandar Puteri, 47100 Puchong, Selangor Darul Ehsan, Malaysia; tel (06) 8061 4929

Boys' Homes
Ipoh Boys' Home: 4367 Jalan Tambun, 31400 Ipoh, PO Box 221, 30720 Ipoh, Perak, Malaysia; tel: [60] (05) 545 7819 (acc 60)

Centre for Special Children
Hopehaven Centre for Special Children: 321 Jalan Parameswara, 75000 Melaka, Malaysia; tel: [60] (06) 283 2101 (acc 100)

Children's Homes
Ipoh Children's Home: 255 Kampar Rd, 30250 Ipoh, Perak, Malaysia; tel: (05) 254 9767; fax: (05) 242 9630 (acc 50)
Penang Children's Home: 8A Logan Rd, 10400 Penang, Malaysia; tel: (04) 227 0162 (acc 58)
Lighthouse Children's Home: 404 Taman Sinn, Jalan Semabok 75050, Melaka, Malaysia; tel: (06) 283 2101 (acc 35)

Day Care Centres for Children
Batang Melaka Day Care Centre: J7702 Main Rd, Batang Melaka 77500, Selandar Malaysia; tel: (06) 446 1601 (acc 80)
Banting Day Care Centre: 30 Jalan Cendana 15, Taman Mihhibah, Banting 42700 (acc 50)
Kuala Lumpur Day Care centre: 1 Lingkungan Hujan, Overseas Union Garden 58200 KL, Malaysia; tel: (03) 7782 4766 (acc 100)

Homes for the Aged
Joyhaven Home for the Elderly: 1 Jalan 12/17, Seksyen 12, 46200 Petaling Jaya, Selangor, Malaysia; tel: (03) 7958 6257 (acc 25)
Perak Home for the Aged: Jalan Bersatu, Jelapang, 30020 Ipoh, Perak, Malaysia; tel: (05) 526 2108 (acc 55)

Corps Community Services
Puchong Community Services: 26-1 Jalan Puteri 4/2, Bandar Puteri 47100, Puchong, Selangor, Malaysia; tel: (03) 8061 4929

Social/Community Services – Melaka State
Melaka Social and Community Services: 321 Jalan Parameswara, 75000 Melaka, Malaysia; tel: (06) 283 1203
Batang Melaka Community Services: J7702 Main Rd, Batang Malaka, 77500 Selander, Melaka West Malaysia; tel: (06) 4461601

MYANMAR REGION
Headquarters: 176-178 Anawrahta St, Botahtaung, East Yangon 11161, Myanmar; Postal address: GPO Box 394, Yangon, Myanmar; tel: [95] (1) 294267/293307; fax: [95] (1) 298067
Regional Officer: Maj Gordon Daly

DISTRICTS
Central: District Office, Mandalay
Kalaymyo: District Office, D-group, Tahan, Kalemyo; tel: [95] (73) 21396
Tamu: District Office, Kanan Corps, Kanan Township

SCHOOL FOR OFFICER TRAINING (Myanmar)
50 Byaing Ye O Zin St, Tarmway, Yangon, Myanmar; tel: [95] (1) 543694

Boys' Home
406 Banyadala Rd, Tarmway, Yangon, Myanmar; tel: 95 1 541462 (acc 50)

Children's Home
50 Bago Rd, Pyu, Myanmar (acc 50)

Girls' Home
50 Byaing Ye O Zin St, Tarmway, Yangon, Myanmar; tel: 95 1 543961 (acc 50)

Day Care Centre for Children
Tarmway Corps

SOUTH AMERICA EAST TERRITORY

Territorial leaders:
Colonels Nestor and Rebecca Nüesch

Territorial Commander:
Colonel Nestor Nüesch (1 Dec 2006)

Chief Secretary:
Lieut-Colonel Ricardo Bouzigues (1 Jul 2008)

**Territorial Headquarters: Avda Rivadavia 3257 (C1203AAE),
Buenos Aires, Argentina**

Postal address: Casilla de Correos 2240 (C1000WAW) Buenos Aires, Argentina

Tel/fax: [54] (11) 4864-9321/9348/9491/1075; email: ejersaljefatura@SAE.salvationarmy.org;
website: www.ejercitodesalvacion.org.ar

Four officers, who knew no Spanish, established The Salvation Army in Buenos Aires in 1890. Operations spread to other South American nations, of which Paraguay (1910), Uruguay (1890) and Argentina now comprise the South America East Territory.

The Salvation Army was recognised as a juridical person in Argentina by the Government Decree of 26 February 1914 (No A 54/909); in Uruguay by the Ministry of the Interior on 17 January 1917 (No 366537); and in Paraguay by Presidential Decree of 28 May 1928 (No 30217).

Zone: Americas and Caribbean
Countries included in the territory: Argentina, Paraguay, Uruguay
'The Salvation Army' in Spanish: Ejército de Salvación
Language in which the gospel is preached: Spanish, Korean, Guaraní
Periodicals: *El Oficial*, *El Salvacionista*

THE territory continues to march from strength to strength as new soldiers are enrolled, ministry is begun in new locations, outposts are elevated to corps status and new programmes find expression in various towns and cities of Argentina, Paraguay and Uruguay.

Territorial and divisional events – youth, music and women's ministries – were supported enthusiastically and attended by increased numbers. For the first time in the territory's history a territorial men's camp was arranged and was a great success.

A celebratory crowd welcomed five new lieutenants and four new captains (commissioned to full rank from being auxiliary-captains) at the ordination and commissioning of the Witnesses For Jesus Session. Only a few months later the 10 cadets of the Ambassadors Of Holiness Session were greeted with enthusiasm as, marching behind the flags of their respective countries, they joined the nine cadets of the

South America East Territory

Prayer Warriors Session to fill the training college to capacity for the first time in many years.

Officers and their families met together at the Officers' Family Retreat, experiencing an inspiring series of meetings and age-appropriate gatherings as well as enjoying wonderful fellowship together.

Although fire destroyed the interior and fixtures of the Salto (Uruguay) corps premises, the officers and local Salvationists quickly raised the flag in a temporary location where they continue to meet while resources are sought to replace all that was lost.

Such enthusiasm and dedication is multiplied around the territory as The Salvation Army seeks to impact the communities in which it operates.

As the implementation of a territorial strategy of self-sufficiency of appointments becomes a reality, numerous charity/thrift shops are being opened where it is deemed feasible to do so. Enthusiasm and deeper understanding of the mission possibilities connected with this strategy was realised through a successful territorial conference on this theme.

STATISTICS
Officers 153 (active 123 retired 30) **Cadets** 19 Employees 152
Corps 41 Outposts 19 Institutions 39
Senior Soldiers 1,714 Adherents 508 **Junior Soldiers** 548

STAFF
Women's Ministries: Col Rebecca Nüesch (TPWM) Lt-Col Sonia Bouzigues (TSWM)
Personnel: Maj Wendy Johnstone
Programme: Maj Pablo Nicolasa
Business Administration: tba
Education: Maj Wendy Johnstone
Finance: Mr Sergio Cerezo (Accountant in charge)
Legal: Mr Rene Menares
Literature and Editor: Lt-Col Sonia Bouzigues
Music and Gospel Arts: S/L Omar Pérez
Pastoral Care: Maj Bartolo Aguirre
Projects/Sponsorship/Missing Persons: Mrs Claudia Franchetti
Property: Mr Rolando Ramírez
Red Shield/Thrift Store Operations: Maj Miguel Del Bello
Social: Maj Bartolo Aguirre
Supplies: tba
Training: Maj John Mowers
Youth and Candidates: Capt William De Jesús

DIVISIONS
Buenos Aires: Avda Rivadavia 3257 – Piso 2 (C1203AAE), Buenos Aires, Argentina; tel: (011) 4861 1930/9499; Maj Estela Nicolasa
Central Argentina: Urquiza 2142, (S2000AOD) Rosario Pcia de Santa Fe, Argentina; tel/fax: (0341) 425 6739
Uruguay: Hocquart 1886, (11800) Montevideo, Uruguay; tel: (598) (2) 409 7581; Majs Danton and Juana Moya

DISTRICTS
Central West Argentina: Felix Frías 434/6, (X5004AHJ) Córdoba, Argentina; tel: (351) 423-3228; Maj Raúl Bernao
North East Argentina: Brignole 126, (H3500BOF) Resistencia, Prov De Chaco, Argentina; tel: (3722) 466-529; Maj Hugo Gutierrez
Paraguay: Héroes de la Independencia y Vietman, Casilla 2008, (CP 2160) San Lorenzo, Paraguay; tel/fax: 595 (21) 577 082; Maj Thore Paulsen
Southern Argentina: Moreno 759 (B8000FWO), Bahía Blanca, Pcia de Buenos Aires; tel/fax: (291) 4533 642; Maj Dimas Joel Barrault

TRAINING COLLEGE
Avda Tte Gral Donato Álvarez 465/67, (C1406BOC) Buenos Aires; tel/fax: (011) 4631 4815

COMMUNITY AND DAY CARE CENTRES
Argentina: Pellegrini 376, (E3200AMF) Concordia (Entre Ríos); tel: (345) 421 1751 (acc 30)

South America East Territory

Uruguay: Sarandí 1573, (60,000) Paysandú; tel: (72) 22709 (acc 30)

CONFERENCE CENTRES AND YOUTH CAMP
Argentina
Parque General Jorge L. Carpenter, Avda Benavídez 115, (Paraguay y Uruguay) (B1621) Benavídez, Pcia de Buenos Aires; tel: (03488) 458644
Parque El Oasis, Ruta 14 Km 7 Camino Público a Rosario – Zona Rural (Santa Fe); tel: (341) 495 0003

SOCIAL SERVICES
Counselling and Labour Exchange
Argentina: Loria 190, (C1173ACD) Buenos Aires; tel: (11) 4865 0074

Boys' Home
Uruguay: El Lucero, J. M. Blanes 62, (50,000) Salto; tel: (732) 32740 (acc 30)

Children's Homes (mixed)
Argentina: Evangelina, Monroe 1166, (B1878IPP) Quilmes, Pcia de Buenos Aires; tel: (11) 4253 0623 (acc 32)
Paraguay: El Redil, Dr Hassler 4402 y MacArthur, Asunción; tel: [595] (21) 600 291 (acc 40)

Eventide Homes
Argentina
Catalina Higgins Home, Calle Mitre, 54 No 2749, (1650) Villa Maipú, San Martín, Pcia de Buenos Aires; tel: (11) 4753 4117 (acc 54)
Eliasen Home, Primera Junta 750, (B1878IPP) Quilmes, Pcia de Buenos Aires; tel: (011) 4254 5897 (acc 37)
Uruguay: El Atardecer, Avda Agraciada 3567, (11800) Montevideo; tel: (2) 308 5227/309 5385 (acc 75)

Industrial Homes
Argentina
Avda Sáenz 580, (C1437DNS) Buenos Aires; tel: (11) 4911 7561/0781/7585
Amenábar 581, (S2000OQK) Rosario; tel: (341) 482 0155
Bustamante 1027, Gerli, Pcia de Buenos Aires; tel: (011) 4203 2133
O'Brien 1272/84, (C1137ABD) Buenos Aires; tel: (11) 4305 5021
Salta 3197, Barrio San Javier, (H3500BOF) Resistencia; tel: (3722) 466 529

Night Shelters
(Men)
Argentina
Copahué 2032, (C1288ABB) Buenos Aires; tel: (11) 438 6750 (acc 75)
Maza 2258 (C1240ADV) Buenos Aires; tel: (11) 4912 0843 (acc 86)

(Women and Children)
Argentina
José I. Rucci 1231, (B1822CJY) Valentín Alsina, Pcia de Buenos Aires; tel: (11) 4228 4328 (acc 34)
O'Brien 1272, (C1137ABD) Buenos Aires; tel: (11) 4304 8753 (acc 38)

Students' Homes
Argentina
Bat de Junín 2921, (S3000ASQ) Santa Fe; tel: (342) 452 0563 (acc 28)
Calle 4, No 711, (1900) La Plata, Pcia de Buenos Aires; tel: (0221) 483 6152 (acc 16)
Félix Frías 434/6, (X5004AHJ) Córdoba; tel: (351) 423 3228 (acc 15)
Godoy Cruz 352, (M5500GOQ) Mendoza, Pcia de Mendoza; tel: (261) 429 6113 (acc 6)
San Martín 964 (U9100BET) Trelew, (Chubut); tel: (2965) 433 125 (acc 20)

Women's Residence
Argentina: Esparza 93, (C1171ACA) Buenos Aires; tel: (11) 4861 3119 (acc 56)

Primary School
Argentina: EEGB No 1027 Federico Held, Barrio ULM, (H3730BQA) Charata, Pcia del Chaco; tel: (3731) 421 292 (acc 450)

Technical School
Argentina: 'Major Juan C. Costen and Friends of Germany', Coronel Bogado s/n, Bo OLM, (H3730BQA) Charata, Pcia del Chaco; tel: (3731) 421 292

Health Centre
Argentina: Pcia del Chaco, Coronel Bogado 4, Barrio ULM, (H3730BQA) Charata; tel: (3731) 421 292

Medical Clinic
Paraguay: Héroes de la Independencia y Vietnam, Villa Laurelty, San Lorenzo; tel: [595] 21 577 082

SOUTH AMERICA WEST TERRITORY

Territorial leaders:
Commissioners Jorge A. and Adelina Ferreira

Territorial Commander:
Commissioner Jorge A. Ferreira
(1 Feb 2007)

Chief Secretary:
Lieut-Colonel F. Bradford Bailey (1 Jul 2008)

Territorial Headquarters: Av. España 44, Santiago, Chile

Postal address: Casilla 3225, Santiago, Chile (parcels/courier service: Avenida España No 44, Santiago Centro, Santiago, Chile)

Tel: [56] (2) 671 8237/695 7005; fax: [56] (2) 698 5560

Salvation Army operations were commenced in Chile soon after the arrival of Brigadier and Mrs William T. Bonnet to Valparaíso on 1 October 1909. The first corps was opened in Santiago on 28 November, with Captain David Arn and Lieutenant Alfred Danielson as officers. Adjutant and Mrs David Thomas, with Lieutenant Zacarías Ribeiro, pioneered the work in Peru in March 1910. The work in Bolivia, started in December 1920, was planned by Brigadier Chas Hauswirth and established by Adjutant and Mrs Oscar E. Ahlm. Quito saw the Army's arrival in Ecuador on 30 October 1985 under the command of Captain and Mrs Eliseo Flores Morales.

Zone: Americas and Caribbean
Countries included in the territory: Bolivia, Chile, Ecuador, Peru
'The Salvation Army' in Aymara: Ejercitunaca Salvaciananaca; in Quechua: Ejercituman Salvacionman; in Spanish: Ejército de Salvación
Languages in which the gospel is preached: Aymara, Quechua, Spanish
Publications: *El Grito de Guerra* (*The War Cry*), *El Trébol* (Women's Ministries annual magazine and programme aids)

DURING the past five years the territory has emphasised strong Bible teaching as the guide for Salvationists' actions in ministry. The territorial theme for 2009 was 'Because Your Word Urges Me To Return To Our Roots'. Rediscovering the origins and motivation as Christians and Salvationists has helped the territory to be more effective in its work, while responding to God's purpose in raising up The Salvation Army.

Guided by this theme, each centre across the territory continued to pursue and accomplish the Army's mission in their city and area of influence.

A territorial music camp was held with a strong emphasis on the connection between worship and the use of creative arts. Music ministry is very important in the territory, and this kind of camp helps the development of its music leaders.

South America West Territory

Activities in a new school in Santiago were initiated, and in Trujillo (northern Peru) property was purchased in order to enhance the services provided there.

Schools are an important Christian influence in the four countries where the Army serves (Ecuador, Bolivia, Peru and Chile) and there are no limitations placed on Christian teaching. In fact, in Chile the Government encourages The Salvation Army in its Christian principles and wants the movement to continue with its ministry of spiritual and moral education.

Various seminars and institutes were held across the territory, many conducted by the Territorial Mobile Team. The Latin American Institute for Officers took place in Santiago, directed by Colonel John Bate (now retired in USA Western Territory).

Celebrations launching the Army's centenary in Chile were held, with Retired General John Larsson and Commissioner Freda Larsson as the special guests. They served in the territory more than 25 years ago.

The year under review has been one of growth, and the territory gives thanks to God for the many men, women and children who have come to faith and joined the ranks of The Salvation Army.

STATISTICS

Officers 301 (active 270 retired 31) **Cadets** (1st Yr) 3 (2nd Yr) 3 **Employees** 778
Corps 84 **Outposts** 25 **Schools** 18 **Day Nurseries** 24 **Community and Development Centres** 38 **Hospital** 1 **Dental Clinic** 1 **Health Clinic (with Mobile Clinic)** 3 **Kindergartens** 11 **Institutions** 28

Senior Soldiers 4,145 **Adherents** 498 **Junior Soldiers** 1,849

STAFF

Women's Ministries: Comr Adelina de Ferreira (TPWM) Lt-Col Heidi Bailey (TSWM)
Business Administration: Lt-Col María de Alarcón
Personnel: Lt-Col David Alarcón
Programme: Maj Antonio Arguedas

Education: Maj Víctor García
  Schools: Capt Eduardo Salinas
Enterprise Development: Capt Mauricio Urzúa
Finance and Legal: Lt-Col María de Alarcón
League of Mercy, Golden Age, SAMF: Maj Antonio Arguedas
Literary and Editor, *The War Cry*: Maj María Flores
Property: Lt-Col María de Alarcón
Public Relations: Maj María Flores
Silver Star and Retired Officers: Col Adelina de Ferreira
Social and Sponsorship: Capt Paulina de Márquez
Trade: Capt Manuel Márquez
Training: Maj Ángela de García
  Candidates: Maj Lilian de Arguedas

DIVISIONS

Bolivia Altiplano: Calle Cañada Strongest 1888, Zona San Pedro, Casilla 926, La Paz, Bolivia; tel: 591 (2) 249 1560; fax: 591 (2) 248 5948; Majs Eliseo and Remedios Flores

Bolivia Central: Calle Rico Toro 773 Zona Queru Queru, Casilla 3594, Cochabamba, Bolivia; tel: 591 (4) 445 4281/468 1147 fax: 591 (4) 411 5887; Majs Sixto and Aída Alí

Chile Central: Agustinas 3020, Casilla 3225, Santiago, Chile; tel/fax: 56 (2) 681 4992/ 681 5277; Maj Cecilia Bahamonde

Chile South: Av. Caupolicán 990, Casilla 1064, Temuco, Chile; tel: 56 (45) 215 850; fax: 56 (45) 271 425; Majs Juan Carlos and Nancy Alarcón

Ecuador: Tomás Chariove 149-144 y Manuel Valdivieso, El Pinar Bajo, Casilla 17,10.7179, Quito, Ecuador; tel/fax: 593 (2) 243 5422/ 244 7829; Majs Jaime and Zaida Herrera

Peru: Calle Zaragoza 215, Urbanización Parque San Martín, Pueblo Libre, Lima 21, Apartado 690, Lima 100, Peru; tel: 51 (1) 653 4965/653 4966; fax: 51 (1) 653 4968; Majs Alex and Luz Nesterenko

South America West Territory

DISTRICT
Chile North: Sucre 872, Casilla 310, Antofagasta, Chile; tel: 56 (55) 280 668/ 224 094; Maj Luis Cisternas

TRAINING COLLEGE
Coronel Souper 4564, Estación Central, Casilla 3225, Santiago, Chile; tel: 56 (2) 776 2425/776 0865; fax: 56 (2) 779 9187

SALVATION ARMY CAMP GROUNDS
Bolivia
'Chapare', Población Chimoré, Chapare, Casilla 3594, Cochabamba; tel: 591 7642 8777
'Eben-Ezer', Puente Villa, Comunidad Tarila, Provincia Nor Yungas, Casilla 926, La Paz

Chile
Complejo Angostura, Panamericana Sur km 55, Paine, Región Metropolitana, Casila 3225, Santiago; tel: 591 (2) 825 0398
Villa Frontera, Parcela 16, Calle San Martín, Villa la Frontera, Arica

EDUCATIONAL WORK
Vocational Institutes
'Lindgren' (Superior), Murillo 436, Barrio Central Viacha, Casilla 15084, La Paz, Bolivia; tel/fax: 591 (2) 280 0969 (acc 200)
'William Booth' (Technical), Sucre 909, Casilla 86, Oruro, Bolivia; tel: 591 (2) 525 1369; fax: 591 (2) 511 3512

Salvationist Bible Institute
(City Campus) Calle Cañada Strongest 1888, La Paz, Bolivia
(Rural Campus) Tiahuanacu – Calle General José Bollivian 377, Oruro – Calle Sucre 909, La Paz, Bolivia

Schools
Bolivia
'William Booth' – Oruro, Sucre 909, Casilla 86, Oruro; tel: 591 (2) 525 1369; fax: 591 (2) 511 3512 (acc 800)
'William Booth' – Viacha, Murillo 436, Barrio Central, Viacha, Casilla 15084, La Paz; tel: 591 (2) 280 0969 (acc 200)
William Booth – Villa Cosmos, Uraciri Patica 2064, Barrio Cosmos 79, Unidad Vecinal C, La Paz; tel: 591 (2) 288 0118 (acc 175)

Chile
Ejército de Salvación – Arica, Av. Cancha Rayada 3839, Segunda Etapa Población Cardenal Silva Henríquez, Casilla 203, Arica; tel/fax: 56 (58) 211 100 (acc 678)
Ejército de Salvación – Calama, Aníbal Pinto 2121, Casilla 62, Calama; tel/fax: 56 (55) 311 216/345 802
Ejército de Salvación Catherine Booth – Calama, Irene Frei 2875, Villa Esmeralda, Casilla 347, Calama; tel/fax: 56 (55) 360 458 (acc 800)
Ejército de Salvación – Santiago, Herrera 185, Casilla 3225, Santiago; tel: 56 (2) 681 7097 (acc 400)
Ejército de Salvación No 1619 Pudahuel, Mapocho 9047, Pudahuel, Casilla 3225, Santiago; tel: 56 (2) 643 1875 (acc 160)
'Naciones Unidas' – Puerto Montt, Séptimo de Línea 148, Población Libertad; Casilla 277; tel/fax: 56 (65) 254 047/ 251 918 (acc 1,600)
'William Booth' – Osorno, Zenteno 1015, Casilla 317, Osorno; tel: 56 (64) 247 449; tel/fax: 56 (64) 233 141 (acc 790 + 89 infants)

Peru
'Eduardo Palací', Av Progreso 1032, Urb. San Gregorio, Vitarte, Lima, Apartado 690, Lima 100; tel/fax: 51 (1) 356 0461 (acc 500)
Miguel Grau, Av. 29 de Diciembre 127, Apartado 759, Trujillo; tel/fax: 51 (44) 255 571 (acc 300)

Ecuador
Ejército de Salvación – Cayambe (Educational Centre), Calle H 1 393 Morales, Urb. Las Orquídeas, Cayambe, Casilla 17.10.7179, Quito; tel: 593 (2) 211 0196 (acc 150)
Ejército de Salvación – Manta, Av. 201 (entre Calles 116 y 117), Barrio La Paz, Casilla 13.05.149, Manta; tel; 593 (5) 292 0147 (acc 40)

Pre-Primary School
Ejército de Salvación No 1562 – El Bosque, Las Vizcachas 858, Población Las Acacias, El Bosque, Santiago, Chile; tel: 56 (2) 529 4242 (acc 45)

MEDICAL WORK
Bolivia
Harry Williams Hospital: Av. Suecia 1038-1058, Zona Huayra K'assa, Casilla 4099, Cochabamba; tel: 591 (4) 422 7778/474 7432; fax: 591 (4) 474 5329 (acc 27 beds)
Community Extension Programme with Mobile Clinic: Av. Suecia 1038-1058, Zona Huayra K'assa, Casilla 4099, Cochabamba; tel: 591 (4) 422 7778/474 7432; fax: 591 (4) 474 5329

South America West Territory

Ecuador
Health Clinic and Dental Clinic: Quito Sur, Calle Apuela S 25-182 y Malimpia, Santa Rita, Casilla 17.107179, Quito; tel: 593 (2) 284 5529
Health Clinic: Calles Uruguay y Ecuador, Barrio Las Américas, Casilla 08.01.73, Esmeraldas; tel: 593 (6) 271 0439

SOCIAL WORK
Social Welfare Office: Chile Central, Mapocho 4130, Quinta Normal, Casilla 3225, Santiago, Chile; tel: 56 (2) 775 1566

Men's Shelters
Bolivia
'Manuel Asín', Calle Prolongación Illampu 1888, Zona San Pedro, Casilla 926, La Paz; tel: 591 (2) 231 1189 (acc 100)

Chile
Prat 1045, Casilla 917, Antofagasta; tel: 56 (55) 223 847 (acc 50)
Villagrán 9, Casilla 1887, Valparasío; tel: 56 (32) 221 4946 (acc 170)

Peru
Colón 138/142, Callao; tel: 51 (1) 429 3128 (acc 24)

Transit House (Women)
Calle Zenteno 1499, Casilla 3225, Santiago, Chile; tel: 56 (2) 554 1767 (acc 15)

Pregnant Teens Refuge
Av, 201, entre calles 116 y 117, Barrio La Paz, Casilla 13-05-149, Manta, Ecuador; tel: 593 (5) 292 0147 (acc 20)

Student Residence Halls
Bolivia
'Remedios Asín' (Girls), Cañada Strongest 1888, Casilla 926, La Paz; tel: 591 (2) 248 0502 (acc 20)
'Tte.-Coronel Jorge Nery Torrico' (Boys), Calle Junin 459, entre 6 de Octubre y Potosí; Casilla 86, Oruro; tel: 591 (2) 528 6885 (acc 22)
'Tte.-Coronel Rosa de Nery' (Girls), Calle Lanza S-0555, Casilla 3198, Cochabamba; tel: 591 (4) 422 6553/422 1491 (acc 30)

Chile
'El Faro' (Boys), Santiago Concha 1333, Casilla 3225, Santiago; tel: 56 (2) 555 3406 (acc 24)

Peru
'Catalina Booth' (Girls), Jirón Huancayo 245 Lima, Apartado 690, Lima 100; tel: 51 (1) 433 8747 (acc 20)
'Las Palmeras' – Tarapoto, Jirón Amoraca 212, Distrito Morales, Apartado 88, Tarapoto, San Martín; tel: 51 (42) 527 540 (acc 20)

Children's Homes
Bolivia
Evangelina Booth (Girls), Francisco Viedma 1054, Villa Montenegro, Casilla 542, Cochabamba; tel: 591 (4) 424 1560 (acc 60)
'María Remedios Asín' (Boys'), Murillo 434, Barrio Central Viacha, Casilla 15084, La Paz; tel/fax: 591 (2) 280 0404 (acc 50)
'Oscar Ahlms' (Boys), Km 19.5 Carretera a Oruro cruce San Jorge, Calle Bolivar s/n, Comunidad de San Jorge, Vinto, Casilla 542, Cochabamba; tel: 591 (4) 435 6264 (acc 48)

Chile
'El Broquel' (Girls), 12 Poniente 8390, La Granja, Casilla 3225, Santiago; tel/fax: 56 (2) 541 6079 (acc 30)
'El Redil' (Boys), Arzobispo Valdivieso 410, Casilla 61, Llo Lleo; tel: 56 (35) 282 054 (acc 52)
'Los Copihues' (Girls), Calle Los Sauces 0202, Población Las Quilas, Casilla 1064, Temuco; tel: 56 (45) 234 028/275 008 (acc 60)
'Tte-Coronel Helmuth Hühner' (Boys), Av. Arturo Allessandri 6342, Lo Valledor Sur, Pedro Aguirre Cerda, Casilla 3225, Santiago; tel: 56 (2) 521 5575 (acc 55)

Eventide Home
'Otoño Dorado', Av. La Florida 9995, La Florida, Casilla 3225, Santiago, Chile; tel: 56 (2) 287 5280; tel/fax: 56 (2) 287 1869 (acc 48)

Day Care Centres for the Aged
Chile
'Los Lagos', Berlín 818, Población Los Lagos, Angol; tel: 56 (45) 712 583 (acc 20)

Ecuador
Cayambe, Calle Montalvo 220, Cayambe, Casilla 1710.7179, Quito; tel: 593 (2) 236 1273 (acc 60)

Day Nurseries/Kindergartens
Bolivia
'Catalina Booth', Lanza S-0555, Zona Central, Casilla 542, Cochabamba; tel: 591 (4) 422 7123 (acc 150)
'Gotitas de Amor', Calle Corumba 2360 (esq.

South America West Territory

Calle Cañada Larga), Barrio Lazareto, Casilla 2576, Santa Cruz; tel: 591 (3) 346 3531 (acc 40)
'La Roca', Calicanto, Comunidad La Serena Calicanto, Kilómetro 8, Carretera antigua a Santa Cruz, Casilla 542, Cochabamba; tel: 591 (4) 433 8338 (acc 35)
'Mi Casita' – El Temporal, Calle J. Mostajo s/n, Zona El Temporal, Casilla 542, Cochabamba; tel: 591 (4) 445 0809 (acc 70)
'Refugio de Amor', Villa 8 de Diciembre, Calle Rosendo Gutiérrez 120, Barrio Alto Sopocachi, Casilla 926, La Paz; tel 591 (2) 241 0470 (acc 25)
'Wawasninchej' – Huayra K'assa, Av. Suecia 1083, Zona Huayra K'assa, Casilla 542, Cochabamba; tel: 591 (4) 422 4808 (acc 50)

Chile:
'Arca de Noé', El Fundador 13678, Población Santiago de la Nueva Extremadura, La Pintana, Casilla 3225, Santiago; tel: 56 (2) 542 4523 (acc 60)
'Catalina Booth', Hipólito Salas 760, Concepción; tel: 56 (41) 223 0447 (acc 24)
'Faro de Ángeles', Calle Santa Martha 443, Cerro Playa Ancha, Casilla 1887, Valparaíso; tel: 56 (32) 228 1160 (acc 75)
'Gotitas', Av. Carlos Condell 1535, Los Salares, Casilla 436, Copiapó; tel: 56 (52) 216 099 (acc 32)
'Hijitos de Dios', Iquique 24, Población San Francisco, Rancagua; tel: 56 (72) 239 028 (acc 20)
'La Estrellita', Maipú 284, Maipú, Casilla 3225, Santiago; tel: 56 (2) 531 2638 (acc 40)
'Las Acacias', Las Vizcachas 858, Población Las Acacias, Comuna El Bosque, Casilla 3225; Santiago; tel: 56 (2) 529 4242 (acc 52)
'Las Estrellitas', Esmeralda 862, Casilla 134, Iquique; tel/fax: 56 (57) 421325 (acc 38)
'Lautarito', Castro 5193, Población Lautaro, Casilla 581, Antofagasta; tel: 56 (55) 380 719 (acc 70)
'Marta Brunet', Montaña Adentro 01650, Puente Alto, Casilla 3225, Santiago; tel: 56 (2) 572 9340 (ac 50)
'Neptuno', Los Aromos 833, Lo Prado, Casilla 3225, Santiago; tel: 56 (2) 773 5154 (acc 60)
'Nido Alegre', Santa Petronila 1048, Quinta Normal, Casilla 3225; tel: 56 (2) 773 8554 (acc 40)
'Padre Las Casas', Los Misioneros 1354, Comuna de Padre Las Casas, Temuco (acc 20)

'Rayito de Luz', Picarte 1894, Valdivia; tel/fax: 56 (63) 214 404 (acc 120)
'Rayitos de Sol', Av. Brasil 73, Casilla 3225, Santiago; tel: 56 (2) 699 3595; fax: 56 (2) 688 4755 (acc 90)
'Soldaditos de Jesús', Santo Domingo 90, Puente Alto, Casilla 3225, Santiago; tel: 56 (2) 850 3331 (acc 86)

Ecuador
'Arca de Noé', Av. 201, entre calles 116 y 117, Barrio La Paz, Casilla 13-05-149, Manta; tel: 593 (5) 292 0147 (acc 30)
Ejército de Salvación – La Colmena, Calle Pomasqui 955 y Pedro Andrade, La Colmena, Casilla 17.10.7179, Quito; tel: 593 (2) 258 1081/228 4776 (acc 60)
'El Ranchito', Manzana 44, lote 801, 802, Rancho Alto, Casilla 7110.7179, Quito; tel: 593 (2) 338 2408/338 2409; (acc 60)
'Gotitas de Miel', Montalvo 220, Cayambe, Casilla 17.10.7179, Quito; tel: 593 (2) 236 1273 (acc 100)
'Mi Casita', Apuela S25-182 y Malimpia, Santa Rita, Casilla 17.1071.79, Quito; tel: 593 (2) 284 5529 (acc 40)
'Mi Hermoso Redil', Urbanización Sierra Hermosa, Calle 5, lotes 237-239, Parroquia de Carapungo, Quito; tel: 593 (2) 282 6835 (acc 100)
'Nueva Esperanza', Av. Martha de Roldós km 5½, Via Daule, Casilla 09.01.10478, Guayaquil; tel: 593 (4) 300 0842 (acc 60)

Food Aid Programme
Chile:
Ancud: Oscar Bonilla 2, Calle Ejército 721, Ancud; tel: 56 (65) 622 045 (acc 80)
Antofagasta: Salón Sala 9684, Población Bonilla, Casilla 581, Antofagasta; (acc 50)

Peru
Emergency Dining Rooms
Chiclayo: PP.JJ. San Christian, Manzana 'A', Lote 17, Chiclayo; tel: 51 (74) 208 216 (neighbour) (acc 100)
El Porvenir: Calle Synneva Vestheim 583, Cacerío El Porvenir, Provincia Rioja, Dpto San Martín; tel: 51 (42) 832 360 (public phone) (acc 50)

Development Integral Centres and Nutritional Centres
Bolivia
Achachicala, La Paz (acc 150, 2 shifts)
'El Tejar', La Paz (acc 245, 2 shifts)

'Nueva Vida' (BO-367), Santa Cruz (acc 250)
Tiahuanacu, La Paz (acc 200)
Viacha, La Paz (acc 250, 2 shifts)
Villa Cantería, Potosí (acc 50, 2 shifts)
Villa Cosmos, La Paz (acc 250)
Villa 8 de Diciembre, La Paz (acc 90)
Zona Este de Oruro, Oruro (acc 150, 2 shifts)

Ecuador
'Bastión Popular', EC-561, Guayaquil (acc 100)
'El Rancho', EC-108, Quito (acc 100)
'Mi Casita', EC-124, Quito (acc 120, 2 shifts)
'Nido Alegre', EC-120, Quito (acc 150)
'Nueva Esperanza', Guayaquil (acc 160)
'Pedacito de Cielo', EC-594, Esmeraldas (acc 200)
'William Booth', EC-129, Cayambe (acc 150)

Community Day Centres/School-Age Day Care Centres (attached to corps/outposts)
Bolivia
'Batallón Colorados', Sucre (acc 60)
Corqueamaya, La Paz (acc 70)
El Temporal, Cochabamba (acc 75)
'El Vergel', Chaparé (acc 60)
'Fortín del Niño', Uspha Uspha, Cochabamba (acc 100)
Huayra K'assa, Cochabamba (acc 50)
La Chimba, Cochabamba (acc 80)
Lacaya, La Paz (acc 75)
'La Roca', Calicanto, Santa Cruz (acc 20)
Pacata, Cochabamba (acc 50)
Parotani, Cochabamba (acc 60)
Pockonas, Sucre (acc 50)
Potosí, (acc 30, 2 shifts)
'Primero de Mayo', Santa Cruz (acc 50)
Tarija (acc 50)
Villa Fátima, La Paz (acc 50, 2 shifts)
Yaurichambi, La Paz (acc 75)

Peru
Buenos Aires, Trujillo (acc 50)
La Esperanza, Trujillo (acc 40)
Moquegua (acc 60)
San Martín de Porras, Lima (acc 40)
Tacna (acc 60)
Vitarte, Lima (acc 80)

Workshop
Ecuador
Tailoring Workshop and Sewing Centre:
   Calle Apuela S25-182 y Malimpia, Santa Rita,
   Casilla 17.10.7179, Quito;
   tel: 593 (2) 284 5529

Enterprise Development
Warehouse: Coronel Souper 4564, Estación
   Central, Casilla 3225, Santiago, Chile;
   tel: 56 (2) 764 1917

Children attending the mobile clinic in Cochabamba, Bolivia, receive a nutritional drink as part of The Salvation Army's health care programme

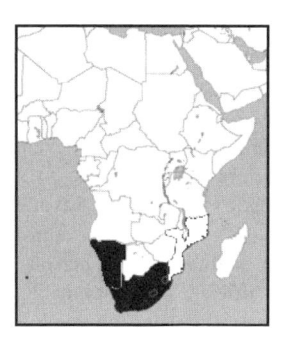

SOUTHERN AFRICA TERRITORY

Territorial leaders:
Commissioners André and Silvia Cox

Territorial Commander:
Commissioner André Cox (1 Oct 2008)

Chief Secretary:
Lieut-Colonel Joash Malabi (1 Feb 2007)

Territorial Headquarters: 119-121 Rissik Street, Braamfontein, Johannesburg 2001

Postal address: PO Box 1018, Johannesburg 2000, South Africa
Tel: [27] (011) 718 6700; fax: [27] (011) 718 6790;
email: CS_SouthernAfrica@SAF.salvationarmy.org; website: www.salvationarmy.co.za

On 4 March 1883 Major and Mrs Francis Simmonds with Lieutenant Alice Teager 'opened fire' in Cape Town. Other officers were sent to the island of St Helena in 1886 to consolidate work commenced (in 1884) by Salvationist 'Bluejackets'. Social services began in 1886. The Salvation Army's first organised ministry among the African people was established in 1888 in Natal and, in 1891, in Zululand. Work in Swaziland was commenced in 1960. Having previously been in Namibia from 1932 to 1939, the Army re-established a presence in the country in January 2008 under the leadership of Major Lenah Jwili, a South African national, and was given official recognition on 11 March 2008.

Zone: Africa
Countries included in the territory: Lesotho, Namibia, Island of St Helena, South Africa, Swaziland
'The Salvation Army' in Afrikaans: Die Heilsleër; in IsiXhosa: Umkhosi wo Sindiso; in IsiZulu: Impi yo Sindiso; in SeSotho: Mokhosi oa Poloko; in SiPedi: Mogosi wa Pholoso; in Tshivenda: Mbi ya u Tshidza; in Tsonga: Nyi Moi Yoponisa
Languages in which the gospel is preached: Afrikaans, English, IsiXhosa, IsiZulu, SeSotho, Shangaan, SiPedi, Tshivenda, Tsonga, Tswana
Periodicals: *Echoes of Mercy*, *Home League Highlights*, *Home League Resource Manual*, *Outer Circle Newsletter*, *SAMF Newsletter*, *The Reporter*, *The War Cry*

THE weekend of 26-28 September 2008 was a time of great celebration as Salvationists from across the territory gathered at Walter Sisulu Square, Kliptown (Soweto), to celebrate the 125th anniversary of The Salvation Army's stepping onto the shores of Cape Town. Under special guests Commissioners Israel and Eva Gaither (USA national leaders and previous territorial leaders in Southern Africa), the anniversary congress was a time to praise God for what he had done in the past, to look forward, and – as indicated by the congress theme – to 'Rejoice And Let Tomorrow Begin!'

Lieut-Colonels Torben and Deise Eliasen (command leaders, Mozambique) joined the celebration.

Southern Africa Territory

Part of the congress was the retirement salute to the territory's leaders, Commissioners Trevor and Memory Tuck, who were commended by Commissioner Israel Gaither on their 83 years' combined service to God. During the beautiful singing of 'Jesus, See Me At Thy Feet' by Soweto Central Youth Chorus, people publicly signified their commitment to Jesus.

The following month saw the welcome to the new territorial leaders, [then] Colonels André and Silvia Cox.

With a vision encapsulated in the slogan 'Code RED' (Reaching, Evangelism, Discipleship), the Youth Department set about providing training, resources and leadership in all aspects of youth and children's ministry.

The department ran with the theme of 'Redefine – It Matters', which followed two years of the 'Revolution' concept. It was seen as a positive means of challenging young people to go deeper in their walk and talk with Jesus.

The territory responded to the needs of foreigners displaced as a result of horrific xenophobic attacks. Officers, soldiers, employees and friends offered shelter and sustenance to victims, and the Army was grateful for generous public support in providing resources for this special relief work.

After a thorough review, the college for officer training is now able to accommodate two sessions of cadets. Six cadets of the Ambassadors Of Holiness Session were accepted for first-year training, joining the seven Prayers Warriors Session cadets.

Responding to the theme 'Living Christ's Values', the territory aims for a greater mobilisation of personnel, a more efficient use of available resources and a greater degree of professionalism.

STATISTICS
Officers 288 (active 182 retired 106) **Auxiliary-Captains** 15 **Cadets** 14 **Employees** 510
Corps 172 **Societies and Outposts** 89 **Mission Team** 1 **Schools** 3 **Hospitals** 2 **Institutions** 24 **Day Care Centres** 18 **Goodwill Centres** 7 **Nursery Schools** 3
Senior Soldiers 28,800 **Adherents** 1,894 **Junior Soldiers** 3,845

STAFF
Women's Ministries: Comr Silvia Cox (TPWM) Lt-Col Florence Malabi (TSWM) Lt-Col Zakithi Mabaso (Ret Officers Sec/Officers' Children)
Business Administration: Lt-Col Timothy Mabaso
  Finance: Maj Daniel Moukoko
  Financial Consultant: Mr John Pugsley
  Audit: Maj Lilia Macayana
  Information Technology: Mr Andrew Geer
  Property: Mr Stan Eland
  Public Relations: Capt Gath Niemand
  Trade: Mr Gavin Blackwood
Programme: Lt-Col Robert Donaldson
  Field Programme: Lt-Col Janine Donaldson
  Youth: Capt Stephen Malins
  Adult Ministries: Lt-Col Zakithi Mabaso
  Medical Ministries: Capt (Dr) Felicia Christians
  Projects and Emergencies: Capt Peter White
  Child Sponsorship: Capt Gail White
  Family Tracing: Lt-Col Veronica Trollip
  Social Programme: Capt Robert Hendricks
  Statistician: Maj Arschette Moukoko
Personnel: Lt-Col William Langa
  Pastoral Care: Maj Jaime Macayana
  Human Resources: Mr Leon Schmahl
Training: Maj Jabulani Khoza
Education: Maj Frankie Burgoyne
Editor: Capt Gail White
Candidates: Maj Jabulani Khoza

Southern Africa Territory

DIVISIONS
Central: PO Box 756, Rosettenville, Johannesburg 2130; tel: (011) 435-0267; fax: (011) 435-2835; Majs Alistair and Marieke Venter
Eastern Cape: PO Box 12514, Centralhill, Port Elizabeth 6006; tel: (041) 585-5363; fax: (041) 586-3521; Majs Daniel and Tracey Kasuso
Eastern Kwa Zulu/Natal: PO Box 1267, Eshowe 3815; tel: (035) 474-1132; fax: (035) 474-1132; Majs Johannes and Veliswa Raselalome
Mid Kwa Zulu/Natal: PO Box 100061, Scottsville, Pietermaritzburg 3209; tel: (033) 386-3881; fax: (033) 386-8019; Majs Bennie and Jenny Harms
Mpumalanga/Swaziland: PO Box 1571, Nelspruit 1200; tel/fax: (013) 741-2869; Majs Solomon and Mercy Mahlangu
Northern: PO Box 3549, Louis Trichardt 0920; tel/fax: (015) 963-6145; Majs Keith and Yvonne Conrad
Northern Kwa Zulu/Natal: PO Box 923, Vryheid 3100; tel: (034) 982-3113; fax: (034) 983-2882; Majs Albert and Peggy Shekwa
Western Cape: PO Box 13079, Mowbray, Cape Town 7705; tel: (021) 689-8915; fax: (021) 689-3023; Majs Patrick and Margaret Booth
St Helena: The Salvation Army, Jamestown, Island of St Helena, South Atlantic Ocean; tel: 09 (290) 2703; fax: 09 (290) 2052; email: salvationarmy@cwimail.sh; Envoy Coral Yon

THQ OUTREACH – NAMIBIA
The Salvation Army, PO Box 26820, Windhoek, Namibia; tel: [00] (264) 61223881; mobile: 264 813087518; email: salvationarmy@iway.na; Maj Lenah Jwili

COLLEGE FOR OFFICER TRAINING
PO Box 32902, Braamfontein 2017, Johannesburg; tel: (011) 718 6762

DAY CARE CENTRES FOR PRE-SCHOOL CHILDREN
Central: Benoni, Eldorado Park, Galashewe, Katlehong, Lethlabile, Mangaung
Mpumalanga/Swaziland: Barberton, Emangweni, Pienaar
Mid Kwa Zulu/Natal: Hammarsdale, Imbali, Kwa Mashu, Umlazi
Northern: Messina
Northern Kwa Zulu/Natal: Ezakheni, Madadeni, Mondlo, Ulundi, Vryheid
Western Cape: Bonteheuwel, Mitchells Plein, Manenburg

DAY CARE CENTRES FOR SENIOR CITIZENS
Central: Benoni, Kimberley, Krugersdorp, Pretoria, Vereeniging
Eastern Cape: East London, Port Elizabeth
Mid Kwa Zulu/Natal: Pietermaritzburg
Western Cape: Goodwood

GOODWILL CENTRES
Benoni West 1503: Benoni Goodwill Centre, PO Box 17299
East London, Vincent 5217: Hind House, PO Box 13012
Kimberley 8300: Kimberley Goodwill Centre, PO Box 1691
Krugersdorp 1740: Family Mission Centre, PO Box 351
Pietermaritzburg, Scottsville 3209: Hope Goodwill House, PO Box 100-213
Vereeniging 1930: Sally Ann Cottage, PO Box 2090

HEALTH SERVICES
Booth Hospital: 32 Prince St, Oranjezicht, Cape Town 8001; tel: (021) 465-4896/46 (acc 84)
Carl Sithole Wellness, VCT and Art Support Centre: PO Box 180, Orlando, Soweto 1840
Mountain View Hospital: PO Salvation 3110, via Vryheid, Natal; tel: (034) 967-1544 (acc 88) (with Mountain View Mobile Clinic)
Msunduza Community and Primary Health Care Centre and Mbuluzi Clinic: Box 2543, Mbabane, Swaziland; tel: (268) 404-5243

RETIRED OFFICERS RESIDENCES
Citadel Court: Vrede St, Gardens, Cape Town 8001
Emmarentia Flats: PO Box 85214, Emmarentia 2029, Johannesburg; tel: (011) 646-2126
Ephraim Zulu Flats: PO Box 49, Orlando 1804, Soweto; tel: (011) 982-1084
Sunset Lodge: 10 World's View Cl, World's View, Doonside 4135, Natal

SOCIAL SERVICES
Crèches
Bridgman Crèche: PO Box 62, Kwa Xuma 1868; 88, 3b White City, Jabavu 1856; tel: (011) 982-5574 (acc 140)
Carl Sithole Crèche: Carl Sithole Centre,

Southern Africa Territory

PO Box 180, Orlando 1804; tel: (011) 986-7417 (acc 40)

Children's Homes
Bethany: Carl Sithole Centre, Klipspruit, PO Box 180, Orlando 1804; tel: (011) 986-7417 (acc 110 children 6-18 yrs)

Bethesda: Zodwa's House, Carl Sithole Centre, PO Box 180, Orlando 1804, Soweto (acc 32 children 2-6 yrs)

Ethembeni (Place of Hope): 63 Sherwell St, Doornfontein, Johannesburg 2094; tel: (011) 402-8101 (acc 60 children 0-3 yrs)

Firlands: Fourth Ave, PO Box 44291, Linden 2104; tel: (011) 782-5556/7 (acc 60 children 3-18 yrs)

Joseph Baynes House: 89 Trelawney Rd, Pentrich, PO Box 212275, Oribi 3205, Natal; tel: (033) 386-2266 (acc 72 children 0-18 yrs)

Strathyre: Eleventh Ave, Dewetshof, PO Box 28240, Kensington 2101, Johannesburg; tel: (011) 615-7327/7344 (acc 50 children 3-18 yrs)

Community Programme
Thusanong/Osizweni: Home-based Community Care and Counselling Programme, Carl Sithole Centre, Klipspruit, Soweto, PO Box 180, Orlando 1804; tel: (011) 986-7417

Street Children's Home
Musawenkosi: PO Box 14794, Madadeni Township 2951 (acc 16 boys 7-18 yrs)

Eventide Home (men)
Beth Rogelim: Cape Town 8005, 22 Alfred St; tel: (021) 425-2138 (acc 52)

Eventide Homes (men and women)
Emmarentia: Johannesburg, PO Box 85214, Emmarentia 2029, 113 Komatie Rd; tel: (011) 646-2126 (acc 40)

Ephraim Zulu Senior Citizen Centre: Orlando 1804, PO Box 49; tel: (011) 982-1084 (acc 100)

Salisbury House: East London, 19 Rhodes St, PO Box 18380; tel: (011) 722-4454

The Salvation Army Albert Baumann Frail Care Home: Doonside, 4135, 10 World's View Cl, PO Box 53, World's View, 4125, South Coast, Natal; tel: (031) 903-3139 (acc 76)

Thembela: Durban 4001, 68 Montpelier Place; tel: (031) 321-6360 (acc 53)

Homes for Abused Women
Beth Shan, PO Box 19713, Pretoria West 0117, Pretoria (acc 15 women)

Care Haven: PO Box 38186, Gates Ville 7766, Cape Town; tel: (021) 638-5511; fax: (031) 637-0226; email: careaid@iafrica.co.za (acc 18 women, 60 children)

Durban Family Care, PO Box 47122, Greyville 4023, Durban; tel: (031) 309-1395 (acc 45)

Haven of Hope Home, PO Box 2304, North End 6056, Port Elizabeth; tel: (041) 373-4317 (acc 32)

Men's Homes
Beth Rogelim: 22 Alfred St, Cape Town 8005; tel: (021) 425-2138 (acc 100)

Bloemfontein Men's Home: 23 Fountain St, Bloemfontein 9301; tel: (051) 447-2626 (acc 28)

Rehabilitation Centres
Hesketh King Treatment Centre: PO Box 5, Elsenburg 7607, Cape; tel: (021) 884-4600 (acc 60)

Mountain Lodge: PO Box 168, Magaliesburg 2805; tel: (014) 577 2155 (acc 60)

Social Centres
Durban Family Care Centre: PO Box 47122, Greyville, Durban 4023; tel: (031) 309-1395 (acc 70)

Haven of Hope Home: PO Box 2304, North End, Port Elizabeth 6056; tel: (041) 373-4317 (acc 60)

Johannesburg Social Services: Simmonds St Ext, Johannesburg 2001; tel: (011) 832-1227; fax: (011) 833-6259 (acc 56)

Pretoria Family Care Centre: PO Box 19713, Pretoria West 0117; tel: (012) 327-3005 (acc 80)

SCHOOLS
Bethany Combined School: Carl Sithole Centre, PO Box 180, Orlando 1804; tel: (011) 986-7417

Mathunjwa High School: PO Box 923, Vryheid 3100

William Booth Primary School: Mountain View, PO Salvation 3110; tel: (034) 967-1533

YOUTH MISSION TRAINING CENTRE
Mission House, 162 High St, Rosettenville 2130; tel/fax: (011) 435-1822

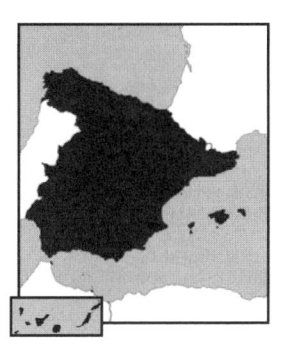

SPAIN COMMAND

Command leaders:
Lieut-Colonels Luis E. and Aída A. Castillo

Officer Commanding:
Lieut-Colonel Luis E. Castillo
(1 Jul 2008)

Command Headquarters: Hermosilla 126 Lc 1, 28028 Madrid

Postal address: Ejército de Salvación, c/ Hermosilla, 126 Local 1, 28028 Madrid, Spain
Tel: [34] 91 356 6644; fax: [34] 91 361 4782; email: Spain_Command@SPA.salvationarmy.org;
website: www.ejercitodesalvacion.es

Following the appointment of Captain and Mrs Enrique Rey to La Coruña on Ascension Day 1971, it was announced on 24 December 1971 that The Salvation Army had been granted the status of a Legal Person, enjoying full legal rights in the country and permitted to carry on its work without let or hindrance.

Zone: Europe
Country and autonomous communities included in the territory: Canary Islands, Mallorca, Spain
'The Salvation Army' in Spanish: Ejército de Salvación
Languages in which the gospel is preached: English (Mallorca, Denia), Filipino, Spanish

YOUTH work has seen good results, with the programmes and activities being appreciated by the young participants. An action plan was drawn up to encourage the young people to get together regularly. The plan, called *Madrid Joven* ('Young Madrid'), has resulted in increased attendances at the youth fellowships being held every three months.

For several years the command has sought to develop music and arts ministries through a music training week. Every year, the National Music School has been a great incentive for musicians and has undoubtedly strengthened the music ministry of many of the command's corps.

Social work undertaken in corps is resulting in a greater involvement in the community. This benefits The Salvation Army's mission as various social services projects gain support from Government authorities and private agencies. During 2008 the Social Department presented 13 small projects to the Government; eight of them were approved.

After several years of planning, a long-distance training programme has begun. The one cadet at present participating in this new experience has shown excellent development.

The celebration of Women's Ministries Week was a good opportunity to win women and their families for the Lord.

As God's Spirit continues to move

Spain Command

in their lives, Spain's Salvationists give thanks that their efforts in evangelism and outreach ministries are resulting in the growth of the Army family in their country.

STATISTICS
Officers 28 (active 26 retired 2) **Employees** 31 **Corps** 11 **Outposts** 5 **Institution** 1 **Thrift Shops** 14
Senior Soldiers 487 **Adherents** 86 **Junior Soldiers** 84
Personnel serving outside command Officers 2

STAFF
Women's Ministries: Lt-Col Aída Castillo (CPWM)
Business Administration: Maj Ambrosio Aycón
Programme and Evangelism: Maj Juan José Arias
Finance: Maj Fortunato Echeverría
Accountant: Fausta Gonzales
Training: Maj Pauline Gruer-Caulfield

SOCIAL SERVICES
Food and/or Clothing Distribution Centres
Alicante 03006: c/ Deportista César Porcel, 11 Bajo
Barcelona 08024: c/ del Rubí 18
Denia, Alicante 03700: c/ San José 14 B
La Coruña 15010: c/ Francisco Añón 9
Las Palmas 35014: Plaza de los Ruiseñores, Local 8 alto, Miller Bajo
Madrid 28028: c/ Hermosilla, 126, Local 4
Madrid 28038: Avda Rafael Alberti, 18 Bis
Mallorca 07015: Cala Mayor, Avda Joan Miró 285
Tenerife 38006: c/ Marisol Marín 10
Valdemoro-Madrid 28340: c/Bretón de los Herreros 10

Emergency Feeding Kitchens
Barcelona 08024: c/ del Rubí 18
La Coruña 15010: c/ Francisco Añón 9

Eventide Home (men and women)
Finca El Apostolado, Vereda del Alquitón 9, Arganda del Rey, Madrid 28500 (acc 35)

Homeless Day Care Centre – 'Sen Teito'
La Coruña 15010: c/ Francisco Añón 9 (acc 25)

Social Emergency Apartments
La Coruña 15010: c/ Francisco Añón 9 (acc 25)

CONFERENCE, RETREAT AND HOLIDAY CENTRE
Camp Sarón, Partida Torre Carrals 64, 03700 Denia, Alicante; tel: 96 578 2152; fax: 96 643 1206; website: www.campsaron.com (acc 61)

Children at the command's Vocational Bible School, hosted by Madrid Central Corps

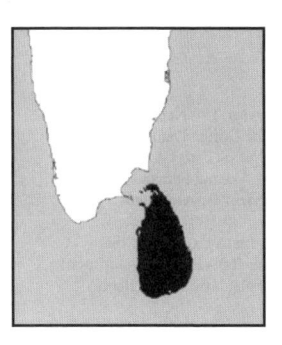

SRI LANKA TERRITORY

Territorial leaders:
Colonels Lalzamlova and Nemkhanching

Territorial Commander:
Colonel Lalzamlova (1 Jun 2006)

Chief Secretary:
Lieut-Colonel Edward Daniel (1 May 2004)

Territorial Headquarters: 53 Sir James Peiris Mawatha, Colombo 2
Postal address: PO Box 193, Colombo, Sri Lanka
Tel: [94] (11) 232 4660/233 2159; fax: [94] (11) 243 6065; website: www.sri.salvationarmy.org

Salvation Army work began in Ceylon (now Sri Lanka) on 26 January 1883 under the leadership of Captain William Gladwin. 'The General of The Salvation Army' is a corporation Sole by Ordinance No 11 of 1924.

Zone: South Asia
Country included in the territory: Sri Lanka
'The Salvation Army' in Sinhala: Galavime Hamudava; in Tamil: Ratchaniya Senai
Languages in which the gospel is preached: English, Sinhala, Tamil
Periodical: *Yudha Handa* (*The War Cry*)

SRI LANKAN Salvationists are united in pleading to God to 'Heal Our Nation', praying for the population's spiritual well-being as well as the country's economic, social and political situation. All Salvation Army centres were provided with relevant Bible passages to be read to congregations in Sunday morning meetings throughout the year.

Work in up-country rural districts progresses well: Sunday schools are under way; home league classes have been commenced in three new areas. Moratumulla became the territory's fourth corps to achieve self-supporting (general maintenance) status.

Five cadets of the Witnesses For Christ Session were ordained and commissioned when South Asia zonal leaders Commissioners Lalkiamlova and Lalhlimpuii led commissioning meetings at Colombo Central in December 2008. Six cadets of the Ambassadors Of Holiness Session were welcomed in April 2009.

The main Indian Ocean Tsunami Response project funded by SAWSO, Canada and Bermuda Territory/CIDA and The Netherlands and Czech Republic Territory was concluded, with 730 houses and 11 community centres having been completed. A thanksgiving celebration was held at Bandarnaike Memorial International Conference Hall on 23 April 2009, when Commissioner William Francis (TC, Canada and Bermuda) was chief

Sri Lanka Territory

guest. The Honourable Minister of Religious Affairs, a representative of the Deputy Minister for Social Services, the Canadian High Commissioner, other dignitaries and church representatives were present.

Territorial representatives attended various conferences. These included the International Missing Persons/Family Tracing Educational Seminar (Chicago, USA); the Ecumenical Theological Education Consultation (Kolkata, India); the Christian Council of Asia's Human Rights Training (Bangkok, Thailand); the Council for World Mission's global consultation on Combating Human Trafficking (Delhi, India); 'Peacemaking, Conflict Resolution and Reconciliation Skills' (Bangalore, India).

An officers' retreat-cum-field session (23-25 July 2008) was a time of spiritual enrichment that deepened delegates' understanding of the Army's faith and practices, its biblical basis and pastoral care. In addition to the territorial leaders, speakers included K. Zohmingthanga, BA, BD, MTh – a soldier from India Eastern Territory – and the Rev Duleep Fernando.

STATISTICS
Officers 151 (active 101 retired 50) Cadets 9 Employees 151
Corps 44 Corps Plants 5 Social Homes and Hostels 11 Community Centres 5 Day Care Centre 1 Corps-based Child Care Centres 6 Health Centre 1 Conference Centre 1
Senior Soldiers 3,768 Adherents 848 Junior Soldiers 559
Personnel serving outside territory Officers 2

STAFF
Women's Ministries: Col Nemkhanching (TPWM) Lt-Col Lalitha Daniel (TSWM) Maj Nilanthi Philip (THLS & WDO)
Candidates: Maj Ajantha Fernando
Community Services Development: tba
Editorial: tba
Evangelism and Field Extension: tba
Field and Human Resources Development: Maj Packianathan Jayaratnasingham
Finance: tba
Combating Human Trafficking Programme: Mrs Swarna De Silva
Information Technology: Miss Coojanie Heendeniya
Projects and Sponsorship: Maj Colleen Marshall
Property: Maj Ian Marshall
Public Relations, Legal and Fund-raising: Maj Alister Philip
Social Services: Maj Nihal Hettiarachchi
Training: Maj Newton Fernando
Youth: Capt Wijenama Wijesinghe

DIVISIONS
Rambukkana: Mawanella Rd, Rambukkana; tel: (035) 226 5179; email: salrambu@sltnet.lk; Majs Ranjit and Vijayashri Senaratne
Western: 53 Sir James Peiris Mawatha, Colombo 2; tel: (11) 232 4660 ext 214; Maj Chandra Jayaratnasingham

DISTRICTS
Kandy: 26 Srimath Bennet Soysa Veediya, Kandy; tel: (08) 223 4804; Maj Kokila Muthusamy
Northern: Kandy Rd, Kaithady; tel: 021 3217450; Maj Newton Jacob

SECTIONS
Eastern: 135 Trincomalee St, Batticaloa; tel: (065) 222 4558; fax: (065) 222 4768 (AST Link Communication & Agency Post Office – Batticaloa); Maj M. Puvanendran
Southern: Weerasooriya Watte, Patuwatha-Dodanduwa; tel: (091) 227 7146; Maj Shelton Fernando

TRAINING COLLEGE
77 Ananda Rajakaruna Mawatha, Colombo 10; tel: (11) 268 6116; email: lankatg@sltnet.lk

SOCIAL SERVICES
Children's Homes
Batticoloa Girls' Home: 135 Trincomalee St, Batticaloa; tel: (065) 222 4558 (acc 16)
Dehiwela Girls' Home: 12 School Ave, Dehiwela; tel: 271 7049 (acc 50)

Sri Lanka Territory

Rajagiriya Boys' Home: Obeysekera Rd, Rajagiriya; tel: 286 2301 (acc 30)
Shalom Children's Home and Centre: Kandy Rd, Kaithady; tel: (021) 321 0779 (acc boys 16, girls 22, remandees 10)
Sunshine Home: 127 E. W. Perera Mawatha, Colombo 10 (acc remandees 34)
Swedlanka Boys' Home: South Pallansena Jaya Mawatha, Kochchikade; tel: (031) 227 7964 (acc 25)
The Haven: 127, E. W. Perera Mawatha, Colombo 10; tel: 269 5275 (acc babies 10, children 10)

Hostels
Dehiwela Eventide Home for Women: 8 School Ave, Dehiwela; tel: 272 8542 (acc 34)
Hope House Home for Employed Disabled Men: 11 Sir James Peiris Mawatha, Colombo 2; tel: (11) 232 4660 ext 200 (acc 12)
Ladies' Hostel (1): 18 Sri Saugathodaya Mawatha, Colombo 2; tel: (011) 311 7783 (acc 82)
Ladies' Hostel (2): 30 Union Pl, Colombo 2; tel: (011) 311 7735 (acc 78)
Rajagiriya Elders' Home and Iris Perera Home: 1700 Cotta Rd, Rajagiriya; tel: 288 5947 (acc men 20, women 22)
Rajagiriya Young Men's Hostel: Obeysekera Rd, Rajagiriya; tel: 286 2301 (acc 10)
Rawathawatte Hostel for Women: 14 Charles Pl, Rawathawatte, Moratuwa; tel: 421 3018 (acc working girls 28)
The Haven: 127 E. W. Perera Mawatha, Colombo 10; tel: 269 5275 (acc unwed mothers 14, elderly women 10, rehabilitation 10)

Community Centres
Dias Place: 16, Dias Place, Colombo 11; tel: 242 3912
Hope House: 11 Sir James Peiris Mawatha, Colombo 2; tel: (11) 232 4660 ext 200
Matale: 147 Trincomalee St, Matale; tel: (066) 223 0844
Rambukkana: Mawanella Rd, Rambukkana; tel: (035) 226 5179
Weerasooriya Centre: 88 Weerasooriya Watta, Patuwatha, Dodanduwa; tel: (091) 227 7146

Child Day Care Centres
Amparai: Main Rd, Amparai; tel: (063) 222 3779
Kudagama: Kudagama, Dombemada
Hewadiwela: Hewadiwela; tel: (035) 226 6785
Talampitiya: Mahagama, Kohilegedera, Talampitiya; tel: (037) 223 8278
Wattegama: 34 Nuwaratenne Rd, Wattegama; tel: (081) 380 3319
Rathmeewela, Menikdiwela

HEALTH SERVICES
Physiotherapy Unit: Colombo; tel (11) 232 4660 ext 204

COMBATING HUMAN TRAFFICKING PROGRAMME
Colombo: Anuradhapura, Hikkaduwa (Advocacy, Home-Based Care Counselling, Community Capacity Development)

COMMUNITY CAPACITY DEVELOPMENT
Hikkaduwa, Southern Section: Weerasooriya Watte, Pathuwatha, Dodanduwa-Hikkaduwa; tel: (091) 227 7146

CONFERENCE CENTRE
Rambukkana Conference Centre for Camp: Mawanella Rd, Rambukkana; tel: (035) 2265179

KALUTARA ESTATE AND CAMP CENTRE
Galapatha, Kalutara

Christian care is given at the Rajagiriya Elders' Home and Iris Perera Home

SWEDEN AND LATVIA TERRITORY

Territorial leaders:
Commissioners Victor and Roslyn Poke

Territorial Commander:
Commissioner Victor Poke (1 Nov 2006)

Chief Secretary:
Colonel Kristina Frisk (1 Aug 2006)

Territorial Headquarters: Östermalmsgatan 71, Stockholm, Sweden

Postal address: Box 5090, SE 102 42 Stockholm, Sweden

Tel: [46] (08) 562 282 00; fax: [46] (08) 562 283 91; email: fralsningsarmen@fralsningsarmen.se;
website: www.fralsningsarmen.se

Commissioner Hanna Ouchterlony, inspired by the first Army meeting held on Swedish soil in Värnamo in 1878 led by the young Chief of the Staff, Bramwell Booth, began Salvation Army work in a Stockholm theatre on 28 December 1882. The first women's home and a men's shelter were opened in 1890. Work among deaf and blind people was inaugurated in 1895. The Salvation Army was re-established in Latvia on 18 November 1990 and two months later, on 23 January 1991, The Salvation Army in Latvia became a juridical person. On 15 November 1994 the Sweden Territory was renamed the Sweden and Latvia Territory.

Zone: Europe
Countries included in the territory: Latvia, Sweden
'The Salvation Army' in Swedish: Frälsningsarmén; in Latvian: Pestíšanas Armija; in Russian: Armiya Spaseniya
Languages in which the gospel is preached: Latvian, Russian, Swedish
Periodical: *Stridsropet*

AN estimated 400,000 children and young people in Sweden are being raised in homes where one of the parents experiences alcohol or drug problems. A similar number grow up with parents who have psychological problems. These youngsters are often called 'the forgotten children'.

The Salvation Army has opened a family centre in Stockholm that provides a place for some of these children to enjoy an environment where play, conversation and healthy activity become important tools for personal development. A similar work is carried out at the Army's family centre in Jönköping, which opened a couple of years ago.

In the annual Confirmation Ceremony, held at Stockholm Temple, 34 teenagers confirmed their Christian faith. They had met for several weeks at Ågestagården to study the Bible and Salvation Army doctrine.

During midsummer, about 200

Sweden and Latvia Territory

people gathered at Högaberg Camp grounds for Roots 08, when the theme was 'The Fire Of God In A New Time'. Seven cadets were welcomed into the Prayer Warriors Session.

As the only voluntary organisation taking part in the Stockholm Marathon, the Army had an excellent opportunity to raise its profile and collect money for the Kenya Water Project. Salvation Army bands and gospel choirs provided music along the route as several Salvationists ran the race.

Because of a keener interest in buying second-hand goods from Salvation Army charity shops – known as Myrorna – income has increased. Myrorna is the oldest chain of charity shops in Sweden, with 28 premises around the country. Their main object is to raise money for the Army's social services, but Myrorna is also keen to provide jobs and practical training. There are 350 employees and a further 400 people undergoing training.

The territory has created a new and effective administrative structure. The process of change began in the spring of 2009, but in the build-up four well-attended 'Hearing Days' gave Salvationists in different locations across the territory opportunity to dialogue with the Territorial Commander on significant matters of concern.

Salvation Army work in Latvia continues to progress. For example, a further Russian-speaking ministry has commenced, this time at Riga 2 Corps. New soldiers have been enrolled and adherents accepted. Several outposts have been opened, with work focusing on children who live in marginalised circumstances.

Under the theme 'Learning To Know The Father', about 100 people from across Latvia spent time in worship and prayer during a day of prayer at Riga 1 Corps.

STATISTICS
Officers 386 (active 174 retired 212) **Cadets** (2nd Yr) 12 **Employees** 1,077
Corps (incl Community and Family Services) 147 **Outposts** 24 **Hotels/Guest Homes** 2
Senior Soldiers 5,321 **Adherents** 864 **Junior Soldiers** 125
Personnel serving outside territory Officers 10

STAFF
Women's Ministries: Comr Roslyn Poke (TPWM)

Business Administration
Sec for Business Administration: Capt Elisabeth Beckman
  Editor-in-Chief: Maj Bert Åberg
  Fundraising: Mr Mats Wiberg
  Legacies: Maj Margaretha Andersson

Personnel
Sec for Personnel: Lt-Col Kenneth Nordenberg
  Human Resources Responsibility: Mrs Eva Malmberg
  Training College: Maj Mona Stockman
  People's High School: Mr Magnus Wetterberg

Programme Office
Sec for Programme: Lt-Col Britt-Marie Alm
  Development Officers: Maj Sonja Blomberg, Col Kehs David Löfgren, Maj Gunilla Olausson, Maj Leif Öberg
  Area Experts:
    Corps Development: Capt Mia-Lisa Alhbin
    Social Work: Maj Kenneth Karlsson
    Youth: Mrs Gunnel Lerne
    Women's Ministries: Comr Roslyn Poke
    International Development: Mr Christian Lerne
    Child Sponsorship: Mrs Anna-Carin Wiberg Löw

Sweden and Latvia Territory

'Sally Ann' – Trading Programme:
Sally Ann Sverige AB:
email: sallyann@fralsningsarmen.se
website: www.sallyann.se
Manager: Mr Lars Beijer
Chair of Board: Comr Christina Kjellgren
Shop: Hornsgatan 98, 118 21 Stockholm

TRAINING
Training College
Frälsningsarméns Officersskola, Ågestagården,
Bonäsvägen, 5, 123 52 Farsta;
tel: (08) 562 281 50; fax: (08) 562 281 70

People's High Schools
Ågesta Folkhögskola: Bonäsvägen 5,
123 52 Farsta; tel: (08) 562 281 00;
fax (08) 562 281 20
Älvsjö Bransch: Älvsjö Gårdsväg 9,
125 30 Älvsjö; tel: (08) 647 52 77;
fax: (08) 556 233 15

CONFERENCE CENTRE/GUEST HOMES
Smålandsgården, Örserum, 563 91 Gränna;
tel: (0390) 300 14; fax: (0390) 304 17
(acc 67)
'Lännerstahemmet', Djurgårdsvägen 7,
132 46 Saltsjö-Boo; tel: (08) 715 11 58;
fax: (08) 747 11 76

SOCIAL SERVICES
Work Among Alcoholics
Treatment Centre for Substance Abusers
'Kurön', 178 92 Adelsö; tel: (08) 560 518 80;
fax: (08) 560 514 05 (acc 63)

Rehabilitation Centres
Göteborg: 'Lilla Bommen', S:t Eriksgatan 4,
411 05 Göteborg; tel: (031) 60 45 56;
fax: (031) 711 83 67 (acc 63)
Göteborg: 'Nylösegården', Skaragatan 3,
415 01 Göteborg; tel: (031) 25 59 59;
fax: (031) 21 99 86 (acc 20)
Örebro: 'Gnistan', Bruksgatan 13, 702 20
Örebro; tel: (019) 32 38 40;
fax: (019) 32 37 72 (acc 11)
Stockholm: 'Värtahemmet', Kolargatan 2;
115 42 Stockholm; tel: (08) 545 835 00;
fax: (08) 545 835 07 (acc 42)
Stockholm Tyresö: 'Källan',
Wättingegårdsväg 1, 135 40 Tyresö;
tel: (08) 448 73 50; fax: (08) 448 73 59
(acc 20)
Sundsvall: 'Klippangården', Fredsgatan 38,
852 38 Sundsvall; tel: (060) 17 31 74;
fax: (060) 17 52 10 (acc 16)
Uppsala: 'Sagahemmet', Storgatan 2 A, 753 31
Uppsala; tel: (018) 10 08 01;
fax: (018) 12 12 39 (acc 26)

Night Shelters
Örebro: 'Gnistan', Bruksgatan 13, 702 20 Örebro;
tel: (019) 32 38 40; fax: (019) 32 37 72
(acc 10)
Stockholm: 'Midsommarkransen',
Midsommarslingan 1-3, 126 32 Hägersten;
tel: (08) 19 13 30; fax: (08) 744 20 78
(acc 27)
Sundsvall: 'Klippangården', Fredsgatan 38,
852 38 Sundsvall; tel: (060) 17 31 74;
fax: (018) 12 12 39
Uppsala: 'Sagahemmet', Storgatan 2 A,
753 31 Uppsala; tel: (018) 10 08 01;
fax: (018) 12 12 39 (acc 10)

Drop-in Centre
Stockholm: Bergsundsstrand 51, 117 38
Stockholm; tel: (08) 34 85 98;
fax: (08) 31 97 85

Harbour Light Corps
'Fyrbåkskåren', S:t Eriksgatan 4, 411 05
Göteborg; tel: (031) 19 82 18

Advisory Services
Stockholm: 'Eken' Counselling Centre,
Hornsgatan 98, 118 21 Stockholm;
tel: (08) 55 60 80 76
Uppsala: 'Brobygget', S:t Persgatan 20,
753 20 Uppsala; tel: (018) 71 05 44;
fax: (018) 14 84 59

Work Among Children and Families
Pre-Schools
Jönköping: 'Vårsol', Von Platensgatan 10,
553 13 Jönköping; tel: (036) 71 15 02;
fax: (036) 71 21 90 (acc 17)
Umeå: 'Krubban', N Slevgränd 123,
906 27 Umeå; tel: (090) 18 05 90;
fax: (090) 18 27 88 (acc 18)
Västra Frölunda: 'Morgonsol', Poppelgatan 11,
426 74 Västra Frölunda; tel/fax: (013) 29 10 29
(acc 34)

Work Among Mother and Children
Stockholm: Frälsningsarméns Mamma –
barnarbete, Gotlandsgatan 73 C,
116 38 Stockholm; tel: (08) 21 47 92

Sweden and Latvia Territory

Some of the 34 teenagers who met for several weeks at Ågestagården to study the Bible and Salvation Army doctrine before they confirmed their Christian faith in the territory's annual Confirmation Ceremony held at Stockholm Temple

School and Treatment Centre for Adolescents
'Sundsgården', 179 96 Svartsjö;
tel: (08) 560 428 21; fax: (08) 560 425 00
(acc 27)

Treatment Centre for Families
'FAM-Huset', Hagvägen 1, 513 32 Fristad;
tel: (033) 21 01 62; fax: (033) 21 01 63
(acc adults 8, babies 8)

Emergency Diagnostic and Short-term Treatment Centre
'Vårsol', Von Platensgatan 10,
553 13 Jönköping; tel: (036) 16 74 58;
fax: (036) 71 21 90 (acc 6)

Group Homes for Adolescents
Jönköping: 'Vårsols Ungdomsboende',
V:a Storgatan 21, 553 15 Jönköping;
tel: (036) 17 32 75; fax: (036) 17 32 74 (acc 6)

Stockholm: 'Locus', Grev Turegatan 66,
114 38 Stockholm; tel: (08) 667 21 82;
fax: (08) 667 21 87 (acc 14)

Family Centres with Advisory Service
'Vårsols Familjecenter', V:a Storgatan 21,
553 15 Jönköping; tel: (036) 17 32 72;
fax: (036) 17 32 74
393:s Familjecenter, Södermannagatan 46,
116 40 Stockholm; tel: (08) 664 60 32

Salvation Army Refugee Aid
Jönköping SARA: V:a Storgatan 21,
553 15 Jönköping; tel: (036) 17 32 75;
fax: (036) 17 32 74

Vacation Centres for Children
Gävle: 'Rörberg', Hedesundavägen 89,
818 91 Valbo; tel: (026) 330 19 (acc 15)
Luleå: Sunderbyvägen 323, 954 42 Södra
Sunderbyn; tel: (0920) 26 57 25 (acc 15)

Sweden and Latvia Territory

Malmö: Klockarevägen 20, 236 36 Höllviken;
tel: (040) 45 05 24 (acc 15)

Centre for Elderly People
'Dalen', Kapellgatan 14, 571 31 Nässjö;
tel: (0380) 188 11 (acc 20)

Recreation Centre for Elderly People
Malmö: 'Furubo', Klockarevägen 22, 236 36
Höllviken; tel: (040) 45 39 13

Multicultural Ministries
'Akalla', Sibeliusgången 6, 164 73 Kista; tel:
(08) 750 62 16; fax: (08) 751 71 61

Women Emergency Residence
Stockholm: 'Skogsbo', Box 112, 132 23 Saltsjö
Boo; tel: (08) 21 47 92

Second-hand Shops
Head office: Stensätravägen 3B,
127 39 Skärholmen; tel: (08) 563 169 50;
fax: (08) 563 169 60
Shops: Borås, Eskilstuna, Falun, Gävle,
Göteborg, Halmstad, Jönköping, Karlstad,
Linköping, Luleå, Malmö (2), Norrköping,
Skellefteå, Stockholm (8), Sundbyberg,
Sundsvall, Trollhättan, Umeå, Uppsala (2),
Västerås, Örebro

LATVIA REGION (under THQ)
Regional Headquarters: Bruninieku iela 10A,
LV 1001 Riga; tel: [371] 673 10037;
fax: [371] 673 15266;
email: info@pestisanasarmija.lv;
website: www.pestisanasarmija.lv
Regional leaders: Lts Peter and Rut Baronowsky
Training: Maj Lisbeth Månsson

STATISTICS
Officers 14 (active 13 retired 1) **Cadets** (1st yr)
1 (2nd yr) 2 **Envoys** 3 **Employees** 122
Corps 6 **Outposts** 6 **Institutions** 4
Senior Soldiers 274 **Adherents** 215 **Junior Soldiers** 99

SOCIAL SERVICES
Leontine Gorkša Children's Home: Agenskalna
iela 3, LV 1048 Riga; tel: [371] 760 17 00
Maternity and Child Health Centre: Bruninieku
iela 10A, LV 1001 Riga;
tel/fax: [371] 672 71384
'Patverums' Day Centre for Children at Risk:
Bruninieku iela 10 A, LV 1001 Riga;
tel: [371] 731 14 63
Skangale School Home: Liepa pag, Césu
rajons, LV 4128 Liepa; tel: [371] 641 02220;
fax: [371] 641 02221

SOUTHERN AFRICA: Responding to a call to help meet the needs of foreigners displaced as a result of xenophobic attacks, Salvationists and generous supporters provided shelter and sustenance to many of the victims (*see page 232*). The photograph shows the ministry carried out at Gill Camp.

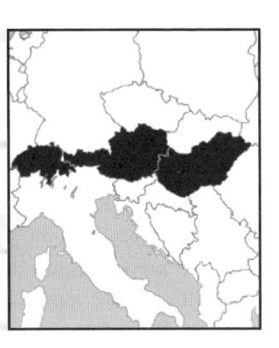

SWITZERLAND, AUSTRIA AND HUNGARY TERRITORY

Territorial leaders:
Commissioners Kurt Burger and Alicia Burger-Pedersen

Territorial Commander:
Commissioner Kurt Burger (1 Sep 2007)

Chief Secretary:
Colonel Franz Boschung (1 Oct 2007)

Territorial Headquarters: Laupenstrasse 5, Bern, Switzerland
Postal address: Die Heilsarmee, Postfach 6575, 3001 Bern, Switzerland
Tel: [41] (31) 388 05 91; fax: [41] (31) 388 05 95; email: info@swi.salvationarmy.org
websites: www.heilsarmee.ch; www.armeedusalut.ch; www.salvationarmy.ch

On 10 December 1882 Salvation Army operations were commenced in the Salle de la Réformation, Geneva, by the Maréchale, Catherine Booth, and Colonel Arthur S. Clibborn. Bitter opposition was encountered but now the Army is recognised as an evangelical and social force throughout the Confederation. The Salvation Army's constitution consists of Foundation Salvation Army Switzerland; Cooperative Salvation Army Social Organisation; Salvation Army Immo Ltd.

Work first commenced in Austria on 27 May 1927 in Vienna. Unofficial meetings had been held earlier, but the official opening was conducted by Lieut-Commissioner Bruno Friedrich and Captain Lydia Saak was the officer-in-charge. 'Verein der Heilsarmee' was legally recognised by the Austrian Federal Ministry on 8 May 1952.

The Salvation Army's operations in Hungary were commenced on 24 April 1924 by Colonel Rothstein with two German women-officers. The evangelistic and social activities were maintained until suppressed in 1950. After the opening of the central European borders, The Salvation Army was officially re-established on 3 November 1990 by General Eva Burrows.

Zone: Europe
Countries included in the territory: Austria, Hungary, Switzerland
'The Salvation Army' in German: Die Heilsarmee; in French: Armée du Salut; in Hungarian: Az Üdvhadsereg; in Spanish: Ejército de Salvación
Languages in which the gospel is preached: French, German, Hungarian, Spanish
Periodicals: *Espoir* (French), *Dialog* (German), *Dialogue* (French), *IN* (French and German), *Just 4 U* (French), *Klecks* (German), *Trampoline* (French), *Trialog* (German)

EUROPE'S economic crisis and an unusually severe winter created a difficult year for the territory as it sought to minister to many needy people in various places. For example, The Open Heart Social Services Centre in the heart of Zurich responded to the bad weather conditions by expanding its bed capacity in order to accommodate more homeless men and women.

The territory's refugee services

were faced with an unexpected influx of people. Three new shelters had to be opened. Even a former nuclear bomb shelter was used to house refugees. The average number that The Salvation Army takes care of at any given time is 650 people. The unexpected 'flood' raised the count to 1,000.

This is a ministry the Army has been engaged in for more than 20 years, and the number of people seeking a better life seems to be continually rising.

A milestone of a different kind was the reopening of Basel Children's Home. After a two-year construction period, 25 children moved into a bright and spacious facility where they receive professional, Christian-based care. There is always a waiting list; demand to take children out of troubled homes never seems to lessen.

The thrift stores (charity shops) are a particular source of pride in the territory. The stores are clean, well-stocked and customer friendly. In spite of the difficult economic climate, sales revenue rose again to 20.1 million Swiss francs and a surplus of two million Swiss francs was distributed among Salvation Army projects.

The Swiss are generous donors – for example, about 65 tons of clothing is donated every month to thrift stores. This creates jobs and job training for men and women who would otherwise have difficulty finding work.

In October 2008 Commissioner Robin Dunster became the first Chief of the Staff in 75 years to visit The Salvation Army in Hungary. She spent a weekend encouraging the small but devoted and growing Army of God in that part of the territory.

Visits to the social services centres in Budapest, holiness and praise meetings on Sunday, officers councils and a reception with church and civic leaders were part of the Chief's busy schedule. Hearing about the Army's extensive work, church leaders pledged increased support.

Everyone appreciated the Chief's visit, renewed in their commitment to serve God and suffering humanity in this often difficult part of the Salvation Army world.

STATISTICS
Officers 429 (active 187 retired 242) **Cadets** (1st Yr) 1 (2nd Yr) 1 **Employees** 1,524
Corps 65 **Outposts** 5 **Institutions** 45 **Thrift Stores** 24
Senior Soldiers 3,030 **Adherents** 856 **Junior Soldiers** 379
Personnel serving outside territory Officers 14 Layworkers 1

STAFF
Dept of Evangelisation: Maj Fritz Schmid
Society and Family: Comr Alicia Burger-Pedersen (TPWM) Col Hanny Boschung (TSWM) Maj Christianne Winkler (Territorial Women's Ministries & Seniors Sec) Capt Barbara Bösch (Territorial Family Work)
Music and Gospel Arts: Sgt Phillip Manger
Youth: Capt Thomas Bösch

Dept of Social Work: Sgt Erhard Meyner-Dätwyler
Social French Part: Mr Michel Bonjour
Social German Part: Mr Christian Rohrbach
Prison Work: Maj Samuel Winkler
Family Tracing: Maj Martha Mosimann
Refugees: Mr Jakob Amstutz
Thrift Stores: Mr David Küenzi

Switzerland, Austria and Hungary Territory

Dept of Personnel: Maj Marianne Meyner-Stettler
Candidates: Maj Daniela Zurbrügg-Jäggi
Training: Maj Hervé Cachelin
Personnel Administration: Sgt Christian Hefti

Dept of Finance and Business Administration: Sgt Philip Bates
Finance + Controlling Evangelisation: Maj Peter Zurbrügg
Finance + Controlling THQ: Sgt Kenneth Hofer
Finance + Controlling Social: Mr Michael Lippuner
Property: Mr Marc Hendry
Mission and Development: Sgt Markus Muntwiler

Dept of Communication: tba
Editor-in-Chief: tba
Editor and Publishing: Mrs Gabrielle Keller
Fundraising: Sgt Christoph Bitter
Information Technology: Mr Martin Schweizer
Museum and Archives: Maj Heidi Scheurer
Trade Shop: Mrs Hanni Butler

DIVISIONS

Bern: Gartenstrasse 8, 3007 Bern;
tel: (031) 380 75 45; fax: (031) 380 75 42;
Majs Bernhard and Regina Wittwer
Division Romande: Rue de l'Ecluse 16,
2000 Neuchâtel; tel: (032) 729 20 81;
Majs Jacques and Claude-Evelyne Donzé
Nordwestschweiz : Breisacherstrasse 45,
4057 Basel; tel: (061) 691 11 50;
fax: (061) 691 12 59; Majs August and Ruth Martin
Ost-Division: Eidmattstrasse 16, 8032 Zürich;
tel: (044) 383 69 70; fax: (044) 383 52 48;
Majs Allan and Fiona Hofer

SCHOOL FOR OFFICER TRAINING

4012 Basel, Habsburgerstrasse 15, Postfach 410,
CH-4012 Basel; tel: (061) 387 91 11;
fax: (061) 381 77 63

SOCIAL WORK

Social Services Advice Bureaux

4053 Basel: Frobenstrasse 18; tel: (061) 272 00 07;
fax: (061) 273 29 00
3007 Bern: Gartenstrasse 8; tel: (031) 380 75 40;
fax: (031) 380 75 42
2503 Biel-Bienne: Oberer Quai 12;
tel: (032) 322 53 66; fax: (032) 322 60 64
1018 Lausanne: Rue de la Borde 22;
tel: (021) 646 46 10
8400 Winterthur: CASA, Wartstrasse 9;
tel: 052 202 77 80
8032 Zürich: Eidmattstrasse 16; tel: 044 383 16 96
8005 Zürich: Luisenstrasse 23; tel: 044 272 85 20

Adult Rehabilitation Centres

1201 Genève: Centre-Espoir, Rue Jean-Dassier 10;
tel: (022) 338 22 00; fax: (022) 338 22 01
(acc 109)
3098 Köniz: Buchseegut, Buchseeweg 15;
tel: (031) 970 63 63; fax: (031) 970 63 64
(acc 40) (with gardening and workshop)
1003 Lausanne: Foyer Féminin, Avenue
Ruchonnet 49; tel: (021) 310 40 40;
fax: (021) 310 40 42 (acc 23)
1005 Lausanne: La Résidence, Place du Vallon 1a;
tel: (021) 320 48 55; fax: (021) 310 39 34
(acc 38)
5022 Rombach (Aarau): Obstgarten,
Bibersteinstrasse 54; tel: (062) 839 80 80;
fax: (062) 839 80 89 (acc 34)
2024 St-Aubin: Le Devens, Socio-medical Home;
tel: (032) 836 27 29; fax: (032) 836 27 28
(acc 34)
9205 Waldkirch: Hasenberg; tel: (071) 434 61 61;
fax: (071) 434 61 71 (acc 48) (agriculture and workshop)

Community Centres

Hochfeld, Bern; Eidmattegge, Zürich; Gelber
Stern, Zürich; Open Heart, Zürich; Genève.

Emergency Shelters

1201 Genève: Accueil de Nuit, Chemin
Galiffe 4; tel: (022) 388 22 00;
fax: (022) 338 22 01 (acc 40)
1005 Lausanne: La Marmotte, Rue du
Vallon 17; tel: (021) 311 79 12 (acc 30)

Holiday Flats

3715 Adelboden: Chalet Bethel;
tel: (033) 673 21 62 (acc 20)

Homes for the Aged

3013 Bern: Lorrainehof, Lorrainestrasse 34-38;
tel: (031) 330 16 16; fax: (031) 330 16 00
(acc 50 + 10 flats) (health care)
1814 La Tour-de-Peilz: Le Phare-Elim, Avenue
de la Paix 11, case postale 444;
tel: (021) 977 33 33; fax: (021) 977 33 90
(acc 44) (health care)
1201 Genève: Résidence Amitié (health care),
Rue Baudit 1; tel: (022) 919 95 95;
fax: (022) 740 30 11 (acc 52) (health care)
2000 Neuchâtel: Le Foyer, Rue de l'Ecluse 18;
tel: (032) 729 20 20 (acc 30) (health care)

Switzerland, Austria and Hungary Territory

Homes for Children
8344 Bäretswil: Sunnemätteli Home for
Handicapped Children, Wirzwil,
Rüggenthalstrasse 71; tel: (044) 939 11 88;
fax (044) 979 10 45 (acc 16)
4054 Basel: Kinderhaus Holee,
Nenzlingerstrasse 2; tel: (061) 301 24 50;
fax: (061) 301 24 44 (acc 24)
8932 Mettmenstetten: Kinderheim Paradies;
tel: (044) 768 58 00; fax: (044) 768 58 19
(acc 24)
3110 Münsingen: Kinderheim Sonnhalde,
Standweg 7; tel: (031) 721 08 06;
fax: (031) 721 42 72 (acc 24)

Hostels for Men
4058 Basel: Rheinblick, Rheingasse 80;
tel: (061) 666 66 77; fax: (061) 666 66 78
(acc 53)
8004 Zürich: Dienerstrasse 76; tel: (044) 298 90 80;
fax: (044) 242 41 71 (acc 26)
8005 Zürich: Geroldstrasse 27;
tel: (043) 204 10 20; fax: (043) 204 10 21
(acc 25)

Hostels for Men and Women
3006 Bern: Passantenheim, Muristrasse 6;
tel: (031) 351 80 27; fax: (031) 351 46 97
(acc 43)
2503 Biel: Haus am Quai, Oberer Quai 12;
tel: (032) 322 68 38; fax: (032) 322 60 64
(acc 24)
3600 Thun: Passantenheim, Waisenhausstrasse 26;
tel: (033) 222 69 20; fax: (033) 222 69 25
(acc 15)
8400 Winterthur: Wartstrasse 40;
tel: (052) 208 90 50; fax: (052) 208 90 59
(acc 34)
8026 Zürich: Molkenstrasse 6; tel: (044) 298 90 00;
fax: (044) 242 38 97 (acc 85)

Hostel for Women
4058 Basel: Frauenwohnheim, Alemannengasse 7;
tel: (061) 681 34 70; fax: (061) 681 34 72
(acc 37)

Young Women's Residence
4059 Basel: Schlössli, Eichhornstrasse 21;
tel: (061) 335 31 10; fax: (061) 335 31 29
(acc 14)

Refugee Work
Main Office: 3008 Bern: Effingerstrasse 67;
tel: (031) 380 18 80; fax: (031) 398 04 28
(12 centres, 6 coordination offices)

Social Flats
3012 Bern: Begleitetes Wohnen,
Waldheimstrasse 16; tel: (031) 302 02 35
(acc 25 flats)

HOTELS
4055 Basel: Alegria B&B, Habsburgerstrasse 15;
tel: (061) 387 91 10; fax: (061) 381 77 63
1204 Genève: Bel' Espérance, Rue de la
Vallée 1; tel: (022) 818 37 37;
fax: (022) 818 37 73 (acc 65 beds, 40 rooms)
3852 Ringgenberg: Guesthouse, Vordorf 264;
tel: (033) 822 70 25; fax: (033) 822 70 74
(acc 24 beds, 12 rooms)

YOUTH CENTRES
Under THQ
3715 Adelboden (acc 75)

Under DHQ
Nordwestschweiz: 4462 Rickenbach, Waldegg
(acc 100)
Division Romande: 1451 Les Rasses (acc 150)
Ost-Division: 8712 Stäfa (acc 55)

AUSTRIA
City Command: AT-1020 Vienna Salztor-
Zentrum, Grosse Schiffgasse 3;
tel: [43] (1) 214 48 30; fax: [43] (1) 214 48 30 55;
City Commander: Maj Hans-Marcel Leber

Hostel for Men
AT-1020 Vienna: SalztorZentrum, Grosse
Schiffgasse 3; tel: [43] (1) 214 48 30 27;
fax: [43] (1) 214 48 30 55 (acc men 60,
sheltered housing 42, external flats 21)

HUNGARY REGION
Regional Headquarters: Bajnok utca 25,
HU-1063 Budapest VI, Hungary;
tel: [36] (1) 332 3324; fax: [36] (1) 373 0010
Regional Officer: Capt Andrew Morgan

Hostel for Men
'Új Remenység Háza', HU-1086 Budapest VIII,
Dobozi utca 29; tel: [36] (1) 314 2775
(acc 98)

Hostel for Women
'A Válaszút Háza', HU-1171 Budapest XVII,
Lemberg utca 38-42; tel: [36] (1) 259 1095
(acc 24)

Refuge for Maltreated Women and Children
'Fény Hazá', IV utca 16, HU-1172 Budapest XVII;
tel/fax: [36] (1) 257 9461 (acc mothers with
children 5)

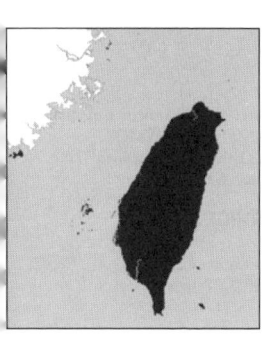

TAIWAN REGION

Regional leaders:
Majors Michael and Annette Coleman

Regional Commander:
Major Michael Coleman (1 May 2008)

Regional Headquarters: 3/F, 273 Tun Hwa South Road, Section 2, Da-an District, Taipei 106

Postal address: PO Box 44-100, Taipei, Taiwan

Tel: [886] (02) 2738 1079/1171; fax: [886] (02) 2738 5422; email: taiwan@taw.salvationarmy.org;

website: www.salvationarmy.org.tw

Pioneered in 1928 by Colonel Yasowo Segawa, Salvation Army work in Taiwan was curtailed by the Second World War. Following initiatives by two American servicemen, operations were officially re-established in October 1965 by Colonel and Mrs George Lancashire. Formerly linked with Hong Kong, Taiwan became a separate region on 1 January 1997.

Zone: South Pacific and East Asia
Country included in the region: Taiwan
'The Salvation Army' in Taiwanese (Hokkien): Kiu Se Kuen; in Mandarin: Chiu Shih Chun
Languages in which the gospel is preached: English, Hakka, Mandarin, Taiwanese (Hokkien)
Periodical: *Taiwan Regional News*

SALVATIONISTS embarked on discovering a fresh vision for Salvation Army work in Taiwan with a day of prayer (30 November 2008). Ideas were collated and further refined during an all-day workshop held in March 2009.

The launch of the Regional Mission Team (14 February 2009) helped to create a greater outreach culture and provided a response to the growing desire to develop mission skills. The team will continue to support the outreach ministry of corps around Taiwan.

On 11 May 2008 Colonels Malcolm and Irene Induruwage (territorial leaders of The Philippines) conducted the installation of Majors Michael and Annette Coleman as regional leaders.

Thanks to generous financial and helpful personnel support from Australia Southern Territory, a children's gospel camp and a music camp took place during July 2008. Eight young people accepted Christ for the first time, and many were linked up to corps.

In September 2008 three holiness seminars led by Lieut-Colonels Wayne and Myra Pritchett (IHQ) were a significant high point in the spiritual life of the region. The mercy seat was used frequently and many delegates expressed a greater commitment in their Salvationism.

As part of the Taipei Homeless Persons Photography Project, a public exhibition was held during November. Those clients who carried out photography assignments gained a sense of purpose, developing new skills and producing professional-quality photographs.

STATISTICS
Officers 16 (active 14 retired 2)
Corps with Community Centres 5 **Social Services Centres** 3
Senior Soldiers 178 **Adherents** 91 **Junior Soldiers** 33

STAFF
Women's Ministries: Maj Annette Coleman (RPWM) Maj Mary Tsou (WMO)
Administration Officer: Maj Stephen Tsou
Youth: Capt Grace Weng

SOCIAL SERVICES
Homeless
Taipei Homeless Caring Centre: c/o 1/F, No 42, Lane 65, Jin Si St., Taipei 103

Youth
Puli Youth Services Centre: No 192 Pei Hwang Rd, Puli Town, Nantou County 545 (acc 60)

COMMUNITY SERVICES
Puli Community Development Centre: c/o No 62-1, Shueitou Rd, Puli Town, Nantou County 545

UNITED KINGDOM: Free copies of the new-look *War Cry* – 'the people's paper' – are given away in London's Oxford Street. This exciting initiative in literature evangelism was welcomed enthusiastically in the territory (*see page 256*).

Junior soldiers from Finland sing about the Bible during the annual Salvation Army congress in Helsinki

Above: at Mapangazya Divisional Congress in Zambia, League of Mercy members bring gifts for The Salvation Army's Chikankata Hospital

Below: the study of Bible superheroes caught the imaginations of children the Central Bible and Leadership Institute in USA Central Territory

Left: while visiting The Philippines, Major Eirwen Pallant (International Health Services) meets girls who live in The Salvation Army's care in Bethany Home, Quezon City

These soldiers were enrolled in two of The Salvation Army's newest openings – Mali and Burundi – at corps in Bamako (right) and Bujumbura (below)

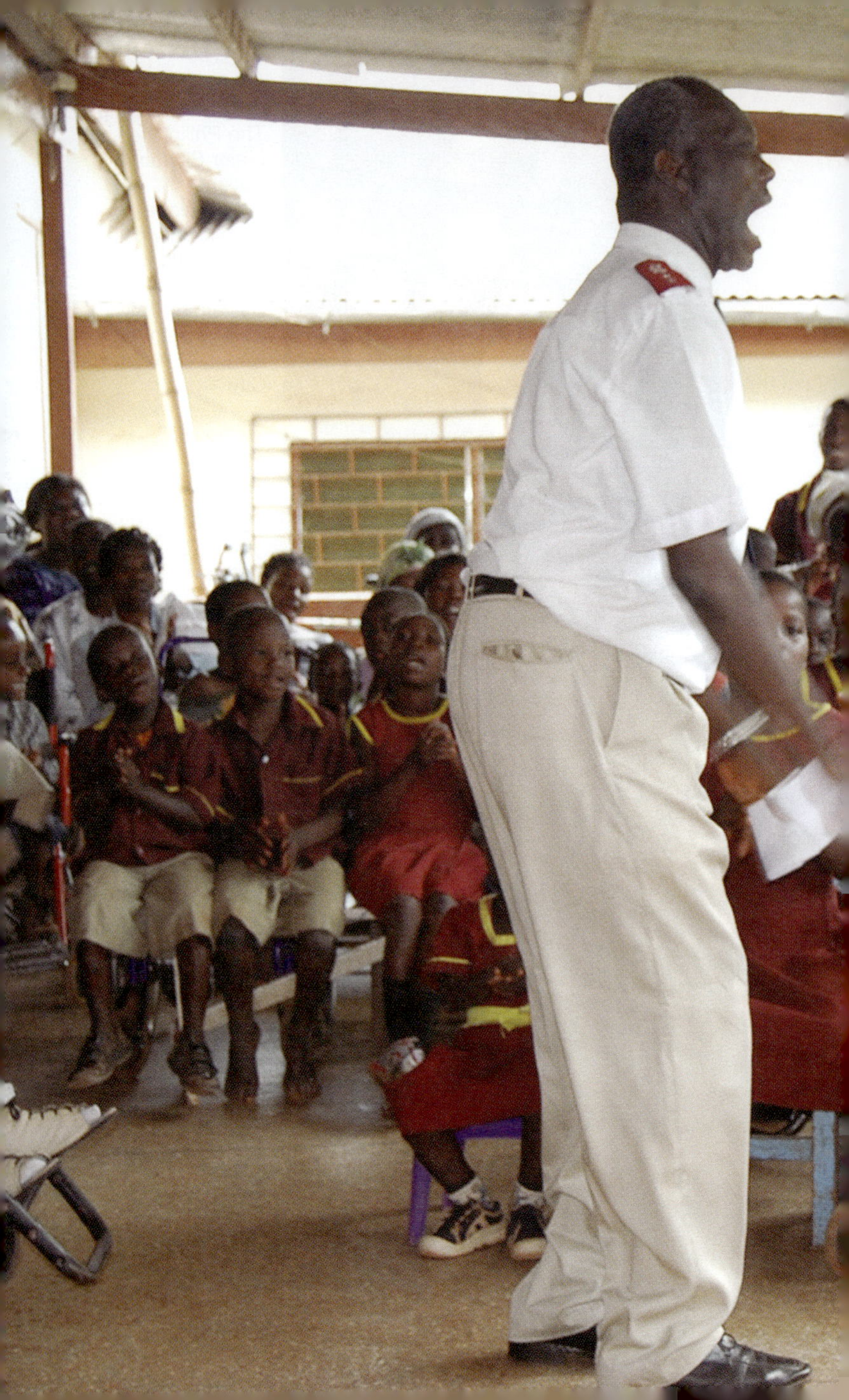

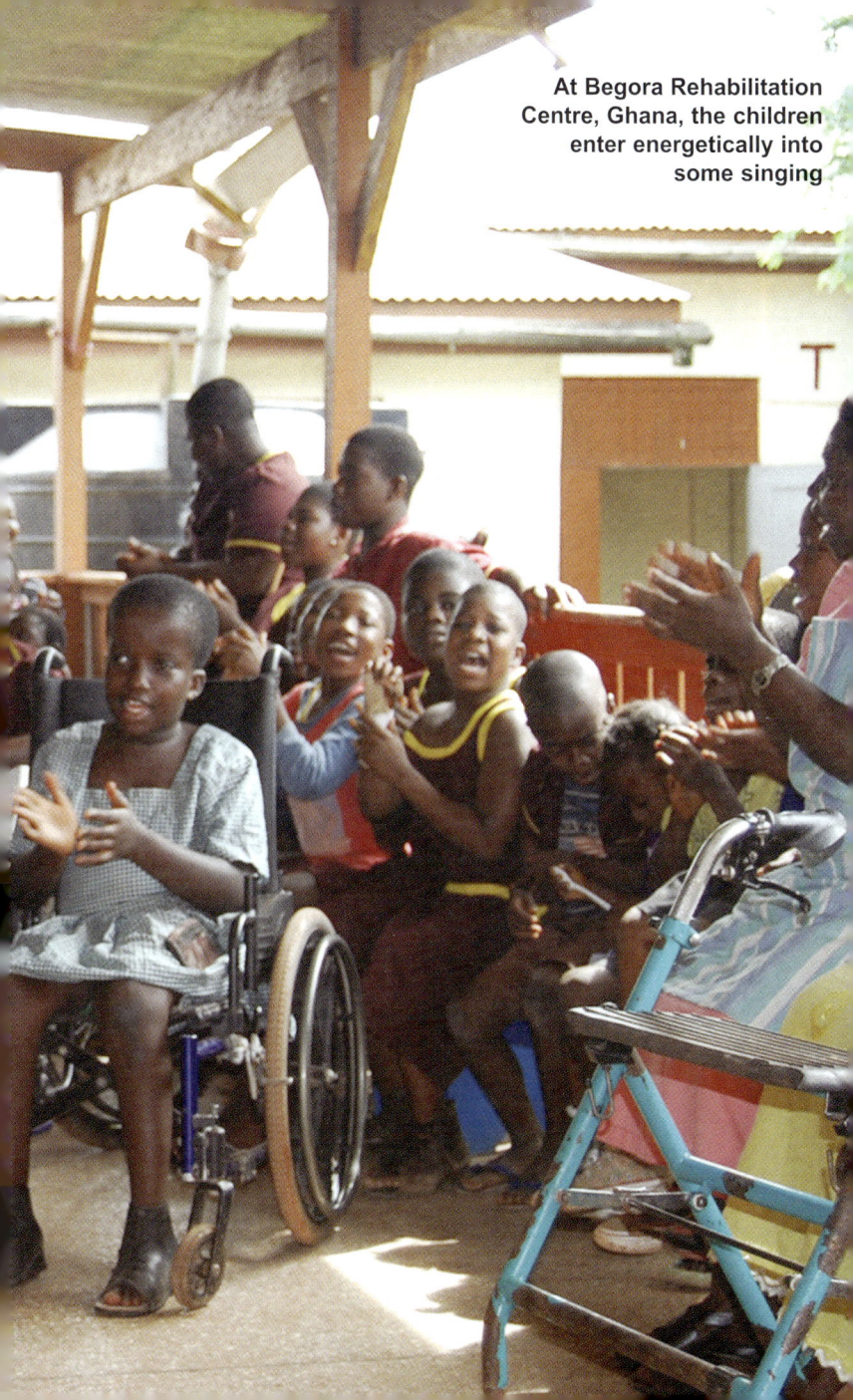

At Begora Rehabilitation Centre, Ghana, the children enter energetically into some singing

During an evangelical campaign in São Paulo, Brazil, young Salvationists perform street theatre (top) to attract children and young people. Some joined the Central Corps Sunday school and (above) took part in a Christmas meeting.

A Salvationist clown proves popular during a children's evangelism programme in Krnov, Czech Republic, while (top) a village open-air meeting in Machilipatnam, India Central Territory, also attracts attention

Above: a Salvation Army team in Indonesia takes essential supplies to a village affected by an earthquake that hit the island of Java

Below: in India South Western Territory, Salvationists assess how assistance can best be given to a widow who spends much of each day breaking and selling rocks by the roadside to raise a meagre income for her family

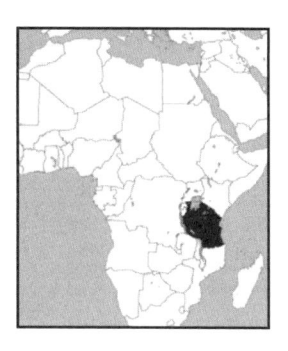

TANZANIA TERRITORY

Territorial leaders:
Colonels Hezekiel and Mirriam Mavundla

Territorial Commander:
Colonel Hezekiel Mavundla (1 Feb 2008)

Chief Secretary:
Lieut-Colonel Benjamin Mnyampi
(1 Feb 2008)

Territorial Headquarters: Kilwa Road, Dar es Salaam

Postal address: PO Box 1273, Dar es Salaam, Tanzania

Tel/fax: [255] (22) 2850468/2850542

Adjutant and Mrs Francis Dare began Salvation Army work in Tabora, Tanzania (formerly known as Tanganyika), in November 1933, as part of the East Africa Territory. In 1950, at the request for assistance from the Colonial Governor, The Salvation Army set up Mgulani Camp, where the Tanzania Headquarters is now located. Tanzania became a separate command on 1 October 1998 and was elevated to territory status on 1 February 2008.

Zone: Africa
Country included in the territory: Tanzania
'The Salvation Army' in Kiswahili: Jeshi la Wokovu
Languages in which the gospel is preached: Kiswahili and various tribal languages

THERE were encouraging signs of progress during 2008-09, for which the territory is grateful to God. With the Lord's help 468 new senior soldiers, 431 junior soldiers and 489 Home League members were enrolled in 2008. Salvationists raised 55 per cent more money for the International Self-Denial Fund and the Home League Helping-Hand Scheme also realised an increase on the 2007 total.

Twelve corps leaders (a group of long-time accepted candidates who for one reason or another never entered the training college) were offered an alternative training programme to equip them for future service. After three years of flexible training, largely on the field but with residential sessions for four to five weeks each year, the six couples were commissioned as officers on 10 August 2008.

After a year without a training session, the officers' training college was opened on 15 January 2009 and the welcome meeting for 12 cadets of the Ambassadors Of Holiness Session took place 10 days later.

THQ, divisions, districts and social centres were represented at a women officers' administration course, where 15 delegates were trained to help improve their ministry. Christian leadership, management, effective planning and good office practice were among subjects covered.

Seven women from Canada and Bermuda, a Partners In Mission territory, paid a 10-day visit (21-30 September 2008) and took part in the Coastal District Home League Rally.

During May and August 2008 all the territory's officers had an opportunity to attend one of two retreats held in Mbeya and Mwanza (for the south and north respectively). These were times of wonderful fellowship and much encouragement.

In June, staff from the International Projects and Development Services, IHQ, gave a week's training on the new Community Project Management System.

STATISTICS
Officers 133 (active 126 retired 7) **Employees** 150
Corps 65 **Outposts** 64 **Schools** 2 **Day Care Centres** 17 **Hostel** 1
Senior Soldiers 5,372 **Junior Soldiers** 3,567

STAFF
Women's Ministries: Col Mirriam Mavundla (TPWM) Lt-Col Grace Mnyampi (TSWM) Maj Tamali Mwalukani (LOMS/ SAMF)
Education: Maj Musa Magaigwa
Field: Maj Wilson Mwalukani
Finance: Maj Yesuvadian Manoharan (Finance Sec) Maj Hosea Kindi (Asst Finance Sec)
Projects: Mr Frederick Urembo
Property: Capt Peter Tingo
Social Services: Maj Joy Paxton
Sponsorship: Maj Vethamony Manoharan
Training: Maj Lynda Levis
Youth and Candidates: Maj Fanuel Ndabila

DIVISIONS
Mbeya: PO Box 1214, Mbeya; tel: (025) 2560009; Majs Samuel and Mary Mkami
Tarime: PO Box 37, Tarime; tel: (028) 2690095; Majs Yohana and Jesinala Msongwe

DISTRICTS
Coastal: PO Box 7622, Dar es Salaam; tel: (022) 2860365; Capt James Mwita
Mwanza: PO Box 11267, Mwanza; tel: (028) 40123; Capt James Gitangita
Serengeti: PO Box 28, Mugumu; tel: (028) 2621434; Capt Christopher Ighoty

TRAINING COLLEGE
PO Box 1273, Dar es Salaam

AGRICULTURE DEVELOPMENT PROGRAMME
PO Box 1273, Dar es Salaam

EDUCATIONAL WORK
College for Business Management and Administration
Shukrani International College for Business Management and Administration, PO Box 535, Mbeya; tel: (00255) (0)25 2504404; fax: (00255) (0)25 2500202

Primary School for the Physically Handicapped
Matumaini School, PO Box 1273, Dar es Salaam; tel: (022) 2851861 (acc 175)

Secondary School
Itundu School, PO Box 2994, Mbeya

SOCIAL SERVICES
Kwetu Counselling and Psycho-Social Support Services: PO Box 1273, Dar es Salaam
Mbagala Girls' Home: PO Box 1273, Dar es Salaam
Mgulani Hostel and Conference Centre: PO Box 1273, Dar es Salaam; tel: (022) 2851467 (acc 110)
Vocational Training Workshop: PO Box 1273, Dar es Salaam

Anti-Human Trafficking Programmes

Rehabilitation and Reunification Services for Orphans and Vulnerable Children

PROJECTS
Community counselling, Community psycho-social support programme for orphans and vulnerable children, Gardening and farming activities, Goats banking schemes, Home-based care services, Literacy classes, Micro-credit schemes, Nutrition programmes, Primary health care, Training and economic empowerment for rural women, Water and sanitation programmes

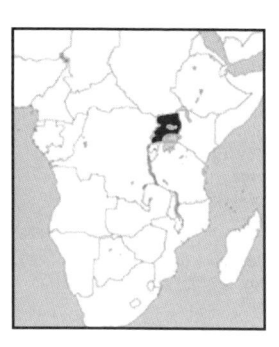

UGANDA COMMAND

Command leaders:
Lieut-Colonels Moses and Sarah Wandulu
Officer Commanding:
Lieut-Colonel Moses Wandulu (1 Jul 2007)

General Secretary:
Major Stephen Moriasi (1 Jul 2007)

Command Headquarters: Plot 78-82 Lugogo Bypass, Kampala
Postal address: PO Box 11776, Kampala, Uganda
Tel: [256] 41 533901; Kampala mobile: [256] 752 375782

The Salvation Army opened fire in Uganda in 1931 when Captain and Mrs Edward Osborne unfurled the flag in Mbale, as part of the East Africa Territory. In September 1977 the Army's religious teaching was banned and in June 1978 its ministry, including social work, was proscribed. In 1980 Majors Leonard and Dorothy Millar began work with the persecuted Salvationists to re-establish The Salvation Army. Uganda became a separate command on 1 November 2005.

Zone: Africa
Country included in the command: Uganda
'The Salvation Army' in Kiswahili: Jeshi La Wokovu; in Luganda: Eje Liobulokozi
Languages in which the gospel is preached: English, Kiswahili, Luganda and a number of tribal languages

SALVATION Army work continues to expand in such a way that new areas have been reached and evangelised. Two districts were upgraded to division status; two new districts were opened; five societies became corps and 10 new units were opened.

The visit of Chief of the Staff Commissioner Robin Dunster (9-12 April 2009) for the Easter Congress began with the opening of a new three-storey Command Headquarters building. On Good Friday, Salvationists gathered in Kampala to remember Christ's crucifixion. A women's rally at Buwambingwa was attended by thousands of Home League members.

Tropical rain did not deter thousands of Salvationists tramping through mud on Easter Sunday morning to celebrate the Risen Lord at Bumbo. At the conclusion of the meeting crowds flocked to stand by a cross to pray. Growing respect for The Salvation Army in Uganda was shown by the presence of national and local government representatives.

The Orphans and Vulnerable Children (OVC) programme is strengthening communities as it meets the needs of OVCs and people affected by HIV/Aids. Community Action Team members, trainers and regional coordinators followed up on 600 food and nutrition initiatives.

Uganda Command

Uganda Salvationists were encouraged by the visit of a Partners In Mission team from Georgia Division (USA Southern) who visited the command during November 2008. Their ministry reached as far as some of the corps in rural areas.

Twenty-four members of the Ambassadors Of Holiness Session were welcomed as 'pioneer' cadets in the command's newly opened training college.

STATISTICS
Officers 61 (active 56 retired 4) **Envoys** 2
Corps leaders 94 **Cadets** 24 **Employees** 86
Corps 75 **Outposts and Outreach Centres** 18
Pre-primary Schools 2 **Day Care Centre** 1
Primary Schools 11 **Vocational Centres** 3
Institutions 3
Senior Soldiers 5,646 **Junior Soldiers** 6,512

STAFF
Women's Ministries: Lt-Col Sarah Wandulu (CPWM) Maj Rose Moriasi (CSWM) Maj Aidah Nabiswa (CCM)
Field: Maj Eliud Nabiswa
Finance: Capt Patrick Sithole
Projects: Maj Emmanuel Sichibona
Property: tba
Social Services: Maj Rose Moriasi (acting)
Statistics: Capt Jesline Sithole
Training: Maj Trustmore Muzorori
Youth: Maj Elizabeth Soita
   Candidates: Capt Jesline Sithole

DIVISION
Eastern: PO Box 168, Tororo; Majs Joseph and Alice Wandulu
Southern: PO Box 2012, Busia; Majs Bramwell and Margaret Simiyu
West: PO Box 73, Kigumba via Masindi; Majs Emmanuel and Irene Sichibona

DISTRICTS
Central: PO Box 11776, Kampala; Maj Peter Soita
Mbale: PO Box 2214, Mbale; Maj Moses Itwalume
Mulimani: c/o PO Box 168, Tororo; Capt Christine Ambenge

Sebei: c/o PO Box 2214, Mbale; Maj Esau Wekalao

SOCIAL SERVICES
Children's Home
Tororo: PO Box 48, Tororo; tel: 045-45244 (acc 54)

Community Centre
Kampala: PO Box 11776, Kampala; tel: 041-532517

Home for Children with Physically Disabilities
Home of Joy, PO Box 1186, Kampala; tel: 041-542409 (acc 30)

Vocational Training Workshops
Kampala (carpentry, catering, tailoring): PO Box 11776, Kampala
Lira (carpentry, tailoring, building): PO Box 13, Lira
Mbalala (carpentry, tailoring): PO Box 11776, Mbalala

PROJECTS
'Peace for African Child' (Education Programme)
PO Box 11776, Kampala

SAU-OVC Programme
HIV/Aids Education for Orphans and Vulnerable Children: PO Box 11776, Kampala; tel: 041-533113

WORTH Programme
Income Generation for Women: PO Box 2214, Mbale; tel: 045-79295

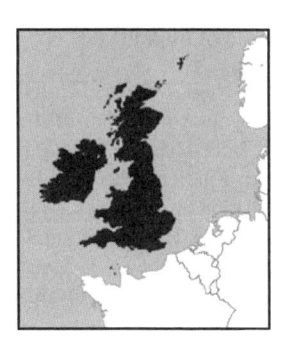

UNITED KINGDOM TERRITORY WITH THE REPUBLIC OF IRELAND

Territorial leaders:
Commissioners John and Elizabeth Matear

Territorial Commander:
Commissioner John Matear (2 Apr 2006)

Chief Secretary:
Colonel Brian Peddle (1 Jun 2009)

Territorial Headquarters: 101 Newington Causeway, London SE1 6BN, UK

Tel: [44] 20 7367 4500; email: thq@salvationarmy.org.uk;
website: www.salvationarmy.org.uk

The foundation of the territory dates from the earliest formation of The Salvation Army – prior to the adoption of that title in 1878 – when in July 1865 the Founder, William Booth, took charge of a mission to the East End of London. Certain UK corps were first established as Christian Mission stations.

Throughout the Army's history its work in this geographical area has been organised in a variety of forms and territories, but before 1990 these were all part of International Headquarters administration. However, on 1 November 1990 a restructuring occurred so that now the United Kingdom Territory is separate from International Headquarters and under a single command similar to that of the Army's other territories.

Zone: Europe
Countries included in the territory: Channel Islands, Isle of Man, Republic of Ireland, United Kingdom of Great Britain and Northern Ireland
Languages in which the gospel is preached: English, Korean, Urdu, Welsh
'The Salvation Army' in Welsh: Byddin Yr Iachawdwriaeth Cymru
Periodicals: *Kids Alive!*, *Salvationist*, *The War Cry*

IF public recognition were the criterion to judge achievement, then the territory claims some success. For example, in the ComRes Charity Awards (October 2008) it was voted by MPs and peers as having presented the Best Social, Religious or Family Campaign. In June 2008 it won nearly £50,000 through Spark – a nationwide social enterprise competition – which helped establish a commercial business for clients of its Employment Plus programme.

In April 2009 *Together* – a recording by the International Staff Band on the mainstream Universal label – was shortlisted for Best Album Of The Year in the Classical BRIT Awards.

Local programmes were honoured too. The Investors In People Award was given to Liverpool's Darbyshire House centre for the homeless in

February 2009, for instance, and in June 2008 The Haven Community Project in Portsmouth became the first-ever Salvation Army project to win the Queen's Award For Voluntary Service for its 'practical, innovative and hands-on approach to social needs'. That description could well apply to similar local programmes across the British Isles.

But awards tell little of the real story. The Army raised its voice in continued campaigning against human trafficking and unregulated gambling. It presented new research into causes of social exclusion and homelessness in its July 2008 report *The Seeds of Exclusion*, based on research in Salvation Army centres across the territory, and in October promoted a public symposium involving members of the Government and parliamentary opposition.

Salvationists attended the three main party conferences in the autumn of 2008, and joined the Put People First march ahead of the G20 summit in March 2009.

The effects of the 'credit crunch' on families could be measured in an increased number of debt management services operated from local corps. But in spite of the global recession, social programmes continued with support from the public.

The results of the 2007 Annual Appeal published in August 2008 showed more than £2.5 million raised, with 91p in every pound going directly to social and community work. Other fundraising schemes included the New Covent Garden Food Co dedicating its 'Soup of the Month' for December 2008 and a 'Soup Kitchen Challenge' to resettlement and nutrition programmes.

Meanwhile a new HostelPlus initiative scheme was launched in social services centres, with its first awards made in March 2009.

William Booth College awarded its first-ever degrees in pastoral care and psychology in October 2008, in partnership with Havering College. It is also expanding its distance-learning programme, including its officer training for cadets.

In February 2009 planning permission was received for the redevelopment of the William Booth College site at Denmark Hill, London. Once completed, the redevelopment will result in a 21st-century facility comprising an entirely upgraded and well-resourced worship, training and learning environment. Such investment confirms a strong commitment to the training and development of all involved in Salvation Army work and service.

A major change of size and style of *The War Cry* – 'the people's paper' – in January 2009 was universally welcomed. The book *God, the Big Bang and Bunsen Burning Issues*, based largely on *War Cry* interviews with eminent scientists, was published in the summer of 2008.

Below the radar of recognition God is working through faithful Salvationists and in mostly unsung situations to maintain and advance

United Kingdom Territory with the Republic of Ireland

his work throughout the territory. Some are in new or refurbished premises – in Aberdeen, Bedlington, Berwick, Birmingham, Chelmsford, Macclesfield and Romford, for example – while others are creating brand-new opportunities in places such as Gibbonsdown, South Wales, where youth programmes regularly attract government endorsement.

THE SALVATION ARMY TRUSTEE COMPANY
Registered Office: 101 Newington Causeway, London SE1 6BN

THE SALVATION ARMY (REPUBLIC OF IRELAND)
Registered Office: PO Box 2098, Lwr Abbey St, Dublin 1, Republic of Ireland

STATISTICS
Officers 2,717 (active 1,247 retired 1,470)
Cadets (1st Yr) 23 (2nd Yr) 37 (+19 distance learning cadets) **Employees** 4,890
Corps/Outreach Centres/New Plants 704
Social Services Centres 112 **Red Shield Defence Services Clubs** 28 **Mobile Units for Servicemen** 12
Senior Soldiers 31,575 **Adherents** 9,818 **Junior Soldiers** 5,022
Personnel serving outside territory Officers 76 Layworkers 8

STAFF
Women's Ministries: Comr Elizabeth Matear (TPWM) Col Rosalie Peddle (TSWM)

Asst Chief Sec: Lt-Col Sylvia Hinton
Asst Chief Sec: Lt-Col Roland Sewell (Special Services)
  Executive Sec to Territorial Leadership: Lt-Col Sylvia Hinton
  International Staff Band: B/M Dr Stephen Cobb
  International Staff Songsters: S/L Mrs Dorothy Nancekievill

Sec for Business Administration: Lt-Col David Hinton
  Asst Sec for Business Administration (Risk and Research): Mr David Rice
  Company Sec: Maj Alan Read
  Finance: Maj Alan Read
  Internal Audit: Mr Phil Goss
  Property: Mr Keith Manners
  Strategic Information: Mr Martyn Croft
  SAGIC: Mr John Mott
  Trade: Mr Trevor Caffull

Sec for Communications: Lt-Col Marion Drew
  Editor-in-Chief and Publishing Sec: Maj Christine Clement
    Editors: *Salvationist*: Maj Christine Clement *The War Cry*: Maj Nigel Bovey *Kids Alive!*: Mr Justin Reeves
  Head of Media: Cathy Le Feuvre
  Public Affairs Officer: Mr Tim Stone
  Territorial Ecumenical Officer: Maj John Read
  International Heritage Centre: Maj Stephen Grinsted (Director)
  Schools and Colleges Unit: Maj Stephen Grinsted (Director)
  Marketing and Fundraising: Mr Julius Wolff-Ingham

Sec for Personnel: Lt-Col George Pilkington
  Asst Sec for Personnel: Maj Angela Irving
  Asst Sec for Personnel (Development): Maj Carol Telfer
  Human Resources (Employees): Mr Ian Hammond
  Overseas Services Sec: Maj Pam Cameron
  Pastoral Care Unit: Maj Colin Cowdery
  Retired Officers Sec: Maj James Williams
  Safeguarding: Mr Dean Juster

Sec for Programme: Lt-Col Ian Barr
  Asst Sec for Programme: Maj Ivor Telfer
  Anti-Trafficking Response: Maj Anne Read
  Employment Plus: Lt-Col Roland Sewell
  Evangelism: Maj Paul Main
  Adult and Family Ministries: Majs John and Lorna Smith
  Children's and Youth Ministries: Majs Mark and Andrea Sawyer (ALOVE) Capt Janet Robson
  Mission Development Unit: Maj Noel Wright
  Music Ministries: B/M Dr Stephen Cobb
  International Development: Maj Mary Capsey
  Family Tracing: Lt-Col Mike Williams
  Research and Development: Mr Mitch Menagh
  Social Services: Maj Ray Irving (Director) Maj Jane Cowell (Deputy – Head of Operations)
    Compliance and Monitoring: Mrs Jacqui King (SAHA secondment)
      Homelessness Services: Mr Maff Potts

United Kingdom Territory with the Republic of Ireland

Older People's Services: Mrs Elaine Cobb
Red Shield Defence and Emergency Services: Maj Muriel McClenahan
Special Events: Mr Melvin Hart

WILLIAM BOOTH COLLEGE

Denmark Hill, London SE5 8BQ;
tel: (020) 7326 2700; fax: (020) 7326 2750
Principal: Maj Norman Ord
Directors of School for Officer Training:
  Training Programme: Capt Sheila Dunkinson
  Spiritual Programme: Capt Gordon Cotterill
Director of School for In-Service Training and Development: Maj Judith Payne
Territorial Candidates Director: Maj Mark Herbert

INTERNATIONAL HERITAGE CENTRE (including The William Booth Birthplace Museum, Nottingham) AND SCHOOLS AND COLLEGES UNIT

Denmark Hill, London SE5 8BQ;
tel: (020) 7737 3327;
email: heritage@salvationarmy.org.uk;
Director: Maj Stephen Grinsted

SCOTLAND SECRETARIAT

12a Dryden Rd, Loanhead, Midlothian EH20 9LZ; tel: (0131) 440 9100;
fax: (0131) 440 9111;
Scotland Sec: Lt-Col Alan Burns

DIVISIONS

Anglia: 2 Barton Way, Norwich NR1 1DL; tel: (01603) 724 400; fax: (01603) 724 411; Maj David Jackson (DC) Maj Irene Draycott (DDWM)

Central North: 80 Eccles New Rd, Salford, Gtr Manchester M5 4DU; tel: (0161) 743 3900; fax: (0161) 743 3911; Majs Melvyn and Kathleen Jones

Central South: 16c Cowley Rd, Uxbridge, Middlesex UB8 2LT; tel: (01895) 208800; fax: (01895) 208811; Maj Christine Bailey

East Midlands: Paisley Grove, Chilwell Meadows Business Park, Nottingham NG9 6DJ; tel: (0115) 983 5000; fax: (0115) 983 5011; Majs Jonathan and Jayne Roberts

East Scotland: 12a Dryden Rd, Loanhead, Midlothian EH20 9LZ; tel: (0131) 440 9100; fax: (0131) 440 9111; Lt-Cols Alan and Alison Burns

Ireland: 12 Station Mews, Sydenham, Belfast BT4 1TL; tel: (028) 9067 5000; fax: (028) 9067 5011; Majs Alan and Linda Watters

London Central: 1 Tiverton St, London SE1 6NT; tel: (020) 7378 1021; fax: (020) 7378 1026; Lt-Cols Michael and Joan Parker

London North-East: Maldon Rd, Hatfield Peverel, Chelmsford, Essex CM3 2HL; tel: (01245) 383 000; fax: (01245) 383 011; Maj Carol Bailey

London South-East: 1 East Court, Enterprise Rd, Maidstone, Kent ME15 6JF; tel: (01622) 775000; fax: (01622) 775011; Lt-Cols Anthony and Gillian Cotterill

North Scotland: Deer Rd, Woodside, Aberdeen AB24 2BL; tel: (01224) 496000; fax: (01224) 496011; Maj Martin Hill (DC) Maj Catherine Wyles (DDWM)

North-Western: 16 Faraday Rd, Wavertree Technology Park, Liverpool L13 1EH; tel: (0151) 252 6100; fax: (0151) 252 6111; Majs Michael and Lynn Highton

Northern: Balliol Business Park West, Newcastle upon Tyne NE12 8EW; tel: (0191) 238 1800; fax: (0191) 238 1811; Majs Melvin and Suzanne Fincham

South and Mid Wales: East Moors Rd, Ocean Park, Cardiff CF24 5SA; tel: (029) 2044 0600; fax: (029) 2044 0611; Majs Peter and Sandra Moran

South-Western: 6 Marlborough Court, Manaton Close, Matford Business Park, Exeter, Devon EX2 8PF; tel: (01392) 822100; fax: (01392) 822111; Majs Clifford and Jean Bradbury

Southern: 6-8 Little Park Farm Rd, Segensworth, Fareham, Hants PO15 5TD; tel: (01489) 566800; fax: (01489) 566811; Majs Neil and Christine Webb

West Midlands: 102 Unett St North, Hockley, Birmingham B19 3BZ; tel: (0121) 507 8500; fax: (0121) 507 8511; Maj Samuel Edgar (DC) Maj Amanda White (DDWM)

West Scotland: 4 Buchanan Court, Cumbernauld Rd, Stepps, Glasgow G33 6HZ; tel: (0141) 779 5000; fax: (0141) 779 5011; Majs Victor and Miriam Kennedy

Yorkshire: 1 Cadman Court, Hanley Rd, Morley, Leeds LS27 0RX; tel: (0113) 281 0100; fax: (0113) 281 0111; Lt-Cols William and Gillian Heeley

CONFERENCE CENTRES

Carfax: Bath BA2 4BS; tel: (01225) 462089
St Christopher's (small): 15 Sea Rd, Westgate-on-Sea, Kent; tel: (01932) 782196
Sunbury Court (incl Recreation Centre and Log

United Kingdom Territory with the Republic of Ireland

Cabin): Lwr Hampton Rd, Sunbury-on-Thames, Middlesex TW16 5PL; tel: (01932) 782196

CONFERENCE AND YOUTH CENTRE
Sunbury Court, Log Cabin and Recreational Centre: Lwr Hampton Rd, Sunbury-on-Thames, Middlesex TW16 5PL; tel: (01932) 782196

SELF-CATERING ACCOMMODATION
Caldew House: Sebergham, Cumbria; tel: (01225) 462089 (large house)
St Christopher's: Westgate-on-Sea, Kent; tel: (01932) 782196 (5 flats)
Sunbury Court, Log Cabin and Recreational Centre: Lower Hampton Rd, Sunbury-on-Thames, Middlesex TW16 5PL; tel: (01932) 782196

FAMILY TRACING SERVICE
101 Newington Causeway, London SE1 6BN; tel: (020) 7367 4747; fax: (020) 7367 4723

FARM
Hadleigh: Castle Lane, Hadleigh, Benfleet, Essex; tel: (01702) 558550

HOTELS
Bath: Carfax Hotel, Gt Pulteney St, Bath BA2 4BS; tel: (01225) 462089
Bournemouth: Cliff House, 13 Belle Vue Rd, Bournemouth, Dorset BH6 3DA; tel: (01202) 424701 (office); (01202) 425852 (guests)
Westgate-on-Sea: St Christopher's, 15 Sea Rd, Westgate-on-Sea, Kent CT8 8SA; tel: (01932) 782196

INSURANCE CORPORATION
The Salvation Army General Insurance Corporation Ltd, Faith House, 23-24 Lovat Lane, London EC3R 8EB; tel: 0845 634 0260; fax: 0845 634 0263

PASTORAL CARE UNIT
Administration (inc Trauma Care Programme): 101 Newington Causeway, London SE1 6BN; tel: (020) 7367 6580;
After-office hours mobile: 0779 699 1579
Counselling Services: 1 Water Lane, Stratford, London E15 4LU; tel: (020) 8536 5480; fax: (020) 8536 5489
Pastoral Support:
London Central, London North-East, UKT personnel departing/arriving from overseas; tel: (020) 7367 6580; mobile: 07796 991579

Central South, London South-East, Southern, South-Western; tel: (01895) 252794
Central North, North-Western, South and Mid Wales, West Midlands; tel: (01282) 697378
Northern, Yorkshire, East Midlands, Anglia: tel: (01924) 420407
Scotland and Ireland: tel: (01506) 854474
Director: Maj Colin Cowdery

TRADE (SP&S)
Head Office (and shop): 66-78 Denington Rd, Denington Industrial Estate, Wellingborough, Northants NN8 2QH; tel: (01933) 445445 (mail order); fax: (01933) 445415
Shop: 1 Tiverton St, London SE1 6NT

TRADING (SA TRADING CO LTD)
66-78 Denington Rd, Denington Industrial Estate, Wellingborough, Northants NN8 2QH
Textile Recycling Division:
    tel: (01933) 441086; fax: (01933) 445449; email: paul.ozanne@satradingco.org
Charity Shops Division:
    tel: (01933) 441807; fax: (01933) 442942; email: reception@satradingco.org

SOCIAL SERVICES DEPARTMENT
Centres for Older People
Bath: Smallcombe House, Bathwick Hill, BA2 6EJ; tel: (01225) 465694; fax: (01225) 465769 (acc men and women 31, sheltered flat 1)
Buxton: The Hawthorns, Burlington Rd, SK17 9AR; tel: (01298) 23700 (office) (01298) 28768 (residents); fax: (01298) 29761 (acc 34)
Coventry: Youell Court, Skipworth Rd, Binley CV3 2XA; tel: (024) 76561300; fax: (024) 76561306 (acc 40)
Edinburgh:
    Davidson House, 266 Colinton Rd, EH14 1DT; tel: (0131) 441 2117 (acc 40)
    Eagle Lodge, 488 Ferry Rd, EH5 2DL; tel: (0131) 551 1611; fax: (0131) 551 1644 (acc 32)
Glasgow: Eva Burrows Day Centre, Clyde Place, Halfway, Cambuslang G72 7QT; tel: (0141) 646 1461 (day centre places 112)
Hassocks: Villa Adastra, 79 Keymer Rd, BN6 8QH; tel: (01273) 842184 (office); (01273) 845299 (residents) (acc 40, day centre places 20)
Holywood: The Sir Samuel Kelly Memorial Home, 39 Bangor Rd, Co Down BT18 0NE; tel: (028) 9042 2293; fax: (028) 9042 7361 (acc 40)

United Kingdom Territory with the Republic of Ireland

London:
   Alver Bank, 17 West Rd, Clapham SW4 7DL;
     tel: (020) 7627 8061 (office)
     (020) 7498 0119 (residents) (acc 27)
   Glebe Court, 2 Blackheath Rise, Lewisham
     SE13 7PN; tel: (020) 8297 0637 (office)
     (020) 8463 0508 (residents);
     fax: (020) 8852 7298 (acc 42)
   Rookstone, Lawrie Park Cres, Sydenham
     SE26 6HH; tel: (020) 8778 0317 (office)
     (020) 8778 0314 (residents);
     fax: (020) 8778 0349 (acc 32)
North Walsham: Furze Hill House,
   73 Happisburgh Rd, NR28 9HD;
   tel: 01692 502703 (acc 40, day centre
   places 22)
Nottingham: Notintone House, Sneinton Rd,
   NG2 4QL; tel: (0115) 950 3788 (office)
   (0115) 950 2060 (public call box) (acc 40)
Prestwich: Holt House, Headlands Dr, Hilton
   Lane, Gtr Manchester M25 9YF;
   tel: (0161) 773 0220 (office)
   (0161) 798 5843 (residents);
   fax: (0161) 798 6428 (acc 32)
Sandridge: Lyndon, 2 High St, Sandridge, St
   Albans AL4 9DH; tel: (01727) 851050 (office)
   (01727) 837741 (residents) (acc 32)
Southend-on-Sea: Bradbury Home, 2 Roots Hall
   Drive, SS2 6DA; tel: (01702) 435838 (acc 34)
Tunbridge Wells: Sunset Lodge, Pembury Rd,
   TN2 3QT; tel: (01892) 530861 (office)
   (01892) 533769 (residents) (acc 27)
Weston-super-Mare: Dewdown House,
   64 Beach Rd, BS23 4BE; tel: (01934) 417125
   (acc 40)

Centres for Families (Residential)

Belfast:
   Glen Alva, 19 Cliftonville Rd, BT14 6JN;
     tel: (028) 9035 1185 (acc family units 20,
     max 77 residents)
   Thorndale Parenting Assessment/Family Centre,
     Duncairn Ave, Antrim Rd, BT14 6BP;
     tel: (028) 9035 1900 (acc family units 34,
     single bedsits 4, max 125 residents)
Leeds: Mount Cross, 139 Broad Lane,
   Bramley LS13 2JP; tel: (0113) 257 0810
   (acc flats 28, max 78 residents)
Portsmouth: Catherine Booth House, 23 St Paul's
   Rd, Southsea PO5 4AE; tel: (023) 9273 7226
   (acc family units 21, max 40 residents)

Refuge from Domestic Abuse (women with children)

Birmingham: Shepherd's Green House; address
   and telephone confidential; contact via West
   Midlands DHQ (acc 16 families, 4 single
   women, max 83 residents)

Centres for People with Learning Difficulties

Kilbirnie: George Steven Centre, Craigton Rd,
   KA25 6LJ
Plymouth: Pilgrim House, Courtfield Rd,
   PL3 5BB; tel: (01752) 823435
Stoke: Lovatt Court, Lovatt St, Stoke-on-Trent
   ST4 7RL; tel: (01782) 415621

Centres for the Single Homeless

Accrington: Accrington Crossroads, Empress St,
   BB5 1SG; tel: (01254) 389157 (acc 11)
Belfast:
   Centenary House, 2 Victoria St, BT1 3GG;
     tel: (02890) 320320 (acc direct access 80)
   Calder Fountain (attached to Centenary House)
     (registered care 28, resettlement 12)
Birmingham: William Booth Centre,
   72 Shadwell St, B4 6HA; tel: (0121) 236 6554;
   fax: (0121) 236 7135 (acc 74)
Blackburn: Bramwell House, Heaton St,
   BB2 2EF; tel: (01254) 677338 (acc 54)
Bradford: Lawley House, 371 Leeds Rd,
   BD3 9NG; tel: (01274) 731221 (acc direct
   access 51, resettlement 12)
Braintree: New Direction Centre, David
   Blackwell House, 25-27 Bocking End,
   CM7 9AE; tel: (01376) 553373 (acc 14)
Bristol: Logos House, Wade St, BS2 9EL;
   tel: (0117) 955 2821 (acc 69)
Cardiff: Ty Gobaith, 240 Bute St, CF1 5TY;
   tel: (029) 2048 0187 (acc 50)
Cardiff: Northlands, 202 North Rd, CF4 3XP;
   tel: (029) 2061 9077 (acc 26)
Coventry: 1 Lincoln St, CV1 4JN;
   tel: (024) 7625 1437 (acc 99)
Darlington: Tom Raine Court, Coburg St,
   DL1 1SB; tel: (01325) 489242 (acc 37)
Dublin: Granby Centre, 9-10 Granby Row,
   Dublin 1, Eire; tel: [353] (1) 872 5500
   (acc units 106)
Dundee:
   Strathmore Lodge, 31 Ward Rd, DD1 1NG;
     tel: (01382) 225448 (acc 39)
   Burnside Mill, Milnes East Wynd, DD1 5BA
     (acc 20)
Edinburgh:
   Ashbrook, 492 Ferry Rd, EH5 2DL;
     tel: (0131) 552 5705 (acc 24)
   The Pleasance, EH8 9UE; tel: (0131) 556 9674
     (acc 37)
Glasgow:
   Hope House, 14 Clyde St, G1 5JH;

United Kingdom Territory with the Republic of Ireland

tel: (0141) 552 0537 (acc 98)
Wallace of Campsie House, 30 East
Campbell St, G1 5DT; tel: (0141) 552 4301;
fax: (0141) 552 7856 (acc 52)
William Hunter House, 70 Oxford St, G5 9EP;
tel: (0141) 429 5201 (acc 43)
Grimsby: Brighowgate, DN32 0QW;
tel: (01472) 242648 (acc 46)
Hull: William Booth House, 2 Hessle Rd,
HU1 2QQ; tel: (01482) 225521 (acc 113)
Huntingdon: Kings Ripton Court, Kings
Ripton Rd, PE17 2NZ; tel: (01480) 423800
(acc 36)
Ipswich: Lyndon House, 107 Fore St, IP4 1JZ;
tel: (01473) 251070 (acc 39)
Isle of Man: David Gray House, 6 Drury Tce,
Douglas, IM2 3HY; tel: (01624) 662814
(acc 4)
Leamington Spa: Eden Villa, 13 Charlotte St,
CV31 3EB; tel: (01926) 450708 (acc 11)
Liverpool:
Ann Fowler House, Fraser St, L3 8JX;
tel: (0151) 207 3815 (acc 38)
Darbyshire House, 380 Prescot Rd, L13 3DA;
tel: (0151) 228 0925 (acc 45)
London:
David Barker House, Blackfriars Rd, SE1
(acc 40)
Booth House, 153-157 Whitechapel Rd,
E1 1DF; tel: (020) 7392 9490 (acc 150)
Cambria House, 37 Hunter St, WC1N 1BJ;
tel: (020) 7841 0230; fax: (020) 7841 0239
(acc 48)
Edith Road, 10-12 Edith Rd, Hammersmith,
W14 9BA; tel: (020) 7603 1692 (acc 25)
Edward Alsop Court, 18 Great Peter St,
Westminster, SW1 2BT;
tel: (020) 7233 0296 (acc 108)
Hopetown, 60 Old Montague St, Whitechapel,
E1 5LF; tel: (020) 7539 9240;
fax: (020) 7539 3810 (acc 116)
Riverside House, 20 Garford St, West India
Dock Rd, E14 8JG; tel: (020) 7068 0950;
fax: (020) 7068 0959 (acc 20)
Manchester: 1 Wilmott St, Chorlton-on-Medlock,
M15 6BD; tel: (0161) 236 7537 (acc 113)
Newcastle upon Tyne:
39 City Rd, NE1 2BR; tel: (0191) 233 9150
(acc 66)
Cedar House, Denmark St, Byker, NE6 2UH;
tel: (0191) 224 1509 (acc direct access 18,
resettlement flats 6)
Nottingham:
Acorn Lodge, Campbell St, NG3 1GZ (acc 12)
Sneinton House, 2 Boston St, NG1 1ED;
tel: (0115) 950 4364 (acc 70)

Perth: 16 Skinnergate, PH1 5JH;
tel: (01738) 624360 (acc 36)
Plymouth: Devonport House and Zion House,
Park Ave, PL1 4BA;
tel: (01752) 562170/564545 (acc 72)
Reading: Willow House, Willow St, RG1 6AB;
tel: (0118) 959 0681 (acc 38)
Rochdale: Providence House, High St, OL12 0NT;
tel: (01706) 645151 (acc 73)
St Helens: Salisbury House, Parr St, WA9 1JU;
tel: (01744) 744800 (acc 68)
Salford: James St (off Oldfield Rd), M3 5HP;
tel: (0161) 831 7020/7040 (acc 38)
Sheffield: 161 Fitzwilliam St; Office and postal
address: 126 Charter Row, S1 4HK;
tel: (0114) 272 5158 (acc 51)
Skegness: Witham Lodge, Alexandra Rd,
PE25 3TL; tel: (01754) 899151 (acc 30)
Southampton: The Booth Centre, 57 Oxford St,
SO14 3DL
Stoke-on-Trent: Vale St, ST4 7RN;
tel: (01782) 744374 (acc 64 + 4 training
flats)
Sunderland: Swan Lodge, High St East, SR1 2AU;
tel: (0191) 565 5411 (acc 65)
Swindon: Booth House, 1 Spring Close, SN1 2BF;
tel: (01793) 401830 (acc 50)
Warrington: James Lee House, Brick St, Howley,
WA1 2PD; tel: (01925) 636496 (acc 54)

Children's Homes/Centres (Residential)
Dublin:
Lefroy Night Light, 12-14 Eden Quay,
Dublin 1, Eire; tel: [353] (1) 874 3762
(acc 7 overnight emergency beds)
Lefroy Support Flats, 12-14 Eden Quay,
Dublin 1, Eire; tel: [353] (1) 874 3762
(acc 7)
Leeds: Spring Grove, 139 Broad Lane,
Bramley, LS13 2JP; tel: (0113) 257 7552
(acc 6 female care leavers)
London: The Haven, Springfield Rd, SE26 6HG;
tel: (020) 8659 4033/4 (acc 12)

**Day Care, Early Years Education and
Contact Centres for Children**
Bath: The Mews Nursery, The Mews Out of
School Club and Green Park Out of School
Club, Carfax Hotel, Henrietta Mews,
BA2 6LR; tel: (01225) 332 593
(registered for 88 total)
Birmingham: Sally Ann's Pre-School and
Out of School Club @ Elmwood Church,
45 Hamstead Hill, B20 1BU;
tel: (0121) 523 734 (registered for 64 total)
Leeds: Copper Beech Day Nursery and

United Kingdom Territory with the Republic of Ireland

Rainbow After-School Club, 137 Broad Lane, Bramley, LS13 2JP; tel: (0113) 256 5820 (registered for 84 total)

There are a further 5 Day Nurseries, 23 Pre-schools/ Playgroups, 2 Crèches, 10 Out-of-School Clubs and 8 Child Contact Centres attached to social centres and corps

Domiciliary Care (elderly)
Community Care Service (Angus): Chapel St, Forfar, DD8 2AB; tel: (01307) 469574

Drop In Centres
Edinburgh: 25 Niddry St, Edinburgh EH1 1LG
Glasgow: Laurieston Centre, 39 South Portland St, G5 9JL; tel: (0141) 429 6533
London: 97 Rochester Row, SW1P 1LJ; tel: (020) 7233 9862
Norwich: Pottergate Arc, 28 Pottergate, NR2 1DX; tel: (01603) 663496
Southampton: H2O Project, Princess St, Northam, SO14 5RP; tel: (023) 8022 4632

Employment Training Centre
Hadleigh: Castle Lane, Hadleigh, Benfleet, Essex SS7 2AP; tel: (01702) 552963

Night Shelter
Dublin: Cedar House, Marlborough Pl, Dublin 2, Eire; tel: [353] (1) 873 1241 (acc 48)

Outreach Teams
Bristol: Logos House, Bridge Project, Little George St, BS2 9EL; tel: (0117) 955 2821
Cardiff: Bus Project, Ty Gobiath, 240 Bute St, CF1 5TY; tel: (029) 2048 0187
London: Faith House, 11 Argyle St, King's Cross, WC1H 8EJ; tel: (020) 7837 5149
York: Homeless Prevention/Resettlement, Gillygate, YO31 7EA; tel: (01904) 630470

Prison Ministries
Prison Ministries Officer, 101 Newington Causeway, London SE1 6BN; tel: (020) 7367 4866

Probation Hostel
Isle of Man: David Gray House, 6 Drury Tce, Douglas, IM2 3HY; tel: (01624) 662814 (acc 9)

Red Shield Services
UK THQ: 101 Newington Causeway, London SE1 6BN; tel: (020) 7367 4851
HQ Germany: SAHQ/CVWW, Block 1, NAAFI Complex, BFPO 15; tel: [49] (5221) 24627

Sheltered Housing
London: Alver Bank, 17 West Rd, Clapham, SW4 7DL; tel: (020) 7627 8061 (acc single 6, double 2)
Tunbridge Wells: Charles Court, Pembury Rd, TN2 3QY; tel: (01892) 547439 (acc single 9, double 8)

Addiction Service
Bristol: Bridge Project, Little George St, BS2 9EL; tel: (0117) 935 1255 (acc 24)
Cardiff: Bridge Project, Ty Gobiath, 240 Bute St, CF1 5TY; tel: (029) 2048 0187 (acc 23)
Dublin: York House, Alcohol Recovery Unit (inc short-term intervention), Longford St Little, Dublin 2, Rep of Ireland; tel: (00 353-1) 476 3337 (acc 24)
Highworth: Gloucester House (Residential Rehabilitation Centre), 6 High St, Swindon, SN6 7AG; tel: (01793) 762365 (acc 12, halfway house 3, day programme 4)
London:
  Greig House, 20 Garford St, West India Dock Rd, E14 8JG; tel: (020) 7987 5658 (acc 25)
  Riverside House 'Specialist' Homeless Centre for People with Addiction Issues, 20 Garford St, West India Dock Rd, E14 8JG; tel: (020) 7068 0950 (acc 31)
  Riverside House Harbour Recovery Project (inc detoxification), 20 Garford St, West India Dock Rd, E14 8JG; tel:(020) 7068 0950 (acc 8)
Stirling: Harm Reduction Service, SA Hall, Drip Rd, FK8 1RA; tel: (01786) 448923

Offering Hope to Trafficked Women
The Jarrett Community

Biomedical Services
Biomedical Support Services are provided across social work disciplines in partnership with the University of Kent, Canterbury

THE UNITED STATES OF AMERICA

National leaders:
Commissioners Israel L. and Eva D. Gaither

National Commander:
Commissioner Israel L. Gaither (1 May 2006)

National Chief Secretary:
Colonel David Jeffrey (1 Jul 2007)

National Headquarters: 615 Slaters Lane, PO Box 269, Alexandria, VA 22313-0269, USA

Tel: [1] (703) 684 5500; fax: [1] (703) 684 3478; website: www.salvationarmyusa.org

The Salvation Army began its ministry in the United States in October 1879. Lieutenant Eliza Shirley left England to join her parents who had migrated to America in search of work. She held meetings that were so successful that General William Booth sent Commissioner George Scott Railton and seven women officers to the United States in March 1880 to formalise the effort. Their initial street meeting was held on the dockside at Battery Park in New York City the day they arrived.

In only three years, operations had expanded into California, Connecticut, Indiana, Kentucky, Maryland, Massachusetts, Michigan, Missouri, New Jersey, New York, Ohio and Pennsylvania. Family services, youth services, elderly services and disaster services are among the many programmes offered in local communities throughout the United States, in Puerto Rico, the Virgin Islands, the Marshall Islands and Guam.

The National Headquarters was incorporated as a religious and charitable corporation in the State of New Jersey in 1982 as 'The Salvation Army National Corporation' and is qualified to conduct its affairs in the Commonwealth of Virginia.

Zone: Americas and Caribbean
Periodicals: *The War Cry*, *Women's Ministries Resources*, *Word & Deed – A Journal of Theology and Ministry*, *Young Salvationist*

SALVATIONISTS continue to serve throughout America with passion and integrity. A recent survey revealed 84 per cent of Americans believe The Salvation Army is the nation's most productive non-profit organisation.

Individuals and corps are reaching people for Christ in creative ways and engaging them in salvation warfare. Since the 'Come, Join Our Army' campaign was launched in June 2007, almost 11,500 new senior and junior soldiers have been enrolled.

The National Commander was the commencement speaker at Taylor University in Upland, Indiana, when he was bestowed an Honorary Doctorate of Divinity in recognition of his extensive career in practical evangelical ministry. Commissioner Israel L. Gaither challenged students to 'show up' spiritually and evangelically as they take their new degrees out into the world of business and seek to develop their careers.

In a year of severe economic recession the American public responded to the annual Red Kettle

USA National

American boy band Jonas Brothers and Mr Jerry Jones (owner of the Dallas Cowboys and chair of The Salvation Army Christmas campaign) join the USA National Commander to kick off the 12th annual Kettle Appeal

Appeal by donating more than $130 million. This represents an all-time national record of giving for the campaign and a $12 million increase on the previous year.

The campaign was chaired by Mr Jerry Jones, owner of the Dallas Cowboys, and he hosted the 12th annual national kettle kick-off event at Texas Stadium on Thanksgiving Day. The Jonas Brothers' half-time show entertainment generated new levels of media and public interest.

The National Advisory Board, under the leadership of Chairman Rob Pace (Goldman Sachs), continued its progressive work on a national strategic plan to deepen the impact of the Army's mission in America.

NATIONAL STATISTICS
(incorporating all USA territories)
Officers 5,348 (active 3,443 retired 1,905) **Cadets** (1st Yr) 141 (2nd Yr) 121 **Employees** 62,746
Corps 1,252 **Outposts** 24 **Institutions** 790
Senior Soldiers 82,012 **Adherents** 15,837 **Junior Soldiers** 24,902

STATISTICS
(National Headquarters)
Officers (active) 28 **Employees** 64 **SAWSO Employees** 16

STAFF
Women's Ministries: Comr Eva D. Gaither (NPWM); tel: (703) 684 5503; Col Barbara Jeffrey (NSWM, NRVAVS); tel: (703) 684 5504
Asst Nat Chief Sec: Maj Joan Canning; tel: (703) 684 5508
Nat Treasurer and Nat Sec for Business Administration: Lt-Col Gary W. Haupt; tel: (703) 684 5507
Nat Financial Sec: Maj Randall W. Sjogren; tel: (703) 684 5155; fax: (703) 519 5887
Nat Sec for Personnel: Lt-Col Suzanne H. Haupt; tel: (703) 684 5512
Nat Sec for Programme: Lt-Col Mark Israel; tel: (703) 684 5527; fax: (703) 519 5880
Nat Social Services Sec: Maj Betty A. Israel; tel: (703) 684 5533; fax: (703) 519 5889
Nat Community Relations and Development Sec: Maj George Hood; tel: (703) 684 5526; fax: (703) 684 5538
Nat Editor-in-Chief and Literary Sec: Maj Edward Forster; tel: (703) 684 5523; fax: (703) 684 5539
Salvation Army World Service Office (SAWSO): Lt-Col Daniel L. Starrett, jr; tel: (703) 684-5524; fax: (703) 684 5536

ARCHIVES AND RESEARCH CENTRE
Email: Archives@usn.salvationarmy.org

USA CENTRAL TERRITORY

Territorial leaders:
Commissioners Barry C. and E. Sue Swanson

Territorial Commander:
Commissioner Barry C. Swanson
(1 Oct 2008)

Chief Secretary:
Colonel Paul R. Seiler (1 Jul 2006)

Territorial Headquarters: 10 W Algonquin Rd, Des Plaines, IL 60016-6006, USA

Tel: [1] (847) 294-2000; fax: [1] (847) 294-2295; website: www.usc.salvationarmy.org

The Salvation Army was incorporated as a religious and charitable corporation in the State of Illinois in 1913 as 'The Salvation Army' and is qualified to conduct its affairs in all of the states of the territory.

Zone: Americas and Caribbean
USA states included in the territory: Illinois, Indiana, Iowa, Kansas, Michigan, Minnesota, Missouri, Nebraska, North Dakota, South Dakota, Wisconsin
'The Salvation Army' in Spanish: Ejército de Salvación; in Swedish: Frälsningsarmén
Languages in which the gospel is preached: English, Korean, Laotian, Russian, Spanish, Swedish
Periodical: *Central Connection*

THE second year of the 'Come, Join Our Army' initiative in the territory produced much fruit. Each monthly issue of the territorial publication *Central Connection* reported corps and centres blossoming with new enrolments – almost 800 senior soldiers, more than 600 junior soldiers and nearly 300 adherents.

A territorial writers' conference – 'Right Here, Write Now' – in May 2008 attracted nearly 100 delegates who learned from a variety of writing and publishing professionals.

The next month, 'iConnect' was held in conjunction with commissioning weekend to help 2,300 attendees personally connect with the Army mission. Centralites learned they had raised a record $7.1 million for World Services.

Commissioner Ken Baillie (then Territorial Commander) ordained, commissioned and appointed 22 officers of the God's Fellow-Workers Session. The commissioner's message and appeal resulted in almost 300 seekers at the mercy seat.

Forty adults on four week-long Global Mission teams renovated

Salvation Army facilities in Chile and Jamaica in 2008, while 39 young adults served on summer teams in Malawi, Moldova/Russia, Peru, South Africa, Spain, the Bahamas and the Central Territory.

The annual Central Bible and Leadership Institute in July 2008 gathered 550 campers and featured Dr Roger Green. A month later, the Central Music Institute attracted 303 campers from all divisions, other US territories, South America, Sweden and the UK. The Territorial Music and Gospel Arts Department developed two worship series on personal finances and staying pure – *Good $ense* and *Risk It*.

In October 2008 the territory welcomed back home Commissioners Barry and Sue Swanson as territorial leaders, succeeding Commissioners Ken and Joy Baillie, who retired the previous month. National leaders Commissioners Israel L. and Eva D. Gaither conducted the Baillies' retirement after welcoming 30 cadets of the Prayer Warriors Session the night before.

A few weeks later the Gaithers installed the Swansons who – in support of 'Come, Join Our Army' – had two new soldiers as flag-bearers.

In January 2009 the TC called a Territorial Economic Summit at which 64 delegates strategised more-efficient mission and service delivery, cost containment and revenue generation.

As resources tightened during the national recession, requests for services increased dramatically. Many people seeking help had never before needed assistance. While challenging, it presented endless opportunities to show God's love in practical ways.

Many social services programmes continued to achieve certification. Caring Partners Adult Day Care in Rochester, Minnesota, received the territorial award for programme excellence.

The TC also designated youth ministry a top priority in 2009. The annual 're:Generation' conference in February drew more than 250 delegates and encouraged young adults to pursue intentional, mission-driven lives.

Progress continued on Ray and Joan Kroc corps community centres throughout the territory. Groundbreaking for the centre at Grand Rapids, Michigan, took place in October 2008 and construction in Omaha, Nebraska, neared completion.

Year-round, the territory's Emergency Disaster Services (EDS) teams provided relief, comfort and hope in response to floods, blizzards, tornadoes and severe storms. Half the states within the territory dealt with historic flooding during summer and fall 2008; the EDS response was substantial, from massive feeding and clean-up services to long-term support.

STATISTICS
Officers 1,177 (active 755 retired 434) **Cadets** (1st Yr) 30 (2nd Yr) 15 **Employees** 8,158 **Corps** 272 **Institutions** 172

USA Central Territory

Senior Soldiers 16,637 **Adherents** 2,560 **Junior Soldiers** 3,660
Personnel serving outside territory Officers 35

STAFF
Women's Ministries: Comr E. Sue Swanson (TPWM) Col Carol Seiler (TSWM) Maj Dorene Jennings (TCCMS)
Personnel: Lt-Col James Nauta
Programme: Lt-Col Richard E. Vander Weele
Business: Lt-Col Merle Heatwole
Adult Rehabilitation Centres: Maj Graham Allan
Audit: Maj David Clark
Candidates: Lt-Col Dawn Heatwole
Community Relations and Development: Maj John Wilkins
Corps Mission and Adult Ministries: Maj Joseph Wheeler
Evangelism and Corps Growth: Capt Carol J. Lewis
Finance: Maj Robert Doliber
Information Technology: Mr Ronald E. Shoults
Legal and Legacy: Maj James C. Hoskin
Multicultural Ministries: Maj Mary Hammerly
Music and Gospel Arts: B/M William F. Himes, jr, OF
Pastoral Care Officers: Majs Larry and Margo Thorson
Property: Maj Cheryl Lawry
Resource and Development: Lt-Col Janice Nauta
Resource Connection Dept: Mr Robert Jones
Risk Management: Maj Norman R. Nonnweiler
Social Services: Maj Geoffrey Allan
Training: Maj Paul Fleeman
Youth: Maj Gail Aho

DIVISIONS
Eastern Michigan: 16130 Northland Dr, Southfield, MI 48075-5218; tel: (248) 443-5500; Lt-Cols Norman S. and Diane Marshall
Heartland: 401 NE Adams St, Peoria, IL 61603-4201; tel: (309) 655-7220; Majs Charles and Sharon Smith
Indiana: 3100 N Meridian St, Indianapolis, IN 46208-4718; tel: (317) 937-7000; Majs Richard and Vicki Amick
Kansas and Western Missouri: 3637 Broadway, Kansas City, MO 64111-2503; tel: (816) 756-1455; Majs Jeffrey and Dorothy Smith
Metropolitan: 5040 N Pulaski Rd, Chicago, IL 60630-2788; tel: (773) 725-1100; Lt-Cols David E. and Sherry Grindle
Midland: 1130 Hampton Ave, St Louis, MO 63139-3147; tel: (314) 646-3000; Majs Lonneal and Patty Richardson
Northern: 2445 Prior Ave, Roseville, MN 55113-2714; tel: (651) 746-3400; Lt-Cols Daniel and Rebecca Sjogren
Western: 3612 Cuming St, Omaha, NE 68131-1900; tel: (402) 898-5900; Majs Paul and Renea Smith
Western Michigan and Northern Indiana: 1215 E Fulton, Grand Rapids, MI 49503-3849; tel: (616) 459-3433; Majs Ralph and Susan Bukiewicz
Wisconsin and Upper Michigan: 11315 W Watertown Plank Rd, Wauwatosa, WI 53226-0019; tel: (414) 302-4300; Majs Robert E. and Nancy Thomson, jr

COLLEGE FOR OFFICER TRAINING
700 W Brompton Ave, Chicago, IL 60657-1831; tel: (773) 524-2000

UNDER THQ
Conference Centre
10 W Algonquin, Des Plaines, IL 60016-6006

SOCIAL SERVICES
Adult Rehabilitation Centres
Chicago (Central), IL 506: N Des Plaines St; tel: (312) 738-4367 (acc 200)
Chicago (North Side), IL 60614: 2258 N Clybourn Ave; tel: (773) 477-1771 (acc 135)
Davenport (River Valley), IA 52806: 4001 N Brady St; tel: (563) 323-2748 (acc 96)
Des Moines, IA 50309-4897: 133 E 2nd St; tel: (515) 243-4277 (acc 58)
Flint, MI 48506: 2200 N Dort Highway; tel: (810) 234-2678 (acc 121)
Fort Wayne, IN 46802: 427 W Washington Blvd; tel: (260) 424-1655 (acc 75)
Gary, IN 46402: 1351 W 11th Ave; tel: (219) 882-9377 (acc 110)
Grand Rapids, MI 49507-1601: 1491 S Division Ave; tel: (616) 452-3133 (acc 126)
Indianapolis, IN 46202-3915: 711 E Washington St; tel: (317) 638-6585 (acc 97)
Kansas City, MO 64106: 1351 E 10th St; tel: (816) 421-5434 (acc 132)
Milwaukee, WI 53202-5999: 324 N Jackson St; tel: (414) 276-4316 (acc 100)
Minneapolis, MN 55401-1039: 900 N 4th St; tel: (612) 332-5855 (acc 125)
Omaha, NE 68131-2642: 2551 Dodge St; tel: (402) 342-4135 (acc 95)

USA Central Territory

Rockford, IL 61104-7385: 1706 18th Ave;
  tel: (815) 397-0440 (acc 76)
Romulus, MI 48174-4205: 5931 Middlebelt;
  tel: (734) 729-3939 (acc 111)
St Louis, MO 63108-3211: 3949 Forest Park
  Ave; tel: (314) 535-0057 (acc 102)
South Bend, IN 46601-2226: 510-18 S Main St;
  tel: (574) 288-2539 (acc 63)
Southeast, MI:
  Main Campus: 1627 W Fort St, Detroit,
    MI 48216; tel: (313) 965-7760;
    toll-free: (866) GIVE-TOO
  North Campus: 118 W Lawrence, Pontiac,
    MI 48341; tel: (248) 338-9601 (acc 360)
Springfield, IL 62703-1003: 221 N 11th St;
  tel: (217) 528-7573 (acc 89)
Waukegan, IL 60085-6511: 431 S Genesee St;
  tel: (847) 662-7730 (acc 100)

UNDER DIVISIONS
Emergency Lodges
Alton, IL 62002: 525 Alby
Alton, IL 62002: 14-16 E 5th St
Ann Arbor, MI 48108: 3660 Packard Rd
Appleton, WI 54914: 124 E North St
Belleville, IL 62226: 4102 W Main St
Benton Harbor, MI 49022: 645 Pipestone St
Bloomington, IL 61701: 601 W Washinton St
Champaign, IL 61820: 2212 N Market St
Chicago, IL 60640: 800 W Lawrence
Columbia, MO 65203: 602 N Ann St
Davenport, IA 52803-5101: 301-307 W 6th St
Decatur, IL 62525: 229 W Main St
Detroit, MI 48208-2517: 3737 Humboldt
Detroit, MI 48208-2517: 3737 Lawton
Grand Island, NE 68801-5828; 818 W 3rd St
Grand Rapids, MI 49503: 143 Lakeside Dr SE
Hutchinson, KS 67504-0310: 200 S Main
Independence, MO 64050-2664: 14704 E
  Truman Rd
Indianapolis, IN 46204: 540 N Alabama St
Iron Mountain, MI 49801: 114 W Brown St
Jefferson City, MO 65101: 907 Jefferson St
Kankakee, IL 60901: 148 N Harrison
Kankakee, IL 60901: 541 E Court Ave
Kansas City, KS 66102: 6721 State Ave
Kansas City, MO 64127: 6935 Bell Rd
LaCrosse, WI 54601: 223 N 8th St
Lafayette, IN 47904-1934: 1110 Union St
Lawrence, KS 66044: 946 New Hampshire St
Madison, WI 53703: E 630 Washington Ave E
Mankato, MN 56001-2338: 700 S Riverfront Dr
Milwaukee, WI 53205: 1730 N 7th St
Monroe, MI 48161: 815 E 1st St
O'Fallon, MO 63366-2938: 1 William Booth Dr
Olathe, KS 66061: 400-402 E Santa Fe

Omaha, NE 68131: 3612 Cuming St
Peoria, IL 61603: 417 NE Adams St
Peoria, IL 61603; 414 NE Jefferson St
Quincy, IL 62301: 400 Broadway
Rockford, IL 61104: 1706 18th Ave E
St Cloud, MN 56304: 400 Highway 10
St Joseph, MO 64501: 618 S 6th St
St Louis, MO 63132: 10740 W Page Ave
Sheboygan, WI 53081: 710 Pennsylvania Ave
Sioux Falls, SD 57103-0128: 800 N Cliff Ave
Somerset, WI 54025: 203 Church Hill Rd
Springfield, IL 62701: 100 N 9th St
Springfield, MO 65802: 636 N Boonville
Warren, MI 48091: 24140 Mound Rd
Waterloo, IA 50703: 218 Logan Ave
Waterloo, IA 50703: 229 Logan Ave
Waterloo, IA 50703: 603 S Hanchett Rd
Waukesha, WI 53188: 445 Madison St
Wichita, KS 67202-2010: 350 N Market

Senior Citizens' Residences
Chicago, IL 60607: 1500 W Madison
Columbus, IN 47201: 300 Gladstone Ave
Grandview, MO 64030: 6111 E 129th St
Indianapolis, IN 46254-2738: 4390 N High
  School Rd
Kansas City, KS 66112: 1331 N 75th St
Minneapolis, MN 55403-2116: 1421 Yale Pl
Oak Creek, WI 53154: 150 W Centennial Dr
Oak Creek, WI 53154: 180 W Centennial Dr
Omaha, NE 68131: 923 38th St
St Louis, MO 63118: 3133 Iowa St

Harbour-Light Centres
Chicago, IL 60607: 1515 W Monroe St;
  tel: (312) 421-5753
Clinton Township, MI 48043: 42590 Stepnitz
Detroit, MI 48201: 3737 Lawton;
  tel. (313) 361-6136
Indianapolis, IN 46222: 2400 N Tibbs Ave;
  tel: (317) 972-1450
Kansas City, KS 66102: 6721 State Ave;
  tel: (913) 232-5400
Minneapolis, MN 55403: 1010 Currie;
  tel: (612) 338-0113
Monroe, MI 48161: 3580 S Custer
St Louis, MO 63188: 3010 Washington Ave

Substance Abuse Centres
Detroit, MI 48216: 3737 Humboldt
Grand Rapids, MI 49503: 72 Sheldon Blvd SE:
  tel: (616) 742-0351
Kansas City, MO 64127: 5100 E 24th;
  tel: (816) 483-3679
Minneapolis, MN 55403: 1010 Currie Ave;
  tel: (612) 338-0113

USA Central Territory

Transitional Housing
Appleton, WI 54914: 105 S Badger Ave
Champaign, IL 61820: 502 N Prospect
Cheboygan, MI 49712: 444 S Main St
Duluth, MN 55806: 215 S 27th Ave W
Grand Rapids, MI 49503: 1215 E Fulton St
Green Bay, WI 54301: 626 Union Ct
Jefferson City, MO 65101: 907 Jefferson St
Joplin, MO 64801: 320 E 8th St
Kansas City, KS 66102: 6723 State Ave
Kansas City, MO 64111: 101 W Linwood Blvd
Kansas City, MO 64127: 6935 Bell Rd
Lawrence, KS 66044: 946 New Hampshire
Minneapolis, MN 55403: 1010 Currie
New Albany, IN 47151: 2300 Green Valley Rd
Olathe, KS 66061: 400 E Santa Fe
Omaha, NE 68131: 3612 Cuming St
Pekin, IL 61554: 243 Derby R
Pine Lawn, MO 63120: 4210 Peyton Ln
Rochester, MN 55906: 20 First Ave NE
Rockford, IL 61104: 416 S Madison
Steven's Point, WI 54481: 824 Fremont
St Louis, MO 63118: 2740 Arsenal
St Paul, MN 55108: 1471 Como Ave W
Sioux Falls, SD 57103-0128; 800 N Cliff Ave
Springfield, MO 65802: 10740 W Chestnut Expwy
Waterloo, IA 50703: 149 Argyle St
Wausau, WI 54401-4630: 113 S Second St
Wichita, KS 67202-2010: 350 Market

Child Day Care
Benton Harbor, MI 49023: 1840 Union St
Bloomington, IN 47404-3966: 111 N Rogers St
Chicago, IL 60621: 845 W 69th St
DeKalb, IL 60115-0442: 830 Grove St
Emporia, KS 66801: 327 Constitution St
Kansas City, KS 66117: 500 N 7th St
Kansas City, MO 64111: 500 W 39th St
Kokomo, IN 46902: 1105 S Waugh St
Lansing, MI 48901-4176: 525 N Pennsylvania Ave
Madison, WI 53703: 630 Washington Ave
Menasha, WI 54911: 1525 Appleton Rd
Mishawaka, IN 46544: 1026 Dodge Ave
Oak Creek, WI 53154: 8853 S Howell Ave
Olathe, KS 66051: 420 E Santa Fe
Omaha, NE 68131: 3612 Cuming St
Pekin, IL 61554: 243 Derby St
Peoria, IL 61603: 210 Spalding Ave
Plymouth, MI 48170: 9451 S Main St
Rockford, IL 61101: 210 N Kilburn
Rockford, IL 61104: 220 S Madison
Royal Oak, MI 48073: 3015 N Main St
St Paul, MN 55102: 401 W 7th St
Sheboygan, WI 53081: 1125 N 13th
Topeka, KS 66601: 1320 E 6th St
Traverse City, MI 49685-0063: 1239 Barlow St

Emergency Diagnostic and Short-term Treatment Centre
Edwin Denby Memorial Children's Home:
  20775 Pembroke Ave, Detroit, MI 48219;
  tel: (313) 537-2130 (acc 40)
Wilcox Residential Programmes: North Platte,
  NE 69101-2268, 1121 W 18th St;
  tel: (308) 534-4164

Youth Group Homes
North Platte, NE 69101-2258: 1121 W 18th St
Omaha, NE 68131-1998: 3612 Cuming St

Emergency Shelter Care of Children
Kansas City, MO 64111: 101 W Linwood Blvd
North Platte, NE 69101: 704 S Welch Ave
Oak Park, IL 60302-1713: 924 N Austin
Omaha, NE 68131: 3612 Cuming St
St Paul, MN 55108-2542: 1471 Como Ave W
Wichita, KS 67202-2010: 350 N Market

Head Start Programmes
Chicago, IL 60651: 4255 W Division
Chicago, IL 60644: 500 S Central
Chicago, IL 60651: 1345 N Karlov
Chicago, IL 60607: 1 N Ogden
Chicago, IL 60621: 945 W 69th St
Chicago, IL 60649: 1631 E 71st St
Saginaw, MI 48602: 2030 N Carolina St

Homes (each of the following have facilities for unmarried mothers)
Detroit, MI 48219-1398: 20775 Pembroke Ave
Grand Rapids, MI 49503: 1215 E Fulton St;
  tel: (616) 459-9468 (Teen-parent centre)
Omaha, NE 68131-1998: 3612 Cuming St

Latchkey Programmes
DeKalb, IL 60115-0442: Camp 'I Can Do It'
DeKalb, IL 60115-0442: 830 Grove St
Evanston, IL 60201-4414: 1403 Sherman Ave
Gary-Merrillville, IN 46408-4420: 4800 Harrison St
Huntingdon, IN 46750: 1424 E Market St
Huron, SD 57350: 237 Illinois St SW
Indianapolis, IN 46203-1944: 1337 Shelby St
Kokomo, IN 46902: 1101 S Waugh
Jacksonville, IL 62650: 331 W Douglas St
Newton, IA 50208: 301 N 2nd Ave E
North Platte, NE 69101: 421 E 6th St
Omaha, NE 68131: 3612 Cuming St
Pekin, IL 61554: 243 Derby St

USA Central Territory

Royal Oak, MI 48073: 3015 N Main Sts
Springfield, MO 65802: 1707 W Chestnut Expway
St Louis, MO 63113: 2618 N Euclid Ave
St Louis, MO 63143: 7701-15 Rannells Ave
Wyandotte, MI 49192-3498: 1258 Biddle Ave

Residential Services for Mentally Ill
Omaha, NE 68131: 3612 Cuming St

Permanent and/or Supportive Housing
Coon Rapids, MN 55433: 10347 Ibis Ave
Jefferson City, MO 65101: 907 Jefferson St
Joplin, MO 64801: 320 E 8th St
Kansas City, KS 66102: 6723 State Ave
Kansas City, MO 64111: 101 W Linwood
Minneapolis, MN 55403: 53 Glenwood Ave
Rochester, MN 55906: 120 S Broadway
St Louis, MO 63103: 205 N 18th St
St Louis, MO 63132: 10740 W Page Ave
St Paul, MN 55108: 1471 Como Ave W

Foster Care
Wichita, KS 67202: Kock Center, 350 N Marat

Medical/Dental Clinics (SA owned and occupied)
Grand Rapids, MI 49503: 1215 E Fulton St
Rochester, MN 55906: 120 S Broadway
Sheboygan, WI 53081: 710 Pennsylvania Ave

In addition, a number of fresh-air camps, youth centres, community centres, red shield clubs, day nurseries, family service and emergency relief bureaux are attached to corps and divisions

New senior soldiers are enrolled at The Bridge Outpost during the 'Come, Join Our Army' recruitment campaign. The outpost is run from Cicero Templo Laramie Corps in suburban Chicago, Illinois. The second year of the territory's 'Come, Join Our Army' initiative saw almost 800 senior soldiers, more than 600 junior soldiers and nearly 300 adherents enrolled.

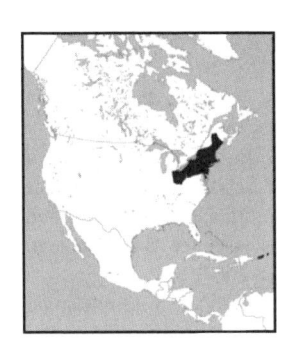

USA EASTERN TERRITORY

Territorial leaders:
Commissioners Lawrence R. and Nancy A. Moretz

Territorial Commander:
Commissioner Lawrence R. Moretz
(13 Nov 2002)

Chief Secretary:
Colonel R. Steven Hedgren (1 Oct 2008)

Territorial Headquarters: 440 West Nyack Road, PO Box C-635, West Nyack, New York 10994-1739, USA
Tel: [1] (845) 620-7200; fax: [1] (845) 620-7756; website: www.salvationarmy-usaeast.org

The Salvation Army was incorporated as a religious and charitable corporation in the State of New York in 1899 as 'The Salvation Army' and is qualified to conduct its affairs in all of the states of the territory.

Zone: Americas and Caribbean
USA states included in the territory: Connecticut, Delaware, Kentucky, Maine, Massachusetts, New Hampshire, New Jersey, New York, Ohio, Pennsylvania, Rhode Island, Vermont
Other countries included in the territory: Puerto Rico, Virgin Islands
'The Salvation Army' in Korean: Koo Sei Kun; in Norwegian: Frelsesarmeen; in Spanish: Ejército de Salvación; in Swedish: Frälsningsarmén
Languages in which the gospel is preached: Creole, English, Korean, Laotian, Portuguese, Russian, Spanish, Swedish
Periodicals: *¡Buenas Noticias!* (Spanish), *Cristianos en Marcha* (Spanish), *Good News!* (English and Korean), *Priority!*, *Ven a Cristo Hoy* (Spanish)

THE territory launched a three-year journey of evangelism and spiritual growth with the theme 'Holiness Ablaze'. Focusing on a Scripture text in *The Message* paraphrase, the Territorial Commander challenged officers and soldiers to live 'as obedient children ... pulled into a life shaped by God's life, a life energetic and blazing with holiness' (1 Peter 1:14).

Every major event in 2009 was stamped with the 'Holiness Ablaze' theme, concentrating on God the Father's 'Perfect Love'. These included commissioning weekend, which featured a 'Praise Ablaze' interactive concert, and the Old Orchard Beach camp meetings under the leadership of General Shaw Clifton and Commissioner Helen Clifton.

Stressing the Trinitarian aspect of holiness, the three-year programme will continue with reflections on the 'Perfect Example' of God the Son and, in 2011, the 'Perfect Power' of God the Holy Spirit.

During the year under review the territory held its first Hispanic Brengle Institute and an African-American Empowerment Conference. Both were well attended as part of the territory's spiritual formation mission objectives.

The territory published a new book, *Will You Choose Joy?* by Captain Normajean Honsberger. The book's editor, Lieut-Colonel Lois Rader, has brought together the author's sermons on Philippians and her 'closer to home' reflections.

Despite fiscal challenges the territory continued in faith to open new facilities. A state-of-the-art conference centre, located at territorial headquarters, has already become a resource for the entire territory. The new Western Pennsylvania DHQ, built 'green', will be a 'beacon on a hill'. Montclair, New Jersey, and Ponce, Puerto Rico, corps facilities will be 'lighthouses to their communities'. The territory's first Ray and Joan Kroc Community Centre in Ashland, Ohio, will be 'a place of welcome and hope'.

Continued emphasis on the national 'Come, Join Our Army' soldier enrolment campaign has seen more than 3,000 senior and junior soldiers enrolled in the territory, with progress being made toward the 2010 goal of a 10 per cent increase.

The Territorial Commander is excited by the enrolment of new soldiers. While attending a soldiers weekend in Western Pennsylvania Division he heard many timely stories of mission advance and blessing. He reports that 200 senior and junior soldiers have been enrolled in that division since the campaign began in June 2007.

In keeping with the five missional objectives outlined in his vision statement, the TC issued a call to prayer and challenged every officer in the territory to send him at least one name of a prospective candidate for officership. The names would be entered into the prayer journal in the THQ Prayer Room. A total of 1,400 names were submitted and the territory is now praying that the Lord of the Harvest will send forth labourers into the vineyard.

The territory launched an 'Introduction To Officership' course which will be required for all accepted candidates. This online course strengthens the pre-training programme and allows candidates a measured plan of study and practical experience before entrance into the school for officer training.

In prayerful covenant and active witness, the territory's Salvationists accept the challenge to live 'blazing with holiness' as God's obedient servants.

STATISTICS
Officers 1,692 (active 1,071 retired 621) **Cadets** 72 **Employees** 12,188

Corps 382 **Outposts** 1 **Institutions** 96

Senior Soldiers 20,975 **Adherents** 7,531 **Junior Soldiers** 8,116

Personnel serving outside territory Officers 31 Layworker 1

USA Eastern Territory

STAFF
Women's Ministries: Comr Nancy A. Moretz (TPWM) Col Judith A. Hedgren (TSWM) Lt-Col Sharon Tillsley (TMFS) Lt-Col Judy LaMarr (TCCM, TWAS) Lt-Col Susan Gregg (OCS)
Personnel: Lt-Col Mark W. Tillsley
Programme: Lt-Col Kenneth W. Maynor
Business: Lt-Col James W. Reynolds
Asst Chief Sec: Lt-Col Tito E. Paredes
Territorial Ambassadors for Evangelism: Lt-Cols Howard and Patricia Burr
Territorial Ambassadors for Holiness: Majs David and Jean Antill
Territorial Ambassador for Prayer/Spiritual Formation: Lt-Col Cheryl A. Maynor
ARC Commander: Lt-Col Timothy Raines
Audit: Maj John Cramer
Community Relations/Development: Maj Karla Clark
Education: Maj Edward Russell
Finance: Maj Glenn C. Bloomfield
Information Technology: Mr Paul Kelly
Legal: Maj Thomas A. Schenk
Literary: Linda D. Johnson
Mission and Culture: Maj William R. Groff
Music: B/M Ronald Waiksnoris
  New York Staff Band: B/M Ronald Waiksnoris
  Territorial Songsters: S/L William Rollins
Officers' Services/Records: Maj Deborah K. Goforth
Pastoral Care and Spiritual Special: Lt-Col R. Eugene Pigford
Property/Mission Expansion: Maj Hubert S. Steele III
Risk Management: Mr Samuel C. Bennett
Social Services: Maj John Cheydleur
Supplies/Purchasing: Maj Frank Klemanski
Training: Maj Stephen Banfield
Youth and Candidates: Maj Kevin Stoops

DIVISIONS
Eastern Pennsylvania and Delaware: 701 N Broad St, Philadelphia, PA 19123; tel: (215) 787-2800; Lt-Cols William R. and Marcella Carlson
Empire State: 200 Twin Oaks Dr, PO Box 148, Syracuse, NY 13206-0148; tel: (315) 434-1300; Maj Donald W. and Capt Renee P. Lance
Greater New York: 120 West 14th St, New York, NY 10011-7393; tel: (212) 337-7200; Lt-Cols Guy D. and Henrietta Klemanski
Massachusetts: 147 Berkeley St, Boston, MA 02116-5197; tel: (617) 542-5420; Majs William H. and Joan I. Bode
New Jersey: 4 Gary Rd, Union, NJ 07083-5598, PO Box 3170, Union, NJ 07083; tel: (908) 851-9300; Majs Donald and Vicki Berry
Northeast Ohio: 2507 E 22nd St, 44115-3202, PO Box 5847, Cleveland, OH 44101-0847; tel: (216) 861-8185; Majs William A. and G. Lorraine Bamford
Northern New England: 297 Cumberland Ave, PO Box 3647, Portland, ME 04104; tel: (207) 774-6304; Majs David E. and Naomi R. Kelly
Puerto Rico and Virgin Islands: 306 Ave De La Constitución 00901-2235, PO Box 71523, San Juan PR, 00936-8623; tel: (787) 999-7000; Capts Ricardo J. and Mirtha N. Fernandez
Southern New England: 855 Asylum Ave, PO Box 628, Hartford, CT 06142-0628; tel: (860) 543-8400; Lt-Col Barbara A. Hunter
Southwest Ohio and Northeast Kentucky: 114 E Central Parkway, PO Box 596, Cincinnati, OH 45201; tel: (513) 762-5600; Majs Ronald R. and Dorine M. Foreman
Western Pennsylvania: 700 N Bell Ave, Carnegie, PA 15106; tel: (412) 446-1500; Majs Robert J. and Lynette Reel

SCHOOL FOR OFFICER TRAINING
201 Lafayette Ave, Suffern, NY 10901-4798; tel: (845) 357-3501

THE SALVATION ARMY RETIREMENT COMMUNITY
1400 Webb St, Asbury Park, NJ 07712; tel: (732) 775-2200; Maj Jean Booth (Administrator) (acc 32)

SOCIAL SERVICES
Adult Rehabilitation Centres
(*Includes facilities for women)
Akron, OH 44311: 1006 Grant St, PO Box 1743; tel: (330) 773-3331 (acc 83)
Albany, NY 12206: 452 Clinton Ave, PO Box 66389; tel: (518) 465-2416 (acc 90)
Altoona, PA 16602: 200 7th Ave, PO Box 1405, 16603 (mail); tel: (814) 946-3645 (acc 39)
Binghamton, NY 13904: 3-5 Griswold St; tel: (607) 723-5381 (acc 62)
*Boston (Saugus), MA 01906: 209 Broadway Rte 1; tel: (781) 231-0803 (acc 125)
Bridgeport CT 06607: 1313 Connecticut Ave; tel: (203) 367-8621 (acc 50)
Brockton, MA 02301: 281 N Main St; tel: (508) 586-1187 (acc 56)
Brooklyn, NY 11217: 62 Hanson Pl; tel: (718) 622-7166 (acc 136)

USA Eastern Territory

Buffalo, NY 14217-2587: 1080 Military Rd, PO Box 36, 14217-0036; tel: (716) 875-2533 (acc 90)

Cincinnati, OH 45212: 2250 Park Ave, PO Box 12546, Norwood, OH 45212-0546; tel: (513) 351-3457 (acc 175)

Cleveland, OH 44103: 5005 Euclid Ave; tel: (216) 881-2625 (acc 159)

Columbus, OH 43207: 1675 S High St; tel: (614) 221-4269 (acc 122)

*Dayton, OH 45402: 913 S Patterson Blvd; tel: (937) 461-2769 (acc 72)

Erie, PA 16501: 1209 Sassafras St, PO Box 6176, 16512; tel: (814) 456-4237 (acc 50)

*Harrisburg, PA 17110: 3650 Vartan Way, PO Box 60095, 17106-0095; tel: (717) 541-0203 (acc 100)

*Hartford, CT 06132: 333 Homestead Ave, PO Box 320440; tel: (860) 527-8106 (acc 110)

Hempstead, NY 11550: 194 Front St; tel: (516) 481-7600 (acc 100)

Jersey City, NJ 07302: 248 Erie St; tel: (201) 653-3071 (acc 75)

Mount Vernon, NY 10550: 745 S Third Ave; tel: (914) 664-0800 (acc 80)

Newark, NJ 07101: 65 Pennington St, PO Box 815; tel: (973) 589-0370 (acc 125)

New Haven, CT 06511: 301 George St, PO Box 1413, 06506; tel: (203) 865-0511 (acc 45)

*New York, NY 10036: 535 W 48th St; tel: (212) 757-7745 (acc 140)

Paterson, NJ 07505: 31 Van Houten St, PO Box 1976, 07509; tel: (973) 742-1126 (acc 89)

*Philadelphia, PA 19128: 4555 Pechin St; tel: (215) 483-3340 (acc 138)

Pittsburgh, PA 15203: 44 S 9th St; tel: (412) 481-7900 (acc 127)

Portland, ME 04101: 30 Warren Ave, PO Box 1298, 04104; tel: (207) 878-8555 (acc 60)

Poughkeepsie, NY 12601: 570 Main St; tel: (845) 471-1730 (acc 50)

*Providence, RI 02906: 201 Pitman St; tel: (401) 421-5270 (acc 129)

*Rochester, NY 14611: 745 West Ave; tel: (585) 235-0020 (acc 135)

San Juan, PR 00903: ARC, Fernández Juncos Ave, cnr of Valdés #104, Puerta de Tierra, PO Box 13814, 00908; tel: (787) 722-3301 (acc 36)

Scranton, PA 18505: 610 S Washington Ave, PO Box 3064; tel: (570) 346-0007 (acc 62)

Springfield, MA 01104: 285 Liberty St, PO Box 1569, 01101-1569 (mail); tel: (413) 785-1921 (acc 70)

*Syracuse, NY 13224: 2433 Erie Blvd East; tel: (315) 445-0520 (acc 100)

Toledo, OH 43602: 27 Moorish Ave, PO Box 355, 43697; tel: (419) 241-8231 (acc 60)

Trenton, NJ 08638: 436 Mulberry St, PO Box 5011; tel: (609) 599-9801 (acc 86)

Wilkes-Barre, PA 18702: 163 Hazle St, PO Box 728, 18703-0728; tel: (570) 822-4248 (acc 52)

*Wilmington, DE 19801: 107 S Market St; tel: (302) 654-8808 (acc 81)

*Worcester, MA 01603: 72 Cambridge St; tel: (508) 799-0520 (acc 115)

ATTACHED TO DIVISIONS
Adult Day Care

Buffalo, NY 14202: Golden Age Center, 950 Main St; tel: (716) 883-9800 (acc 300)

Carlisle, PA 17013: 20 East Pomfret St, PO Box 309; tel: (717) 249-1411

Cincinnati, OH 45210: 131 E 12th St; tel: (513) 762-5693 (acc 20)

Lancaster, OH 43130: 228 W. Hubert Ave, tel: (740) 687-1921, ext 111 (acc 50)

Newport, KY 41072: 340 West 10th St, PO Box 271; tel: (859) 291-8107 (acc 15)

Quincy, MA 02169-6932: 6 Baxter St; tel: (617) 472-2345 (acc 27)

Syracuse, NY 13202: 749 S Warren St; tel: (315) 479-1313

Extended In-home Service for the Elderly

Syracuse, NY 13202: 749 S Warren St; tel: (315) 479-1309

Adult Rehabilitation

Kenmore, NY 14217: 1080 Military Rd; tel: (716) 875-2533 (acc 90)

Day Care Centres

Akron, OH 44303: Child Development Center, 135 Hall St; tel: (330) 762-8177 (acc 69)

Boston, MA 02124: 26 Wales St; tel: (617) 436-2480 (acc 70)

Bronx, NY 10451: 425 E 159th St; tel: (718) 742-2346 (acc 45)

Bronx, NY 10457: 2121 Washington Ave; tel: (718) 563-1530 (acc 69)

Brooklyn, NY 11212: Day Care Center, 280 Riverdale Ave; tel: (718) 922-7661 (acc 100)

Brooklyn, NY 11212: Sutter Day Care and Family Day Care, 20 Sutter Ave; tel: (718) 773-3041/(718) 735-6519 (acc 75 and 248)

Brooklyn, NY 11216: 110 Kosciusko St; tel: (718) 857-7264 (acc 39)

Brooklyn, NY 11221: 1151 Bushwick Ave; tel: (718) 455-0100 (acc 60)

USA Eastern Territory

Brooklyn, NY 11231: Family Day Care Redhook and Fiesta Day Care Center, 80 Lorraine St; tel: (718) 834-8755 (acc 62 and 65)
Cambridge, MA 02139: 402 Massachusetts Ave, PO Box 390647; tel: (617) 547-3400 (acc 28)
Cincinnati, OH 45202: 3501 Warsaw Ave; tel: (513) 251-1451 (acc 112)
Cleveland, OH 44103: 6010 Hough Ave; tel: (216) 432-0505 (acc 40)
Danbury, CT 06813-0826: 15 Foster St, PO Box 826; tel: (203) 792-7505 (acc 30)
Darby, PA 19023: 22 N Ninth St; tel: (610) 583-3720 (acc 25)
Hartford, CT 06105: 121 Sigourney St; tel: (860) 543-8488 (acc 69)
Hempstead, NY 11550: 65 Atlantic Ave; tel: (516) 485-4980 (acc 103)
Jersey City, NJ 07034: 562 Bergen Ave, PO Box 4237, Bergen Stn; tel: (201) 435-7355 (acc 70)
Lexington, KY 40508: 736 W Main St; tel: (859) 252-7709 (acc 80)
Meriden, CT 06450-0234: 23 St Casimir Dr, PO Box 234; tel: (203) 235-6532 (acc 27)
Morristown, NJ 07960: 95 Spring St, PO Box 9150; tel: (973) 538-0543 (acc 95)
New York, NY 10034: 3732 10th Ave; tel: (212) 569-4300 (acc 63)
Philadelphia (Germantown), PA 19133: 2601 North 11th St; tel: (215) 225-2700 (acc 131)
Providence, RI 02905: 20 Miner St; tel: (401) 781-7238 (acc 110)
Syracuse, NY 13202: Cab Horse Commons, 677 S Salina St; tel: (315) 479-1305
Syracuse, NY 13202: 749 S Warren St; tel: (315) 479-1334
Syracuse, NY 13202: South Salina Street Infant Care Center, 667 S Salina St; tel: (315) 479-1329
Syracuse, NY 13207: Elmwood Day Care Center, 1640 S Ave; tel: (315) 701-2750
Syracuse, NY 13202: School Age Day Care, 749 S Warren St; tel: (315) 479-1334
Wilmington, DE 19899: 107 W 4th St; tel: (302) 472-0712 (acc 110)

Family Centres
Newark, NJ 07102: Newark Area Services Kinship Care, 45 Central Ave; tel: (973) 623-5959

Development Disabilities Services
Bronx, NY 10457: Topping Ave Residence, 1638-1640 Topping Ave; tel: (718) 466-1503 (acc 8)
Brooklyn, NY 11220: Centennial House, 426 56th St; tel: (718) 492-4415 (acc 9)
Brooklyn, NY 11237: Decade House, 315 Covert St; tel: (718) 417-1583 (acc 10)
Brooklyn, NY 11206: Millennium House, 13 Pulaski St; tel: (718) 222-0736 (acc 13)
Glendale, NY 11385: Glendale House, 71-29 70th St; tel: (718) 381-7329 (acc 13)
Jamaica, NY 11423: Family Care, 90-23 161st St; tel: (718) 206-9171 (acc 15)
Philadelphia, PA 19123: Developmental Disabilities Program, 701 N Broad St, Administrative Offices; tel: (215) 787-2804 (community homes 46, acc 100)
South Ozone Park, NY 11420: Hope House, 115-37 133rd St; tel: (718) 322-1616 (acc 9)
Springfield, OH 45501: Hand N'Hand Activity Center for Adults with Disabilities, 15 S Plum St; tel: (937) 322-3434
St Albans, NY 11412: Pioneer House, 104-14 186th St; tel: (718) 264-8350 (acc 12)

Evangeline Residence
New York, NY 10011: 123 W 13th St (Markle Memorial Residence); tel: (212) 242-2400; fax: (212) 229-2801 (acc 286)

Family Counselling
Boston, MA 02118: Family Service Bureau, 1500 Washington St; tel: (617) 236-7233; fax: (617) 236-0123
Bronx, NY 10458: Bronx Belmont Center for Families, 601 Crescent Ave; tel: (718) 329-5410
Bronx, NY 10453: Morris Heights Center for Families, 7 W Burnside Ave; tel: (718) 561-3190; fax: (718) 561-3856
Brooklyn, NY 11207: Williamsburg Center for Families, 295 Division St; tel: (718) 782-4587
Buffalo, NY 14202: Emergency Family Assistance, Family Court Visitation Program, Spouse Abuse Education Workshop, 960 Main St; tel: (716) 883-9800
Cincinnati, OH 45210: Cincinnati Family Service Bureau, 131 E 12th; tel: (513) 762-5660
Covington, KY 41014: N Kentucky Family Service Bureau, 1806 Scott Blvd; tel: (859) 261-0835
Manhattan, NY 10011: Bushwick Center for Families, 132 W 14th St; tel: (212) 337-7200
Newport, KY 41072: N Kentucky Family Service Bureau, 340 W 10th St; tel: (859) 431-1063
Rochester, NY 14604-4310: Rochester Emergency Family Assistance, 70 Liberty Pole Way, PO Box 41210; tel: (716) 987-9540
San Juan, PR 00921-2118: Family Services for Victims of Crime, 1327 Americo Miranda

USA Eastern Territory

Ave, PO Box 10601, 00922-0601;
tel: (787) 749-0027, 0029
Syracuse, NY 13202: Family Services,
749 S Warren St; tel: (315) 479-3651
Syracuse, NY 13207: Family Place Visitation
Center, 350 Rich St; tel: (315) 474-2931

Foster Home Services

Allentown, PA 18109: Foster Care In-Home
Placement Services, Adoption Services and
Administrative Services, 425 Allentown Dr,
Suite 1; tel: (610) 821-7706
Jamaica, NY 11432: Jamaica Homes for
Children, 163-18 Jamaica Ave;
tel: (718) 558-4486; fax: (718) 558-5799
Manhattan, NY 10011: Bushwick Homes for
Children, 132 W 14th St; tel: (212) 337-7200
Mineola, NY 11501: Nassau Therapeutic
Program: 85 Willis Ave; tel: (516) 746-1484;
fax: (516) 746-1488
New York, NY 10011: 132 W 14th St;
tel: (212) 807-6100; fax: (212) 620-3096

Group Homes for Adolescents

Bronx, NY 10451: Glover House, 301 E 162nd St;
tel: (718) 992-4020 (acc men 12)
Bronx, NY 10453: West Bronx Group Homes,
121 W 179th St; tel: (718) 716-2609
(acc females 12)
Bronx, NY 10469: North Bronx Group Home,
1268 Adee Ave; tel: (718) 515-6600
(acc men 12)
Fall River, MA 02720: Gentle Arms of Jesus
Teen Living Center, 429 Winter St;
tel: (508) 324-4558 (acc 15)
Lefrak City, NY 11368: Lefrak City Group Home,
96-04 57th Ave, Apt 3K; tel: (718) 271-8318
(acc women 10)
Manhattan, NY 10027: Manhattan West Group
Home, 136 West 127th St; tel: (212) 678-6121
(acc men 12)
Manhattan, NY 10031: Manhattan East Group
Home, 241 East 116th St; tel: (212) 534-5455
(acc men 12)
New York, NY 10027: Lenox House, 131 W
132nd St; tel: (212) 334-1394 (acc men 12)

Harbour Light Centres

Boston, MA 02118: Adult Women's Programme,
407-409 Shawmut Ave, PO Box 180130;
tel: (617) 536-7469 (acc 74)
Cleveland, OH 44115-2376: Harbor Light
Complex, 1710 Prospect Ave;
tel: (216) 781-3773 (acc 177)
Pittsburgh, PA 15233: 865 W North Ave;
tel: (412) 231-0500 (acc 50)

Hotels, Lodges, Emergency Homes

Akron, OH 44302: Booth Manor Emergency
Lodge, 216 S Maple St; tel: (330) 762-8481
ext 194 (acc 38)
Allentown, PA 18102: Hospitality House,
344 N 7th St; tel: (610) 432-0128 (acc 65)
Bellaire, OH 43906: 315 37th St;
tel: (740) 676-6810 (acc 40)
Brooklyn, NY 11207: Bushwick Family
Residence, 1675 Broadway; tel: (718) 574-2701
(acc families 87)
Brooklyn, NY 11203: Kingsboro Men's Shelter,
681 Clarkson Ave; tel: (718) 363-7738
(acc 80)
Bronx, NY 10456: Franklin Women's Shelter
and Referral, 1122 Franklin Ave;
tel: (347) 417- 8200 (acc 200)
Buffalo, NY 14202: 960 Main St, Emergency
Family Shelter; tel: (716) 884-4798 (acc 96)
Cambridge, MA 02139-0008: Day Drop-in Shelter
for Men and Women/Night Shelter for Men,
402 Mass Ave, PO Box 390647;
tel: (617) 547-3400 (acc 200/50)
Carlisle, PA 17013: Stuart House (Women's
Transitional Housing), 125-127 S Hanover St;
tel: (717) 249-1411 (acc 41)
Carlisle, PA 17013: Genesis House (Men's
Emergency Housing), 24 E Pomfret St;
tel: (717) 249-1411
Chester, PA 19013: Stepping Stone Program,
151 W 15th St; tel: (610) 874-0423 (acc 35)
Cincinnati, OH 45210: Emergency Shelter,
131 E 12th St; tel: (513) 762-5655 (acc 24)
Cleveland, OH 44115: Zelma George Family
Shelter, 1710 Prospect Ave;
tel: (216) 641-3712 (acc 110)
Concord, NH 03301: McKenna House (Adult
Shelter), 100 S Fruit St; tel: (603) 228-3505
(acc 29)
Dayton, OH 45402: Women and Children's
Homeless Shelter, 138 S Wilkinson St;
tel: (937) 228-8241 (acc 27)
Dayton, OH 45402: Men's Homeless Shelter,
624 S Main St; tel: (937) 228-8210 (acc 55)
East Stroudsburg, PA 18301: 226 Washington St;
tel: (570) 421-3050
Elizabeth, NJ 07201: 1018 E Grand St;
tel: (908) 352-2886 (acc 45)
Elmira, NY 14902: 414 Lake St, PO Box 293;
tel: (607) 732-0314 (24-hour Domestic
Violence Hotline); Victims of Domestic
Violence Safe House (acc 15)
Elmira, NY 14901: Our House, 401-403
Division St; tel: (607) 734-0032 (acc 20)
Hartford, CT 06105: Family Shelter,
225 S Marshall St; tel: (860) 543-8423 (acc 27)

USA Eastern Territory

Jamaica, NY 11434: Springfield Family Residence, 46-80 Guy r. Brewer Blvd; tel: (718) 521-5090 (acc families 90)

Jamestown, NY 14702: ANEW Center Shelter for Domestic Violence, Residential/Non-Residential Program, PO Box 368; tel: (716) 483-0830; 24-hour Hotline tel: (800) 252-8748

Johnstown, PA 15901: Emergency Shelter; tel: (814) 539-3110 (acc 24)

Laconia, NH 03801: The Carey House, 6 Spring St; tel: (603) 528-8086 (acc 30)

Lexington, KY 40508: Early Learning Center Families, 736 W Main St; tel: (859) 252-7706 (acc 129)

Montclair, NJ 07042-2776: 68 N Fullerton Ave; tel: (973) 744-8666 (acc 18)

Newark, OH 43055: 250 E Main St; tel: (740) 345-3289 (acc 18)

New Britain, CT 06050: 78 Franklin Sq; tel: (860) 225-8491 (acc 25 men)

Norristown, PA 19404: 533 Swede St; tel: (610) 275-9225 (acc 41)

Northport, NY 11768-0039: Northport Veterans' Residence, 79 Middleville Rd, Bldg 11, PO Box 300 (mail); tel: (631) 262-0601 (acc 87)

Perth Amboy, NJ 08862-0613: Care House, 433 State St; tel: (732) 826-7040 (acc men 9)

Philadelphia, PA 19107: Eliza Shirley House, 1320 Arch St; tel: (215) 568-5111 (acc 125)

Philadelphia, PA 19123: Red Shield Family Residence, 715 N Broad St; tel: (215) 787-2887 (acc 100)

Pittsburgh, PA 15206: Family Caring Center, 6017 Broad St; tel: (412) 362-0891 (acc 40)

Pittsburgh, PA 15233: Homeless Drop In Center, 100 W North Ave; tel (412) 321-0290

Pottstown, PA 19464: Lessig-Booth Family Residence, 137 King St; tel: (610) 327-0836 (acc 32)

Queens (Jamaica), NY 11435: Briarwood Family Residence, 80-20 134th St; tel: (718) 268-3395 (acc 91)

Rochester, NY 14604-4310: Men's Emergency Shelter, Booth Haven, 70 Liberty Pole Way, PO Box 41210; tel: (585) 987-9500 (acc 84)

Rochester, NY 14604-4310: Women's Shelter, Hope House, 100 West Ave, PO Box 41210; tel: (585) 697-3430 (acc 19)

Rochester, NY 14604-4310: Safe Haven Emergency Shelter, 70 Liberty Pole Way, PO Box 21210; tel: (585) 987-9540 (acc 16)

San Juan, PR 00903: Homeless Shelter, Proyecto Esperanza, Fernández Juncos, cnr Valdés; tel: (787) 722-2370

Schenectady, NY 12305: Evangeline Booth Home and Women's Shelter, 168 Lafayette St; tel: (518) 370-0276

Syracuse, NY: Parenting Center, 667 S Salina St; tel: (315) 479-1330

Syracuse, NY 13202: Emergency Lodge, 749 S Warren St; tel: (315) 479-1332

Trenton, NJ 08601: Homeless Drop In Center, 575 E State St; tel: (609) 599-9373

Waterbury, CT 06720: 74 Central Ave; tel: (203) 756-1718 (acc 29)

West Chester, PA 19380: Railton House, 101 E Market St; tel: (610) 696-7434 (acc 17)

Wilkes Barre, PA 18701: Kirby Family House, 35 S Pennsylvania Ave; tel: (570) 824-8380 (acc 50)

Wilmington, DE 19899: Booth Social Service Center, 104 W 5th St; tel: (302) 472-0764 (acc 52)

Wooster, OH 44691: 24-Hour Open Door Emergency Shelter, 437 S Market St; tel: (330) 264-4704 (acc 44)

Zanesville, OH 43701: 515 Putnam Ave; tel: (740) 454-8953 (acc 35)

HIV Services

Bronx, NY 10458: 601 Crescent Ave; tel: (718) 329-5410; fax: (718) 329-5409

Bronx, NY 10453: 7 West Burnside Ave; tel: (718) 561-3190,; fax: (718) 367-6720

Newark, NJ 07102: 45 Central Ave; tel: (973) 623-5959; fax: (973) 848-1556

New York, NY 10011: 132 West 14 St; tel: (212) 352-5644; fax: (646) 335-6311

Homeless Youth and Runaways

Rochester, NY 14604-1210: Genesis House, 35 Ardmore St, PO Box 41210; tel: (585) 235-2600 (acc 14)

Syracuse, NY 13205: Barnabas House, 1912 S Salina St; tel: (315) 475-9720 (acc 8)

Syracuse, NY 13205: Booth House and Host Home, 264 Furman St; tel: (315) 471-7628 (acc 8)

Transitional Housing Programme

Arlington, MA 02474-6597: Wellington House, 8 Wellington St (Single Resident Occupancy); tel: (781) 648-2636 (acc 20)

Buffalo, NY 14202: 984 Main St; tel: (716) 884-4798

Cincinnati, OH 45210: (families with children) 19 & 21 E 15th St; tel: (513) 762-5660

Cleveland, OH 44103: Railton House, 6000 Woodland; tel: (216) 361-6778 (acc 50)

Cleveland, OH 44115: Pass Programme,

USA Eastern Territory

1710 Prospect Ave; tel: (216) 619-4727 (acc 75)
Cleveland, OH 44115: Project Share, 2501 E 22nd St; tel: (216) 623-7492 (acc 38)
Lancaster, PA 17603: 131 South Queen St; tel: (717) 397-7565 (acc 21)
Perth Amboy, NJ 08862-0613: Care House Transitional Shelter for Homeless Veterans, 433 State St; tel: (732) 826-7040 (acc 11)
Philadelphia, PA 19103: Mid-City Apartments Permanent Housing, 2025 Chestnut St; tel: (215) 569-9160 (acc 60)
Philadelphia, PA 19147: Reed House Permanent Housing, 1320 S 32nd St; tel: (215) 755-6789 (acc 66)
Syracuse, NY 13205: Transitional Family Apartments, 1482 S State St; tel: (315) 475-7663
Syracuse, NY 13205: Transitional Living Project Apartments (youth), 1941 S Salina St; tel: (315) 475-9720
Syracuse, NY 13205: Women's Shelter, 1704 S Salina St; tel: (315) 472-0947
West Chester, PA 19380: William Booth Initiative, 101 E Market St; tel: (610) 696-8746 (acc7)

Youth Service and Emergency Shelter
Syracuse, NY 13205: Barnabas, 1941 S Salina St; tel: (315) 475-9744

Senior Citizens' Residences
Cincinnati, OH 45224: Booth Residence for the Elderly and Handicapped, 6000 Townvista Dr; tel: (513) 242-4482 (acc 150)
New York, NY 10025: Williams Residence, 720 West End Ave; tel: (212) 316-6000; fax: (212) 280-0410 (acc 367)
Philadelphia, PA 19139: Booth Manor, 5522 Arch St; tel: (215) 471-0500 (acc 50)
Philadelphia, PA 19131: Ivy Residence, 4051 Ford Rd; tel: (215) 871-3303 (acc 75)

Continued emphasis on the 'Come, Join Our Army' recruitment campaign saw more than 3,000 senior and junior soldiers enrolled in the territory

USA SOUTHERN TERRITORY

Territorial leaders:
Commissioners Maxwell and Lenora Feener

Territorial Commander:
Commissioner Maxwell Feener
(1 Jul 2006)

Chief Secretary:
Colonel Terry W. Griffin (2 Jul 2007)

Territorial Headquarters: 1424 Northeast Expressway, Atlanta, GA 30329-2088, USA

Tel: [1] (404) 728 1300; fax: [1] (404) 728 1392; website: www.salvationarmysouth.org

The Salvation Army was incorporated as a religious and charitable corporation in the State of Georgia in 1927 as 'The Salvation Army' and is qualified to conduct all its affairs in all of the states of the territory.

Zone: Americas and Caribbean
USA states included in the territory: Alabama, Arkansas, Florida, Georgia, Kentucky, Louisiana, Maryland, Mississippi, North Carolina, Oklahoma, South Carolina, Tennessee, Texas, Virginia, West Virginia, District of Columbia
Languages in which the gospel is preached: English, Haitian-Creole, Korean, Laotian, Spanish, Vietnamese
Periodical: *Southern Spirit*

INSPIRED by the General's call to holiness, the territorial leaders called all officers and soldiers to 'Go Deeper With God'. This sought-after spiritual experience was the theme of the 2008 Holiness Congress held in Gwinnett Arena, Georgia.

More than 6,000 Salvationists gathered for a weekend of immeasurable inspiration with USA national leaders Commissioners Israel L. and Eva D. Gaither as special guests. Each session was linked to the 'Go Deeper' theme.

'Go Deeper Into His Wonder' began with a challenge: 'Let our daily prayer be that God may "sanctify us wholly; and our whole spirit and soul and body be preserved blameless unto the coming of our Lord Jesus Christ"' (1 Thessalonians 5:23).

'Go Deeper Into His World' saw a re-enactment of the Founder preaching, followed by a parade of flags and costumes representing every country of Army service. The 2008 World Services Ingathering reported a record $8.2 million of personal giving.

'Go Deeper Into His Way' acknowledged new senior and junior

soldiers, followed by the premier of Lieut-Colonel W. Eddie Hobgood's new musical *Brengle: My Life's Ambition*, which included amazing special effects as well as outstanding drama and music.

'Go Deeper Into His Will' included the ordination and commissioning of the God's Fellow-Workers Session. During his Bible message the National Commander's charismatic style and the Holy Spirit's presence filled the huge auditorium. Every inch became hallowed ground. Hundreds of people made spiritual decisions, many offering for full-time service.

The 2008 Territorial Bible Conference had as its special guests General Shaw Clifton and Commissioner Helen Clifton. In his closing Bible message the General challenged the newly arrived Prayer Warriors Session of cadets – the largest session in the territory for many years.

In the late summer three major hurricanes made landfall within the territory – Dolly, Gustav and Ike. The latter two made the most impact across the states of Alabama, Mississippi and Louisiana (Gustav); and Louisiana, Texas, Oklahoma and Kentucky (Ike).

The East Texas coast was the most devastated area after Ike, and was served for several weeks by a large number of Emergency Disaster Services canteens (mobile kitchens) and shelters which involved many hundreds of officers, employees and volunteers.

Galveston Island received the most damage, a reminder of the first official Salvation Army response in 1900. Texas State Emergency Management invited the Army to accompany the first response team on a search and rescue operation along the East Texas coast.

In spite of the dramatic downturn in the world's economy, the territory's Christmas fundraising Red Kettle Appeal realised an increase. Out of the top 10 divisions in the nation, six were in the Southern Territory. In 2009, donors continued to be supportive – such is the public's confidence in the Army's daily promise of 'Doing the Most Good'.

Family stores reported an increase in public interest, but also noted a small decline in donations of quality goods, reflecting the overall trend by everyone to 'make do' during harder economic times. Overall, the Army's social services were stretched even further as more and more people sought help.

STATISTICS
Officers 1,426 (active 959 retired 467) **Cadets** (1st Yr) 39 (2nd Yr) 43 **Employees** 17,043
Corps 347 **Societies/Outposts** 9 **Institutions** 251
Senior Soldiers 27,264 **Adherents** 2,717 **Junior Soldiers** 7,641
Personnel serving outside territory Officers 33

STAFF
Women's Ministries: Comr Lenora Feener (TPWM) Col Linda Griffin (TSWM)
Maj Susan Ellis (CCMS/Outreach) Maj Teresa Tanner (TWAS)
Personnel: Lt-Col Charles White
Programme: Lt-Col Edward Hobgood
Business: Lt-Col Kenneth Johnson
Adult Rehabilitation Centres Command: Lt-Col Larry White

USA Southern Territory

Audit: Maj Eugene Broome
Community Relations and Development: Maj Mark Brown
Evangelism and Adult Ministries: Maj John White
Employee Relations: Dr Murray Flagg
Finance: Maj Stephen Ellis
Legal: Maj Charles Powell
Multicultural Ministries: Maj Victor Valdes
Music: Mr Nicholas Simmons-Smith
Officers' Health Services: Maj Jeanne Johnson
Property: Mr Robert L. Taylor
Retired Officers: Maj Hilda Howell
Social Services: Mr Kevin Tompson-Hooper
Supplies and Purchasing: Maj Robert Bagley
Training: Maj Willis Howell
Youth: Maj Kelly Igleheart
  Candidates: Maj Susan Brown

DIVISIONS

Alabama-Louisiana-Mississippi: 1450 Riverside Dr, PO Box 4857, 39296-4857, Jackson, MS 39202; tel: (601) 969 7560; fax: (601) 968-0273; Majs John R., Jr and Arduth Jones

Arkansas and Oklahoma: 5101 N Pennsylvania Ave, PO Box 12600, 73157, Oklahoma City, OK 73112; tel: (405) 840 0735; fax: (405) 840 0460; Majs Kenneth and Dawn Luyk

Florida: 5631 Van Dyke Rd, Lutz, FL 33558, PO Box 270848, 33688-0848, Tampa, FL; tel: (813) 962 6611; fax: (813) 962 4098; Lt-Cols Vernon and Martha Jewett

Georgia: 1000 Center Pl, NW, 30093, PO Box 930188, 30003 Norcross, GA 30003; tel: (770) 441-6200; fax: (770) 441-6214; Majs William and Debra Mockabee

Kentucky and Tennessee: 214-216 W Chestnut St, Box 2229, 40201-2229, Louisville, KY 40202; tel: (502) 583 5391; fax: (502) 625 1199; Majs John and Marthalyn Needham

Maryland and West Virginia: 814 Light St, Baltimore, MD 21230; tel: (410) 347 9944; fax: (410) 539 7744; Maj Sandra Defibaugh

National Capital and Virginia: 2626 Pennsylvania Ave NW, PO Box 18658, Washington, DC 20037; tel: (202) 756 2600; fax: (202) 756 2660; Majs Mark and Alice Bell

North and South Carolina: 501 Archdale Dr, Box 241808, 28224-1808, Charlotte, NC 28217-4237; tel: (704) 522 4970; fax: (704) 522 4980; Majs Dalton and Wanda Cunningham

Texas: 6500 Harry Hines Blvd, PO Box 36607, 75235, Dallas, TX 75235; tel: (214) 956 6000; fax: (214) 956 9436; Lt-Cols Henry and M. Dorris Gonzalez

SCHOOL FOR OFFICER TRAINING

1032 Metropolitan Pkwy, SW Atlanta, GA 30310; tel: (404) 753 4166; fax: (404) 753 3709

ATTACHED TO DIVISIONS

Alcoholic Rehabilitation
Fort Worth, TX 76103: 1855 E Lancaster (women only, acc 13)
Greenville, SC 29609: 419 Rutherford St (acc 40)
Mobile, AL 36604: 1009 Dauphin St (acc 30)

Child Care Centres
Annapolis, MD 21403: 351 Hilltop Lane (acc 80)
Austin, TX 78767: 4523 Tannehill Hill (acc 26)
Clearwater, FL 34625: 1625 N Belcher Rd (acc 54)
Charlottesville, VA 22204: 207 Ridge St (acc 50)
Daytona Beach, FL 32117: 1555 LPGA Blvd (acc 355)
Decatur, AL 36604: 100 Austinville Rd SW
Freeport, TX 77541-2620: 1618 Ave J (acc 85)
Irving, TX 75061: 250 E Grauwyler (acc 62)
Jacksonville, FL 32202: 318 N Ocean St (acc 125)
Lakeland, FL 33801: 835 N Kentucky (acc 45)
Lakeland, FL 33810: 2620 Kathleen Rd (acc 100)
Lynchburg, VA 24501: 2215 Park Ave (acc 40)
Memphis, TN 38105: 696 Jackson Ave (acc 60)
Naples, FL 34104: 3180 Estey Ave (acc 124)
Nashville, TN 37207: 631 Dickerson Rd (acc 37)
Princeton, WV 24740: 300 Princeton Ave (acc 102)
Salisbury, MD 21804: 415 Oak St (acc 52)
San Antonio (Southside), TX 78211: 1034 Fenfield Ave (acc 92)
West Pasco, FL 34673: PO Box 1050, Port Richey (acc 161)
Winston-Salem, NC 27101: 1255 N Trade St (acc 30)

Children's Residential Care
Birmingham, AL 35212: Youth Emergency Services, 6001 Crestwood Blvd (acc 33)
Dallas, TX, 75220: Casa Youth Runaway Shelter, 2640 Webb Chapel Ext (acc 16)
St Petersburg, FL 33733: Children's Village, PO Drawer 10909 (acc 24)
St Petersburg, FL 33733: Sallie House Emergency Shelter, PO Drawer 10909 (acc 18)

USA Southern Territory

Family Resident Programme
Alexandria, VA 22301: 2525 Mt Vernon Ave (acc 40)
Albany, GA 31721: 304 W 2nd Ave (acc 12)
Amarillo, TX 79105: 400 S Harrison (acc 15)
Arlington, TX 76013: 711 W Border (acc 30)
Athens, GA 30606: 484 Hawthorne Ave (acc 20)
Atlanta, GA 30310: 400 Luckie St NW (acc 106)
Augusta, GA 30904: 2020 Gardner St (acc 30)
Austin, TX 78701: 501 E 8th St (acc 60)
Austin, TX 78767: 4523 Tannehill Ln (Women and Children Shelter) (acc 26)
Baltimore, MD 21030: 1114 N Calvert St (acc 75)
Beaumont, TX 77701: 1078 McFadden (acc 10)
Bradenton, FL 34205: 1204 14th St W (acc 102)
Cambridge, MD 21613: 200 Washington St (acc 10)
Charleston, WV 25302: 308, 308A, 310, 312 Ohio St (16)
Charlottesville, VA: 207 Ridge St NW (acc 36)
Chattanooga, TN 37403: 800 N McCallie Ave (acc 72)
Clearwater, FL 33756: 1527 East Druid Rd (acc 64)
Corpus Christi, TX 78401: 513 Josephine (acc 28)
Dalton, GA 30720: 1101 A North Thorton Ave (acc 24)
Daytona Beach, FL 32114: 560 Ballough Rd (acc 49)
Ft Lauderdale, FL 33312: 1445 W Broward Blvd (acc 251)
Ft Myers, FL 33901: 2163 Stella St (acc 134)
Fort Worth, TX 76103: 1855 E Lancaster Ave (acc 62)
Gainesville, FL 32601: 639 E University Ave (acc 24)
Hagerstown, MD 21740: 534 W Franklin St (acc 30)
Harrisonburg, VA 22801: 895 Jefferson St (acc 72)
Hollywood, FL 33020: 1960 Sherman St (acc 140)
Houston, TX 77004: 1603 McGowen (acc 42)
Jacksonville, FL 32201: PO Box 52508 (acc 108)
Lakeland, FL 33801: 835 N Kentucky Ave (acc 166)
Louisville, KY 40203: 209 E Breckinridge (acc 35)
Louisville, KY 40203: 817 S Brook St (acc 18)
Lynchburg, VA 24501: 2215 Park Ave (acc 22)
Macon, GA 31206: 2312 Houston Ave (acc 9)
Melbourne, FL 32901: 1080 S Hickory St (acc 48)
Memphis, TN 38105: 696 Jackson Ave (acc 120)
Miami, FL 33142: 1907 NW 38th St (acc 244)
Nashville, TN 37207-5608: 631 Dickerson Rd (acc 53)
Newport News, VA 23602: 11931 Jefferson Ave (acc 30)
N Central Brevard, Cocoa, FL 32922: 919 Peachtree St (acc 33)
Norfolk, VA 23220: 2097 Military Highway, Chesapeake (acc 65)
Ocala, FL 34475: 320 NW 1st Ave (acc 108)
Orlando, FL 32804: 400 W Colonial Dr (acc 198)
Panama City, FL 32401: 1824 W 15th St (acc 48)
Parkersburg, WV 24740: 534-570 Fifth St (acc 32)
Pensacola, FL 32505: 1310 North S St (acc 28)
Richmond, VA 23220: 2 W Grace St (acc 52)
San Antonio, TX 78212: 515 W Elmira 78212 (acc 300)
Sarasota, FL 34236: 1400 10th St (acc 226)
Savannah, GA 31405: 3100 Montgomery St (acc 9)
St Petersburg, FL 33733: PO Drawer 10909 (acc 96)
Tampa, FL 33602: 1603 N Florida (acc 192)
Texarkana, TX 71854: 316 Hazel (acc 46)
Thomasville, GA 31792: 208 South St (acc 9)
Titusville, FL 32796: 1212 W Main (acc 16)
Tyler, TX 75701: 633 N Broadway 75702
Washington, DC 20009: 1434 Harvard St NW (acc 60)
West Palm Beach, FL 33402: PO Box 789 (acc 86)
Wheeling, WV 26003: 140 16th St (acc 32)
Winter Haven, FL 33882: PO Box 1069 (acc 24)
Williamsburg, VA 7131: Merrimac Trail (acc 17)

Harbour Light Centres
Atlanta, GA 30313: 400 Luckie St (acc 324)
Dallas, TX 75235: 5302 Harry Hines Blvd (acc 309)
Houston, TX 77009: 2407 N Main St (acc 308)
Washington, DC 20002: 2100 New York Ave, NE (acc 207)

Senior Citizens' Centres
Arlington, TX 76013: 712 W Abrams
Beaumont, MS 1502: Bolton Ave
Birmingham, '614 Birmingham' AL 35203: 2410 8th Ave N
Brooklyn, MS: Carnes Rd
Dallas Cedar Crest, TX 75203: 1007 Hutchins Rd
Dallas Oak Cliff, TX 75208: 1617 W Jefferson Blvd

USA Southern Territory

Dallas Pleasant Grove, TX 75217-0728: 8341 Elam Rd
Ft Worth, TX 76106: 3023 NW 24th St
Houston Aldine/Westfield, TX 77093: 2600 Aldine Westfield
Houston Pasadena, TX 77506: 45/6 Irvington Blvd
Houston Temple, TX 77009: 2627 Cherrybrook Ln 77502
Jacksonville, FL 32202: 17 E Church St
Lufkin, TX 75904: 305 Shands
Montgomery, AL 36107: 900 Bell St
Oklahoma City, OK 73109: 311 SW 5th St (includes 5 drop-in centres)
San Antonio Citadel, TX 78201: 2810 W Ashby Pl
San Antonio Dave Coy Center, TX 78202: 226 Nolan St
San Antonio Hope Center, TX 78212: 521 W Elmira
Sarasota, FL 34236: 1400 10th St
Shreveport, LA 71163: 200 E Stoner
St Petersburg, FL 33713: 3800 9th Ave N
Washington (Sherman Ave), DC 20010: 3335 Sherman Ave NW
Washington (Southeast), DC 20003: 1211 G St SE

Senior Citizens' Residences

Atlanta, GA 30306: Wm Booth Towers, 1125 Ponce de Leon Ave NE (acc 99)
Charlotte, NC 28202-1727: Wm Booth Gardens Apts, 421 North Poplar St (acc 130)
Cumberland, MD 21502-0282: Wm Booth Tower, 220 Somerville Ave (acc 113)
Fort Worth, TX 76119-5813: Catherine Booth Friendship House, 1901 E Seminary Dr (acc 157)
Gastonia, NC 28054: Catherine Booth Gardens Apts, 1336 Union Rd (acc 82)
High Point, NC 27263: William Booth Gardens Apts, 123 SW Cloverleaf Place (acc 76)
Houston, TX 77009: Wm Booth Garden Apts, 808 Frawley (acc 62)
Ocala, FL 34470: Evangeline Booth Garden Apts, 2921 NE 14th St (acc 64)
Orlando, FL 32801: Wm Booth Towers, 633 Lake Dot Circle (acc 168)
Orlando, FL 32801: Catherine Booth Towers, 625 Lake Dot Circle (acc 125)
Pasadena, TX 77502: Evangeline Booth, 2627 Cherrybrook Ln. (acc 62)
San Antonio, TX 78201-5397: William Booth Gardens Apts, 2710 W Ashby Pl (acc 95)
San Antonio, TX 78201: Catherine Booth Apts, 2810 W Ashby Pl (acc 62)

Tyler, TX 75701: Wm Booth Gardens Apts, 601 Golden Rd (acc 132)
Waco, TX 76708-1141: Wm Booth Gardens Apts, 4200 N 19th (acc 120)
Waco, TX 76708-1141: Catherine Booth, N 19th

Service Centres

Alexander City, AL 35010: 823 Cherokee Rd
Americus, GA 31709: 204 Prince St
Bainbridge, GA 39819: 600 Scott St
Bay City, TX 77414: 1911 7th St
Borger, TX 79007-4252: 1090 Coronado Center Cir 79007-2502
Bogalusa, LA 70427: 400 Georgia Ave
Brownwood, TX 76801: 405 Lakeway
Bushnell, FL 33513: PO Box 25 (Sumter County)
Carrollton, GA 30112: 115 Lake Carroll Blvd
Carthage, MS 39051: 610 Hwy 16 West, Suite A
Cleburne, TX 76031: 111 S Anglin
Columbia, MD 21045 (Howard County): PO Box 2877
Corinth, MS 38835: 2200 Lackey Dr
Covington, GA 30014: 5193 Washington St
Culpeper, VA 22701: 14300 Achievement Dr
Douglas, GA 31533: 110 S Gaskin Ave
Dublin, GA 31021: 1617 Telfair St
East Pasco, Dade City, FL 33523: 14445 7th St
Eden, NC 27288: 314 Morgan Rd
Elberton, GA 30635: 262 N McIntosh St
Elizabethtown, KY 42701: 1006 N Mulberry
Enterprise, AL 366331: (Coffee County) 1919-B E Park Ave
Fernandina Beach, FL 32034: 421 S 9th St
Fort Payne, AL 35967: (Dekalb County) 450 Gault Ave N
Frankline, VA, 23851: 50l N Main St
Fulton, MS 38843: 414 E Main St
Glen Burnie, MD 21061: 511 S Crain Hwy
Gonzales, LA 70737: 218 Bayou Narcisse
Guntersville, AL 35976: (Marshall County) 1336 Gunter Ave
Hopewell, VA 23860: 222 N Main St, Suite 218
Houma, LA 70363: 1414 E Tunnel Blvd.
Houston, MS 38851: 114 Washington St
Immokalee, FL 34142: 2050 Commerce Ave, Unit 3A
Jackson, GA 30233 (Jackson/Butts County): 178 N Benton St
Jacksonville, FL 32256: 10940 Beach Blvd.
Jacksonville, FL 32204: Towers, 900 W Adams St
Jasper, AL 35502: (Walker County) 207 20th St E
Lake City, FL 32055: 934 NE Lake DeSoto Circle, Ste 104
Lebanon, TN, 37087: 215 University Ave
Lenoir, NC 28645: 108 Morganton Blvd

USA Southern Territory

Lewisburg, WV 24901: (Greenbriar Valley) 148 Maplewood Ave
Lewisville, TX 75067: 207 Elm St 75057
McDonough, GA 30253: 401 Race Track Rd
McGehee, AR 71654: (Desha County) 202 N 2nd
Milledgeville, GA 31061: 420 S Wilkinson St
Mocksville, NC 27028: (Davie County) 279 N Main St
Morganton, NC 28655: 420-B West Fleming Dr
Nacogdoches, TX 75963: 118 E Hospital Suite 101
Natchez, MS 39120: 509 N Canal St
New Braunfels, TX 78130: 373 B Landa St
Newnan, GA 30264: 670 Jefferson St
Okmulgee, OK 74447-0123: 105-111 E 8th St
Oneonta, AL 35121: (Blount County) 333 Valley Rd
Opelika, AL 36801: (Lee County) 720 Columbus Pkwy
Oxford, MS 38655: 2617 W Oxford Loop, Ste 4
Ozark, AL 36360: (Dale County) 154 E Broad St
Pontotoc, MS 38863: 187 Hwy 15 N
Putnam County, WV 25177: 720 N Winfield Rd, St Albans, WV
Sallisaw, OK: PO Box 292 Fort Smith, AR 72902
San Marcos, TX 78667: 1658 I-35 S
Scottsboro, AL 35768: (Jackson County) 1501 E Willow St
Spencer, WV 25276: (Roane County) 145 Main St
Starksville, MS 39759: 501 Hwy 12 W
St Mary's, GA 31558: 1909 Osborne Rd
Sylacauga, AL 35150: (Talledega South) 100 E 3rd St
Talladega, AL 35160: (Talledega North) 215 E Battle St
Tarpon Springs, FL 34689: 209 S Pinellas Ave
Thomasville, AL 36784: 122 W Wilson Ave
Troy, AL 36081: 509 S Brundidge St
Vidalia, GA 30475: 204 Jackson St
Warrenton, VA 20186: 26 S Third St
Wellsburg, WV 26070: 491 Commerce St
Westminster, MD 21157: 300 Hahn Rd
Winchester, VA 22604: 300 Fort Collier Rd
Yadkinville, NC 27055: 111 W Main St

Spouse House Shelters

Cocoa, FL: 919 Peachtree St 32922 (PO Box 1540, 32923) (acc 16)
Panama City, FL 32401: 1824 W 15th St (PO Box 540, 32412) (acc 12)
Port Richey, FL 34673: PO Box 5517 Hudson, FL 34674-5517 (acc 32)
Roanoke, VA 24016 (acc 60)
Warner Robins, GA 31093: 96 Thomas Blvd (acc 15)

SOCIAL SERVICES
Adult Rehabilitation Centres (including industrial stores)

Alexandria, VA 22312: Northern Virginia Center, 6528 Little River Turnpike (acc 120)
Atlanta, GA 30318-5726: 740 Marietta St, NW (acc 132)
Austin, TX 78745: 4216 S Congress (acc 118)
Baltimore, MD 21230: 2700 W Patapsco Ave (acc 115)
Birmingham, AL 35234: 1401 F. L. Shuttlesworth Dr (acc 107)
Charlotte, NC 28204: 1023 Central Ave (acc 118)
Dallas, TX 75235-7213: 5554 Harry Hines Blvd (acc 137)
Fort Lauderdale, FL 33312-1597: 1901 W Broward Blvd (acc 99)
Fort Worth, TX 76111-2996: 2901 NE 28th St (acc 109)
Houston, TX 77007-6113: 1015 Hemphill St (acc 167)
Hyattsville, MD 20781: (Washington, DC, and Suburban Maryland Center) 3304 Kenilworth Ave (acc 151)
Jacksonville, FL 32246: 10900 Beach Blvd 32216 (acc 121)
Memphis, TN 38103-1954: 130 N Danny Thomas Blvd (acc 86)
Miami, FL 33127-4981: 2236 NW Miami Court (acc 134)
Nashville, TN 37213-1102: 140 N 1st St (acc 86)
New Orleans, LA 70121-2596: 200 Jefferson Highway (acc 50)
Oklahoma City, OK 73106-2409: 2041 NW 7th St (acc 81)
Orlando, FL 32808-7927: 3955 W Colonial Dr (acc 105)
Richmond, VA 23220-1199: 2601 Hermitage Rd (acc 81)
San Antonio, TX 78204: 1324 S Flores St (acc 110)
St Petersburg, FL 33709-1597: Suncoast Area Center, 5885 66th St N (acc 119)
Tampa, FL 33682-2949: 13815 N Salvation Army Lane (acc 131)
Tulsa, OK 74106-5163: 601-611 N Main St (acc 86)
Virginia Beach, VA 23462: Hampton Roads Center, 5560 Virginia Beach Blvd (acc 123)

In addition, 10 fresh-air camps and 332 community centres, boys'/girls' clubs are attached to the division

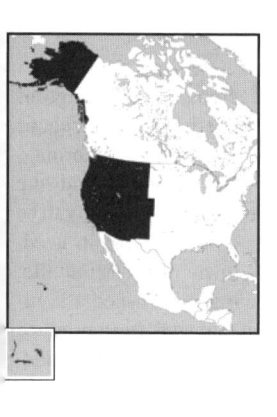

USA WESTERN TERRITORY

Territorial leaders:
Commissioners Philip W. and Patricia L. Swyers

Territorial Commander:
Commissioner Philip W. Swyers
(1 Jan 2005)

Chief Secretary:
Colonel William Harfoot (1 Jul 2008)

**Territorial Headquarters: 180 E Ocean Boulevard,
PO Box 22646 (90801-5646), Long Beach, California 90802-4709, USA**

Tel: [1] (562) 436-7000; website: www.usw.salvationarmy.org

The Salvation Army was incorporated as a religious and charitable corporation in the State of California in 1914 as 'The Salvation Army' and is qualified, along with its several affiliated separate corporations, to conduct its affairs in all of the states of the territory.

Zone: Americas and Caribbean
USA states included in the territory: Alaska, Arizona, California, Colorado, Hawaii, Idaho, Montana, Nevada, New Mexico, Oregon, Utah, Washington, Wyoming, Texas (El Paso County), Guam (US Territory)
Other countries included in territory: Republic of the Marshall Islands, Federated States of Micronesia
'The Salvation Army' in Cantonese: Kau Shai Kwan; in Japanese: Kyu-sei-gun; in Mandarin (Kuoyo): Chiu Shi Chuen; in Spanish: Ejército de Salvación
Languages in which the gospel is preached: Cantonese, Chamarro, Chuukese, English, Hmong, Korean, Laotian, Mandarin, Marshallese, Philipino, Pohnpeian, Portuguese, Spanish, and Tlingit
Periodicals: *Caring*, *New Frontier*, *Nuevas Fronteras* (Spanish)

IN September 2008 the territory welcomed the 30 cadets of the Prayer Warriors Session and the Territorial Commander installed Colonels William and Susan Harfoot as the new Chief Secretary and Territorial Secretary for Women's Ministries.

Hawaiian and Pacific Islands Divisional Commander Major Edward Hill officially opened Saipan Corps (5 October 2008) and in Honolulu the TC dedicated to God's glory a new transitional housing facility for women in recovery. As part of 'Revolution Hawaii', eight young adults participated in an urban mission programme serving the homeless and addicted.

A Latino version of the musical *Spirit* premiered to a sell-out crowd at Los Angeles Central Corps (May 2008). Conceived by brothers Bandmaster Kevin Larsson and Karl Larsson, *Espiritu* featured Latin-style music and was set in a present-day city like Los Angeles.

San Francisco's new Ray and Joan Kroc Corps Community Centre was dedicated to God by National Commander Commissioner Israel L. Gaither (June 2008). Members of the Kroc family were present for the celebration.

The first-ever Western Bible Conference took place (25 June-5 July 2008) at Asilomar near Monterey, California, with the theme 'Refresh'. More than 500 delegates from across the territory listened to Commissioner Israel L. Gaither. Morning Bible studies were provided by Dr Bill Ury, Professor of Systematic and Historical Theology, Wesley Biblical Seminary.

Celebrating 115 years of ministry, Pasadena Tabernacle Band proclaimed the gospel on a 10-day tour of USA Southern Territory.

In January 2009 the Territorial Youth Chorus debuted in San Francisco. The following month, 140 delegates attended the second Worship Arts Retreat at which Colonels Robert and Gwenyth Redhead (Canada and Bermuda) were guest speakers.

The Western Association of Schools and Colleges granted full accreditation to Crestmont College for Officer Training. More than 160 prospective candidates from around the territory gathered at Crestmont for a Future Officers Fellowship retreat.

New soldiers were enrolled in, among other places, the Marshall Islands; Tacoma, Washington; Portland Tabernacle, Oregon; Chinatown and Torrance, California.

Salvation Army units around the territory are applying innovative means to reach people most in need. In the small town of McMinnville, Oregon, the corps established a community garden that adds fresh produce to the food pantry. In Riverside, California, a project in local orange groves provides fresh citrus products to families and supplements the food programme.

Individuals from Riverside County Adult Rehabilitation Centre are successfully integrated in the local corps programmes, and many have become active soldiers. Each week 50-100 people congregate at the local thrift store in El Centro, California, to participate in a chapel service. At the Bell Shelter in Los Angeles, clients can participate in a class to earn pizza-making certification and find work.

STATISTICS
Officers 998 (active 628 retired 360) **Cadets** 44 **Employees** 10,045
Corps 260 **Outposts** 12 **Institutions** 311
Senior Soldiers 16,540 **Adherents** 3,230 **Junior Soldiers** 5,441
Personnel serving outside territory Officers 36 Lay Personnel 6

STAFF
Women's Ministries: Comr Patricia L. Swyers (TPWM) Col Susan Harfoot (TSWM)
Personnel: Lt-Col David E. Hudson
  Asst Sec for Personnel (Officer Development): Maj Charlene Bradley
  Asst Sec for Personnel (Officer Services): Maj Judith Smith
Business: Lt-Col Ron Strickland
Programme: Lt-Col Eda Hokom

USA Western Territory

Assoc Sec for Programme: Lt-Col Pamela Strickland
Asst Sec for Programme: Mr Martin Hunt
ARC Command: Maj Man-Hee Chang
Audit: Maj Joe Frank Chavez
Candidates and Recruitment: Maj John P. Brackenbury
Community Care Ministries: Lt-Col Sharron Hudson
Community Relations/Development: Maj Robert L. Rudd
Education: Maj Linda Manhardt
Finance: Maj Walter J. Fuge
Gift Services: Ms Kathleen Durazo
Human Resources: Ms Margaret (Miki) Webb
Information Technology: Mr Clarence White
Legal: Mr Michael Woodruff
Multicultural Ministries: Maj Elicio Marquez
Music: Mr Neil Smith
Officer Care and Development: Maj William Nottle
Older Adult Ministries: Maj Evelyn Chavez
Property: Maj William Raihl
Risk Management: Mr John McCarthy
Senior Housing Management: Mrs Susan Lawrence
Silvercrest Ministries: Maj Leslie Peacock
Social Services: Maj Allie Laura Niles
Supplies and Purchasing: Mr Robert Jones
Training: Maj Stephen C. Smith
Western Bible Conference Sec: Maj Cathyrn Russell
World Missions: tba
Youth: Major Ivan P. Wild

DIVISIONS

Alaska: 143 E 9th Ave, Anchorage, AK 99501-3618 (Box 101459, 99510-1459); tel: (907) 276-2515; Majs Douglas and Sheryl Tollerud
Cascade: 8495 SE Monterey Ave, Happy Valley, OR 97086; tel: (503) 794-3200; Majs Donald and Arvilla Hostetler
Del Oro: 3755 N Freeway Blvd, Sacramento, CA 95834-1926 (Box 348000, 95834-8000); tel: (916) 563-3700; Majs Douglas F. and Colleen Riley
Golden State: 832 Folsom St, San Francisco, CA 94107-1123 (Box 193465, 94119-3465); tel: (415) 553-3500; Lt-Cols Joe E. and Shawn Posillico
Hawaiian and Pacific Islands: 2950 Manoa Rd, Honolulu, HI 96822-1798 (Box 620, 96809-0620); tel: (808) 988-2136; Majs Edward A. and Shelley Hill
Intermountain: 1370 Pennsylvania St, Denver, CO 80203-2475 (Box 2369, 80201-2369); tel: (303) 861-4833; Majs Victor R. and Joan Doughty
Northwest: 111 Queen Anne Ave N, Seattle, WA 98109-4955 (Box 9219, 98109-0200); tel: (206) 281-4600; Lt-Cols Douglas and Diane O'Brien
Sierra Del Mar: 2320 5th Ave, San Diego, CA 92101-1679 (Box 122688, 92112-2688); tel: (619) 231-6000; Maj Linda Markiewicz
Southern California: 900 W James M. Wood Blvd, Los Angeles, CA 90015-1356 (Box 15899 Del Valle Station 90015-0899); tel: (213) 896-9160; Lt-Cols Victor A. and Rose-Marie Leslie
Southwest: 2707 E Van Buren St, Phoenix, AZ 85008-6039 (Box 52177, 85072-2177); tel: (602) 267-4100; Lt-Cols Douglas and Rhode Danielson

COLLEGE FOR OFFICER TRAINING
30840 Hawthorne Blvd, Rancho Palos Verdes, CA 90275-5301; tel: (310) 377-0481; fax: (310) 541-1697

SOCIAL SERVICES
Adult Rehabilitation Centres (Men)
Anaheim, CA 92805: 1300 S Lewis St; tel: (714) 758-0414 (acc 147)
Bakersfield, CA 93301: 200 19th St; tel: (661) 325-8626 (acc 58)
Canoga Park, CA 91304: 21375 Roscoe Blvd; tel: (818) 883-6321 (acc 52)
Colorado Springs, CO 80903: 505 S Weber St, PO Box 1385, 80901; tel: (719) 473-6161 (acc 37)
Denver, CO 80216: 4751 Broadway; tel: (303) 294-0827 (acc 96)
Fresno, CA 93721: 804 S Parallel Ave; tel: (559) 490-7020 (acc 91)
Honolulu, HI 96817: 322 Sumner St; tel: (808) 522-8400 (acc 75)
Long Beach, CA 90813: 1370 Alamitos Ave; tel: (562) 218-2351 (acc 94)
Lytton, CA 95448: 200 Lytton Springs Rd, Healdsburg, PO Box 668, Healdsburg, 95448; tel: (707) 433-3334 (acc 75)
Oakland, CA 94607: 601 Webster St, PO Box 24054, 94623; tel: (510) 451-4514 (acc 130)
Pasadena, CA 91105: 56 W Del Mar Blvd; tel: (626) 795-8075 (acc 107)
Phoenix, AZ 85004: 1625 S Central Ave; tel: (602) 256-4500 (acc 92)
Portland, OR 97214: 139 SE Martin Luther King Jr Blvd; tel: (503) 235-4192 (acc 72)
Riverside County, CA 92570: 24201 Orange Ave,

USA Western Territory

Perris, PO Box 278, Perris 92570;
tel: (951) 940-5790 (acc 125)
Sacramento, CA 95814: 1615 D St, PO Box 2948, 95812; tel: (916) 441-5267 (acc 85)
San Bernardino, CA 92408: 363 S Doolittle Rd;
tel: (909) 889-9605 (acc 120)
San Diego, CA 92101: 1335 Broadway;
tel: (619) 239-4037 (acc 131)
San Francisco, CA 94110: 1500 Valencia St;
tel: (415) 643-8000 (acc 112)
San Jose, CA 95126: 702 W Taylor St;
tel: (408) 298-7600 (acc 103)
Santa Monica, CA 90404: 1665 10th St;
tel: (310) 450-7235 (acc 60)
Seattle, WA 98134: 1000 4th Ave S;
tel: (206) 587-0503 (acc 100)
Stockton, CA 95205: 1247 S Wilson Way;
tel: (209) 466-3871 (acc 84)
Tucson, AZ 85713: 2717 S 6th Ave;
tel: (520) 624-1741 (acc 85)

Adult Rehabilitation Centres (Women)

Anaheim, CA 92805: 1300 S Lewis St;
tel: (714) 758-0414 (acc 28)
Arvada, CO 80002: Cottonwood, 13455 W 58th Ave; tel: (303) 456-0520 (acc 24)
Fresno, CA 93704: Rosecrest, 745 E Andrews St;
tel: (559) 490-7020 (acc 14)
Pasadena, CA 91107: Oakcrest Women's Program, 180 W Huntington Dr;
tel: (626) 795-8075 (acc 13)
Phoenix, AZ 85003: Lyncrest Manor, 344 W Lynwood St (acc 12)
San Francisco, CA 94116: Pinehurst Lodge, 2685 30th Ave; tel: (415) 681-1262 (acc 26)
Seattle, WA 98102: The Marion-Farrell House, 422 11th Ave E; tel: (206) 587-0503 (acc 14)

UNDER DIVISIONS
Clinics

Kalispell, MT 59901: 110 Bountiful Dr;
tel: (406) 257-4357
Lodi, CA 95240: 525 W Lockeford St;
tel: (209) 367-9560
Oxnard/Port Hueneme, CA: 622 W Wooley Rd;
tel: (805) 483-9235
San Diego, CA 92123: Door of Hope, 2799 Health Center Dr; tel: (858) 279-1100

Family Services

Anchorage, AK 99501: Family Services, 1712 'A' St; tel: (907) 277-2593
Apache Junction, AZ 85219: Apache Junction Service Center, 605 E Broadway Ave;
tel: (480) 982-4110
Denver, CO 80205: Denver Family Services, 2201 Stout St; tel: (303) 295-3366
Honokaa, HI 96727: Ke Kama Pono Outreach Program, 45-511 Rickard Place;
tel: (808) 935-4111 ext 16
Havre, MT 59501: Service Ext, Social Service Center, 605 2nd St, PO Box 418;
tel: (406) 265-6411
Honolulu, HI 96814: Honolulu Family Services Offices, 320 Ward Ave #109; tel (808) 591-5605
Kent, WA 98032: S King County Service Center, 1209 Central Ave #145; tel (253) 852-4983
Los Angeles, CA 90015-1352: Los Angeles Family Service, 832 W James M. Wood Blvd;
tel: (213) 438-0933
Mesquite, NV 89048: Mesquite Service Center, 780 Hafen Ln #D; tel: (775) 751-8199
Moses Lake, WA 98837: Service Ext, Social Service Center, 310 S Cedar, PO Box 1000;
tel: (509) 766-5875
Oakland, CA 94612: Family Services, 379 12th St; tel: (645) 9710
Phoenix, AZ 85034-2177: Family Service Center, 2702 E Washington; tel: (602) 267-4122
Riverside, CA 92501: 3695 1st;
tel: (951) 784-3571
Sacramento, CA 95814: Family Service Center, 1225 North 'B' St; tel: (916) 442-0303
San Diego, CA 92101: Social Services;
tel: (619) 231-6000
San Francisco, CA 94103: Family Service Center, 520 Jesse St; tel: (415) 575-4848
Seattle, WA 98101-1923: Emergency Family Assistance, 1101 Pike St; tel: (206) 447-9944
Tiyan, Guam: Family Service Center, 613-615 E Sunset Blvd; tel: (671) 477-3528
Tucson, AZ 85716: Tucson Family Services, 3525 E 2nd St #1; tel: (520) 546-5969
Walla Walla, WA 99362: Service Ext, Social Service Center, 827 W Alder St;
tel: (509) 529-9470
Yucca Valley, CA 92284: Service Ext, 56659 Twenty-nine Palms Hwy;
tel: (760) 228-0114

Adult Care Centres

Anchorage, AK 99508: Serendipity Adult Day Services, 3550 E 20th Ave;
tel: (907) 279-0501 (acc 35)
Henderson, NV 89015: 830 E Lake Mead Dr;
tel: (702) 565-8836 (acc 49)
Honolulu, HI 96817: 296 N Vineyard Blvd;
tel: (808) 521-6551 (acc 57)
San Pedro, CA 90731-2351: 138 S Bandini;
tel: (310) 832-7228 (acc 30)
Torrance, CA 90503: 4223 Emerald St;
tel: (310) 370-4515 (acc 40)

USA Western Territory

Alcoholic and Drug Rehabilitation Services

Anchorage, AK 99503-7317: Box 190567, 99519-0567 Clitheroe Center; tel: (907) 276-2898 (acc 58)
Bell, CA 90201-6418: Bell Shelter, 5600 Rickenbaker Rd 2a/b; tel: (323) 263-1206
Guam, GU 96910: Lighthouse Recovery Center, 440 E Marine Dr, PO Box 23038, GMF GU 96921, E Agana; tel: (671) 477-7671
Honolulu, HI 96816-4500: Women's Way/Family Treatment Services, 845 22nd Ave; tel: (808) 739-4952 (acc 41)
Honolulu, HI 96817: Addiction Treatment Services, 3624 Waokanaka St; tel: (808) 595-6371 (acc 80)
   Admin Office: 2228 Liliha Street, #304; tel: (808) 529-1480
Honolulu, HI 96822-1757: Therapeutic Living, 845 22nd Ave; tel: (808) 739-4931
Los Angeles, CA 90073: The Haven-Victory Place, 11301 Wilshire Blvd, Bldg 212; tel: (310) 478-3711 ext 48761 (acc 200)

Child Day Care Centres

Aiea (Leeward-Ohana Keiki), HI 96701: 98-612 Moanalua Loop; tel: (808) 487-1636 (acc 75)
Aurora, CO 80011: 802 Quari Ct, Box 31739, 80041-0739; tel: (303) 366-7585 (acc 123)
Boise, ID Booth, 83702: 1617 N 24th, Box 1216 83701; tel: (208) 343-3571 (acc 15)
Bozeman, MT 59715: 32 S Rouse, Box 1307, 59771-1307; tel: (406) 586-5813 (acc 14)
Broomfield, CO 80020: Broomfield After-School Program, PO Box 1058, 1080 Birch St; tel: (303) 635-3018
Colorado Springs, CO 80903-4023: Children's Development Center, 709 S Sierra Madre; tel: (719) 578-9190 (acc 30)
Denver, CO 80205-4547: Denver Red Shield Tutor Program, 2915 High St; tel: (303) 295-2108 (acc 203)
Denver, CO 80219-1859: Denver Citadel Tutor Program, PO Box 280750, 80228-0750, 4505 W Alameda Ave; tel: (303) 922-4540 (acc 15)
Globe, AZ 85501: Box 1743, 85502, 161 E Cedar St; tel: (928) 425-4011 (acc 20)
Greeley, CO 80632: Day Care Center, 1119 6th St, Box 87, 80632; tel: (970) 346-1661 (acc 45)
Honolulu 96816: (FTS-Kula Kokua), (FTS-Therapeutic Nursery), 845 22nd Ave; tel: (808) 739-4922 (acc 24, 12)
Honolulu HI 96817: (Kauluwela-Ohana Keiki) 296 N Vineyard Blvd; tel: (808) 521-6551 (acc 75)
Kailua-Kona, HI 96740: (Ohana Keiki) 75-223 Kalani St, Box 1358 96745; tel: (808) 329-7780 (acc 326)
Los Angeles, CA 90026: Alegria Day/After-School Care, 2737 Sunset Blvd; tel: (323) 454-4200 (acc 90)
Los Angeles, CA 90021: 836 Stanford Ave; tel: (213) 623-9022 (acc 250)
Los Angeles, CA 90025: Bessie Pregerson Childcare, Westwood Transitional Village, 1401 S Sepulveda Blvd; tel: (310) 477-9539 (acc 64)
Los Angeles, CA 90001: Siemen Family Center, 7655 Central Ave; tel: (323) 277-0732 (acc 62)
Modesto, CA 95354: 625 'I' St, PO Box 1663, 95353 (mail); tel: (209) 342-5220 (acc 60)
Monterey, CA 93942: 1491 Contra Costa, Seaside, PO Box 1884, 93955 (mail); tel: (831) 899-4915 (acc 105)
Oakland, CA 94604: Box 510, Booth Memorial, 2794 Garden St; tel: (510) 437-9437
Pomona, CA 91767: Box 2562, 91769, 490 E Laverne Ave; tel: (909) 623-1579 (acc 66)
Portland, OR 97296: 2640 NW Alexandra Ave; tel: (503) 239-1248 (acc 18)
Riverside, CA 92501: 3695 1st St; tel: (909) 784-4495 (acc 108)
Sacramento, CA 95817: 2550 Alhambra Blvd; tel: (916) 451-4230
San Francisco, CA 94103: Harbor House, 407 9th St; tel: (415) 503-3000 (acc 66)
Santa Barbara, CA 93111: Day Care and After-School Latchkey Program, Box 6190, 93160-6190, 4849 Hollister Ave; tel: (805) 683-3724 (acc 100)
Santa Fe Springs, CA 90606: Infant/Pre-School and After-School Care, 12000 E Washington Blvd; tel: (310) 696-7175 (acc 57)
Seattle, WA 98103: Little People Day Care, 9501 Greenwood Ave N, Box 30638, 98103-0638; tel: (206) 782-3142 (acc 65)
Tacoma, WA 98405: Joyful Noise Child Care, 1100 S Puget Sound Ave; tel: (253) 752-1661 (acc 47)
Torrance, CA 90503: 4223 Emerald St; tel: (310) 370-4514 (acc 60)
Tustin, CA 92680: Creator's Corner Pre-School, 10200 Pioneer Rd; tel: (714) 918-0659 (acc 90)

Correctional Services Offices

Los Angeles, CA 90015-1356: 900 W James M. Wood Blvd, Box 15899, Del Valle Station 90015-0899; tel: (213) 896-9185

USA Western Territory

Emergency Shelters, Hospitality Houses

Anchorage, AK 99501: Eagle Crest Transitional Housing, 438 E 9th Ave; tel: (907) 276-5913 (acc 76)

Anchorage, AK 99501: McKinnell House, 1712 'A' Street; tel: (907) 276-1609 (acc 110)

Anchorage, AK 99501: Cares for Kids (Crisis Nursery), 1700 'A' Street; tel: (907) 276-8511 (acc 20)

Bell, CA 90201: 5600 Rickenbacker; tel: (323) 263-1206 (acc 484)

Boise, ID 83702: 1617 N 24th St; tel: (208) 343-3571 (acc 24)

Cheyenne, WY 82001: Sally's House, 1920 Seymour St, PO Box 385, 82003 (mail); tel: (307) 634-2769 (acc 6)

Colorado Springs, CO 80909: Bridge House, 2641 E Yampa St; tel: (719) 227-8773 (acc 7)

Colorado Springs, CO 80909-4037: 2649 E Yampa St, Freshstart Transitional Family Housing; tel: (719) 227-8773 (acc 61)

Colorado Springs, CO 80903-4023: R. J. Montgomery New Hope Center, 709 S Sierra Madre; tel: (719) 578-9190 (acc 200)

Denver, CO 80216: Crossroads Center, 1901 29th St; tel: (303) 298-1028 (acc 294)

Denver, CO 80221-4115: Denver New Hope (Lambuth) Family Center, 2741 N Federal Blvd; tel: (303) 477-3758 (acc 84)

El Centro, CA 92244: 375 N 5th St; tel: (760) 352-8462

El Paso, TX 79905: Box 10756-79997, 4300 E Paisano Dr; tel: (915) 544-9811 (acc 136)

Fresno, CA 93711-3705: Gablecrest Women's Transitional Home, 1107 W Shaw; tel: (559) 226-6110 (acc 52)

Glendale, CA 91204-2053: Nancy Painter Home, 320 W Windsor Rd; tel: (213) 245-2424 (acc 19)

Grand Junction, CO 81502: Women's and Family Shelter, 915 Grand Ave, PO Box 578, 0578 81501 (mail); tel: (907) 242-3343 (acc 10)

Grass Valley, CA 95945: Booth Family Center, 12390 Rough and Ready Hwy; tel: (530) 272-2669 (acc 46)

Helena, MT 59601: Transitional Housing, 1905 Henderson; tel: (406) 442-8244 (acc 8)

Hilo, HI 96720: Interim Home for Youth, 1786 Kinoole St, Box 5085; tel: (808) 935-4411 (acc 18)

Honokaa, HI 96727: Residential Group Home, 45-350 Ohelo St, PO Box 5085, Hilo, HI 96720; tel: (808) 775-0241

Honolulu, HI 96816: FTS-Supportive Living, 845 22nd Ave; tel: (808) 732-2802 (acc 24)

Kahului, HI 96732-2256: Safe Haven Drop-in Center, 45 Kamehameha St; tel: (808) 877-3042

Kailua-Kona, HI 96740: Youth Shelter, 75-235 Kalani St, PO Box 5015, Hilo, HI 96720; tel: (808) 935-4411 (acc 8)

Kodiak, AK 99615-6511: Kodiak, Beachcombers Transitional Housing, 1855 Mission Rd; tel: (907) 486-8740 (acc 10)

Las Vegas, NV 89030: Safehaven Shelter, 31 W Owens Ave; tel: (702) 639-0277 (acc 22)

Las Vegas, NV 89030: Pathways, 37 W Owens Ave; tel: (702) 639-0277 (acc 42)

Las Vegas, NV 89030: Lied Transitional Housing, 45 W Owens Ave; tel: (702) 642-7252 (acc 70)

Las Vegas, NV 89030: Emergency Lodge, 47 W Owens Ave; tel: (702) 639-0277 (acc 167)

Las Vegas, NV 89030: PATH – Petaluma Area Transitional Housing, 33 W Owens Ave; tel: (702) 651-0123 (acc 34)

Las Vegas, NV 89030: Horizon Crest Apts, 13 W Owens Ave; tel (702) 399-3255

Lodi, CA 95240-2128: Hope Harbor Family Service Center, 622 N Sacramento St; tel: (209) 367-9560 (acc 54)

Lodi, CA 95240: Hope Avenue for Men, 331 N Stockton Ave (acc 26)

Long Beach, CA 90810: The Village at Callebrio, 2260 Williams St; tel: (562) 388-7600 (acc 82)

Los Angeles, CA 90073: Naomi House (for women veterans), Exodus Lodge (for mentally ill), The Haven, 11301 Wilshire Blvd, Bldg 212, Los Angeles; tel: (310) 478-3711 ext 48761 (acc 100)

Los Angeles, CA 90013: Safe Harbor, 721 E 5th St; tel: (213) 622-5253 (90013) (acc 56)

Los Angeles, CA 90015: Alegria (HIV/Aids housing) Aids Project, Transitional Housing, 2737 Sunset Blvd; tel: (323) 454-4200 (acc 195); Emergency Shelter, 832 W James M. Woods Blvd; tel (213) 438-0933

Los Angeles, CA 90028: The Way In (teen counselling) Drop In Center/Emergency Housing, 5941 Hollywood Blvd, Box 38668, 90038-0668; tel: (213) 468-8666 (acc 26)

Los Angeles, CA 90025-3477: Westwood Transitional Housing, 1401 S Sepulveda Blvd; tel: (310) 477-9539 (acc 60)

Marysville, CA 95901-5629: The Depot Family Crisis Center, 408 'J' St; tel: (530) 216-4530 (acc 67)

Marysville, CA 95901: Transitional Living Program, 5906 B Riverside Dr; tel: (530) 216-4530 (acc 45)

Medford, OR 97501-4630: 1065 Crews Rd; tel: (541) 773-7005 (acc 43)

Modesto, CA 95354: Berberian Shelter, 320 9th St; tel: (209) 525-9954 (acc 110)

USA Western Territory

Nampa, ID 83651: 1412 4th St South;
tel: (208) 461-3733 (acc 54)

Oakland, CA 94601: Family Emergency Shelter,
2794 Garden St, Box 510, 94604 (mail);
tel: (510) 437-9437 (acc 65)

Olympia, WA 98501: Hans K. Lemcke Lodge,
808 5th Ave SE; tel: (360) 352-8596 (acc 86)

Petaluma, CA 94975: PATH – Petaluma Area
Transitional Housing, PO Box 750684;
tel: (707) 769-0716 (acc 15)

Phoenix, AZ 85008: Kaiser Family Center,
2707 E Van Buren, Elim House, PO Box
52177, 85072; tel: (602) 267-4122 (acc 114)

Portland, OR 97296: Women's Shelter,
2640 NW Alexandra Ave; tel: (503) 239-1248
(acc 10)

Portland, OR 97208: Women and Children's
Family Violence Center, PO Box 2398;
tel: (503) 239-1254 (acc 53)

Sacramento, CA 95814-0603: Emergency Shelter,
1200 N 'B' St; tel: (916) 442-0331 (acc 134)

Salem, OR 97303: 1901 Front St NE;
tel: (503) 585-6688 (acc 83)

Salem, OR 97303: 105 River St NE;
tel: (503) 391-1523 (acc 6)

Salem, OR 97303: 1960 Water St NE;
tel: (503) 566-7267 (acc 10)

San Bernardino, CA 92410: Hospitality House,
845 W Kingman St; tel: (909) 884-2365
(acc 60)

Sand City, CA 93955: Good Samaritan Center,
800 Scott St; tel: (831) 899-4988 (acc 60)

San Diego, CA 92101: STEPS, 825 7th Ave;
tel: (619) 669-2233 (acc 30)

San Francisco, CA 94103: SF Harbor House,
407 9th St; tel: (415) 503-3000 (acc 52)

San Francisco, CA 94102: Railton Place
(Permanent and Transitional Housing),
242 Turk St; tel: (415) 345-3400 (acc 110)

San Jose, CA 95112: Santa Clara Hospitality
House, 405 N 4th St, Box 2-D, 95109-0004
(mail); tel: (408) 282-1175 (acc 78)

Santa Ana, CA 92701 (Orange County): 818 E
3rd St; tel: (714) 542-9576 (acc 52)

Santa Barbara, CA 93101: 423 Chapala St;
tel: (805) 962-6281 (acc 40)

Santa Fe Springs, CA 90606: Transitional
Living Center, 12000 E Washington Blvd,
Box 2009, 90610; tel: (562) 696-9562
(acc 116)

Santa Rosa, CA 95404: Transitionanl Living
Program; tel (707) 535-4271 (acc 33)

Seaside, CA 93955: Casa De Las Palmas
Transitional Housing, 535 Palm Ave;
tel: (831) 392-1762 (acc 54)

Seaside, CA 93955: Two-Step-Two Transitional
Housing, 1430 Imperial St; tel: (831) 899-4988
(acc 16)

Seattle, WA 90101: Women's Shelter
(Emergency Financial Assistance), 1101 Pike St,
PO Box 20128; tel: (206) 447-9944 (acc 20)

Seattle, WA: Catherine Booth House (Shelter for
Abused Women), Box 20128, 98102;
tel: (206) 324-4943 (acc 37)

Seattle, WA 98134: William Booth Center –
Emergency Shelter and Transitional
Shelter/Living, 811 Maynard Ave S;
tel: (206) 621-0145 (acc 183)

Seattle, WA 98136: Hickman House (Women),
5600 Fauntleroy Way SW, Box 20128, 98102;
tel: (206) 932-5341 (acc 35)

Spokane, WA 99201: Family Shelter, 204 E
Indiana Ave, Box 9108, 99209-9108;
tel: (509) 325-6814 (acc 48)

Spokane, WA 99201: Sally's House (Foster
Care Home), Box 9108, 99209-9108,
222 E Indiana; tel: (509) 392-2784 (acc 14)

Spokane, WA 99207-2335: Transitional
Housing, 127 E Nora Ave;
tel: (509) 326-7288 (acc 96)

Tacoma, WA 98405: Jarvie Family/Women's
Emergency Shelter, 1521 6th Ave, Box 1254,
98401-1254; tel: (253) 627-3962 (acc 72)

Tucson, AZ 85705: 1021 N 11th Ave;
tel: (520) 622-5411 (acc 91)

Tucson, AZ 85716: SAFE Housing,
3525 E 2nd St #1; tel: (520) 323-6080

Ventura, CA 93001-2703: 155 S Oak St;
tel: (805) 648-5032 (acc 51)

Watsonville, CA 95076-5048: Supportive
Housing Program for Women, 232 Union St;
tel: (831) 763-0131 (acc 60)

Whittier, CA 90602: 7926 Pickering Ave, PO
Box 954, 90608; tel: (562) 698-8348 (acc 17)

Harbour Light Centres

Denver, CO 80205: Denver Harbor Light,
2136 Champa St; tel: (303) 296-2456 (acc 80)

Los Angeles, CA 90013: Los Angeles Harbor
Light, Harmony Hall, Safe Harbor,
809 E 5th St, PO Box 791, 90053-0791;
tel: (213) 626-4786 (acc 324)

Portland, OR 97204: 30 SW 2nd St, Box 5635,
97228-5635; tel: (503) 239-1259 (acc 143)

San Francisco, CA 94103-4405: 1275 Harrison St;
tel: (415) 503-3000 (acc 109)

**Residential Youth Care and Family
Service Centres**

Anchorage, AK 99508: Booth Memorial Youth
and Family Services, 3600 E 20th Ave;
tel: (907) 279-0522 (acc 20)

USA Western Territory

Anchorage, AK 99501: Cares for Kids Crisis Nursery, 1700 'A' St; tel: (907) 276-8511 (acc 20)

Boise, ID 83702: Family Day Care Center, 1617 N 24th St, Box 1216, 83701; tel: (208) 343-3571 (acc 15)

Los Angeles, CA 90028: The Ways In (teen counselling) Transitional Housing, 5941 Hollywood Blvd, Box 38668, 90038-0668; tel: (213) 468-8666 (acc 20)

Portland, OR 97210: 2640 NW Alexandra Ave, Box 10027; tel: (503) 239-1248 (acc 33)

San Diego, CA 92123: Door of Hope Haven, Transitional Living Center, 2799 Health Center Dr; tel: (858) 279-1100

San Francisco, CA 94102: Railton Place Foster Youth Housing, 242 Turk St; tel (415) 345-3400 (acc 27)

Adult Rehabilitation Programmes (Men)

Albuquerque, NM 87102: 400 John St SE, Box 27690, 87125-7690; tel: (505) 242-3112 (acc 36)

Anchorage, AK 99503: 660 E 48th Ave; tel: (907) 562-5408 (acc 61)

Chico, CA 95973: 13404 Browns Valley Dr; tel: (530) 342-2199 (acc 30)

El Centro, CA 92244: 375 N 5th St; tel (760) 352-8462

Grand Junction, CO 81502: 903 Grand Ave, Box 578, 81502; tel: (970) 242-8632 (acc 32)

North Las Vegas, NV 89030: 211 Judson St, Box 30096; tel: (702) 649-2374 (acc 118)

North Las Vegas, NV 89030: 2035 Yale St; tel (702) 649-2374

Reno, NV 89512-1605: 2300 Valley Rd; tel: (775) 688-4570 (acc 85)

Salt Lake City, UT 84102-2030: 252 South 500 East; tel: (801) 323-5817 (acc 51)

San Bernardino, CA 92411: 925 W 10th St; tel: (909) 888-4880

San Diego, CA 92101-6304: STEPS, 825 7th Ave; tel: (619) 231-6038

Adult Rehabilitation Programmes (Women)

Chico, CA 95973: 13404 Browns Valley Dr; tel: (530) 342-2199 (acc 20)

Grand Junction, CO 81502: Adult Rehabilitation Program – Women's Residence, 915 Grand Ave, PO Box 578, 0578-81501 (mail); tel: (907) 242-8632 (acc 10)

Las Vegas, NV 89030: 39 W Owens; tel: (702) 649-1469 (acc 42)

North Las Vegas, NV 89030: 39 W Owens; tel: (702) 649-1469

Ogden, UT 84401-3610: Women's Rehabilitation Program, 2615 Grant Ave; tel: (801) 621-3580 (acc 29)

Senior Citizens' Housing

Albuquerque, NM: Silvercrest, 4400 Pan Am Fwy NE, 87107; tel: (505) 883-1068 (acc 55)

Broomfield, CO 80020-1876: Silvercrest, 1110 E 10th Ave; tel: (303) 464-1994 (acc 85)

Chula Vista, CA 91910: Silvercrest, 636 3rd Ave; tel: (619) 427-4991 (acc 73)

Colorado Springs, CO 80909-7507: Silvercrest I, 904 Yuma St; tel: (719) 475-2045 (acc 50)

Colorado Springs, CO 80909-5097: Silvercrest II, 824 Yuma St; tel: (719) 389-0329 (acc 50)

Denver, CO 80219-1859: Silvercrest, 4595 W Alameda Ave; tel: (303) 922-2924 (acc 66)

El Cajon, CA 92020: Silvercrest, 175 S Anza St; tel: (619) 593-1077 (acc 73)

El Sobrante, CA 94803-1859: Silvercrest, 4630 Appian Way #100; tel: (510) 758-1518 (acc 63)

Escondido, CA 92026: Silvercrest, 1301 Las Villas Way; tel: (760) 741-4106 (acc 75)

Eureka, CA 95501-1264: Silvercrest, 2141 Tydd St; tel: (707) 445-3141 (acc 152)

Fresno, CA 93721-1041: Silvercrest, 1824 Fulton St; tel: (559) 237-9111 (acc 158)

Glendale, CA 92104: Silvercrest, 323 W Garfield; tel: (818) 543-0211 (acc 150)

Hollywood, CA 90028: Silvercrest, 5940 Carlos Ave; tel: (323) 460-4335 (acc 140)

Lake View Terrace, CA 91354: Silvercrest, 11850 Foothill Blvd; tel: (818) 896-7580 (acc 150)

Los Angeles, CA 90006: Silvercrest, 947 S Hoover St; tel: (213) 387-7278 (acc 120)

Mesa, AZ 85201: Silvercrest, 255 E 6th St; tel: (480) 649-9117 (acc 81)

Missoula, MT 59801: Silvercrest, 1550 S 2nd St W #125; tel: (406) 541-0464 (acc 50)

N Las Vegas, NV 89030: Silvercrest, 2801 E Equador Ave; tel: (702) 643-0293 (acc 60)

Oceanside, CA 92056: Silvercrest, 3839 Lake Blvd; tel: (760) 940-0166 (acc 67)

Pasadena, CA 91106: Silvercrest, 975 E Union St; tel: (626) 432-6678 (acc 150)

Phoenix, AZ 85003: Silvercrest, 613 N 4th Ave; tel: (602) 251-2000 (acc 125)

Portland, OR 97232: Silvercrest, 1865 NE Davis; tel: (503) 236-2320 (acc 78)

Puyallup, WA 98373: Silvercrest, 4103 9th St SW; tel: (253) 841-0785 (acc 40)

Crowds queue to enter the Ray and Joan Kroc Corps Community Centre in San Francisco (Photo Kirk M. Wuest)

Redondo Beach, CA 90277: Mindeman Senior Residence, 125 W Beryl St; tel: (310) 318-2827/0582 (acc 54)
Reno, NV 89512-2448: Silvercrest, 1690 Wedekind Rd; tel: (775) 322-2050 (acc 59)
Riverside, CA 92501: Silvercrest, 3003 N Orange; tel: (951) 276-0173 (acc 72)
San Diego, CA 92101: Silvercrest, 727 E St; tel: (619) 699-7272 (acc 122)
San Francisco, CA 94133-3844: SF Chinatown Senior Citizens' Residence, 1450 Powell St; tel: (415) 781-8545 (acc 9)
San Francisco, CA 94107-1132: Silvercrest, 133 Shipley St; tel: (415) 543-5381 (acc 514)
Santa Fe Springs, CA 90670: Silvercrest, 12015 Lakeland Rd; tel: (562) 946-7717 (acc 25)
Santa Monica, CA 90401: Silvercrest, 1530 5th St; tel: (310) 393-5336 (acc 122)
Santa Rosa, CA 95404-6601: Silvercrest, 1050 3rd St; tel: (707) 544-6766 (acc 186)
Seattle, WA 98103, Silvercrest, 9543 Greenwood Ave N #105; tel: (206) 706-0855 (acc 75)
Stockton, CA 95202-2645: Silvercrest, 123 N Stanislaus St; tel: (209) 463-4960 (acc 84)
Tulare, CA 93274: 350 North 'L' St; tel: (559) 688-0704 (acc 65)
Turlock, CA 95380: Silvercrest, 865 Lander Ave; tel: (209) 669-8863 (acc 82)
Ventura, CA 93004: Silvercrest, 750 Petit Ave; tel: (805) 647-0110 (acc 130)
Wahiawa, HI 96786-1961: Silvercrest Residence, 520 Pine St #101; tel: (808) 622-2785 (acc 159)

Senior Citizens' Nutrition Centres
Anchorage, AK 99501: Older Alaskans' Program (OAP), 1702 'A' Street; tel: (907) 349-0613
Denver, CO 80205-4547: Denver Red Shield, 2915 High St; (tel): (303) 295-2107
Fresno, CA 93712-1041: 1824 Fulton St; tel: (559) 233-0139
Phoenix, AZ: Laura Danieli Senior Activity Center, 613 N 4th Ave; tel: (602) 251-2005
Portland, OR 97232-2822: Rose Centre – Senior Citizens' Program, 211 NE 18th Ave; tel: (503) 239-1221
Salinas, CA 93906-1519: 2460 N Main St; tel: (831) 443-9655
San Diego, CA 92101-1679: Senior Citizens' Program (9 Locations), 2320 5th Ave; tel: (619) 446-0212
San Francisco, CA 94107-1125: Senior Meals Program, 850 Harrison St; tel: (415) 777-5350 (5 locations)
San Jose, CA 95112: 359 N 4th St; tel: (408) 282-1165
Tucson, AZ 85705; Nutrition and Home Delivered Meals, 1021 N 11th Ave; tel: (520) 792-1352
Tulare, CA 93274-4131: 314 E San Joaquin Ave; tel: (559) 687-2520
Turlock, CA 95380-5815: 893 Lander Ave; tel: (209) 667-6091
Watsonville, CA 95076-5203: 29-A Bishop St; tel: (831) 724-0948

In addition there are 14 fresh-air camps and 23 youth community centres attached to divisions, as well as 511 service units in the territory

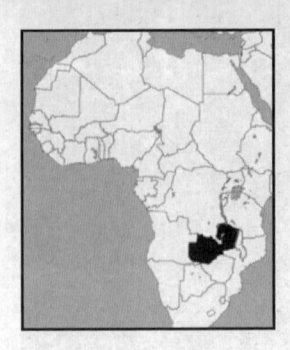

ZAMBIA TERRITORY

Territorial leaders:
Colonels John and Dorita Wainwright

Territorial Commander:
Colonel John Wainwright (1 Mar 2008)

Chief Secretary:
Lieut-Colonel Bislon Hanunka (1 Mar 2008)

Territorial Headquarters: 685A Cairo Road, Lusaka
Postal address: PO Box 34352, Lusaka 10101, Zambia
Tel: [260] 1 238291/228327; fax: [260] 1 226784

In 1922 emigrants from villages on the north bank of the Zambezi River working in a mica mine near Urungwe were converted. They carried home the message of salvation to their chief, and established meeting places in their villages. Two years later, Commandant Kunzwi Shava and Lieutenant Paul Shumba were appointed to command the new opening. The Zambia Division in the Rhodesia Territory became the Zambia Command in 1966. In 1988, the Malawi Division was transferred from the Zimbabwe Territory to form the new Zambia and Malawi Territory. The Zambia and Malawi Territory became the Zambia Territory on 1 October 2002 when Malawi became an independent region.

Zone: Africa
Country included in the territory: Zambia
Languages in which the gospel is preached: Chibemba, Chinyanja, Chitonga, English, Lozi

IN August 2008 the nation was saddened by the death of President Levy Mwanawasa. During a national mourning period, the Council of Churches of Zambia organised prayers by the churches at the National Showgrounds in Lusaka. The Territorial Songsters and cadets were invited to sing. The Territorial Youth Songsters sang on national television.

The Salvation Army was represented at the President's funeral by the Territorial Commander and Chief Secretary. They also attended the inauguration of President Rupiah Banda at Parliament on 2 November.

Zambian Salvationists were greatly encouraged by the visit in November of Africa zonal leaders Commissioners Amos and Rosemary Makina. Three territorial events were held – a Thanksgiving Appeal ingathering and rallies for Home League and Men's Fellowship members. There was great rejoicing at a 61 per cent increase in the Thanksgiving Appeal giving and a 57 per cent increase in giving to the Helping-Hand Scheme.

Also in November the territory's first woman divisional commander was appointed, to Mapangazya Division.

A party of 11 cadets and staff from the Norway, Iceland and The Færoes

Zambia Territory

Territory visited in January 2009. For 12 days they shared in learning, recreation, praise and prayer with cadets and staff of the training college in Lusaka.

Community visits and meeting leadership in Lusaka, Chikankata and Livingstone, and a visit to Victoria Falls, all served to foster a spirit of unity and understanding.

In February, 40 delegates attended a Women's Ministries seminar themed 'Empowered!', which placed an emphasis on prayer and Bible study. Divisional leaders' training was also held in February.

A Community Development seminar in March sought to develop a strategy for the territory's community work for the next five years. The conference brought together delegates from THQ and divisions, as well as from donor territories (the UK and Switzerland, Austria and Hungary), SAWSO, and facilitators from Southern Africa.

Key focus areas identified for future development were health, HIV/Aids, education, water and sanitation, livelihood improvement and anti-human trafficking.

Enthusiasm for music among the territory's youth has grown to such an extent that two music schools were held during the year under review. The first (August 2008) attracted 120 delegates and the other (April 2009) drew more than 400. Both were facilitated by Salvationists from the Zambia and UK Territories.

STATISTICS
Officers 205 (active 185 retired 20) **Cadets** 25 **Employees** 422
Corps 107 **Societies** 44 **Outposts** 156 **New Openings** 13 **Hospital** 1 **High School** 1 **Old People's Home** 1 **Farm** 1
Senior Soldiers 23,035 **Adherents** 2,270 **Junior Soldiers** 5,954
Personnel serving outside territory Officers 4

STAFF
Women's Ministries: Col Dorita Wainwright (TPWM) Lt-Col Melody Hanunka (Asst TPWM) Maj Jessie Magaya (THLS) Capt Rachel Kandama (TJHLS) Lt-Col Marie Mata (TLOMS)
Sec for Personnel: Lt-Col Metson Chilyabanyama
Sec for Programme: Lt-Col Jean-Baptiste Mata
Sec for Business Administration: Lt-Col Davidson Varghese
Community Development and Micro-Credit: Lt-Col Rosemary Chilyabanyama
Extension Training: Capt Aubey Hatukupa
Finance and Audit: Capt Donald Hangoma
Property: Maj Bexter Magaya
Public Relations: Capt Kennedy Mizinga
Projects: Chris and Erin Hann
Social Services and Education: Maj Patricia Hangoma
Sponsorship: Mr Elijah Hazemba
Trade: Maj Ritah Chikoondo
Training: Maj James Weymouth
Youth and Candidates: Capt Ginger Kandama

TRAINING COLLEGE
PO Box 34352, Lusaka, 10101; tel: (01) 261755; email: zsaotc@gmail.com

DIVISIONS
Lusaka North West: PO Box 33934, Lusaka; Majs Frazer and Rodinah Chalwe
Lusaka South East: PO Box 34352, Lusaka; tel: (01) 221960; Majs Bernard and Dorothy Chisengele
Mapangazya: P Bag S2, Mazabuka; Maj Saraphina Milambo (DC) Maj Florence Shavanga (DDWM)
Mazabuka: PO Box 670017, Mazabuka; tel: (032) 30420; Majs Richard and Eunice Mweemba

DISTRICTS
Copperbelt: PO Box 70075, Ndola; tel: (02) 680302; Maj Isaac Kauseni

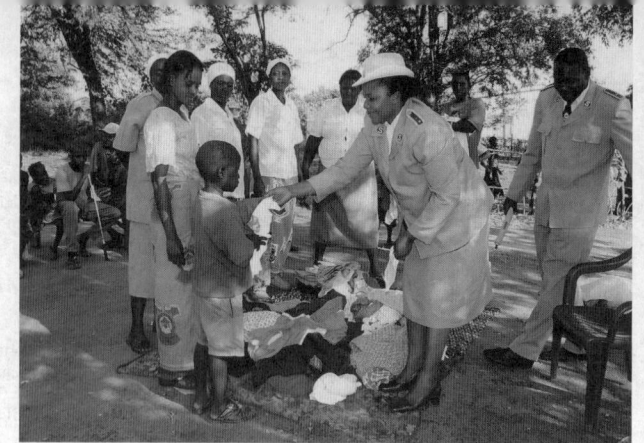

Clothing is distributed to orphans and vulnerable children by Savationists of Chirundu Corps, Siavonga District

Siavonga: PO Box 59, Siavonga; tel: (01) 511362; Capt Clifford Chikondo
Southern: PO Box 630537, Choma; Maj Cason Sichilomba

SECTION (reporting to THQ)
Eastern: PO Box 510199, Chipata; tel: (097) 881828; Capt John Mweene

CHIKANKATA MISSION
P Bag S2, Mazabuka
Mission Director: tba

CHIKANKATA HEALTH SERVICES
P Bag S2, Mazabuka; tel: (01) 222060; email: administration@chikankata.com
Chief Medical Officer: Dr Trevor Kaile
Manager/Administration: Maj Edward Shavanga
Business Manager: Mr Anthony Watson
Manager/Aids Management Training Services: tba
Manager/Community Health and Development: Mr Charles Mang'ombe
Manager/Nursing Education: Mrs Z. Ngalande
Hospital Chaplain: Maj Rotinah Sitwala

Medical Clinics (under Chikankata)
Chaanga, Chikombola, Nadezwe, Nameembo, Syanyolo

Youth Project (under Chikankata)
Chikombola

CHIKANKATA HIGH SCHOOL
P Bag S1, Mazabuka; tel: (01) 220820; email: administration@chikankata.sch.zm
Headmaster: Mr Oscar Mwanza
Matron: Capt Catherine Mukoboto

OLD PEOPLE'S HOME AND VOCATIONAL TRAINING CENTRE
Mitanda Home for the Aged: PO Box 250096, Kansenshi, Ndola; tel: (02) 680460; email: mitanda@zamtel.zm

PRE-SCHOOL GROUPS
Chikankata, Chikanzaya, Chipapa, Chipata, Chitumbi, Choma, Dundu, George, Hapwaya, Ibbwe Munyama, John Laing, Kakole, Kalomo, Kanyama, Kawama, Kazungula, Lusaka Citadel, Maamba, Magoye, Mitchel, Mukwela, Mumbwa, Ngangula, Njomona, Nkonkola, Petauke, Peters, Siavonga, Sikoongo, Sinazongwe, Situmbeko

COMMUNITY SCHOOLS
Chelstone, Chipata (Lusaka), Choma, George, John Laing, Kanyama, Kasiwe, Kawama, Luanshya, Maamba, Mbala, Monze, Petauke

COMMUNITY WORK
Agriculture Projects: Chikankata, Chitumbi, Dundu, Hamabuya, Malala, Ngamgula
Feeding Programme: Lusitu
Fish Farming Projects: George, Kanyama
Health Centres: George, John Laing, Kanyama
HIV/Aids Training, Counselling: Chikankata, THQ
Micro-Credit Projects:
  Eastern: Chipata
  Lusaka North West: Mumbwa
  Mapangazya: Chikankata
  Mazabuka: Magoye, Monze, Nakambala, Njomona

FARM (income-generating)
PO Box 250096, Kansenshi, Ndola; tel: (02) 680460

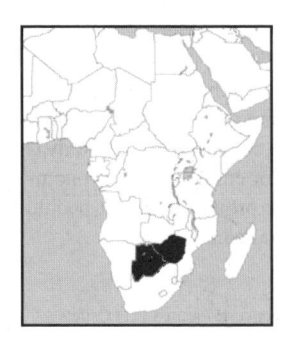

ZIMBABWE TERRITORY

Territorial Commander:
Commissioner Vinece Chigariro
(1 Mar 2008)

Chief Secretary:
Colonel Wilfred Varughese
(1 Aug 2008)

Territorial Headquarters: 45 Josiah Chinamano Avenue, Harare
Postal address: PO Box 14, Harare, Zimbabwe
Tel: [263] (4) 736666/7/8, 250107/8; fax: [263] (4) 726658; email: ZIMTHQ@zim.salvationarmy.org;
website: www.salvationarmy.org/Zimbabwe

A pioneer party led by Major and Mrs Pascoe set out from Kimberley, South Africa, on 5 May 1891 in a wagon drawn by 18 oxen, arriving in Fort Salisbury on 18 November. The then Rhodesia became a separate territory on 1 May 1931. Work spread to Botswana where The Salvation Army was officially recognised in 1997.

Zone: Africa
Countries included in the territory: Botswana, Zimbabwe
'The Salvation Army' in Ndebele: Impi yo Sindiso; in Shona: Hondo yo Ruponiso
Languages in which the gospel is preached: Chitonga, English, Ndebele, Shona, Tswana
Periodicals: *Zimbabwe Salvationist, ZEST* (women's magazine)

AT an officers' Brengle Institute, conducted to instill and enhance the doctrine of sanctification, delegates were encouraged to preach, teach and sing holiness. The officers were lifted to a higher plane of grace and holy living.

Officers' review seminars were held for the deepening of spirituality and the developing of skills, attitudes and commitment to The Salvation Army's mission. Officers were encouraged to continue to give their best in their appointments and to plan for the future.

A 'Servant Leadership' seminar was conducted to empower officers with management skills and help them to be more efficient and effective in their ministry. Colonels John and Dorita Wainwright (territorial leaders, Zambia) facilitated the seminar, emphasising that servant leadership is spiritual leadership and that leaders should have the ability to recognise and develop potential in others.

The Strategic Plan Review for 2007-2012 was conducted to assess what progress was being made and to map a way forward for the territory. Delegates were encouraged to impart more information to the Army's stakeholders.

The territory also launched a business forum for Salvationists involved in business. It was aimed at encouraging Salvationists in business to support the Army's mission and to challenge them to be Kingdom-builders in their corps.

Guest of honour at the training college's Open Day and for the cadets' out-training appointments meeting was Tendai Savanhu, a businessman, politician and Salvationist at Harare Citadel Corps. He 'sponsored' the college for four months, meeting all expenses from September to December 2008.

During August 2008 Zimbabwean youths had participated at the Zambia Territory Music Camp, facilitated by Salvationists from the Zambia and UK Territories. Delegates were taught the purpose and role of music in the lives of people in their corps and communities.

At regional consultative meetings the territorial leadership outlined objectives set to empower the regional group members. They were encouraged to remain mission-focused and continue supporting the Army's work.

During several Women's Ministries rallies conducted at regional level, women were introduced to the Dorcas programme which focuses on sewing. This income-generating scheme seeks to raise Home League funds. Young women in the territory embarked on knitting woollen bedspreads for hospitals while Junior Miss members spent time sewing handkerchiefs for the elderly.

The Territorial Commander officially handed 13 heifers to Chihota Dairy Farmers beneficiaries and presented certificates to other beneficiaries as accepted members. The Chihota community commended The Salvation Army for embarking on economically viable projects to assist people living in rural communities.

STATISTICS

Officers 568 (active 457 retired 111) **Cadets** 40
 Employees 1,430
Corps 404 **Societies** 213 **Outposts** 181
 Institutions/Social Centres 5 **Hospitals** 4
 Schools – Pre-Schools 51 **Primary** 33
 Secondary 13 **Boarding** 4 **Vocational Training** 7
Senior Soldiers 122,513 **Adherents** 4,374
Junior Soldiers 18,882
Personnel serving outside territory Officers 20

STAFF

Women's Ministries: Comr Vinece Chigariro (TPWM) Col Prema Wilfred (TSWM) Maj Martha Chinyemba (TLOMS) Lt-Col Orlipha Ncube (THLS)
Sec for Business: Lt-Col Langton Zipingani
Sec for Personnel: Lt-Col Dubayi Ncube
Sec for Programme: Maj Casman Chinyemba
Audit: Maj Moyo Marasha
Development Services: Capt Criswell Chizengeya
Education: Maj Henry Chitanda
Extension Training: Mrs Rochelle McAlister
Finance: Maj Sheila Chitanda
Human Resources Development: Lt-Col Beauty Zipingani
Literary Sec: tba
Medical and Social: Capt Elizabeth Garland
Property: Capt Lovemore Meda
Public Relations: Maj Itai Mutizwa
Sponsorship: Capt Joice Chizengeya
Statistics: Capt Alice Marondo
Territorial Bandmaster: B/M M. Mtombeni
Territorial Songster Leader: S/L K. E. Mushababiri
Trade: Capt Susan Marere
Training: Maj Abraham Lincoln Mudda
Youth and Candidates: Capt Absolom Makanga

DIVISIONS

Bindura: PO Box 197, Bindura; tel: (071) 6689; Maj Anna Karengesha

Zimbabwe Territory

Chiweshe: PO Box 98, Glendale;
tel: (077) 214524; Majs Last and Margeret Siamoya

Greater Harare: PO Box 1496, Harare;
tel: (04) 747359; Majs Funny and Ellen Nyereyemhuka

Guruve: c/o Box 150, Guruve; tel: (058) 505;
Majs Isiah and Leah Motsi

Harare Central: c/o Highfield Temple,
Stand # 3300, Old Highfield; tel: 663 159;
Majs Friday and Glory Ayanam

Harare Eastern: PO Box 26, Zengeza;
tel: (070) 22639; Majs Sammy and Ellen Nkhoma

Harare West: c/o Dzivarasekwa Corps,
PO Box 37, Dzivarasekwa; tel: (04) 216 293;
Capt Manuel Nhelenhele (Area Coordinator)

Hurungwe: PO Box 269, Karoi;
tel: (064) 629229; Majs Chatonda and Joyce Theu

Kadoma: PO Box 271, Kadoma;
tel: (068) 23338; Majs Isaac and Charity Mhembere

Makonde: PO Box 33, Chinhoyi;
tel: (067) 2107; Majs Frederick and Rosemary Masango

Masvingo: PO Box 314, Masvingo;
tel: (039) 63308; Majs Onai and Deliwe Jera

Matebeleland: PO Box 227 FM, Famona,
Bulawayo; tel: (09) 46934; Majs Tineyi and Rumbidzai Mambo

Midlands: PO Box 624, Kwekwe;
tel: (055) 3992; Majs Edwin and Tambudzai Jeremiah

Mupfure: PO Box 39, Mt Darwin;
tel: (076) 529; Majs Clever and Daphine Kamambo

Semukwe: PO Box Maphisa Township,
Maphisa; tel: (082) 396; Majs Final and Pfumisai Mubaiwa

DISTRICTS

Manicaland: PO Box DV8, Dangamvura,
Mutare; tel: (020) 30014; Capt Sipho Mbangwa

Murehwa: PO Box 268, Murehwa;
tel: (078) 2455; Maj Lovemore Chidhakwa

AREAS

Harare Central: c/o Highfield Temple;
Stand # 3300, Old Highfield; tel: 663 159;
Area Coordinator: Maj Friday Ayanam

Harare West: c/o Dzivarasekwa Corps,
PO Box 37, Dzivarasekwa; tel: (04) 216 293;
Area Coordinator: Maj Tineyi Mambo

Hwange: PO Box 130, Dete; tel: 018 237;
Area Coordinator: Maj Peter Nikisi

TRAINING COLLEGE
PO Box CR95, Cranborne; tel: (04) 742298;
fax: (04) 742575

MASIYE TRAINING CAMP
PO Box AC800 Bulawayo; tel: (09) 60727;
Camp: tel: (0838) 222/261; tel/fax: (0838) 228;
emails: info@masiye.com (camp),
info@byo.masiye.com (town office)

EDUCATION
Boarding Schools
Bradley Secondary School: P Bag 909 Bindura;
tel: (071) 3421 (acc 516)

Howard High School: PO Box 230, Howard;
tel: (0758) 45921 (acc 908)

Mazowe High School: P Bag 211A, Harare;
tel: (075) 25603 (acc 670)

Usher Secondary School: P Bag P5271,
Bulawayo; tel: (083) 2904 (acc 560)

MEDICAL
Athol Evans Hospital Home: Chiremba Rd,
Queensdale, PO Box CR70, Cranborne;
tel: (04) 572121; email: aec.sec@zol.co.zw
(acc 164)

Bumhudzo Hospital Home: St Mary's Township,
PO Box ZG 48, Zengeza, Harare;
tel: (070) 24911; 'C' scheme hospital home
(acc 55); 'B' scheme residential (acc 55)

Howard Hospital: PO Box 190, Glendale;
tel: (0758) 2433; emails:
howard.hospital@africaonline.co.zw,
pthistle@healthnet.zw (acc 144)

Tshelanyemba Hospital: PO Tshelanyemba,
Maphisa; tel: (082) 254; email:
tshelanyemba.hosp@healthnet.zw (acc 103)

SOCIAL SERVICES
Bulawayo
Enterprise House: Josiah Tongogara St/12th Ave,
PO Box 3208; tel: (09) 60012 (acc men 65)

Ralstein Home: Masotsha Ndhlovu Ave;
tel: (09) 61972 (acc mixed 30)

Harare
Braeside Social Complex: General Booth Rd,
Braeside, PO Box CR66, Cranborne;
tel: (04) 742001 (acc women 20, men 64)

Arcadia Girls' Hostel: Jampies St, Arcadia;
tel: (04) 770082 (acc 28)

Howard
Weaving and Dressmaking School: PO Howard;
tel: (0758) 45921

Biographical Information

Based on information received by 30 September 2009

1. The following list contains the names of all active officers with the rank of lieut-colonel and above, and other officers holding certain designated appointments.

2 (a) The place and date in parenthesis immediately following the name denote the place from which the officer entered Army service and the year of service commencement. Officers commissioned prior to 1 January 1973 have their active service dated from the conclusion of the first year of training. After 1 January 1973 active service begins at the date of commissioning following a two-year session of training.

(b) Details of married women officers' entry to active service are shown separately, including maiden name. If a wife was trained separately from her husband the word *and* joins the two entries, but if trained together the word *with* joins them.

(c) At the end of each entry of married officers a joint record of their service in other countries is given. Where applicable this includes countries each served in individually before marriage.

3. Where an officer is serving in a territory/command other than his/her own this is indicated by including the territory/command of origin after the corps from which he/she entered training. In all other instances the information given implies that the officer is serving in his/her home territory.

4. Details of appointments (where not given in this section) may be ascertained under the territorial or departmental headings.

5. A key to abbreviations is given on pages 348-349.

A

ABAYOMI, Ebenezer (Ife Ife, 1988); Maj, Nig. b 4 Apr 60; and
  ABAYOMI, Comfort (Ife Ife, 1990) m 1990; Maj, Nig. b 12 Dec 63.

ABBULU, Sankurati Pedda (Achanta, 1978); Maj, Ind C. b 2 Jan 50; with
  ABBULU, Vimala (née Kumari) m 1970; Maj, Ind C. b 10 Dec 53. Served in Tanz.

ABRAHAM, Puthenparambil T. (Karimala, Ind SW, 1972); Lt-Col, CS, Ind C. b 17 Feb 48; and
  ABRAHAM, Mariyamma (Central Adoor, Ind SW, 1975) m 1975; Lt-Col, TSWM, Ind C. b 30 Mar 52. Served in Ind SW

ADAMS, Clive (Claremont, S Afr, 1983); Col, CS, Nor. b 5 Jan 57; and
  ADAMS, Marianne (née Jokobsen) (Oslo 3, 1985) m 1990; Col, TSWM, Nor. b 10 Feb 60. Served in S Afr, UK and at IHQ.

ADAMS, Shirley Ann (Houston, TX, USA S, 1973); Maj, Mex. b 5 Jan 54. BA (Bus Adm), BA (Chrstn Adm). Served in USA S.

ADDISON, Edward (Swedru, 1981); Maj, Gha. b 24 Jan 54. Ww Lt Margaret, pG 1983; and
  ADDISON, Mercy (née Simpson) (Swedru, 1985) m 1985; Maj, Gha. b 4 Nov 60.

ADEPOJU, Gabriel (Ibadan, 1986); Maj, Nig. b 17 Jul 60. MSc, BA (Relig Studies); and
  ADEPOJU, Comfort (Ibadan, 1994) m 1994; Maj, Nig. b 15 Aug 70.

ADU-MANU, Mike (Jamasi, 1987); Lt-Col, Gha. b 10 Apr 48; with
  ADU-MANU, Theresa (née Asante Pinamang) m 1970; Lt-Col, Gha. b 1 Apr 48.

AGUILERA, Miguel (Lo Valledor, S Am W, 1978); Maj, Brz. b 9 Jul 55; and
  AGUILERA, Angélica (née Cortes) (Lo Valledor, Chile, S Am W, 1978) m 1979; Maj, Brz. b 11 Sep 58. Served in S Am W, Sp and L Am N.

AGUIRRE, Bartolo (Salto, 1972); Maj, S Am E. b 4 May 45. m 1969; Maj Violeta, ret 2009.

AHN, Guhn-shik (Oh Ka, 1985); Maj, Kor. b 23 Dec 57; and
  YANG, Shin-kyong (Sudaemun, 1984) m 1985; Maj, Kor. b 5 Jul 54.

AINSWORTH, Rodney (Mitchelton, 1973); Maj, Aus E. b 26 Nov 49; and
  AINSWORTH, Leonie (née Matthews) (Woonona, 1976) m 1976; Maj, Aus E. b 6 Dec 53.

AKPAN, Joseph (Calabar, 1980); Lt-Col, Nig. b 30 Sep 58; with
  AKPAN, Patience m 1978; Lt-Col, Nig. b 15 May 62.

AKPAN, Mfon Jaktor (Igbobi, Nig, 1969); Comr, TC, Con (Braz). b 21 Jul 49; and
  AKPAN, Ime Johnnie (née Udo) (Ikot Udobia, Nig, 1974) m 1974; Comr, TPWM, Con (Braz). b 9 Nov 53. Served in Nig.

ALARCÓN, David (Punta Arenas, 1980);

Biographical Information

Lt-Col, S Am W. b 24 Jun 56; and
ALARCÓN, María (née Arredondo)
(Rancagua, 1980) m 1982; Lt-Col, S Am W.
b 3 Mar 55.

ALARCÓN, Juan Carlos (Punta Arenas, 1972);
Maj, S Am W. b 25 Jan 51; and
ALARCÓN, Nancy (née Muñoz) (Punta
Arenas, 1971) m 1973; Maj, S Am W.
b 17 Sep 52. Served in USA E.

ALÍ, Sixto (El Tejar, 1990); Maj, S Am W.
b 28 Mar 63; with
ALÍ, Aída (née Cáceres) m 1988; Maj,
S Am W. b 8 Mar 68.

ALLAN, Geoffrey (Detroit Brightmoor, MI,
1977); Maj, USA C. b 27 Feb 46. BA (Ed),
MA (Sec Ed); with
ALLAN, Marian (née Botu) m 1965; Maj,
USA C. b 8 Jun 43. RN (Nursing).

ALLAN, Graham (Kokomo, IN, 1975); Maj,
USA C. b 24 Feb 49. BA (Counselling/Bus
Adm) with
ALLAN, Vickie (née Hardebeck) m 1969;
Maj, USA C. b 26 Jan 50.

ALLEMAND, Carolyn (née Olckers) (Cape
Town Citadel, S Afr, 1980); Lt-Col, UK.
b 4 Oct 55. Served in S Afr, at IHQ and in
S Am E. m 1989; Lt-Col Gustave, ret 2006.

ALLEY, Kelvin (Belconnen, Aus E, 1987); Maj,
PNG. b 3 Apr 54. BA (Adm), BDiv; with
ALLEY, Julie (née Stewart) m 1975; Maj,
PNG. b 19 Jun 56. Served in Aus E.

ALM, Britt-Marie (née Johansson) (Hisingskåren,
1970); Lt-Col, Swdn. b 28 Dec 45.

ALMENDRAS, Eduardo (Puento Alto, S Am W,
1975); Maj, L Am N. b 3 Aug 51, with
ALMENDRAS, Dalia Rosa (née Diaz)
m 1974; Maj, L Am N. b 23 Dec 48. Served
in S Am W and Aus S.

AMAKYE, Francis (Achiase, 1995); Capt, Gha.
b 25 Jul 65; with
AMAKYE, Jemima (née Agyei Yeboah)
m 1992; Capt, Gha. b 3 May 65.

AMBITAN, Harold (Manado 1, 1973); Lt-Col,
Indon. b 9 May 49; and
AMBITAN, Deetje (née Malawau) (Bandung,
1972) m 1975; Lt-Col, Indon. b 8 Jun 49.

AMICK, Richard (Hutchinson, KS, 1978);
Maj, USA C. b 24 Nov 54. BA (Bus Adm);
and
AMICK, Vicki (née Anderson) (Grand
Haven, MI, 1978) m 1979; Maj, USA C.
b 29 Jun 55.

AMPOFO, Jonas (Asiakwa, 1981); Maj, Gha.
b 6 Oct 1950; with
AMPOFO, Constance (née Nyamekye)
m 2004; Capt, Gha. b 14 Apr 57.

ANZEZE, Hezekiel (Naliava, 1980); Comr,
TC, Ken E. b 15 Mar 49. Ww Comr Clerah,
pG 2005.

APPAVOO, William (N Karayankuzhy, 1969);
Lt-Col, Ind SE. b 2 Jun 48; and
APPAVOO, Thavamony William (Booth
Tucker Hall, 1971) m 1972; Lt-Col, Ind SE.
b 18 Mar 47.

APPEATENG, Seth (Manso, 1989); Maj, Gha.
b 9 Jun 62; with
APPEATENG, Janet (née Nkansah) m 1987;
Maj, Gha. b 12 Dec 67.

ARGUEDAS, Antonio (Callao, 1974); Maj,
S Am W. b 9 Sep 53; and
ARGUEDAS, Lilian (née Sánchez) (Lima
Central, 1981) m 1981; Maj, S Am W.
b 24 Nov 58.

ARNAL, Sylvie (Alès, 1977); Maj, Frce.
b 13 Apr 53. Served in Zaï and Con (Braz).

ARNOLD, Wilfred D. (Hamilton, 1973);
Lt-Col, NZ. b 22 May 45. BSoc Sc,
MA (Soc Wk), CQSW; with
ARNOLD, Margaret D. (née Fitness) m 1966;
Lt-Col, NZ. b 6 Jul 45. BN, RGON, Grad Dip
Soc Sc. Served in Aus S and Sing.

ARULAPPAN, Paramadhas (Elanthiady, 1972);
Maj, Ind SE. b 11 May 54; and
ARULAPPAN, Retnam Paramadhas
(Changaneri, 1974) m 1976; Maj, Ind SE.
b 30 May 51.

ASIRVATHAM, Devadhas (Palliyady, 1971);
Maj, Ind SE. b 20 May 51; and
ASIRVATHAM, Jothi Vasanthabai
(Manakarai, 1973) m 1973; Maj, Ind SE.
b 11 Apr 53

ASPERSCHLAGER, Gary C. (Orange, NJ,
1976); Lt-Col, USA E. b 20 Apr 46. BS (Biol),
MA (Div); and
ASPERSCHLAGER, Pearl A. (née Samson)
(White Plains, NY, 1973) m 1976; Lt-Col,
USA E. b 20 Aug 46. BA (Ed).

B

BAAH, Samuel (Duakwa, Gha, 1987); Lt-Col,
Nig. b 13 Mar 63; with
BAAH, Theresa (née Kumi) m 1984; Lt-Col,
Nig. b 10 Sep 64. Served in Gha.

BABU, P. V. Stanly (Chevalloor, 1983); Maj,
Ind SW. b 28 Nov 55; with
BABU, Nirmala (Kanniyakuzhy, 1986)
m 1986; Maj, Ind SW. b 14 Mar 63.

BAHAMONDE, Cecilia (Lo Vial, 1983); Maj,
S Am W. b 23 Mar 63.

BAILEY, Carol (Greenock, 1977); Maj, UK.
b 13 May 57.

BAILEY, Christine (Barking, 1975); Maj, UK.

b 15 Apr 49. BA (Hons) (Soc Sci – Pol), PGCE. Served in S Am E.

BAILEY, F. Bradford (Kansas City [Westport Temple], MO, USA C, 1982); Lt-Col, CS, S Am W. b 4 May 58. BS (Soc Work); with
BAILEY, Heidi J. (née Chandler) m 1978; Lt-Col, TSWM, S Am W. b 17 Jul 54. Served in USA C and Sp (OC/CPWM).

BAKEMBA, Prosper (Mabenga, 1982); Lt-Col, Con (Braz). b 21 Oct 49; with
BAKEMBA, Monique (née Mafoua) m 1980; Lt-Col, Con (Braz). b 28 Jun 52.

BAKER, Gary (Nundah, 1976); Maj, Aus E. b 23 Sep 48. ThA; with
BAKER, Judith (née Wells) m 1969; Maj, Aus E. b 3 Jun 49.

BAMFORD, William A. III (Quincy, MA, 1989); Maj, USA E. b 11 Jun 57. BS (Pharm), MS (Org Ldrshp); with
BAMFORD, G. Lorraine (née Brown) m 1980; Maj, USA E. b 25 Jul 53. BA (Mod Langs).

BANFIELD, Stephen (Quincy MA, 1978); Maj, USA E. b 17 Mar 53. BA (Psych); with
BANFIELD, Janet Mae (née Anderson) m 1976; Maj, USA E. b 27 Apr 55.

BARKAT, Samuel (Thal, 1973); Maj, Pak. b 7 Aug 51; with
SAMUEL, Margaret m 1971; Maj, Pak. b 7 Aug 52.

BARNARD, Rodney (Norwood, 1982); Maj, Aus S. b 7 Apr 49; with
BARNARD, Jennifer (née Rowe) m 1970; Maj, Aus S. b 5 Nov 50. Served in UK.

BARR, John M. (Ian) (Saltcoats, 1972); Lt-Col, UK. b 10 Aug 50. BD (Hons), MA Cert Ed. Served at ITC. m 1974; Lt-Col Christine, ret 2009.

BATEMAN, David (Lower Hutt, 1988); Maj, NZ. b 17 Dec 60. Dip Bus, Cert Mgmt (NZIM); with
BATEMAN, Margaret (née Allott) m 1983; Maj, NZ. b 19 Nov 58. BN, RGON.

BAUTISTA, Estelita (née Baquirin) (Asingan, 1994); Maj, Phil. b 12 Nov 62. BS (Comm); and
BAUTISTA, David (Asingan, 1996) m 1996; Capt, Phil. b 12 May 61. BSc (Industrial Ed).

BECKMAN, Elisabeth (née Sundström) (Stockholm Temple, 2006); Capt, Swdn, b 18 Jan 65.

BELL, Donald C. (Spokane, WA, USA W, 1978); Comr, TC, NZ. b 12 Oct 49. BA (Econ & Hist), JD (Law); and
BELL, Debora K. (née Perry) (Hobbs, NM, 1977) m 1979; Comr, TPWM, NZ. b 6 Feb 56.

Served at USA Nat, in USA W (CS/TSWM) and NZ (CS/TSWM).

BELL, Mark (Hagerstown, MD, 1977); Maj, USA S. b 27 Mar 51; with
BELL, Alice (née Armendariz) m 1975; Maj, USA S. b 26 Sep 54.

BERG, Gro (née Egeland) (Stavanger, 1985); Maj, Nor. b 11 Oct 62; and
BERG, Pål Thomas (Nord Odal II, 1985) m 1985; Maj, Nor. b 12 Aug 62.

BERG, Odd (Harstad, 1969); Lt-Col, Nor. b 4 Mar 47; and
BERG, Grethe (née Knetten) (Ski, 1969) m 1971; Lt-Col, Nor. b 12 May 48. Served in Nor, UK, Den and Ger (CS/TSWM).

BERRY, Donald E. (Kearny, NJ, 1976); Maj, USA E. b 9 Jun 49; with
BERRY, Vicki (née Van Nort) m 1970; Maj, USA E. b 15 Jan 50. BA (Engl), MA (Strategic Comms & Ldrshp)

BIAKLIANA, S. (Hnahthial, 1981); Maj, Ind E. b 15 Feb 56; and
BIAKMAWII (Dolchera, 1982) m 1982; Maj, Ind E. b 10 Aug 62.

BLOMBERG, Sonja (née Waern) (Kristinehamn 1994); Maj, Swdn. b 1 May 56; and
BLOMBERG, Christer (Kristinehamn 1994) Maj, Swdn. b 16 Jul 54.

BLOOMFIELD, Glenn C. (Philadelphia NE, PA, 1972); Maj, USA E. b 25 Feb 50; and
BLOOMFIELD, Carol (née Thompson) (Cleveland Temple, OH, 1971) m 1972; Maj, USA E. b 1 Jun 48.

BOADU, Stephen (Topremang 1985); Maj, Gha. b 17 Jul 61; with
BOADU, Cecilia (née Ofori) m 1983; Maj, Gha. b 4 Apr 63.

BODE, William H. (Alliance, OH, 1970); Maj, USA E. b 6 Sep 49, and
BODE, Joan I. (née Burke) (Brooklyn 8th Ave, NY, 1969) m 1971; Maj, USA E. b 30 Aug 48.

BOND, Eric (St Catharines, ON, 1987); Maj, Can. b 24 Dec 46. BA (Teachers Cert); with
BOND, Donna (née Williams) m 1968; Maj, Can. b 10 Mar 49.

BOND, Linda (St James, Winnipeg, Can, 1968); Comr, TC, Aus E. b 22 Jun 46. BRelig Ed, MTS. Served in UK, Can (CS), USA W (TC) and at IHQ.

BONE, Cilla (South Croydon, UK, 1971); Maj, Aus S. b 24 Jul 49. Served in UK, at IHQ and in Aus E.

BOOTH, Patrick (Paris-Central, Frce, 1989); Maj, S Afr. b 12 Jan 55; with
BOOTH, Margaret (née Miaglia) m 1983;

Biographical Information

Maj, S Afr. b 31 Jul 61. Served in Frce and UK
BOSCHUNG, Franz (Basle 2, 1977); Col, CS, Switz. b 21 Sep 49; with
BOSCHUNG, Hanny (née Abderhalden) m 1971; Col, TSWM, Switz. b 7 Apr 50. Served in Con (Braz).

BOSH, Larry (Mansfield, OH, USA E, 1966); Comr, IHQ (IS Am & Carib). b 9 Jun 46. BS (Acct), MBA; and
BOSH, Gillian (née Reid) (Akron Citadel, OH, USA E, 1960) m 1967; Comr, IHQ (ZSWM Am & Carib). b 4 Dec 40. Served at IHQ, USA Nat (Nat CS/NSWM, NRVAVS) and in USA E (CS/TSWM).

BOUZIGUES, Ricardo (Colegiales, 1976); Lt-Col, CS, S Am E. b 12 Sep 52. BA (Pract Theol), MA (Theol); and
BOUZIGUES, Sonia (née Alvez) (Cordoba, 1979) m 1979; Lt-Col, TSWM, S Am E. b 12 Nov 54.

BOWLES, Marsha-Jean (née Wortley) (Woodstock, ON, Can, 1990); Maj, Ger. b 2 Mar 62; with
BOWLES, David m 1981; Maj, Ger. b 20 Jul 60. Served in Can.

BRADBURY, Clifford (Southsea, 1966); Maj, UK. b 17 Aug 45; and
BRADBURY, Jean (née Curtis) (Dorchester, 1965) m 1968; Maj, UK. b 2 Feb 45.

BREKKE, Birgitte (née Nielsen) (Copenhagen Temple, Den, 1980); Col, IHQ. b 17 Sep 54. SRN. Served in Den, Nor, Sri Lan, Ban (CPWO), UK, E Eur and Pakistan (TPWM). Ww Col Bo, pG 2007.

BRINGANS, David (Albion, Aus E, 1970); Comr, TC, Mex. b 25 May 47; with
BRINGANS, Grace (née Palmer) m 1968; Comr, TPWM, Mex. b 21 Sep 46. Served in NZ, HK, Vietnam, Tai (RC/RPWM) and Sing (GS/CSWO, TC/TPWM), .

BUCKINGHAM, Lyndon (Whangarei, 1988); Maj, NZ. b 13 Feb 62; with
BUCKINGHAM, Bronwyn (née Robertson) m 1986; Maj, NZ. b 21 Jun 65. Served in Can.

BUEYA, Nsoki Joseph (Kavwaya, 1981); Lt-Col, DR Con. b 12 Jul 48; with
BUEYA, Germaine (née Nkenda Mbuku) m 1978; Lt-Col, DR Con. b 10 Jun 52.

BUKIEWICZ, Ralph (Milwaukee West, WI, 1980); Maj, USA C. b 3 Mar 60; and
BUKIEWICZ, Susan (née Cunard) (Dearborn Heights, MI, 1981) m 1981; Maj, USA C. b 9 May 58.

BURGER, Kurt (Los Angeles Congress Hall, CA, USA W, 1972); Comr, TC, Switz. b 26 Aug 46. BS (Bus Adm), BA (Psych), MBA (Bus Adm), Cert CPA; and
BURGER, Alicia (née Pedersen) (San Bernardino, CA, USA W, 1976) m 1988; Comr, TPWM, Switz. b 6 Jul 46. Served in USA W.

BURN, Margaret (née Cain) (Lincoln Citadel, 1966); Lt-Col, UK. b 12 Nov 46.

BURNS, Alan (Harlow, 1976); Lt-Col, UK. b 1 May 54. BSc, BSc (Hons); and
BURNS, Alison (née Hitchin) (Regent Hall, 1979) m 1981; Lt-Col, UK. b 8 Oct 52. MA (Evang). Served at IHQ.

BURR, W. Howard (Lexington, KY, 1973); Lt-Col, USA E. b 8 Nov 47. BA (Psych), MS (Ed Adm); with
BURR, Patricia (née Stigleman) m 1970; Lt-Col, USA E. b 29 Jun 51.

BURRIDGE, Keith (Ealing, UK, 1967); Col, TC, Sing. b 21 Jun 44. MBE, MCIM; with
BURRIDGE, Beryl (née Brown) m 1965; Col, TPWM, Sing. b 11 Nov 44. Served in UK and Sing (CS/TSWM).

BURROWS, David (Skipton, UK, 1970); Lt-Col, IHQ. b 30 Apr 47. SRN. Served in Pak, Tanz (OC) and Mal (OC). m 1972; Lt-Col Jean, ret 2009.

BURTON, Joan (Goole, UK, 1978); Maj, Brz. b 5 Jul 55. Served in UK.

C

CACHELIN, Hervé (Biel, 1979); Maj, Switz. b 16 Feb 57; and
CACHELIN, Deborah (née Cullingworth) (Catford, UK, 1981) m 1983; Maj, Switz. b 2 Jul 57. Served in Aus E and UK.

CAFFULL, Michael (Worthing, UK, 1978) Lt-Col, IHQ. b 20 Dec 55. MA (Miss Ldrshp); and
CAFFULL, Wendy (née Hart) (Southend Citadel, UK, 1977) m 1978; Lt-Col, IHQ. b 24 Mar 57. BA (Pastoral Care with Psych). Served in UK.

CAIRNS, Philip (Campsie, 1982); Lt-Col, Aus E. b 5 Feb 51. Dip Mus Ed, Dip Min, MTh; with
CAIRNS, Janice (née Manson) m 1972; Lt-Col, Aus E. b 7 Oct 48. ATCL, LTCL, Grad Dip Chrstn Counselling.

CALLANDER, Ian (Fairfield, Aus S, 1977); Maj, E Eur. b 7 Aug 55. BTh; and
CALLANDER, Vivien (née Wiseman) (Adelaide Congress Hall, Aus S, 1977) m 1982; Maj, E Eur. b 7 May 53. BPhys. Served in Aus S.

CALVO, Esteban (Concepcion de Rios, 1987); Maj, L Am N. b 23 Jan 63; and
CALVO, Ileana (née Jimenez) (Concepcion de

Rios, 1986) m 1989; Maj, L Am N. b 5 Jun 66.
CAMARGO, Iolanda (Niterói, Brz, 1969); Maj, Asst TSWM, Brz. b 6 Aug 49.
CAMARILLO, Luís (Mexico # 1, 2001); Capt, Mex. b 25 Apr 73; with
CAMARILLO, Nohemí (née Martinez) m 1999; Capt, Mex. b 20 May 73. BA (Adm).
CAMPOS Manuel (Mexicali, 1980); Maj, Mex. b 14 Jun 58; with
CAMPOS Ana (née Flores) m 1978; Maj, Mex. b 26 Jul 57.
CANNING, Joan (Moncton, NB, Can, 1983); Maj, Asst CS, USA Nat. b 27 Sep 62. BA (Bible and Theol). Served in Can and at IHQ.
CAREY, Roderick (Dunedin Fortress, 1982); Maj, NZ. b 13 Mar 58. Dip BRS, BTh; with
CAREY, Jennifer (née Cross) m 1980; Maj, NZ. b 5 Feb 61. Served Aust E.
CARLSON, William (Staten Island Port Richmond, NY, 1971); Lt-Col, USA E. b 9 Jan 48. BA (Soc Studies); and
CARLSON, Marcella (née Brewer) (Staten Island Port Richmond, NY, 1971) m 1971; Lt-Col, USA E. b 18 Sep 49.
CASTILLO, Luis (Antofagasta, S Am W, 1977); Lt-Col, OC, Sp. b 7 Jan 48; and
CASTILLO, Aída (Quinta Normal, 1968) m 1972; Lt-Col, CPWM, Sp. b 5 Nov 49. Served in S Am W (CS/TSWM), Mex (CS/TSWM) and S Am E (CS/TSWM).
CASTOR, Onal (Aquin, Haiti, 1979); Col, TC, Carib. b 20 Jul 55; and
CASTOR, Edmane (née Montoban) (Duverger, Haiti, 1980) m 1980; Col, TPWM, Carib. b 1 Oct 57. Served in USA S, Con (Kin) and Carib (CS/TSWM).
CENECIRO, Joel (Manila, 1989); Maj, Phil. b 23 May 66. BA (Biblical Studies), MA (Chrstn Studies); and
CENECIRO, Susan (née Pudpud) (Tondo, 1989); Maj, Phil. b 31 Oct 66.
CENTENO, César (Mexico # 1, 1988); Maj, Mex. b 24 May 53; with
CENTENO, Guadalupe (née Hernandez) m 1973; Maj, Mex. b 28 Jan 53.
CEREZO, Josué (Monterrey, 1985); Lt-Col, CS, Mex. b 16 May 57. BS; with
CEREZO, Ruth (née Garcia) m 1983; Lt-Col, TSWM, Mex. b 22 Oct 60. BA (Soc Wk). Served in L Am N.
CHAGAS, Edgar (São Paulo Central, 1988); Maj, Brz. b 24 Feb 58. BA (Phys) MA (Sci); with
CHAGAS, Sara (née Parker) m 1982; Maj, Brz. b 26 Aug 60. BA (Psychol).
CHALWE, Frazer (Chikumbi, 1989); Maj, Zam. b 25 Jan 65; with

CHALWE, Rodinah (née Mukunkami) m 1986; Maj, Zam. b 8 May 68.
CHANG, Man-Hee (San Francisco Korean, CA, 1993); Maj, USA W. b 31 Mar 58. BA (Bus Adm), MBA (Bus Adm); with
CHANG, Stephanie (née Shim) m 1983; Maj, USA W. b 1 Jun 59. BA (Math).
CHARAN, Samuel (Rampur, Ind N, 1978); Col, TC, Ind E. b 1 Apr 53; with
CHARAN, Bimla Wati (née Bimla Wati) m 1974; Col, TPWM, Ind E. Served in Ind N, Ind E (CS/TSWM) and Ind SW (CS/TSWM).
CHARLET, Horst (Berlin-Neukölln, 1969); Comr, TC, Ger. b 1 May 46. Dip SW, Dip Soc Pedagogue; with
CHARLET, Helga (née Werner); Comr, TPWM, Ger. b 18 Oct 48. Served in Ger (CS/TSWM)
CHAUHAN, Jashwant Soma (Tarapur, 1979); Maj, Ind W. b 20 Feb 52; with
CHAUHAN, Indiraben m 1976; Maj, Ind W. b 8 Jun 56.
CHELLAIYAN, Anbayan (Perai, 1982); Maj, Ind SE. b 9 Apr 55. BA, BD; and
CHELLAIYAN, Ditch Saroja Bai Anbayan (Vannioor, 1984) m 1984; Maj, Ind SE. b 21 Jun 84.
CHELLIAH, Moni (Oyaravillai, 1976); Maj, Ind SE. b 18 May 55. MA; and
CHELLIAH, Mallika Moni (Alady, 1978) m 1978; Maj, Ind SE. b 6 Mar 57.
CHELLIAH, Swamidhas (Kannankulam, 1977); Maj, Ind SE. b 21 Apr 55; and
CHELLIAH, Joicebai Swamidhas (Kaliancaud, 1973) m 1977; Maj, Ind SE. b 16 Feb 53.
CHEPKURUI, Stephen (Cheptais, Ken, 1982); Maj, RC, Rwa. b 22 Feb 58; and
CHEPKURUI, Grace (née Madolio) (Vigeze, Ken, 1980) m 1985; Maj, RPWM, Rwa. b 15 May 55. Served in E Afr and Tanz (GS/CSWM).
CHEPSIRI, Harun (Toroso, 1995) Capt, Ken W. b 20 Sep 65; with
CHEPSIRI, Beatrice (née Cherop) m 1992; Capt, Ken W. b 6 Jul 68.
CHEYDLEUR, John Reeves (Philadelphia Northeast, PA, 1983); Maj, USA E. b 11 Mar 44. BA (Psych), MA (Counselling/Psych), PhD (Org Psych); with
CHEYDLEUR, Judith Ann (née Kunkle) m 1965; Maj, USA E. b 27 Jul 39. BA (Psych/Soc), MA (Writing).
CHIGARIRO, Vinece (Gunguwe, 1975); Comr, TC, TPWM, Zimb. b 7 Mar 54. Served in Tanz (GS) and Zimb (TC, TPWM).

Biographical Information

CHILYABANYAMA, Metson (Chitumbi, 1987); Lt-Col, Zam. b 30 Oct 55; with
CHILYABANYAMA, Rosemary (née Mboozi) m 1982; Lt-Col, Zam. b 8 Aug 61.

CHINYEMBA, Casman (Chimbumu, 1989); Maj, Zimb. b 7 Jan 62; with
CHINYEMBA, Martha (née Gomo) m 1988; Maj, Zimb. b 16 Oct 63. Served in Tanz.

CHISENGELE, Bernard (Monze, 1983); Maj, Zam. b 1 Jan 51; and
CHISENGELE, Dorothy (née Mweemba) (Kaumba, 1985) m 1985; Maj, Zam. b 14 Nov 59.

CHITANDA, Sheila (née Mvere) (Kwekwe, 1992); Maj, Zimb. b 15 Oct 68; and
CHITANDA, Henry (Chinhoyi, 1991) m 1992; Maj, Zimb. b 6 Apr 66.

CHOO, Seung-chan (Yung Deung Po, 1980); Maj, Kor. b 15 Jun 50; with
LEE, Ok-hee m 1978; Maj, Kor. b 2 Aug 54.

CHOPDE, Surendra S. (Kodoli, 1992); Maj, Ind W. b 2 Sep 65; with
CHOPDE, Helen m 1989; Maj, Ind W. b 1 Jun 64.

CHRISTIAN, Gabriel Ibrahim (Muktipur, 1983); Maj, Ind W. b 24 Dec 59; and
CHRISTIAN, Indumati (née Samual Macwan) (Petlad Central, 1985) m 1986; Maj, Ind W. b 30 Aug 62.

CHRISTIAN, Paul (Bhalej, Ind W, 1978); Lt-Col, CS, Ind N. b 22 Sep 48; and
CHRISTIAN, Anandiben (née Kalidas) (Ghoghawada, Ind W) m 1980; Lt-Col, TSWM, Ind N. b 12 Jul 57. Served at Ind Cent Off and in Ind W (CS/THLS).

CHRISTIAN, Prabhudas Jetha (Sinhuj, 1978); Maj, Ind W. b 23 Jan 52; and
CHRISTIAN, Persis (née Zumal) (Jhalod, 1978) m 1978; Maj, Ind W. b 5 Apr 48.

CHRISTURAJ, Rajamani (Elappara, 1983); Maj, Ind SW. b 27 Dec 61; with
MATHEW, Mary m 1983; Maj, Ind SW. b 11 May 59.

CHRISTIAN, Rasik Paul (Chunel, 1988); Maj, Ind W. b 7 Sep 65; and
CHRISTIAN Ramilaben (née Samuel) (Piplag, 1990) m 1990; Maj, Ind W. b 17 Apr 68.

CHUN, Joon-hung (Yong Dong, 1978); Maj, Kor. b 20 Jun 48; with
SHIN, Myung-ja m 1976; Maj, Kor. b 28 Sep 49.

CHUN, Kwang-pyo (Duk Am, 1971); Comr, TC, Kor. b 15 Sep 41; with
YOO, Sung-ja m 1969; Comr, TPWM, Kor. b 11 Jan 41. Served on Kor (CS/TSWM).

CHUNG, Edmund L. (Manhattan Citadel, USA E, 1976); Lt-Col, IHQ. b 8 Aug 48. BS (Chem), MS (Management); and
CHUNG, Carolynne J. (née Wiseman) (Lexington, KY, USA E, 1976) m 1977. BA, MA (Org Ldrshp); Lt-Col, IHQ. b 28 Jul 46. Served in USA E, USA Nat and UK.

CLIFTON, Shaw (Edmonton, UK, 1973); General (see page 26); with
CLIFTON, Helen (née Ashman) m 1967; Comr, World President of Women's Ministries, IHQ. b 4 May 48. BA (Eng Lang/Lit) (Hons), PGCE. Served at IHQ, in Zimb, USA E, Pak (TC/TPWO), NZ (TC/TPWM) and UK (TC/TPWM).

CLINCH, Ronald (Launceston, Aus S, 1986); Lt-Col, CS, Phil. b 6 Sep 54. BEd; with
CLINCH, Robyn (née Mole) m 1982; Lt-Col, TSWM, Phil. b 8 Nov 60.

COCHRANE, William (Barrhead, 1975); Comr, IHQ (IS to CoS). b 7 Sep 54. Served in UK (CS).

COCKER, James (Cleveland Temple, USA E, 1981), Maj, PNG. b 24 Jan 53. BA (Org Mngmnt); with
COCKER, Marcia (née Kelly) m 1978; Maj, PNG. b 21 Sep 58. BA (Ed), MA (Min & Ldrshp), MDiv. Served in USA E.

COLA, Iliesa (Raiwai, 1995); Capt, NZ. b 7 Nov 55; with
COLA, Litiana (née Vuidreketi) m 1982; Capt, NZ. b 8 Mar 62.

COLEMAN, Michael T. (Kwinana, Aus S, 1986); Maj, RC, Tai. b 4 Nov 54; with
COLEMAN, Annette (née Willey) m 1976; Maj, RPWM, Tai. b 23 Oct 55. BSc. Served in Aus S.

CONDON, James (Shoalhaven 1971), Col, CS, Aus E. b 29 Nov 49; and
CONDON, Jan (née Vickery) (Uralla 1971) m 1972; Col, TWSM, Aus E. b 25 Jan 47. ThA. Served in UK and PNG (CS/TSWM).

CONRAD, Keith (Matroosfontein, 1988); Maj, S Afr. b 31 Mar 62; with
CONRAD, Yvonne (née Jansen) m 1984; Maj, S Afr. b 13 Mar 63. Served in NZ.

COPPLE, Donald (Flin Flon, MB, 1963); Col, CS, Can. b 10 Apr 42; with
COPPLE, Ann (née Cairns) (Point St Charles, QC, 1962) m 1965; Col, TSWM, Can. b 15 Jul 42.

COSTAS, Deisy (Achachicala, Bolivia, S Am W, 1981); Maj, L Am N. b 21 Jan 56.

COTTERILL, Anthony (Regent Hall, 1984); Lt-Col, UK. b 9 Dec 57. BA (Hons); with
COTTERILL, Gillian (née Rushforth) m 1979; Lt-Col, UK. b 15 Sep 57. SRN.

COURT, Stephen (Etobicoke Temple, Can,

1994); Maj, Aus S. b 28 Feb 66; and
STRICKLAND, Danielle (Brampton, Can, 1995) m 1995; Maj, Aus S. b 14 Sep 72. Served in Can.

COWLING, Alison (Macleans, Aus E, 1978); Maj, Asst CS, Can. b 10 Feb 50. Served in Aus E and at IHQ.

COX, André (Geneva 1, Switz, 1979); Comr, TC, S Afr. b 12 Jul 54; with
COX, Silvia (née Volet) m 1976; Comr, TPWM, S Afr. b 18 Nov 55. Served in Switz, Zimb and Fin (TC/TPWM).

CRAIG, Graeme (Rockhampton, Aus E, 1984); Maj, Gha. b 10 Feb 56; and
CRAIG, Heather (née Mackay) (Parramatta, Aus E, 1986) m 1986; Maj, Gha. b 31 Dec 57. Served in Aus E.

CUNNINGHAM, James D. (Gastonia, NC, 1974); Maj, USA S. b 15 Feb 52; with
CUNNINGHAM, Wanda (née Ammons) m 1971; Maj. USA S. b 14 Jul 52.

D

DADDOW, Allan (Adelaide Congress Hall, 1978); Maj, Aus S. b 4 Aug 44; with
DADDOW, Lorraine (née Andrew) m 1965; Maj, Aus S. b 21 Sep 45.

DALI, Peter (Ebushibungo, Ken, 1978); Lt-Col, OC, Lib. b 2 Mar 52; and
DALI, Jessica (née Kavere) (Masigolo, Ken, 1978) m 1979; Lt-Col, CPWM, Lib. b 25 Dec 55. Served in Ken, Tanz, at IHQ, Gha (CS/TSWM) and Zim (CS/TSWM).

DAMOR, Nicolas Maganlal (Jalpa, 1979); Maj, Ind W. b 1 Jun 55; and
DAMOR, Flora (née David) (Dilsar, 1980) m 1980; Maj, Ind W. b 26 Apr 58.

DANIEL, Edward (Meesalai, 1977); Lt-Col, CS, Sri Lan. b 18 Mar 56; and
DANIEL, Lalitha (née Ranchagodage) (Colombo Central, 1981) m 1981; Lt-Col, TSWM, Sri Lan. b 1 Oct 53.

DANIELS, Frank (Katanning, 1967); Lt-Col, Aus S. b 10 Apr 47; and
DANIELS, Yvonne (née Knapp) (Melbourne City Temple, 1972) m 1972; Lt-Col, Aus S. b 4 Oct 47.

DANIELSON, Douglas (El Paso, TX, 1987); Lt-Col, USA W. b 19 Aug 58. BSc (Cmptr Sci), MA (Missiology); with
DANIELSON, Rhode (née Doria) m 1983; Lt-Col, Mex. b 29 Jul 59. BSEd, MA (Maths). Served in S Am E, Carib, L Am N (CS/TSWM) and Mex.

DANSO, Isaac (Asene, 1991); Maj, Gha. b 22 Feb 1960; with

DANSO, Eva (née Amoah) m 1988; Maj, Gha. b 1 Jul 61.

DARSE, Jeevaratnam (Danthuluru, Ind C, 1994); Maj, Ind Nat. b 25 Apr 62. BA, BL, HACDP, ADHA; with
DARSE, Daiva Kumari m 1990; Maj, Ind Nat. b 6 Jun 65. BCom, BEd. Served in Ind C and Ind N.

DAS, Sabita (Angul 1974); Maj, Ind N. b 1 Jan 53; with
DAS, Samuel m 1971; Maj, Ind N. b 22 Oct 51

DASARI, John Kumar (Pathamupparru, 1991); Maj, Ind C. b 7 Jan 61; with
DASARI, Mani Kumari m 1986; Maj, Ind C. b 3 May 66. BTh, MA.

DAVID, K. C. (Puthuchira, Ind SW, 1978); Lt-Col, Ind Nat. b 5 Jan 53. BA; and
DAVID, G. Marykutty (Thevalapuram, Ind SW, 1981) m 1981; Lt-Col, Ind Nat. b 12 Nov 55. Served in Ind SW.

DAVIDSON, Daniel (Trivandrum Central, 1985); Maj, Ind SW. b 6 May 53. BA; with
DAVIDSON, M.V. Estherbai m 1984, Maj, Ind SW. b 1 Jun 61.

DAWNGLIANA, C. (Chhilngchip, 1981); Maj, Ind E. b 1 Oct 55; and
H. MANTHANGI (Champhai, 1982) m 1982; Maj, Ind E. b 20 Sep 61.

DEFIBAUGH, Sandra (Staunton, VA, 1978); Maj, USA S. b 19 Jan 51. Served at USA Nat.

DEN HOLLANDER, Johannes A. (Treebeek, 1990); Maj, Neth. b 21 Nov 56, with
DEN HOLLANDER, Annetje C. (née Poppema) m 1978; Maj, Neth. b 4 May 57.

DEVARAPALLI, Jayapaul (M. R. Nagaram, Ind C, 1974); Col, TC, Ind SW. b 25 Dec 47. MA, BTS, Hon DD: with
DEVARAPALLI, Yesudayamma m 1971; Col, TPWM, Ind SW. b 21 Nov 54. Served in Ind C and Ind E (TC/TPWM).

DEVASUNDARAM, Samuel Raj (Vadasery, 1974); Maj, Ind SE. b 21 Sep 54; and
DEVASUNDARAM, Kanagamony Samuel Raj (Brahmapuram, 1978) m 1978; Maj, Ind SE. b 5 Feb 52.

DIAKANWA, Wante Emmanuel (Kintambo, 1985); Maj, DR Con. b 23 Dec 50; with
DIAKANWA, Madeleine (née Sitwakemba Luzizila) m 1974; Maj, DR Con. b 11 Nov 55.

DIANDAGA, Frédéric (Nzoko, 1988); Maj, Con (Braz). b 26 May 55; and
DIANDAGA, Claudia (née Bayekoula) (Ouenze, 1990) m 1990; Maj, Con (Braz). b 29 Oct 66.

DIJKSTRA, Pieter H. (Amsterdam West, 1979); Col, CS, Neth. b 27 Jan 48; with

Biographical Information

DIJKSTRA, Alida (née Voorn); Col, TSWM, Neth. b 21 Nov 50. Served in Cze R.

DOLIBER, Robert (Champaign, IL, 1978); Maj, USA C. b 15 Jul 54. BS (Bus Adm), MBA; and
DOLIBER, Rae (née Briggs) (Champaign, IL, 1982); Maj, USA C. b 5 Jun 58.

DONALDSON, Robert (Dunedin South, NZ, 1987); Lt-Col, S Afr. b 8 Jul 61. BSc, LTh; with
DONALDSON, Janine (née Hamilton) m 1983, Lt-Col, S Afr. b 23 Sep 62. Served in NZ and Zamb.

DONZÉ, Jacques (St Aubin, 1988); Maj, Switz. b 16 Feb 64; with
DONZÉ, Claude-Evelyne (née Roth) m 1983; Maj, Switz. b 5 Feb 63. Served in Belg.

DOUGHTY, Victor (Seattle Temple, WA, 1984); Maj, USA W. b 25 Mar 54. BA (Soc Anthrplgy), MSW (Soc Wk), CERT (Soc Wk); with
DOUGHTY, Joan (née Ritchie) m 1980; Maj, USA W. b 7 May 55.

DOWNER, Gillian (Great Yarmouth, UK, 1977); Lt-Col, IHQ. b 18 Mar 54. Served in UK, Phil, Vietnam, HK, Tai and Sing (GS, CS).

DRAYCOTT, Irene (née Chase) (Grimsby Citadel, 1984); Maj, UK. b 20 Mar 51; with
DRAYCOTT, Aubrey m 1974; Maj, UK. b 10 Jun 51.

DREW, Marion (Boscombe, 1979); Lt-Col, UK. b 12 Jan 49. BA (French & Law), Dip Inst Linguists. Served at ICO.

DUCHÊNE, Alain (Paris Montparnasse, 1971); Col, TC, Frce. b 1 Jan 45. Served at ESFOT and in Frce (CS). m 1972; Lt-Col Suzette, ret 2002.

DULA, Sangthang T. (Diakkawn 1986); Maj, Ind E. b 2 Jul 63. BTh, MA (Mission), MTh (Missiology), DMiss; with
MALSAWMI m 1984; Maj, Ind E. b 10 Jun 59.

DUNSTER, Robin (Dulwich Hill Temple, Aus E, 1970); Comr, CoS, IHQ. b 12 Jan 44. SRN, SCM, RPN, RMN, IPPF (Ed). Served in Aus E, Zimb (CS), Con (Kin) (TC, TPWO) and Phil (TC, TPWM).

DUSHING, Ashok K. (Byculla Central, Ind W, 1991); Maj, Ind Nat. b 16 Jun 62; with
DUSHING, Sanjivani m 1989; Maj, Ind Nat. b 10 May 68. BA. Served in Ind W.

E

EDGAR, Samuel (Londonderry, 1969); Maj, UK. b 26 Feb 49. Served at ITC and in Ger.

EGGER, Paulette (Vallorbe, 1977); Maj, Switz. b 22 Nov 55.

ELDRIDGE, David (Northcote, 1979); Maj, Aus S. b 25 Jun 50; with

ELDRIDGE, Gloria; Maj, Aus S. b 10 Aug 57. Served in UK.

ELIASEN, Anna Riitta (née Hamalainen) (Erie Central, PA, 1967); Lt-Col, USA E. b 11 Aug 45. BA (Org Mgmt). Served in UK, Brz, S Am E, Sp and Fin (CS). Ww Lt-Col Samuel, pG 1997.

ELIASEN, Torben (Bosque, Brz, 1983); Lt-Col, OC, Moz. b 28 Nov 60; and
ELIASEN, Deise Calor (née de Souza) (Rio Comprido, Brz, 1985) m 1985; Lt-Col, CPWM, Moz. b 22 Feb 66. BA (Jrnlsm). Served in Brz (CS)

ELLIS, Stephen R. (Atlanta Temple, GA, 1989); Maj, USA S. b 25 Oct 62; with
ELLIS, Susan (née Kennedy) m 1984; Maj, USA S. b 27 Apr 62. Served in Ger.

EMMANUEL, Muthu Yesudhason (Neduvaazhy, Ind SE, 1974); Comr, TC, Ind C. b 8 May 51; and
REGINA, Chandra Bai (Valliyoor, Ind SE, 1978) m 1978; Comr, TPWM, Ind C. b 3 Mar 55. Served in Ind SE, Ind N (CS/TSWM) and Ind E (TC/TPWM).

EMMANUEL, Walter (Green Town, 1983); Maj, Pak. b 7 Jul 57; with
WALTER, Mussaraf (née Ullah) m 1981; Maj, Pak. b 1 Dec 65.

EZEKWERE, Chika Boniface (Umuchu, 1978); Maj, Nig. b 1 Jan 49; with
EZEKWERE, Virginia Ete m 1976; Maj, Nig. b 1 Jan 54.

F

FEENER, Maxwell (Port Leamington, NF, Can, 1966); Comr, TC, USA S. b 5 Jul 45, with
FEENER, Lenora (née Tippett) m 1967; Comr, TPWM, USA S. b 26 Dec 45. Served in Can, S Afr (CS/TSWM) and USA S (CS/TSWM).

FERGUSON, Lester (Nassau, Bahamas, 1988); Maj, Carib. b 1 Sep 65. BA (Bible and Theol), MA (Chrstn Ed); and
FERGUSON, Beverely (née Armstrong) (Bridgetown Central, Barbados, 1999) m 1999; Capt, Carib. b 12 Dec 64.

FERNANDEZ, Ricardo J. (Caparra Temple, PR, 1996); Capt, USA E. b 3 Jun 60; with
FERNANDEZ, Mirtha N. (née Benitez) m 1979; Capt, USA E. b 4 Jan 57.

FERNANDO, Newton (Handugala, 1981); Maj, Sri Lan. b 30 Aug 60; and
FERNANDO Ajantha (née Marasinghalage) (Talampitiya, 1984) m 1984; Maj, Sri Lan. b 8 Jun 61.

FERREIRA, Jorge Alberto (Cordoba, S Am E,

Biographical Information

1972); Comr, TC, S Am W. b 24 Jun 53; and
FERREIRA, Adelina (née Solorza) (Lauis, S Am E, 1974) m 1979; Comr, TPWM, S Am W. b 19 Sep 55. Served in S Am E (CS/TSWM) and L Am N (TC/TPWM).

FINCHAM, Melvin (Croydon Citadel, 1981); Maj, UK. b 20 May 56; and
FINCHAM, Suzanne (née Kenny) (Stockport Citadel, 1981) m 1981; Maj, UK. b 19 Jan 59.

FINGER, Raymond (Hawthorn, 1974); Col, CS, Aus S. b 11 Jul 51; and
FINGER, Aylene (née Rinaldi) (Maylands, 1974) m 1976; Col, TSWM, Aus S. b 17 Apr 53.

FLEEMAN, W. Paul (Royal Oak, MI, 1976); Maj, USA C. b 23 Dec 48. BA (Psychol), MA (Relig), MDiv (Counselling/Ed); with
FLEEMAN, Paula (née Cloyd) m 1973; Maj, USA C. b 14 Jun 54.

FLINTOFF, Ethne (Dunedin North, NZ, 1971); Lt-Col, OC, Ban. b 11 Nov 46. RN, RM. Served in NZ, Ind W, Ind N and Pak.

FLORES, Eliseo (Cochabamba, 1977); Maj, S Am W. b 28 Jul 56; and
FLORES, Remedios (née Gutiérrez) (Oruro, 1977) m 1978; Maj, S Am W. b 6 Apr 55.

FLORES, Myline Joy (Lebe, 1988); Maj, Phil. b 2 May 63. BMin.

FOREMAN, Ronald R. (Concord, NH, 1978); Maj, USA E. b 17 Sep 1952. BA (Sociol), MSW (Soc Wk), EJD (Gen Law); with
FOREMAN, Dorine (née Long); m 1972; Maj, USA E. b 6 Apr 1955. BSW (Soc Wk), MSW (Soc Wk). Served at USA Nat.

FORSTER, Malcolm (St Helier, UK, 1971); Lt-Col, S Afr. b 26 Mar 51; and
FORSTER, Valerie (née Jupp) (Croydon Citadel, UK, 1978) m 1979; Lt-Col, S Afr. b 5 Jun 55. Served in UK, at ITC, in Zam & Mal, Gha & Lib, Mal (OC/CPWM) and Tanz (OC/CPWM).

FORSYTH, Robin W. (Edinburgh Gorgie, UK, 1968); Comr, IHQ (IS Prog Res). b 30 Aug 1946; with
FORSYTH, Shona (née Leslie) m 1966; Comr, IHQ (Chaplain). b 25 Mar 1948. Served in Aus S, Mex, UK, L Am N (TC/TPWM) and NZ (CS/TSWM).

FOSEN, Jan Peder (Haugesund, 1976); Maj, Nor. b 18 Nov 55; and
FOSEN, Birgit (née Taarnesvik) (Trondheim, 1981) m 1979; Maj, Nor. b 27 Aug 49.

FRANCIS, William (Paterson, NJ, USA E, 1973); Comr, TC, Can. b 5 Mar 44. BA (Mus/Hist), MDiv, Hon DD; with
FRANCIS, Marilyn (née Burroughs) m 1965;

Comr, TPWM, Can. b 3 Feb 43. BA (Mus), MA. Served in USA E (CS/TSWM) and at IHQ (IS/SWM Am and Carib).

FRANS, Roy (Surabaya, Indon, 1977); Comr, TC, Neth. b 30 Oct 50; and
FRANS, Arda (née Haurissa) (Jakarta 1, Indon, 1978) m 1978; Comr, TPWM, Neth. b 10 May 44. Served in Indon, Aus E, Sing, Ban, Sri Lan (TC/TPWM) and at IHQ (IS/ZSWM SPEA).

FREIND, John (Floreat Park, 1981); Maj, Aus S. b 11 Dec 55; with
FRIEND, Wendy (née Morris) m 1977; Maj, Aus S. b 5 Aug 53.

FRIEDL, Jörg (Munich, 1994); Maj, Ger. b 4 Jun 60. Dip SW, Dip Soc Pedagogue; with
FRIEDL, Susann (née Harm) m 1982; Maj, Ger. b 25 Jul 62.

FRISK, Kristina M. (née Larsson) (Örebro 1, 1965); Col, CS, Swdn. b 22 May 45. m 1977; Lt-Col Anders, ret 2004.

FUGE, Walter J. (Anacortes, WA, 1972); Maj, USA W. b 18 Aug 52. MBA (Bus Adm), BS (Bus & Mngmnt), CERT (Data Analyst) (Internal Audit); with
FUGE, Ardis (née Muus) (Monterey, CA, 1974) m 1974; Maj, USA W. b 31 Jan 53.

G

GABRIEL, K. M. (Kaithaparambu, 1981); Maj, Ind SW. b 15 Nov 55; with
GABRIEL, Molamma K. m1986; Maj, Ind SW. b 10 May 67.

GAIKWAD, Benjamin Yacob (Bodhegaon, 1974); Maj, Ind W. b 3 Oct 48; and
GAIKWAD, Sudina P. (née Makasare) (Bodhegaon, 1975) m 1975; Maj, Ind W. b 23 Oct 57.

GAITHER, Israel L. (New Castle, PA, USA E, 1964); Comr, NC, USA Nat. b 27 Oct 44. Hon LHD, Hon DD; and
GAITHER, Eva D. (née Shue) (Sidney, OH, USA E, 1964) m 1967; Comr, NPWM, USA Nat. b 9 Sep 43. Served in USA E (CS/TSWO), S Afr (TC/TPWO), USA E (TC/TPWM) and at IHQ (CoS/WSWM).

GALVÁN, Guadalupe (Savo Loredo, 1975); Maj, Mex; b 28 Mar 51. Served in USA S and L Am N.

GARCÍA, Ángela (née Sanguinetti) (Lima, 1982); Maj, S Am W. b 15 Oct 1953; and
GARCÍA, Victor (Trujillo, 1982) m 1983; Maj, S Am W. b 21 Jan 1955. Served in USA C and L Am N.

GARCÍA, Humberto (Monterrey, 1990); Maj, Mex. b 19 Jan 57. LLM; with

Biographical Information

GARCÍA, Leticia (née Castañeda) m 1981; Maj, Mex. b 9 Mar 59. BA (Primary Ed).

GARLAND, Elizabeth (Dulwich Hill, Aus E, 1998); Capt, Zimb. b 23 May 68. BN (Nursing), MPHC (Masters Primary Health Care), RN (Nursing). Served in Aus E and Gha.

GARRAD, Rob (Skegness, UK, 1971); Lt-Col, IHQ. b 16 Jan 52. Served in UK and Rus.

GENABE, Alexander (Cebu, 1981); Maj, Phil. b 27 Mar 58; and
GENABE, Jocelyn (née Willy) (Baguio 1993) m 1993; Maj, Phil. b 10 Feb 60. BSN, BSSW.

GEORGE, N. J. (Moncotta, 1978); Maj, Ind SW. b 24 Dec 51; with
GEORGE, Ruth M. C. m 1979, Maj, Ind SW. b 23 Apr 48.

GEORGE, N. S. (Vayala, 1980); Maj, Ind SW. b 19 Mar 50; and
GEORGE, A. Annamma (Kunnathoor, 1983) m 1983; Maj, Ind SW. b 10 Apr 61.

GERA, Thomas (EBLH, Bapatla, Ind C. 1988); Maj, Ind N. b 12 Jul 65; with
GERA, Sion Kumari m 1984; Maj, Ind N. b 9 Oct 67. Served in Ind C.

GHULAM, Yousaf (Lahore, 1975); Lt-Col, CS, Pak. b 4 Jan 55; and
YOUSAF, Rebecca (née Charn Masih) (Shantinagar, 1975) m 1976; Lt-Col, TSWM, Pak. b 6 May 56.

GILL, Daniel (Alidullapur, 1980); Maj, Ind N. b 5 Apr 57; and
GILL, Parveen Daniel (Mukerian 1981) m 1981; Maj, Ind N. b 3 Apr 62.

GJERULDSEN, Frank (Brevik, 1981); Maj, Nor. b 21 Jan 58; and
GJERULDSEN, Tone (née Olsen) (Templet, Oslo, 1984) m 1983; Maj, Nor. b 11 Feb 1959.

GLORIES, Pascale (née Alquier) (Ganges, 1981); Maj, TSWM, Frce. b 4 Apr 58; with
GLORIES, Dominique m 1978; Maj, Frce. b 23 Jul 54.

GLUYAS, Miriam (Wauchope, 1981); Lt-Col, Aus E. b 3 Jun 59. Dip Min.

GOA, Christian (Lae, 1994); Capt, PNG. b 9 Feb 69; with
GOA, Tilitah (née Shong); Capt, PNG. b 6 Apr 69.

GONÇALVES, Adão (Pelotas, 1997); Capt, Brz. b 3 Sep 65; and
GONÇALVES, Vilma (née Rosa) (Bosque, 1996) m 1986; Capt, Brz. b 8 Nov 51. BA (SocS).

GONZALEZ, Henry (Orange, TX, 1967); Lt-Col, USA S. b 18 Aug 46. BS (Sociol); and
GONZALEZ, Mary Dorris (née McCollum) (Meridian, MS, 1967) m 1969; Lt-Col, USA S. b 13 Sep 48.

GOWER, Ross Richardson (Christchurch City, NZ, 1980); Col, CS, Indon. b 15 Dec 50; with
GOWER, Annette Veronica (née Knight) m 1972; Col, TSWM, Indon. Served in NZ and UK.

GRAVES, Lee (Tillsonburg, ON, 1983); Lt-Col, Can. b 8 Aug 61. MBA; with
GRAVES, Deborah (née Smith) m 1984; Lt-Col, Can. b 24 Feb 1960. BA (Bible and Theol), BSW.

GREEN, Lynette (née Marion) (Bendigo, Aus S, 1965); Lt-Col, Aus E. b 30 Mar 44. Ww Maj Frederick, pG 1998. Served in Aus S, E Afr and Port (OC).

GRIFFIN, Stanley (St John's, Antigua, 1979); Maj, Carib. b 20 Feb 54; and
GRIFFIN, Hazel (née Whyte) (St John's, Antigua, 1980) m 1981; Maj, Carib. b 23 Sep 57. Served in L Am N.

GRIFFIN, Terry W. (Seattle Temple, WA, USA W, 1970); Col, CS, USA S. b 2 Nov 46. BA (Bib Lit), MA (Relig); with
GRIFFIN, Linda (née Bawden) m 1967; Col, TSWM, USA S. b 28 Aug 46. Served in USA W.

GRINDLE, David E. (Detroit Brightmoor, MI, 1966); Lt-Col, USA C. b 5 Mar 44; with
GRINDLE, Sherry (née McNabb) m 1964; Lt-Col, USA C. b 25 Jul 45.

GYIMAH, William (Wiamoase, 1976); Lt-Col, CS, Gha. b 31 Dec 47; with
GYIMAH, Mary (née Pokuaa) m 1974; Lt-Col, TSWM, Gha. b 14 Aug 48. Served in Lib and Uga.

H

HAGGAR, Kerry (née Geers) (Rockdale, 1982); Maj, Aus E, b 30 Nov 59. ThA, BComm, MAL; and
HAGGAR, Colin (Rockdale 1983) m 1983; Maj, Aus E. b 16 Mar 59. BE, ATh

HAMILTON, Ian E. (Clayton, Aus E, 1971); Lt-Col, Aus S. b 8 Jun 47. Dip Theol; with
HAMILTON, Marilyn (née Rawiller) m 1968; Lt-Col, Aus S. b 6 Aug 48. Served in Aus E.

HANGOMA, Donald (Munali, 1995); Capt, Zam. b 15 Jan 70; and
HANGOMA, Patricia (née Michelo) (1993); Maj, Zam. b 19 Mar 70.

HANUNKA, Bislon (Chibbuku, 1985); Lt-Col, CS, Zam. b 10 Jun 58; with
HANUNKA, Melody m 1979; Lt-Col, Asst TPWM, Zam. b 15 Dec 62.

HARFOOT, William (Detroit Brightmoor, MI, 1977); Col, CS, USA W. b 6 Sep 48. BS (Ed), MA (Relig); with

Biographical Information

HARFOOT, Susan (née Stange) m 1969; Col, TSWM, USA W. b 21 Oct 48. AA. Served in USA E.

HARITA, Naoko (Shibuya, 1968); Maj, Jpn. b 19 Jul 43. BA (Sociol).

HARMS, Bennie (Johannesburg City, 1974); Maj, S Afr. b 15 Apr 52; with
HARMS, Jennifer (née Hall) m 1972; Maj, S Afr. b 21 Oct 48. Served in Zimb.

HARRY, Kervin (Kingstown, St Vincent, 1987); Maj, Carib. b 14 Sep 64. BA (Chrstn Ed); and
HARRY, Lucia (née De Randamie) (Rotterdam North, Neth, 1982) m 1993; Maj, Carib. b 9 May 54. RN.

HARTVEIT, Jørg Walter (Langesund, 1971); Lt-Col, Nor. b 22 Jun 47. m 1971; Lt-Col Rigmor, ret 2006.

HAUGHTON, Devon (Port Antonio, Jamaica, 1981); Maj, Carib. b 22 Jul 59; and
HAUGHTON, Verona Beverly (née Henry) (Havendale, Jamaica, 1976) m 1982; Maj, Carib. b 15 Apr 54. BA (Guidance and Counselling).

HAUPT, Gary W. (New Orleans, LA, USA S, 1982); Lt-Col, USA Nat. b 27 Nov 53. BS (Bus Adm); with
HAUPT, Suzanne H. (née Hogan); m 1979; Lt-Col, USA Nat. b 3 May 56. BS (Ed). Served in USA S.

HEATWOLE, Merle D. (Milwaukee Citadel, WI, 1984); Lt-Col, USA C. b 7 Jan 60. BS (Maths); with
HEATWOLE, Dawn Idell (née Lewis) m 1981; Lt-Col, USA C. b 26 Nov 62.

HEDGREN, R. Steven (Chicago Mont Clare, IL, USA C, 1978); Col, CS, USA E. b 7 Mar 50. BS (Bus Adm); with
HEDGREN, Judith Ann (née White) m 1975; Col, TSWM, USA E. b 14 Feb 49. Served in USA C and USA S. AS (Bus).

HEELEY, William (Rock Ferry, 1974); Lt-Col, UK. b 6 May 48; and
HEELEY, Gillian (née Lacey) (Rock Ferry, 1975) m 1975; Lt-Col, UK. b 18 Apr 52.

HEGGELUND, Brith-Mari (Harstad, 1972); Maj, Nor. b 22 Jul 49.

HENDRICKS, Robert E. (Claremont Temple, 2005); Capt, S Afr. b 25 Mar 54; with
HENDRICKS, Felicia (neé Christian) m 1983; Capt, S Afr. b 11 Jul 57.

HENNE, Ingrid Elisabeth (Bergen 1, 1982); Maj, Nor. b 6 Sep 52.

HERIVEL, Richard (Dearborn Heights, MI. USA C, 1984); Maj, E Eur. b 4 Oct 51. BS (Bus Adm), MA Relig; with
HERIVEL, Brenda (née Rhoads) m 1976; Maj, E Eur. b 26 Dec 54. BA Relig, MA Relig, MSoc Wk. Served in USA C.

HERRERA, Jaime (Hualpencillo, 1981); Maj, S Am W; b 27 Jul 59; and
HERRERA, Zaida (née Lopizic) (Santiago Central, 1983) m 1983; Maj, S Am W; b 12 Feb 58. Served in Braz.

HERRING, Alistair Chapman (Wellington City, NZ, 1975); Lt-Col, CS, E Eur. b 4 Mar 51. DipSW; with
HERRING, Verna Astrid (née Weggery) m 1971; Lt-Col, TSWM, E Eur. b 29 Oct 51. Served in NZ

HETTIARACHCHI, Nihal (Colombo, 1985); Maj, Sri Lan. b 20 Jun 64; and
HETTIARACHCHI, Rohini Swarnalatha (née Wettamuni) (Colombo Central, 1994) m 1994; Maj, Sri Lan. b 18 Oct 64.

HIGHTON, Michael (Hinckley, 1985); Maj, UK. b 27 May 53; with
HIGHTON, Lynn (née Edwards) m 1975; Maj, UK. b 10 Mar 53.

HIGUCHI, Kazumitsu (Nagoya, 1976); Maj, Jpn. b 9 Apr 51; and
HIGUCHI, Aiko (née Kutomi) (Shibuya, 1979) m 1982; Maj, Jpn. b 25 Sep 53.

HILL, Edward (Pasadena Tabernacle, CA 1993); Maj, USA W. b 7 Nov 59. BA (History), MA (Chrstn Ed); with
HILL, Shelley (née Chandler) m 1985; Maj, USA W. b 11 Jul 63.

HILL, Martin (Northampton Central, 1984); Maj, UK. b 3 Jul 55. BA (Hons) (Soc Sci), MTh (Ap Theol).

HINTON, David (Blackheath, 1975); Lt-Col, UK. b 28 Oct 53; and
HINTON, Sylvia (née Brooks) (Bedlington, 1975) m 1977; Lt-Col, UK. b 2 Dec 53.

HIRAMOTO, Naoshi (Ueno, 1971); Lt-Col, CS, Jpn. b 24 Oct 46. BA (Law); and
HIRAMOTO, Seiko (née Kobayashi) (Kyobashi, 1968) m 1973; Lt-Col, TSWM, Jpn. b 7 Oct 43. BA (Eng Lit).

HIRAMOTO, Nobuhiro (Ueno, 1979); Maj, Jpn. b 28 Dec 51. BA (Chinese Lit); and
HIRAMOTO, Yasuko (née Kinoshita) (Ueno, 1979) m 1979; Maj, Jpn. b 7 Dec 51.

HISCOCK, David G. (Corner Brook Citadel, NF, 1965); Lt-Col, Can. b 11 May 45; and
HISCOCK, Margaret (née Brown) (Bay Roberts, NF, 1966) m 1967; Lt-Col, Can. b 27 Mar 45.

HOBGOOD, W. Edward (Greenville, NC, 1983); Lt-Col, USA S. b 6 Apr 58; with
HOBGOOD, M. Kathryn (née Hathaway) m 1978; Lt-Col, USA S. b 12 Jun 54.

Biographical Information

HODDER, Kenneth G. (Pasadena Tabernacle, CA, USA W, 1988); Comr, IHQ (IS Int Pers). b 16 Jun 58. BA (Hist), JD (Law); with
HODDER, Jolene (née Lloyd) m 1982; Comr, IHQ (Assoc IS Int Pers). b 30 Jul 61. BA (Home Econ). Served in USA W, USA S, Ken (CS/TLWM) and Ken E (CS/TLWM).

HODGE, John (Wollongong, 1972); Lt-Col, Aus E. b 27 Aug 45. BA (Relig Studies and Ed), Dip Teach, MBA. Ww Lt Marie, pG 1974. Served in PNG; and
HODGE, Pamela (née Henry) (Bankstown, 1972) m 1975; Lt-Col, Aus E. b 29 Oct 49. Served in Carib (CS/TSWO), Phil (TC/TPWO) and NZ.

HOFER, Allan (Sissach Basel, 1986); Maj, Switz. b 30 Mar 61; and
HOFER, Fiona (née Pressland) (Barking, UK, 1987) m 1987; Maj, Switz, b 15 Apr 64. Served in Port, UK, Brz and USA S.

HOKOM, Eda M. (Caldwell, ID, 1974); Lt-Col, USA W. b 19 Mar 48. BA (Soc Sci), BS (Relig Ed). Served in PNG.

HOLLEY, Peter (Bankstown, 1969) Maj, Aus E. b 23 Mar 1946; and
HOLLEY, Eileen (née Lodge) (Narrabri, 1971) m 1971; Maj, Aus E. b 7 Nov 1947.

HONSBERG, Frank (Cologne, 1987); Maj, Ger. b 24 Jan 63. Grad Bus Mgmt; with
HONSBERG, Stefanie (née Gossens) m 1985; Maj, Ger. b 17 Dec 65.

HOOD, Brian (Bundaberg, 1974); Lt-Col, Aus E, b 23 Mar 44; with
HOOD, Elaine (née Toft) m 1970; Lt-Col, Aus E. b 19 Apr 51. Served in Aus S and PNG.

HOOD, George (Hamilton, OH, USA W, 1983); Maj, USA Nat. b 31 Jan 47. BS (Mgmt), MS (Mgmt); and
HOOD, Donna J. (née Morrison) (Newport, KY, USA W, 1984) m 1969; Maj, USA Nat. b 25 Oct 47. BS (Org Mgmt), MA (Theol). Served in USA E and USA W.

HOOD, Sallyann (née Carpenter) (San Diego Citadel, CA, USA W, 1977); Maj, Mex. b 12 Nov 45. BA (Pre-med Zoology), MD (Ob/Gyn); with
HOOD, James m 1971; Maj, Mex. b 27 Oct 46. BS (Agric Eng), MS (Civil Eng), Served in USA W and Ind SE.

HOSTETLER, Donald D. (Cincinnati Citadel, OH, 1971); Maj, USA W. b 2 Jan 49. BA (Soc), MA (Public Adm); with
HOSTETLER, Arvilla J. (née Marcum) m 1969; Maj, USA W. b 14 Aug 50.

HOWARD, Steven (Hamilton, OH, USA E, 1983); Col, CS, Ken E. b 21 May 57.

BS (Architecture), MSc (Bus Adm); with
HOWARD, Janice (née Collopy) m 1979; Col, TLWM, Ken E. b 18 Mar 59. BS (Bus Ed). Served in USA E and at ICO.

HOWELL, Willis (Hyattsville, MD, 1985); Maj, USA S. b 3 Mar 56; with
HOWELL, Barbara (née Leidy) m 1978; Maj, USA S. b 3 Apr 57.

HUDSON, David E. (Portland Tabernacle, OR, 1975); Lt-Col, USA W. b 28 Jun 54. BS (Bus Mgmt); and
HUDSON, Sharon (née Smith) (Santa Ana, CA, 1975) m 1976; Lt-Col, USA W. b 14 Jun 52.

HULSMAN, Everdina (Nijverdal, 1975); Lt-Col, Neth. b 21 Dec 47.

HUNTER, Barbara (née Booth) (Tucson, AZ, USA W, 1967); Lt-Col, USA E. b 17 Mar 47. BS (Org Mgmt). Served in USA W and Rus (CSWO). Ww Lt-Col William, pG 2001.

HWANG, Sun-yup (Ah Hyun, 1985); Maj, Kor. b 28 Dec 55; with
CHOI, Myung-soon m 1982; Maj, Kor. b 9 Sep 59. Served in USA S and UK.

HYNES, Junior (Happy Valley, NL, 1971); Maj, Can. b 6 Jan 51; and
HYNES, Verna (née Downton) (Windsor, NL, 1971) m 1973; Maj, Can. b 27 Aug 50. Served in UK.

I

IP KAN, Ming-chun Connie (Kwai Chung, 1985); Maj, CSWM, HK. b 16 Jul 62.

ILUNGA, Bidwaya Clément (Salle Centrale, 1987); Maj, DR Con. b 16 Nov 62; with
ILUNGA, Béatrice (née Kalenga Monga) m 1988; Maj, DR Con. b 12 Sep 60.

IMBIAKHA, Daniel (Musingu, 1992); Maj, Ken W. b 14 Aug 60; with
IMBIAKHA, Nolega (née Clera) m 1988; Maj, Ken W. b 21 Mar 69.

IMMANUEL, Sam (Thulickal, 1984); Maj, Ind SW. b 27 May 59; with
IMMANUEL, Rachel P. C. m 1982; Maj, Ind SW. b 15 Jun 57.

INDURUWAGE, Malcolm (Colombo Central, Sri Lan, 1977); Col, TC, Phil. b 24 Sep 50; and
INDURUWAGE, Irene (née Horathalge) (Colombo Central, Sri Lan, 1977) m 1977; Col, TPWM, Phil. b 29 Nov 55. Served in Sri Lan and Phil (CS/TSWM).

IRVING, Ray (Shiremoor, 1989); Maj, UK. b 20 Apr 51. MVA, MCMI; and
IRVING, Angela (née Richards) (Torquay, 1972) m 1989; Maj, UK. b 12 Feb 51.

ISRAEL, Betty A. (née Sheinfeldt) (Waltham, MA, USA E, 1971); Maj, USA Nat. b 6 Jan 47.

Biographical Information

BA (Sociol), MA (Counselling/Human Services), PG Dip (Supervision & Training). Served in USA E and at IHQ. Ww Capt James, pG 1988.

ISRAEL, Mark H. (Warner Robbins, GA, USA S, 1982); Lt-Col, USA Nat. b 8 May 58. BA (Bible), MA (Theol Studies); and
ISRAEL, Carolee J. (née Zarfas) (Des Moines Citadel, IA, USA C, 1981); m 1982; Lt-Col, USA Nat. b 30 Mar 58. BS (Pract Min). Served in USA S.

J

JACKSON, David (Romford, 1976); Maj, UK. b 10 Nov 52. Served at IHQ.

JADHAV, Philip Baburao (Vishrantwadi, 1986); Maj, Ind W. b 6 May 63; and
JADHAV, Rebecca (Byculla Marathi, 1992) m 1988; Maj, Ind W. b 11 Nov 65.

JAMES, M. C. (Monkotta, Ind SW, 1979); Comr, TC, Ind SE. b 20 Oct 54. MA Soc; and
JAMES, L. Susamma (Pothencode, Ind SW, 1983) m 1983; Comr, TPWM, Ind SE. b 1 Mar 61. Served in Ind SW, Ind N and Ind C (CS/TSWM, TC/TPWM).

JAYARATNASINGHAM, Packianathan (Jaffna, 1973); Maj, Sri Lan. b 4 Nov 52; and
JAYARATNASINGHAM, Delankage Chandralatha (née Delankage) (Siyambalangamua, 1979) m 1980; Maj, Sri Lan. b 28 Oct 59. Served at IHQ.

JEBAMONY, Jayaseelan (Maharajaduram 1982); Maj, Ind SE. b 20 May 57; and
JEBAMONY, Gnanaselvi Jayaseelan (Nattalam, 1985) m 1980; Maj, Ind SE. b 30 Dec 57.

JEYARAJ, Daniel Jebasingh Raj (Booth Tucker Hall, Nagercoil, 1987); Maj, Ind SE. b 10 Jun 61. BA (Eng), MA (Social), BTh, BD, MTh; with
JEYARAJ, Rajam Daniel Jebasingh Raj (Kuzhikalai, 1992) m 1992; Maj, Ind SE. b 12 Mar 64. BA (Eng), MA (History), BTh PM, MTh PM. Served in Ind SE and at Ind Nat.

JEFFREY, David (Morgantown, WV, USA S, 1973); Col, Nat CS, USA Nat. b 2 Aug 51. BS, MA (Relig); and
JEFFREY, Barbara (née Garris) (Morgantown, WV, USA S, 1966) m 1969; Col, NSWM, USA Nat. b 1 Jan 46. Served in USA S (CS/TSWM).

JERA, Onai (Marowa, 1992); Maj, Zimb. b 10 Sep 67; and
JERA, Deliwe (née Gasa) (Gunguhwe, 1992) m 1994; Maj, Zimb. b 18 Jun 68.

JEREMIAH, Edwin (Mupfure, 1990); Maj, Zimb. b 30 Jun 60; with
JEREMIAH, Tambudzai (née Kabaya) m 1979; Maj, Zimb. b 10 Feb 62.

JEWETT, Vernon Wayne (Atlanta Temple, GA, 1980); Lt-Col, USA S. b 11 Dec 47. BA, MA; with
JEWETT, Martha Gaye (née Brewer) m 1975; Lt-Col, USA S. b 22 Oct 52. BA.

JOB, William (Manalikarai, 1981); Maj, Ind SE. b 8 Dec 51. BA; and
JOB, Daizy Bai William (Poottetty, 1982) m 1982; Maj, Ind SE. b 17 Apr 59.

JOHN, Morris (Rancho Lines, 1975); Lt-Col, Pak. b 1 Jan 53. Ww Lt-Col Salma, pG 2007.

JOHN, Rajan K. (Parayankerry, 1979); Maj, Ind SW. b 26 Mar 52; with
JOHN, Susamma m 1977; Maj, Ind SW. b 17 Oct 52.

JOHNSON, Kenneth (Charlotte Temple, NC, 1984); Lt-Col, USA S. b 10 Aug 56. BS (Bus Mgmt); with
JOHNSON, Paula (née Salmon) m 1981; Lt-Col, USA S. b 23 Nov 62.

JOHNSTONE, Wendy (London South, ON, Can, 1980); Maj, S Am E. b 31 Oct 57. Served in Can and at IHQ.

JONAS, Dewhurst (St John's, Antigua, 1982); Maj, Carib. b 20 May 56; and
JONAS, Vevene (née Gordon) (Rae Town, Jamaica, 1980) m 1983; Maj, Carib. b 1 Jun 57.

JONES, John Roy, Jr (Gastonia, NC, 1971); Maj, USA S. b 2 Feb 49; and
JONES, Arduth Eleanor (née Johnson) (Charlotte Temple, NC, 1971), m 1973; Maj, USA S. b 1 Jan 50.

JONES, Melvyn (Hoxton, 1976); Maj, UK. b 21 Nov 51. MA (Nat Sci); with
JONES, Kathleen (née Hall) m 1974; Maj, UK. b 15 Mar 51. SRN, SCM.

JOSHI, Devadasi (Musunuru, 1981); Maj, Ind C. b 1 Oct 54; with
JOSHI, Leelamani m 1977; Maj, Ind C. b 1 Jun 53.

JUNG, Verônica (Cachoeira Paulista, 1984); Maj, Brz. b 15 Sep 59. BA (Trans and Interp).

K

KAKI, Sundara Rao (Denduluru, 1978); Maj, Ind C. b 9 May 55; with
KAKI, Dasaratna Kumari m 1974; Maj, Ind C. b 12 Sep 55.

KALAI, Andrew (Koki, 1981); Comr, TC, PNG. b 18 Jan 56. BA (Psych). Ww Capt Napa, pG 1994; Ww Col Julie, pG 2006. Served in UK.

Biographical Information

KALE, Ratnakar Dinkar (Ahmednagar Central, 1977); Maj, Ind W. b 1 Jul 53; and
KALE, Leela (née Magar) (Byculla, 1981) m 1981; Maj, Ind W. b 1 Mar 60.
KAMAMBO, Clever (Chrome Mine, 1979); Maj, Zimb. b 28 Dec 57; and
KAMAMBO, Daphne (née Mhlanga) (Mufakose, 1981) m 1984; Maj, Zimb. b 16 Dec 59.
KAMBLE, Pramod (Fariabagh, 1992); Maj, Ind W. b 30 Apr 57; with
KAMBLE, Shanta m 1981; Maj, Ind W. b 1 Jun 68.
KANG, Jik-koo (Pu Sang, 1978); Maj, Kor. b 25 Aug 48; with
KIM, Chung-sook m 1976; Maj, Kor. b 5 May 57.
KANIS, Jacob (Kampen, 1968); Lt-Col, Neth. b 12 Oct 46; and
KANIS, Wijna (née Arends) (Kampen, 1968) m 1969; Lt-Col, Neth. b 21 Apr 47.
KARENGESHA, Annah (née Meda) (Kandeya, 1973); Maj, Zimb. b 1 Jun 50. Ww Maj Micah, pG 1993.
KARTODARSONO, Ribut (Surakarta, 1975); Comr, TC, Indon. b 13 Dec 49. BA (Relig Ed), MA (Relig Ed & Public Societies); and
KARTODARSONO, Marie (née Ticoalu) (Bandung 3, 1975) m 1979; Comr, TPWM, Indon. b 30 Nov 52. Served in Indon (CS/TSWM) and UK.
KASAEDJA, Jones (Kulawi, 1982); Maj, Indon. b 22 Jun 68; and
KASAEDJA, Mariyam (née Barani) (Salupone, 1982) m 1989; Maj, Indon. b 10 Oct 54.
KASBE, Devdan (Ahmednagar Central, 1970); Maj, Ind W. b 9 Feb 49; and
KASBE, Maryabai (née Devhe) (Dapodi, 1972) m 1972; Maj, Ind W. b 16 Oct 52.
KASUSO, Daniel (Pearson, Zimb, 1986); Maj, S Afr. b 15 Jul 65; and
KASUSO, Tracey (née Mashiri) (Torwood, Zimb, 1986); Maj, S Afr. b 19 Oct 64. Served in Zimb.
KATHENDU, Johnstone Njeru (Siakago, 1988); Maj, Ken E. b 22 Jun 63; with
KATHENDU, Nancy (née Turi) m 1984; Maj, Ken E. b 26 Feb 64.
KATHURI, Gabriel (Mombasa, 1982); Lt-Col, Ken E. b 13 Jan 51; with
KATHURI, Monica (née Minoo) m 1977; Lt-Col, Ken E. b 22 Feb 54.
KATSUCHI, Jiro (Hamamatsu, 1984); Maj, Jpn. b 3 May 49; and
KATSUCHI, Keiko (née Munemori) (Nagoya, 1969) m 1986; Maj, Jpn. b 30 Jun 47.
KELLY, David E. (Cincinnati, OH, 1980); Maj, USA E. b 30 Nov 59. AS (Bus Adm), MA (Ldrshp & Min); and
KELLY, Naomi R. (née Foster) (Tonawanda, NY, 1977) m 1981; Maj, USA E. b 14 Sep 56. BA (Org Mgmt).
KENNEDY, Anthony (Gander, NL, Can, 1998); Capt, E Eur. b 24 Dec 53; with
KENNEDY, Patricia (née Snow) m 1975; Capt, E Eur. b 17 Jul 55. BA, BE, BSc. Served in Can.
KENNEDY, Victor (Fulham, 1974); Maj, UK. b 3 May 45; with
KENNEDY, Miriam (née Smith) m 1967; Maj, UK. b 30 Nov 46. BD (Hons), DipTh. Served at ITC.
KHAIZADINGA (Bukpui, 1974); Maj, Ind E. b 20 Jan 50; with
RAMTHANMAWII m 1970; Maj, Ind E. b 23 Nov 53.
KHAMALISHI, Frederick (Shavahiga, 1990); Maj, Ken E. b 22 Feb 63; with
KHAMALISHI, Jescah (née Khavele) m 1988; Maj, Ken E. b 12 Mar 65.
KHOZA, Jabulani (Mbabane, 1985); Maj, S Afr. b 8 Jun 62; and
KHOZA, Fikile (née Mkhize) (Ezakheni, 1986) m 1986; Maj, S Afr. b 28 Aug 66.
KIM, Kyung-kwang (Do Bong, 1991); Maj, Kor. b 16 Jul 57; with
BAI, You-kyeong m 1989; Maj, Kor. b 4 Jul 68.
KIM, Nam-sun (Ah Hyun, 1983); Maj, Kor. b 11 Sep 54.
KIM, Un-ho (Eum Am, 1979); Maj, Kor. b 31 Jan 52; with
LEE, Ok-kyung m 1977; Maj, Kor. b 9 Jun 53.
KIM, Young-tae (Chin Chook, 1986); Maj, Kor. b 23 Mar 56. BAdm, MBA; with
PYO, Choon-yun m 1977; Maj, Kor. b 30 Aug 53.
KING, Charles (New Barnet, UK, 1975); Lt-Col, IHQ. b 29 Nov 48. Served in UK.
KITHOME, Lucas (Mwala, 1986); Maj, Ken E. b 10 Feb 59; with
KITHOME, Agnes (née Nduku) m 1984; Maj, Ken E. b 15 Jan 63.
KIVINDYO, Isaac (Kanzalu, 1982); Maj, Ken W. b 1 Aug 56; with
KIVINDYO, Naomi (née Loko) m 1970; Maj, Ken W. b 1 May 60.
KJELLGREN, Hasse (Östra Kåren, 1971); Comr, Swdn. b 1 Nov 45. BSc; and
KJELLGREN, Christina (née Forssell) (Hisingskaren, 1971) m 1971; Comr, Swdn.

b 21 May 47. Served in S Am E (TC/TPWO), Switz (TC/TPWM), Swdn (TC/TPWM) and at IHQ (IS/ZSWM Eur).

KLARENBEEK, Elsje (Amsterdam Zuid, 1979); Maj, Neth. b 2 Jun 52.

KLEMAN, Johnny (Boras, Swdn, 1982); Maj, Fin. b 29 Jul 59; and
KLEMAN, Eva (née Hedberg) (Motala, Swdn, 1981) m 1982; Maj, Fin. b 6 Sep 60. Served in Swdn.

KLEMANSKI, Guy (Lewiston-Auburn, ME, 1970); Lt-Col, USA E. b 21 Nov 50; and
KLEMANSKI, Henrietta (née Wallace) (Cleveland, West Side, OH, 1970) m 1972; Lt-Col, USA E. b 27 Jul 47.

KNAGGS, James (Philadelphia Roxborough, PA, USA E, 1976); Comr, TC, Aus S. b 5 Dec 50. MPS (Urban Min); with
KNAGGS, Carolyn (née Lance) m 1972; Comr, TPWM, Aus S. b 19 Sep 51. Served in USA E (CS/TSWM).

KNAPP, Jocelyn (Camberwell, 1969); Lt-Col, Aus S. b 7 Apr 44. Served in Aus E.

KNEDAL, Jan Øystein (Templet, Oslo, 1974); Maj, Nor. b 25 Aug 52; and
KNEDAL, Brit (née Kolloen) (Templet, Oslo, 1976) m 1978; Maj, Nor. b 27 Apr 58

KOMBO, Blaise (Makelekele, 1996); Capt, Con (Braz). b 15 Oct 68. MA Psych; with
KOMBO, Evelynne (née Missamon) (Sangolo, 1996) m 1992; Capt, Con (Braz). b 6 Jan 75.

KORNILOW, Petter (Parkano, 1981); Maj, Fin. b 21 Aug 53; and
KORNILOW, Eija Hellevi (née Astikainen) (Tampere Kaleva, 1981) m 1981; Maj, Fin. b 28 Jun 56.

KROMMENHOEK, Dick (Amsterdam Congress Hall, Neth, 1983); Comr, TC, Fin. b 18 Jun 52. MA (Music); with
KROMMENHOEK, Vibeke (née Schou Larsen) m 1978; Comr, TPWM, Fin. b 27 Nov 56. MA (Theol). Served in Neth, Den (TC/TPWM), Frce (TC/TPWM) and at IHQ.

KUMAR BABU, K. Y. Raj (Kahjipalem, 1981); Maj, Ind C. b 11 Jun 55; with
KRUPA, Bai m 1976; Maj, Ind C. b 6 Jan 55.

KUMAR, K. Y. Dhana (Khajipalem, Bapatla, 1980); Maj, Ind C. b 21 Sep 57. BCom; with
KUMAR, Yesamma (née Dasari) m 1978; Maj, Ind C. b 18 May 1961.

KUMAR, Raj (Mukerian, 1989); Maj, Ind N. b 7 Aug 64. BA, BD; with
KAUR, Mohinder m 1987; Maj, Ind N. b 5 May 64.

KWENDA, Peter (Mutondo, Zimb, 1976); Lt-Col, Nig. b 10 Apr 57; and
KWENDA, Norma (née Nyawo) (Dombwe-Makonde, Zimb, 1977) m 1977; Lt-Col, Nig. b 10 Jul 55. Served in Zimb.

KWON, Sung-dal (Son Chi, 1977); Maj, Kor. b 17 Apr 47; with
KIM, Moon-ok m 1973; Maj, Kor. b 29 Oct 53.

L

LAHASE, Kashinath V. (Chapadgaon, Ind W, 1972); Comr, TC, Ind N. b 1 Nov 49; with
LAHASE, Kusum K. m 1970; Comr, TPWM, Ind N. b 7 Jun 49. Served in Ind W, Ind SW and Ind N (CS/TSWM).

LALBULLIANA (Darlawn, Ind E, 1987); Maj, Ken E. b 20 Sep 64; and
LALBULLIANA, Lalnunhlui (Thingsulthliah, Ind E, 1990) m 1990; Maj, Ken E. b 12 Dec 65. Served in Ind E.

LALHMINGLIANA (Chaltlang, 1994); Maj, Ind E. b 29 Sep 71. BA (Hons) (Hist); and
LALHLIMPUII (Bethel, 1994) m 1994; Maj, Ind E. b 28 Oct 71. Served at IHQ.

LALKIAMLOVA (Kahrawt, 1971); Comr, IHQ (IS S Asia). b 7 Mar 49. BA; and
LALHLIMPUII (Saitual, 1973) m 1973; Comr, IHQ (ZSWM S Asia). b 25 Sep 53. Served in Ind E, Ind SW (CS/TSWO) and Ind C (TC/TPWM).

LALNGAIHAWMI, Naomi (Aizawl Central, 1978); Lt-Col, CS, Ind E. b 1 Jan 54. MA. Served at Ind Nat

LALRAMHLUNA (Chaltlang, Ind E, 1981); Lt-Col, CS, Ind W. b 9 May 51; and
KAWLRAMTHANGI (Chaltlang, Ind E, 1981) m 1972, Lt-Col, TSWM, Ind W. b 14 Nov 52. Served in Ind E.

LALRAMLIANA, Hnamte (Govt Complex, Aizawl, Ind E, 1996); Capt, Ind Nat. b 3 Jan 67. BA, BD; with
C. LALHRIATPUII m 1994; Capt, Ind Nat. b 15 Sep 69. Served in Ind E.

LALZAMLOVA (Tuinu, Ind E, 1986); Col, TC, Sri Lan. b 1 Feb 62. BA; with
NEMKHANCHING (Nu-i) m 1984; Col, TPWM, Sri Lan. b 23 Feb 63. Served in Ind E and Ind N.

LAMARR, Armida Joy (Old Orchard Beach, ME, USA E, 2002); Capt, Ken E. b 10 Jul 75. Served in USA E.

LAMARR, William (Yonkers Citadel, NY, 1967); Lt-Col, USA E. b 8 Apr 45; and
LAMARR, Judy (née Lowers) (East Liverpool, OH, 1962) m 1968; Lt-Col, USA E. b 14 Sep 41. LPN (Nursing)

Biographical Information

LAMARTINIERE, Lucien (Petit Goave, Haiti, 1992); Maj, Carib. b 13 Jun 57; with
LAMARTINIERE, Marie (née Bonhomme) m 1980; Maj, Carib. b 26 May 57. Served in Can.

LANCE, Donald W. (Philadelphia Roxborough, PA, 1980); Maj, USA E. b 7 Feb 53. BA (Bus); and
LANCE, Renee (née Hewlett) (Scranton, PA, 2002) m 2003; Capt, USA E. b 3 Jun 53. RN (Nursing).

LANGA, William (Witbank, 1977); Lt-Col, S Afr. b 15 Jul 49; with
LANGA, Thalitha (née Themba) m 1973; Lt-Col, S Afr. b 1 Sep 50.

LANTO, Sadrackh (Bandung 2, 1976); Maj, Indon. b 15 Aug 49; and
LANTO, Patricia (née Likenono) (Palu 1982) m 1984; Maj, Indon. b 26 Feb 57.

LAUKKANEN, Arja (Turku 2, 1975); Lt-Col, CS, Fin. b 29 Apr 46.

LAWS, Peter (Wauchope, 1973); Lt-Col, Aus E. b 23 Oct 1950. BAL, MBA; with
LAWS, Jan (née Cook) m 1970; Lt-Col, Aus E. b 18 Jun 50.

LEAVEY, Wendy (Street, UK, 1980); Lt-Col, Gha. b 17 Feb 53. SRN, SCM. Served in UK.

LEE, Ki-yong (Chun Yun, Seoul 1982); Maj, Kor. b 9 Aug 52; and
KIM, Sun-ho (Eum Am, 1985); m 1985; Maj, Kor. b 19 Jan 54.

LEE, Kong Chew (Bob) (Balestier, 1983); Lt-Col, CS, Sing. b 8 Oct 57. BDiv; and
LEE, Teoh Gim Leng (Wendy) (Penang, 1983) m 1982; Lt-Col, TSWM, Sing. b 24 Aug 57.

LESLIE, Victor A. (Port-of-Spain, Carib, 1980); Lt-Col, USA W. b 5 Nov 56. BA (Mgmt), MA (Relig Studies), CERT (Chem Dpndnce), JD (Law), MBA (Mgmt); and
LESLIE, Rose-Marie (née Campbell) (Lucea, Carib, 1977) m 1980; Lt-Col, USA W. b 15 Aug 57. BS (Soc Wk), AS (Nursing), RN (Nursing), BS (Nursing), CERT (Public Health Nurse). Served in Carib.

LEVIS, Linda (Harrow, UK, 1980); Maj, Tanz. b 2 Nov 49. Served in UK and at ITC.

LEWIS, Douglas (Toronto Temple, 1972); Maj, Can. b 14 Jan 47; with
LEWIS, Elizabeth (née Legge) m 1966; Maj, Can. b 30 Jul 46. Served in Ger and Carib.

LIANHLIRA (Ratu, 1979); Maj, Ind E. b 28 Apr 51, with
THANZUALI m 1975; Maj, Indon. b 20 Jan 57.

LIANTHANGA (Darlawn, 1974); Maj, Ind E. b 1 Mar 50; and
RINGLIANI (Darlawn, 1974) m 1975; Maj, Ind E. b 10 Jan 52.

LIGT de, Jacoba (née Oosterheerd) (Nieuwegein, Neth, 1987); Maj, Ken W. b 24 Apr 58; and
LIGT de, Cornelis (Nieuwegein, Neth, 1990) m 1988; Maj, Ken W. b 23 Sep 61. Served in Neth, E Afr and Ken.

LIM, Hun-taek (Kunsan, 1979); Lt-Col, Kor. b 24 Aug 50; with
CHUN, Soon-ja m 1977; Lt-Col, Kor. b 9 Mar 50. Served in Aus S.

LIM, Young-shik (Shin An, 1975); Lt-Col, Kor. b 26 Jun 49; with
YEO, Keum-soo m 1972; Lt-Col, Kor. b 14 Dec 50.

LINARES, Orestes (Camaguey, 1997); Capt, L Am N. b 13 Aug 60; with
LINARES, Sandra (née Fernández) m 1986; Capt, L Am N. b 26 Jun 63.

LÖFGREN, Kehs David (Norrköping, 1968); Col, Swdn. b 8 Nov 45; and
LÖFGREN, Edith (née Sjöström) (Borlänge, 1974) m 1977; Col, Swdn. b 2 Mar 51. Served in UK and Nor (CS/TSWO).

LOSSO, Mesak (Jakarta 2, 1968); Lt-Col, Indon. b 12 Nov 45; and
LOSSO, Mona (née Warani) (Turen, 1971) m 1972; Lt-Col, Indon. b 13 Jun 44.

LOUZOLO Dieudonnee (Nzoko, 1992); Maj, Con (Braz). b 20 Apr 67. BA Lang; with
LOUZOLO Edith (née Goudzoumou) m 1990; Maj, Con (Braz). b 25 Jul 69.

LUDIAZO, Jean Bakidi (Salle Centrale, Kinshasa, Con (Kin), 1971); Comr, TC, Nig. b 19 Nov 45; with
LUDIAZO, Véronique (née Lusieboko Lutatabio) m 1970; Comr, TPWM, Nig. b 26 Sep 53. Served in Con, Can and Con (Kin) (TC/TPWM).

LUFUMBU, Enock (Londiani, Nakuru, 1982); Maj, Ken E. b 10 Feb 52; with
LUFUMBU, Beatrice (née Kageha) m 1978; Maj, Ken E. b 22 Feb 57.

LUKAU, Joseph (Kimbanseke 1, Con (Kin), 1977); Lt-Col, IHQ. b 18 Sep 53; with
LUKAU, Angélique (née Makiese) m 1975; Lt-Col, IHQ. b 1 Sep 54. Served in Con (Kin) and Frce (CS/TPWM).

LUTHER, Lise (Harstad, 1992); Maj, Nor. b 20 May 65.

LUYK, Kenneth E. (Columbus, GA, 1985); Maj, USA S. b 2 Oct 55. MA (Relig); with
LUYK, Dawn M. (née Busby) m 1981; Maj,

USA S. b 5 Jun 60. BA (Chrstn Min).
LYDHOLM, Carl A. S. (Gartnergade, Den, 1966); Comr, TC, Nor. b 14 Nov 45; and
LYDHOLM, Gudrun (née Arskog) (Odense, Den, 1967) m 1967; Comr, TPWM, Nor. b 5 Aug 47. MTh. Served in Den, UK, Rus/CIS (GS/CSWM) and Fin (TC/TPWM).

M

MABASO, Timothy John (Witbank, 1988); Lt-Col, S Afr. b 18 May 60. BA (Bus Adm); with
MABASO, Zakithi (née Zulu) m 1983; Lt-Col, S Afr. b 16 Dec 57.

MABUTO, Christopher (Chaanga, Zam, 1979); Lt-Col, Ken W. b 2 Jan 54; with
MABUTO, Anne (née Hamayobe) m 1974; Lt-Col, Ken W. b 25 Feb 58. Served in Zam & Mal.

MABWIDI, Malonga Philippe (Salle Centrale, 1985); Maj, DR Con. b 25 Jan 53; with
MABWIDI Marie-Thérèse (née Biyela Lukimwena), m 1986; Maj, DR Con. b 13 Mar 63.

MACMILLAN, M. Christine (North York, Can, 1975); Comr, IHQ. b 9 Oct 47. Served in UK, Aus E, PNG (TC, TPWM) and Can (TC, TPWM).

MACWAN, Jashwant Trikam (1986); Maj, Ind W. b 11 Jun 63; and
MACWAN, Sunita J. (1986) m 1986; Maj, Ind W. b 5 Sep 61.

MACWAN, Phulen W. (Poona, 1981); Maj, Ind W. b 21 Apr 51.

MACWAN, Punjalal Ukabhai (Lingda, 1980); Maj, Ind W. b 8 Jul 51; with
MACWAN, Margaret m 1975; Maj, Ind W. b 17 May 55.

McCLIMONT, Graeme, (Brighton, 1977); Maj, Aus S. b 29 Jan 48. BSW; with
McCLIMONT, Helen (née Clee) m 1969; Maj, Aus S. b 1 Dec 49. Served in UK and PNG.

McKENZIE, Sydney (Havendale, Jamaica, 1970); Lt-Col, Carib. b 24 Dec 47; and
McKENZIE, Trypheme (née Forrest) (Bluefields, Jamaica, 1971) m 1973; Lt-Col, Carib. b 14 Jan 50.

McMILLAN, Susan (Montreal Citadel, Can, 1979); Lt-Col, IHQ. b 20 Oct 54. BAS, MBA, CGA. Served in Can, Mex & Central Am, S Am E and S Am W (CS).

MAELAND, Erling Dag (Bryne, Nor, 1964); Col, TC, Den. b 9 Oct 43; and
MAELAND, Signe Helene (née Paulsen) (Bryne, Nor, 1964) m 1965; Col, TPWM, Den. b 12 Jun 45. Served in UK, at IHQ and in Nor (CS/TSWM).

MAFUTA, Mavana Denis (Kamina, 1993); Capt, DR Con. b 18 Oct 54; with
MAFUTA Modestine (née Lumwanga Ngoy); Maj, DR Con. b 18 Oct 1962.

MAGANLAL, Paul (Vaso, 1979); Maj, Ind W. b 7 Jan 54; with
MAGANLAL, Febiben m 1973; Maj, Ind W. b 11 Jun 52.

MAGAR, Bhausaheb J. (Dahiphal, 1977); Maj, Ind W. b 2 Jun 53; and
MAGAR, Pushpa (née Gajbhiv) (Dahiphal, 1978) m 1979; Maj, Ind W. b 2 Jun 54.

MAHIDA, Jashwant D. (Vishrampura, 1984); Maj, Ind W. b 12 Jun 60; and
MAHIDA, Ruth (née Maganlal) (Anand Central, 1990) m 1990; Maj, Ind W. b 12 Nov 67.

MAHLANGU, Solomon (Brits, 1983); Maj, S Afr. b 29 Oct 60; and
MAHLANGU, Mercy (née Razwinani) (Khubvi, 1983) m 1985; Maj, S Afr. b 30 Jun 63. BA Soc Studies. Served at IHQ.

MAKINA, Amos (Gwelo, Zimb, 1971); Comr, IHQ (IS Afr). b 28 Jun 47; and
MAKINA, Rosemary (née Chinjiri) (Mutonda, Zimb, 1973) m 1973; Comr, IHQ (ZSWM Afr). b 8 Aug 52. Served in Gha and Zimb (TC/TPWM).

MALABI, Joash (Mulatiwa, Ken, 1984); Lt-Col, CS, S Afr. b 17 May 55; and
MALABI, Florence (née Mutindi) (Webuye, Ken, 1988) m 1988; Lt-Col, TSWM, S Afr. b 26 Jun 64. Served in E Afr and Rwa (RC/RPWM).

MANGIWA, Indra (Bandung 2, 1976), Maj, Indon. b 14 Mar 52; and
MANGIWA, Helly (née Salainti) (Surabaya, 1977) m 1982; Maj, Indon. b 16 Jun 56.

MANOHARAN, Yesudian (Nantikuzhy, Ind SE, 1987); Maj, Tanz. b 14 May 64. MCom; and
MANOHARAN, Vethamony (Ettamadai, Ind SE, 1987) m 1987; Maj, Tanz. b 20 Mar 64. Served in Ind SE and Ind N.

MARKIEWICZ, Linda V. (Rome, NY, USA E, 1981); Maj, USA W. b 15 Oct 50. BA (Arts/ Engl). Served in USA E and at IHQ and ICO.

MÁRQUEZ, Paulina (née Condori) (Viacha, 1987); Capt, S Am W. b 2 Mar 1964; and
MÁRQUEZ, Manuel (La Esperanza, 1995) m 1997; Capt, S Am W. b 12 Feb 1971.

MARSEILLE, Gerrit W. J. (Ribe, Den, 1978); Lt-Col, CS, Con (Braz). b 8 Jun 51. MSc, MEd; with
MARSEILLE, Eva (née Larsen) m 1976; Lt-Col, TSWM, Con (Braz). b 18 Jun 52.

Biographical Information

Cand Odont. Served in Neth, Zai, Den and S Afr.

MARSHALL, Norman Stephen (Chicago Mont Clare, IL, 1978); Lt-Col, USA C. b 17 Jun 45. BA (Sociol), MS (Human Services Adm), MA (Org Dev); with
MARSHALL, Diane Bernice (née Hedgren) m 1974; Lt-Col, USA C. b 30 Sep 47. BS (Ed).

MARTI, Paul William (Templet, Oslo, 1980), Maj, Nor. b 24 Jan 61; and
MARTI, Margaret Saue (née Saue) (Voss, 1980) m 1983, Maj, Nor. b 29 Aug 58. Served in Switz.

MARTIN, August (Biel, 1977); Maj, Switz. b 24 Oct 52; with
MARTIN, Ruth (née Beyeler) m 1974; Maj, Switz. b 22 Oct 51.

MARTIN, Larry R. (Edmonton Northside, AB, 1980); Maj, Can. b 31 Jul 1950. BA, MA, MTS; with
MARTIN, Velma (née Ginn) m 1972; Maj, Can. b 4 Oct 50. Served in UK.

MASANGO, Frederick (Mangula, 1971); Maj, Zimb. b 24 Jul 49; with
MASANGO, Rosemary (née Handiria) (Karambazungu, 1981) m 1981; Maj, Zimb. b 13 Feb 56.

MASIH, Edwin (Bareilly, Ind N, 1979); Maj, Carib. b 6 Oct 57; with
MASIH, Sumita (Gurdaspur, Ind N, 1983) m 1983; Maj, Carib. b 9 Oct 63. Served in Ind N.

MASIH, Gian (Jalalabad, 1972); Maj, Ind N. b 1 Oct 50; and
MASIH, Salima (Barnala, 1978) m 1978; Maj, Ind N. b 1 Dec 54.

MASIH, Gurnam (Kaler Kalan, 1991); Maj, Ind N. b 7 Jan 68; and
MASIH, Razia (Durangla, 1987); m 1992; Maj, Ind N. b 1 Apr 65.

MASIH, Joginder (Bhoper, 1982); Maj, Ind N. b 13 Jul 58; with
MASIH, Shanti m 1980; Maj, CSWM, Ban. b 15 May 59. Served in Ban (GS/CHQ).

MASIH, Lazar (Rampur, 1974); Maj, Ind N. b 20 May 52; with
MASIH, Sharbati m 1969; Maj, Ind N. b 15 Jun 53.

MASIH, Makhan (Shahpur Guraya, 1990); Maj, Ind N. b 30 Mar 68; and
MASIH, Sunila Makhan (City Corps, Amritsar, 1992) m 1992; Maj, Ind N. b 5 May 66.

MASIH, Manga (Bhandal, 1979); Maj, Ind N. b 1 May 54; and
MASIH, Roseleen (Batala Central, 1980) m 1980; Maj, Ind N. b 2 Jun 59.

MASIH, Manuel (Amritsar, 1994); Maj, Ind N. b 1 Apr 64; with
MASIH, Anita m 1991; Maj, Ind N. b 22 Apr 62.

MASIH, Parkash (Khunda, 1984); Maj, Ind N. b 10 Mar 58; with
MASIH, Mariam Parkash m 1981; Maj, Ind N. b 2 Apr 62.

MASIH, Piara (Kathane, 1982); Maj, Ind N. b 3 Mar 61; with
MASIH, Grace (Babri Jiwanwal, 1984) m 1985; Maj, Ind N. b 6 Feb 64.

MASIH, Salamat (Shantinagar, 1989); Maj, Pak. b 12 Aug 64; with
SALAMAT, Grace (née Sardar) m 1987; Maj, Pak. b 18 Apr 64.

MASIH, Shafqat (Rehimabad, 1981); Maj, Pak. b 30 Oct 48; with
SHAFQAT, Parveen (née Sardar) m 1979; Maj, Pak. b 26 Jun 51.

MASIH, Swinder (Jammu, Ind N, 1994); Maj, Ind Nat. b 4 May 64; with
MASIH, Sudesh m 1991; Maj, Ind Nat. b 17 Sep 69. Served in Ind N.

MASON, Winsome (Burnie 1987); Maj, Aus S. b 2 Feb 1958. Served in UK.

MASSIÉLÉ, Antoine (Yaya, 1982); Maj, Con (Braz). b 20 Feb 53; with
MASSIÉLÉ, Marianne (née Ngoli) m 1978; Maj, Con (Braz). b 2 Jan 50.

MATA, Mayisilwa Jean-Baptiste (Kisenso, DR Con, 1983); Lt-Col, Zam. b 21 Oct 51; with
MATA, Marie (née Mundele Kisokama) m 1981; Lt-Col, Zam. b 22 Mar 58. Served in Con (Kin).

MATEAR, John (Whifflet, 1978); Comr, TC, UK. b 26 Apr 47; and
MATEAR, Elizabeth (née Kowbus) (Greenock Citadel, 1977) m 1978; Comr, TPWM, UK. b 16 Aug 52. Dip Youth, Commun and Soc Wk, Emp Law. Served in Carib (TC/TPWM).

MATONDO, Gracia Victor (Kimpese, 1985); Maj, DR Con. b 23 May 60; with
MATONDO, Isabel (née Lydia) m 1982; Maj, DR Con. b 8 Sep 1962.

MATONDO, Isidore Mayunga (Boma, 1989); Maj, DR Con. b 6 Jul 56; with
MATONDO, Marthe (née Nlandu Luzoladio) m 1987; Maj, DR Con. b 7 Dec 62.

MAVOUNA, Nkouka François (Nzoko, 1988); Maj, Con (Braz). b 15 Mar 60; with
MAVOUNA, Louise (née Matondo) m 1986; Maj, Con (Braz). b 11 Dec 62.

MAVUNDLA, Hezekiel (Barberton, S Afr, 1970); Col, TC, Tanz. b 19 Jan 47; and
MAVUNDLA, Mirriam (née Maphanga)

(Barberton, S Afr, 1970) m 1970; Col, TPWM, Tanz. b 2 Aug 52. Served in S Afr (CS/TSWM).

MAXWELL, Wayne (Canberra City Temple, 1984); Maj, Aus E. b 31 May 58. DipMin, BMin, MAL; with
MAXWELL, Robyn (née Alley) m 1980; Maj, Aus E. b 14 Feb 60. Dip Pastoral Counselling

MAYNOR, Kenneth (Cleveland South, OH, 1980); Lt-Col, USA E. b 1 Feb 59. BS (Org Mgmt); with
MAYNOR, Cheryl Ann (née Staaf) m 1977; Lt-Col, USA E. b 27 Sep 58. BS (Church Mgmt).

MAYORGA, Max (Central, Costa Rica, 1989); Maj, L Am N. b 1 Feb 62; with
MAYORGA, Julia (née Obando); m 1981; Maj, L Am N. b 23 Oct 61.

MBAJA, Tiras Atulo (Kibera, 1986); Maj, Ken W. b 13 Jul 54; with
MBAJA, Mebo (née Mukiza) m 1983; Maj, Ken W. b 25 Mar 60.

MBALA, Lubaki Sébastien (Kifuma, 1987); Maj, DR Con. b 23 Jun 58, and
MBALA, Godette Mboyo (née Moseka) (Kintambo, 1987) m 1988; Maj, DR Con. b 26 Sep 62.

MBAKAYA, Herman (Nairobi Central, 1986), Maj, Ken W. b 11 Jan 57; with
MBAKAYA, Lucia (née Manduu) m 1992; Maj, Ken W. b 13 Oct 67.

MBIZI, Gabin (Ouenze, 1988); Maj, Con (Braz). b 30 Jan 63; with
MBIZI, Philomene (née Nkounkou) m 1986; Maj, Con (Braz). b 22 Aug 67.

MEITEI, Shamu (Leizhangphai Manipur, 1988); Maj, Ind E. b 1 Jan 61. BCom; with
HOIHNIANG m 1983; Maj, Ind E. b 10 Jun 59.

MENDES, Marcio (Belo Horizonte, 1980); Maj, Brz. b 24 Feb 57. BA (Theol); and
MENDES, Jurema (née Mazzini) (Quarai, 1979) m 1981; Maj, Brz. b 4 Aug 57. BA (Ed).

MENDEZ, Jorge (El Faro, 1988); Maj, L Am N. b 5 Oct 51; with
MENDEZ, Idali (née Jiminez) m 1973; Maj, L Am N. b 24 Aug 52.

MENIA, Virgilio (Asingan, 1990); Maj, Phil. b 2 Jun 61. BEd. b 7 Jan 62.
MENIA, Ma Luisa (née Araneta) (Negros Occ, 1984) m 1990; Maj, Phil. b 7 Jan 62.

MERAS, Marja (Turku 2, 1977); Maj, Fin. b 6 Sep 49.

MERRETT, Kelvin (Renown Pk, 1983); Maj, Aus S. b 6 Sep 58. Assoc Theol; and
MERRETT, Winsome (née Morris)

(Kempsey, 1987) m 1987; Maj, Aus S. b 21 Sep 58. MA (Theol Studies).

MEYNER, Marianne (née Stettler) (Basle 2, 1983); Maj, Switz. b 14 Apr 57; with
MEYNER, Urs m 1978; Maj, Switz. b 30 Jan 51.

MGBEBUIHE, Benson (Amauzari, 1990); Maj, Nig. b 1 Aug 64; with
MGBEBUIHE, Celine m 1988; Maj, Nig. b 1 Aug 66.

MHASVI, Evan (née Mhizha) (Shirichena, 1977); Lt-Col, Zimb. b 1 Feb 55. Served in Zam. Ww Lt-Col Henry, pG 2006.

MHEMBERE, Isaac (Mukwenya 1989); Maj, Zimb. b 5 May 69; and
MHEMBERE, Charity (née Muchapondwa) (Muchapondwa, 1990) m 1991; Maj, Zimb. b 2 Jan 67.

MILAMBO, Saraphina (née Shikawala) (Kafue, 1989); Maj, TSWM, Zam. b 1 Feb 55. Ww Maj Vincent, pG 2007.

MILLAR, Ronald (Winnipeg Cit, Can, 1978); Maj, Carib. b 22 Oct 50. BA, BEd, MTS; with
MILLAR, Donna (née Barkwell) m 1973; Maj, Carib. b 12 Dec 51. BA. Served in Can and Aus E.

MKAMI, Samuel Chacha (Kitagutiti, 1988); Maj, Tanz. b 16 Apr 65; with
MKAMI, Mary (née Kibera) m 1985; Maj, Tanz. b 20 Jul 66.

MNYAMPI, Benjamin (Mgulani, 1985); Lt-Col, CS, Tan. b 1 Mar 54; with
MNYAMPI, Grace (née Sage) m 1984; Lt-Col, TSWM, Tan. b 3 Jun 63. Served in E Afr, Rwa and Zimb.

MOCKABEE, William (Anniston, AL, 1975); Maj, USA S. b 1 Nov 54; and
MOCKABEE, Debra (née Salmon) (Oklahoma City, OK, 1976) m 1976; Maj, USA S. b 9 Sep 54.

MORAN, Peter (Bradford West Bowling, 1979); Maj, UK. b 11 Feb 51; with
MORAN, Sandra (née Clapham) m 1971; Maj, UK. b 16 Jul 49.

MORETZ, Lawrence R. (Sunbury, PA, 1964); Comr, TC, USA E. b 22 Jul 43; and
MORETZ, Nancy A. (née Burke) (Kingston, NY, 1964) m 1965; Comr, TPWM, USA E. b 29 Nov 44. Served in S Am W (TC/TPWO) and USA C (TC/TPWM).

MORIASI, Stephen (Keng'uso, Ken, 1984); Maj, GS, Uga. b 7 Jun 60; and
MORIASI, Rose Mmbaga (née Onchari) (Embago, Ken, 1988) m 1990; Maj, CSWM, Uga. Served in E Afr and at IHQ.

Biographical Information

MOTSI, Isiah (Tomlinson, 1989); Maj, Zimb. b 9 Sep 68; and
MOTSI, Leah (née Mupfeki) (Braeside, 1993) m 1993; b 15 Dec 73.

MOUKOKO, Daniel (Bacongo, Con (Braz), 1990); Maj, S Afr. b 1 Dec 60; with
MOUKOKO, Arschette (née Nguitoukoulou) m 1988; Maj, S Afr. b 30 Oct 62. Served in Con (Braz) and Rwa.

MOWERS, John D. (Kansas City [Westport Temple], MO, USA C, 1976); Maj, S Am E. b 25 Sep 52. BA (Sociol); with
MOWERS, Nancy J. (née Hultin) m 1970; Maj, S Am E. b 26 Apr 49. BA (Psychol). Served in USA C and L Am N.

MOYA, Danton (Lo Valledor, 1989); Maj, S Am E. b 17 Jun 58; with
MOYA, Juana (neé Balboa) m 1979, Maj, S Am E. b 24 Jun 60. Served in S Am W.

MPANZU, Manu Emmanuel (Kimbanseke 1, 1979); Maj, DR Con. b 20 Jul 54; with
MPANZU, Albertine (née Luzayadio Yema) m 1977; Maj, DR Con. b 27 Dec 58.

MSONGWE, Yohana (Ilembo, 1985); Maj, Tanz. b 1 Jan 62; with
MSONGWE, Jesinala m 1985; Maj, Tanz. b 15 Jun 64.

MUASA, Jackson (Kivaku, 1980); Lt-Col, Ken E. b 9 Jan 56; and
MUASA, Ciennah (née Mwandi) (Kee, 1980) m 1982; Lt-Col, Ken E. b 10 Oct 57.

MUBAIWA, Final (Nyarukunda, 1990); Maj, Zimb. b 29 June 60, with
MUBAIWA, Pfumisai (née Ngwenya) m 1988; Maj, Zimb. b 12 May 69.

MUDDA, Abraham Lincoln (Nellore Central, Ind C, 1991); Maj, Zim. b 12 Sep 64. MA, MDiv; with
MUDDA, Mercy Manjula m1988; Maj, Zim. b 22 May 66. BA, BEd, BTS. Served in Ind C.

MUIKKU, Aino (Turku II, Fin, 1985); Lt-Col, CS, Den. b 3 May 56. Served in Fin.

MUKOKO, Mamfweni Pierre (Mbanza-Nsundi, 1979); Maj, DR Con. b 3 Feb 49; with
MUKOKO, Marie-José (née Sansa Mundele) m 1981; Maj, DR Con. b 25 Feb 59.

MUKONGA, Julius (Kwa Kyambu, 1978); Lt-Col, Ken E. b 10 Mar 53; with
MUKONGA, Phyllis (née Mumbua) m 1976; Lt-Col, Ken E. b 28 Mar 57.

MUKUBWA, James (Lwanda, 1980) Maj, Ken W. b 23 Jul 54; with
MUKUBWA, Grace (née Nandako) m 1979; Maj, Ken W. b 8 Apr 55.

MUNN, Richard (Lexington, KY, USA E, 1987); Lt-Col, IHQ (Principal, ICO). b 16 Jan 56.
BA (Ed), MDiv (Theol), DM (Chrstn Ldrshp); with
MUNN, Janet (née White) m 1980; Lt-Col, IHQ. b 22 Oct 60. BA (Psych/Spanish), MA (Ldrshp & Min). Served in USA E.

MUÑOZ, Manuel (Limón, 1989); Maj, L Am N. b 25 Mar 57; and
MUÑOZ, Nancy (née Letóna) (Central Corps, Guatemala, 1984) m 1985; Maj, L Am N. b 29 Dec 62.

MUNYEKHE, Boniface (Kithituni, 1977); Maj, Ken E. b 21 Mar 50; with
MUNYEKHE, Esther (née Mumbe) m 1973; Maj, Ken E. b 12 May 52.

MUTUKU, Peter (Kamuthanga, 1980) Maj, Ken W. b 5 Aug 53; with
MUTUKU, Ann (née Ndunge) m 1978; Maj, Ken W. b 19 Mar 53.

MUTUNGI, William (Kawaethei, 1990) Maj, Ken W. b 2 Nov 62; with
MUTUNGI, Florence (née Mbithe) m 1988; Maj Ken W. b 12 Dec 66.

MWALUKANI, Wilson (Maendeleo, 1984); Maj, Tanz. b 1 Aug 59; with
MWALUKANI, Tamali (née Sanya) m 1983; Maj, Tanz. b 1 Jan 63.

MWEEMBA, Richard (Choma, 1989); Maj, Zam. b 24 Feb 54; with
MWEEMBA, Eunice (née Chiyalamanza) m 1975; Maj, Zam. b 15 Apr 60.

N

NAMAI, Kiyoshi (Wakamatsu, 1984); Maj, Jpn. b 20 Apr 42; with
NAMAI, Fumiko (née Isago) m 1971; Maj, Jpn. b 1 Jan 48.

NALLATHAMBI, Edwin Sathyadhas (Kolvey, 1981); Maj, Ind SE. b 10 Aug 55; with
NALLATHAMBI, Gnana Jessibell Edwin Sathyadhas m 1980; Maj, Ind SE. b 15 Jun 57

NANGI, Masamba Henri (Kinzadi, 1979); Lt-Col, DR Con. b 21 May 53; with
NANGI, Josephine (née Nsimba Babinga); Lt-Col, DR Con. b 30 Dec 53.

NANLABI, Priscilla (San Jose, Phil, 1980); Maj, GS, HK. b 15 Nov 58. Served in Phil.

NAUD, Daniel (Paris-Montparnasse, Frce, 1979); Lt-Col, OC, It. b 8 Mar 54; and
NAUD Eliane (née Volet) (Strasbourge, Frce, 1980) m 1980; Lt-Col, CPWM, It. b 3 Apr 60. Served in Frce and Belg.

NAUD, Patrick (Paris Villette, Fra, 1987); Lt-Col, CS, Ger. b 15 Mar 57; with
NAUD, Anne-Dore (nèe Kaiser) (Hamburg, 1987) m 1987; Lt-Col, TSWM, Ger. b 26 Nov 59. Served in Fra and Belg.

Biographical Information

NAUTA, James (Grand Rapids Heritage Hill, MI, 1989); Lt-Col, USA C. b 18 Apr 44. BA (Psych), MSW; with
NAUTA, Janice B. (née Rager) m 1964; Lt-Col , USA C. b 28 Jul 42.

NCUBE, Dubayi (Ndola, 1972); Lt-Col, Zimb. b 8 Jun 52; and
NCUBE, Orlipha (née Ndlovu) (Mpopoma, 1976) m 1976; Lt-Col, Zimb. b 25 Dec 54.

NEEDHAM, John (Atlanta, GA, 1977); Maj, USA S. b 11 Aug 51. MTS; with
NEEDHAM, Marthalynn (née Ling) m 1973; Maj, USA S. b 5 Jun 52. Served in UK.

NESTERENKO, Alex (Vitarte, 1986); Maj, S Am W. b 13 Dec 63; and
NESTERENKO, Luz (née Henríquez) (Santiago Central, 1990) m 1991; Capt, S Am W. b 10 May 67. Served in Rus.

NGANDA, Francis (Kanzalu, 1978); Maj, Ken E. b 11 Jan 52; with
NGANDA, Lucy (née Njioka) m 1976; Maj, Ken E. b 8 Apr 59.

NGOY, Wa Mande Hubert (Kamina, 1989); Maj, DR Con. b 5 Jul 60; with
NGOY, Mbayo Célestine (née Mbayokidi) m 1983; Maj, DR Con. b 21 Nov 62. Served in Tanz.

NGWANGA, Kakinanatadiko Madeleine (Matadi, 1979); Col, TC and TPWM, DR Con. b 25 Nov 55. Served in DR Con (CS and TSWM).

NICOLASA, Pablo (Buenos Aires Central, 1989); Maj, S Am E. b 20 Feb 61; with
NICOLASA, Estela (née Ocampo) m 1984; Maj, S Am E. b 4 Jul 66.

NICOLSON, Clive (Dunedin Fortress, 1990); Maj, NZ. b 31 Jul 47; with
NICOLSON, Lesley (née Ide) m 1970; Maj, NZ. b 20 Mar 52.

NILES, Allie Laura (Pasadena Tabernacle, CA, 1985); Maj, USA W. b 24 Oct 56. BA (Psych), BA (Soc Wk).

NJIRU, Nahashon Kidhakwa (Mombasa, 1984); Maj, Ken W. b 30 Apr 53; with
NJIRU, Zipporah (née Ndeleve) m 1976; Maj, Ken W. b 22 Feb 56.

NKANU, Bintoma Norbert (Kavwaya, 1981); Maj, DR Con. b 29 Jun 54, with
NKANU, Hèléne (née Makuiza Lutonadio) m 1978; Maj, DR Con. b 18 Nov 61.

NKHOMA, Sammy (Zhombe, 1990); Maj, Zimb. b 7 Jul 61; with
NKHOMA, Ellen (née Mandizvidza) m 1987; Maj, Zimb. b 27 Sep 66.

NOAKES, David (Edendale, 1980); Maj, NZ. b 21 Sep 53. BA, DipTchg, DipGrad, PG DipTh; with
NOAKES, Vyvyenne (née Melhuish) m 1974; Maj, NZ. b 16 Mar 53. DipTchg (ECE).

NORDENBERG, Kenneth (Hisingskåren 1973); Lt-Col, Swdn. b 3 Jan 47; with
NORDENBERG, Ewa (née Landström); Lt-Col, Swdn. b 1 Sep 49.

NSUMBU, Fwadiabana Jean-Jacques (Kavwaya, 1977); Maj, DR Con. b 16 Aug 47; with
NSUMBU, Alice (née Muila Luvengika) m 1970; Maj, DR Con. b 24 Apr 51.

NSUMBU, Mambueni Emmanuel (Kingudi, 1981); Maj, DR Con. b 14 Aug 52; with
NSUMBU, Clémentine (née Mbimbu Bamba) m 1978; Maj, DR Con. b 10 Jun 59.

NTEMBI, Lukombo Esaïe (Mvuila, 1987); Maj, DR Con. b 15 Sep 57; and
NTEMBI, Marie-José (née Yoka Nzakimuena) m 1983; Maj, DR Con. b 6 Oct 62.

NTOYA, Kapela (Kinshasa IV, Con, 1983); Maj, IHQ (Principal, SALT Afr). b 2 Apr 55. BA, ThA; and
NTOYA, Rose-Nicole (née Makuena) (Kinshasa IV, Con, 1983); m 1983; Maj, IHQ (SALT Afr). b 21 Nov 60. Served in Con (Kin).

NUESCH, Nestor (New York Temple, NY, USA E, 1977); Col, TC, S Am E. b 1 Dec 49. BA (Bus Adm), MBA; and
NUESCH, Rebecca (née Brewer) (Ithaca, NY, USA E, 1977) m 1977; Col, TPWM, S Am E. b 17 Jan 55. Served in USA E.

NYAGAH, Henry Njagi (Kagaari, 1986); Lt-Col, CS, Ken W. b 21 Feb 54; with
NYAGAH, Catherine (née Njoki) m 1984; Lt-Col, TSWM, Ken W. b 3 Sep 59.

NYAMBALO, Francis (Migowi, 1982); Maj, GS, Mal. b 15 Aug 51; with
NYAMBALO, Jamiya (née Khumani) m 1970; Maj, CSWM, Mal. b 14 Aug 56. Served in Zam.

NYEREYEMHUKA, Funny (Dombwe, 1973); Maj, Zimb. b 15 Dec 50; and
NYEREYEMHUKA, Ellen (née Mpofu) (Gandiwa Society, 1978) m 1978; Maj, Zimb. b 9 Jul 55.

NZILA, Luyeye Barthélemy (Lemba-Ngaba, 1987); Maj, DR Con. b 16 Mar 61; and
NZILA, Bibisky (née Ntombo Nsosa) m 1985; Maj, DR Con. b 6 Oct 66.

NZINGOULA, Victor (Loussala, 1988); Maj, Con (Braz). b 27 Mar 63; with
NZINGOULA, Emma (née Malonga) m 1986; Maj, Con (Braz). b 27 Apr 68.

Biographical Information

NZITA, Jerôme (Bakongo, 1977); Maj, Con (Braz). b 15 Oct 48; with
NZITA, Jeanne (née Nsongala Jeanne) m 1976; Maj, Con (Braz). b 26 Jun 52.

O

OALANG, David (Sta Barbara, 1995); Capt, Phil. b 20 Feb 66. BSc (Bus Adm); and
OALANG, Elsa (née Gallna) (Quezon City 1, 1988) m 1995; Maj, Phil. b 25 May 62. BSc (Mass Comm), MA (Theol).

OBANDO, Maria Eugenia (née Vanegas) (Sagrada Familia, Costa Rica, 1991); Maj, L Am N. b 21 Apr 65; with
OBANDO, Javier m 1988; Maj, L Am N. b 2 Mar 66.

OBENG-APPAU, Richmond (Suame, 1989); Maj, Gha. b 1 Nov 61; with
OBENG-APPAU, Dora (née Kwane) m 1986; Maj, Gha. b 26 Jun 60.

ÖBERG, Leif (Centrumkåren, 1986); Maj, Swdn. b 17 Dec 60; and
ÖBERG, Helena (née Gezelius); Maj, Swdn. b 25 May 61.

O'BRIEN, Douglas G. (San Francisco Citadel, 1976); Lt-Col, USA W. b 1 Aug 49. BA (Speech), MA (Relig); and
O'BRIEN, Diane (née Lillicrap) (Staines, UK, 1975) m 1988; Lt-Col, USA W. b 8 Nov 50. FTCL, GTCL. Served in UK.

ODURO, Godfried (Kyekyewere, 1981); Maj, Gha. b 17 Jul 54; with
ODURO, Felicia (née Obeng) m 1978; Maj, Gha. b 25 Jun 60.

ODURO, Rockson (Kwao Nartey, 1993); Maj, Gha. b 29 Jan 63; with
ODURO, Emelia (née Lamtei) m 1991; Maj, Gha. b 12 Mar 64.

ODURO-AMOAH, Peter (Achiase, 1989); Maj, Gha. b 26 Aug 58; with
ODURO-AMOAH, Grace (née Fosua) m 1984; Maj, Gha. b 11 Feb 64.

OGUNDAHUNSI, Raphael (Ogbagi, 1986); Maj, Nig. b 10 Jul 59; with
OGUNDAHUNSI, Esther m 19; Maj, Nig. b 13 Apr 64.

OKOROUGO, Edwin Rapurnchukwu (Amesi, 1982); Maj, Nig. b 2 Aug 49. BA (Relig Studies), MA (Eth and Phil); with
OKOROUGO, Agnes (née Nwokekwe) m 1978; Maj, Nig. b 5 Apr 52.

OLAUSSON, Gunilla (née Lind) (Helsingborg, 1986) Maj, Swdn. b 23 Aug 60 and
OLAUSSON, Kjell Edor (Hisingskår, 1978) m 1986; Maj, Swdn. b 12 Nov 56.

OLEWA, John (Mukhombe, 1986); Maj, Ken E. b 12 Nov 54; with
OLEWA, Mary (née Kadzo) m 1982; Maj, Ken E. b 19 Sep 1960.

OLORUNTOBA, Festus (Supare, 1976); Lt-Col, CS, Nig. b 7 Jul 55. Ww Lt-Col Gloria, pG 2009.

ONYEKWERE, Paul (Umuogo, 1984); Maj, Nig. b 27 Jul 58; with
ONYEKWERE, Edinah; Maj, Nig. b 29 Oct 61.

ORASIBE, Patrick (Akokwa, 1988); Maj, Nig. b 9 Oct 58; with
ORASIBE, Blessing (née Chituru) Maj, Nig. b 5 Dec 58.

ORD, Norman (Peterborough Citadel, 1992); Maj, UK. b 28 Sep 55. MA (Hons) (French and Music), PGCE, CDRS. Ww Capt Christine, pG 2009.

ØRSNES, Bernt Olaf (Bergen 1, 1983); Maj, Nor. b 22 Apr 59; and
ØRSNES, Hildegard (née Anthun) (Bergen 1, 1984) m 1986; Maj, Nor. b 29 Sep 61. Served in Carib.

OTA, Haruhisa (Hamamatsu, 1973); Maj, Jpn. b 30 Jan 50; and
OTA, Hiromi (née Nakatsugawa) (Hamamatsu, 1973) m 1976; Maj, Jpn. b 21 Jun 48.

OWEN, Graham (Nuneaton, 1977); Lt-Col, UK. b 8 Jul 53; and
OWEN, Kirsten (née Jacobsen) (Copenhagen Temple, Den, 1977) m 1978; Lt-Col, UK. b 2 May 56. Served in Den (CS/THQ).

OYESANYA, Michael (Iperu, 1984); Maj, Nig. b 17 May 61; and
OYESANYA, Roseline (Iperu, 1988) m 1988; Maj, Nig. b 21 Jun 65.

P

PANG, Kie-chang (Yung Chun, 1975); Maj, Kor. b 7 Oct 44; and
PARK, Keum-ja (Ah Hyun, 1973) m 1975; Maj, Kor. b 16 Mar 44.

PAONE, Massimo (Naples, It, 1977); Lt-Col, CS, Frce. b 8 Jun 52; and
PAONE, Elizabeth Jane (née Moir) (Nunhead, UK, 1982) m 1982; Lt-Col, TPWM, Frce. b 17 Dec 58. BA (Hons). Served in UK and It (OC/CPWM).

PARDO, Zoilo B. (Hollywood, CA, USA W, 1989); Lt-Col, CS, L Am N. b 9 Dec 53. BA (Acct); with
PARDO, Magali (née Pacheco) m 1980; Lt-Col, TSWM, L Am N. b 20 Apr 56. BA (Gen Ed), BA (Acct). Served in USA W and Mex.

PAREDES, Tito E. (La Paz, S Am W, 1976); Lt-Col, Asst CS, USA E. b 14 Aug 54; and
PAREDES, Martha (née Nery) (Cochabamba, S Am W, 1976) m 1977; Lt-Col, USA E. b 3 Jun 54. Served in S Am W and L Am N (CS/TSWM).

PARK, Chong-duk (Pupyung, 1977); Lt-Col, Kor. b 22 May 50. ThM, DipMin; with
YOON, Eun-sook m 1975; Lt-Col, Kor. b 23 Oct 50.

PARK, Man-hee (Chung Ju, 1975); Col, CS, Kor. b 11 Aug 47; with
KIM, Keum-nyeo m 1973; Col, TSWM, Kor. b 13 Jun 51.

PARK, Nai-hoon (Syn Heung, 1978); Maj, Kor. b 23 Oct 46; with
KIL, Soon-boon m 1971; Maj, Kor. b 26 Nov 49.

PARKER, Michael (Hucknall, 1977); Lt-Col, UK. b 28 Jul 50; with
PARKER, Joan (née Brailsford) m 1971; Lt-Col, UK. b 16 Jan 52. Served at ITC.

PARMAR, Kantilal K. (Ode, 1983); Maj, Ind W. b 1 Jun 53. BA, BEd; and
PARMAR, Eunice K. (née Gaikwad) (Mohmedwadi, 1977) m 1983; Maj, Ind W. b 30 Oct 52.

PAWAR, Suresh S. (Ahmednagar Evangeline Booth Hall, 1981); Maj, Ind W. b 10 Feb 60; and
PAWAR, Martha (née Shirsath) (Ahmednagar Central, 1981) m 1981; Maj, Ind W. b 17 Nov 63.

PAXTON, Joy (Rosyth, UK, 1976); Maj, Tanz. b 16 Aug 50. Served in UK.

PAYNE, Godfrey (Goff) (Tunbridge Wells, UK, 1980); Lt-Col, OC, Mal. b 15 Oct 51; with
PAYNE, Diane (née Harris) m 1975; Lt-Col, CPWM, Mal. b 28 Dec 52. Served in UK, E Afr, Zam & Mal and Uga (OC/CPWM).

PEARCE, Lynette J. (Parkes, Aus E, 1971); Comr, IHQ (WSWM). b 13 Jan 45. BA. Served in Aus E and ICO.

PEDDLE, Brian (Dildo/New Harbour, NF, Can, 1977); Col, CS, UK. b 8 Aug 57; and
PEDDLE, Rosalie (née Rowe) (Carbonear, NF, Can, 1976) m 1978; Col, TSWM, UK. b 17 Jan 56. Served in Can and NZ.

PERINBANAYAGAM, Suthananthadhas (Booth Tucker Hall, Nagercoil, 1986); Maj, Ind SE. b 14 Oct 56. MA, HACDP; and
PERINBANAYAGAM Esther Evangelin Suthananthadhas (Attoor, 1986) m 1986; Maj, Ind SE. b 18 Apr 63. BSc.

PETTERSEN, Per Arne (Sarpsborg, 1969); Maj, Nor. b 20 Mar 47; and
PETTERSEN, Lillian (née Madsø) (Namsos, 1969) m 1971; Maj, Nor. b 5 Jun 45.

PHILIP, P. K. (Thottamon, 1975); Maj, Ind SW. b 12 Dec 48; and
PHILIP, Rachel (Kottarakara Central, 1980) m 1979; Maj, Ind SW. b 10 Nov 54.

PHO, Samuel (Altona, Aus S, 1983); Lt-Col, OC, HK. b 17 Jun 57. BTh; with
PHO, Donni (née Kkuu) (Altona, Aus S, 1985) m 1985; Lt-Col, CPWM, HK. b 30 May 58.

PIGFORD, R. Eugene (Wellsville, NY, 1970); Lt-Col, USA E. b 26 Jun 44. BA (Sci), MA (Ed Adm); with
PIGFORD, Edith Helen (née Waldron) m 1966; Lt-Col, USA E. b 12 May 45. BA (Chrstn Ed & Fr). Served in Can.

PILKINGTON, George A. (Lamberhead Green, 1972); Lt-Col, UK. b 11 Apr 50. SRN. Served at ITC. m 1974; Maj Vera, ret 2007.

POA, Selly Barak (Jakarta, 1979); Lt-Col, Indon. b 25 Sep 55; and
POA, Anastasia (née Djoko Slamet) (Surakarta 2, 1984) m 1985; Lt-Col, Indon. b 29 Jun 62.

POBJIE, Barry R. (Paddington, Aus E, 1965); Comr, IHQ (IS Eur). b 25 Jan 45. Ww Capt Ruth, pG 1978. Served in PNG; and
POBJIE, Raemor (née Wilson) (Port Kembla, Aus E, 1971) m 1980; Comr, IHQ (ZSWM Eur). b 22 Sep 48. Served in NZ, Aus E, Rus (GS/CSWO), E Eur (OC/CPWM, TC/TPWM) and at IHQ (IS/ZSWM SPEA).

POKE, Victor (Burnie, Aus S, 1968); Comr, TC, Swdn. b 8 Jan 46; and
POKE, Roslyn (née Pengilly) (Maylands, Aus S, 1968) m 1970; Comr, TPWM, Swdn. b 20 Jun 45. Served in Aus S and UK (CS/TSWM).

PONNIAH, Masilamony (Periavilai, Ind SE, 1969); Lt-Col, CS, Ind SW. b 2 Jun 49; and
PONNIAH, Sathiyabama (Layam, Ind SE, 1974) m 1974; Lt-Col, TSWM, Ind SW. b 14 Apr 56. Served in Ind SE, Ind W and Ind N.

POSADAS, Leopoldo (Dagupan City, Phil, 1981); Maj, GS, Ban. b 18 Aug 58. BSc; and
POSADAS, Evelyn (née Felix) (Hermoza, Phil, 1982) m 1982; Maj, CSWM, Ban. b 2 Aug 57. Served in Phil.

POSILLICO, Joseph E. (Los Angeles Lincoln Heights, CA, 1972); Lt-Col, USA W. b 29 Dec 50; and
POSILLICO, Shawn L. (née Patrick) (San Francisco, CA, 1984) m 1988; Lt-Col, USA W. b 3 Aug 57. BS (Bus Econ).

PRASAD, P. C. (Annavaram, 1981); Maj, Ind C. b 9 Sep 58; with
PRASAD, Krupamma m 1979; Maj, Ind C. b 4 Jun 59.

Biographical Information

PRITCHETT, Wayne (Deer Lake, NF, Can, 1970); Lt-Col, IHQ. b 13 Aug 46. BA, BEd, MTS; and
PRITCHETT, Myra (née Rice) (Roberts Arm, NF, Can, 1969) m 1972; Lt-Col, IHQ. b 19 Jun 50. BA, MTS. Served in Can.
PULULU, Celestino Pepe (Makala, DR Con, 1985), Maj, GS, Moz. b 15 Oct 52; with
PULULU, Veronica Lukombo (née Nkenge) m 1978; Maj, CSWM, Moz. b 4 Dec 57. Served in Con (Kin).
PUOTINIEMI, Tella (née Juntunen) (Helsinki IV, 1983); Maj, Fin. b 17 Oct 52; and
PUOTINIEMI, Antero (Oulu, 1981) m 1983; Maj, Fin. b 15 Oct 48.

R

RAINES, Timothy (Mt Vernon, NY, 1971); Lt-Col, USA E. b 30 Dec 47. BS (Org Mgmt); and
RAINES, Lynda Lou (née Swingle) (Zanesville, OH, 1969) m 1969; Lt-Col, USA E. b 23 Aug 48. BS (Org Mgmt).
RAJAKUMARI, P. Mary (née Desari) (New Colony, Bapatla, Ind C, 1978); Comr, TC, TPWM, Ind W. MA (Engl), MA (Hist). Served in Ind M & A, at IHQ, at Ind Cent Off, in Ind W (THLS), Ind N (TPWM) and Ind SE (TPWM). Ww Comr P. D. Krupa Das, pG 2007
RAJU, K. Samuel (Kakulapadu, 1980); Maj, Ind C. b 5 May 58; and
RAJU, K. Raja (née Kumari) (Pedaparapudi, 1980) m 1981; Maj, Ind C. b 3 May 64.
RAJU, M. Daniel (M. R. Nagaram, 1984); Maj, Ind C. b 20 Jun 54. MA (Econ); with
RAJU, Rachel (née Kondamudi) m 1982; Maj, Ind C. b 15 Jun 62.
RANDIVE, Benjamin B. (Shevgaon, 1981); Maj, Ind W. b 11 Jan 60; and
RANDIVE, Ratan S. (née Teldune) (Shenegaon Central, 1981) m 1981; Maj, Ind W. b 17 Aug 62.
RANGI, Gidion (Kulawi, 1990), Maj, Indon. b 7 Aug 60; with
RANGI, Lidia (née Norlan) m 1985; Maj, Indon. b 25 Nov 65.
RAO, S. Jayananda (Madras Central, 1981); Maj, Ind C. b 29 Oct 52; with
RAO, S. Christiansen m 1976; Maj, Ind C. b 22 Dec 60.
RASELALOME, Johannes (Seshego, 1982); Maj, S Afr. b 3 May 60; and
RASELALOME, Veliswa Atalanta (née Mehu) (Tshoxa, 1982) m 1985; Maj, S Afr. b 16 Jul 62.

RATHAN, P. Samuel (Mandavalli, 1974); Maj, Ind C. b 3 May 51; with
KUMARI, P. Ananda m 1976; Maj, Ind C. b 1 Oct 57.
RATNAM, Guddam Venkata (Guraza, 1973); Maj, Ind C. b 5 Apr 49; with
RATNAM, Gaddam Rajakumari m 1969; Maj, Ind C. b 15 Mar 52.
READ, Alan (Newcastle Byker, 1980); Maj, UK. b 10 Apr 58. MSc, FCIS. Served at IHQ; and
READ, Janet (née Rumble) (Redhill, 1977) m 1982; Maj, UK. b 22 Mar 55. BA (Hons) (Relig Studies).
REDDISH, Graeme John (Thames, 1974); Col, CS, NZ. b 28 Aug 49. Ww Maj Nola, pG 2002; and
REDDISH, Wynne (née Jellyman) (Miramar, 1982) m 2005; Col, TSWM, NZ. b 22 Apr 57. Dip BRS, BBus, Dip Mgmt (NZIM). Served at IHQ.
REEL, Robert J. (Wilkes-Barre, PA, 1970); Maj, USA E. b 28 Dec 44. BA (Org Mgmt); with
REEL, Lynette M. (née Hufford) m 1964; Maj, USA E. b 2 Sep 45. BA (Org Mgmt).
REES, David H. (Rockdale, Aus E, 1976); Lt-Col, IHQ. b 29 Jun 47; with
REES, Christine F. (née Cairns) m 1969; Lt-Col. IHQ. b 11 Apr 49. Served in Aus E and Sri Lan.
REES, John (Ipswich, 1974); Maj, Aus E. b 29 Jun 47; with
REES, Narelle (née Lehmann) m 1969; Maj, Aus E. b 27 Jun 48. Served in PNG and Rus.
REFSTIE, Peder R. (Mandal, Nor, 1965); Comr, TC, Brz. b 13 Jul 43; and
REFSTIE, Janet M. (née Dex) (Bedford, UK, 1966) m 1969; Comr, TPWM, Brz. b 7 Jul 43. Served in UK, S Am W, Port, Nor, Sp (OC/CPWM), at IHQ and in S Am E (TC/TPWM).
REYNOLDS, James (Canton Citadel, OH, 1976); Lt-Col, USA E. b 2 Jun 48. BS (HRM); with
REYNOLDS, Blanche Louise (née Labus) m 1972; Lt-Col, USA E. b 16 Dec 49.
RICE, Sandra (Roberts Arm, NF, 1980); Lt-Col, Can. b 16 Feb 58. BEd, BA, MTS.
RICHARDSON, Alfred (Mount Dennis, ON, 1967); Lt-Col, Can. b 5 Dec 44; with
RICHARDSON, Ethel (née Howell) m 1964; Lt-Col, Can. b 2 Apr 43.
RICHARDSON, Lonneal (Bloomington, IN, 1983) Maj, USA C. b 3 Mar 59. BA (Bus Adm); and
RICHARDSON, Patty (née Barton) (Omaha South, NE, 1979) m 1983; Maj, USA C. b 30 Jan 57. BA (Bus Adm).

Biographical Information

RIEDER, Beat (Basle 1, Switz, 1989); Maj, Ger. b 8 Oct 58; and
RIEDER, Annette (née Pell) (Cologne, 1986) m 1989; Maj, Ger. b 9 May 64. Served in Switz and Can.

RIGLEY, Graeme (Norwood, 1988); Maj, Aus S. b 10 Aug 54. BMd, BS; with
RIGLEY, Karyn (née Whitehead) m 1981; Maj, Aus S. b 8 Apr 59.

RILEY, Douglas F. (Pasadena Tabernacle, CA, 1995); Maj, USA W. b 6 Feb 59. BS (Fin), MBA (Bus Adm), MA (Theol); with
RILEY, Colleen R. (née Hogan) m. 1991; Maj, USA W. b 14 Aug. 68.

ROBERTS, Campbell (New Brighton, 1969); Maj, NZ. b 15 Feb 47. BTh; and
ROBERTS, Gay (née Robertson) (Naenae, 1969) m 1971; Maj, NZ. b 26 Oct 46.

ROBERTS, Jonathan (Leicester Central, 1986); Maj, UK. b 20 Feb 62. BA (Hons) (Theol), BA (Hons) (Econ); and
ROBERTS, Jayne (née Melling) (Southend Citadel, 1985) m 1986; Maj, UK. b 23 Apr 58. BA (Hons) (Eng).

ROBERTS, William A. (Detroit Citadel, MI, USA C, 1971); Comr, TC, Ken W. b 26 Feb 46; BS, MA; with
ROBERTS, Nancy Louise (née Overly) m 1968; Comr, TPWM, Ken W. b 27 Oct 43. BS, MA. Served in USA C, S Am E (TC/TPWM) and at IHQ (IS Bus Adm/Sec for Staff Dev).

RODWELL, Heather (Dunedin South, 1990); Maj, NZ. b 24 Sep 55.

ROTONA, Kabona (Boregaina, 1983); Maj, PNG. b 10 Jan 59; with
ROTONA, Margaret (née Michael) m 1978; Maj, PNG. b 14 Jan 62.

ROUFFET, Jacques (Regent Hall, UK, 1972) Maj, Frce. b Oct 49; and
ROUFFET, Yvonne (née Chislett) (New Barnet ,UK ,1972) m 1974; Maj, Frce. b 20 Nov 50. Served UK and Belg.

ROWE, Dennis (Norwood, 1971); Maj, Aus S. b 25 Jun 48; and
ROWE, Patricia (née Muir) (Woodville Gardens, 1970) m 1972; Maj, Aus S. b 18 Mar 48. Served in HK and Tai.

ROWE, Lindsay (Chance Cove, NF, Can, 1972); Lt-Col, CS, Carib. b 21 Sep 51. BA (Hon), MDiv; and
ROWE, Lynette (née Hutt) (Winterton, NF, Can, 1971) m 1974; Lt-Col, TSWM, Carib. b 13 Feb 52. Served in Can and S Afr.

S

SAKAMESSO, Jean-Aléxis (Ouenze, 1979); Lt-Col, Con (Braz). b 25 May 50; with
SAKAMESSO, Pauline (née Louya) m 1976; Lt-Col, Con (Braz). b 19 Jan 56.

SALVE, Jaiprakash P. (Karegoan, 1984); Maj, Ind W. b 1 Jun 56; with
SALVE, Hemalata m 1980; Maj, Ind W. b 4 May 61.

SAMUEL, Johns (Central Corps, Trivandrum, 1984); Maj, Ind SW. b 22 May 53. Ww Maj Annamma, pG 2007.

SAMUEL, M. (Central, Kottarakara, 1974); Maj, Ind SW. b 15 Dec 51; and
SAMUEL, K. Thankamma (Ommanoor, 1977) m 1976; Maj, Ind SW. b 15 Oct 53.

SÁNCHEZ, José (Mexico # 1, 1967); Maj, Mex. b 27 May 45.

SANCHEZ, Oscar (Lima Central, S Am W, 1982); Col, TC, L Am N. b 21 Nov 56; and
SANCHEZ, Ana Rosa (née Limache) (Huayra K'assa, S Am W, 1985) m 1987; Col, TPWM, L Am N. b 12 Jun 60. Served in Sp, S Am W, USA W and Brz.

SANGCHHUNGA (Ratu, 1974); Maj, Ind E. b 15 Mar 52; and
VANLALAUVI (Ngopa, 1975) m 1975; Maj, Ind E. b 10 Jun 55.

SANTIAGO, José (Guayama, PR, USA E, 1987); Maj, L Am N. b 8 Aug 50; with
SANTIAGO, Hilda (née Amill); m 1975; Maj, L Am N. b 15 Nov 53.

SATHIYASEELAN, D. (Kanacode, 1974); Maj, Ind SW. b 10 May 51; and
SATHIYASEELAN, Aleyamma (Adoor Central,1975) m 1980; Maj, Ind SW. b 29 Jun 50.

SATTERLEE, Allen (Lakeland, FL, USA S, 1977); Maj, Carib. b 21 Apr 53. BS Psych, MTS; and
SATTERLEE, Esther (née Sands) (Laurel, MS, USA S, 1979) m 1982; Maj, Carib. b 9 Mar 55 BS Bus Adm. Served in USA S, Sing and PNG.

SAYUTI, Yohannes (Surabaya 2, 1975); Lt-Col, Indon. b 28 Jul 51; and
SAYUTI, Asya (née Tonta) (Bandung 3, 1974) m 1979; Lt-Col, Indon. b 5 Jan 51.

SCHMID, Fritz (Adelboden/Thun, 1980); Maj, Switz. b 20 Nov 53; and
SCHMID, Margrit (née Dössegger) (Seon, 1981) m 1981; Maj, Switz. b 4 Dec 52.

SCHOLTENS, Teunis (Zwolle, 1980); Maj, Neth. b 28 Aug 52; with
SCHOLTENS, Hendrika (née Stuurop) m 1977; Maj, Neth. b 28 May 56.

SCHWARTZ, Barry Richard (Goodwood, S Afr, 1973); Lt-Col, CS, DR Con. b 17 Apr 48; with

Biographical Information

SCHWARTZ, Anja Jacoba (née Kamminga) m 1967; Lt-Col, TSWM, DR Con. b 28 Jul 48. Served in S Afr.

SEILER, Paul R. (Hollywood Tabernacle, CA, USA W, 1981); Col, CS, USA C. b 23 May 51. MBA, BS (Bus Adm); with
SEILER, Carol (née Sturgess) m 1978; Col, TSWM, USA C. b 6 Apr 52. RN, BS (Nursing), MPH. Served in USA W.

SENARATNE Ranjit (Siyambalanguwa, 1994) Maj, Sri Lan. b 7 Jan 63; and
SENARATNE Vijayashri (née Kandasamy) (Jaffna, 1994) m 1995; Maj, Sri Lan. b 3 Oct 70.

SERÈM, Alberto (Lisbon Central, 1985); Maj, OC, Port. b 27 Nov 56; and
SERÈM, Maria José (née Leitão) (Picheleira, 1977) m 1980; Maj, CPWM, Port. b 13 Dec 52. Served in UK and It.

SEVAK, David Keshav (Sokhada, 1981); Maj, Ind W. b 15 Nov 50; and
SEVAK, Vimalaben (Bharoda, 1983) m 1983; Maj, Ind W. b 5 Jun 63.

SEWELL, Roland (Buckingham, 1976); Lt-Col, UK. b 26 Dec 44. MBE, BSc (Hons) (Eng), CEng, MICE. Served in Zam, Nig (CS) and at IHQ. m 1967; Lt-Col Dawn, ret 2009.

SEYMOUR, Geanette (Belmore, Aus E, 1973); Lt-Col, IHQ. b 20 Feb 50. BA (Soc Wk). Served in Aus E (CS)

SHAKESPEARE, David (Catford, UK, 1981); Lt-Col, IHQ. b 8 Oct 59; and
SHAKESPEARE, Karen (née Grainger) (Catford, UK, 1980) m 1981; Lt-Col, IHQ. b 2 Aug 54. BEd (Hons), MA (Pastoral Theol), MA (Adult Ed with Theol Reflection). Served in UK

SHAROVA, Svetlana (née Blagodirova) (Chisinau Botannica, 1999); Capt, E Eur. b 18 Jun 65; with
SHAROV, Alexander m 1986; Capt, E Eur. b 6 Jul 57.

SHAVANGA, Edward (Matunda, Ken W, 1982); Maj, Zam. b 9 Mar 58; with
SHAVANGA, Florence (née Vulehi) m 1979; Maj, Zam. b 11 Oct 60. Served in E Afr and Ken.

SHAVANGA, Moses (Musudzuu, 1984); Maj, Ken W. b 10 Jun 57; with
SHAVANGA, Gladys (née Sharia) m 1982; Maj, Ken W. b 18 Mar 61. Served in Tanz.

SHEKWA, Albert Zondiwe (Emangweni, 1974); Maj, S Afr. b 12 Mar 51; and
SHEKWA, Peggy (née Maimela) (Louis Trichardt, 1974) m 1974; Maj, S Afr. b 3 Jun 54.

SIAGIAN, Pieter (Solo, 1973); Lt-Col, Indon. b 5 May 45; and

SIAGIAN, Sukarsih (née Sosromihardjo) (Turen, 1972) m 1975; Lt-Col, Indon. b 2 Aug 49.

SIJUADE, Michael A. (Ife Ife, 1992); Maj, Nig. b 13 Jun 64; with
SIJUADE, Comfort m 1990; Maj, Nig. b 11 Nov 67.

SIMON, T. J. (Perumpetty, 1977); Maj, Ind SW. b 15 Nov 52; with
SIMON, Ammini, m 1979; Maj, Ind SW. b 1 Feb 60.

SINGH, Dilip (Simultala, 1990); Maj, Ind N. b 4 Nov 68; and
SINGH, Nivedita (née Christian) (Fatapukur, 1992) m 1992; Maj, Ind N. b 14 Sep 71.

SINGH, Vijayapal (Batala City, 1994); Maj, Ind N. b 25 Oct 66; with
SINGH, Roseleen m 1993; Maj, Ind N. b 10 Apr 67.

SJOGREN, Daniel (St Paul (Temple), MN, 1972); Lt-Col, USA C. b 12 Nov 51; and
SJOGREN, Rebecca (née Nefzger) (Hibbing, MN, 1973) m 1973; Lt-Col, USA C. b 11 Jun 53.

SJOGREN, Randall W. (St Paul Temple, MN, USA C, 1975); Maj, USA Nat. b 6 Dec 53; and
SJOGREN, Deborah (née Garrington) (Chicago Irving Park, IL, USA C, 1976) m 1976; Maj, USA Nat. b 8 Aug 54. AA (Pract Min). Served in USA C and at IHQ.

SMITH, Charles (Kansas City (Blue Valley), MN, 1978]; Maj, USA C. b 22 Aug 57; with
SMITH, Sharon (née Cockrill) m 1975; Maj, USA C. b 7 Mar 54.

SMITH, Jeffrey (Flint Citadel, MI, 1986); Maj, USA C. b 19 Jan 54. BA (Bible), MRE; with
SMITH, Dorothy R. (née Kumpula) m 1974; Maj, USA C. b 22 Oct 54. BA (Psychol/Sociol), MA (Soc Wk).

SMITH, Paul (Milwaukee Citadel, WI, 1985); Maj, USA C. b 23 Jun 56. BA (Psychol), MA (Theatre); and
SMITH, Renea (née Bonifield) (Grand Rapids Centennial Temple, MI, 1984) m 1985; Maj, USA C. b 16 Nov 57.

SMITH, Stephen C. (Renton, WA, 1988); Maj, USA W. b 12 Jun 58. MA (Music Comp), BA (Music Perf); with
SMITH, Marcia (née Harvey), m 1981, Maj, USA W. b 23 Jan 59. BS (Chrstn Ldrshp).

SONDA, Jean-Pierre (Mahita, 1990); Maj, Con (Braz). b 28 Nov 56; with
SONDA, Jeannette (née Ndoudi) m 1988; Maj, Con (Braz). b 25 Jan 67.

SOUZA, Maruilson (Petrolina, 1987); Maj, Brz.

b 6 May 64. BA (Acct), MBA, BA (Theol), MA (Theol), PhD; with
SOUZA, Francisca (née Rodrigues) m 1982; Maj, Brz. b 15 Oct 66.

SPILLER, Lyndon S. (Springvale, 1970); Lt-Col, Aus S. b 26 May 45; with
SPILLER, Julie (née King) m 1968; Lt-Col, Aus S. b 7 Aug 47. Served in Pak, Zam, Gha (CS/TSWO) and E Afr (CS/TSWM).

STARRETT, Daniel L. (Roswell, NM, USA W, 1973); Lt-Col, USA Nat. b 1 Jun 52. BS (Appl Bus & Mgmt), MBA; and
STARRETT, Helen (née Laverty) (San José, CA, USA W, 1973) m 1974; Lt-Col, USA Nat. b 20 Jul 48. Served in USA W and at IHQ.

STOCKMAN, Mona Valborg (née Ericson) (Uppsala, 1978); Maj, Swdn. b 24 Nov 46. BA (Sociol); and
STOCKMAN, Björn (Kalmar, 1981) m 1984; Maj, Swdn. b 12 Nov 51.

STRASSE, Wilson S. (Rio Grande, 1988); Maj, Brz. b 20 Jul 63; with
STRASSE, Nara (née Charão) m 1985; Maj, Brz. b 12 Feb 68.

STREET, Robert (Stotfold, UK, 1968); Comr, IHQ (IS SPEA). b 24 Feb 47; with
STREET, Janet (née Adams) m 1967; Comr, IHQ (ZSWM SPEA). b 19 Aug 45. Served in UK, Aus E (CS/TSWM) and at IHQ (IS to CoS/WSWM).

STRICKLAND, Ron (Santa Barbara, CA, 1978); Lt-Col, USA W. b 7 Aug 45. BS (Bus Mgmt); and
STRICKLAND, Pamela (née Fuss) (Minot, ND, 1969) m 1970; Lt-Col, USA W. b 1 Dec 48.

STRISSEL, Dennis L. (St Louis Northside, MO, USA C, 1974); Col, TC, Gha. b 4 Mar 52; and
STRISSEL, Sharon (née Olson) (Sioux City, IA, USA C, 1974) m 1975; Col, TPWM, Gha. b 7 Oct 51. Served in USA C and S Afr.

SUMARTA, Mulyati (Surakarta, 1983); Maj, Indon. b 14 Apr 59.

SUNDARAM, Motchakan (Aramboly, 1974); Maj, Ind SE. b 17 Mar 50; and
SUNDARAM, Selvabai Motchakan (Kaliancaud, 1974) m 1975; Maj, Ind SE. b 2 May 50.

SUSEELKUMAR, John (Pallickal, 1978); Maj, Ind SW. b 11 Oct 51. Ww Maj Aleyamma, pG 2007.

SWANSBURY, Charles (Croydon Citadel, UK, 1983); Maj, GS, Lib. b 7 Dec 52. BA, MBA; with
SWANSBURY, Denise (née Everett) m 1974; Maj, CSWM, Lib. b 9 Nov 53. BA. Served in UK, Zim and at IHQ.

SWANSON, Barry C. (Chicago Mt Greenwood, IL, 1978); Comr, TC, USA C. b 22 Apr 50. BS (Marketing); with
SWANSON, E. Sue (née Miller) m 1975; Comr, TPWM, USA C. b 13 Aug 50. BA (Soc Wk). Served in USA C (CS/TSWM), at USA Nat (Nat CS/NSWM) and at IHQ (IS/ZSWM Am and Carib).

SWYERS, Philip W. (Dallas Temple, TX, USA S, 1968); Comr, TC, USA W. b 22 Apr 44. BBA; and
SWYERS, Patricia Lyvonne (née Lowery) (Charlotte, NC, USA S, 1968) m 1968; Comr, TPWM, USA W. b 26 Aug 41. Served in USA C (CS/TSWM) and USA S (CS/TSWM)

T

TADI, Patrick (Bimbouloulou, 1984); Maj, Con (Braz). b 17 Apr 59; with
TADI, Clémentine (née Bassinguinina) m 1982; Maj, Con (Braz). b 4 Apr 58.

TAMPAI, Yusak (Turen, 1993); Maj, Indon. b 25 Feb 66; and
TAMPAI, Widiawati (Anca, 1995) m 1997; Maj, Indon. b 19 Apr 73. Served at ICO.

TAN, Thean Seng (Penang, 1966); Lt-Col, Sing. b 24 Jul 45; and
LOO, Lay Saik (Penang, 1966) m 1969; Lt-Col, Sing. b 12 Jul 47. Served at IHQ and in Sing (OC/CPWM) and HK (OC/CPWM).

TANAKA, Teiichi (Omori, 1983); Maj, Jpn. b 19 Feb 52; and
TANAKA, Chieko (née Hirose) (Nishinari, 1977) m 1984; Maj, Jpn. b 22 Apr 48.

TANDAYAG, Susana (née Organo) (Santiago Isabela, 1989); Maj, Phil. b 26 Feb 60. BSc (Home Tech), BSSW; and
TANDAYAG, Miguel (Pasig, 1980) m 1982; Capt, Phil. b 30 Sep 58.

TARI, Samuel (Shantinagar, 1970); Maj, Pak. b 7 Sep 49; and
SAMUEL, Victoria (née Khurshid) (Khanewal, 1971) m 1973; Maj, Pak. b 15 Oct 52.

TATY, Daniel (Pointe-Noire, 1982), Maj, Con (Braz). b 14 Feb 54; with
TATY, Angèle m 1980; Maj, Con (Braz). b 6 Dec 56.

TEMINE, David (Lembina, 1992); Maj, PNG. b 12 May 70; and
TEMINE, Doreen (née A'o) (Kamila, 1999) m 2002; Capt, PNG. b 24 Feb 73.

THANHLIRA (Ratu, 1971); Maj, Ind E. b 15 Feb 49; and

Biographical Information

THANTLUANGI (Central, 1975) m 1975; Maj, Ind E. b 5 Jan 50.

THARMAR, Alfred (Arumanai, 1977); Maj, Ind SE. b 23 May 54; and
THARMAR, Rajabai Alfred (Pottetty, 1975) m 1977; Maj, Ind SE. b 16 Apr 53.

THEODORE, Sinous (Luly, Haiti, 1981); Maj, Carib. b 20 Oct 52; and
THEODORE, Marie Lourdes (née Doralus) (Port-au-Prince, Haiti, 1981) m 1982; Maj, Carib. b 22 Sep 57.

THEU, Chatonda (Migowi, Mal, 1987); Maj, Zimb. b 3 Mar 59; with
THEU, Joyce (née Banda) m 1986; Maj, Zimb. b 5 Mar 65. Served in Mal.

THOMAS, Darrell (Southend Citadel, UK, 1975); Maj, Sing. b 28 Jun 53; and
THOMAS, Katrina (née Lagunowitsch) (Royston, UK, 1976) m 1976; Maj, Sing. b 27 Sep 51. Served in UK.

THOMSON, Robert E. (Evansville Asplan Citadel, IN, 1971); Maj, USA C. b 20 Nov 50. BS (Soc Wk), MSW; with
THOMSON, Nancy (née Philpot) m 1972; Maj, USA C. b 4 May 50.

THUMATI, Vijayakumar (Denduluru, Ind C, 1970); Lt-Col, CS, Ind SE. b 10 Jun 49; and
THUMATI, Keraham Manikyam Vijayakumar (née Karuhu) (Denduluru, Ind C, 1970) m 1971; Lt-Col, TSWM, Ind SE. b 17 Apr 53. Served in Ind C, Ind SE, Ban (GS/CSWM) and at Ind Nat.

TIDD, Floyd (Sudbury, ON, 1986); Lt-Col, Can. b 11 Mar 61. BSc, MTS; with
TIDD, Tracey (née Blacklock) m 1982; Lt-Col, Can. b 9 Jan 61.

TILLSLEY, Mark W. (East Northport, NY, 1987); Lt-Col, USA E. b 20 Nov 57. BA (Psychol/Sociol), MSW; with
TILLSLEY, Sharon (née Lowman) m 1979; Lt-Col, USA E. b 21 Jun 57. BS (Nursing).

TOLLERUD, Douglas (Santa Ana, CA, 1983); Maj, USA W. b 16 Mar 57; with
TOLLERUD, Sheryl (née Smith) m 1978; Maj, USA W. b 12 Jan 59. BS (Org Mngmnt).

TRAINOR, Iain (Orillia, Can, 1974); Maj, Aus S. b 18 Jan 45; with
TRAINOR, Dawn (née McCormack) m 1965; Maj, Aus S. b 19 Jun 44. Served in Can.

TRIM, Kester (Scarborough Citadel, ON, 1983); Maj, Can. b 16 Jun 53. BA, MDiv; with
TRIM, Kathryn (née Webster) m 1976; Maj, Can. b 2 Jun 54. BA. Served in Zai and at IHQ (SALT College).

TURSI, Massimo (Naples, 1983); Maj, GS, It. b 14 Nov 57; and

TURSI, Anne-Florence (née Cachelin) (Bern 1, Switz, 1983) m 1983; Maj, CSWM, It. b 25 Mar 59. Served in Switz and Ger.

TVEDT, Hannelise (née Nielsen) (Copenhagen Temple, 1976); Maj, Den. b 13 Dec 55. Served in Nor.

U

UNDERSRUD, Anne Lise (née Bendiksen) (Finnsnes, 1969); Maj, Asst CS, Nor. b 12 Feb 48; and
UNDERSRUD, Arne (Drammen, 1968) m 1974; Maj, Nor. b 15 Mar 44. Served in UK.

URBIEN Elnora (Manila Central, 1980); Lt-Col, Phil. b 4 Apr 50. BSc (Element Ed). Served in PNG.

UWAK, Udoh (Ikot Obio Inyang, 1992); Maj, Nig. b 2 Oct 66; with
UWAK, Esther m 1990; Maj, Nig. b 12 Dec 73.

UZOHO, Stephen (Umuobom, 1974); Maj, Nig. b 22 Sep 49; with
UZOHO, Edith; Maj, Nig. b 2 Jul 53.

V

VAN DER HARST, Willem (Scheveningen, Neth, 1966); Comr, TC, E Eur. b 13 Mar 44. Ww Capt Suzanne, pG 1985; and
VAN DER HARST, Netty (née Kruisinga) (Amsterdam Congress Hall, Neth, 1984) m 1985; Comr, TPWM, E Eur. b 15 Feb 58. Served in Cze R and Neth (TC/TPWM).

VAN DUINEN, Susan (née Jewers) (Mississauga, ON, 1978); Maj, Can. b 11 Mar 50. BA, MDiv; with
VAN DUINEN, Dirk m 1970; Maj. b 13 Jun 49. Served Ger and Cze Rep.

VAN HOUDT, Fernanda (Solingen, 1983); Maj, Ger. b 10 Oct 57. Served at ESFOT.

VAN VLIET, Johan C. J. (Baarn, Neth, 1975); Lt-Col, CS, PNG. b 17 Jul 52. Dip SocS Adm; with
VAN VLIET, Maria (née de Ruiter) m 1971; Lt-Col, TSWM, PNG. b 9 May 51. Served in Neth.

VANDER WEELE, Richard E. (Kalamazoo, MI, 1976); Lt-Col, USA C. b 19 May 48. BS (Soc), MSW.

VANLALTHANGA (Ruallung, 1979); Maj, Ind E. b 4 Jul 57; with
HMUNROPUII m 1977; Maj, Ind E. b 25 Oct 59.

VARGHESE, Davidson (Trivandrum Central, Ind SW, 1986); Lt-Col, Zam. b 13 Dec 58. BA; and
DAVIDSON, Mariamma (née Chacko)

(Adoor Central, Ind SW, 1985) m 1988; Lt-Col, Zam. b 1 May 65. Served in Ind SW.
VARUGHESE, Wilfred (Trivandrum Central, Ind SW, 1985); Col, CS, Zim. b 25 Mar 58. BSc, BTS; and
WILFRED, Prema (née Prema) (Anayara, Ind SW, 1987) m 1987; Col, TSWM, Zim. b 25 May 60. BA, BD. Served in Ind SW and at Ind Nat.
VELE, David (Hohola, 1997); Capt, PNG . b 9 May 66; with
VELE, Rita (née Pisin) m 1994; Capt, PNG. b 26 Sep 73.
VENTER, Alistair (Cape Town Citadel, 1981); Maj, S Afr. b 19 Aug 58. ThA, BTh; and
VENTER, Marieke (née van Leeuwen) (Benoni, 1988) m 1987; Maj, S Afr. b 31 Dec 62, BCur (Hons), MTh.
VIRU, Zarena (Bhogiwal, 1973); Lt-Col, Pak. b 1 Jan 52.
VOORHAM, Christina (The Hague South, 1970); Lt-Col, Neth. b 2 Sep 46.
VYLE, Bruce (Hamilton City, 1995); Maj, NZ. b 5 Jun 46. MA, BA, DipT; with
VYLE, Elaine (née French) m 1968; Maj, NZ.
b 9 Jul 48.

W

WAINWRIGHT, John (Reading Central, UK, 1979); Col, TC, Zamb. b 13 Mar 51; with
WAINWRIGHT, Dorita (née Willetts) m 1976; Col, TPWM, Zamb. b 19 Oct 51. Served in UK, E Afr and Zimb.
WALKER, Peter (Morley, 1982); Lt-Col, Aus S. b 2 Mar 54. BA (Soc); with
WALKER, Jennifer (née Friend) m 1975; Lt-Col, Aus S. b 26 Feb 56. BEd. Served in Mlys.
WANDULU, Moses (Bumbo, 1986); Maj, OC, Uga. b 5 Aug 60; with
WANDULU, Sarah (née Rwolekya) m 1982; Maj, CPWM, Uga. b 30 Aug 1964. Served in E Afr
WANJARE, Sanjay (Vithalwadi, 1994); Capt, Ind W. b 10 Oct 67, with
WANJARE Sunita m 1992; Capt, Ind W. b 1 Jun 70.
WANYAMA, Sarah (Wabukhonyi, 1978); Lt-Col, Ken E. b 3 Mar 56.
WARD, H. Alfred (Atlanta Temple, GA, USA S, 1971); Lt-Col, CS, Brz. b 2 Aug 46. BA (Chem), MBA; with
WARD, Mary M. (née Busby); Lt-Col, TSWM, Brz. b 13 Nov 47. BVA. Served in USA S and Aus E.

WARD, Robert (Brock Avenue, TO, Can, 1970); Col, TC, Pak. b 22 Feb 48. MHSc (Health Mgmt), BA (Adm); and
WARD, Marguerite (née Simon) (Swift Current, SK, Can, 1970) m 1971; Col, TPWM, Pak. b 13 May 48. Served in Can, S Afr, Zimb (CS/TSWM) and USA C.
WATERS, Frederick (Mississauga, ON, 1983); Maj, Can. b 24 Dec 56; with
WATERS, Wendy (née Kitney) m 1979; Maj, Can. b 22 Jul 57.
WATSON, Ritchie (Darwin, Aus S, 1988); Maj, PNG. b 6 Apr 51; with
WATSON, Gail (née Hogan) m 1972; Maj, PNG. b 20 Feb 52. Served in Aus S.
WATT, Neil (Montreal Citadel, 1977); Lt-Col, Can. b 4 Nov 48. BTh; with
WATT, Lynda (née Westover) m 1968; Lt-Col , Can. b 5 May 46. Served in UK.
WATTERS, Alan (Cape Town Citadel, S Afr/ Brighton East, 1987); Maj, UK. b 2 May 53. BD; with
WATTERS, Linda (née Farrier) m 1980; Maj, UK. b 13 Nov 56. Served in S Afr.
WATTS, Gavin (Carina, 1994); Maj, Aus E. b 30 Oct 69. Dip Min, Dip Bus; with
WATTS, Wendy (née Wallis) m 1990; Maj, Aus E. b 27 Apr 68. DipTeach, DipMin. Served in NZ.
WEBB, Neil (Nottingham New Basford, 1983); Maj, UK. b 6 Sep 58; and
WEBB, Christine (née Holdstock) (Bromley, 1983) m 1983; Maj, UK. b 1 Mar 55. BA, CQSW, Dip RS.
WEBER, Stephan (Nuremberg, 1987); Maj, Ger. b 5 Jul 59; with
WEBER, Andrea (née Mueller) m 1982; Maj, Ger. b 21 Mar 63.
WELANDER, Knud David (Copenhagen Temple, Den/Oslo Temple, 1984); Nor. b 20 May 61; and
WELANDER, Lisbeth (née Wederhus) (Florø, 1984) m 1984; Maj, Nor. b 29 Nov 63.
WESTRUPP, Andrew (Dunedin South, 1980); Maj, NZ. b 4 Oct 54; with
WESTRUPP, Yvonne (née Medland) m 1974; Maj, NZ. b 13 Jul 54.
WEYMOUTH, James (Adelaide Congress Hall, Aus S, 1976); Maj, Zam. b 14 Nov 51. BA, BTh; and
WEYMOUTH, Marion (née Campbell) (Adelaide Congress Hall, Aus S, 1977); m 1977; Maj, Zam. b 3 Feb 50. Served in Aus S and HK.
WHITE, Amanda (née Smith) (Woolwich, 1984); Maj, UK. b 16 Feb 61; and

Biographical Information

WHITE, Stephen (Hillingdon, 1987) m 1987; Maj, UK. b 13 Dec 61. Served in Aus E.

WHITE, Charles (Owensboro, KY, 1967); Lt-Col, USA S. b 7 May 46; with
WHITE, Shirley (née Sanders) m 1962; Lt-Col, USA S. b 24 Apr 43.

WHITE, Larry Wayne (Orlando, FL, 1972); Lt-Col, USA S. b 27 Aug 45; and
WHITE, Shirley Anne (née Knight) (Lake Charles, LA, 1967) m 1969; Lt-Col, USA S. b 7 Mar 42.

WICKINGS, Margaret (Welling, UK, 1976); Maj, Gha. b 15 Apr 51. BEd, MTh. Served in UK, Zam and E Afr.

WIDYANOADI, Wayan (Semarang 2, 1990); Maj, Indon. b 2 Jan 68; and
WIDYANOADI, Herlina (née Ayawaila) (Jemba, 1995) m 1995; Maj, Indon. b 30 Jan 65.

WILKINSON, Darrell (Long Bay, Barbados, 1985); Maj, Carib. b 1 Apr 55; and
WILKINSON, Joan (née Marshall) (Carlton, Barbados, 1985) m 1986; Maj, Carib. b 18 Sep 58.

WILLERMARK, Marie (Göteborg 1, Swdn, 1980); Maj, E Eur. b 18 Jun 54. Served in Swdn and Den.

WILLIAMS, John (Murukondapadu, 1991); Maj, Ind C. b 7 May 66. Ww Capt K. Mary Rani; and
WILLIAMS, Ratna Sundari (Murukondapadu, 2000) m 1999; Capt, Ind C. b 2 Nov 67.

WILLIAMS, Michael (Bristol Easton Road, 1967); Lt-Col, UK. b 16 Dec 46. Served at IHQ. m 1969; Lt-Col Ruth, ret 2004.

WITTWER, Bernhard (Brienz, 1988); Maj, Switz. b 1 Feb 61; with
WITTWER, Regina (née Mäder) m 1983, Maj, Switz. b 22 May 63.

WOLTERINK, Theo (Hengelo, 1974); Lt-Col, Neth. b 16 Jun 47; with
WOLTERINK, Albertine (née Riezebos) m 1970; Lt-Col, Neth. b 17 Feb 46. Served at IHQ, in Cz R and Neth (CS/TSWM).

WOODALL, Ann (Croydon Citadel, UK, 1969); Comr, IHQ (IS Bus Adm). b 3 Feb 50. MA, MSc, FCCA, PhD. Served in Con, Zam, Zaï and UK.

WOODWARD, Cecil (Coorparoo, 1969); Maj, Aus E. b 3 Jun 46. BSW (Hons), MSWAP, MBA; and
WOODWARD, Catherine (née Lucas) (Miranda, 1969) m 1970; Maj, Aus E. b 20 Jan 48

WYLES, Catherine (née Dolling) (Hillindon, 1986); Maj, UK. b 29 Dec 63; and
WYLES, Russell (Hillindon, 1986) m 1986; Maj, UK. b 14 Mar 64.

Y

YAMANAKA, Masaru (Fukuoka, 1970); Maj, Jpn. b 10 Jul 44; and
YAMANAKA, Machiko (née Matsui) (Tenma, 1963) m 1973; Maj, Jpn. b 21 Jan 39.

YANDERAVE, Borley (Lembina, 1991); Maj, PNG. b 7 Oct 58; with
YANDERAVE, Iveme (née John) m 1985; Maj, PNG. b 25 Oct 66.

YANG, Tae-soo (Chun Yun, 1978); Lt-Col, Kor. b 14 Feb 47; with
CHUN, Ok-kyung m 1968; Lt-Col, Kor. b 14 Jul 47. Served in Sing.

YESUDAS, Kancherla (Pedapalli, 1984); Maj, Ind C. b 13 Apr 54. BA (Econ); with
YESUDAS, Hemalatha (née Devi) m 1979; Maj, Ind C. b 16 Jul 58.

YOHANNAN, C. S. (Kaithaparambu, 1975); Maj, Ind SW. b 8 Jan 54; and
YOHANNAN, L. Rachel (Pathanapuram, 1979) m 1978; Maj, Ind SW. b 31 Jul 55.

YOHANNAN, P. J. (Oollayam Kangazha, 1978); Maj, Ind SW. b 17 May 49; and
YOHANNAN, Annamma (Oollayam Kangazha, 1981) m 1981; Maj, Ind SW. b 31 Aug 55.

YOSHIDA, Makoto (Shibuya, 1969); Comr, TC, Jap. b 7 Dec 45. BS (Engin); and
YOSHIDA, Kaoru (née Imamura) (Omori, 1971) m 1974; Comr, TPWM, Jap. b 13 Jan 45. Served in Jpn (CS/TSWM) and at IHQ (IS/ZSWM SPEA).

YOSHIDA, Tsukasa (Shibuya, 1982); Maj, Jpn. b 26 Nov 54; and
YOSHIDA, Kyoko (née Tsuchiya) (Kiyose, 1980) m 1982; Maj, Jpn. b 13 Oct 53.

YOUSAF, Javed (Amritnagar, 1988); Maj, Pak. b 2 Nov 66; with
JAVED, Surriya (née Zaffar) m 1987; Maj, Pak. b 18 May 69.

Z

ZIPINGANI, Langton (Pearson, 1987); Lt-Col, Zimb. b 22 Nov 61; and
ZIPINGANI, Beauty (née Chimunda) (Mutonda, 1987) m 1989; Lt-Col, Zimb. b 2 Aug 66.

ZOLA, Ambroise (Kingudi, DR Con, 1979); Lt-Col, OC, Ang. b 6 Sep 52; with
ZOLA, Alphonsine Kuzoma (née Nsiesi) m 1976; Lt-Col, CPWM, Ang. b 2 Jan 57. Served in Con (Kin) and Con (Braz) (CS/TSWM)

Retired Generals and Commissioners

The following list contains the names of retired Generals, commissioners and lieut-commissioners, and widows of lieut-commissioners and above, as at 30 September 2009

A

ADIWINOTO, Lilian E. (Malang, Indon, 1954); Comr b 31 Jul 27. Served in UK, Indon (TC) and at IHQ.

ASANO, Hiroshi (Shizuoka, Jpn, 1950); Comr b 5 May 27; and Mrs Comr **Tomoko** (née Ohara) (Kyoto, 1953) m 1955. Served in Jpn (TC/TPWO).

B

BAILLIE, Kenneth (Warren, USA E, 1966); Comr b 3 Nov 42. BA (Soc); with Comr **Joy M.** (née Gabrielsen) m 1962; b 30 May 41. BA (Biochem). Served in Can, USA E, E Eur (OC/CPWO) and USA C (TC/TPWM).

BANKS, Keith (Wokingham, UK, 1963); Comr b 5 Nov 42. Served in UK, PNG (OC), Jpn (CS) and at IHQ (IS Int Per). Ww Comr Pauline, pG 2008.

BASSETT, W. Todd (Syracuse Citadel, NY, USA E, 1965); Comr b 25 Aug 39. BEd; with Comr **Carol A.** (née Easterday) m 1960; b 10 Dec 40. BEd. Served in USA E, at IHQ (IS to CoS/Mission Res Sec) and at USA Nat (NC/NPWM).

BATH, Vida (née McNeill) (Moree, Aus E, 1945); Mrs Comr. Served in Sri Lan, Ind W, Ind NE, Ind SW, at IHQ and in Aus E. Ww Comr Robert, pG 2006.

BAXENDALE, David A. (Pittsburgh, PA, USA E, 1954); Comr b 23 Apr 30. MA (Col), BSc (Sprd); with Mrs Comr **Alice** (née Chamberlain); BMus Ed (Syra). Served in USA E, USA W (CS/THLS), Carib (TC/TPWO), S Am W (TC/TPWO), at ICO (Principal) and IHQ (IS/SWO Am and Carib).

BIMWALA, Zunga Mbanza Etienne (Central Hall, Kinshasa 1, Zaï, 1959); Comr b 29 Sep 32. Served in Zaï (TC) and Switz. Ww Mrs Comr Alice, pG 2004.

BIRD, Patricia (Fulham, UK, 1958); Comr b 7 Aug 35. Served in Nig, UK, Zam (TC) and at IHQ (IS Fin, IS Afr).

BOVEN van, Johannes (The Hague, Neth, 1955); Comr b 9 Jan 35; and Comr **Klazina** (née Grauwmeijer) (Rotterdam, 1959) m 1960; b 22 Sep 35. Served in Neth (TC/TPWO).

BRAUN, Edouard (Vevey, Frce, 1968); Comr b 16 Aug 42; with Comr **Françoise** (née Volet) m 1966; b 8 Dec 43. Served in Frce (TC/TPWM) and Switz (TC/TPWM).

BROWN, Jean (née Barclay) (Montreal Citadel, Can, 1938); Mrs General. Served at IHQ and in Can. Ww General Arnold Brown, pG 2002.

BUCKINGHAM, Lorraine (née Smith) (Waimate, NZ, 1960); Comr. Served in Aus S, NZ (TSWO) and Aus E (TPWO). Ww Comr Hillmon, pG 2009.

BURROWS, Eva Evelyn General (1986-93) (see page 25).

BUSBY, John A. (Atlanta Temple, GA, USA S, 1963); Comr b 14 Oct 37. BA (Asbury); with Comr **Elsie Louise** (née Henderson) m 1958; b 11 Jun 36. Served in Can (CS/TSWO), USA S (TC/TPWO) and USA Nat (NC/NPWM).

C

CACHELIN, Genevieve (née Booth) (Paris Central, Frce, 1947); Mrs Comr. MA. Served in Switz, Belg, Frce, Ger, BT and at IHQ. Ww Comr Francy, pG 2007

CAIRNS, Alistair Grant (West End, Aus E, 1942); Comr b 12 Dec 16. AM, Order of Australia (1996). Served in Kor, Aus E (CS), at ITC and in S Afr (TC). Ww Mrs Comr Margery, pG 2006.

CAIRNS, Beulah (née Harris) (Parramatta, NSW, Aus E, 1959); Mrs Comr. Served in Aus E and at IHQ. Ww Comr William, pG 2008.

CALVERT, Ruth (Port Hope, ON, 1955); Mrs Comr b 8 Feb 35. Served in Aus E. Ww Comr Roy, pG 1994.

CAMPBELL, Donald (Highgate, WA, Aus S, 1945); Comr b 31 Oct 23. Served in NZ (TC) and Aus S (TC). Ww Comr Crystal, pG 2008.

CHANG, Peter Hei-dong (Seoul Central, Kor, 1960); Comr b 12 May 32. BD, STm (Union, NY), BTh MEd (Columbia, NY); and Comr

Retired Generals and Commissioners

Grace **Eun-Shik** (née Chung) (Seoul, Kor, 1963) m 1963. BA, BMus (Seoul Nat). Served in UK, Sing, HK, USA E, Kor (CS/THLS, TC/TPWO), USA W (TC/TPWO) and at IHQ.

CHEVALLY, Simone (née Gindraux) (Lausanne 1, Switz, 1947); Mrs Comr. Served in Switz (TPWO) and at IHQ. Ww Comr Robert, pG 1989.

CHIANGHNUNA (Ngupa, Ind W, 1951); Comr b 10 Jun 29; and Mrs Comr **Barbara** (née Powell) (Ware, UK, 1948) m 1968. Served in Ind N (CS/THLS), Ind E (CS/THLS) and Ind W (TC/TPWO).

CLAUSEN, Siegfried (Catford, UK, 1958); Comr b 4 Mar 38; and Comr **Inger-Lise** (née Lydholm) (Valby, 1958) m 1961; b 1 Oct 39. Served in UK, S Am W, Sp (OC/CPWO), L Am N (TC/TPWO), Ger (TC/TPWO) and at IHQ (IS/SWM Am and Carib).

CLINCH, John H. (Fairfield, Vic, Aus S, 1956); Comr b 30 Nov 30; with Comr **Beth** (née Barker). Served in Aus S, Aus E (CS/THLS), at IHQ (IS/SWO SPEA) and in Aus S (TC/TPWO).

COLES, Alan C. (Harrow, UK, 1953); Comr b 2 Feb 25. ACIB. Ww Heather, pG 1978; and Mrs Comr **Brenda** (née Deeming) (Tipton, UK, 1959) m 1980. Served in Zimb (TC) and at IHQ.

COLES, Dudley (North Toronto, ON, Can, 1954); Comr b 22 Mar 26; and Mrs Comr **Evangeline** (née Oxbury) (Powell River, BC, Can, 1954) m 1956. Served in Can, Ind Audit, Ind W, Sri Lan (TC/TPWO) and at IHQ (IS/SWO S Asia).

COOPER, Raymond A. (Washington Georgetown, DC, USA S, 1956); Comr b 24 May 37; and Comr **Merlyn S.** (née Wishon) (Winston Salem Southside, NC, USA S, 1957) m 1959; b 2 Sep 36. Served in USA C and USA S (TC/TPWO).

COX, Hilda (née Chevalley) (Geneva, 1949); Mrs Comr. Served in UK, Zam, Zimb, Frce (THLS), Neth (THLS) and at IHQ (WSHL). Ww Comr Ron, pG 1995.

CUTMORE, Ian (Tamworth, Aus E, 1954); Comr b 27 Sep 33; and Comr **Nancy** (née Richardson) (Atherton, Aus E, 1957). Served in Aus E, PNG, UK (CS/TSWO), ICO (Principal) and NZ (TC/TPWO).

D

DAVIS, Douglas E. (Moreland, Aus S, 1960); Comr b 12 Feb 37; with Comr **Beverley J.** (née Roberts) m 1958; b 23 Feb 38. Served in NZ, UK (CS/TSWO) and Aus S (TC/TPWO).

DELCOURT, Raymond Andre (Montpellier, Frce, 1935); Comr b 25 Oct 14. Croix de Guerre (1939-40), Medaille Penitentiaire (1973), Medaille d'Honneur de la Ville de Paris (1976), Chevalier de la Legion d'Honneur (1978); and Mrs Comr **France** (née Bardiaux) (Lyon 1, Frce, 1943) m 1943. Served in BT and Frce (TC/TPWO).

DEVAVARAM, Prathipati (New Colony, Ind C, 1964); Comr b 15 Nov 46. MBBS, BSc; and Comr **P. Victoria** (Bapatla Central, Ind C, 1970) m 1974; b 25 Nov 49. BSc, BEd, BLSc. Served in Ind C, at Ind Nat, in Ind E and Ind SE (TC/TPWM).

DIAKANWA, Mbakanu (Poste Francais, Kin, Zaï, 1949); Comr b 1923. Officier de l'Ordre du Leopard (1981). Served in Zaï (TC). Ww Comr Situwa, pG 1998.

DITMER, Anne (née Sharp) (Dayton Central, OH, USA E, 1957) Mrs Comr. Served in USA S, USA C (TPWO) and USA E (TPWO). Ww Comr Stanley, pG 2003.

DU PLESSIS, Paul (Salt River, S Afr, 1968); Comr b 3 Jul 41. MB, ChB, MRCP, DTM&H; with Comr **Margaret** (née Siebrits); m 1964; b 17 Jul 42. BSoc Sc. Served in Zam, Ind C (TC/TPWO), S Afr (TC/TPWO) and at IHQ.

DURMAN, David C. (Bromley, UK, 1940); Comr b 21 Aug 20; and Mrs Comr **Vera** (née Livick) (South Croydon, UK, 1942) m 1949. Served in UK, Ind W (TC/TPWO) and at IHQ (Chancellor of Exchequer, IS/SWO S Asia).

DWYER, June M. (Windsor, NS, Can, 1952); Comr. b 28 Aug 32. Served at USA Nat, in S Afr (CS) and at IHQ (IS Admin).

E

EDWARDS, David (New Market Street, Georgetown, Guyana, Carib, 1962); Comr b 15 May 41; and Comr **Doreen** (née Bartlett) (Wellington St, Barbados, Carib, 1957) m 1966; b 4 Mar 35. Served in USA E, Carib (TC/TPWO), at IHQ (IS/SWO Am and Carib) and in USA W (TC/TPWO).

EGGER, Verena (née Halbenleib) (Solothurn, Switz, 1945); Mrs Comr. Served in Carib and C Am, Zaï, Mex and C Am, S Am E and Switz. Ww Comr Jacques E., pG 2001.

ELIASEN, Carl S. (Gartnergade, Den, 1951); Comr b 28 Mar 32. Served in Port (OC), Brz (TC), S Am W (TC) and at IHQ (IS Americas). Ww Comr Maria, pG 2003.

EVANS, Willard S. (Greenville, SC, USA S, 1949), Comr b 2 Sep 24. BA (Bob Jones Univ); with Mrs Comr **Marie** (née Fitton).

Served in USA S, USA E (CS/THLS) and USA W (TC/TPWO).

F

FEWSTER, Lilian (née Hunt) (Hanwell, UK, 1931); Mrs Comr. Served in UK, Can and Zimb. Ww Comr Ernest F., pG 1973.

FREI, Werner (Rorbas, Switz, 1965); Comr b 6 Mar 40; and Comr **Paula** (née Berweger) (Heiden, Switz, 1965) m 1967; b 19 Mar 36. Served in Switz (CS/TSWO) and Ger (TC/TPWM).

FULLARTON, Frank (Bromley, UK, 1955); Comr b 3 Mar 31. BSc, DipSoc; and Comr **Rosemarie** (née Steck) (Croydon Citadel, UK, 1958) m 1959. BEd (Hons), MITD. Served at IHQ (CS to CoS, IS/SWO Eur), Soc S (GBI) (Ldr) and in Switz (TC/TPWO).

G

GAUNTLETT, Marjorie (née Markham) (Wood Green, UK, 1952); Mrs Comr. Served at ITC, in Zimb, Frce, Ger (THLS), Switz (THLS) and at IHQ (WSHL). Ww Comr Caughey, pG 2009.

GOODIER, William Robert (Atlanta Temple, GA, USA S, 1941) Comr b 23 May 16; with Mrs Comr **Renee** (née Tilley). Served in USA S (CS/THLS), at USA Nat (CS/NHLS), in Aus S (TC/TPWO) and USA E (TC/TPWO).

GOWANS, John General (1999-2002) (see page 26);
and Comr **Gisèle** (née Bonhotal) (Paris Central, Frce, 1955) m 1957. Served in USA W, Frce (TPWO), Aus E (TPWO), UK (TPWO) and at IHQ (WPWM).

GRIFFIN, Joy (née Button) (Tottenham Citadel, UK, 1957); Mrs Lt-Comr. Served in BT. Ww Lt-Comr Frederick, pG 1990.

GRINSTED, Dora (née Bottle) (Sittingbourne, UK, 1950); Mrs Comr. Served in UK, Zam, Zimb, Jpn and at IHQ. Ww Comr David Ramsay, pG 1992.

GULLIKSEN, Thorleif R. (Haugesund, Nor, 1967); Comr b 26 Apr 40; with Comr **Olaug** (née Henriksen) m 1962; b 25 Jan 38. Served in Nor, Neth (TC/TPWO) and at IHQ (IS/SWM Eur).

H

HANNEVIK, Anna (Bergen 2, Nor, 1947); Comr b 9 Aug 25. Served in Nor, UK (Ldr SocS), Swdn (TC) and at IHQ (IS Eur). Paul Harris Medal (1987), Commander of the Royal Order of the Northern Star (Sweden).

HANNEVIK, Edward (Oslo 3, Nor, 1954); Comr b 6 Dec 32; and Comr **Margaret** (née Moody) (Newfield, UK, 1956) m 1958. Served in UK, Den (TC/TPWO), Nor (TC/TPWO) and at IHQ (IS/SWO Eur).

HARITA, Nozomi (Shibuya, Jap, 1966); Comr b 10 May 39. BA (Mus); and Comr **Kazuko** (née Hasegawa) (Shibuya, Jap, 1966) m 1969; b 19 Dec 37. BA (Ed). Served in Aus E and Jap (TC/TPWM).

HARRIS, Bramwell Wesley (Cardiff Stuart Hall, UK, 1948); Comr b 25 Nov 28; and Mrs Comr **Margaret** (née Sansom) (Barking, UK, 1949), m 1955. Served in UK, at IHQ, in Aus S (CS/THLS), Scot (TC/THLP), NZ (TC/TPWO) and Can (TC/TPWO).

HAWKINS, Peter (Croydon Citadel, UK, 1948); Comr b 16 Oct 29. FCIS; and Mrs Comr **Mary** (née McElroy) (Partick, UK, 1949) m 1952. Served in UK and at IHQ (IS Finance).

HEDBERG, Lennart (Nykoping, Swdn, 1954); Comr b 12 Oct 32; and Comr **Ingvor** (née Fagerstedt) (Nykoping, Swdn, 1955) m 1956. Served in Den, Swdn (TC/TPWO) and at IHQ (IS/SWO Eur).

HINSON, Harold D. (High Point, NC, USA S, 1955); Comr b 7 Sep 35; and Comr **Betty M.** (née Morris) (New Orleans, LA, USA S, 1955); b 1 Jun 35. Served in USA S (CS/THLS) and USA C (TC/TPWO).

HODDER, Kenneth L. (San Francisco Citadel, CA, USA W, 1958); Comr b 30 Oct 30. BA (Richmond), DSS (Hons) (Richmond), JD (California); and Comr **Marjorie J.** (née Fitton) (San Francisco Citadel, CA, USA W, 1958). Served in USA W, USA C, Aus S (CS), USA S (TC/TPWO) and at USA Nat (NC/NPWM).

HOLLAND, Louise (née Cruickshank) (Invercairn, UK, 1958); Mrs Comr. Served in UK, E Afr, Nig, Gha, Pak and at IHQ. Ww Comr Arthur, pG 1998.

HOOD, H. Kenneth (Denver Citadel, CO, USA W, 1954); Comr b 27 Jan 33; and Comr **Barbara** (née Johnson) (Pasadena, CA, USA W, 1952) m 1957. Served in USA W (CS/THLS), at USA Nat (CS/Asst NPWO) and in USA S (TC/TPWO).

HOUGHTON, Raymond (Woodhouse, UK, 1967); Comr b 12 Apr 44. MCMI; with Comr **Judith** (née Jones) m 1965; b 15 Nov 45. Served in UK (CS/TSWO), at IHQ (IS to CoS/Mission Resources Sec) and in Carib (TC/TPWM).

HOWE, Norman (Dartford, UK, 1957); Comr b 13 Aug 36; and Comr **Marian** (née Butler) (Boscombe, UK, 1953) m 1959; b 9 Feb 30.

Retired Generals and Commissioners

Cert Ed. Served in UK, at ITC (Principal), in Aus S (TC/TPWO), Can (TC/TPWO) and at IHQ (IS Prog Res/SWO Eur, General's Travelling Representative).

HUGHES, Alex (Paisley West, UK, 1960); Comr b 29 Jan 42; and Comr **Ingeborg** (née Clausen) (Catford, UK, 1964) m 1971; b 2 Jan 42. Served in L Am N, S Am E (CS/THLS, TC/TPWO), S Am W (TC/TPWO), at IHQ (IS/SWO Am and Carib) and in UK (TC/TPWM).

HUGUENIN, Willy (Le Locle, Switz, 1954); Comr b 22 Sep 31; and Mrs Comr **Miriam** (née Luthi) (La Chaux-de-Fonds, Switz, 1953) m 1955. Served in Zaï (GS), Con (TC/TPWO), Switz (TC/TPWO) and at IHQ (IS/SWO Afr).

I

IRWIN, Ronald G. (Philadelphia, PA, USA E, 1957); Comr b 4 Aug 33. BS (Rutgers), MA (Columbia); and Comr **Pauline** (née Laipply) (Cincinnati, OH, USA E, 1953) m 1967. Served in USA W (CS/THLS) and USA E (TC/TPWO).

ISRAEL, Jillapegu (Peralipadu, Ind N, 1957); Comr b 31 May 32. BA, BEd; with Comr **Rachel** (née Amarthaluri); Served in Ind M & A (CS/THLS), Ind N (TC/TPWO) and Ind SW (TC/TPWO).

K

KANG, Sung-hwan (Noh Mai Sil, Kyung Buk, Kor, 1973); Comr b 15 Dec 39; with Comr **Lee, Jung-ok** m1970; b 10 Nov 49. Served in Aus S and Kor (TC/TPWM).

KELLNER, Paul S. (Miami Citadel, FL, USA S, 1963); Comr b 1 Sep 35. BMus; with Comr **Jajuan** (née Pemberton); b 23 Feb 39. Served in USA S, Carib, Con (Braz) and Zimb (TC/TPWO).

KENDREW, K. Ross (Sydenham, NZ, 1962); Comr b 7 Dec 38; and Comr **M. June** (née Robb) (Wanganui, NZ, 1961) m 1964; b 8 Oct 39. Served in NZ (TC/TPWO) and Aus S (TC/TPWO).

KERR, Donald (Vancouver Temple, BC, Can, 1955); Comr b 25 Oct 33; and Comr **Joyce** (née Knaap) (Mt Dennis, ON, 1955) m 1957; b 12 Jan 35. Served in UK (CS) and Can (TC/TPWO).

KIM, Suk-tai (Choon Chun, Kor, 1957); Comr b 23 Jan 26. ThB, BA, MSoc; and **Lim, Jung-sun** (Sudaemun, Kor, 1969) m 1975. BMus. Served in Kor (TC/TPWO).

KING, Margaret (née Coull) (Fairview, S Afr, 1936); Mrs Comr. Served in S Afr (TPWO). Ww Comr Hesketh, pG 1990.

L

LALTHANNGURA (Ratu, Ind E, 1963); Comr b 15 Sep 38. BA; with **Kaphliri**; b 9 Sep 43. Served in Ind C (CS/THLS) and Ind E (TC/TPWM).

LANG, Ivan B. (Auburn, Aus S, 1967); Comr b 18 Jul 40. AM, Order of Australia (2007), with Comr **Heather C.** (née Luhrs) m 1961; b 8 Dec 42. Served in Sing (OC/CPWO), Aus E (CS/TSWO), at IHQ (IS/SWM SPEA) and in Aus S (TC/TPWM).

LARSSON, John General (2002-06) (see page 26); and Comr **Freda** (née Turner) (Kingston-upon-Thames, UK, 1964) m 1969. Served in S Am W (THLS), at ITC, in UK (TPWO), NZ (TPWO), Swdn (TPWO) and at IHQ (WSWM, WPWM).

LEE, Sung-duk (Cho Kang, Kor, 1963); Comr b 10 Jun 35; with Comr **Cho, In-sun** (Taejon Central, Kor, 1963) m 1961; b 8 May 40. Served in Kor (TC/TPWO).

LIM, Ah Ang (Balestier Rd, Sing, 1954); Comr b 30 May 32; and Comr **Fong Pui Chan** (Singapore Central, 1954) m 1958. Served in Sing, HK (OC/CPWO), Phil (TC/TPWO) and at IHQ (IS/SWO SPEA).

LINDBERG, Ingrid E. (Norrköping, Swdn, 1951); Comr b 12 Dec 25. Served in Swdn, Zimb, Phil (OC), Den (TC) and Fin (TC).

LINNETT, Merle (née Clinch) (Hindmarsh, Aus S, 1947); Mrs Comr. Served in NZ, at IHQ, ITC, ICO and in Aus S. Ww Comr Arthur, pG 1986.

LOVATT, Olive (née Chapman) (Doncaster, UK, 1949); Mrs Comr. Served in UK, Aus S, Aus E & PNG and at IHQ. Ww Comr Roy, pG 2000.

LUTTRELL, Bill (Greeley, CO, USA W, 1958); Comr b 4 Jul 38. BA Soc; and Comr **Gwendolyn** (née Shinn) (Long Beach, CA, USA W, 1961) m 1962; b 3 Sep 38. BA Soc. Served at IHQ (IS/SWO Am and Carib), in Can (TC/TPWM) and USA W (CS/TSWO, TC/TPWM).

LYSTER, Ingrid (Valerenga, Nor, 1947); Comr b 7 Apr 22. BA (S Afr). Served in Nig, Zimb, Nor (CS) and at ICO (Principal).

M

MABENA, William (Bloemfontein, S Afr, 1959); Comr b 23 May 40; and Comr **Lydia** (née Lebusho) (Bloemfontein, S Afr, 1959) m 1960; b 25 Jun 39. Served in UK, S Afr (CS/THLS, TC/TPWM), Gha (TC/TPWO) and at IHQ (IS/SWO Afr).

MAILLER, Georges (Neuchatel, Switz, 1961); Comr b 9 Nov 36. BTh; with Comr **Muriel** (née Aeberli) m 1959; b 15 Apr 35. Served at ESFOT, in Frce and Switz (TC/TPWO).

MAKOUMBOU, Antoine (Bacongo, Con (Braz), 1968); Comr b 2 Mar 40; with Comr **Véronique** (née Niangui) m 1967; b 30 Aug 46. Served in Con (Braz) (TC/TPWM).

MANNAM, Samuel (Duggirala, Ind N, 1946); Comr b 3 Jun 21. Ww Mrs M., pG 1974; and Mrs Comr **Ruby** (née Manuel) (Leyton Citadel, UK, 1953) m 1975. Served in Ind M & A (TC/TPWO), Ind W (TC/TPWO), Ind SW (TC/TPWO), Ind E (TC/TPWO) and Ind N (TC/TPWO).

MARSHALL, Marjorie (née Kimball) (New York Temple, USA E, 1944); Mrs Comr. Served in USA C, USA E (TPWO), at IHQ (SWO Am and Carib) and at USA Nat (NPWO). Ww Comr Norman S., pG 1995.

MASIH, Mohan (Khundi, 1961); Comr b 29 Sep 39; with Comr **Swarni** m 1958; b 14 Mar 42. Served in Ind N (CS/THLS), Ind C (TC/TPWO), Ind SW (TC/TPWO) and Ind W (TC/TPWO).

MAXWELL, Earle Alexander (Orange, Aus E, 1954); Comr b 8 Jul 34. FCIS, ASA, CPA; and Comr **Wilma** (née Cugley) (Camberwell, Aus S, 1956) m 1957. Served in Aus E, Sing (OC/CPWO), Phil (TC/TPWO), NZ (TC/TPWO) and at IHQ (CoS/WSWO).

McKENZIE, Garth (Wellington City, NZ, 1975); Comr b 19 Feb 44; with Comr **Merilyn** (née Probert) m 1968; b 20 Jul 46. Served in Aus S and NZ (TC/TPWM).

MILLER, Andrew S. (Newark, NJ, USA E, 1943); Comr b 14 Oct 23. BSc (Akron), Hon LLD (Asbury), Hon LHD (Akron); and Mrs Comr **Joan** (née Hackworth) (Hamilton, OH, USA E, 1945) m 1946. Hon LHD (Wesley Biblical Seminary, MS). Served in USA E, USA C (CS/THLS), USA S (TC/TPWO) and at USA Nat (NC/NPWO).

MORGAN, K. Brian (Bairnsdale, Aus S, 1958); Comr b 5 Oct 37; and Comr **Carolyn** (née Bath) (Melville Park, Aus S, 1958) m 1961; b 5 Mar 38. Served in Rus/CIS (OC/CPWO), Aus S (CS/TSWO) and Aus E (TC/TPWM).

MORRIS, Louise (née Holmes) (Charleston, W VA, USA S, 1953) Comr. Served in USA S and Jpn (TPWO). Ww Comr Ted, pG 2004.

MOYO, Gideon (Chikankata, Zam, 1963); Comr b 3 May 33. Served in Zam (GS) and Zimb (TC). Ww Comr Lista, pG 2001.

MOYO, Selina (née Ndhlovu) (Bulayao Central, 1951); Mrs Comr. Served in Zimb (TPWO). Ww Comr David, pG 2005.

MUNGATE, Stuart (Mabvuku, Zimb, 1970); Comr, b 15 Nov 46. BA, Grad Cert Ed, Dip Bus Admin; and Comr **Hope** (née Musvosvi) (Mucherengi, Zimb, 1974) m 1974; b 23 Mar 53. Dip Journ. Served in Zimb, Con (Kin) (CS/TSWM, TC/TPWM), Nig (TC/TPWM) and DR Con (TC/TPWM).

MUTEWERA, Stanslous (Sinoia, Zimb, 1970); Comr b 25 Dec 47; and Comr **Jannet** (née Zinyemba) (Tsatse, Zimb, 1973) m 1973; b 11 Nov 52. Served in UK and Zimb (TC/TPWM).

N

NEEDHAM, Philip D. (Miami Citadel, USA S, 1969); Comr b 5 Dec 40. BA (Rel), MDiv, ThM, DMin; with Comr **Keitha** (née Holz) m 1963; b 9 Oct 41. BA (Ed). Served at ICO (Principal), in USA W and USA S (TC/TPWM).

NELSON, John (Victoria Citadel, BC, Can, 1952); Comr b 19 Aug 32; and Comr **Elizabeth** (née McLean) (Chatham, Ont, Can, 1953) m 1956. Served in Can, at IHQ (IS/SWO S Asia), in Carib and Pak (TC/TPWO).

NELTING, George L. (Brooklyn, Bushwick, NY, USA E, 1942); Comr b 20 Jun 18. Ww Mrs Kathleen (née McKeag), pG 1976; and Mrs Comr **Juanita** (née Prine) (Cincinnati Cent, OH, USA E, 1962) m 1977.Served in USA E, at USA Nat (CS), Neth (TC/TPWO), at IHQ (IS/SWO Afr and IS Far East) and in USA C (TC/TPWO).

NGUGI, Joshua (Nakuru, 1945); Comr. b 29 Jan 16. Served in E Afr (TC). Ww Comr Bathisheba, pG 2005.

NILSON, Birgitta K. (Boone, IA, USA C, 1964); Comr. b 2 Oct 37. AB (Chicago), MSW (Loyola). Served in USA C, Swdn (TC) and at IHQ (IS Eur).

NILSSON, Sven (Vansbro, Swdn, 1940); Comr b 27 Jul 19. King's Medal (12th size) Sweden (1983). Served in Nor (CS), Den (TC) and Swdn (TC). Ww Mrs Comr Lisbeth, pG 2007.

NOLAND, Joseph J. (Santa Ana, CA, USA W, 1965); Comr b 17 Jul 37. BA, MS; and Comr **Doris** (née Tobin) (Los Angeles Congress Hall, CA, USA W, 1965) m 1966. RN. Served

Retired Generals and Commissioners

in USA W, Aus E and USA E (TC/TPWO).
NTUK, Patience (née Ekpe) (Ibadan, Nig, 1969); Comr. Served in Nig (TPWM). Ww Comr Joshua, pG 2007.
NUESCH, Ruben D. (Rosario Cent, Brz, 1946); Comr b 28 Feb 21; and Mrs Comr **Rosario** (née Legarda) (Bahia Blanca, 1946) m 1948. Served in Brz (TC/TPWO), S Am W (TC/TPWO) and S Am E (TC/TPWO).

O

ØDEGAARD, B. Donald (Oslo 3, Nor, 1966); Comr b 18 Dec 40. Cand Mag; and Comr **Berit** (née Gjersøe) (Tønsberg, Nor, 1964) m 1967; b 27 Sep 44. SRN. Served in Zimb, S Afr, Nig (TC/TPWO), E Afr (TC/TPWO), Nor (TC/TPWM) and at IHQ (IS Prog Resources/'Sally Ann' Coordinator).
OLCKERS, Roy (Uitenhage, S Afr, 1952); Comr b 16 Jul 29; and Mrs Comr **Yvonne** (née Holdstock) (Fairview, S Afr, 1952) m 1955. Served in S Afr (TC/TPWO).
ORD, John (Easington Colliery, UK, 1948); Comr b 7 Sep 29 and Mrs Comr **Lydie** (née Deboeck) (Brussels, Belg, 1951) m1953. Served in Frce, Belg (OC/OPWO), at ITC, ICO, in UK and Nor (TC/TPWO).
ORSBORN, Amy (née Webb) (Adelaide North, Aus S, 1951); Mrs Comr. Served in Aus S, NZ, UK, Swdn (TPWO) and Aus E (TPWO). Ww Comr Howard, pG 2008.
OSBORNE, James (Washington 3, DC, USA S, 1947); Comr b 3 Jul 27; with Mrs Comr **Ruth** (née Campbell, Served in USA W (CS), USA S (TC) and at USA Nat (NC).

P

PARKINS, May (née Epplett) (Seattle Citadel, WA, USA W, 1951); Mrs Lt-Comr. Served in USA E, USA S and USA W (TPWO). Ww Lt-Comr William, pG 1990.
PATTIPEILOHY, Blanche (née Sahanaja) (Djakarta 1, Indon, 1955); Mrs Comr. Served in Indon (TPWO). Ww Comr Herman G., pG 2000.
PATRAS, Gulzar (Punjgarian, Pak, 1973); Comr b 19 Aug 47; and Comr **Sheila** (née John) (Amritnagar, Pak, 1973) m 1973; b 22 Sep 46. Served in Pak (TC/TPWM).
PENDER, Winifred (née Dale) (Godmanchester, UK, 1954); Comr. Served in NZ (THLS), S Afr (THLS, TPWO), Scot (TPWO), at IHQ, in Aus S (TPWO) and UK (TPWO). Ww Comr Dinsdale, pG 2006.
PINDRED, Gladys (née Dods) (Kitsilano, BC, Can, 1941); Mrs Comr. Served in Can and Carib. Ww Comr Leslie, pG 1990.
PITCHER, Arthur Ralph (St John's, NF, Can, 1939); Comr b 30 Oct 17. Served in S Afr (CS), Carib (TC), USA S (TC) and Can (TC). Ww Mrs Comr Elizabeth, pG 2009.
PRATT, William (Ilford, UK, 1947); Comr b 8 May 25; and Mrs Comr **Kathleen** (née Lyons) (Harlesden, UK, 1948) m 1949. Served at IHQ, in BT (CS), USA W (TC/TPWO) and Can (TC/TPWO).

R

RADER, Paul A. General (1994-1999) (see page 25);
with Comr **Kay F.** (née Fuller) (Cincinnati, OH, USA E, 1995) m 1956. BA (Asbury), Hon DD (Asbury Theol Seminary), Hon LHD (Greenville), Hon DD (Roberts Wesleyan). Served in Kor (THLS), USA E (THLS), USA W (TPWO) and at IHQ (WPWO).
RANGEL, Paulo (Rio Comprido, Brz, 1968); Comr b 19 Nov 41, Hon DD, and Comr **Yoshiko** (née Namba) (São Paulo, Brz, 1967) m 1969; b 1 Sep 44. Served in Brz (TC/TPWM).
READ, Harry (Edinburgh Gorgie, UK, 1948); Comr b 17 May 24. Served in UK, at IHQ, ITC (Principal), in Can (CS), Aus E (TC) and BT (Brit Comr). Ww Mrs Comr Winifred, pG 2007
RIGHTMIRE, Robert S. (Cincinnati, OH, USA E, 1946); Comr b 23 Jun 24; and Comr **Katherine** (née Stillwell) (Newark Citadel, USA E, 1942) m 1947. Served in USA E, S Afr (CS), Jpn (TC/TWPWO, Kor (TC/TPWO) and USA C (TC/TPWO).
RIVERS, William (Hadleigh Temple, UK, 1952); Comr b 22 Dec 27; and Mrs Comr **Rose** (née Ross) (Aberdeen Torry, UK, 1956) m 1957. Served in UK and at IHQ (IS Admin).
ROBERTS, William H. (Detroit Brightmoor, MI, USA C, 1943); Comr b 27 May 22; and Mrs Comr **Ivy** (née Anderson) (Marshalltown, IA, USA C, 1943) m 1945. BA (Wayne State). Served in USA C, Aus S (CS) and at IHQ (IS Am and Carib, IS for Dev).
ROOS, Rolf (Uppsala, Swdn, 1962); Comr b 13 Nov 40; and Comr **Majvor** (née Ljunggren) (Uppsala, Swdn, 1964) m 1965; b 15 Sep 38. Served in Fin (TC/TPWO) and Swdn (TC/ TPWM).
RUTH, Fred L. (Shawnee, OK, 1955); Comr b 21 Aug 35. BA (Georgia State), Dip Ed, MA (Counselling and Psychol Studies) (Trinity). Served in Kor, USA W, USA S,

at USA Nat and IHQ (IS SPEA). Ww Mrs Col Sylvia, pG 1990.

S

SAUNDERS, Robert F. (Philadelphia Pioneer, PA, USA E, 1962); Comr b 16 Jan 37. C Th (Fuller); and Comr **Carol J.** (née Rudd) (Seattle Temple, WA, USA W, 1966) m 1967; b 10 Sep 43. Served in Carib, USA E, USA W, Kor (CS/TSWO), Phil (TC/TPWO) and at IHQ (IS/SWO SPEA).

SCHURINK, Reinder J. (Zutphen, Neth, 1947); Comr b 2 Dec 27. Officer Order of Orange Nassau (1987). Ww Mrs Capt Henderika (née Hazeveld), pG 1961. Served in Ger (CS), Neth (TC) and Rus (Cmndr). Ww Mrs Comr Wietske (née Kloosterman), pG 1997. m Lt-Col Dora Verhagen, 1998.

SCOTT, Albert P. (Lawrence, MA, USA E, 1941); Comr b 15 Oct 18. Ww Mrs Dorothy, pG 1970; and Mrs Comr **Frances O.** (née Clark) (Concord, NH, USA E, 1953) m 1971. Served in USA E (CS) and at IHQ (IS Am and Carib, and IS Dev).

SHIPE, Tadeous (Mukakatanwa, Zimb, 1969); Comr b 13 Jul 43. Served in Zimb, Zam & Mal (TC/TPWM) and Zam (TC/TPWM). Ww Comr Nikiwe, pG 2008.

SHOULTS, Harold (St Louis Tower Grove, MO, USA C, 1949); Comr b 6 Mar 29; and Mrs Comr **Pauline** (née Cox) (St Louis Tower Grove, MO, USA C, 1951) m 1952. Served in USA E (CS/TSWO), USA N (CS/Asst NPWO) and USA C (TC/TPWO).

SKINNER, Verna E. (West End, Aus E, 1957); Comr b 5 May 36. Served in Aus E, HK, Sri Lan (TC), Aus S (CS), at IHQ (IS Resources) and in E Afr (TC).

SOLHAUG, Karsten Anker (Sandvika, Nor, 1936); Comr b 9 Nov 14. Kt, St Olav. Served in UK, Den (CS) and Nor (TC). Ww Comr Else, pG 2006.

STRONG, Leslie J. (Kalbar, Aus E, 1965); Comr. b 5 Apr 43. BAL and Comr **Coral** (née Scholz) (Kalbar, Aus E, 1966) m 1967; b 30 Mar 44. Served in Aus S (CS/TSWM) and Aus E (TC/TPWM).

SUNDARAM, Thota Gnana (Denduluru, Ind SE, 1963); Comr b 1 Oct 35; with Comr **Suseela** m 1955; b 16 Apr 36. Served in Ind C, Ind SE (TC/TPWO) and Ind W (TC/ TPWO).

SUTHERLAND, Margaret (Sleaford, UK, 1968); Comr b 22 Jul 43. MA, ARCO. Served in Zam, UK, Zimb (CS), at IHQ (IS Afr) and ICO (Principal).

SWINFEN, John M. (Penge, UK, 1955); Comr b 24 Jan 31. BA, Cert Ed, Chevalier de l'Ordre du Merite Exceptionnel (Congo); with Comr **Norma** (née Salmon). Served in Zimb, ITC, UK, E Afr (CS/THLS), Con (TC/TPWO) and at IHQ (IS/SWO Afr).

SWYERS, B. Gordon (Atlanta Temple, GA, USA S, 1959); Comr b 25 Jul 36. BBA (Georgia State); and Comr **Jacqueline** (née Alexander); b 25 Dec 29. Served in USA S and at IHQ (IS Admin/SWO SPEA).

T

TAYLOR, Margaret (née Overton) (Aylsham, UK, 1962); Comr b 13 Feb 40. Served in UK, E Afr (THLS), Pak (TPWO) and at IHQ (SWO SAsia, SWO Afr, IS Prog Resources). Ww Comr Brian E., pG 2004.

TAYLOR, Orval A. (Seattle Citadel, WA, USA W, 1940); Comr b 21 May 19; and Mrs Comr **Muriel** (née Upton) (Long Beach, USA W, 1937) m 1943. Served in USA W, USA S, USA N (CS/TSWO), Carib (TC/TPWO), at IHQ (IS Planning and Dev) and USA E (TC/TPWO).

THOMPSON, Arthur T. (Croydon Citadel, UK, 1961); Comr b 23 Dec 32. BSc, PhD, PGCE, Freeman of the City of London' and Comr **Karen** (née Westergaard) (Camberwell, UK, 1961) m 1962. BA, PGCE. Served in Zimb, Zam, UK, NZ (CS/THLS) and at IHQ (IS Admin/IS Resources, SWO Eur).

THOMSON, Robert E. (Racine, WI, USA C, 1951); Comr b 21 Feb 28. BM (St Olaf); with Mrs Comr **Carol** (née Nielsen); BA (St Olaf). Served at USA Nat, in USA C (CS/TSWO), at IHQ (IS/SWO Am and Carib) and in USA E (TC/TPWO).

TILLSLEY, Bramwell Howard General (1993-94) (see page 25); with Mrs General **Maud** (née Pitcher). Served in Can, at ITC, in USA S, Aus S (TPWO) and at IHQ (WSWO, WPWO).

TONDI, Roos (née Mundung) (Sonder, Indon, 1958); Comr. Served in Aus S and Indon (TPWO). Ww Comr Victor, pG 2002.

TUCK, Trevor M. (Kensington Citadel, S Afr, 1969); Comr b 11 Sep 43, and Comr **Memory** (née Fortune) (Benoni, S Afr, 1965) m 1968; b 28 Apr 45. Served in PNG (TC/TPWM) and S Afr (CS/TSWM, TC/TPWM).

V

VERWAAL, Sjoerdje (née Zoethout) (Zaandam, Neth, 1947); Mrs Comr. Served at IHQ (SWO Eur) and in Neth (TPWO). Ww Comr Cornelis, pG 2002.

Retired Generals and Commissioners

W

WAGHELA, Chimanbhai Somabhai (Ratanpura, Ind W, 1968); Comr b 1 Jun 47; with Comr **Rahelbai** m 1972; b 1 May 52. Served in Ind W, Ind SE (CS/TSWO), Ind E (CS/TSWO) and Ind SW (TC/TPWM).

WAHLSTRÖM, Maire (née Nyberg) (Helsinki 1, Fin, 1944); Mrs General. Served in Fin (TPWO), Swdn (TPWO), Can (TPWO) and at IHQ (WPWO). Ww General Jarl Wahlström, pG 1999.

WALTER, Alison (née Harewood) (Calgary Citadel, AB, Can, 1955); Mrs Comr. Served in Zimb, E Afr, Can (TSWO), S Afr (TPWO) and at IHQ. Ww Comr Stanley, pG 2004.

WATERS, Margaret (née Eastland) (Niagara Falls, Can, 1953); Comr b 1 Mar 34. Served in Can (TSWO) and at IHQ. Ww Comr Arthur W., pG 2002.

WATILETE, Johannes G. (Bandung 3, Indon, 1963); Comr b 9 Sep 41. BA, MTh, DTh, DMin (HC); and Comr **Augustina** (née Sarman) (Bandung 3, Indon, 1962) m 1966; b 16 Aug 39. Served in Sing (GS/CHLS), Phil (CS/THLS and TC/TPWO) and Indon (TC/TPWM).

WATSON, Robert A. (Philadelphia Pioneer, PA, USA E, 1955); Comr b 11 Aug 34, and Comr **Alice** (née Irwin) (Philadelphia Pioneer, PA, USA E, 1956) m 1957. Served in USA E (CS/THLS) and at USA Nat (NC/NPWO).

WICKBERG, Eivor (née Lindberg) (Norrköping 1, Swdn, 1946); Mrs General. Ww General Erik Wickberg, pG 1996.

WILLIAMS, Harry William (Wood Green, UK, 1934); Comr b 13 Jul 13. OBE (1970), FRCS (Edin), FICS. Served in Ind W, Ind NE, Ind S (TC), NZ (TC), Aus E (TC) and at IHQ (IS Am, IS Australasia, IS Planning and Dev). Ww Mrs Comr Eileen M., pG 2002.

Y

YOHANNAN, Paulose (Kalayapuram, Ind SW, 1974); Comr b 1 Dec 45. MA (Sociol), DD, PhD; with Comr **Kunjamma** (née Jesaiah) m 1966; b 15 Jun 47. Served in Ind SW, Ind E, Ind SE (TC/TPWM) and Ind N (TC/TPWM).

FROM Angola to Australia, from Ukraine to the USA, The Salvation Army is being used by God to change people's lives. For evidence and eye-witness reports, pick up a copy of *All the World*, The Salvation Army's international magazine.

Published four times a year, *All the World* contains in-depth features on emergency relief, development and community work undertaken by Salvationists across the globe. Where there's a soup run, a house-building project, a rehabilitation scheme or a community programme *All the World* aims to be there, witnessing the often miraculous transformations brought about through the power of God and the dedication and sheer hard work of his people in The Salvation Army.

Copies of *All the World* can be purchased from any Salvation Army headquarters and subscriptions are available through Salvationist Publishing and Supplies, UK Territory. The online version of the magazine, including downloadable artwork, can be accessed at: www.salvationarmy.org/alltheworld

Retirements from Active Service

AUSTRALIA EASTERN
Maj Pamela Johns from THQ on 1 Dec 2008
Maj Beryl Lingard from Booth College on 7 Jan 2009
Capt Errol Hart from Ayr on 8 Jan 2009
Maj Edwin Phillips from Forster/Tuncurry on 8 Jan 2009
Capt Mary Timperley from Maclean on 8 Jan 2009
Maj Ray Proud from THQ on 12 Jan 2009
Maj Ray Allen from Chaplain, Employment Plus on 1 Feb 2009
Maj Jenny Allen from Recovery Services on 1 Feb 2009
Maj Innes Stiles from The Greater West DHQ on 1 May 2009
Lt-Cols Graham and Rhondda Durston from The Philippines (CS/TSWM) on 30 Apr 2009
Lt-Cols Mervyn and Elaine Rowland from Hong Kong and Macau (OC/CPWM) on 30 Jun 2009

AUSTRALIA SOUTHERN
Maj Valma Thomas from Melbourne Central DHQ on 8 Jan 2009
Maj John Vale from THQ on 1 Feb 2009
Maj Helen Brunt from THQ on 1 Feb 2009
Majs David and Janet Button from Western Australia DHQ on 1 Mar 2009
Maj Arthur Ford from THQ on 1 Mar 2009
Majs Bryce and Barbara Mouchemore from THQ on 1 Apr 2009
Maj Keith Cheng from Western Australia DHQ on 1 Apr 2009

BRAZIL TERRITORY
Maj Linda Campos from Lar do Outono on 31 Mar 2009

CANADA AND BERMUDA
Majs Warrick and Lucy Pilgrim from Stratford, ON on 1 Oct 2008
Majs Edwin and Ruth Kimmins from Toronto, ON on 1 Dec 2008
Maj Jane Archer from Toronto, ON on 1 Jan 2009
Maj Gail Norton from DHQ Orillia, ON on 1 Jan 2009
Maj Carletta Thornhill from Charlottetown, PE on 1 Feb 2009

Maj Lorraine Simpson from THQ on 1 May 2009
Maj Maureen Voce from Wingham, ON on 1 May 2009
Majs Lloyd and Ellen Boone from North York, ON on 1 Jun 2009
Maj Gloria Fudge on 1 Jul 2009
Maj John Norton from Ontario North DHQ on 1 Jul 2009
Maj Linda Bulmer from THQ on 1 Aug 2009
Maj Brenda Holnbeck from Ontario North DHQ on 1 Aug 2009
Lt-Col Jean Moulton from THQ on 1 Aug 2009
Lt-Cols Raymond and Audrey Rowe from Newfoundland and Labrador East DHQ on 1 Aug 2009
Majs Eric and Gillian Walker from Belleville, ON on 1 Sep 2009
Majs Harry and Elaine Banfield from Hamilton ON on 1 Sep 2009
Majs Harvey and Doreen Canning from Toronto, ON on 1 Sep 2009

CARIBBEAN
Majs Metelus and Adeline Charles on 4 Jul 2008
Majs Bryon and Joycelyn Maxam from All Saints Corps and Sunshine Girls' Home, Antigua, on 30 Nov 2008
Majs Denzil and Nora Walcott from Point Corps/Fern Outpost, Western Jamaica, on 31 Dec 2008
Maj Lynette Walkins from Josephine Shaw House and Belmont Corps, Trinidad, on 31 Dec 2008
Majs Jean St Jean and Rosalie Charles from Arcahaie, Haiti, on 28 Feb 2009
Majs Rudolph and Jean Richards Hanbury Children's Home, Jamaica, on 20 Jul 2009
Majs Errol and Sheila Robateau from Belize RHQ on 5 Jul 2009

DENMARK
Maj Aud Berntsen from THQ on 1 Sep 2008

EASTERN EUROPE
Maj Natalia Landyrev from Training College, Moscow, on 1 May 2009
Capt Lidia Prisiazhny from Pesotchin, Ukraine, on 1 Aug 2009

Retirements from Active Service

FRANCE AND BELGIUM
Maj Robert Muller from THQ on 1 Nov 2008

GERMANY AND LITHUANIA
Maj Ivor Edwards from Cologne on
30 Sep 2008
Capt Heidrun Harbeke from Barmstedt on
30 Apr 2009

GHANA
Aux-Capts Samuel and Sarah Dadzi from
Kofiase on 12 Oct 2008
Majs Joseph and Comfort Nkansah from
Abekoase on 19 Oct 2008

INDIA EASTERN
Majs K. Chhuanvawra and Zalawmi from
Kawnpui on 3 May 2009

INDIA NORTHERN
Majs Nabh Kishore and Zeena Nayak from
Angul on 1 Nov 2008
Majs Kallan and Sheela Masih from Bareilly
on 30 Apr 2009

INDIA SOUTH WESTERN
Majs K. C. Peter and Annamma Peter on
30 Apr 2009
Maj P. Y. Mary on 30 Apr 2009
Maj M. Elcybai on 30 Apr 2009

INDONESIA
Lt-Col Mina Laua from Palu 2 on 1 Jul 2008
Maj Andina Manik from Sibedi Outpost on
1 Mar 2009

JAPAN
Majs Masakatsu and Tomoko Miyamoto from
Obihiro and Kushiro on 30 Jun 2009

KOREA
Maj Shin, Moon-ho and Maj Cho, In-sook
from Officer Training College on 31 May 2009

THE NETHERLANDS AND CZECH REPUBLIC
Maj Mieke Kuijpers from Harlingen on
1 Aug 2008
Maj Wil Graafland from Arnhem on
31 Aug 2008
Maj Lida Cornelisse from THQ on 20 Dec 2008
Maj Cobi Inge from Amsterdam Goodwill on
15 Jun 2009
Majs Henk and Mary van Essen from
Amsterdam West on 9 Jun 2009

Maj Marian Poppema from Apeldoorn/
Deventer on 9 Jun 2009

NEW ZEALAND, FIJI AND TONGA
Maj Merilyn Goldsack from THQ on
29 Feb 2008
Capt Judith Christensen from THQ on
30 Apr 2008
Maj Joyce Langdon from THQ on
31 May 2008
Maj Janee Sawyer from THQ on 16 Jul 2008
Maj Bernie Knowles from Auckland Bridge on
31 Jul 2008
Majs Jack and Rosalie Miller from Blenheim
on 31 Aug 2008
Maj Val Townsend from THQ on 30 Nov 2008
Majs William and Alison Millar from
Whangarei Community Ministries on
30 Nov 2008
Lt-Col Raeline Savage from Christchurch City
on 8 Jan 2009
Maj Raewyn Fridd from Homecare on
18 Jan 2009
Capts John and Beryl Billington from
Tokoroa on 28 Feb 2009
Comrs Garth and Mel McKenzie from THQ
(TC/TPWM) on 28 Feb 2009
Maj Haydn Rive from Pukekohe on
31 May 2009

NIGERIA
Maj Ruth Attabong from Orphans' and
Vulnerable Children's Home, Akai, on
29 Mar 2009
Majs Cornelius and Caroline Ajubiga from
THQ on 30 Aug 2009

NORWAY, ICELAND AND THE FÆROES
Maj Anne Lise Børstad from Gjøvik on
1 Nov 2008
Maj Margot Krokeda from Hamar on
31 Dec 2008
Maj Gerd Østhu from THQ on 1 Jan 2009
Maj Marit Endresen from THQ on
30 Apr 2009
Maj Julie Wærne from THQ on 30 Jun 2009
Maj Rolf Stackbo from Kopervik on 31 Jul
2009

PAKISTAN
Aux-Capts James Sardar and Naziran James
from Chak 118 on 15 Nov 2008
Maj Barkat Masih from Youhanabad on
30 Apr 2009
Maj Eric Prem from Liddar on 30 Apr 2009

Retirements from Active Service

Majs Zaki Jacob and Parveen Zaki from Nawabanwala on 30 Apr 2009

PAPUA NEW GUINEA
Capts Patrick and Maggie Wasku from Nawei on 9 Jan 2009
Majs Lapu and Araga Rawali from THQ on 27 Jul 2009

SOUTH AMERICA EAST
Majs Carlos and Isabel Bembhy from Santa Fe on 31 Dec 2008
Maj Violeta Aguirre from THQ on 10 Jun 2009
Maj Lidia Saavedra from THQ on 30 Jun 2009
Majs Juan and Maria Vazquez from Buenos Aires on 30 Jun 2009
Capt Juana Ortiz from Nueva Chicago on 31 Jul 2009

SOUTHERN AFRICA
Maj Jeremiah Dlamini from Witbank on 31 Oct 2008
Majs Douglas and Poppy Makhanya from Peart Memorial on 31 Jan 2009

SWEDEN AND LATVIA
Lt-Col Ing-Britt Hansson from THQ on 31 Dec 2008
Maj Britt Alhbin from THQ on 30 Jun 2009
Maj Birgitta Kjellqvist from THQ on 1 Jul 2009
Maj Ingrid Albinsson from THQ on 1 Aug 2009

SWITZERLAND, AUSTRIA AND HUNGARY
Comrs Edouard and Françoise Braun-Volet from THQ (TC/TPWM) on 31 Aug 2007
Col Ines Adler from THQ (CS) on 30 Sep 2007
Maj Dieter Ringger from Frauenfeld on 30 Sep 2007
Maj Heidi Braun from THQ on 30 Nov 2007
Maj Hanna Frutiger from Northwest Division on 30 Nov 2007
Maj Susanne Bürki-Illi from Moudon/Payerne on 29 Feb 2008
Maj Jean-Pierre Geiser from Vevey on 30 Sep 2008
Maj Hans Knecht from Northwest DHQ on 31 Jan 2008
Capts Ádám and Rozália Macher from Debrecen, Hungary, on 31 Aug 2008
Maj Susanne Wildi-Wildi from Bern Division on 30 June 2009
Maj Paul Schaffner from Buchs on 31 Aug 2009
Maj Werner Schwendener from Arbon on 30 Sep 2009
Maj Ruth Tschopp from Regional Officer, Hungary, on 31 Oct 2009
Maj Ernst Kugler from THQ on 30 Nov 2009
Maj Heidi Scheurer from THQ on 31 Dec 2009

UNITED KINGDOM WITH THE REPUBLIC OF IRELAND
Maj Elizabeth Burns from THQ on 1 Sep 2008
Maj Richard Hope from Barnet on 1 Sep 2008
Majs Anthony and Phyllis Martin from Swadlincote on 1 Sep 2008
Maj Janet Thompson from Chaplain, Heathrow Airport on 1 Sep 2008
Maj Lesley Baker from William Booth College on 1 Oct 2008
Maj Malcolm Watkins from THQ on 1 Nov 2008
Capt Judith Morgans from Skewen on 1 Dec 2008
Maj Mary Boyd from THQ on 1 Jan 2009
Capt Marilyn Warmington from Bradford Citadel on 1 Jan 2009
Majs Ernest and Susanna Benson from Ballymena and Ballymoney on 1 Feb 2009
Maj Christine Marriott from Buckhaven on 1 Feb 2009
Maj Brenda Stones from Attercliffe on 1 Mar 2009
Maj Alma Thomas from Edinburgh Homelessness Project on 1 Mar 2009
Maj Olive Drake from William Booth College on 1 Apr 2009
Maj Rosemary Randall from Brighton (Bevendean and Congress Hall) on 1 Apr 2009
Capt Peter Simpson from Maldon on 1 Apr 2009
Maj Raymond Ebden from Yorkshire DHQ on 1 May 2009
Comrs Raymond and Judith Houghton from Caribbean (TC/TPWM) on 1 May 2009
Majs Keith and Gillian Manning from Letchworth on 1 May 2009
Majs John and Ann Thomas from Yeovil on 1 May 2009
Lt-Col Royston Bartlett from THQ on 1 Jun 2009
Maj John Boyd from Littleport on 1 Jun 2009
Maj Ellen Cushing from East Midlands DHQ on 1 Jun 2009
Maj Margaret Dockerill from Croydon Citadel on 1 Jun 2009
Maj Joy McIntosh from Maidstone on 1 Jun 2009

Retirements from Active Service

Lt-Col Jean Burrows from IHQ on 1 Jul 2009
Maj Brian Griffin from Central South DHQ on 1 Jul 2009
Maj Katharine Howard from Zimbabwe on 1 Jul 2009
Maj Sandra Wills from IHQ on 1 Jul 2009
Lt-Col Christine Barr from THQ on 1 Aug 2009
Majs James and Helen Bryden from THQ and IHQ respectively on 1 Aug 2009
Maj Linda Cordner from Southern DHQ on 1 Aug 2009
Lt-Col Trevor Davis from Leicester South on 1 Aug 2009
Majs Gordon and Ruth Downey from THQ on 1 Aug 2009
Maj Christine Edwin from Nuneaton on 1 Aug 2009
Maj Alan Ford from Chaplain, Riverside House on 1 Aug 2009
Maj Valerie Hart from Deal on 1 Aug 2009
Maj Rita Jepson from Tidworth Red Shield Club on 1 Aug 2009
Maj Malcolm Jones from London Central DHQ on 1 Aug 2009
Maj Kingsley Layton from William Booth College on 1 Aug 2009
Maj Mary McDonald from East Scotland DHQ on 1 Aug 2009
Maj Robin McIntosh from Chaplain, Gatwick Airport on 1 Aug 2009
Maj Norma Paget from Pokesdown on 1 Aug 2009
Maj Ann Powell from THQ on 1 Aug 2009
Lt-Col Dawn Sewell from THQ on 1 Aug 2009
Capt Sheila Smith from Leicester Central on 1 Aug 2009
Maj Cherry Umasanthiram from Sunset Lodge, Tunbridge Wells on 1 Aug 2009
Maj Susan Waddington from Morley on 1 Aug 2009
Maj Susan Woollacott from Alton on 1 Aug 2009

USA CENTRAL

Comrs Ken and Joy Baillie from THQ (TC/TPWM) on 1 Oct 2008
Majs Charles and Lila Lieurance from Fort Wayne ARC, IN on 1 Oct 2008
Maj Patricia Kiddoo from US NHQ on 1 Feb 2009
Maj Rosemary Matson from Superior, WI on 1 Jul 2009
Lt-Cols Mickey and June McLaren from THQ on 1 Jul 2009
Maj Deborah Doliber from Eastern Michigan DHQ on 1 Jul 2009
Majs Patrick and Carmella McPherson from Flint, MI on 1 Jul 2009

USA EASTERN

Majs Kenneth and Shirley Kristiansen from Massachusetts DHQ on 1 Sep 2008
Majs Harold and Helen Robbins from THQ on 1 Sep 2008
Majs Joseph and Rose Marie White from Scranton ARC, PA on 1 Sep 2008
Majs Richard and Joyce Kuhl from THQ on 1 Nov 2008
Majs David and Alice Hathorn from Marietta, OH on 31 Dec 2008
Majs Clyde and Judith Jones from Toledo, OH on 1 Jan 2009
Majs Thomas and Patricia Mack from THQ on 1 Mar 2009
Maj Mary West from Wooster, OH on 1 Apr 2009
Majs Frederick and Melissa Hagglund from Rochester, PA on 1 May 2009
Maj Harriet Mendez from THQ on 1 May 2009
Maj Elizabeth Butts from THQ on 1 Jul 2009
Majs Robert and Mary Carney from Beaver Falls, PA on 1 Jul 2009
Majs Randall and Patricia Davis from Williams Memorial Residence, NY on 1 Aug 2009
Maj Veronica Demeraski from Northeast Ohio DHQ on 1 Aug 2009
Maj Brian Figueroa from THQ on 1 Aug 2009
Maj Kellus and Marcia Vanover from School for Officer Training on 1 Aug 2009

USA SOUTHERN

Lt-Cols William and LaVerne Crabson from National Capital and Virginia DHQ on 1 Aug 2008
Capts John and Shirley Chapman from Hickory, NC on 1 Aug 2008
Majs Allen and Lorraine Hausner from Eden, NC on 1 Aug 2008
Majs Michael and Beverly Waters from Nashville ARC, TN on 1 Sep 2008
Majs Oliver and Joyce Michels from Maryland and West Virginia DHQ on 1 Feb 2009
Majs Roy and Judy Ward from Atlanta ARC, GA on 1 Apr 2009
Capts Kenneth and Sandra Bagley from Leesburg, FL on 1 Jul 2009
Lt-Cols Donald and Constance Canning from THQ on 1 Jul 2009

Retirements from Active Service

Lt-Cols Donald and Marian Faulkner from THQ on 1 Jul 2009
Maj Patricia Johnson from Booth Towers Atlanta, GA on 1 Jul 2009
Majs William and Mary Ann Madison from St Petersburg ARC, FL on 1 Jul 2009
Majs Alvin and Bobbie Sue Smith from Raleigh, NC on 1 Jul 2009
Capts Marvin and Wanda Trayler from San Antonio, TX on 1 Jul 2009
Majs Jack and Sharon Owens from North Central Brevard, FL on 1 Jul 2009
Maj Joanne Senft from Texas DHQ on 1 Jul 2009

USA WESTERN

Maj Katrina Grundahl from Anchorage, AK on 1 Sep 2008
Majs Bounmy and Manivene Luangamath from Whittier, CA on 1 Sep 2008
Maj Patricia Jolley from Rancho Palos Verdes, CA on 1 Oct 2008

Majs Robert and Leslie Souders from Happy Valley, OR on 1 Oct 2008
Majs Lanny and Noreen French from Riverside, CA on 1 Nov 2008
Maj Benia Meyer from San Francisco, CA on 1 Nov 2008
Lt-Cols Don and Jan Mowery from Phoenix, AZ on 1 Nov 2008
Majs Leonard L. and Barbara Blix from Happy Valley, OR on 1 Jul 2009
Majs Keith C. and Linda Bottjen from Billings, MT on 1 Jul 2009
Cols Olin O. and Dianne C. Hogan from Mexico (TC/TPWM) on 1 Jul 2009
Majs Erik W. and Angeline Sholin from Honolulu, HI on 1 Jul 2009
Majs R. Hal and Sheri Hads from Port Angeles, WA on 1 Aug 2009
Majs J. Robert and Marjorie Hall from Denver, CO on 1 Aug 2009
Maj Joyce Stevenson from THQ on 1 Aug 2009

Retirements from Active Service

Promotions to Glory

AUSTRALIA EASTERN
Brig Thelma Entwistle on 5 Aug 2008
Maj Harold Pearson on 9 Aug 2008
Mrs Brig Anne Reece on 15 Aug 2008
Mrs Brig Ida Palmer on 26 Sep 2008
Mrs Lt-Col Olive Lynn on 7 Oct 2008
Mrs Comr Crystal Campbell on 8 Oct 2008
Maj Maisie Beasey on 16 Oct 2008
Brig Lester Wright on 17 Oct 2008
Lt-Col Dudley Schoupp on 13 Dec 2008
Maj Melva Doncaster on 30 Dec 2008
Mrs Brig Coral Smith on 20 Apr 2009
Maj Bill Redwood on 21 May 2009
Brig Edna Earle on 1 Jun 2009
Brig Isobel Clark on 15 Jun 2009
Capt Denise Pillinger on 22 Jun 2009
Brig John McCabe on 4 Jul 2009
Mrs Maj May Edwards on 23 Jul 2009
Capt Bill Rutherford on 5 Aug 2009

AUSTRALIA SOUTHERN
Mrs Col Ellen Novell on 30 Mar 2008
Brig Laurel Watson on 18 Apr 2008
Maj Mavis Webb on 21 Apr 2008
Mrs Brig Susanne Thomas on 22 Apr 2008
Maj Douglas Young on 5 Jul 2008
Mrs Maj Jean Parker on 28 Aug 2008
Maj Frank Corlass on 7 Sep 2008
Mrs Comr Crystal Campbell on 8 Oct 2008
Mrs Maj Maisie Beasley on 16 Oct 2008
Mrs Brig Alma Findlay on 3 Nov 2008
Mrs Capt June Newman on 20 Feb 2009

BRAZIL
Brig Jakob Stalder on 18 Jun 2008

CANADA AND BERMUDA
Mrs Lt-Col Hazel Smith on 25 Aug 2008
Maj Neil Voce on 30 Aug 2008
Maj Eva Duffett on 22 Sep 2008
Maj Harold Cull on 15 Oct 2008
Maj Lillian Thompson on 15 Oct 2008
Maj Zeversa Richards on 25 Oct 2008
Maj Robert Hammond on 7 Nov 2008
Maj William Davies on 5 Dec 2008
Maj William Boone on 5 Dec 2008
Maj Ruth Foote on 6 Dec 2008
Maj Robert Wilson on 12 Jan 2009
Maj Marie Hansen on 21 Jan 2009
Maj Johanna (Evangeline) Loucks on 6 Feb 2009
Maj Beulah Cole 15 Feb 2009
Mrs Comr Elizabeth Pitcher on 24 Apr 2009
Lt-Col Isabel Armstrong on 27 Apr 2009
Maj Baxter Davis on 30 Apr 2009
Lt-Col Howard Moore on 8 May 2009
Capt Wilson Simms on 11 May 2009
Maj Maritza Suarez on 30 May 2009
Maj Ross Cole on 12 Jun 2009
Maj Bernard Wiseman on 8 Jul 2009
Maj Edward Amos on 27 Jul 2009
Capt Frank Phelps on 17 Aug 2009
Capt Douglas Butt on 11 Sep 2009
Maj William Stoodley on 1 Oct 2009
Maj Archie Peat on 15 Oct 2009

CARIBBEAN
Brig Samuel Daley on 10 Dec 2008

DENMARK
Comr Rigmor Østergaard on 3 Feb 2009

EASTERN EUROPE
Capt Mark Prisiazhny (A) from Pestochin, Ukraine, on 12 Oct 2008

FINLAND AND ESTONIA
Capt Kirsti Thusberg on 17 Feb 2009
Maj Marita Salmi on 5 Jul 2009

FRANCE AND BELGIUM
Capt Olive Braquehais Bais on 24 Sep 2008
Maj Daniel Russier on 20 Nov 2008
Lt-Col Martial Castelli on 10 Jan 2009
Maj Elise Delon on 16 Feb 2009
Maj Bernard Chastagnier on 17 Feb 2009
Maj Marie Bouneau on 14 Mar 2009

GERMANY AND LITHUANIA
Mrs Maj Irma Dietz on 30 Oct 2008
Maj Rudolf Schollmeier (A) from Northern DHQ on 24 Feb 2009

GHANA
Maj Felicia Danquah on 21 Dec 2008
Maj Mary Duodu on 28 Jun 2009

INDIA NORTHERN
Capt Pargat Masih (A) from Khushalpur on 19 Nov 2008
Maj Iqbal Bibi Mukhtar Masih on 21 Dec 2008
Maj Ram Kali Masih on 12 Jan 2009

Promotions to Glory

Maj Anwer Bibi Majid Masih on 23 Feb 2009
Brig S. L. Joseph on 8 Mar 2009
Maj Nawab Din on 16 Apr 2009

INDIA SOUTH WESTERN

Maj Manuel J. Lukose (A) from Perumpazhuthoor on 19 Jul 2008
Maj C. J. Rachel Abraham on 2 Aug 2008
Maj P. Joseph on 29 Oct 2008
Lt-Col Y. Gracy David on 3 Nov 2008
Maj R. Yohannan on 28 Nov 2008
Maj K. C. Aleyamma Davidson on 2 Dec 2008
Maj V. J. Yesudasan on 6 Dec 2008
Maj Y. Joseph on 13 Dec 2008
Maj V. J. Yesudasan on 13 Dec 2008
Maj P. J. Snehamony Paulose on 4 Jan 2009
Brig M. K. Joseph on 8 Feb 2009
Maj P. P. Thankamma Paul on 20 Mar 2009
Maj P. A. Rachel Samuel on 26 May 2009
Maj M. S. Sarah David on 16 Jun 2009
Maj T. Kamalam (A) from Kakode on 26 Jul 2009
Maj M. Manuel on 30 Jul 2009

INDIA WESTERN

Maj John Mirpagare on 18 Sep 2008
Maj Babu Unhawane on 19 Oct 2008
Maj Madhusudan Jacob (A) from Muktipur on 20 Nov 2008
Maj Ranjit Limba on 25 Dec 2008
Col Jaikumar Makanji on 9 Jan 2009
Maj Ramanlal Dunger on 7 Mar 2009
Maj Khemchand Mahida on 9 Apr 2009
Capt Monalisa Joliph (A) from Matar on 29 Apr 2009

INDONESIA

Brig Rachel Misatia Losso on 17 Apr 2008
Maj Markus Djido Lesso on 1 May 2008
Lt-Col Saiman Hadisukirna on 8 Jul 2008
Maj Tuti S. Tjondrowikarto on 25 Sep 2008
Maj Alberth Mangiwa (A) from East Palu Division on 9 Nov 2008
Maj Daniel Hetta on 23 Nov 2008
Mrs Comr Blanche Pattipeilohy on 13 Dec 2008
Maj Alberth M. Manik (A) from Kulawi Division on 3 Jan 2009
Maj Yoseph Rigo on 11 Apr 2009

ITALY

Maj Giovanni Iannarone on 26 Jan 2009

JAPAN

Brig Harue Miki on 11 Sep 2008
Mrs Brig Tomoko Takeshita on 7 Nov 2008
Maj Akiyo Kawano on 7 Jan 2009
Maj Yukuo Takehana on 21 Feb 2009
Mrs Brig Yukiko Tsuda on 4 Jul 2009
Mrs Brig Fumiko Koyano on 10 Jul 2009
Mrs Comr Ai Yoshida on 29 Jul 2009

KENYA WEST

Maj Trufosa Muiruri on 24 Apr 2008
Maj Thomas Kiplagat on 18 Dec 2008
Maj Rachel Andolo (A) from Wabukhonyi, Bungoma, on 18 Mar 2009
Lt-Col Annah Makhanu on 29 Apr 2009

KOREA

Maj Park, Kyeah-won on 6 Jan 2009
Capt Kim, Choon-ok (A) on 5 Mar 2009

MALAWI

Envoy Olivia Phiri (A) from Ulongwe on 1 Nov 2008

THE NETHERLANDS AND CZECH REPUBLIC

Capt Elizabeth Davidsz on 25 Jul 2008
Col Geertruida Krommenhoek on 29 Aug 2008
Maj Gezina Ranselaar on 10 Oct 2008
Maj Rinske Brandsma on 15 Feb 2009
Maj Aukje Antje Koopmans on 16 Feb 2009
Maj Anthonia van der Werf on 18 Feb 2009
Brig Louise Brouwer on 19 Mar 2009
Lt-Col Adriana Mast on 28 Mar 2009
Brig Jozina Veenendaal on 13 Apr 2009
Maj Jacobtje Zuidema on 4 May 2009
Maj Herman Wielenga on 18 May 2009
Maj Frederik Zuidema on 29 May 2009

NEW ZEALAND, FIJI AND TONGA

Maj Robert Millar on 15 Apr 2008
Maj Hazel Sutton on 17 Apr 2008
Maj Elizabeth Major on 8 Jul 2008
Maj Gladys Winwood on 2 Nov 2008
Lt-Col Beatrice Palmer on 25 Dec 2008
Brig Elizabeth (Betty) Roberts on 11 Feb 2009
Maj Lawrence Daly on 28 Mar 2009
Maj Doreen Bell on 10 Apr 2009
Brig Lucia Parkinson on 16 Apr 2009
Comr Hillmon Buckingham on 19 Apr 2009
Brig Grace Tong on 2 Jun 2009
Maj Thelma Smith on 22 June 2009

NIGERIA

Maj Smart N. Umoh (A) from Ibadan DHQ on 10 Nov 2008
Capt Justina Obot (A) from Akwa Ibom South West DHQ on 29 Sep 2008

Promotions to Glory

Capt Uchechukwu Ezeofor (A) from Badagry District on 4 May 2008
Capt Angelina Metuh (A) from Okoko on 17 Jul 2008
Capt Nseobong Udobong (A) from Afaha Eket on 15 Jan 2009
Lt-Col Gloria Oloruntoba (A) from THQ (TSWM) on 24 Mar 2009

NORWAY, ICELAND AND FÆROES
Maj Alf Helge Skogly on 6 Nov 2008
Maj Peder Werner Johansen on 16 Dec 2008
Mrs Col Julie Staveland on 18 Jan 2009
Maj Per Rekdal on 1 Feb 2009
Mrs Comr Eili Dahlstrøm on 16 Jun 2009

PAKISTAN
Capt Dilshad Rafiq (A) from Chappa, Sheikhupura, on 3 Dec 2008
Aux-Capt Rafique Masih on 10 Jul 2009
Maj Gulzar Sana Ullah on 29 Jul 2009
Maj Gabriel Morris on 2 Aug 2009

PAPUA NEW GUINEA
Maj Rosemary Danagi on 1 Sep 2008
Capt Davera Kila on 12 Nov 2008
Maj Mea Peter on 7 Jul 2009

THE PHILIPPINES
Brig Florie Urbien on 12 Mar 2009

SOUTH AMERICA EAST
Maj Juan Carlos Costen (A) from Charata on 30 Mar 2008
Capt Alejandro Amaya (A) from Goya on 18 Oct 2008
Lt-Col Carlos Bembhy on 15 Nov 2008
Maj Raquel Gallego on 16 Apr 2009
Maj Mariel de los Santos on 18 May 2009
Maj Clelia Alvez on 26 May 2009

SOUTHERN AFRICA
Maj Herbert Lovick on 5 Mar 2009

SRI LANKA
Col William Perera on 8 Aug 2008
Maj G. Edwards on 4 Dec 2008
Maj Mrs R. Melder on 18 Aug 2009
Maj Ananda Subasinghe on 22 Aug 2009

SWEDEN AND LATVIA
Envoy Gunhild Åkerblom on 10 Sep 2008
Maj Sten Sandin on 30 Sep 2008
Maj Anne Kristoffersson on 26 Oct 2008
Brig Gulli Janson on 2 Nov 2008
Maj Kerstin Wendt on 20 Nov 2008
Capt Ture Danielsson on 21 Nov 2008
Brig Gärd Johansson on 14 Dec 2008
Brig Karin Malmqvist 17 Dec 2008
Lt-Col Lewi Högberg on 20 Dec 2008
Maj Gunborg Jonsson on 28 Dec 2008
Maj Bo Sandqvist on 24 Jan 2009
Brig Elsie Jonelid on 1 Feb 2009
Maj Britta Wallander on 1 Feb 2009
Maj Stina Ahlstrand on 19 Feb 2009
Mrs Brig Gerd Gelotte on 28 Mar 2009
Brig Fannie Sjögren on 30 Mar 2009
Brig Margit Erikson on 20 Apr 2009
Maj Elsa Fredriksson on 1 May 2009

SWITZERLAND, AUSTRIA AND HUNGARY
Maj Mina Anderegg on 6 Jul 2007
Comr Francy Cachelin on 16 Aug 2007
Maj Arthur Rutschmann on 10 Sep 2007
Maj Heinz Gossauer on 23 Sep 2007
Maj Melanie Kohl on 1 Oct 2007
Lt-Col Samuel Holland on 12 Jan 2008
Brig Nelly Porret-Roulier on 23 Jan 2008
Maj Jeanne Millioud-Cardis on 24 Feb 2008
Maj Rösli Roggli on 9 Mar 2008
Maj Freida Siebenmann on 27 Apr 2008
Maj Emma Chappuis on 15 May 2008
Brig Margaretha Bindschädler on 10 Oct 2008
Maj Johann Meier on 15 Nov 2008
Brig Gertrud Bühler on 6 Feb 2009
Brig Martha Rohr-Burger on 24 Mar 2009
Maj Paul Schweizer on 22 Apr 2009

TANZANIA
Maj Anna Mnyampi on 7 Jan 2009

UNITED KINGDOM WITH THE REPUBLIC OF IRELAND
Comr Pauline Banks on 4 Sep 2008
Lt-Col Roy Smith 12 Sep 2008
Maj Margaret Seymour on 15 Sep 2008
Maj Robert Cullingworth on 16 Sep 2008
Maj Ron Holmes on 20 Sep 2008
Maj Edward Williams on 7 Oct 2008
Brig Kathleen Ramsey on 17 Oct 2008
Maj William Spriggs on 21 Oct 2008
Maj Beryl Thomas on 25 Oct 2008
Lt-Col Muriel Linkins 28 Oct 2008
Lt-Col Fred Crowhurst on 3 Nov 2008
Brig Peggy Park on 5 Nov 2008
Maj Stanley Gravestock on 8 Nov 2008
Maj Maureen Sands on 22 Nov 2008
Maj Brenda Fleming on 27 Nov 2008
Maj Evelyn Smith on 2 Dec 2008

Promotions to Glory

Maj Margaret Evans on 12 Dec 2008
Maj Brenda England on 21 Dec 2008
Maj Georgina Rennie on 31 Dec 2008
Maj Kenneth Taylor on 4 Jan 2009
Maj David Murray on 8 Jan 2009
Capt Christine Ord (A) from William Booth College on 9 Jan 2009
Aux-Capt Florence Tidswell on 15 Jan 2009
Maj Florence Baker on 23 Jan 2009
Maj Brenda Taylor on 23 Jan 2009
Mrs Col Daisy Dennis on 25 Jan 2009
Maj Edna Callaway on 29 Jan 2009
Brig Lily Spencer on 5 Feb 2009
Maj Stephen Norman on 6 Feb 2009
Brig Winifred Gilmore on 10 Feb 2009
Maj Thomas Bailey on 11 Feb 2009
Mrs Aux-Capt Muriel Sims on 16 Feb 2009
Brig Mrs Kate Fleming on 21 Feb 2009
Aux-Capt Pearl Getty on 4 Mar 2009
Maj Marjorie Roberts on 4 Mar 2009
Mrs Col Eva Fenwick on 7 Mar 2009
Mrs Brig Ivy Day on 16 Mar 2009
Mrs Lt-Col Eva Cooper on 23 Mar 2009
Comr Denis Hunter on 26 Mar 2009
Col Brindley Boon on 28 Mar 2009
Maj Christina Green on 5 Apr 2009
Maj June Young on 18 Apr 2009
Mrs Brig Mary Johnson on 19 Apr 2009
Maj Christine Hamilton on 27 Apr 2009
Maj Muriel Lund on 29 Apr 2009
Brig Mrs Mary Cumming on 15 May 2009
Brig George Stoner on 8 Jun 2009
Brig Ella Cutler on 17 Jun 2009
Maj Steven Booth 1975 on 26 Jun 2009
Maj Josephine Norton (A) from Wandsworth on 27 Jun 2009
Maj Anthony Martin on 1 Jul 2009
Capt Christine Budding (A) from Carshalton on 14 Jul 2009
Brig Phyllis Whittle on 30 Jul 2009
Brig Alfred Mitchell on 31 Jul 2009
Maj Cyril Wood on 2 Aug 2009
Brig Kenneth Nutty on 3 Aug 2009
Capt Maurice Tones on 7 Aug 2009
Brig Charles Martin on 10 Aug 2009
Mrs Lt-Col Avril May on 17 Aug 2009
Maj Frank Rattenbury on 23 Aug, 2009
Maj Marion Reeves on 23 Aug 2009
Lt-Col Harold Hobson on 29 Aug 2009

USA CENTRAL
Mrs Maj Elsie Nelson on 11 Aug 2008
Mrs Maj Gertrude Ball on 21 Aug 2008
Brig Rodney Sharp on 29 Aug 2008
Maj Mary Garrison on 5 Sep 2008
Col Franklyn Thompson on 27 Sep 2008
Maj Ehlert Wallin on 16 Nov 2008
Mrs Maj Jewell Kiddoo on 26 Nov 2008
Mrs Lt-Col Jeanette Brigman on 4 Dec 2008
Maj Ralph Metz on 19 Dec 2008
Mrs Maj Ida Hogg on 28 Dec 2008
Maj Dale Horn on 10 Jan 2009
Lt-Col Darlene Winkler on 26 Jan 2009
Mrs Col Elsie Franzen on 2 Feb 2009
Maj William D. Stuart on 24 Apr 2009
Mrs Col Marie Koerner on 28 Apr 2009
Maj C. Paul Wilson on 2 May 2009
Maj Harold Thomas on 5 May 2009
Mrs Brig Emma Matheson on 24 May 2009
Maj H. Leilon Ball on 7 Jul 2009
Maj Elizabeth Yoder on 17 Jul 2009
Maj Lullah Logan on 31 Jul 2009
Lt-Col Herbert H. Lodge on 12 Aug 2009

USA EASTERN
Brig Dorothy Ellis on 9 Sep 2008
Maj Edward Taylor, Jr (A) from Philadelphia ARC, PA on 3 Oct 2008
Brig Maude Staples on 11 Oct 2008
Maj Charles Sargent on 30 Oct 2008
Maj Arthur F. Ferreira on 19 Nov 2008
Maj Camilla M. Pfeiffer on 9 Dec 2008
Mrs Brig Ellen Churchill on 18 Dec 2008
Maj Mrs A. Catherine King on 23 Jan 2009
Mrs Brig Ruth E. Banta on 15 Feb 2009
Mrs Lt-Col A. Audrey Seiler on 2 Mar 2009
Mrs Brig Eunice M. Bloethe on 12 Mar 2009
Mrs Lt-Col Dorothy M. Oldford on 14 Mar 2009
Brig William D. Hazzard on 16 Mar 2009
Maj Ralph S. Michaels on 23 Mar 2009
Maj Michael C. Sharpe (A) from Bridgeport, CT on 9 Apr 2009
A/Capt Iris G. Hawkins on 9 Apr 2009
Maj Naomi E. Shaffer (A) from Columbus ARC, OH on 18 Apr 2009
Maj Irving Cranford on 23 Apr 2009
Maj Elsie Marie Brown on 21 May 2009
Brig Stanley H. Wright on 29 May 2009
Maj Beatrice M. Clinton on 2 Jun 2009
Maj William B. Simons on 15 Jun 2009
Mrs Brig Barbara Wheatley on 27 Jun 2009
Capt Jill L. Wallace on 16 Jul 2009
Mrs Maj Sandra B. Senak on 20 Jul 2009
Brig Oscar L. Auchmoody on 3 Aug 2009
Mrs Lt-Col Doris Berry on 10 Aug 2009
Mrs Brig Minnie E. Leggett on 11 Aug 2009

USA SOUTHERN
Mrs Maj Florence Brewer on 15 Oct 2008

Promotions to Glory

Maj James E. Brogden on 29 Nov 2008
Col Leon Ferraez on 7 Dec 2008
Mrs Brig Florence Bergren on 22 Dec 2008
Maj Nellie Hussey on 26 Dec 2008
Maj James E. Snelson on 12 Jan 2009
Maj Louise Smith Shreveport on 10 Feb 2009
Maj Duane B. Greer on 16 Feb 2009
Mrs Maj Irene Proctor on 14 Mar 2009
Mrs Maj Bernice White on 26 Mar 2009
Maj Fern Williford on 8 Apr 2009
Maj Charles I. Anderson, Jr on 15 Apr 2009

USA WESTERN
Maj Charles W. Griffin on 17 Sep 2008
Maj Donald Pack on 16 Oct 2008
Maj Max Garza on 9 Nov 2008
Maj Myrtle Griffin on 21 Dec 2008
Maj Maria Yepez on 27 Jan 2009
Maj Gloria Utrera on 11 Feb 2009
Maj Gertrude Angel 16 Feb 2009

Comr Lawrence Smith on 2 Mar 2009
Maj Edward Scriven on 28 Mar 2009
Brig Edith McDonald on 19 Apr 2009
Maj Stephen Sutter on 24 Jun 2009

ZAMBIA
Capt Patrick Cheelo (A) from Lungae on 2 Sep 2008
Maj Sunday Hamuzembo on 28 Apr 2009
Maj Bryson Sitwala (A) from Mission Director, Chikankata on 8 Jun 2009

ZIMBABWE
Maj Orpha Ndlovu on 16 Sep 2008
Capt Chipo Madombwe (A) from Nyakudya, Chiweshe, on 11 Nov 2008
Maj Mpofu on 26 Dec 2008
Maj Lot Moyo on 9 Mar 2009
Brig Usinganete Nhari on 26 Mar 2009
Maj Florah Hlabangani on 24 Jun 2009

PROMOTED TO GLORY

THERE are many descriptions to soften the harshness of the word 'death' but one of the most radical is the Army's descriptive phrase, 'promoted to Glory'. It sounds a triumphant, positive note in support of the Army's belief in eternal life, Heaven and an unending period in Glory with the Father. It declares incontrovertibly that death is not the end, but the beginning of a new and glorious experience for those redeemed by the blood of Jesus Christ.

The term was first used in *The War Cry* of 14 December 1882, at a time when so many other military phrases were being introduced following the advent of the name 'The Salvation Army' four years earlier. It seems to have found ready acceptance and soon entered common usage.

It was also consistent with the Founder's dislike of sombre black clothing as a sign of mourning. He believed that, while Christ sympathises with sorrow, he desires to make personal tragedy a stepping stone to greater faith by seeing death as a victory.

Abbreviations used in *The Year Book*

A
(A) (active officer pG); Acc (Accommodation); Adj (Adjutatnt); Afr (Africa); Am (America); Ang (Angola); AO (Area Officer); Apt (Apartment); Appt (Appointment); ARC (Adult Rehabilitation Centre); Asst (Assistant); Aus (Australia); A/Capt, Aux-Capt (Auxiliary-Captain).

B
b (born); Ban (Bangladesh); Belg (Belgium); B/M (Bandmaster); Braz (Brazzaville); Brig (Brigadier); Brz (Brazil); BT (British Territory).

C
Can (Canada and Bermuda); Capt (Captain); Carib (Caribbean); CIDA (Canadian International Development Agency); CO (Commanding Officer); Col (Colonel); Comr (Commissioner); Con (Congo); CoS (Chief of the Staff); CS (Chief Secretary); C/S (Corps Secretary); CSM (Corps Sergeant-Major); C/T (Corps Treasurer); CWMO (Command Women's Ministries Officer); Cze R (Czech Republic).

D
DC (Divisional Commander); Den (Denmark); Dis O (District Officer); DO (Divisional Officer); DR Con (Democratic Republic of Congo).

E
E Afr (East Africa); E Eur (Eastern Europe); Ens (Ensign); Env (Envoy); ESFOT (European School for Officers' Training).

F
Fin (Finland and Estonia); Frce (France and Belgium).

G
Ger (Germany and Lithuania); Gha (Ghana); GS (General Secretary).

H
HK (Hong Kong and Macau); HL (Home League); Hun (Hungary).

I
ICO (International College for Officers and Centre for Spiritual Life Development); IES (International Emergency Services); IHQ (International Headquarters); IHS (International Health Services); Ind C, E, etc (India Central, Eastern, etc); Ind M&A (India Madras and Andhra); Indon (Indonesia); Internl (International); IPDS (International Projects and Development Services); IS (International Secretary); It (Italy); ITC (International Training College).

J
JHLS (Junior Home League Secretary); Jpn (Japan).

K
Ken (Kenya); Kin (Kinshasa); Kor (Korea).

L
L Am N (Latin America North); Lat (Latvia); Lib (Liberia); Lt, Lieut (Lieutenant); Lt-Col, Lieut-Colonel (Lieutenant-Colonel); LOM (League of Mercy).

M
m (married); Maj (Major); Mal (Malawi); Mlys (Malaysia); Mol (Moldova); Moz (Mozambique); My (Myanmar).

N
Nat (National); NC (National Commander); Neth (The Netherlands and Czech Republic); NHQ (National Headquarters); Nor (Norway, Iceland and The Færoes); NZ (New Zealand, Fiji and Tonga).

O
OC (Officer Commanding); ODAS (Order of Distinguished Auxiliary Service); OF (Order of the Founder); O&R (Orders and Regulations).

P
Pak (Pakistan); pG (promoted to Glory); Phil (The Philippines); PINS (Persons in need of supervision); PNG (Papua New Guinea); Port (Portugal); PO (Provincial Officer); Pres (President); PRD (Public Relations Department); PS (Private Secretary).

R
RC (Regional Commander); RDWM (Regional Director of Women's Ministries); ret (retired); RO (Regional Officer); ROS (Retired Officers Secretary); RPWM (Regional President of Women's Ministries); Rtd (Retired); Rus (Russia); Rwa (Rwanda and Burundi).

S
S/, Snr (Senior); SAAS (Salvation Army Assurance Society); SABAC (Salvation Army

Abbreviations

Boys' Adventure Corps); S Afr (Southern Africa); SALT (Salvation Army Leadership Training); S Am E (South America East); SAMF (Salvation Army Medical Fellowship); S Am W (South America West); SAWSO (Salvation Army World Service Office); Scot (Scotland); Sec (Secretary); Sen (Senior); SFOT (School for Officers' Training); Sgt (Sergeant); Sing (Singapore, Malaysia and Myanmar); S/L (Songster Leader); Soc S (Social Services); Sp (Spain); SP&S (Salvationist Publishing and Supplies); Sri Lan (Sri Lanka); Supt (Superintendent); Swdn (Sweden and Latvia); Switz (Switzerland, Austria and Hungary).

T

Tai (Taiwan); Tanz (Tanzania); tba (to be appointed); TC (Territorial Commander); tel (telephone); TCCMS (Territorial Community Care Ministries Secretary); THQ (Territorial Headquarters); TLWM, TPWM, TSWM (Territorial Leader of, President of, Secretary for Women's Ministries); TPWO, TSWO (Territorial President of, Secretary for Women's Ministries); TWMS (Territorial Women's Ministries Secretary).

U

Uga (Uganda); UK (United Kingdom); Uk (Ukraine); USA (United States of America); USA Nat, USA C, etc (USA National, Central, etc).

W

WI (West Indies); WPWM WSWM (World President of, Secretary for Women's Ministries); Ww (Widow).

Z

Zai (Zaïre); Zam (Zambia); Zimb (Zimbabwe).

International Direct Dialling

Telephone country codes to territorial and command headquarters are listed below

In *The Year Book* the international prefix, which varies from country to country, is indicated by [square brackets]. Local codes are indicated by (round brackets)

Angola	[244]	
Argentina	[54]	
Australia	[61]	
Bangladesh	[880]	
Belgium	[32]	
Brazil	[55]	
Canada	[1]	
Chile	[56]	
Congo (Democratic Republic)	[243]	
Congo (Republic)	[242]	
Costa Rica	[506]	
Denmark	[45]	
Finland	[358]	
France	[33]	
Germany	[49]	
Ghana	[233]	
Hong Kong	[852]
India	[91]
Indonesia	[62]
Italy	[39]
Jamaica	[1876]
Japan	[81]
Kenya	[254]
Korea	[82]
Liberia	[231]
Mexico	[525]
Malawi	[265]
Mozambique	[258]
Netherlands (The)	[31]
New Zealand	[64]
Nigeria	[234]
Norway	[47]
Pakistan	[92]
Papua New Guinea	[675]
Philippines (The)	[63]
Portugal	[351]
Russia	[7]
Rwanda	[250]
Singapore	[65]
South Africa	[27]
Spain	[34]
Sri Lanka	[94]
Sweden	[46]
Switzerland	[41]
Taiwan	[886]
Tanzania	[255]
United Kingdom	[44]
USA	[1]
Zambia	[260]
Zimbabwe	[263]

INDEX

A

Abraham, Lt-Col C. Mariamma, 129
Abraham, Lt-Col P. T., 128
Adams, Col Clive, 199
Adams, Col Marianne, 200
Africa, 8, 21, 40, 47, 49, 93, 96, 117, 158, 161, 174, 176, 182, 196, 216, 231, 251, 253, 294, 297
Africa Development Centre, 43
Africa Zonal Facilitation Resources Office, 43
Akpan, Comr Ime, 93, 94
Akpan, Comr Mfon, 93
Alaska, 17
Algeria, 18
All-Africa Congress, 20
All the World, 16, 18, 31, 40, 337
Americas and Caribbean, 40, 74, 78, 88, 169, 178, 222, 225, 263, 265, 271, 279, 285
Amsterdam Staff Band and Songsters, 187
Andaman and Nicobar Islands, 135
Angola, 19, 21, 27, 47, 49-50, *see also* Democratic Republic of Congo 96-99
Antigua, 17, 27, 79, *see also* Caribbean 88-92
Anzeze, Comr Hezekiel, 158
Argentina, 7, 17, 27, *see also* South America East 222-224
Australia, 8, 10, 16, 17, 20, 23, 27, 48, 51, 52, 60
    National Secretariat, 31, 51
    Eastern, 21, 23, 24, 26, 31, 33, 36, 37, 46, 48, 51, 52-59, 60, 206, 207
    Southern, 21, 23, 25, 31, 33, 46, 51, 52, 60-71, 249
Australian Agency for International Development (AusAID), 48, 51
Austria, 18, 27, 47, *see also* Switzerland, Austria and Hungary 245-248

B

Bahamas, 18, 27, 266, *see also* Caribbean 88-92
Bailey, Lt-Col Bradford, 225
Bailey, Lt-Col Heidi, 226
Baillie, Comr Joy, 266
Baillie, Comr Kenneth, 265, 266
Band of Love, 17
Bangladesh, 19, 27, 46, 47, 50, 72-73
Barbados, 17, 27, *see also* Caribbean 88-92
Bate, Col John, 226
Belgium, 17, 27, 46, *see also* France and Belgium 109-113
Belize, 18, 27, *see also* Caribbean 88-92
Bell, Comr Debora, 189, 190
Bell, Comr Donald, 189
Bermuda, 17, 27, *see also* Canada and Bermuda 78-87
Bolivia, 18, 27, *see also* South America West 225-230
Bond, Comr Linda, 52, 53
Booth, Bramwell, 13, 16, 18, 22, 35, 240
    Catherine, 5, 6, 11, 13, 16, 109
    Evangeline, 5, 6, 16, 18, 22, 23, 178
    William, 5, 11, 13, 16, 18, 22, 32, 33, 41, 107, 109, 121, 185, 216, 219, 255, 263
Boschung, Col Franz, 245
Boschung, Col Hanny, 246
Bosh, Comr Gillian, 41
Bosh, Comr Larry, 40, 45
Botswana, 20, 27, 297
Bouzigues, Lt-Col Ricardo, 222
Bouzigues, Lt-Col Sonia, 223
Brazil, 18, 27, 31, 33, 46, 47, 74-77
Brekke, Col Birgitta, 3, 39, 100
Bringans, Comr David, 178, 219
Bringans, Comr Grace, 178, 179, 219
British Guiana, 17
British Honduras, 18
Brown, General Arnold, 19, 22, 24

Index

Burger, Comr Kurt, 245
Burger-Pedersen, Comr Alicia, 245, 246
Burma, 18, 218, *see also* Myanmar
Burridge, Col Beryl, 218, 219
Burridge, Col Keith, 218
Burrows, General Eva, 5, 19, 22, 25, 199
Burundi, 20, 21, 27, 47, *see also* Rwanda and Burundi 216-217

C

Canada, 16, 17, 20, 23, 24, 25, 27, 34, 46, 48, 185
Canada and Bermuda, 24, 25, 31, 78-86, 88, 237, 252
Canadian Staff Band, 86
Canary Islands, *see* Spain 235-236
Caribbean, 31, 33, 46, 47, 88-92
Carpenter, General George Lyndon, 18, 22, 23, 37
Carpenter, Mrs General Minnie, 34
Castillo, Lt-Col Aída, 235, 236
Castillo, Lt-Col Luis, 235
Castor, Col Edmane, 88, 89
Castor, Col Onal, 88
Celebes, 18
Central Africa Development Office, 43
Central Africa Women's Development Office, 43
Cerezo, Lt-Col Josué, 178
Cerezo, Lt-Col Ruth, 179
Chan, Maj Tommy, 87, 120, 121
Chandra Bai, Comr T. Regina, 128, 129
Channel Islands, 16, *see also* United Kingdom, 255-262
Charan, Col Bimla, 132, 133
Charan, Col Samuel, 132
Charlet, Comr Helga, 114, 115
Charlet, Comr Horst, 114
Chepkurui, Maj Grace, 216, 217
Chepkurui, Maj Stephen, 216
Chigariro, Comr Vinece, 297, 298
Chile, 18, 27, 266, *see also* South America West 225-230
China, 18, 21, 27, 87, *see also* Hong Kong and Macau 120-125

Christian Mission, The, 11, 16, 39, 255
Christian, Lt-Col Anandi, 136
Christian, Lt-Col Paul, 135
Chun, Comr Kwang-pyo, 164
Clifton, Comr Helen, 1, 21, 26, 39, 50, 72, 117, 154, 164, 165, 203, 271, 280
Clifton, General Shaw, 1, 2, 3, 4, 20, 21, 22, 26, 28, 33, 38, 41, 50, 72, 117, 119, 148, 153, 164, 165, 168, 203, 271, 280
Clinch, Lt-Col Robyn, 210
Clinch, Lt-Col Ronald, 209
Cochrane, Comr William, 39, 45
Coleman, Maj Annette, 249, 250
Coleman, Maj Micael, 249
Colombia, 18, 19, 27, *see also* Latin America North 169-173
Community Care Ministries, 34, 182
Community Development Projects, 48
Condon, Col James, 52
Condon, Col Jan, 53
Congo (Brazzaville), 18, 27, 31, 33, 46, 47, 93-95, 185
Congo (Kinshasa) and Angola, 18, 27, 46, 47, 49, 96, *see also* Democratic Republic of Congo 96-99
Copple, Col Ann, 80
Copple, Col Donald, 78
Costa Rica, 18, 27, *see also* Latin America North 169-173
Coutts, General Frederick, 19, 22, 24
Cox, Comr André, 231
Cox, Comr Silvia, 231, 232
Cuba, 18, 27, *see also* Latin America North 169-173
Curacao, 18, 184
Czech Republic (Czechoslovakia), 18, 19, 20, 27, 46, 47, *see also* Netherlands, The, and Czech Republic 184-188

D

Dali, Lt-Col Jessica, 174, 175
Dali, Lt-Col Peter, 174
Daniel, Lt-Col Edward, 237
Daniel, Lt-Col Lalitha, 238
David, Lt-Col K.C., 126

Index

Democratic Republic of Congo, 31, 33, 49, 94, 95, 96-99, 185
Denmark, 17, 27, 31, 33, 46, 94, 100-102, 103
Devarapalli, Col Jayapaul, 142
Devarapalli, Col Yesudayamma, 142, 143
Devil's Island (French Guiana), 18
Dijkstra, Col Alida, 185
Dijkstra, Col Pietre, 184, 186
Doctrines of The Salvation Army, 12, 16
Dominican Republic, 20, 27, *see also* Latin America North 169-173
Downer, Lt-Col Gillian, 41, 87
Duchêne, Col Alain, 109, 110, 112
Dunster, Comr Robin, 38, 45, 87, 206, 214, 246, 253
Durston, Lt-Col Graham, 150, 212
Durston, Lt-Col Rhondda, 150

E

East Africa, 20, 24, 251, 253
East Germany, 19
Eastern Europe, 20, 21, 31, 33, 46, 47, 102, 103-105
Ecuador, 19, 27, *see also* South America West 225-230
Egypt, 18
Eliasen, Lt-Col Deise, 182, 183, 231
Eliasen, Lt-Col Torben, 182, 231
El Salvador, 19, 27, *see also* Latin America North 169-173
Emmanuel, Comr Muthu Yesudhason, 128
England, *see* United Kingdom 255-262
Estonia, 18, 20, 27, 46, 47, *see also* Finland and Estonia 106-108
Europe, 21, 41, 47, 100, 103, 106, 109, 114, 153, 184, 199, 214, 235, 240, 245, 255
European Youth Congress, 20

F

Færoes, The, 18, 27, *see also* Norway, Iceland and The Færoes 199-202
Family Tracing Service, 16, 259
Feener, Comr Lenora, 79, 179, 279, 280

Feener, Comr Maxwell, 79, 179, 279
Fellowship of the Silver Star, 18, 34, 72
Ferreira, Col Adelina, 225, 226
Ferreira, Col Jorge, 225
Fiji, 19, 27, 46, 47, *see also* New Zealand, Fiji and Tonga, 189-195
Finger, Col Aylene, 61
Finger, Col Raymond, 60
Finland, 17, 25, 27, 103
Finland and Estonia, 31, 33, 46, 106-108
Flintoff, Lt-Col Ethne, 72, 73
Forsyth, Comr Robin, 40, 45
Forsyth, Comr Shona, 39
Founders of The Salvation Army, 13
France, 16, 26, 27, 46
France and Belgium, 31, 109-112
Francis, Comr Marilyn, 41, 78, 80
Francis, Comr William, 39, 41, 78, 237
Frans, Comr Arda, 184, 185
Frans, Comr, Roy, 184, 186
French Guiana, 18, 19, 27, *see also* Caribbean 88-92
Frisk, Col Kristina, 240

G

Gaither, Comr Eva D., 231, 263, 264, 266, 279
Gaither, Comr Israel L., 231, 232, 263, 264, 266, 279, 286
General's Consultative Council, The, 39
Georgia, 27, *see also* Eastern Europe 103-105
German Staff Band, 114
Germany, 4, 17, 24, 27, 48
Germany and Lithuania, 20, 31, 46, 47, 114-116, 215
Ghana, 8, 18, 27, 31, 33, 46, 47, 117-119
Ghulam, Lt-Col Rebecca Yousef, 203, 204
Ghulam, Lt-Col Yusaf, 203
Gibraltar, 17
Gowans, General John, 20, 22, 26
Greece, 21, 27, *see also* Italy 153-154
Grenada, 17, 27, *see also* Caribbean 88-92
Griffin, Col, Linda, 280

Index

Griffin, Col, Terry, 279
Guam, 20, 27, 263, *see also* USA Western 285-294
Guatemala, 19, 27, *see also* Latin America North 169-173
Guernsey, 27
Guyana, 17, 28, *see also* Caribbean 88-92
Gyimah, Lt-Col Mary, 118
Gyimah, Lt-Col William, 117

H

Haiti, 19, 28, *see also* Caribbean 88-92
Hanunka, Lt-Col Bislon, 294
Hanunka, Lt-Col Melody, 295
Harfoot, Col Susan, 285, 286
Harfoot, Col William, 285
Hawaii/Hawaiian Islands, 17, 209, 285
Hedgren, Col Judith, 273
Hedgren, Col R. Steven, 271
Herring, Lt-Col Alistair, 103
Herring, Lt-Col Astrid, 104
Higgins, General Edward J., 18, 22, 23
High Council, 18, 19, 20, 22, 23, 39
Hill, Maj Edward, 285
Hiramoto, Lt-Col Naoshi, 155
Hiramoto, Lt-Col Seiko, 156
Hodder, Comr Jolene, 40
Hodder, Comr, Kenneth, 39, 40, 45
Holly, Maj Peter, 51
Holy Land, 17
Home League, 13, 17, 34
Home League Helping-Hand Scheme, 89, 129, 143, 154, 203, 251, 294
Honduras, 20, 28, *see also* Latin America North 169-173
Hong Kong, 18, 20, 21, 28, 52, 249
Hong Kong and Macau, 21, 31, 33, 46, 47, 87, 120-125
Hong Kong Staff Band, 21, 52, 121
'Hope For Life' (suicide prevention programme), 52
Houghton, Comr Raymond, 88
Howard, Comr Henry, 41
Howard, Col Janice, 159
Howard, Col Steven, 158

Hungary, 18, 19, 28, 47, *see also* Switzerland, Austria and Hungary 245-248

I

Iceland, 17, 28, *see also* Norway, Iceland and The Faeroes, 199-202
In Darkest England and the Way Out, 13, 17, 185
India, 16, 17, 28, 126-148
  National Secretariat, 31, 33, 47, 126
  Central, 31, 33, 46, 47, 127, 128-131
  Eastern, 21, 31, 33, 46, 47, 127, 132-134, 238
  Northern, 31, 46, 47, 135-138
  South Eastern, 31, 46, 47, 127, 139-141
  South Western, 31, 46, 47, 127, 142-144
  Western, 31, 33, 46, 47, 145-148
Indian Ocean Tsunami, 20, 136, 150, 237
Indonesia, 17, 18, 28, 46, 47, 149-152, 184
Induruwage, Col Irene, 209, 210, 249
Induruwage, Col Malcolm, 209, 212, 249
International College for Officers, 17, 19, 21
International College for Officers and College for Spiritual Life Development, 41, 44
International Commission on Officership, 20
International Conference of Leaders, 19, 20, 21
International Conference for Personnel Secretaries, 20
International Conference for Training Principals, 20
International Congress, 16, 17, 18, 19, 20
International Corps Cadet Congress, 19
International Doctrine Council, 39, 42
International Education Symposium, 20
International Emergency Services, 40, 96
International Headquarters, 14, 18, 19, 20, 21, 23, 24, 26, 31, 32, 38-48, 255
  Administration Department, 39
  Administrative Structure, 44
  Business Administration Department, 40

Index

International Management Council, 39
International Personnel Department, 40
Programme Resources Department, 40
Zonal Departments, 40-41
International Health Services, 7-8, 40
International Heritage Centre, 258
International Literary and Publications Conference, 20
International Literature Programme, 33, 40
International Moral and Social Issues Council (IMASIC), 39, 42
International Music and Other Creative Ministries Forum (MOSAIC), 20
International Poverty Summit, 20
International Projects and Development Services, 40, 48, 94, 252
International Self-Denial Fund, 9-10, 46, 158, 251
International Social Justice Commission, 20, 42
International Staff Band, 17, 255, 257
International Staff Songsters, 19, 257
International Training College, 18, 24, 25, 26
International Youth Congress, 19
International Youth Forum, 20
Ireland, Republic of, 16, 23, 28, *see also* United Kingdom, 255-262
Isle of Man, 16, 28, *see also* United Kingdom, 255-262
Italy, 17, 28, 31, 33, 46, 47, 148, 153-154

J

Jamaica, 17, 28, 266, *see also* Caribbean 88-92
James, Comr Susamma, 139, 140
James, Comr M. C., 126, 139
Japan, 17, 28, 32, 33, 46, 155-157, 164
Java, 17, 18, *see also* Indonesia 149-152
Jeffrey, Col Barbara, 264
Jeffrey, Col David, 263
Jersey, 28
Johnson, Lt-Cols Kenneth/Paula, 216

K

Kalai, Comr Andrew, 206

Kartodarsono, Comr Marie, 149, 150
Kartodarsono, Comr Ribut, 149
Kawlramthangi, Lt-Col, 146
Kenya, 18, 20, 21, 28, 241
Kenya East, 21, 32, 46, 47, 158-160, 161, 162
Kenya West, 21, 32, 46, 47, 158, 160, 161-163
Kim, Col Keum-nyeo, 166
Kitching, General Wilfred, 19, 22, 23
Kjellgren, Comr Christina, 100, 109, 154
Kjellgren, Comr Hasse, 100, 109, 112, 154
Knaggs, Comr Carolyn, 60, 61
Knaggs, Comr James, 60
Korea, 18, 21, 25, 28, 32, 33, 46, 47, 164-168
Korea, Democratic People's Republic of, 21, 164
Krommenhoek, Comr Dick, 106
Krommenhoek, Comr Vibeke, 106, 107
Kuwait, 21, 28, 47

L

Lahase, Comr Kashinath, 135
Lahase, Comr Kusum, 135, 136
Lalhlimpuii, Comr, 41, 132, 135, 237
Lalkiamlova, Comr, 41, 45, 132, 135, 237
Lalngaihawmi, Lt-Col, 132, 133
Lalramhluna, Lt-Col, 145
Lalzamlova, Col, 237
Lang, Comrs Ivan/Heather, 219
Larsson, Comr Freda, 114, 226
Larsson, General John, 20, 22, 26, 32, 114, 226
Latin America North, 19, 32, 46, 47, 169-173, 185
Latvia, 18, 19, 28, 47, *see also* Sweden and Latvia 240-244
Laukkanen, Lt-Col Arja, 106
League of Mercy, 15, 17, 34, 129, 205
Lee, Lt-Col Bob, 218
Lee, Lt-Col Wendy, 219
Lesotho, 19, 28, *see also* Southern Africa 231-234
Liberia, 19, 28, 46, 47, 174-175

Index

Lithuania, 20, 28, *see also* Germany and Lithuania 114-116
Ludiazo, Comr Jean B., 196
Ludiazo, Comr Véronique, 196, 197
Lydholm, Comr Carl, 199
Lydholm, Comr Gudrun, 199, 200

M

Macau, 20, 28, *see also* Hong Kong and Macau 120-125
MacMillan, Comr M. Christine, 39, 42, 200
McKee, Maj Pamela, 175
Maeland, Col Erling, 100
Maeland, Col Signe Helene, 100, 101
Makina, Comr Amos, 40, 45, 294
Makina, Comr Rosemary, 40, 94, 294
Malabi, Lt-Col Florence, 232
Malabi, Lt-Col Joash, 231
Malawi, 10, 19, 28, 46, 47, 176-177, 266, 294
Malaysia, 18, 28, 46, 47, *see also* Singapore, Malaysia and Myanmar 218-221
Mali, 21, 47, *see also* Nigeria 196-198
Mallorca, *see* Spain 235-236
Malta, 17
Manikyam, Lt-Col Keraham, 140
Marseille, Lt-Col Eva, 94
Marseille, Lt-Col Gerrit, 93
Marshall Islands, 19, 28, 263, *see also* USA Western 285-294
Matear, Comr Elizabeth (Betty), 204, 255, 256, 257
Matear, Comr John, 204, 255
Mavundla, Col Mirriam, 251, 252
Mavundla, Col Hezekiel, 251
Melbourne Staff Band, 165
Mexico, 18, 19, 28, 32, 46, 47, 86, 169, 178-181
Micronesia, Federated States of, 19, 28, *see also* USA Western 285-294
Migration Department, 17
Mnyampi, Lt-Col Benjamin, 251
Mnyampi, Lt-Col Grace, 252

Moldova, 28, 266, *see also* Eastern Europe 103-105
Mongolia, 21, 28, *see also* Korea 164-168
Moravia, 188
Moretz, Comr Lawrence, 271
Moretz, Comr Nancy, 271, 273
Moriasi, Maj Rose, 254
Moriasi, Maj Stephen, 253
Mozambique, 18, 21, 28, 32, 46, 47, 182-183, 185
Muikku, Lt-Col Aino, 100
Mumford, Catherine, 13, 16
Mungate, Comr Hope, 216
Mungate, Comr Stuart, 216
Munn, Lt-Col Janet, 39, 42
Munn, Lt-Col Richard, 39, 41
Myanmar, 18, 28, 46, 47, *see also* Singapore, Malaysia and Myanmar 218-221

N

Namibia, 18, 21, 28, *see also* Southern Africa 231-234
Nanlabi, Maj Priscilla, 87, 120
Naud, Lt-Col Anne-Dore, 115
Naud, Lt-Col Daniel, 153, 154
Naud, Lt-Col Eliane, 153, 154
Naud, Lt-Col Patrick, 114
Nemkhanching, Col, 237, 238
Nepal, 21, 28, *see also* India Eastern 132-134
Netherlands, The 17, 20, 28, 46, 48
Netherlands, The, and Czech Republic, 32, 48, 94, 184-188, 237
Newfoundland, 16, 25, *see also* Canada and Bermuda 78-87
New Zealand, 16, 17, 23, 28, 46
New Zealand, Fiji and Tonga, 26, 32, 33, 183, 189-195
Ngwanga, Col Madeleine, 96, 97
Nigeria, 18, 28, 32, 33, 46, 47, 196-198
NORAD (Norway), 48
Norway, 17, 28, 35, 46, 48
Norway, Iceland and The Færoes, 32, 199-202, 219, 294

Index

Nuesch, Col Nestor, 222
Nuesch, Col Rebecca, 222, 223
Nyagah, Col Catherine, 162
Nyagah, Col Henry, 161
Nyambalo, Maj Francis, 176
Nyambalo, Maj Jamiya, 177

O

Officer, The, 17, 31, 40
Oloruntoba, Lt-Col Festus, 196
Order of Distinguished Auxiliary Service, 18, 37
Order of the Founder, 18, 35-37
Order of the Silver Star, 18, *see also* Fellowship of the Silver Star
Orsborn, General Albert, 18, 22, 23, 41

P

Pakistan, 2, 16, 21, 26, 28, 32, 46, 47, 203-205
Pallant, Maj Dean, 7, 40
Panama, 17, 28, *see also* Latin America North 169-173
Paone, Lt-Col Jane, 110
Paone, Lt-Col Massimo, 109, 110
Papua New Guinea, 19, 28, 32, 33, 46, 47, 155, 157, 206-208
Paraguay, 2, 18, 28, *see also* South America East 222-224
Pardo, Lt-Col Magali, 170
Pardo, Lt-Col Zoilo, 169
Park, Col Man-hee, 164
Payne, Lt-Col Diane, 176, 177
Payne, Lt-Col Godfrey, 176
Pearce, Comr Lyn, 40
Peddle, Col Brian, 45, 255
Peddle, Col Rosalie, 257
Peru, 18, 28, 266, *see also* South America West 225-230
Philippines, The, 18, 28, 32, 33, 46, 47, 209-213
Pho, Lt-Col Donni, 120, 121
Pho, Lt-Col Samuel, 120
Pobjie, Comr Barry, 41, 45, 87, 149
Pobjie, Comr Raemor, 41, 149, 152

Poke, Comr Roslyn, 240, 241
Poke, Comr Victor, 240
Poland, 20, 28, 47, *see also* Germany and Lithuania 114-116
Ponnaih, Lt-Col Masilamony, 142
Ponnaih, Lt-Col Sathiabama, 143
Portugal, 5, 19, 28, 46, 47, 110, 214-215
Portuguese East Africa, 18
Posadas, Maj Evelyn, 73
Posadas, Maj Leopoldo, 72
Pritchett, Lt-Col Myra, 249
Pritchett, Lt-Col Wayne, 140, 249
Project Warsaw, 20, 114
Puerto Rico, 19, 28, 263, *see also* USA Eastern 271-278
Pululu, Maj Celestino Pepe, 182
Pululu, Maj Veronica, 183

R

Rader, Comr Kay, 200
Rader, General Paul A., 20, 22, 25, 200
Railton, Comr George Scott, 164, 199, 263
Rajakumari, Comr P. Mary, 145, 146
Reddish, Col Graeme, 189
Reddish, Col Wynne, 190
Redhead, Cols Robert/Gwenyth, 286
Refstie, Comr Janet, 74, 75
Refstie, Comr Peder, 74
Reliance Bank Ltd, 17, 45
Revive, 21, 31, 40
Roberts, Comr Nancy, 161, 162
Roberts, Com William, 161
Romania, 20, 28, 102, *see also* Eastern Europe 103-105
Rowe, Lt-Col Lindsay, 88
Rowe, Lt-Col Lynette, 89
Russia (Russian Federation), 18, 19, 20, 21, 28, *see also* Eastern Europe 103-105
Rwanda, 20, 28, 46, 47
Rwanda and Burundi, 216-217

S

Sabah (East Malaysia), 20
St Helena, 16, 28, *see also* Southern Africa 231-234

Index

St Kitts, 18, 28, *see also* Caribbean 88-92
St Lucia, 17, 28, *see also* Caribbean 88-92
St Maarten, 28, *see also* Caribbean 88-92
St Vincent, 17, 28, *see also* Caribbean 88-92
'Sally Ann' trading, 73, 204,
Salvation Army
  Blue Shield Fellowship, 35
  International Trustee Company, 45
  Leadership Training College (SALT) of Africa, 43, 47
  Medical Fellowship, 18, 34
  Scouts and Guides Jamboree, 20
  Students' Fellowship, 19, 35
Salvation Army Act 1931, 18, 22
Salvation Army Act 1980, 11, 19, 22
Salvation Army Australia Development Office (SAADO), 51
Salvation Army World Service Office (SAWSO), 46, 48, 174, 237, 264, 295
Salvation Story, 20
Sanchez, Col Ana Rosa, 169, 170
Sanchez, Col Oscar, 169
Schwartz, Lt-Col Barry, 96
Schwartz, Lt-Col Anja, 97
Scotland, 16, 23, 24, 25, 26, *see also* United Kingdom, 255-262
Seiler, Col Carol, 267
Seiler, Col Paul, 265
Self-Denial Appeal, 9, 15, 162, 196, 207 *see also* International Self-Denial Fund
Serém, Maj Alberto, 214
Serém, Maj Maria José, 214, 215
Singapore, 18, 28, 46, 47
Singapore, Malaysia and Myanmar, 20, 32, 218-221
Soldier's Covenant, 15
Soper, Capt Florence, 13, *see also* Booth, Florence
South Africa, 16, 17, 20, 28, 182, 266, 297, *see also* Southern Africa 231-234
South America East, 23, 32, 46, 47, 222-224
South America West, 26, 32, 33, 46, 47, 225-230

South Asia, 21, 41, 47, 72, 128, 132, 135, 139, 142, 145, 203, 237
South Pacific and East Asia (SPEA), 21, 41, 47, 52, 60, 87, 120, 149, 155, 164, 189, 206, 209, 218, 249
Southern Africa, 20, 32, 33, 46, 47, 231-234, 244, 295
SP&S Ltd, 259
Spain, 19, 28, 46, 47, 235-236, 266
Sri Lanka, 16, 25, 28, 32, 33, 46, 47, 237-239
Street, Comr Janet, 41, 45, 93, 209, 210
Street, Comr Robert, 33, 41, 45, 209
Strissell, Col Dennis, 117, 174
Strissell, Col Sharon, 117, 118, 174
Sumatra, 18
Sunbury Court, 22, 258, 259
Suriname, 18, 28, 184, *see also* Caribbean 88-92
Swanbury, Maj Charles, 174, 175
Swanbury, Maj Denise, 175
Swanson, Comr Barry C., 265, 266
Swanson, Comr E. Sue, 265, 266, 267
Swaziland, 28, *see also* Southern Africa 231-234
Sweden, 3, 16, 17, 20, 23, 24, 25, 28, 46, 48, 185, 266
Sweden and Latvia, 26, 32, 33, 240-244
Switzerland, 16, 24, 28, 48, 114
Switzerland, Austria and Hungary, 32, 46, 48, 204, 245-248, 295
Swyers, Comr Patricia, 179, 285, 286
Swyers, Comr Philip, 179, 210, 212, 285

T

Taiwan, 19, 28, 32, 46, 47, 52, 249-250
Tanzania, 18, 28, 46, 47, 79, 216, 251-252
Tillsley, General Bramwell H., 19, 22, 25
Tobago, 28, *see also* Caribbean 88-92
Togo, 117
Tonga, 19, 28, *see also* New Zealand, Fiji and Tonga 189-195
Trinidad, 17, 28, *see also* Caribbean 88-92
Tuck, Comrs Trevor/Memory, 232

Index

Tursi, Maj Anne-Florence, 154
Tursi, Maj Massimo, 153

U

Uganda, 18, 20, 28, 46, 47, 216, 253-254
Ukraine, 28, *see also* Eastern Europe 103-105
United Kingdom with the Republic of Ireland, 19, 26, 28, 32, 33, 46, 48, 250, 255-262, 266, 295, 298
United Nations, 21, 42
United States of America, 16, 17, 18, 23, 28, 34, 48, 78, 263-294
    National, 19, 32, 33, 48, 263-264
    Central, 32, 46, 265-270
    Eastern, 25, 26, 32, 46, 271-278
    Southern, 25, 32, 46, 88, 162, 170, 179, 200, 254, 279-284, 286
    Western, 25, 26, 32, 33, 46, 161, 210, 285-294
USA Eastern Territorial Arts Ministry, 79, 85
Uruguay, 17, 28, *see also* South America East 222-224
USAID, 48, 176

V

Van der Harst, Comr Netty, 103, 104
Van der Harst, Comr Willem, 103, 105
Van Vliet, Lt-Col Hans, 206
Van Vliet, Lt-Col Marja, 207
Varguhese, Col Prema, 5, 298
Varguhese, Col Wilfred, 297
Venezuela, 19, 28, *see also* Latin America North 169-173
Vijayakumar, Lt-Col Thumati, 139
Virgin Islands, 18, 28, 263, *see also* USA Eastern 271-278

W

Wahlström, General Jarl, 19, 22, 25
Wainwright, Col Dorita, 294, 295, 297
Wainwright, Col John, 294, 297
Wales, 16, *see also* United Kingdom, 255-262

Wandulu, Lt-Col Moses, 253
Wandulu, Lt-Col Sarah, 253, 254
Ward, Lt-Col Alfred, 74
Ward, Lt-Col Mary, 75
Ward, Col Marguerite, 203, 204
Ward, Col Robert, 203
West Germany, 19
Wickberg, General Erik, 19, 22, 24
William Booth College (UK), 18, 39, 256, 258
Williams, Comr Harry, 32, 33
Wiseman, General Clarence, 19, 22, 24, 32
Women's Ministries, 34, 39
Women's Social Work, 13, 16
Woodall, Comr Ann, 9, 40, 45
Words of Life, 31, 40
World Youth Convention, 3-4, 39

Y

Yoo, Comr Sung-ja, 164, 166
Yoshida, Comr Kaoru, 155, 156
Yoshida, Comr Makoto, 155
Yugoslavia, 18

Z

Zambia, 10, 18, 28, 46, 47, 176, 294-296, 298
Zimbabwe, 17, 20, 25, 26, 28, 32, 33, 46, 47, 176, 294, 297-299
Zola, Lt-Col Alphonsine, 49, 50
Zola, Lt-Col Ambroise, 49
Zululand, 17, 231

NOTES

NOTES

NOTES

TERRITORIES (T), COMMANDS (C) AND REGIONS (R) WITHIN EACH ZONE

AFRICA
Angola (C)
Congo (Brazzaville) (T)
Democratic Republic of Congo (T)
Ghana (T)
Kenya East (T)
Kenya West (T)
Liberia (C)
Malawi (C)
Mozambique (C)
Nigeria (T)
Rwanda and Burundi (R)
Southern Africa (T)
Tanzania (T)
Uganda (C)
Zambia (T)
Zimbabwe (T)

AMERICAS AND CARIBBEAN
Brazil (T)
Canada and Bermuda (T)
Caribbean (T)
Latin America North (T)
Mexico (T)
South America East (T)
South America West (T)
USA Central (T)
USA Eastern (T)
USA Southern (T)
USA Western (T)

EUROPE
Denmark (T)
Eastern Europe (T)
Finland and Estonia (T)
France and Belgium (T)
Germany and Lithuania (T)
Italy (C)
The Netherlands and Czech Republic (T)
Norway, Iceland and The Færoes (T)
Portugal (C)
Spain (C)
Sweden and Latvia (T)
Switzerland, Austria and Hungary (T)
United Kingdom with the Republic of Ireland (T)

SOUTH ASIA
Bangladesh (C)
India Central (T)
India Eastern (T)
India Northern (T)
India South Eastern (T)
India South Western (T)
India Western (T)
Pakistan (T)
Sri Lanka (T)

SOUTH PACIFIC AND EAST ASIA
Australia Eastern (T)
Australia Southern (T)
Hong Kong and Macau (C)
Indonesia (T)
Japan (T)
Korea (T)
New Zealand, Fiji and Tonga (T)
Papua New Guinea (T)
The Philippines (T)
Singapore, Malaysia and Myanmar (T)
Taiwan (R)